LEIBNIZ

Of all the thinkers of the century of genius that inaugurated modern philosophy, none lived an intellectual life more rich and varied than Gottfried Wilhelm Leibniz (1646–1716). Trained as a jurist and employed as a counsellor, librarian, and historian, he made famous contributions to logic, mathematics, physics, and metaphysics, yet viewed his own aspirations as ultimately ethical and theological, and married these theoretical concerns with politics, diplomacy, and an equally broad range of practical reforms: juridical, economic, administrative, technological, medical, and ecclesiastical.

Maria Rosa Antognazza's pioneering biography not only surveys the full breadth and depth of these theoretical interests and practical activities; it also weaves them together for the first time into a unified portrait of this unique thinker and the world from which he came.

At the centre of the huge range of Leibniz's apparently miscellaneous endeavours, Antognazza reveals a single master project lending unity to his extraordinarily multifaceted life's work. Throughout the vicissitudes of his long life, Leibniz tenaciously pursued the dream of a systematic reform and advancement of all the sciences, to be undertaken as a collaborative enterprise supported by an enlightened ruler. These theoretical pursuits were, in turn, ultimately grounded in a practical goal: the improvement of the human condition and the celebration thereby of the glory of God in His creation.

As well as tracing the threads of continuity that bound these theoretical and practical activities to this all-embracing plan, this illuminating study also follows these threads back to the intellectual traditions of the Holy Roman Empire in which Leibniz lived and throughout the broader intellectual networks that linked him to patrons in countries as distant as Russia and to correspondents as far afield as China.

Maria Rosa Antognazza is Reader in the Philosophy of Religion at King's College London. A recipient of research fellowships from the British Academy, the Herzog August Bibliothek, and the Leverhulme Trust, she is the author of *Leibniz on the Trinity and the Incarnation: Reason and Revelation in the Seventeenth Century* and has contributed to *The Cambridge History of Eighteenth-Century Philosophy*.

Leibniz
An Intellectual Biography

Maria Rosa Antognazza

CAMBRIDGE
UNIVERSITY PRESS

CAMBRIDGE UNIVERSITY PRESS

Cambridge, New York, Melbourne, Madrid, Cape Town, Singapore, São Paulo, Delhi

Cambridge University Press
32 Avenue of the Americas, New York, NY 10013-2473, USA

www.cambridge.org
Information on this title: www.cambridge.org/9780521806190

First published 2009

Printed in the United States of America

A catalog record for this publication is available from the British Library.

Library of Congress Cataloging in Publication Data

Antognazza, Maria Rosa, 1964–
Leibniz : an intellectual biography / Maria Rosa Antognazza.
p.   cm.
Includes bibliographical references and index.
ISBN 978-0-521-80619-0 (hardback)
1. Leibniz, Gottfried Wilhelm, 1646–1716.   I. Title.
B2597.A68   2008
193–dc22   [B]   2007048443

ISBN   978-0-521-80619-0 hardback

To my husband, Howard Hotson,
and our children, John, Sophia, and Francesca

"[A]ll these things are connected and have to be directed to the same aim, which is the glory of God and the advancement of the public good by means of useful works and beautiful discoveries." (Leibniz to Duke Johann Friedrich of Hanover, 1678)

"Tranquillity is a step on the path toward stupidity . . . One should always find something to do, to think, to plan, concerning ourselves for the community and for the individual, yet in such a way that we can rejoice if our wishes are fulfilled and not be saddened if they are not." (Leibniz to Louise von Hohenzollern, 1705)

"Sometimes so many thoughts occur to me in the morning during an hour in which I am still in bed, that it takes me all morning, and sometimes all day and more, to write them down accurately." (In Bodemann, *Handschriften*, p. 338)

Contents

Acknowledgements

Work on this book began during the tenure of a British Academy Post-doctoral Fellowship and was subsequently supported by the Leverhulme Trust with a two-year research fellowship, which included a grant for research in Germany. I am deeply grateful to these two institutions for allowing me, first, to take up the challenge of this project, and, second, to liberate enough time to see it to completion.

The University of Aberdeen and King's College London provided the research-friendly environments necessary for the flourishing of academic work. Over the years I have become indebted to a great many people who in different ways have contributed to the completion of this book. My husband, Howard Hotson, has supported and advised me during all stages of this project. Without him this book could never have been written. In particular, I have enormously benefited from his deep understanding of the intellectual history of the period. With extraordinary scholarly generosity, Massimo Mugnai and Paul Lodge have carefully read and commented on a complete draft of this book. I owe them many insightful suggestions and sincere gratitude for sharing with me their profound knowledge of Leibniz. Heinrich Schepers, Robert M. Adams, Knud Haakonssen, and Udo Thiel read the initial prospectus of the book and encouraged me to embark on this venture. Their support at various stages of my work, together with the sympathy and encouragement of Maria Grazia Zaccone Sina and Mario Sina, have meant a great deal to me. Niccolò Guicciardini has provided invaluable advice, especially on mathematics. I am grateful to Sean Greenberg for his feedback on some aspects of my work, and to an anonymous reader who reviewed the manuscript for a number of helpful suggestions. Vincenzo De Risi, François Duchesneau, Laurent Jaffro, Arnaud Pelletier, Lidia Ripamonti, Christoph Selzer, and Stephan Waldhoff have advised me on specific points and/or sent me rare literature from Germany. I am grateful to Daniel Garber, Brandon Look, Michael Murray, and Donald Rutherford for sharing with me their work in progess or in press. With great kindness and expertise, Herbert Breger helped me resolve a number of biographical riddles during my visits to the Leibniz-Archiv. My sincere thanks also go to the editors of the Akademie-Ausgabe and to the staff of the Gottfried Wilhelm Leibniz Bibliothek/Niedersächsische Landesbibliothek for their cordiality and help over many years.

A more abstract but no less profound debt of gratitude is owed to generations of past and contemporary Leibniz scholars without whose work this present contribution would be utterly unthinkable. Müller and Krönert's *Leben und Werk von Gottfried Wilhelm Leibniz* has provided an indispensable chronological framework which has guided my own research and assisted inestimably in locating many key primary sources. The classic biography by G. E. Guhrauer has likewise provided a still valuable point of departure, supplemented by the more recent work of E. J. Aiton and Heinrich Schepers, an illuminating entry in the *Neue Deutsche Biographie*. My enormous debt to a great many excellent individual studies large and small is recorded in the footnotes and bibliography. It has been a delight and a privilege to attempt to stitch these together, and I hope that at least a majority of these authors will feel that I have done their research justice.

In 2004, in the midst of the writing of this book, I was diagnosed with an advanced stage of breast cancer. I would like to thank my family, extended family, and friends for fighting with me during the ten months of intensive treatment which followed. Without the expert care of Dr. A. W. Hutcheon, Professor Liliana Colombo, and the British National Health Service I would not be here to tell this story. My debt to all these people, and to this publicly funded institution, is greater than words can say. I would also like to remember the relatives and friends who lost their battles while I was fighting mine: Jennifer Hotson, Mariuccia Ferrario, Liliana Corti, Patrizio Dagrada, and, especially, two mothers of young children, Anna Negri and Gabriella Bizzotto. Finally, there are two people to whom in particular I would have liked to present this book: the late Terence Moore of Cambridge University Press, who entrusted me with this challenging and fascinating project, and the late Albert Heinekamp, who with great cordiality guided the first steps of an eager but ignorant Ph.D. student into the labyrinth of the Leibniz-Archiv.

Abbreviations

A: Leibniz, G. W. *Sämtliche Schriften und Briefe*. Ed. by the Academy of Sciences of Berlin. Series I–VIII. Darmstadt, Leipzig, and Berlin, 1923 ff. Cited by series, volume, and page. "N." followed by an Arabic numeral indicates the number assigned to the text by the editors.

    I: *Allgemeiner, politischer und historischer Briefwechsel*
   II: *Philosophischer Briefwechsel*
  III: *Mathematischer, naturwissenschaftlicher und technischer Briefwechsel*
  IV: *Politische Schriften*
   V: *Historische und sprachwissenschaftliche Schriften*
  VI: *Philosophische Schriften*
 VII: *Mathematische Schriften*
VIII: *Naturwissenschaftliche, medizinische und technische Schriften*

Bodemann, *Briefwechsel*: Bodemann, Eduard. *Der Briefwechsel des Gottfried Wilhelm Leibniz*. Hanover, 1889. Reprint, Hildesheim: Olms, 1966.

Bodemann, *Handschriften*: Bodemann, Eduard. *Die Leibniz-Handschriften der Königlichen öffentlichen Bibliothek zu Hannover*. Hanover and Leipzig, 1895. Reprint, Hildesheim: Olms, 1966.

Couturat: Leibniz, G. W. *Opuscules et fragments inédits*. Ed. by Louis Couturat. Paris: F. Alcan, 1903. Reprint, Hildesheim: Olms, 1988.

Deutsche Schriften: Leibniz, G. W. *Deutsche Schriften*. Ed. by G. E. Guhrauer. 2 vols. Berlin, 1840.

Dutens: Leibniz, G. W. *Opera omnia, nunc primum collecta, in classes distributa, praefationibus et indicibus exornata*. Ed. by L. Dutens. 6 vols. Geneva: De Tournes, 1768. Cited by volume, part (if relevant), and page.

Erdmann: Leibniz, G. W. *Opera philosophica quae extant Latina Gallica Germanica omnia*. Ed. by J. E. Erdmann. Berlin, 1839–40.

FC, *Oeuvres*: *Oeuvres de Leibniz*. Ed. by A. Foucher de Careil. 7 vols. Paris: Firmin Didot frères, 1861–75 (vols. I and II have also appeared in 2nd ed.: Paris: Firmin Didot frères, 1867–9; unless otherwise stated I refer to the first edition).

Feller: Feller, Joachim Friedrich. *Otium Hanoveranum sive Miscellanea ex ore et schedis Illustris Viri, piae memoriae Godofr. Guilielmi Leibnitii.* Leipzig: Impensis Johann. Christiani Martini, 1718.

GB: *Der Briefwechsel von Gottfried Wilhelm Leibniz mit Mathematikern.* Ed. by C. I. Gerhardt. Berlin: Mayer & Müller, 1899.

GM: Leibniz, G. W. *Mathematische Schriften*. 7 vols. Ed. by C. I. Gerhardt. Berlin and Halle: A. Asher and H. W. Schmidt, 1849–63.

GP: Leibniz, G. W. *Die Philosophischen Schriften*. Ed. by C. I. Gerhardt. 7 vols. Berlin: Weidmannsche Buchhandlung, 1875–90. Reprint, Hildesheim: Olms, 1960–61. Cited by volume and page.

Grua: Leibniz, G. W. *Textes inédits d'après les manuscrits de la Bibliothèque Provinciale de Hanovre*. Ed. by G. Grua. 2 vols. Paris: PUF, 1948.

Klopp: Leibniz, G. W. *Die Werke*. Ed. by O. Klopp. 11 vols. Hanover: Klindworth, 1864–84.

LBr: Leibniz – Briefwechsel. Hanover, Gottfried Wilhelm Leibniz Bibliothek / Niedersächsische Landesbibliothek.

LH: Leibniz – Handschriften. Hanover, Gottfried Wilhelm Leibniz Bibliothek / Niedersächsische Landesbibliothek.

Pertz: Leibniz, G. W. *Gesammelte Werke*. Ed. by Georg Heinrich Pertz. 4 vols. Hanover: Hahnschen Hof-Buchhandlung, 1843–7. Reprint, Hildesheim: Olms, 1966.

Ravier: *Bibliographie des oeuvres de Leibniz*. Ed. by Émile Ravier. Paris: F. Alcan, 1937. Reprint, Hildesheim: Olms, 1966.

AG: Leibniz, G. W. *Philosophical Essays*. Ed. and trans. by R. Ariew and D. Garber. Indianapolis: Hackett, 1989.

L: Leibniz, G. W. *Philosophical Papers and Letters*. Ed. and trans. by Leroy E. Loemker. 2nd ed. Dordrecht and Boston: Reidel, 1969.

NE: Leibniz, G. W. *New Essays on Human Understanding*. Ed. and trans. by Peter Remnant and Jonathan Bennett. Cambridge: Cambridge University Press, 1981.

WF: *Leibniz's New System and Associated Contemporary Texts*. Ed. and trans. by R. S. Woolhouse and Richard Francks. Oxford: Clarendon Press, 1997.

Dating

N.S.: New Style.
O.S.: Old Style.

All dates are given in the New (Gregorian) Style unless otherwise indicated. The so-called Gregorian calendar was introduced in 1582 in Catholic countries following a papal bull issued by Pope Gregory XVIII. In February 1700 the Gregorian style was also introduced into the Protestant states of Germany: after the 18th of February ten days were cancelled to make the following date the 1st of March. Great Britain and her colonies did not adopt the new calendar until 1752. Because 1700 was a leap year in the old (Julian) calendar, after 29 February 1700 (O.S.) the difference between the two systems became eleven days.

Asterisks after dates indicate probable dating.

Chronological Table

1 July (21 June [O. S.]) 1646: Gottfried Wilhelm Leibniz is born in Leipzig (Saxony).

July 1653–Easter 1661 Leibniz attends the Nikolaischule, one of Leipzig's two main Latin schools and one of the best preparatory schools in Saxony.

April 1661: Leibniz begins his studies at the University of Leipzig.

2 December 1662: Bachelor's degree in philosophy.

9 June 1663: Discussion of the dissertation written for his Bachelor's degree in philosophy (*Disputatio Metaphysica de Principio Individui*).

20 June 1663: Enrolment for the summer semester at the University of Jena (Saxony).

October 1663: Return to Leipzig for the beginning of the winter semester.

7 February 1664: Master's degree in philosophy.

December 1664: Discussion of the dissertation written for his Master's degree in philosophy (*Specimen Quaestionum Philosophicarum ex Jure collectarum*).

24 July and 27 August 1665: Discussion of the first and second parts of his dissertation on conditional judgements in law (*De conditionibus*) for his Bachelor's degree in law.

28 September 1665: Bachelor's degree in law.

1666: *Dissertatio de Arte Combinatoria*. Discussion on 17 March 1666 of its first part under the title of *Disputatio arithmetica de Complexionibus* for Leibniz's habilitation in the faculty of philosophy.

End of September 1666: Leibniz leaves Leipzig.

xvii

4 October 1666: Enrolment in the law faculty of the University of Altdorf, situated within the territories of the imperial free city of Nuremberg.

15 November 1666: Discussion of the thesis for the licence and the doctorate in law (*Disputatio de Casibus perplexis in Jure*).

1666–7: Leibniz's first paid position: secretary of a Nuremberg alchemical society.

Autumn of 1667: Leibniz leaves Nuremberg, intending to undertake a European grand tour via the Rhine and Holland.

November 1667: Leibniz in Frankfurt; visit to the nearby Catholic archiepiscopal seat in Mainz.

End of 1667: Publication of the *Nova Methodus Discendae Docendaeque Jurisprudentiae*.

End of 1667–early 1668: First encounters with Baron Johann Christian von Boineburg.

1668: Employment by the elector and prince-archbishop of Mainz, Johann Philipp von Schönborn, as collaborator on the reform and reorganisation of the *corpus juris*; *Confessio Naturae contra Atheistas*.

1668–9: *Demonstrationum Catholicarum Conspectus*.

April 1669: Letter to his former teacher, Jakob Thomasius.

1669–71: *Elementa Juris naturalis*.

1670: New edition (with introduction by Leibniz) of Mario Nizolio, *Antibarbarus seu de veris principiis et vera ratione philosophandi contra pseudophilosophos*.

1670–1: *Theoria motus abstracti* and *Hypothesis physica nova*.

1671: *Grundriß eines Bedenkens von aufrichtung einer Societät in Deutschland zu aufnehmen der Künste und Wissenschaften*.

May 1671: Letter to Magnus Wedderkopf.

20 June 1671: Letter from Pierre de Carcavy to Leibniz, containing the first known mention of Leibniz's calculating machine.

1671–2: *Directiones ad rem Medicam pertinentes*.

19 March 1672: Departure for Paris, where Leibniz arrives at the end of March.

Autumn of 1672: First meeting with Christiaan Huygens. Intensive mathematical work, especially on the summation of series.

Autumn of 1672–early 1673: *Confessio Philosophi.*

November 1672: Supervision of the education of Baron Boineburg's son.

15 December 1672: Death of Leibniz's patron, Baron Boineburg.

End January–end February 1673: First visit to London. First personal encounter with Heinrich Oldenburg, secretary to the Royal Society.

1 February 1673: Demonstration of Leibniz's calculating machine at a meeting of the Royal Society.

Beginning of March 1673: Leibniz back in Paris.

19 April 1673: Leibniz elected Fellow of the Royal Society.

13 September 1674: Leibniz dismissed by the widow of the late Baron Boineburg.

21 January 1675: Leibniz accepts the offer of Duke Johann Friedrich of Hanover to enter his service.

October 1675: Invention of the infinitesimal calculus, prepared by a series of mathematical studies and results achieved after his return from London.

1675–6: *De Summa Rerum* (including the dialogue *Pacidius Philaleti*).

Summer of 1676: *De Arcanis Motus.*

4 October 1676: Leibniz leaves Paris.

18–29 October 1676: Second visit to London.

November 1676: Leibniz in Holland; extended conversations with Baruch Spinoza in The Hague.

Mid-December 1676: Arrival in Hanover to assume the duties of court counsellor and librarian to Duke Johann Friedrich.

May 1677: Letter to Duke Johann Friedrich: justice as *caritas sapientis* ("charity of the wise").

June–October 1677: *Caesarini Fürstenerii de Jure Suprematus ac Legationis Principum Germaniae.*

August 1677: Leibniz suggests the investigation of a possible link between the Guelf house and the ancient Italian noble family of Este.

1678–9: Leibniz relaunches his encyclopaedic plan of the *Demonstrationes Catholicae* (letter of the autumn of 1679 to Duke Johann Friedrich); introduces the idea of a *scientia generalis* and a demonstrative or inventive encyclopaedia; writes a ground-breaking study on the notion of force in which he quantifies force as the product of mass (m) and the square of speed (v^2) (*De corporum concursu*, January 1678); starts developing a *characteristica geometrica* or *analysis situs* and a dyadic or binary arithmetic; writes a cluster of key logical papers providing the basis of a logical calculus (April 1679); lays the foundations for an advanced philosophy of probability (*De incerti aestimatione*, September 1678); proposes the creation of new ways of organising scientific research and learned societies to collaborate on the encyclopaedic task.

Autumn of 1678: Beginning of his involvement in the Harz mines.

28 December 1679: Death of Duke Johann Friedrich. The duchy of Hanover passes to the late duke's youngest brother, Ernst August, married to Sophie von der Pfalz.

1680–83: Series of practical proposals to Ernst August, including the introduction of an official medical system and state provision of education.

1680–86: Heavy involvement in the Harz mines: Leibniz makes thirty-one separate trips to the Harz and spends at least 165 weeks there out of a total of 365.

1683: Hanoverian negotiations on reunification between Catholics and Protestants, led by Bishop Cristobal de Rojas y Spinola and Gerhard Wolter Molanus. By this time Leibniz has proved Fermat's little theorem.

August–September 1683: *Mars Christianissimus seu Apologia armorum Regis Christianissimi contra Christianos.*

January 1684: Invention of determinants and discovery of their properties.

October 1684: Publication in the *Acta Eruditorum* of the *Nova Methodus pro Maximis et Minimis* (that is, Leibniz's first public presentation of the infinitesimal calculus); later complemented by *De Geometria Recondita et Analysi Indivisibilium et infinitorum*, published in the *Acta Eruditorum* of July 1686.

November 1684: Publication in the *Acta Eruditorum* of the *Meditationes de Cognitione, Veritate et Ideis.*

April 1685: Collapse of the Harz project.

June 1685: Leibniz charged with writing the Guelf history.

Autumn 1685: First memorandum for Ernst August providing historical and legal arguments in support of the duke's claim to electoral status.

1686: Leibniz writes four fundamental texts in physics, metaphysics, theology, and logic: (1) *Brevis demonstratio erroris memorabilis Cartesii et aliorum circa legem naturae*; (2) *Discours de Métaphysique*; (3) *Examen Religionis Christianae*; (4) *Generales Inquisitiones de Analysi Notionum et Veritatum*.

1686–90: Correspondence with Antoine Arnauld on the topics discussed in the *Discours de Métaphysique*.

End of October 1687: Departure for southern Germany.

November 1687: Two-week stay in Rheinfels, visiting one of his most trusted friends and correspondents, Landgraf Ernst von Hessen-Rheinfels.

January 1688: Leibniz hosted for several days by Christian Knorr von Rosenroth in Sulzbach.

End of March 1688: After a number of stops and detours (including a meeting in Graupen, Bohemia, with his long-standing friend, Johann Daniel Crafft, and two weeks in Regensburg), Leibniz arrives at his original main destination: Munich.

April 1688: Leibniz finds proof of the dynastic connection between the Este family and the Braunschweig-Lüneburg house in a manuscript codex in Augsburg.

End of April 1688: Leibniz decides to visit the Este archives in Modena (Italy). On 29 April he leaves Munich for Vienna.

8 May 1688: Leibniz arrives in Vienna where he stays until February 1689; audience with Emperor Leopold I (October 1688) and several meetings on ecclesiastical reunification with Bishop Rojas.

Autumn–winter of 1688–9: *Mars christianissimus ou Reflexions sur la declaration de la guerre, que la France fait à l'Empire.*

February 1689: Publication in the *Acta Eruditorum* of the *Tentamen de Motuum caelestium Causis*.

16 January 1689: Leibniz receives permission from the duke of Modena to visit the Este archives.

11 February 1689: Departure for Italy.

4 March 1689: Leibniz in Venice until the end of the month.

14 April 1689: Leibniz arrives in Rome.

Beginning of May 1689: Leibniz visits Naples.

Mid-May 1689: Leibniz back in Rome, where he stays until 20 November 1689; participation in meetings of the Accademia Fisico-Matematica.

Second half of July 1689: *Phoranomus seu de potentia et legibus naturae.*

August 1689–90: *Dynamica de Potentia et Legibus Naturae Corporeae.*

Spring–autumn of 1689: *Tentamen de Physicis Motuum Coelestium Rationibus* and *Principia Logico-Metaphysica* (also known as *Primae Veritates*).

November 1689: Departs Rome for Florence, where he meets Rudolf Christian von Bodenhausen; first appearance of the word 'dynamica' in his correspondence with Bodenhausen (31 December 1689).

22 December 1689: Leibniz leaves Florence for Bologna.

28 December 1689: Leibniz leaves Bologna, finally headed for the official destination of his Italian trip: the Este court in Modena.

January 1690: Consultation of the Este archives. Leibniz leaves Modena on 2 February.

10 February 1690: Visit to the tombs of the ancient Este family in the monastery of Vangadizza at Badia Polesine, near Rovigo. Leibniz discovers the exact connection between the Este and Guelf houses.

February–March 1690: Leibniz in Venice. Meetings with Michel Angelo Fardella. Leibniz leaves Venice on 24 March.

End of April–mid-May 1690: Leibniz in Vienna.

Mid-June 1690: Leibniz back in Hanover.

1690–91: Correspondence with Paul Pellisson-Fontanier on religious toleration.

Autumn 1690–92: Several outlines of the Guelf history, notably a *Brevis synopsis historiae Guelficae*. Leibniz plans to complete the history by 1693.

14 January 1691: Leibniz assumes additional duties at the court of Wolfenbüttel as director of the impressive ducal library; in the second half of 1691 he supervises the creation of a new catalogue (completed by 1699). Wolfenbüttel becomes his second regular place of residence, where he maintains permanent quarters.

15 February 1692: Letter of Nicolas Fatio de Duillier to Huygens, claiming that Leibniz has derived his calculus from Newton without acknowledging his debt.

March 1692: Emperor Leopold I grants the status of ninth electorate to the territories of Calenberg (Hanover) and Celle, crowning years of efforts by Leibniz in preparing historical and legal documents in support of Duke Ernst August's electoral claim.

May 1692: Leibniz declines an invitation, received via Jacob Auguste Barnabas Comte Des Viviers, to join the service of Louis XIV.

1692–6: Renewed involvement in the Harz mines.

1693: Publication of the *Codex Juris Gentium Diplomaticus.*

March 1694: Publication in the *Acta Eruditorum* of *De Primae Philosophiae Emendatione, et de Notione Substantiae.*

End of 1694: The *Protogaea* (Leibniz's treatise on the origin and history of the earth) is complete but remains unpublished.

1695: Publication of the first part of a *Specimen Dynamicum* in the *Acta Eruditorum* (April); publication of the *Système nouveau de la nature et de la communication des substances* in the *Journal de Sçavans* (June and July); first appearance of the expression 'pre-established harmony' and of the term 'monad', used to indicate 'real unities' or 'simple substances'.

Mid-1690s: *Mémoire pour des Personnes éclairées et de bonne intention.*

5 February 1695: Antonio Alberti (alias Amable de Tourreil) informs Leibniz that he could be offered the custodianship of the Vatican Library if he converts to Catholicism. Leibniz declines.

July 1696: Elevation to the position of privy counsellor of justice (*Geheimer Justizrat*).

1696–7: *Unvorgreiffliche Gedancken betreffend die Ausübung und Verbesserung der Teutschen Sprache.*

23 November 1697: *De rerum originatione radicali.*

1697: Publication of the *Novissima Sinica*; especially from 1697 onward Leibniz's focus shifts from the reconciliation of Catholicism and Lutheranism to the reunion of Lutherans and Calvinists, Evangelicals, and Reformed.

1697–1700: Leibniz comments on the dispute between John Locke and Edward Stillingfleet.

Early 1698–early 1699: *Unvorgreiffliches Bedencken über eine Schrift genandt "Kurtze Vorstellung"*, written in collaboration with Molanus.

2 February 1698: Death of Ernst August. His oldest son, Georg Ludwig, becomes the new Elector and Duke of Hanover.

September 1698: Publication of *De ipsa natura* in the *Acta Eruditorum*; *Tentamen Expositionis Irenicae*.

November 1698–February 1705: Leibniz spends extended periods of time in Berlin (some twenty-four months in total), establishing an exceptionally close bond with Sophie Charlotte, electress of Brandenburg and sister of Georg Ludwig.

December 1698–January 1706: Correspondence with Burchard de Volder.

1698 and 1700: Publication of two volumes of *Accessiones Historicae* and of a *Mantissa Codicis Juris Gentium Diplomatici*.

1699: A mathematical treatise by Nicolas Fatio de Duillier raises the suspicion that Leibniz plagiarized his calculus from Newton.

1699–1705: Leibniz writes to Gilbert Burnet asking for the support of the English church on the issue of Protestant reunification (January 1699); commentary on Article 17 of Burnet's *Exposition of the Thirty-Nine Articles of the Church of England*.

February 1700: Leibniz elected foreign member of the Parisian Académie Royale des Sciences.

19 March 1700: Friedrich III of Brandenburg approves the foundation of the Berlin Society of Sciences under Leibniz's presidency; on 11 July 1700 the Elector signs the Society's *Stiftungbrief* (decree of foundation); on 12 July 1700 Leibniz is officially named President of the Society and privy counsellor of justice (*Geheimer Justizrat*) in Brandenburg.

End of October–mid-December 1700: Leibniz in Vienna following a summons from Emperor Leopold for further talks on the reunification of the Catholic and Protestant churches.

18 January 1701: The Brandenburg elector crowned Friedrich I, King in Prussia.

8 August 1701: *Annotatiunculae Subitaneae ad Tolandi Librum De Christianismo Mysteriis Carente.*

14 August 1701: The Act of Settlement is presented to the dowager Electress Sophie, sanctioning the Protestant succession to the English crown through the Hanoverian line.

11 June 1702–May 1703: Leibniz in Lützenburg and Berlin. During the summer of 1702, discussions in Lützenburg with Sophie Charlotte and her entourage provide the basis for the *Theodicy.*

1702: *Lettre touchant ce qui est independant des Sens et de la Matiere*, addressed to Sophie Charlotte.

April 1703: *Explication de l'Arithmetique Binaire* commenting on the parallel between the hexagrams of the *I Ching* and Leibniz's dyadic, discussed in his correspondence with Joachim Bouvet.

Beginning of June 1703: Leibniz back in Hanover.

Summer of 1703–summer of 1705: *Nouveaux Essais.*

Summer of 1703: *Méditation sur la notion commune de la justice.*

30 January–2 February 1704: Leibniz in Dresden to promote the idea of founding a Society of Sciences in Saxony.

12 April 1704: Death of Jacques-Bénigne Bossuet, with whom Leibniz intermittently corresponded from 1679 onward on the issue of ecclesiastical reunification.

27 August 1704: Arrival at Lützenburg for a sojourn in Brandenburg of more than six months; Leibniz meets Wilhelmine Caroline von Ansbach.

December 1704–16: Correspondence with Christian Wolff.

1 February 1705: Death of Sophie Charlotte in Hanover, while Leibniz is still in Berlin.

March 1705: Leibniz back in Hanover.

2 September 1705: The son and heir of Georg Ludwig, Georg August, marries Wilhelmine Caroline von Ansbach.

January 1706–16: Correspondence with Bartholomew Des Bosses, including (from 1712) discussion of the *vinculum substantiale.*

Mid-November 1706–mid-May 1707: Leibniz in Berlin.

June 1707: Publication of the first volume of *Scriptores rerum Brunsvicensium*; two further volumes follow in 1710 and 1711.

December 1708: Leibniz in Vienna.

Early January–early March 1709: Short visit to Leipzig (early January); sojourn in Berlin.

9 March 1709: Back in Hanover.

1710: Publication in Amsterdam of the *Essais de Théodicée sur la bonté de Dieu, la liberté de l'homme et l'origine du mal*; publication of the first volume of the *Miscellanea Berolinensia* by the Berlin Society of Sciences; on 7 August Friedrich I nominates Marquard Ludwig von Printzen as honorary president of the Society, thereby compromising Leibniz's role as president; the *Philosophical Transactions* for 1708 (actually published in 1710) includes a paper by the Scottish mathematician John Keill in which Leibniz is openly accused of having plagiarized Newton's calculus.

October 1710: In a letter to Thomas Burnett, Leibniz presents the *Theodicy* as the "forerunner" of a broader enterprise reminiscent of the *Demonstrationes Catholicae*, later reconceived as the *scientia generalis*, and finally envisaged in this letter as "Elements of general philosophy and of natural theology."

25 February–beginning of May 1711: last sojourn in Berlin.

30 October 1711, 6–10 November 1712: audiences with Peter the Great, tsar of Russia, in Torgau (Saxony) and Carlsbad (Bohemia).

11 November 1712: Leibniz nominated Russian privy counsellor of justice as well as adviser to the tsar on mathematical and scientific matters.

1712: *Epistolica de historia etymologica dissertatio.*

Mid-December 1712–early September 1714: Leibniz in Vienna.

January 1713: Publication in London of the *Commercium Epistolicum.*

April 1713: Nomination (back-dated to 2 January 1712) of Leibniz as member of the Imperial Aulic Council (*Reichshofrat*), one of the two supreme courts of appeal of the Empire.

14 August 1713: Emperor Charles VI names Leibniz director of a planned Imperial Society of Sciences in Vienna, which is never realised.

Summer 1713: Leibniz writes the so-called *Charta Volans* anonymously.

1714: Leibniz writes the *Principes de la nature et de la grâce fondés en raison* for Prince Eugene of Savoy (completed in Vienna by August 1714) and works in Vienna and Hanover on a paper published after his death as *Monadologie*.

8 June 1714: Death of the dowager Electress Sophie, Leibniz's long-standing friend and protector in Hanover.

August 1714: Death of Queen Anne of Great Britain and Ireland; passage of the throne to Georg Ludwig of Hanover (George I).

3 September 1714: Departure from Vienna.

14 September 1714: Leibniz arrives in Hanover, three days after the elector and his court have left for London.

12 October 1714: Caroline, now Princess of Wales, leaves Hanover.

Late 1714–16: Leibniz tries unsuccessfully to secure the office of historiographer of Great Britain in order to follow the court in London; he considers moving to Vienna or Paris; intensive work on the Guelf history (*Annales Imperii Occidentis Brunsvicenses*).

15 March 1715: Leibniz criticizes Berkeley's philosophy in a letter to Des Bosses.

Spring-early summer of 1715: Ἀποκατάστασις.

November 1715–October 1716: Correspondence between Leibniz and Samuel Clarke mediated by Princess Caroline.

Late 1705–early 1716: *Discours sur la Theologie naturelle des Chinois*.

Summer 1716: Meetings with Peter the Great in Bad Pyrmont (Lower Saxony).

3 August 1716: Leibniz reports satisfactory improvements on the most recent model of his calculating machine.

3 November 1716: Leibniz's last dated letter, conveying his hopes for the flourishing of the Society of Sciences of Berlin.

6–14 November 1716: Leibniz bedridden, plagued by gout and arthritis, and unable to write.

Evening of 14 November 1716: Leibniz dies in Hanover, where his funeral takes place on 14 December 1716.

Introduction

ON 13 NOVEMBER 1717, the secretary of the Académie Royale des Sciences, Bernard Le Bovier de Fontenelle, presented to his colleagues in Paris a eulogy of Gottfried Wilhelm Leibniz, who had died a year and a day earlier. Fontenelle had corresponded with the German philosopher on numerous occasions, and his "Éloge" could also draw on the biographical sketch provided by Leibniz's secretary, Johann Georg Eckhart. Informed by such personal knowledge, the French savant naturally identified at the outset the aspect of his subject most worthy of a eulogy: the extraordinary range of Leibniz's intellectual achievements. "In somewhat the same way that ancients could manage simultaneously up to eight harnessed horses," he observed in the classicising vein still fashionable even in scientific circles in Paris, "Leibniz could manage simultaneously all the sciences." Yet this very intellectual range confronted Fontenelle with seemingly insuperable difficulties in composing an intelligible biographical sketch. Leibniz, he lamented, "wrote about different matters during the same years, and . . . this almost perpetual jumble, which did not produce any confusion in his ideas, these abrupt and frequent transitions from one subject to another completely opposite subject, which did not trouble him, would trouble and confuse this history."[1] Confronted by the difficulty of keeping eight rampant lines of intertwining intellectual development from getting hopelessly tangled with one another, Fontenelle abandoned "the customary chronological order" and organised his eulogy thematically.

During the almost three centuries since Leibniz's death, the difficulty first confronted by Fontenelle has multiplied many times over. Leibniz himself confided to another contemporary that those who knew him only from his published works did not know him at all;[2] and the immense mountain of his private papers – placed under seal even before

I

his body had been removed from his house on the Schmiedestraße the evening after his death – eventually revealed that the published writings available to Fontenelle represented only a tiny fraction of Leibniz's intellectual output. The size of the archive was enormous: thousands upon thousands of letters and hundreds upon hundreds of draft treatises, fragments, sketches, and notes, which once collected in the ongoing edition of the Berlin Academy of Sciences will eventually extend to some one hundred twenty large quarto volumes organized in eight distinct series (three devoted to Leibniz's correspondence and five to his other writings).[3] No less remarkable than their quantity was their intellectual quality. Far from broadcasting his views indiscriminately, Leibniz had kept many of his most profound convictions and most remarkable conclusions to himself and a few most trusted correspondents. Preserved essentially intact in the royal library in Hanover (recently renamed the Gottfried Wilhelm Leibniz Bibliothek), his papers have yielded a fresh supply of intellectual gems to virtually every generation between Leibniz's and our own in an almost unmanageable stream of fresh works and partial editions of previously unpublished writings.[4] Perhaps most impressive of all was their thematic scope. From philosophy and mathematics narrowly construed they extended across the encyclopaedia of the sciences and beyond: to astronomy, physics, chemistry, and geology; to botany, psychology, medicine, and natural history; to jurisprudence, ethics, and political philosophy; to history and antiquities, German, European and Chinese languages; to linguistics, etymology, philology, and poetry; to theology both natural and revealed; and beyond contemplative pursuits altogether to a wide range of practical affairs: from legal reform to the reunification of the churches, from diplomacy and practical politics to institutional reform, technological improvement, and the organisation of scientific societies, libraries, and the book trade.

Despairing of treating the many strands of Leibniz's intellectual life in a single, chronologically organised narrative, Fontenelle decided "to split him up or, speaking philosophically, to analyze him." Again a classical analogy suggested itself: "Antiquity made only one person from several Hercules; we will make several savants from a single Leibniz." Already within a year of his death, Leibniz's system was being broken up into several distinct fields and his contributions to them narrated one by one. When the textual difficulties of dealing with such an unwieldy mass of papers and publications was added to the technical challenge of grasping such complex and wide-ranging thought, Leibniz inevitably became the domain of the specialist. The corpus of his writings was clinically dissected and portioned out to specialists for further study; and the coherent intellectual world which he had worked so long and hard to create was unceremoniously dismembered and divided amongst an entire army of scholars studying the complete encyclopaedia of the disciplines.

As if this intellectual disintegration were not damaging enough, not all of these disciplines have historically treated their share of his Nachlaß with equal regard. His enduring contributions to mathematics have never lacked admirers. His brilliant innovations in logic and remarkable conclusions in metaphysics have attracted even more attention. In many other sciences, however, his work inevitably proved less enduring. His rapidly consolidating reputation as a mathematician and a rationalist may have deflected attention from his contribution to other fields while deterring specialists who lacked facility with the supposed core of logic, metaphysics, and mathematics from investigating many crucial aspects of his life and work. However precisely it came about, the resulting imbalance is clearly reflected in the huge mass of secondary literature which has gradually accumulated around Leibniz's published and unpublished writings since his death. The standard bibliography of literature on Leibniz before 1980 lists 806 items on metaphysics and ontology, 552 on mathematics, 430 on logic, 282 on epistemology, and 220 on the physical sciences. Ethics and practical philosophy in the same bibliography, by contrast, share only 154 items. Political philosophy and law – the discipline in which Leibniz was formally trained – rate a mere 135. Theology and the philosophy of religion – arguably at the very centre of his lifelong project – score only 122. Linguistics and literary studies attracted a meagre 98 studies. Historiography – Leibniz's chief profession for the latter half of his career – and the philosophy of history a paltry 79. Medicine an anaemic 54.[5] Whether or not these figures are an accurate index of Leibniz's enduring contributions to these fields – or indeed of the somewhat readjusted emphases of the most recent quarter century[6] – they are clearly unrepresentative of the importance of these fields in his own mind and of his own efforts to contribute to them.

Moreover, the dismemberment of Leibniz's intellectual system and the unbalanced attention to its individual components has inevitably bred misunderstandings; and key features of Leibniz's writings have exacerbated this tendency. Leibniz, famously, was a man who sought to reconcile apparent antitheses, often in extremely subtle and sophisticated ways. Leibniz, no less famously, corresponded with a great variety of contemporaries and displayed different facets of his thought to different people. Confronted by strikingly different emphases in diverse works and letters, some scholars hastily concluded that Leibniz was disingenuous, a timeserver, a courtier, willing to placate opposing parties by misrepresenting his principles, or a man without principles at all. Indeed, many of his more small-minded contemporaries formed similar conclusions even during his lifetime: some worried he would convert to Calvinism, others that he had already converted to Catholicism, others still that he was a closet atheist. Reductionist characterisations continued to proliferate after his death, ranging from deist and hard rationalist on the one hand to Kabbalist, alchemist, or Rosicrucian on the other. This tendency to question Leibniz's intellectual and personal integrity and to divide him – in the manner only metaphorically suggested by Fontenelle – into two quite separate philosophers reached its apex in the interpretation of perhaps the most eminent philosopher ever to dedicate a monograph specifically to Leibniz. No less a figure than Bertrand Russell concluded that Leibniz had not one philosophy but two: a bad, public philosophy or "fantastic fairy tale" designed to please and divert his courtly patrons, and a good, private philosophy centred around the nuggets of logic and mathematics which Russell himself so much admired.[7]

In recent decades, reductionistic interpretations such as these have generally been waning; and it is unlikely that any serious scholar now fully embraces Russell's dualistic account of Leibniz's philosophical *oeuvre*. Instead of resorting to *ad hominem* arguments such as these, Leibniz scholars have become increasingly adept at patiently teasing out the consistencies underlying apparently diverse formulations or interpreting genuine inconsistencies as part of a gradual process of philosophical exploration and development. A man like Leibniz, supremely capable of seeing the harmonies underlying seeming antitheses, was equally capable of presenting his single, coherent position in apparently incompatible ways; and a man pursuing practical as well as theoretical objectives often had good grounds for displaying the very different facets of his single, coherent position to correspondents from opposing theological, philosophical, or political camps.[8] The key to interpreting even Leibniz's clearly philosophical texts consistently, in other words, is often to be found in his nonphilosophical commitments, in his broader intellectual projects, or in the political and confessional contexts in which individual texts were written and intended to be read. There were unquestionably many different faces to Leibniz's philosophy, and an intensely private as well as an engagingly public side to his intellectual life; but the difference between the two is more like the two sides of a coin than a Janus face with sincere private and false public philosophies.

Through returning texts to their intellectual and historical contexts, in short, considerable progress has been made in recent decades in dispelling misconceptions, in redressing imbalances, and in working out the many ways in which the various aspects of Leibniz's thought fit and in fact evolved together. Against the backdrop of this work, the full unity of Leibniz's seemingly heterogeneous activities has begun to become apparent for the first time. Born two years before the end of the Thirty Years War, Leibniz was a man of synthesis and reconciliation. He was deeply convinced of the unity of knowledge and of the universality of truth to be discovered through ongoing intellectual exchange and conversation as well as excavated from millennia of human thought. At the same time, he was a 'blue-sky' thinker, ready to depart from common notions in order to develop striking new insights in an amazing variety of fields. The problem at hand, whether philosophical, mathematical, scientific, or practical, was for him always part of an all-encompassing, systematic plan of development of the whole encyclopaedia of the sciences, to be pursued as a collaborative enterprise publicly supported by an enlightened ruler. His final aim was the improvement of the human condition and thereby the celebration of the glory of God in His creation. Even the most theoretical reflections on logic, mathematics, metaphysics, physics, ethics, and theology were therefore, ultimately, *ad usum vitae* (in the service of life) and aimed at the happiness of humankind. In Leibniz's striking motto for the Society of Sciences of Berlin, his regulative ideal was to wed *Theoria cum Praxi*. Indeed, for all the heights of his logical, mathematical, and metaphysical thinking, Leibniz kept his feet sufficiently firmly on the ground to understand that political stability, health, and social security contributed more to the happiness of human beings than many elevated meditations. Leibniz was a man who, more than anything else, wanted to *do* certain things. If he perceived that some of his most striking philosophical views would have bred disagreement and misunderstanding rather than contributing to his main objectives, he preferred to keep them to himself.

Despite the potentially confusing kaleidoscope of his theoretical and practical activities, the breadth, length, and depth of Leibniz's intellectual life converged in a master project which unified most of his apparently miscellaneous endeavours and therefore provides a key to distilling from his innumerable and wide-ranging fragments a central objective consistently if episodically pursued. Throughout his life Leibniz nursed essentially the same dream: the dream of recalling the multiplicity of human knowledge to a logical, metaphysical, and pedagogical unity, centred on the theistic vision of the Christian tradition and aimed at the common good. This project was formulated in a series of texts which outlined his comprehensive plan to reform and improve the whole encyclopaedia of the sciences. In his youth this project was conceived as the plan of the *Demonstrationes Catholicae* ("Catholic Demonstrations"); later it was reformulated as a *Scientia Generalis* ("General Science"), to be expounded in a "demonstrative" encyclopaedia; and finally, in his very last years, it was restated as the *Éléments de la philosophie générale et de la théologie naturelle* ("Elements of General Philosophy and Natural Theology").[9] If read in the light of Leibniz's all-embracing plan, many of the fragments and drafts of his Nachlaß take on a surprisingly coherent shape, and many of his more concrete efforts at political engagement or institutional reform can also be related to a cluster of core principles and objectives.

Despite increased awareness of the unity underlying Leibniz's wide-ranging thought, a general synthetic statement has been lacking. Studies of the highest quality have appeared in recent years dealing with important aspects of the big picture. Some have treated important themes of Leibniz's thought systematically, placing key philosophical convictions in their broader intellectual context. Others have traced the development of individual aspects of Leibniz's thought over a considerable portion of his lifetime. Others have dwelt extensively – even exhaustively – with the full range of Leibniz's activities during particular periods: his youth in Saxony, for instance; his years in Paris; or his trip to Italy. In other crucial thematic areas, invaluable works and collections of edited documents have appeared. Yet a truly synoptic work surveying in some detail Leibniz's life and thought in the light of recent research is wanting. The classic biography remains that of Gottschalk Eduard Guhrauer, published in Breslau in 1842.[10] The most important life to appear in the last century was the briefer work of the mathematician E. J. Aiton, which supplemented Guhrauer chiefly on the scientific and mathematical aspects of Leibniz's thought.[11] The recent lively narration of Leibniz's life by Eike Christian Hirsch, written in a popular style for the general public, should also be mentioned.[12] Given the difficulties which have confounded biographers since Fontenelle, it is perhaps not difficult to understand why the field is not awash with scholarly biographies of Leibniz; but as perspectives have broadened and deepened, the need for a fresh synopsis has grown irresistible.

Equally apparent is the need to attempt this intellectual reunification in narrative fashion. Common sense alone suggests the need for a narrative approach. If the exceptionally various domains of Leibniz's thought were interconnected in a coherent synthesis, it stands to reason that this immense system did not come into being in an instant but must have evolved from a few basic intuitions, assumptions, or aspirations over a considerable period of time. The experience of reading Leibniz's mature texts also confirms this need. Even mature presentations of Leibniz's metaphysics such as the *Monadology* often appear bewildering, not simply because they lack the full apparatus of supporting argumentation, but also because that argumentation is intertwined with a pattern of intellectual development ranging over several decades and many disciplines. His conclusions often become far more intelligible – and his results appear far more powerful – when viewed as the outcome of a long process of intellectual evolution. Historical investigation has also demonstrated the indispensable need for a genetic approach. Since Willy Kabitz at least, specialists have been aware that many of Leibniz's most fundamental philosophical commitments were established remarkably early.[13] But if a narrative account is indispensable, this narrative cannot be restricted to philosophy. The problems which Leibniz attempted to solve ranged far beyond the realm of philosophy – even the broadly defined philosophy of the seventeenth century – to embrace the entire encyclopaedia of the arts and sciences. Indeed, they spread beyond theoretical considerations to embrace practical concerns as well, including politics, ethics, law, medicine, practical, social and institutional reform, and technological innovation. Just as a comprehensive presentation of Leibniz's thought requires a narrative dimension, that narrative must expand from philosophy to embrace his whole world.

Here we encounter one further difficulty; for Leibniz inhabited a complex and unfamiliar entity – the now vanished world of the Holy Roman Empire of the German nation – and that entity exercised a profound influence over every stage of his life and every aspect of his work. The problems of ecclesiastical, political, and cultural fragmentation, particularly acute in central Europe, had exercised several generations of central European intellectuals before Leibniz, and these figures provided some of the earliest and most enduring influences on his all-embracing synthetic project. It was these early aspirations which filtered the influences he later received and which provided the intellectual context which unified his seemingly miscellaneous endeavours. It was likewise these fundamental aspirations and unifying projects which so sharply distinguished Leibniz from his most celebrated western European contemporaries and which explain the broad shape of his reception: the incredulity of contemporary Englishmen to his ideas, the ridicule of a later generation of Frenchmen, and his great influence within eighteenth-century central Europe and Scandinavia. Last but by no means least, the concrete circumstances of Leibniz's Germany also provide the key to understanding his extensive nonphilosophical interests and activities in politics, diplomacy, institutional reform, and ecclesiastical reunification, as well as the means for understanding the coherence of these activities with his more narrowly philosophical concerns. Returning Leibniz to his central European context thus provides the opportunity to portray him, not as a 'modern' Western intellectual unaccountably marooned in the politically and intellectually 'backward' petty states of central Europe, but as a distinctively central European variant of early modern thought which in fact draws upon a long and fruitful if largely neglected tradition. Many of the keys to the unity of Leibniz's life and thought are therefore to be found in the relatively uncelebrated places where few have thought to look for them: not merely or even primarily in Paris, London, and The Hague, but in Leipzig, Altdorf, and Nuremberg; in Herborn, Helmstedt, and Wolfenbüttel; and more obviously in Mainz, Hanover, Vienna, and Berlin – a further challenge, if any were needed, to decipher Leibniz's Nachlaß.

Stated in properly Leibnizian terms, the riddle first confronted by Fontenelle is how to reduce the multiplicity of Leibniz's activities to a biographical unity. Applying the approach to this problem outlined above is intended to produce an intellectual biography unified by four basic, underlying theses. The first of these theses is that Leibniz's life and work need to be assessed as a whole. In contrast to the tendency to characterise his philosophy exclusively in terms of his logic or metaphysics, or his thought exclusively in terms of his philosophy, or his life exclusively in terms of his thought, this thesis argues that a full appreciation of Leibniz must embrace his life and work, his theoretical reflections and his practical activities. Hence the need for a comprehensive account.

A second, related thesis is that this whole is a remarkably unified one. This thesis confronts the tendency to see Leibniz's practical affairs as a tragic distraction from his philosophical investigations, or to judge some of his intellectual projects retrospectively as more precious than others. Instead, this thesis assumes for heuristic purposes that Leibniz's life was rather like his thought: that his intellectual and practical affairs were unified by a small number of basic principles or objectives, and that everything was connected with everything else. Stated more prosaically, this thesis assumes that the last universal genius was no fool, that Leibniz was not a bad judge of which options, amongst those actually available to him, were most likely to advance his central projects, and that all of his major undertakings have something important to tell us about his major objectives. Hence the need for an account which is reasonably systematic as well as comprehensive.

The third thesis is that the most basic of these unifying principles and aspirations were established remarkably early and that the outlines of Leibniz's life and thought emerged organically from them. Although by no means discounting the importance of his mature philosophy, this approach emphasizes that the seeds of that philosophy were planted in his youth. In a manner reminiscent of his monads, it almost seems as if the most basic features of Leibniz's intellectual system were implicit from the beginning. At the same time, since his theoretical projects were ultimately dedicated to practical objectives, he did not resist – indeed he positively pursued – involvement in the world of practical affairs. And while new developments refashioned and changing circumstances reshaped the means in which he sought to obtain his objectives, Leibniz preserved and pursued his original vision with remarkable tenacity. Hence the need for a narrative account.

Finally, these distinctive commitments were established so early and preserved so tenaciously because they were not created *ex nihilo* but were deeply rooted in the environment of his native country. Against those tempted to portray Leibniz as a progressive westerner stranded in an intellectual backwater, this thesis argues that Leibniz was in essence a German philosopher – or, far more precisely and adequately, a philosopher of the Holy Roman Empire. Although the territorial and confessional fragmentation of his homeland ultimately deprived him of the resources needed to realise many of his audacious aspirations, it was precisely those

fragmented conditions which had generated and sustained those aspirations in the first place; and it was these aspirations which sharply distinguished Leibniz from most of his western European intellectual contemporaries. Hence the need for an exposition set as firmly as possible in
its concrete historical context.

None of these four theses is entirely novel, of course. The second
and third in particular have been implicit or explicit in a good deal of
the best recent Leibniz literature. But the only way to bring them all
together and to develop them extensively is in a single large book which is
reasonably comprehensive, systematic, narrative, and historically contextualised. The general purpose of this book, then, is to stitch back together
the man dismembered by Fontenelle and his successors by emphasizing
the organic development of a generally harmonious system of thought
and action within a particular historical context. In doing so it also seeks
to capture some of the key intellectual features of seventeenth- and early
eighteenth-century Europe which were both emblematically represented
and dramatically transcended by Leibniz himself. By mediating complex
ideas through the vehicle of a biographical narrative, it aims to illustrate
how thought can only be understood fully in the context of a life, as a life
can only be understood fully in the context of its time and space.

This general strategy still leaves the more prosaic problem of how to
deal with Leibniz's lifelong ability to pursue several distinct lines of intellectual investigation simultaneously. A purely chronological method of
organisation is obviously unworkable. A detailed chronology of Leibniz's
life and work in fact already exists in the invaluable *Leben und Werk von
Gottfried Wilhelm Leibniz*, published in 1969 by Kurt Müller and Gisela
Krönert; but this is a "Nachschlagewerk" ("reference work"), conceived
not as a biography but as a "point of departure for a scholarly biography"
of Leibniz, "which has long been wanting".[14] If there were any doubt
about the seriousness of the problem originally confronted by Fontenelle,
this *Chronik* displays it *in extenso*: on every page we see "the almost perpetual jumble" of "different matters," the "abrupt and frequent transitions
from one subject to another completely opposite subject," which render
any strictly chronological narrative of Leibniz's life and thought almost
unintelligible and entirely unreadable.

In order to recast Leibniz's life in a form intelligible to those of us who
are not universal geniuses, chronological science must, therefore, yield
to narrative art. While the series of chapters which follows is arranged

chronologically, within that framework concrete and abstract developments are woven together in a variety of ways. Generally speaking, each chapter (with the exception of the first) begins by setting the scene with a brief overview of the period in question. There then follows a considered account of the concrete circumstances of this phase of Leibniz's career and their impact on aspects of his intellectual work. This typically gives way in turn to an account of other features of his intellectual development within that context, broken down further in places in order to keep the multiple strands of narrative moving forward. Within these accounts care has been taken not to dwell long on the exposition of well-known texts and doctrines: there is already a large and admirable literature to which the reader can turn for illumination on these matters. While no mechanical principle of exposition could apply to all the challenges encountered along the way, the result is an approach which subordinates systematic exposition to the narrative of intellectual development and places that development firmly within its evolving local, imperial, European, and occasionally even global contexts.

The resulting intellectual biography is divided into two unequal parts. The opening section deals with the first thirty years of Leibniz's life, when he was relatively free of professional responsibility and even parental oversight to range at will, physically and intellectually, and thereby to develop in his youth the visions, aspirations, and great projects which he would pursue for the rest of his life. To an astonishing extent, these aspirations can be traced back to his earliest youth in the unpromising circumstances of provincial Leipzig, where access to his deceased father's professorial library provided the precocious young boy with the means to reap extraordinary fruit from an otherwise conventional formal education. Travels to Jena and Altdorf during his university studies and especially to the Catholic court of Mainz thereafter broadened and consolidated the theological, philosophical, jurisprudential, and political dimensions of this vision. Precious further years in the intellectual capitals of Paris and London were dedicated above all to acquiring the latest sophisticated mathematical and philosophical tools needed to execute his ambitious plans.

At the end of this period Leibniz was forced reluctantly to abandon his dream of settling permanently in Paris; and the second main phase of his life, covering his final four decades, saw a clash between dreams and reality, with him struggling to fulfil his youthful aspirations from an inadequate base as court counsellor in the provincial capital of Hanover. Physically this struggle manifested itself as the tension between his desire to range freely throughout the contemporary *république des lettres* and his employers' increasingly inflexible demand that he remain accessible and accountable at his desk in Hanover. Intellectually it was mirrored no less clearly in the tension between his incessant desire to push forward his ambitious intellectual plans and his employers' equally intransigent insistence that he serve the narrower interests of the Braunschweig-Lüneburg dynasty. Far from fickle, Leibniz responded to these difficulties with imagination and determination. Throughout his travels he sought the means for collectively pursuing his aims by courting powerful patrons, whether in Hanover itself, in neighbouring principalities, in the imperial capital, or outside the empire in leading cultural and political centres to the east, south, and west. Back in Hanover, he persistently bent his official duties into means of pursuing his personal aspirations: legal consultations, diplomatic negotiations, political pamphleteering, technical innovation, and historical research were all transformed into means of pursuing one component or another of his longstanding plans. Whether at home or abroad, in the courts of Europe or the mines of the Harz, Leibniz also continued privately to articulate the theoretical dimension of his programme through striking new conceptions in logic, metaphysics, mathematics, physics, theology, law, and ethics and to communicate glimpses of his system to innumerable correspondents spread across Europe and beyond it. Within such a complex story, tragic and comic narratives inevitably intertwine: on the one hand circumstantial difficulties at every level, disagreements with employers, disputes with rivals, inevitable and avoidable distractions, flawed working methods, and the relentless pursuit of unrealisable aspirations; on the other the steady stream of stunning results generated despite these difficulties, and the unquenchable optimism and good humour of the main protagonist himself. In the end Leibniz was dragged back from Vienna (where he sojourned for a protracted period during his last years) to Hanover only to discover that the bulk of the court had abandoned the city for London; and he died two years later with his official project, the Guelf history, still incomplete and his private programme only partially developed in tens of thousands of fragments of his unpublished papers. Yet whether or not his world had progressed in the direction he had wished, Leibniz himself remained unflinchingly convinced until the end that he lived in the best of all possible worlds, created by the supreme wisdom and goodness of God, and progressing towards a better state of things in the future.

The resulting portrait of Leibniz is deliberately unrepresentative of him in one important respect. Leibniz spent decades expanding a brief history of the Guelf dynasty into an enormous series of historical annals, prefaced by two extensive treatises and buttressed by a thousand pages of historical documents. Given the volume, intrinsic interest, and intricacy of this historical work and all the other material left at his death, any diligent biographer could easily devote a lifetime to researching Leibniz's life and then leave a mammoth draft incomplete. As tempting as it might be to imitate Leibniz in this respect, my objective has been instead to pull together an account along the lines indicated above within a finite and very clearly demarcated period of time. Needless to say, the impressive, ongoing critical edition of Leibniz's works and correspondence provided an inexhaustible mine of material, supplemented by the great wealth of major or minor editions and translations and the vast riches still held by the Leibniz-Archiv. Until the massive project of the critical edition is finished, of course, no biography of Leibniz can possibly claim to be definitive. Until the historical imbalances of the Leibniz literature have also been in some measure corrected and more attention directed to the immense nonphilosophical aspects of his life and thought, no one work will be able to provide a fully rounded picture. But it is most unlikely, in any case, that work on Leibniz will ever reach the point beyond which no further improvement is possible. A far more pleasing prospect is to regard the world of Leibniz studies, like Leibniz's best of all possible worlds, as in a state of unending progress towards better things. In this case, the most any one book can aspire to is to inch it a bit further along its rightful path.

Notes

1. Bernard Le Bovier de Fontenelle, "Éloge de M. Leibnitz." In *Histoire de l'Académie Royale des Sciences. Année 1716.* Paris: Impr. Royale, 1718, pp. 94–128. Also in Dutens I, xix–liii (here p. xx). Trans. by R. Ariew in "G. W. Leibniz, Life and Works." In *The Cambridge Companion to Leibniz.* Ed. by Nicholas Jolley. New York and Cambridge: Cambridge University Press, 1995, p. 19.
2. Leibniz to Vincentius Placcius, March 1696 (Dutens VI, 65).
3. For the ms. archive, see Eduard Bodemann, *Der Briefwechsel des Gottfried Wilhelm Leibniz der Königlichen öffentlichen Bibliothek zu Hannover.* Hanover, 1889; repr. Hildesheim: Olms, 1966 and Eduard Bodemann, *Die Leibniz-Handschriften der*

Königlichen öffentlichen Bibliothek zu Hannover. Hanover, 1895; repr. Hildesheim: Olms, 1966. The titles of the eight series which compose the critical edition of Leibniz's writings and correspondence are listed in the Abbreviations.

4. For the complex printing history see Émile Ravier, *Bibliographie des œuvres de Leibniz*. Paris: F. Alcan, 1937; repr. Hildesheim: Olms, 1966; supplemented by Paul Schrecker, "Une bibliographie de Leibniz." *Revue philosophique de la France et de l'étranger* 126 (1938): 324–46.

5. Albert Heinekamp, ed., *Leibniz-Bibliographie. Die Literatur über Leibniz bis 1980*. Frankfurt am Main: Vittorio Klostermann, 1984.

6. For more recent literature see Albert Heinekamp, ed., *Leibniz-Bibliographie. Die Literatur über Leibniz 1981–1990*. Frankfurt am Main: Vittorio Klostermann, 1996; and the on-going bibliography at http://www.leibniz-bibliographie.de.

7. See Bertrand Russell, *A Critical Exposition of the Philosophy of Leibniz*. 2nd ed. London: G. Allen & Unwin, 1937, pp. vi, xiii–xiv.

8. See Donald Rutherford, "Demonstration and Reconciliation: The Eclipse of the Geometrical Method in Leibniz's Philosophy." In *Leibniz's 'New System' (1695)*. Ed. by Roger S. Woolhouse. Florence: Olschki, 1996, pp. 181–201.

9. See Heinrich Schepers's entry on Leibniz in the *Neue Deutsche Biographie*, vol. 14, p. 125 and his "Einleitung" to A VI, 4 (esp. pp. xlvii, liii, lxxxi). On the relation between the *Demonstrationes Catholicae* and the *scientia generalis* see chap. II. 4.

10. Gottschalk Eduard Guhrauer, *Gottfried Wilhelm Freiherr von Leibnitz. Eine Biographie*. 2 vols. Breslau: Hirt, 1842. 2nd enlarged ed. Breslau: Hirt, 1846; repr. Hildesheim: Olms, 1966.

11. E. J. Aiton, *Leibniz: A Biography*. Bristol and Boston: Adam Hilger, 1985.

12. Eike Christian Hirsch, *Der berühmte Herr Leibniz: Eine Biographie*. Munich: Beck, 2000 (cf. p. 627).

13. Willy Kabitz, *Die Philosophie des jungen Leibniz. Untersuchungen zur Entwicklungsgeschichte seines Systems*. Heidelberg: Carl Winter's Universitätsbuchhandlung, 1909.

14. Kurt Müller and Gisela Krönert, *Leben und Werk von G. W. Leibniz. Eine Chronik*. Frankfurt am Main: Vittorio Klostermann, 1969, p. ix (the final phrase is taken from the slipcover).

PART I

Youthful Vocations (1646–1676)

The Birth of a Vision: Background, Childhood, and Education (July 1646 – February 1667)

War and Peace: Problems and Prospects

W HEN GOTTFRIED Wilhelm Leibniz was born in Leipzig on the first day of July 1646, representatives of the princes of Germany and the great powers of Europe had already been meeting for three years in Münster and Osnabrück, three hundred kilometres to the west, where they would continue to negotiate for another two years and more.[1] The purpose of these protracted negotiations was to bring to an end an even more protracted war: a war which raged for thirty years, the most destructive conflict of an era plagued by virtually incessant warfare. The product of these negotiations was the Peace of Westphalia, perhaps the most important treaty signed in the early modern period. But the difficulties which had prolonged first the war and then the peace negotiations lay several layers deep; the deeper strata lay well below the Westphalian diplomats' immediate concerns or responsibilities; and the solutions to the more superficial problems which they hammered out in Münster and Osnabrück in any case brought further problems in their wake. The provisions of the treaty would structure the political life of the Holy Roman Empire until the Empire itself was swept away by the armies of Napoleon a century and a half later. Small wonder then that the terms of the peace, and the intractable problems which underlay it, would also structure a great deal of the intellectual life of the generation born in Germany as the Thirty Years War came to a close.

The most obvious dimension of these difficulties was political; and the most obvious level of political difficulties was the imperial one.[2] The Thirty Years War (1618–48) originated as an internal revolt and was fought out for the most part within the Holy Roman Empire. Over the following three decades this conflict involved in one way or another virtually all of the hundreds of imperial estates which made up the Empire; and because they had all played a part in the war, they all had a stake in the peace. Beyond this myriad of particular claims and counter claims, moreover, the domestic level of the war and of the peace negotiations revolved around one overriding issue: the question of what balance of power was to be struck between the unifying authority of the imperial institutions, most particularly the emperor himself, and the centrifugal forces of the individual principalities. The Habsburgs' determination to impose their authority on the largest territory in the Empire – the still nominally elective kingdom of Bohemia – had helped precipitate the conflict in 1618; and the emperor's attempt in the Edict of Restitution of 1629 to impose something like monarchical authority over the Empire as a whole had provoked the most unstable period of the entire conflict, ushered in by the dramatic Swedish invasion of the Empire in 1631, which permanently internationalised and greatly protracted the war. In arrangements finalised in 1648, the balance of power within the Reich tilted decisively against the emperor and in favour of the larger principalities. Monarchical authority was consolidated, in effect, at the territorial rather than the imperial level. Not only was the princes' liberty of religion confirmed and extended; they also gained unprecedented control over their territories' domestic and even foreign politics. The emperor's power, by contrast, now rested primarily not on the imperial office or its resources but on the Habsburg dynasty's hereditary lands in the southeast corner of the Empire, now enhanced by permanent accession to the Bohemian crown and, towards the end of the century, by the reconquest of the huge kingdom of Hungary as well, outside the boundaries of the Empire itself. From 1648 onward, in short, the Empire was definitively set on a *Sonderweg*, a more or less federal course of political development very different from the increasingly centralised and absolutist monarchies typified *par excellence* by contemporary France under the 'Sun King', Louis XIV (1638–1715). The divergence of political models gave an even greater urgency to the crucial practical question already raised in the final phases of the war: namely, whether such a loosely integrated entity as the Empire could defend itself effectively against far more unified neighbours. And to this practical challenge was joined a theoretical one for the next generation of German intellectuals: to develop a conception of the Empire, not as an antiquated, dilapidated entity resulting from a political accident, but as the embodiment of a European ideal which could and should be reformed, consolidated, and valiantly defended philosophically, politically, and militarily against narrow dynastic interest, resurgent confessionalism, and rampant militarism both within and outside it.

The reason for these urgent practical and theoretical questions was straightforward. On the battlefield, the individual German princes were outgunned by the European monarchs; at the negotiating table, the representatives of the German princelings were outranked by those of the crowned heads of Europe; and as a direct consequence of this further imbalance, the war which had begun in 1618 as a domestic dispute had rapidly escalated into an international affair intersecting with longstanding struggles on all sides.[3] The Austrian Habsburgs, with relatively few resources and military experience of their own at the start of the war, immediately called upon their cousins in Spain – the most belligerent nation in Europe during the previous century – for assistance in the Rhineland. From the outset, therefore, the conflict in central Europe was linked in various ways with the eighty-year-long Dutch revolt from Spanish rule in the northwest corner of the continent. Denmark, threatened by the arrival of the second stage of the conflict within its sphere of influence in the Protestant north, was lured into an ill-conceived and ultimately disastrous intervention in 1625. Sweden, worried by the prospect of Habsburg hegemony extending as far north as the Baltic, entered the war with far greater success in 1631, thereby linking the war in the Empire with the Northern Wars taking place to its northeast. The rulers of England, Scotland, and Ireland attempted to remain neutral, but the Stuart dynasty was directly involved in the fray from the outset: Elisabeth Stuart, daughter of James VI and I and sister of Charles I, had married the Elector Palatine, Friedrich V, whose election as king of Bohemia in 1619 made him the emperor's principal enemy in the opening phase of the conflict. Defence of the honour of the ancient house of Stuart therefore drew thousands of English and particularly Scottish soldiers and diplomats into the affair, tangentially connecting the civil wars in Germany with those which plagued the British Isles from 1639 onward. France, eager as she had been for a century to frustrate the consolidation of Habsburg power, first subsidised rebels and foreign interlopers financially and then entered directly into the field in 1635, after it appeared that the emperor might pacify the situation on terms favourable to himself. And these principal combatants were supplemented by minor ones: northern Italy, still notionally within the Empire, Poland, directly affected by imperial and Swedish affairs, the

militantly Protestant principality of Transylvania, even the distant colos-
sus of Russia, all played a part in the conflict. What had begun as a civil
war therefore rapidly escalated into an international conflict; and the final
phase of the war proved particularly protracted because the exhausted
and fragmented participants from within the Empire no longer had the
strength to evict the two main foreign combatants, France and Sweden,
from large swaths of imperial territory. All the foreign powers involved
in the war also had to be placated by the peace: Denmark received the
bishoprics of Bremen and Oldenburg for her pains; Sweden the duchy of
Mecklenburg; England gained the return of the Rhineland Palatinate to
the grandson of James VI and I, the son of the 'Winter King and Queen of
Bohemia'; and the Dutch won a formal recognition of their independence
from the Empire. France, on the face of it, appeared to get very little:
just Metz, Toul, and Verdun, three small cities inside the western frontier of the Empire. But this paltry outcome masked a far more important
strategic shift: while the French monarchy consolidated its political and
military strength in the postwar period, the terms of the Peace of Westphalia permanently undermined the capacity of its rivals on the imperial
throne to do the same; and in the decades which followed the war France
would prove all too able to exploit this weakness and use its tiny imperial
possessions as stepping stones in the piecemeal annexation of the left bank
of the Rhine.

As if these political circumstances were not intricate enough, both the
imperial and the international dimensions of the situation were further
complicated by confessional considerations.[4] The issue which ostensibly
provoked the Bohemian revolt in 1618 was religious: the determination
of the kingdom's overwhelmingly Protestant estates to defend their religious liberties against efforts to reimpose Catholicism undertaken by a
new generation of Habsburgs steeled by the new ethos of the Counter
Reformation. The considerations which prompted the Calvinist Palatine elector to accept the Bohemian crown in 1619 were likewise largely
religious: seizing Bohemia from the Habsburgs would decisively tip the
balance of forces within the Empire in favour of his confession. The early
entry of Lutheran Saxony on one side of the conflict, and the later entries
of Lutheran Denmark and Sweden on the other side, were also prompted
by confessional as well as political considerations, as were the diplomatic
and military efforts of the Dutch Republic and Transylvania throughout the war. Even at the outset of the conflict, to be sure, such religious

motives had masked or reinforced political ones; and by its end confessional politics had long since become subordinate to political and military considerations. But religious differences were never forgotten during the war, nor were they fully resolved in the peace. The religious resolutions of the Peace of Westphalia officially recognised the right, provisionally granted in the Peace of Augsburg in 1555, of Lutherans to practice their religion in Lutheran territories and extended similar rights for the first time to Calvinists as well. But while these provisions laid to rest one of the issues which had helped provoke the conflict, they only confirmed a deeper reality established in Germany almost a century earlier: the Empire was now officially divided confessionally into three religious groups. Compounding as it did the Empire's territorial fragmentation, this religious division was an obvious source of weakness which in the past had brought the cumbersome machinery of imperial government grinding to a halt. If such problems were to be avoided in the future, and if the Empire was to compete with confessionally as well as politically unified absolutist states, it would need to reconcile to some degree these differences which had proved so disruptive in the past. Politically the time was ripe to pursue ecclesiastical reconciliation within the Empire. With the existential anxieties of Lutherans and Calvinists substantially laid to rest, Germans of all three confessions had begun to see for the first time that the gravest threat to their material if not spiritual wellbeing lay not with their confessional enemies within the Empire but with their political enemies outside it. The end of the war therefore saw the beginning of the kind of serious efforts at broad-based ecclesiastical reconciliation which Germany had not witnessed for a century. But religious issues, still more than political ones, proved impossible to settle on a national or imperial basis: the fragmentation of the Protestant churches at the territorial level made negotiations at the imperial level difficult, while the universal claims of the Roman church made it even more difficult to prevent such negotiations spilling over onto the international plane.[5]

Moreover, this project of ecclesiastical unification was complicated by a fresh and daunting intellectual challenge. Confessional reconciliation depended to some degree on theological reconciliation; and theological discussions were complicated in this period by the fact that they took place in a period of philosophical revolution. During the generation in which central Europe had been thrown into military and political turmoil, western Europe had begun a period of equally disorientating intellectual upheaval. The limited problem of the competing world systems of Ptolemy, Copernicus, and Tycho Brahe had broadened into a clash of basic approaches to natural philosophy, pitting Galileo, Bacon, Gassendi, and Descartes against the revered authority of Aristotle. In an era still riven by theological controversies, the theological implications of these philosophical developments went far beyond the obvious questions of whether the heliocentric cosmos, the infinite universe, or the mechanical philosophy could be reconciled with traditional Christian doctrine. An even more profound consequence was to undercut the philosophical foundations of the theological controversies themselves. During the previous era, crucial theological controversies had proved irresolvable despite the fact that all the disputing parties shared, with varying degrees of conviction, a reliance on Aristotelian logic, physics, and metaphysics. Now that the very rules of scientific method and the basic principles of philosophy had been thrown into question, the complicated process of resolving theological differences could only become more complicated still. In central Europe, these intellectual developments enormously compounded the difficulties of ecclesiastical reconciliation. How were theological differences to be resolved when philosophical tools, methods, assumptions, and doctrines had all been thrown into doubt? How was a consensus on theological questions to be achieved when even a basic consensus on philosophical questions and intellectual methods had suddenly vanished?

To the cautious, conservative majority, therefore, the intellectual crisis of the mid-seventeenth century only deepened the dangers of Europe's longstanding political and confessional difficulties. The threat of institutional annihilation by immediately obvious, hostile military forces had been replaced by the threat of intellectual extinction by insidious and dimly understood philosophical and theological trends. For an inveterate optimist with extraordinary reserves of intellectual imagination and self-confidence, however, this crisis also represented an opportunity. In a period of profound intellectual flux, new solutions to previously intractable intellectual problems were bound to emerge. As the philosophical substructure of theological controversies was modified or dismantled, perhaps the controversies themselves would finally prove capable of resolution. The most fundamental doctrinal differences, after all, had now all been formulated in a technical, philosophical language which was rapidly being rendered obsolete. The varying understandings of holy communion, for instance – the 'transubstantiation' of the Catholics, the 'real presence' of the Lutherans, and the 'spiritual' communion emphasized by the Reformed[6] – were all formulated in terms derived from Aristotelian metaphysics. The no less intractable problem of free will and divine determination in human salvation – the problem which had split Lutherans from Catholics, Calvinists from Lutherans, and Arminians from Calvinists – was likewise couched largely in terms derived from traditional ethics and psychology. Although the proliferation of philosophical systems greatly complicated these ongoing debates, it also held out fresh hope of resolving them. Perhaps controversies which had proved irresolvable in the traditional language of Aristotelian scholasticism might be resolved in terms derived from one or another of the new philosophies. Perhaps fresh philosophical insight could demonstrate that supposedly opposing points of view could be reconciled, that previous disagreements were based on misunderstandings, that the truths implacably defended by warring camps could in fact be harmonised with one another. Perhaps the language central to the new, mechanical philosophy – the language of mathematics – could even provide the prototype of a new philosophical language capable of resolving disputes of all kinds conclusively. Clearly this project would entail reaping the best fruits of the fertile intellectual traditions which had been developing outside the Empire over the past generation; but it also meant harnessing those traditions to new uses, or rather to old uses, to purposes deeply rooted in the conditions of the Empire. The point was not to pursue philosophy as a purely theoretical exercise, withdrawn from the world in splendid isolation; nor was the intention to use the new philosophies to sweep aside the intellectual rubbish accumulated over the centuries, as Bacon and Descartes had proposed. Rather, if employed as a practical means of bettering the human condition and resolving the national and international, political and confessional problems which plagued the Empire, the certainties which the new science seemed capable of delivering might be used to reform, harmonise, bolster, and defend all that was best in the old theological, ecclesiastical, and political order.

Preoccupied as they were with the political dimension of this problem, it is unlikely that many of the delegates meeting in Münster and Osnabrück spared a thought for these dawning theoretical opportunities. Only a member of the coming generation, further removed from the negotiation table, with more perspective on the traumas of the wartime generation, more familiarity with the intellectual breakthroughs of mid-century, and extraordinary breadth of vision and intellectual confidence would be able to glimpse the fresh potential nascent in this tangle of interrelated problems. But the potential for a fresh assault on all these problems was there. The political problems plaguing Europe and the Empire could be addressed not only on their own level but also by addressing the underlying theoretical and confessional ones. The confessional differences could be resolved not only through political means but by resolving the underlying theological issues. And theological disagreements could be tackled afresh by approaching them with the powerful new logical, physical, metaphysical, and mathematical tools currently being forged by Europe's most creative and disciplined philosophical minds. No one person could hope to carry this whole agenda forward alone. Indeed, only an *Universalgelehrter*, a man of deep intellectual insight and comprehensive intellectual competence, could hope even to coordinate the enormous collective efforts which would be needed to address all the dimensions of this daunting campaign. But some of the resources needed to confront these problems had already been assembled by others. While the soldiers had been fighting and the diplomats negotiating, several schools of central European thought had been addressing the various dimensions of this central European dilemma. The postwar generation confronting this thicket of inter-related problems would therefore not need to begin entirely *de novo*. Their challenge was rather to use the intellectual traditions well established in various quarters of the Empire, updated by recourse to the latest intellectual developments imported from western Europe, to address problems central to seventeenth-century Europe as a whole and nowhere more acute than in its politically fragmented centre. In cities scattered across the Empire – and indeed in places far outside it to which refugees from the great war had been displaced – central European thinkers had been developing related lines of thought for some time. The chief paradox of Leibniz's earliest years is that Leipzig was not among them.

Leibniz's Family and Leipzig's Religion

The conservatism of Leibniz's birthplace is, ironically, very largely a product of the fact that the principality of which it was part had had a pretty good war. If any German territory can be regarded as a winner at the end of such a bloody and protracted conflict, then one of the winners of the Thirty Years War was Electoral Saxony; and this outcome was the product of pursuing an extremely conservative confessional and political strategy throughout the conflict. Saxony was the birthplace of Luther and Lutheranism. Politically, the dukes of Saxony, as one of only four secular electors in the Empire, were for most of the period since the Reformation the most senior Lutheran princes in the Empire. It was only natural, therefore, that in the decades before the outbreak of war the theologians of Saxony's universities, the clergy of its churches, and above all the court preachers at the electors' residence in Dresden came to see themselves as the most valiant and vigilant defenders of true Evangelical belief and practice.[7] More surprisingly, perhaps, their vigilance was directed not so much against the well-known dangers of Catholicism, which, until recently, had been on the retreat in Germany, as against the creeping spread of what they called 'sacramentarianism', the 'Zwinglian heresy', or simply 'Calvinism', which had infiltrated one princely court after another and from which it had then been forcibly imposed on previously Lutheran subjects. In political as well as confessional terms, the Saxon dukes came to see Calvinism's confessional innovations and the Palatinate's political machinations as endangering the delicate ceasefire between Lutheranism and Catholicism established in the Peace of Augsburg in 1555, which had preserved an increasingly precarious peace in the Empire for generations.[8] When the Palatine elector Friedrich V accepted the offer of the crown of Bohemia in 1619 and entered the Bohemian revolt against the Habsburgs, Saxony had, therefore, thrown in its lot with the Catholic emperor and sought to suppress the leader of the Calvinists in the Empire once and for all.

In the negotiations in Westphalia, this conservative political and religious posture had been richly rewarded. The Habsburgs had lured Saxony onto their side of the conflict at the outset with the offer of the adjacent principality of Lusatia, the smallest of four territories which made up the kingdom of Bohemia; and in 1635 the Peace of Prague ceded both Upper and Lower Lusatia to Saxony, greatly expanding the dominions of the Saxon elector. Such a lavish reward naturally consolidated Saxony's conservative posture, confessional as well as political. The intransigent defence of orthodox Lutheranism so characteristic of Leipzig, Wittenberg, and Jena before the war was therefore scarcely less evident afterwards. The public exercise of Roman Catholicism or the Reformed religion remained strictly forbidden in Saxony and any sign of sympathy towards them was met with the gravest suspicion.[9] In the mid-seventeenth century, theologians at Leipzig's university such as Johannes Hülsemann (1602–61) and Johann Benedikt Carpzov (1607–57) were at the forefront of the fight against Georg Calixt (1586–1656) and his followers at the University of Helmstedt, who sought means of repairing the divisions between Lutheranism and Catholicism.[10] This might seem an unlikely place to produce one of the most broadminded ecumenists of his day, especially since Leibniz's own family was deeply rooted in the academic world in which this theological orthodoxy was defined and defended.

Leibniz's own belief in the Slavic origin of his family probably overestimated a possible Slavic component in the ancestry of a family rooted in northeastern Germany. There is no firm evidence either of a noble component in Leibniz's lineage or even of his subsequent elevation to the peerage,[11] as would be suggested by the use of the surname 'von Leibniz' in his German correspondence.[12] But the ties linking Leibniz to the academic, legal, and clerical stratum of Leipzig society are manifold. His father, Friedrich Leubnitz or Leibnütz (as he signed himself),[13] was born on 24 November 1597 in Altenberg (Erzgebirge), the son of a civil servant, Ambrosius Leubnitz (1569–1617), and of Anna Deuerlein. In 1617 he enrolled at the University of Leipzig, from which he earned a Master's degree five years later. At the death of his patron, the professor of ethics Johannes Müller, he took his place as actuary of the university, and thus joined other university representatives in the civic delegation which negotiated the surrender of Leipzig in 1633.[14] In 1640 he was appointed to the chair of moral philosophy. As well as serving four times as dean of the faculty, he also acted as university notary. His contemporaries prized him especially for this latter office, which he exercised with "integrity" and "industry". In general he was described as a thorough, virtuous, and conscientious person. From what is known of his activity as a professor of moral philosophy, there emerges the picture of a strongly traditionally oriented Lutheran scholar who based his teaching on the Nicomachean Ethics of Aristotle and saw a struggle between the "Christian philosophy" and the "Diabolic philosophy" led by Apollo (alias Lucifer). The studies conducted in the faculty of philosophy were conceived by him above all as a preparation for the study of theology with the final aim of serving the *respublica Christiana*.[15]

Friedrich married three times, knitting his family still further into Leipzig's academic, clerical, and juridical networks in the process. By his first wife, Anna Fritzsche (d. 1634), he had two children: Anna Rosine (1629–66), who married a doctor of theology and later ecclesiastical superintendent, Heinrich Freiesleben of Altenburg; and Johann Friedrich (1632–96), who studied theology before settling down as a teacher at the Thomasschule in Leipzig. Two years after the death of his first wife, Friedrich Leubnitz married Dorothea Voigt, the daughter of a Leipzig publisher and bookseller, who died childless in 1643. On 21 May 1644 a third marriage joined him with Catharina (1621–64), the daughter of the prominent Leipzig jurist and law professor Wilhelm Schmuck (1575–1634). After the death of her mother, Gertraude Lindner, in 1631 and of her father in 1634, Catharina Schmuck had first joined the household of the theology professor Johannes Höpner, and then that of her guardian, the law professor Quirinius Schacher, extending her familial relations still further.

Two years after marrying Friedrich Leubnitz, Catharina gave birth to her first child on 1 July 1646. As the nearly fifty year-old father recorded the event in a now lost family chronicle, "on Sunday 21 June 1646 [O.S.] my son Gottfried Wilhelm was born at 6.45 p.m." The baby's baptism two days later by deacon M. Daniel Moller in the Church of St Nikolai assembled yet further Leipzig churchmen and academics: his godparents were the theologian, court chaplain, and university professor of Hebrew Martin Geier, the jurist Johann Fritsch, and Catharina Scherl. No less evident on this occasion was the fervent public piety characteristic of these circles: the family chronicle reported that, at the moment of baptism, the new-born child raised his head with wide open eyes, and Leibniz's father triumphantly regarded this suggestive episode as a clear sign of the infant's exceptional future contribution to the glory of God and the advancement of the church. Precisely the same attitude is displayed in another anecdote reported by Leibniz himself: having witnessed his lively toddler falling badly from a table and emerging smiling and completely unhurt, Friedrich regarded this narrow escape from danger both as a special sign of God's grace and as a premonition of great things to come. So frequent did the father's prognostications of his son's future greatness become, in fact, that his friends soon began to poke fun at these great expectations.[16] Sadly, Friedrich Leubnitz did not live long enough to see his parental hopes vindicated: he died on 15 September 1652, leaving the six-year-old Gottfried Wilhelm and his younger sister Anna Catharina (1648–72) in the care of their mother.

Little is known about Catharina Schmuck, and next to nothing by the hand of her son. She seems to have been a woman of some determination and independence, who did not remarry but devoted herself instead to raising her two children. Her ability to maintain primary responsibility for them without entering into a new marriage was a sign of at least moderate economic affluence, based in part on the estate left by her father. On the other hand, since the city of Leipzig did not generally permit women to exercise wardship, there must have been an officially nominated guardian for whom the widow had to produce an annual financial report – possibly Heinrich Freiesleben, the husband of Leibniz's much older half-sister, Anna Rosine. At any rate, a relative of Heinrich Freiesleben, Christian Freiesleben, served as administrator of Catharina's paternal inheritance until his death in 1680.[17]

Leibniz's mother died on 16 February 1664 of a respiratory infection.[18] The trait of her personality which emerges most forcefully from her funeral sermon was her unyielding devotion and religiosity.[19] This, of course, is precisely what one would expect to hear at the funeral of the daughter, wife, and step-mother of leading Leipzig professors and clergymen; yet all the other available evidence corroborates the impression that the young Gottfried Wilhelm grew up surrounded by committed Lutherans, many of whom passionately opposed the contamination of orthodoxy by any contact or compromise with other confessions. On 22 January 1672, while Leibniz was employed at the Catholic court of Mainz, his younger sister, Anna Catharina, wrote to express her concern at the rumours circulating in Leipzig that he had converted to Calvinism – something even worse for strict Lutherans than conversion to Catholicism. Her fervent exortation to her brother to return to Leipzig left no doubt as to the dangers she saw in such a change of confession.[20] Her husband, the Leipzig theologian Simon Löffler (1627–74), would probably have used still stronger language, given his uncompromising commitment to the preservation of the purity of the Lutheran doctrine against "Papists" and, even more, Calvinists: in his view, whatever did not agree with the Lutheran orthodoxy was of evil origin and therefore anathema.[21] As for the more numerous letters over thirty years from Leibniz's half-brother, Johann Friedrich, the image they convey is of a strict Lutheran who regarded the ways of the wider world with suspicion, who interpreted the plague which struck Leipzig in 1680 as divine punishment,[22] and who rejected efforts at Protestant reconciliation as a dangerous syncretism

designed to seduce Lutherans from the true faith into Calvinism.[23] Even
the weakening of Johann Friedrich's devotion to sterile academic orthodoxy by the advent of German Pietism in the early 1690s did not increase
his breadth of vision: he greeted the intense religiosity of the new movement as a last defence of the true religion against dead intellectual faith
within the official church and the atheism incipient outside it.[24]

Gottfried Wilhelm's attitude towards Lutheranism in particular and
Christianity in general were soon to develop along very different lines.
In 1669, only three years after leaving Leipzig, he responded to his half-
brother's attack on theological syncretism with a vision of religious reconciliation utterly uncharacteristic of what we know of Leibniz's extended
family and of the educated stratum of Leipzig society from which they
came: "I hold and with God's help will continue to hold fast to the Evangelical truth as long as I live, but I am deterred from condemning others
both by my own personal inclination and by the stern command of Christ:
'Judge not, that ye be not judged'." [25] Leibniz promised to remain an
"Evangelical", in other words, not because he believed that the Lutheran
church possessed a monopoly of religious truth, but because he conceived
of it as one part, alongside all the other particular churches, of the truly
universal or catholic church. Having been born in a church whose fundamental tenets he shared, he regarded as unwise to abandon it to embrace
the creed of another Christian confession whose fundamental beliefs he
could have also shared.[26] Far better instead to work toward reconciling all
these particular churches within a reunified universal church. Given this
divergence of views, it is perhaps unsurprising that Leibniz was to have
little interaction with his family or his native city for the rest of his career.

By the time he recorded these views, of course, Leibniz's outlook
had no doubt been modified by two years' exposure to the strong irenical
atmosphere prevailing at the Catholic court of Mainz.[27] It is no less certain,
however, that his sister, his half-brother, his brother-in-law, and most of
the Leipzig intelligentsia with whom they associated and intermarried
would not have responded in a similar way even if they had strayed from
the safety of Leipzig to risk their eternal souls in an extended stay in
one of Germany's most potent archiepiscopal seats. Frustratingly but
perhaps inevitably, no such explicit contemporary testimony survives to
indicate whether these irenical tendencies so characteristic of Leibniz and
so uncharacteristic of Leipzig were established before he left his native
city; nor do we know for certain how they managed to take root. The

memory of death and destruction still fresh in his city might well have impressed upon Leibniz at an early age the necessity of solving simmering political and religious conflicts by dialogue and negotiation rather than fire and sword; but such speculations explain little, since the older generation of Leipzigers responded to a far more vivid experience of the horrors of war by redoubling their efforts to guard the walls of their Lutheran stronghold from any corrupting influence from the confessions outside it against which they had fought. The contrast between Leibniz's only slightly later views and those so clearly manifest in his family and so firmly rooted in his native city is striking enough to raise the crucial questions of when and how and why these personal views developed. No perfectly adequate answers to these questions are available; but the germ of an indirect answer can be found in Leibniz's earliest intellectual development, which also prepared the ground for his intellectual life more generally even before his formal schooling began.

Formal Schooling and Independent Learning

The issue of the origin of Leibniz's strikingly un-Saxon irenicism is bound up with a broader question. In his autobiographical reminiscences, Leibniz described himself as an autodidact.[28] Most of his biographers, keen to establish his intellectual originality and generally unappreciative of the environment in which he grew up, were happy to take him at his word.[29] Recent scholarship has undermined this judgement in two significant respects.[30] First, the readily established fact has been noted that Leibniz attended one of the best preparatory schools in Saxony and the largest university in Germany. Second, historians have begun to uncover fertile currents of philosophical and theological innovation in Germany which nurtured and influenced his earliest intellectual development.

The most nuanced formulation must concede, in good Leibnizian fashion, that all of these views have their justification and that the most accurate assessment results from harmonizing these seemingly divergent theses. In the specific case of his theological irenicism and the more general one of his precocious philosophical development, Leibniz drew on fertile traditions of German thought firmly institutionalised elsewhere; but none of these traditions were deeply established in his family, in his native city, or in the school and university in which he predominantly studied. If Leibniz reaped extraordinary fruit from a fairly ordinary and highly orthodox education, it was because he approached it in an extraordinary, pedagogically unorthodox fashion.

In July 1653, within a few weeks of his seventh birthday, Leibniz entered one of Leipzig's two main Latin schools, the Nikolaischule, where he remained for almost eight years, until Easter 1661. Founded in 1511, the institution was a fairly distinguished example of the preparatory schools which multiplied in the sixteenth century within the larger German Protestant states. Its purpose was not to provide an elementary or intermediate education to a broad cross-section of the population but to prepare a small cohort of male students for future study at the local university.[31] Indeed, the direct link between the school and the university could scarcely have been more apparent: the rector during Leibniz's school years, Johann Hornschuch (1600–1663), simultaneously occupied the chairs of dialectic and Greek at the university; and Leibniz himself, as the son of a (now deceased) former professor at the university, enjoyed the privilege of marking his entrance into school by matriculating simultaneously at the university at the advanced age of seven.[32] The most important consequence of this intimate link with the university, however, was its impact on the syllabus. Rather than providing a well-rounded education useful in its own right, the school's curriculum was strictly propaedeutic and 'trivial': it was designed to prepare students for university by concentrating overwhelmingly on the classical *trivium* – that is, on the first three of the seven liberal arts: grammar, rhetoric, and logic – to the exclusion of virtually everything else aside from the rudiments of Lutheran theology. Formally, the school was divided into six distinct classes, numbered from sixth (lowest) to first (highest), and not necessarily corresponding to a single year of study each. The first three classes were devoted to Latin grammar, studied through texts on a variety of topics. Greek was introduced in the third-highest class, rhetoric in the second, and logic in the first. The exposure to the *quadrivium* (arithmetic, geometry, astronomy, and music) was at best fleeting. Whereas some twenty hours per week were devoted to Latin (by far the most important discipline), the teaching of arithmetic was limited to two hours per week in the last four classes. Whereas teacher and pupils were required to speak Latin within the confines of the school, instruction in such disciplines as ethics, physics, and astronomy was restricted to four hours per week during the final year. In short, the study of the *quadrivium* and of *realia* such as natural philosophy and history was postponed almost entirely to the undergraduate 'arts' or 'philosophy' course at university.[33] The only subject outside the *trivium* given sustained attention was Lutheran theology, a solid grounding in which was prepared by intensive study of Luther's shorter catechism, the widely used *Compendium locorum theologicorum* of the former Wittenberg professor of theology, Leonhard Hutter (1563–1616), and the reading of the Gospels.[34]

Although this basic curriculum had remained essentially unchanged for over a century, some attempts had recently been made to update the manner in which it was delivered. The school's previous rector, Zacharias Schneider (1630–38), was one of the earliest enthusiastic followers of the leading pedagogical thinker of the seventeenth century, the Moravian Jan Amos Comenius (Komenský, 1592–1670), whose inspired textbook for introducing young students to Latin, the *Januae linguarum reseratae aureae vestibulum*, was used in the first and second classes in Leipzig.[35] But once inserted into this conservative setting, this innovation too quickly became restrictive: in an ironic interpretation of Comenius's conviction that the most efficient and effective pedagogy was a highly 'methodical' one, Leibniz's earliest teachers actively discouraged his independent, exploratory, and therefore disorderly approach to learning and attempted to restrict his reading to the formulas and methods of Comenius's work.[36] Although Leibniz was not an autodidact in the strict sense of the term, and although the formal education he received at school and especially university was not without its genuine stimuli, the pace and trajectory of his earliest intellectual development would clearly be established outside formal educational institutions rather than within them.

Even before he arrived in the Nikolaischule, in fact, the young Leibniz's first steps into the world of learning had been guided by his father. Through narrating histories and reading them aloud to his son, Friedrich had instilled in the young boy a love of both sacred and secular history; and he watched with pride and evident expectation as the child precociously learned in this way to read in the vernacular for himself.[37] The death of his father when Gottfried was six years old deprived him of this paternal tutor; but far from ending this pattern of early and informal learning, it deepened it in two significant respects: from now on Leibniz's extracurricular education was still more free of formal supervision than it had been initially; and the loss of his father may even have deepened the boy's passion for the interests which they had shared. From very early on, in any case, Leibniz took enormous pleasure in the study of history and would not put down a German book on the subject until he had finished it.[38] By the time he began formal schooling at the age of seven, the young boy was already more inclined to sit and read than to play.[39] Simple as it may seem, and impervious as it is to further historical investigation, this early independent study foreshadows both the pattern of Leibniz's formal education and the respect for the past which differentiated him so clearly from most of his great philosophical contemporaries. For anyone familiar with the last decades of Leibniz's life, these earliest studies are also freighted with dramatic irony: Leibniz's intellectual life was to end as it had begun, with a book of German history which he was unable to put down until it was finished.

As he began to be drilled in the rudiments of Latin grammar in the Nikolaischule during the following year, further opportunities for unauthorised reading presented themselves, apparently by accident. Academic households in seventeenth-century Germany often supplemented their income by taking student lodgers. Such an expedient may have been inevitable for a widow raising a family without a regular source of income; and this may account for the young Gottfried's discovery at a very early stage in his formal schooling of two volumes of Latin history misplaced by a student in his house. One was the driest reading matter imaginable: the voluminous *Opus Chronologicum* compiled by Sethus Calvisius. Yet the subject matter of this arid compendium was close to Leibniz's heart, and its straightforward grammar provided the perfect stepping stone for moving from German to Latin historical literature. The second book was an illustrated edition of Livy's Roman history. Here the treatment was far more detailed and the classical prose far more intricate; but the pictures fired his imagination and provided clues to the content; and working from one clue to another while applying the grammar learned in his formal schooling, he gradually built up a clear understanding of the book without even the aid of a dictionary, racing ahead of his classmates in his command of Latin as a result.[40]

Far from being delighted, Leibniz's teacher warned that this "unseasonable and precipitate" reading would throw the young boy's education into confusion; and they therefore sought to return his attention exclusively to the set texts. But at this juncture the situation was transformed – and Leibniz's intellectual world was radically expanded – by the intervention of a figure from beyond the Leipzig academic world. Struck by the exceptional intellectual gifts of the boy, a learned and widely travelled nobleman of the neighbourhood managed to persuade his family to allow him access to his father's library which, in accordance with the advice of his teachers, had been kept locked since its owner's death two years before. For the delighted eight-year-old, this was like discovering a treasure trove hidden in his own house,[41] and small wonder, for in his father's library he entered the arena in which Leipzig had the greatest riches to offer. Lacking a princely court, Leipzig was culturally inferior to nearby Dresden, the glittering residence of the Saxon dukes. Remote from major cultural borders and international thoroughfares, the city was also by no means cosmopolitan. But Leipzig was exceptionally well furnished with two things: books and students; and the first of these in particular played a crucial role in establishing Leibniz's basic intellectual orientation.

Situated at the centre of a prosperous region and at the intersection of major medieval trade routes, Leipzig had long hosted one of the Empire's most important semiannual fairs. A century before Leibniz's schooldays, this fair had emerged behind Frankfurt am Main as the second main German centre for trading one of the most important new commodities of the sixteenth century: printed books. Initially Frankfurt's centrality to the Rhineland corridor and proximity to France and the Netherlands gave it decided advantages; but from the Swedish invasion of 1631 to the French occupations of the region at the end of the war, Frankfurt proved woefully central to the military traffic of the period as well; and around the time of Leibniz's youth Leipzig seized the dominant position within the German book-trade. Such commercial centrality did not immediately transform the city into a hotbed of intellectual innovation; but it did flood the environment of the young Leibniz with books, and by all accounts these became his principal teachers.[42]

Both the commercial and the academic dimension of Leipzig's book culture were reflected in the collections unlocked for the eight-year-old to explore. The core of the library was assembled by Leibniz's father, a professor, as noted above, of moral philosophy. Alongside these philosophical collections, the library included a second set of predominantly legal books inherited from Leibniz's mother's father, the jurist Wilhelm Schmuck. Still more intriguing may have been a third component: the mass of unbound material deriving from the father of Friedrich Leubnitz's second wife, the bookseller and publisher, Bartholomäus Voigt.[43] This was material directly linked with the Leipzig book-trade, not purchased for personal, professional, or domestic use but for resale to buyers from across

Germany and beyond; and it may therefore have been more various and up-to-date even than his father's collection. What is certain is that this collection as a whole included authors doctrinally at variance with strict Lutheranism, who would certainly not have been recommended reading for an impressionable Leipzig schoolboy.

The contrast between the strictly controlled 'method' of Leibniz's formal schooling and the chaotic freedom of his informal learning could scarcely have been more striking. At school he was drilled for hours in textbook fashion on a tiny canon of established authorities in a restrictive elementary curriculum. At home he spent entire days wandering freely in the intellectual *terra incognita* of his father's library, exposed to a dizzying variety of teachings on advanced philosophical and theological problems, which he was left to sort out for himself. At first he simply browsed with curiosity through books he could not yet properly read, given his still rudimentary knowledge of Latin. He then instinctively proceeded to apply to the vastly greater domain of his father's library the methods he had recently developed for groping his way through Livy's Rome: first identifying a few basic conceptual landmarks, and then navigating between them to map out a whole new intellectual world. The experience was clearly formative, and Leibniz himself later recognized it as such. In what appears to be an authentic early echo of his father's providentialism, he interpreted the fact that he had gained so much from his unaccompanied wandering through the forest of his father's books in the absence of proper supervision as a sign of divine guidance: it was as if the voice once heard by Augustine had urged him to "Take, read."[44]

Leibniz's recollection of the order in which he explored this treasure trove of books and authors, on the other hand, is in all likelihood the product of a retrospective reconstruction of his early intellectual awakening. First of all, he later maintained, his interest was captured by "the Ancients": the greatest of the writers of classical Greece and Rome, together with the Latin and Greek Fathers of the early church.[45] Thereafter, during his final years in school, he began devouring works of scholastic philosophy and theology: the final fruits of Renaissance Aristotelianism and Spanish scholasticism on the one hand, and the burgeoning literature of the European reformations on the other. Finally, upon leaving school around the age of fifteen, he "fell upon the moderns"[46] and read the work of the "great men" of recent times. For someone supposedly groping his way unguided around his father's library, there is something

suspiciously programmatic about this recollection: revisiting first antiquity and its revival in the renaissance, then the theological approach
pioneered in the middle ages and revised in the reformation era, and
finally the bold new philosophical developments of his own day. Still
more suspicious is the restriction of this list to great writers, fit for mature
readers, and the absence from it of the anthologies, compendia, textbooks,
and other cribs from which contemporary students (and their teachers)
derived so much of what they knew. The chronology of this programme
of home schooling also remains unclear: much of this advanced reading in
the sources must have taken place (if at all) in Leibniz's university years.
Not entirely clear either is how much of this material was in his father's
library, or precisely why it might have been there.

What is immediately evident, however, is that this unstructured
programme of avid, independent, and wide-ranging reading informed
Leibniz's approach to learning from the very outset of his schooling and
played the crucial role in producing his extraordinary educational results.
Its first consequence was to accelerate his mastery of the subject still foun-
dational to all higher learning: by the age of twelve he was proficient in
the Latin language.[47] The test of such proficiency in seventeenth-century
Germany remained occasional poetry, that is, the rapid composition of
verses, long and learned or short and pithy, which redeployed the forms
of and allusions to classical Latin poetry to add lustre to ephemeral social
occasions or public events. Many years later Leibniz still recalled with
evident pleasure how at a mere thirteen years of age he had embellished
a school celebration with no less than three hundred hexameters of Latin
verse composed in the space of a single morning, a feat which earned
lavish praise from his astonished teachers.

Even more impressive and consequential for his later life was a second
result: Leibniz was accustomed from a very early stage to learn not merely
by memorizing or even mastering a set text but by comparing and contrasting a variety of positions on any topic and a range of solutions to
any intellectual problem. When for the first time he was presented in his
formal schooling with serious intellectual fare, he was therefore not content merely to master what was presented to him but immediately began
seeking alternatives to and refinements of it. For Leibniz, this took place
with his exposure to logic upon arriving in the first or uppermost class of
the Nikolaischule at the age of thirteen. The interest which this subject
immediately awakened in the adolescent was in several respects the most

remarkable feature of his formal schooling. In the first place, while his classmates recoiled from the abstraction and inherent difficulty of the subject, Leibniz found it fascinating and intellectually stimulating from the outset – a testimony not only to his intellectual gifts but also perhaps to the fact that his independent reading had already familiarised him with some of the tasks to which this basic intellectual tool could be put and provided examples of how logical principles could be applied. Second, while many of his philosophical contemporaries later rejected traditional logic and bemoaned the labours they had wasted in school attempting to master it, Leibniz, in a letter written almost forty years later to Gabriel Wagner, defended the fecundity of the Aristotelian logic he had learned in school from the unwarranted contempt of other celebrated "moderns" such as Descartes.[48] Third and most remarkably, if Leibniz was exceptional in his fascination with and appreciation of Aristotelian logic, he was still more precocious in the independence of mind with which he challenged and sought to improve it. From the very outset of his logical studies he bombarded his teachers with queries regarding the adequacy of the ten categories devised by the Aristotelian tradition for grasping all the different orders of things.[49] Moreover, he sought to go beyond the received logic by proposing a new set of categories for ordering not only simple notions (as in Aristotelian logic) but also complex propositions and truths.[50] He also immediately put these logical categories to use by assembling systems of topics or commonplaces which aided him in organising what he had learned, recalling it later, and assembling it in written compositions – nets of divisions and subdivisions, as he explained to one astonished classmate, which he used to catch fleeting thoughts before they could escape.[51] Finally and most important of all, this exposure to logic immediately initiated a series of intellectual developments which spilled over into Leibniz's early years at university and provided one of the basic impulses propelling his intellectual career.

The Rudiments of Logic and the Alphabet of Human Thoughts

One can well imagine that the young Leibniz's teachers and classmates were astonished by displays of this kind. No sooner had the thirteen-year-old been introduced to Aristotelian logic – or to what passed for it in the textbooks which mediated the Stagyrite's original doctrines in terms accommodated to the teaching of teenagers – than he subjected this

tradition to penetrating criticism, suggested a variety of ways of improving
it, and even proposed a bold scheme for going well beyond it. In his most
extended autobiographical fragments Leibniz gives no hint of how he
produced these precocious results; but more candid passages in other
texts reveal something of the methods and sources which generated the
Wunderkind's intellectual pyrotechnics. The "so called *praedicamenta*," he
explained to Wagner in 1696, "struck me as an inventory of all things of
the world, and I searched through all manner of logics to see where such
a general list could best and most completely be found." His "exhaustive
tables" of *praedicamenta*, in other words, were not simply generated by the
autonomous reflections of a thirteen year-old genius on the ancient text of
Aristotle: they had been "gathered together out of all manner of logics,"[52]
that is, collected from the innumerable textbooks produced above all in
Germany during the sixteenth and early seventeenth centuries which
sought not merely to expound but to complete and improve the *Organon*
of Aristotle.[53] From the very outset, it appears, Leibniz's intellectual
innovation and experimentation was born of eclecticism: of the wide and
independent reading he was avidly pursuing in his father's library and of
his precocious desire to explore the world of learning independent of his
teachers and to put the pieces together for himself.

Moreover, the same letter reveals that both this general intellectual
method and at least some of his novel *praedicamenta* had been drawn
from one philosophical and pedagogical tradition in particular. As he
explained to Wagner, "By such tabulation of knowledge I arrived at the
practice of dividing and subdividing as a basis of organization and as a
train of thoughts. On this point the Ramists and semi-Ramists must be
preserved."[54] Although the use of *praedicamenta* and other systems of
categories to organise the fruits of one's reading and to strengthen one's
memory was not unique to any one philosophical school or pedagogical
programme,[55] Leibniz also attributed them in 1711 to the Ramist and
semi-Ramist tradition, which had developed and institutionalised them
most fully: "I certainly did not disregard the worthy things in the Ramist
tradition. I recall that, when I was a teenager, these things helped me to
write on a certain matter in such a way that, upon reading what I had
written, my friends wondered how I had managed to think of all these
things. They had been supplied by a method not much different from the
Ramist one."[56]

The 'semi-Ramist' pedagogical and philosophical tradition which developed with unique fertility in Germany during the latter sixteenth and early seventeenth century represents the first of a series of domestic intellectual traditions crucial to Leibniz's earliest formation. In the course of his campaign to simplify and reform Aristotelian logic, the French humanist pedagogue Petrus Ramus (or Pierre de la Ramée, 1515–72) had himself rejected the Aristotelian *praedicamenta* and sought to provide an alternative system of basic topics or commonplaces (*loci*). The stream of alternative *praedicamenta* with which the young Leibniz bedazzled his teachers and classmates were drawn in all likelihood, not primarily from the works of Ramus himself, but from the numerous German 'semi-Ramists' who had sought to improve on the Frenchman's often inept or inadequate reform of dialectic by reintroducing into it elements of Aristotelianism and other logical and philosophical traditions. Indeed, the post-Ramist tradition of conciliatory eclecticism approached the enterprise of philosophy by establishing a system of topics or commonplaces, collecting within it a wide variety of opinions, comparing and contrasting the full range of opinions on every topic, isolating points of agreement and disagreement, and then searching for ways of distinguishing truth from falsity and reconciling apparent contradictions. A very similar technique generated the young Leibniz's approach to the logical *praedicamenta*, which produced such astonishingly precocious results. Similarly characteristic of Ramism was the young Leibniz's pedagogical application of these categories: his use of logic to divide and subdivide these categories, to order one's thoughts and to aid one's memory. These too were techniques absolutely central to the long tradition of German Ramism. Clearly, by the time he began the formal study of Aristotelian logic at thirteen years of age, Leibniz had not only encountered Ramist and post-Ramist dialectic but also absorbed many of the basic pedagogical techniques developed by the Ramist tradition in Germany.[57]

It is not difficult to understand why this literature, once discovered, should have appealed to the young Leibniz. Ramist pedagogy had been institutionalised in Germany in states very different from Saxony and had been developed to pursue pedagogical ends very different from those fostered in the Nikolaischule. Lacking the means to support full-fledged universities of their own, many of the smallest states and semi-independent cities in northern, Protestant Germany had adopted Ramism as the basis of an intermediate education which was well-rounded in scope, useful in content, and efficient and therefore cost-effective in method. The resulting formula – clear, readily intelligible introductions to useful learning in a broad range of disciplines – was uniquely well adapted to the needs of a young 'autodidact' exploring the middle ranges of an encyclopaedic curriculum on his own, far in advance of his formal education. Moreover, this strictly Ramist tradition had given rise to a series of subsequent pedagogical and philosophical innovations which collectively constituted perhaps the most fertile tradition of academic philosophy pursued in Germany – or indeed anywhere else in the Protestant world – in the later sixteenth and early seventeenth centuries. From a philosophical point of view, to be sure, Ramus's *loci* were clearly inferior to the Aristotelian categories they were intended to supersede: the chief value of Ramism lay not in its technical, logical content but in its pedagogical effectiveness and utility as a means of systematically digesting knowledge in orderly fashion. Precisely in order to avoid the technical limitations of Ramist dialectic, a second generation of post-Ramist philosophers in central Europe, led by Bartholomäus Keckermann (1571–1609) in Heidelberg and Danzig, had sought to improve and eventually supersede Ramus by recombining him with Aristotle; and this in turn had generated a flourishing tradition of philosophical eclecticism which later practitioners further enriched by adding other philosophical influences into this semi-Ramist mix. The editor of Keckermann's philosophical works and professor of philosophy at the Herborn Academy (in the tiny German county of Nassau-Dillenburg), Johann Heinrich Alsted (1588–1638), not only capped the German post-Ramist tradition with the greatest encyclopaedia of the era but also sought to develop a still more powerful pedagogical engine by replacing the static commonplaces of Ramist dialectic with a combinatorial logic inspired by Ramon Lull.[58] In pursuit of this combinatorial encyclopaedia, Alsted's student and son-in-law, Johann Heinrich Bisterfeld (c. 1605–55) – displaced by the warfare in his homeland to the Reformed outpost in Transylvania – had generated conceptual innovations strikingly similar to some of Leibniz's most fundamental and characteristic conceptions. Finally, Alsted's second brilliant student, Jan Amos Comenius – likewise exiled from his Moravian homeland – had attempted to harness this efficient, effective, useful, and encyclopaedic pedagogy to a general instauration of human affairs, including the reconciliation of Europe's churches and the pacification of Europe's states through the advancement and dissemination of a perfect, all-embracing system of pansophic knowledge.[59]

Although flourishing in the gymnasia and academies of some of the Empire's smallest states, Ramus's streamlined pedagogy had been despised from the outset in the leading Protestant universities of larger territories both inside and outside Germany. Leipzig, as the largest of the Lutheran universities, had in fact led the rejection of Ramism in the 1580s and 1590s;[60] and the university seems to have played no part in the rapid generation of the highly eclectic post-Ramist traditions of the Reformed academies and universities in the immediately subsequent decades: during the following seventy years, no explicitly Ramist works appeared from the city's otherwise productive presses.[61] Yet post-Ramist works and pedagogical innovations percolated in still poorly understood ways into Lutheran Germany as well – as witnessed by the presence of Comenius's *Vestibulum* in the Nikolaischule and of related traditions in the university.[62] And some of the most important works of this tradition found their way by two separate channels into the young Leibniz's household: major philosophical works presumably purchased by his father himself, and legal writings from his maternal grandfather, the jurist Wilhelm Schmuck.

Little is known about the precise contents of Friedrich's library; but works from this tradition bulk large amongst the books from within it which his son is known to have studied in his youth and which he still remembered and treasured decades later. In 1684 Leibniz reluctantly agreed to help settle the debts incurred by his lengthy period of youthful study and travel by selling his father's library; but before doing so he expressly requested that a handful of books first be extracted and retained for his own use. These included works by five figures closely related to the post-Ramist tradition and the Herborn school – most notably Keckermann's voluminous *Opera omnia*, the juridical encyclopaedia of the famous Herborn political theorist, Johannes Althusius (1557–1638), and the brilliant logical and encyclopaedic works of Johann Heinrich Bisterfeld,[63] several of which the young Leibniz had annotated, apparently between 1663 and 1666.[64] Miscellaneous sources also document Leibniz's familiarity with other key writers in this tradition around the same time. By 1664 he was acquainted with some of Alsted's writings; in 1667 he quoted several works by Comenius; and by the latter date he had read works by Johannes Piscator (1546–1625), the longstanding rector of the Herborn academy and pioneer of its Ramist approach to philosophy and theology.[65] Later still, his private library included works of Alsted, Althusius, Keckermann, Johann Rudolph Lavater, and Anton Matthaeus, as well as Clemens Timpler (1563/4–1624), Keckermann's teacher in Heidelberg, and Matthias Martinius (1572–1630), Alsted's philosophical tutor in Herborn.[66]

Upon closer inspection, Leibniz's exposure to Ramism appears to have begun not long after the opening of his father's library, when Leibniz was only eight. Upon gaining access to his father's books, Leibniz recollected, he "first fell upon the ancients" and feasted his eyes on writers whom he had previously known only by name: Plato, Aristotle, Herodotus, Xenophon, Archimedes, Hipparchus, Diophantus, Cicero, Quintillian, Seneca, Pliny, Plotinus, the Roman historians, and many Latin and Greek Church Fathers.[67] These were of course the chief authorities for the first, humanistic stage of his formal education; and their names might well have been a source of fascination. But for an eight-year-old, still learning the rudiments of Latin, they were initially incomprehensible: in these authors, he recalled, "at the beginning he [Leibniz] understood nothing, and then something, and at last as much as was needed".[68] Clearly he was proceeding, at least in part, by employing the same methods used to decipher Livy. According to his later recollection, what impressed him above all in these ancient writers was the clarity of their style and the profundity of their content; and after finding these qualities sadly lacking in many later writers he established for himself while still very young "two axioms" which would guide his later study. The first was to seek "clarity in words" and in the other "signs of the soul" such as mathematical notations; the second was to seek "usefulness in things". Only later, however, did the full significance of these two axioms become clear to him. The first axiom, he later realised, constituted the basis of judgement; the second one, the basis of discovery (*inventio*).[69] In reflecting retrospectively on his intellectual awakening, Leibniz recognised in these two the first seeds of his intellectual programme. His search for clarity and for an *ars judicandi* developed into his pursuit of an "alphabet" of human thoughts, which would contain the first intellectual elements from the combination of which all other concepts could be derived in a manner which would eliminate misconceptions and guarantee the certainty of our judgements. His search for utility and for an *ars inveniendi* generated in time an intellectual programme dedicated in the last analysis to the pursuit of knowledge useful for the improvement of the human condition. Yet these two axioms of clarity and utility, and these two arts of judgement and invention – which Leibniz adopted at the very outset of his intellectual life even without fully understanding them and which set the stage for so much that followed – were central to and characteristic of Ramism. Utility, for Ramus, was a fundamental criterion for determining what should be contained in a basic treatment of any art or science; and Ramists were parodied by their peripatetic contemporaries for harping on incessantly about utility. Clarity was an equally basic precondition for effective and efficient teaching of any art or science and one of the basic reasons for preferring Ramist texts and methods to their traditional alternatives. Invention and judgement were likewise the two mains sections into which Ramus's *Dialectica* was famously divided; and the *ars inveniendi* and *ars judicandi* were in effect extensions or elaborations of these. Unless one is to suppose that the schoolboy Leibniz independently formulated both the axioms and the programme of the German Ramist tradition without fully understanding either, one must conclude that his earliest reading in the ancient philosophers, like his earliest formal study of logic, was prepared for and shaped by a previous independent reading in Ramist pedagogical literature – precisely the philosophical literature, in any case, which would have been most immediately accessible to a brilliant young autodidact only eight to twelve years old.

As Leibniz's recollection in this passage suggests, the chief significance of his early exposure to this tradition lay in establishing at an astonishingly early stage some of the key intellectual aspirations which he would pursue for the rest of his life and even in furnishing him with some of the philosophical means for pursuing them. What impressed the teenager Leibniz above all in his earliest exposure to logic was apparently the notion – shared with Ramus and the post-Ramist tradition – that logic provided a powerful tool for the rigorous ordering of thoughts, which reflect in turn the division of things themselves. In other words, Leibniz saw logic as a mirror of reality which allowed the human mind to grasp the order of things. The tables which Leibniz recalled composing to derive all possible notions from the combination of a few simple elements were intended not merely to aid his memory or even rigorously to order his thoughts but as a map of reality itself.[70] The youthful challenge of reforming Aristotle's *praedicamenta* was likewise the search for a new set of categories able to capture not only simple notions (*termini simplices*) but also complex propositions and truths (*termini complexi*). These tables of terms and systems of categories represented the very first germs of Leibniz's work towards the *ars combinatoria* and the development of an alphabet of human thoughts, which were to become some of the key aims of his intellectual career. Just as an infinite number of words, phrases, sentences, and discourses can be generated from the combinations of a finite number of letters, the infinite variety apparent in the world might be reduced to a finite "alphabet" of human thoughts, the rigorously controlled combination of which might allow us to judge conclusively of all things. Leibniz confessed later on that, upon first encountering this wonderful idea as an enthusiastic teenager, he did not recognise the difficulty of this enterprise; but far from abandoning it in more mature years, his advancement in knowledge only confirmed the decision to pursue this extremely ambitious project.[71]

What these later recollections of his early intellectual development failed to mention was that he was not the first to conceive such a project or even to devote a lifetime to pursuing it. Although Leibniz developed these combinatorial aspirations in the most brilliant, thorough, and consistent fashion, he had inherited them from a previous generation of central European thinkers. Alsted's great *Encyclopaedia* not only constituted the most orderly and comprehensive summary of knowledge produced in the generation before Leibniz; it also contained a formula for converting it into a combinatorial form derived from the author's youthful fascinating with Lullism, and as such it provided both a point of departure and an enduring benchmark for Leibniz's encyclopaedic efforts. The "most solid Bisterfeld" exercised an even greater fascination and influence on the Leipzig student.[72] On the title page of his copy of Bisterfeld's *Phosphorus Catholicus*, the young Leibniz described it as an "Ingeniosissimus Libellus" ("a most ingenious little book"). On the title page of Bisterfeld's *Philosophiae Primae Seminarium* he expanded a similar judgement further: "A most brilliant little work and a like one of this kind I have not seen".[73] In these concise and sharp works Leibniz found a conception of reality with two fundamental features which would become hallmarks of his own philosophy: the idea of universal harmony as union and communion of everything with everything,[74] and the extraordinary thesis, central to the theory of monads later developed by Leibniz, that all beings are endowed with perception and appetite.[75] Especially in Bisterfeld, but also in the other authors of the Herborn school, Leibniz therefore encountered a conception of reality which celebrated the variety and multiplicity which he had already come to treasure in his private reading while suggesting a way to recall this multiplicity to unity. The key to this reunification was to be found at the epistemological level in a combinatorial encyclopaedia of all human knowledge and at the metaphysical level in a theologically grounded conception of universal harmony in which Platonic elements enhanced a basic Aristotelianism. This fascinating theoretical construction, moreover, was not conceived as an end in itself. On the contrary, this intellectual tradition had grafted onto the drive for further reformation fundamental to the central European Reformed community, first, the Ramist emphasis on the application of all arts and sciences to the practical purposes of human life, and then, the Baconian call for a new philosophy dedicated to the restoration of man's dominion over nature. In the minds of Alsted and Bisterfeld, therefore, this reduction of epistemological and metaphysical variety to unity was intended to prepare the way for the more concrete resolution of religious and political differences; and Comenius in particular came to see it as a means of improving the human condition still more generally.

Beginning from the opening of his father's library when he was barely eight years old, intensified by his formal introduction to logic five years later, and spilling over from the Nikolaischule into Leipzig's university when he was fifteen, Leibniz had browsed his way to a fertile academic tradition in which aspirations strikingly similar to his own had been nurtured and developed in the gymnasia, academies, and universities of central Europe for several generations. It was above all the adoption of these aspirations at the very outset of his career and the consistent pursuit of them throughout it which unified the apparently miscellaneous intellectual undertakings so strikingly apparent in Leibniz's later life. The distance of this tradition from the educational institutions of his native city justifies Leibniz's description of himself as an "autodidact" within the narrow context of Leipzig. Yet from a broader perspective he was clearly continuing a fertile tradition of philosophical and pedagogical innovation which had been institutionalised in Germany like nowhere else for over a century. It was this basic intellectual agenda deeply rooted in the conditions of the Holy Roman Empire which strikingly distinguished Leibniz from his western European contemporaries and marked him off as a central European philosopher. And if this applies to the conciliatory eclecticism of his basic approach to philosophy, it applies no less to the broadminded irenicism of his theology.

Scholastic Philosophy and Irenical Theology

As history, post-Ramist philosophy, and the classics mingled together to form the earliest conglomerate stratum of Leibniz's independent reading, other sedimentary layers quickly accumulated on top of them. In his early teens, while discovering logic at school, Leibniz began privately to devour works of scholastic philosophy and theology at home as if they were engaging novels. The first name listed in his recollection of this stage of his reading is highly significant: Jacopo Zabarella (1533–89), a leader of the flourishing tradition of Renaissance Aristotelianism in sixteenth-century Padua, had been rapidly imported into Germany in the close of the century as a more sophisticated alternative to Ramist method and incorporated firmly into the post-Ramist tradition by Keckermann.[76] Scarcely less influential in Lutheran philosophical circles were the leading works of Iberian scholasticism, which Leibniz also studied, notably the Jesuits Pedro de Fonseca (1528–99), Antonio Rubio (1548–1615), Gregorius de Valentia (d. 1603), and Francisco Suarez (1548–1617).[77]

Even more significant than this further philosophical literature, however, was the extension of Leibniz's programme of independent reading from philosophy to theology. Here he may have moved by easy stages from the basic instruction in Lutheran theology which complemented the *trivium* in the Nikolaischule. From Luther's shorter catechism it was a short step to his famous diatribe *De servo arbitrio*: Luther's adamant assertion against Erasmus of the absolute sovereignty of the divine will in human salvation. Leibniz later recalled both greatly admiring the book in his youth and believing at the same time that it needed to be "softened."[78] So "hard" were Luther's formulations in this work, in fact, that *De servo arbitrio* had been adopted by Calvinist proponents of predestination; and this may have led the young Leibniz to follow it by reading the records of the debates in which predestination emerged as a third main point of doctrine (alongside the Eucharist and Christology) separating the Lutheran and Reformed confessions: the acts of the colloquy held at Mömpelgard (now French Montbéliard) in 1586 between the Lutheran architect of the Formula of Concord, Jakob Andreae (1528–90), and Calvin's successor as head of the Genevan church, Theodore Beza (1519–1605).[79] Further literature in controversial theology followed: within the Lutheran camp he devoured orthodox authors such as Aegidius Hunnius (1550–1603) and the *Kommentar zur Konkordienformel* by Leonhard Hutter (1563–1616); from the Reformed tradition, the controversial writings of the leading Herborn theologian, Johannes Piscator; from Italy the *De libertate dialogi* of the eminent humanist Lorenzo Valla (1407–57); and finally statements of the Catholic position by the Jesuit Martin Becan (1563–1624).[80] Unsatisfied by canvassing only the views of mainstream theologians, he also studied the writings of figures judged unorthodox by their own confessions: the Jansenists on the one hand, who strained relations with their Catholic coreligionists by gravitating towards an allegedly Augustinian conception of salvation, and the Arminians on the other, who in directly contrary fashion were formally evicted from the Dutch Reformed church for watering down Calvinist predestinarianism with an emphasis on human cooperation reminiscent of Erasmus.[81]

Taken together, this programme of theological reading suggests that the young Leibniz – far from plunging in over his head and paddling around aimlessly in the deep waters of polemical theology – had proceeded in an astonishingly orderly fashion. He had immediately focussed on the central theological issue which precipitated the Lutheran reformation – the question of divine versus human agency in the process of redemption – and had then taken systematic soundings both of the mainstream doctrines and of the principal countercurrents of the three main Christian confessions: Catholic, Lutheran, and Reformed. Intellectually, this survey provided him at the very outset with first-hand familiarity with the full spectrum of authentic, mainstream theological opinions, as articulated not by their confessional enemies but by some of their most distinguished advocates. Personally, this comprehensive survey confirmed his basic allegiance to the "moderate sentiments of the churches of the confession of Augsburg," which he could regard with some justification as lying midway between the Catholic camp on the one hand and the Reformed party on the other and in sympathy with elements of Arminianism and Jansenism.[82] But the specific strand of Lutheranism which he had come most to favour in this process was not the unyielding orthodoxy characteristic of Leipzig but the moderate, irenical school of Georg Calixt, based primarily in Helmstedt and fiercely opposed in Saxony, which sought to reconcile the essentials of Lutheranism with a reformed Roman Catholicism.

This youthful preference for Calixt – expressed retrospectively many years later but in keeping with Leibniz's mature position – raises again in more focussed terms the crucial confessional questions of Leibniz's earliest youth: the questions of whether his later ecumenism, so uncharacteristic of Leipzig, was nevertheless established during his early years there and, if so, how it managed to take root in such an alien environment. Calixt was the most important representative in the wartime generation of the species of irenicism most strikingly similar to Leibniz's longstanding ecumenical vision. Irenicists of a rather different sort had proliferated in all the main Reformed intellectual centres in the Empire before and during the war; but the purpose of the Reformed irenical tradition had been a more limited one: to join Lutherans and Calvinists into a confessional, political, and ultimately military alliance capable of withstanding the onslaught of the Habsburg-led central European Counter Reformation. Unlike this large company of Reformed irenicists, Calixt had pursued in relative isolation the far broader project of reconciling Lutheranism not only with Calvinism but also, and indeed primarily, with a reformed Catholicism.[83] For this he had been castigated in the great majority of more conservative Lutheran universities as a traitor and a "syncretist", polluting the pure springs of Lutheran doctrine with Roman filth and seeking security in a fragile reunion with Rome rather than in the granite verities of gnesio-Lutheran theology. Leipzig theologians such as Johannes Hülsemann (1602–61) and Johann Benedikt Carpzov (1607–57) were amongst Calixt's most implacable opponents.[84] Leibniz's extended family, as we have seen, shared the city's aversion to such "syncretism"; and there is no reason to suppose that the head of his family had not shared in this consensus as well.

Yet there was a particular reason that Calixt's deeply unfashionable works should nevertheless have found their way into Leibniz's father's library. One of the most important and controversial features of Calixt's thought was his moral philosophy. As a professor of moral philosophy, Friedrich Leubnitz would therefore have been virtually compelled to study his works intensively, not because he saw redeeming value in them, but because he needed to fortify himself and his students against pernicious doctrines insinuated into the heart of his discipline by a wayward professor at a neighbouring Lutheran university. By parity of argument, in an age riven with confessional and doctrinal controversies, the presence of a given book in a professor's library by no means indicated that he was

in agreement with all or any of its contents. Friedrich had assembled his
library as an advanced tool for his own professional purposes, not for the
education of his son; and in browsing freely through it the young Leibniz
was, from a narrow confessional point of view, blithely wandering through
a theological minefield. A conservative professor would never have given a
precocious eight- or ten- or fifteen-year-old unrestricted access to such
a dangerous site. In the absence of such close and competent paternal
supervision, the equally prudent teachers of the Nikolaischule urged his
widow to exclude her son from her late husband's library. In this respect,
the father's early death was a crucial precondition for the son's intellectual
precocity. It was not merely the presence of the books but the absence of
their owner which allowed the young Leibniz the freedom to begin his
intellectual odyssey prematurely and to establish at so tender and impressionable an age basic intellectual reflexes strikingly at odds with those of
his family and his birthplace, which would remain with him until the end
of his life.

If this situation explains how Leibniz was able to encounter Calixt's
works so early, it still does not explain why, once he had encountered
them, he responded so differently to their irenicism than his closest relations. It is tempting for those who know Leibniz to rely at this point
on his deep-seated desire to restore multiplicity to unity. But this too,
in the ecclesiastical sphere at least, can be rooted concretely in Leibniz's
earliest reading – and earliest experience – of German history. In the
Lutheran historiographical tradition, stretching back from Calvisius via
Johann Sleiden and Charion's chronicles to medieval imperial historiography, the Holy Roman Empire was portrayed in the most elevated terms
imaginable: it was at once the successor to the Roman *res publica* described
by Livy, the direct heir of the European Empire forged by Charlemagne,
and the fourth of the great Empires prophesied in the Book of Daniel
and destined to shelter and protect the Christian faith until the end of
time.[85] In short, the Empire was one of the central pillars of the ideal of
Christendom, of a unified, harmonious Christian civilisation. The contrast between these visions of imperial greatness and the reality which
Leibniz saw around him in a city emerging from the ruins of a protracted
war was all too apparent. Instead of the successor of Rome, the German
Empire had seemed for a generation before Leibniz's birth more like a
failed state, embroiled inwardly in perennial civil war and preyed upon
at will by its ruthless neighbours. It was no less evident, however, that if

the Empire was to be restored to its former glory and equipped to play its rightful role, the rifts which had so divided and weakened it would have to be mended. And if the religious divisions which cut through the heart of Germany were ever to be healed, this could only be accomplished along the general lines delineated by Calixt. The institutional ideal glimpsed in the earliest, historical phase of Leibniz's reading and the intellectual methods absorbed through the second, philosophical phase of his private and public studies both inclined him to sympathize with the irenical project encountered in the third, theological stage of his private reading. In theology as in philosophy, the young Leibniz's free-ranging explorations within his father's library had led him to an important tradition of German academic thought, vigorously resisted in Leipzig but firmly institutionalised in other German institutions, which provided a central component of the intellectual agenda which he would consistently pursue throughout his long and varied intellectual life. Although strikingly independent within his domestic, scholastic, and civic contexts, he was once again drawing his deepest and most characteristic motivations, not from alien traditions derived at second hand from a western Europe which he had not yet visited, but from seventeenth-century Germany's most vital and creative intellectual traditions, deeply rooted in the unique circumstances of the Empire. Much the same applies to the fourth phase of Leibniz's youthful reading, which occurred on the eve of his graduation from the Nikolaischule to Leipzig's ancient and prospering university.

Ancient Metaphysics and Modern Physics: The Universities of Leipzig and Jena, April 1661–October 1663

As well as books, Leipzig was exceptionally well provided with students. During the 1620s average annual matriculations had peaked at over eight hundred students, well above any German rival, leading the Saxon elector to boast that Leipzig occupied the "first place" amongst German universities. Thereafter warfare had devastated the institution: the first and last great battles of Gustavus Adolphus's German campaign – Breitenfeld on 17 September 1631 and Lützen on 17 November 1632 – took place within a few kilometres of Leipzig; a second main battle at Breitenfeld followed in 1642; and with each main conflict Leipzig was besieged. The juridical faculty in which Leibniz was to study was quite literally caught in the crossfire: its buildings offered a semifortified position with a clear line of fire on Leipzig's citadel, the Pleißenburg; repeated artillery duels between the two positions left these premises, according to one faculty memo in 1634, "fit only as a nesting-place for owls"; and in 1641 even these ruins were swept away to make room for soldiers' barracks. Such miseries notwithstanding, Leipzig fared no worse than most German universities; its recapture and retention by the Swedes in 1642 allowed its recovery to begin a decade before some of its competitors; and in the decade after the war matriculations had already recovered their numbers *ante bellum*.[86] With students as with books, mere numbers did not transform Leipzig into a great centre of intellectual innovation: the conservatism evident in church and school was no less apparent in the university. But Leipzig shared in the fruitful intellectual traditions which circulated through the German universities; and for someone like Leibniz who knew how to find and make use of these currents, the university had much to offer.

Chief amongst these currents was a variant of the philosophical eclecticism which Leibniz had privately encountered and had been publicly practicing with considerable success in his formal logical studies for two years. Although Leipzig had officially rejected Ramism, student demand had forced Lutheran institutions to react to the development of eclectic post-Ramist traditions in Reformed academies, and through still unknown channels similar eclectic tendencies had manifested themselves in the Saxon universities, although generally in much attenuated form. In Leibniz's day, the chief eclectics in Leipzig were the philosophy professor Johann Adam Scherzer (1628–83) and especially the professor first of moral philosophy and then of rhetoric and dialectic Jakob Thomasius (1622–84). In them Leibniz encountered a brand of Aristotelianism which not only was open to other voices but made of the search for truth in different philosophical traditions a precise programme aimed at the achievement of a superior synthesis centred around the fundamental tenets of Lutheran theology.[87] Like innumerable thinkers before them, these two sought to synthesize elements of classical philosophy with Christian doctrine in an effort to articulate and defend their conception of orthodoxy. Rather than overthrowing philosophical authority altogether, therefore, Thomasius in particular firmly rejected the doctrine of double truth (one philosophical, the other theological) which had recently been defended by other controversial Lutheran thinkers.[88] Instead they employed Christian doctrine as a touchstone for distinguishing acceptable from unacceptable philosophical doctrines. The philosophical component of this synthesis was in essence Aristotelianism tinctured with an admixture of Platonism: with an Aristotelian-based theory of substance they combined a prominent strand of Platonic, Neoplatonic, and Augustinian teaching, particularly the thesis (shared by a long line of Christian thinkers) that the ideas of things in the mind of God functioned as archetypes of God's creation.[89]

Around the time that he began to study under these Leipzig professors, the young Leibniz began a fourth, crucially important phase of reading when he discovered and "fell upon the moderns". Leibniz recalled reading at this stage the "great men" of recent times: Francis Bacon, Girolamo Cardano, Tommaso Campanella, and "specimens of the best philosophy of Kepler, Galileo, and Descartes." Clearly this programme of reading was not completed overnight: Leibniz himself admitted that he did not gain an in-depth first-hand knowledge of Galileo and Descartes until the mid-seventies.[90] Yet no later than 1663 he must have stumbled upon Hobbes and Gassendi as well, as shown by his marginal notes in two textbooks of Aristotelian orientation (one of them by his own teacher in Leipzig, Jakob Thomasius).[91] Chronological uncertainties notwithstanding, it would appear that in the months immediately after his graduation from school to university the young Leibniz encountered for the first time the philosophical crisis that had coincided with the political and military crises in his native country; and his attention very quickly came to focus on the key physical and metaphysical points central to it. What had begun as a revolution in astronomy and cosmology in the writings of Copernicus, Tycho Brahe, and Kepler had spread in the works of Galileo, Descartes, and Gassendi to physics and metaphysics. In searching for a new physics consistent with Copernican cosmology, these philosophers attempted to explain the nature and behaviour of terrestrial matter in the quantitative terms which had proved increasingly successful in describing the heavens. Breaking completely with the qualitative physics of Aristotle, which explained physical phenomena ultimately in terms of incorporeal "substantial forms", the mechanical philosophers sought to explain terrestrial and celestial physics exclusively in terms of the geometrical properties of bodies in motion.[92] To the young Leibniz, this seemed to demand a choice between the qualitative physics of Aristotle deeply institutionalised in the universities and the new mechanistic physics breaking in from outside them.

The necessity of taking this crucial decision precipitated the most significant intellectual crisis of the young Leibniz's life of which a record is preserved. In two well-known letters to Thomas Burnett of Kemney (28 May 1697) and Nicolas Rémond (10 January 1714), Leibniz recalled wandering for entire days in a grove on the outskirts of Leipzig called the Rosental, trying to decide whether to keep the Aristotelian substantial forms or to embrace mechanism.[93] The earlier of these recollections dates this incident at the precise interval in which the young man began his studies at the University of Leipzig in April 1661, some three months before his fifteenth birthday.[94] The second account also links it with the completion of his formal schooling but leaves open the possibility that it took place slightly later, once his university studies had already begun.[95] The conclusion reached during these meditations is also described somewhat differently in the various accounts. One recollection states simply that "Mechanism finally prevailed and led me to apply myself to mathematics,"[96] the very sap of the new mechanical philosophy.[97] A more nuanced passage suggests that he may have rejected, not substantial forms as such, but only "those [philosophers] who use *only* forms or faculties" in explaining physical phenomena.[98] A third recollection clearly implies that he intended from the outset not to reject but merely to "reform" the substantial forms.[99] Whatever precisely Leibniz concluded while roaming in the Rosental, it was this third option which eventually prevailed.[100] What Leibniz rejected, in the slightly longer term at least, was not the Aristotelian philosophy as such but the employment of Aristotelian substantial forms in the explanation of the phenomena of physics proper.[101] As he made clear in the *Confessio Naturae contra Atheistas* (1668) not many years later, in the letter to Rémond (1714) toward the end of his life, and in numerous texts in between, the adoption of mechanistic physics was not incompatible with elements of Aristotelian metaphysics properly understood.[102] Firmly embracing the new mathematically based science of nature for the scientific explanation of phenomena, in other words, did not answer for Leibniz more fundamental questions about the ultimate principles of reality. Rather it pointed towards the necessity of a further level of explanation, the search for which became another main line of Leibniz's philosophical development. In his more strictly scientific work, Leibniz came to regard the "foundations and principles" or the "ultimate reasons" of mechanism as principles of a meta-physical nature:

principles which were implicit in but not reached by physics itself, and which were very close to the fundamental philosophical intuitions underlying the substantial forms or entelechies of the Aristotelian–Scholastic tradition.[103]

Rather than simply choosing between Aristotle and mechanism, therefore, the young Leibniz set out to reconcile what was best in new and old. Given its close coincidence with the beginnings of Leibniz's university studies, it is tempting to regard this decision as an effect of Leibniz's exposure to the conciliatory eclecticism of Thomasius. Yet viewed against the backdrop of the young man's earliest intellectual development, this crucial strategic decision is better understood as a further extension of an eclectic intellectual method which had already become virtually habitual. An "autodidact" in the limited sense that his main intellectual adventures were private, informal, and self-generated, the young Leibniz was accustomed to reading what he wanted and putting the pieces together for himself. From the moment he was exposed to logic, he immediately began comparing the textbook learning with what could be gleaned from all the other sources to which he had access. Loyal to his Lutheran roots, he was unafraid to seek inspiration in pagan writers or medieval, Catholic, or Reformed traditions or to reconcile the traditions in which he had been raised with those he had encountered on his own. Highly appreciative of the ancients, he was nevertheless eager to improve them by recourse to ideas and methods which had proliferated in the central European post-Ramist tradition of Keckermann, Alsted, and Bisterfeld. And when he became aware of a more recent and bolder generation of philosophical innovators, he immediately applied the same approach to the most challenging thinkers of his age: the "moderns". Although the cautious eclecticism of Scherzer and Thomasius harmonised in a general way with the young Leibniz's developing intellectual aims and method, it is unlikely that any of its features were novel to him in 1661. Far more advanced versions of all of these features – and versions far closer to Leibniz's developing approach – were readily apparent in the major figures of the post-Ramist tradition in Germany with whom he was already familiar. Whereas the Leipzig philosophers devoted their modest synthesis to the narrow defence of Lutheran orthodoxy,[104] post-Ramist eclectics such as Comenius pursued the far broader goal of reconciling the Christian churches with one another.[105] Whereas Leipzig's philosophical eclecticism was distinguished primarily by a modest admixture of

Platonism, a far more pronounced Platonic thread ran from Ramus himself through all the major figures of the post-Ramist philosophical and
theological tradition of Reformed Germany.[106] Whereas Leibniz's teachers condemned the "wicked" philosophical syncretism of those tempted by
more exotic philosophical doctrines with the same vehemence with which
they rejected the theological syncretism of Calixt and his school,[107] post-
Ramist philosophers such as Alsted and Bisterfeld had experimented with
a far wider range of philosophical traditions for half a century, including
Lullism, Kabbalism, Paracelsianism, and alchemy.[108] Whereas Thomasius and Scherzer restricted themselves to a narrow canon of ancient
authorities,[109] the direct and indirect followers of Ramus had, *ipso facto*,
introduced recent philosophers into the mix. Finally and most importantly, while Thomasius and Scherzer rejected Descartes's philosophy
as inconsistent with the Christian religion and vigorously opposed the
atheistic dangers which they saw lurking in ancient as well as in modern philosophics,[110] the latest generation of post-Ramist professors across
Europe had already begun incorporating elements of Cartesianism into
their highly eclectic philosophies. In opting to combine the best of old
and new, Leibniz was in fact adopting a position already being developed especially by the so-called *novantiqui* in the Dutch universities and
on the western border of Germany by Johannes Clauberg (1622–65).[111]
Whether or not, as he later claimed, Leibniz's own synthetic approach was
arrived at independent of Clauberg, it was clearly rooted in the intellectual
methods which they shared and was essentially independent of his formal
education.

From the very outset of his university studies in Leipzig, therefore,
Leibniz – drawing yet again on a philosophical tradition deeply rooted
elsewhere in Germany – had already graduated to a far bolder and more
fruitful form of philosophical eclecticism than his professors there. This
much is clear, in fact, from Leibniz's own testimony:

As soon as I arrived in the university, I had the good fortune to have as my teacher
the famous Jacob Thomasius who, though he did not share my doubts and was not
inclined to allow me to proceed with such a reform of the substantial, incorporeal
forms of bodies, strongly enjoined me to read Aristotle, assuring me that, when I
had read this great philosopher, I would have an opinion wholly different from that
provided by his scholastic interpreters. I soon acknowledged the wisdom of this advice
and perceived that there was the same difference between Aristotle and the scholastics
as between a great man versed in the affairs of state and a monk dreaming in his cell.

I thereby formed an idea of Aristotle's philosophy quite different than the common one. I did not accept all his hypotheses, but I approved of them as principles. Aristotle seemed to me to admit – more or less like Democritus or, in my time, like Descartes and Gassendi – that there is no body which is moved by itself.[112]

Clearly Leibniz had formed his doubts about Aristotelian physics before encountering Thomasius. Indeed, he had already decided how to resolve these doubts as well: not by rejecting "the substantial, incorporeal forms of bodies" altogether to become a thoroughgoing mechanist, but by reforming them and meeting the moderns halfway. Equally clearly, Thomasius did not share his student's doubts and actively discouraged Leibniz from resolving them in this way. Instead he hoped to divert the young man from this dangerous course by steering him from the derivative philosophical textbooks, by which most contemporary students were introduced to Aristotelian philosophy, to the text of Aristotle himself. The dutiful young student took his teacher's advice, set aside the epigones, and immersed himself – in all likelihood for the first time – directly in Aristotle. Moreover, this immersion evidently convinced him that his teacher was right in at least one crucial respect: there was a world of difference between Aristotle himself and the later Aristotelians. But the conclusion Leibniz drew from this discovery was precisely the opposite of what his teacher had intended: he rejected the 'common' conception of Aristotle (shared by Thomasius) that he was irreconcilable with mechanism and adopted instead the uncommon but by no means unique conclusion (shared with the *novantiqui*) that at a deeper level Aristotle and the mechanists could be reconciled to produce a synthesis superior to either on its own.

More generally, by immersing his student more deeply in Aristotle and deepening as well his familiarity with the rigours of scholastic philosophy, Thomasius helped fashion one of the foundations upon which Leibniz's far bolder philosophical synthesis would rest. For this purpose Thomasius's genuine erudition – his sophisticated knowledge of the history of philosophy and his deep understanding of Aristotle – combined with an at least partial convergence with Leibniz regarding the aims and methods of philosophy, was very well adapted; and this combination of attributes generated the closest relationship which Leibniz shared with any of his teachers. In the seventeen extant letters exchanged between September 1663 and January 1672,[113] the two men carried out the most fecund and intellectually stimulating correspondence of Leibniz's early youth, the key topic of which was precisely the vexed issue of the relationship between "ancients" (especially Aristotle) and "moderns". Although Thomasius predictably rejected Leibniz's thesis of a possible complementarity between Aristotelian metaphysics and mechanical physics, he could have recognised in his pupil his best lesson: the search for a philosophical synthesis which employed elements of different and apparently opposed traditions with the aim of building a new system which agreed with the Christian religion and could help support it.

A similar impression is gained from the first of Leibniz's published disputations – another conventional feature of German university instruction which Leibniz was to put to exceptional use. Like most of his learned countrymen, Leibniz's first published works were versions of the academic disputations required to mark the various major stages of his higher education. Although many of the students who matriculated in seventeenth-century universities chose to sidestep formal degree studies for one reason or another, the ordinary formal course of study began with a Bachelor's degree in the general 'arts' or 'philosophy' course and then followed this with higher degrees in philosophy or – far more normally – with Bachelor's, Master's and Doctoral degrees in one of the three 'higher faculties' of theology, law, or medicine. Scarcely nineteen months after commencing his university studies, Leibniz marked the first of these stages by taking a Bachelor's degree in philosophy on 2 December 1662. Six months later, on 9 June 1663, he defended his *Disputatio Metaphysica de Principio Individui* (*Metaphysical Disputation on the Principle of Individuation*) under the presidency of Jakob Thomasius. It was a brilliant piece of academic philosophy, handling one of the most complex and controversial topics of scholastic metaphysics: the issue of the principle of individuation. Thomasius's preface to the published version presented Aristotle's doctrine regarding individuals as a distinction between "monadic" and "sporadic" individuals. A monadic individual, he wrote, constituted a species on its own (such as, in Thomas Aquinas's interpretation, each angel), whereas a sporadic individual was just one of the many individuals embraced by the same species.[114] As early as 1663 this eclectic Aristotelian therefore presented Leibniz with a variation of the term which would become the very hallmark of his doctrine of substance – the term of "monad" – applied in the context of a metaphysical discussion of individuals. Later on Leibniz even proposed his doctrine of individual substance as an extension of Aquinas's teaching regarding angels: from a metaphysical point of view each individual constitutes a species.[115]

Leibniz began his disputation proper by listing the four standard positions on the principle of individuation: "the principle of individuation either is reckoned to be the *entire Entity* (1) or not the entire Entity. If not the entire Entity, either it expresses a *Negation* (2), or something positive. This something positive either has a Physical function of determining the essence, *Existence* (3); or a Metaphysical function of determining the species, *Haecceitas* (4)." He then declared himself in favour of the first one: "every individual is individuated by his complete Entity"[116] In other words, the young Leibniz embraced a nominalist–conceptualist option which firmly refused to ascribe to the principle of individuation any kind of reality distinct from the individual itself. Needless to say, this position was not novel, nor did Leibniz claim it to be: on the contrary, he listed diligently the "authorities" in its favour, including the champion of the recent Catholic scholastics, Francisco Suarez. All the same, in his very first philosophical work the young Leibniz had come upon a problem which was to be central to his metaphysics – the issue of individual substance – and the nominalist–conceptualist position adopted in his youth regarding the principle of individuation remained the background of his own original conception. In short, the *Disputatio de Principio Individui* marked the end of Leibniz's formal philosophical apprenticeship under Thomasius in remarkable fashion: although he would continue to correspond with his former teacher for another half-dozen years, it was time for Leibniz to move on.

Ten days after the defence of his dissertation, on 20 June 1663, Leibniz enrolled for the summer semester at the University of Jena. Apart from the desire to study for a period in another flourishing Saxon institution, it is not certain why he decided to move; but the principal attraction of Jena was probably the presence there of Erhard Weigel (1625–99), whose lectures in mathematics Leibniz would certainly have found more stimulating than those of his Leipzig teacher, Johann Kühn.[117] Weigel shared the conviction of Thomasius and Scherzer that Aristotelian philosophy could be reconciled with Christian philosophy by recourse to the Platonic conception that the ideas (or, in Weigel's view, the attributes) of things in the divine mind functioned as archetypes of God's creation.[118] But whereas his colleagues in Leipzig declined to broaden this cautious eclecticism further, Weigel embraced the challenge of the "moderns" and attempted to integrate into this conception elements of the mechanical philosophy. Given the suspicions widespread in Lutheran Germany that Cartesianism had atheistic implications, Weigel (like Leibniz) was highly critical of Descartes himself; but this did not preclude leaving room in his Platonized Aristotelianism for explaining physical properties mechanistically, and his consequent application of mathematics to philosophy represented Leibniz's first formal opportunity to explore a field in which he was destined to make some of his most significant contributions.[119]

Another notable feature of this stay in Jena, perhaps not unrelated to the bolder eclecticism of his teacher there, was Leibniz's membership in the local *Societas Quaerentium*, a group of students and professors which met weekly to discuss old and new books. Once back in Leipzig Leibniz became involved in a similar association, the *Collegium Conferentium*, founded in 1664 as the most recent of a series of similar organisations in Leipzig which had served as a model for the Jena society.[120] In 1665 he served as treasurer of the *Collegium* and probably during the same year he gave a paper *De Collegiis*.[121] *Collegia* in this sense were groups of students meeting to study a particular book or subject, normally informally, privately, and without direct professorial supervision.[122] In one form of these *collegia* – the so-called *collegia Gelliana* frequently recommended by post-Ramist philosophers such as Keckermann, Alsted, and Comenius – the group leader assigned to each of up to half a dozen members one passage from a different author on a single topic; and when the group reconvened each member presented the most salient arguments raised by each author, which were then examined and debated by the group as a whole.[123] Leibniz's interest in such meetings is therefore not difficult to understand: such *collegia* effectively institutionalised the eclectic search for the best doctrines in a host of ancient, medieval, and modern authorities which was central to his intellectual method. Some twenty years later he asked his half-brother Johann Friedrich to keep for him his manuscript records of the Leipzig society's discussions[124] – impressive testimony both of his awareness that his thought had developed organically from seeds planted at the very outset of his studies and of the role played at every stage of that development by the eclectic study and collective discussion of parallel intellectual traditions.

The Legal Studies of an Encyclopaedist: Leipzig and Altdorf, October 1663–February 1667

Upon returning to Leipzig in October 1663 for the beginning of the winter semester with his first degree in philosophy in hand, Leibniz faced a parting of the ways: should he continue to study for higher degrees in philosophy, or should he take the far more usual course and progress to one of the three higher faculties? It is a mark of his intellectual self-confidence and ambition as well as of the essentially encyclopaedic nature of his interests that he decided to pursue both of these academic options at once. Unwilling to study one thing to the exclusion of all else and convinced that the various branches of learning were organically interconnected and mutually sustaining, from this point onward – audaciously but characteristically – Leibniz would simultaneously pursue higher degrees in philosophy and further degrees in the higher faculty of law, the latter under the guidance of Quirinus Schacher and Bartholomaeus Leonhard Schwendendörffer.[125] It is also noteworthy that he chose to study law rather than the theology so deeply engrained in his parents' household and so near to his own heart. No doubt he had read enough of Leipzig's orthodox academic divinity to recognize its problematic relationship with his own theological inclinations. No doubt family tradition and connections also played a part: his maternal grandfather, Wilhelm Schmuck, was a jurist of considerable renown, and other family friends were available to help him on his way. It is also unlikely, in light of his subsequent career, to have escaped his notice that the career prospects of a jurist in Lutheran Germany were considerably more attractive than those of a theologian or churchman.

Thanks to his wide reading in history and his thorough immersion in philosophy, Leibniz found his legal studies undemanding. He did not spend much time on theory, which he mastered without difficulty, and focused instead on practice. A family friend who was an assessor of the High Court of Leipzig – possibly Leibniz's godfather Johann Fritsch[126] – often took the young law student with him, gave him legal acts to read, and taught him through examples how to arrive at verdicts. Leibniz enjoyed the office of judge but not that of trial lawyer, and for this reason he never desired to lead trials despite his interest in legal practice and his proficiency in German prose.[127] His general judgement regarding the organisation of legal studies, moreover, was not particularly flattering. In his proposal for a *Nova Methodus Discendae Docendaeque Jurisprudentiae* (*New Method for Learning and Teaching Jurisprudence*), written only four years later in 1667, he argued that the five-year law course could have been much more efficiently covered in two years – an emphasis on pedagogical efficiency again typical of the post-Ramist tradition.[128] And if legal instruction was unnecessarily protracted on the one hand, it was also far too narrow in conception and application on the other.

What he meant by this second criticism is partially evident in the dissertation he defended and published in December 1664 after taking his Master's degree in philosophy on 7 February of that year. The disputation was entitled *Specimen Quaestionum Philosophicarum ex Jure collectarum*, and the purpose of this *Specimen of Collected Philosophical Questions Concerning Law* was to argue for a tight theoretical, practical, and pedagogical relationship between philosophy and law.[129] Once again, Leibniz was employing the ordinary institutions of the German universities to produce something quite extraordinary. To dispute on a series of loosely related philosophical questions was commonplace. To draw these from the higher discipline of law was more unusual. And to employ these related philosophical questions as a "specimen" of the way in which that higher discipline should be studied, taught, and practiced was bolder still. Yet without reference to philosophy, Leibniz argued, it was impossible to resolve many legal questions, such as whether the notions of justice and injustice apply to animals or whether future contingents are true or false. Jurisprudence, he demanded, should therefore be built on a solid metaphysical foundation, and the study of law should be prepared by rigorous and extensive training in philosophy.[130] Similar broadmindedness was evident in the range of authors which buttressed his argument, sources ranging from "ancients" such as Protagoras, Plato, and Aristotle to "moderns" such as Grotius, Hobbes, and Gassendi, with a still more dizzying array of thinkers in between: from scholastic authors such as Sanchez, to Renaissance Aristotelians such as Zabarella, and a diverse range of recent eclectics such as his teacher Weigel, the Jesuit Athanasius Kircher, and the Reformed encyclopaedist Alsted. Not for the last time, Leibniz seemed to have distilled the entire history of human thought into his little dissertation. Similar specimens of this interdisciplinary and eclectic approach were pursued in his following legal and philosophical disputations; and a few years later he arranged for them to be reprinted under the telling new title: *Specimen Encyclopaediae in Jure* (*Specimen of a Juridical Encyclopaedia*).[131]

Nine days after his graduation as a master of philosophy, Leibniz lost his mother.[132] In order to settle the rather complex details related to a modest inheritance, he travelled in March to Braunschweig to visit his uncle Johann Strauch, a distinguished jurist married to his mother's sister. Strauch was very impressed by his bright nephew, and later wrote on 16 July 1665 to congratulate him on his first juridical dissertation.[133] Written for Leibniz's Bachelor's degree in law, this piece was once again on an issue spanning law and philosophy – that of conditional judgements in law (*De conditionibus*) – and the outstanding law student had again approached the problem in a novel way by attempting to resolve it by means of a mathematical demonstration. As such this little disputation represented his first attempt at the development of a rational jurisprudence or, as he retitled the dissertation a few years later, his first "Specimen certitudinis seu demonstrationum in Jure [Specimen of certainty or demonstrations in jurisprudence]".[134] Since he did not have the time to complete it by the date fixed for the formal disputation (24 July 1665), he presented only a first part on that occasion. The discussion of the second part followed on 27 August.[135] On 28 September 1665, two years after beginning his legal studies, he was awarded the Bachelor's degree in law – the earliest that the university statutes would allow.

By this time he was probably already thinking about his *Nova Methodus Discendae Docendaeque Jurisprudentiae* and was certainly working on his most original early work: the *Dissertatio de Arte Combinatoria*.[136] With the first part, disputed on 17 March 1666 and published under the title of *Disputatio arithmetica de Complexionibus*, Leibniz earned his habilitation in the faculty of philosophy, a mere five years after the commencement of his university studies.[137] The whole work was published shortly afterward and went well beyond what could have been expected even from an outstanding student dissertation. Its background was the *ars combinatoria* (combinatorial art) of the medieval Catalan philosopher Ramon Lull (c. 1232–1316).[138] Lull had devised a mechanical method for finding all the possible combinations between a limited number of simple and general terms. For the purpose of arriving at the formulation of all conceivable propositions, he had constructed a sort of table of categories divided into six series, each containing nine terms represented by nine letters of the alphabet.[139] The nine terms of each series were arranged on six concentric circles, the rotation of which displayed all the possible combinations of all the terms in the six series. The early modern period saw the proliferation of attempts to expound and improve Lull's combinatorial art or *Ars Magna*, notably by Bernard de Lavinheta, Heinrich Cornelius Agrippa, Giordano Bruno, Johann Heinrich Alsted (who, in addition to publishing his own combinatorial works, edited those of Lavinheta and Bruno), and, last but not least, Athanasius Kircher. The *Deliciae physico-mathematicae* published between 1636 and 1653 by Daniel Schwenter and Georg Philipp Harsdörffer constituted an important source of Leibniz's youthful dissertation. Here again the influence of Herborn was strikingly apparent – virtually the only Protestant institution in Germany where these aspirations had penetrated deep into an academic setting.[140]

Although Leibniz appreciated the intuitions of Lull and the efforts of this diffuse Lullist tradition, in his view the *ars combinatoria* could offer far more than had been envisaged by the Catalan master. Lull lacked a formal theory of combinatorial calculus and was not interested in applying his *ars combinatoria* to traditional logic. For Leibniz, by contrast, as for Alsted and Bisterfeld, application to logic – both traditional syllogistic logic and a new *logica inventiva* or logic of discovery – was at the heart of his interest in the *ars combinatoria*; and the scope of his project was therefore far broader than the more narrowly mathematical one of Schwenter and Harsdörffer as well.[141] In April 1666, sending a copy of his newly published dissertation to the rector in Zwickau, Christian Daum, he indicated the scope of his project by describing the *ars combinatoria* as the "key of all sciences," in the rules of which "the whole logic of discovery was contained."[142] In October 1671, summarising his achievements to a prospective employer, he likewise proudly labelled his *ars combinatoria* the "mother of all inventions" and claimed that through it "all the composite notions in the entire world could be reduced to a few simple notions as if to their alphabet; and conversely, from the combination of [the letters of] such an alphabet a way could be paved to the discovery of all things, together with their theorems and everything that could in time be discovered from them by means of an orderly method."[143]

The *Dissertatio de Arte Combinatoria* constituted in fact Leibniz's most striking early attempt at the construction of an alphabet of human thoughts. In this youthful work he outlined for the first time his project of developing a universal language on the basis of this alphabet. The idea was to start with the analysis of concepts in order to arrive at primitive concepts in a way analogous to the mathematical reduction of numbers into prime numbers. Primitive concepts would then have been associated with appropriate signs or characters; and finally a set of rules for the combination of primitive concepts would be established in order to derive from them all other possible concepts. Although Leibniz later began to doubt that it was possible for the human mind to reach concepts which were absolutely primitive,[144] he continued to maintain that we could operate in this fashion with concepts which were primitive for us.[145] Further momentous features of the *Dissertatio de Arte Combinatoria* included its nascent distinction between truths of reason and truths of fact, its reference to the novel equation of thinking with calculating introduced by Hobbes in his *Computatio sive Logica* (1655),[146] its development of a systematic treatment of the syllogism which would remain a central feature of other logical writings, and its formulation of correct rules of combinatorial calculus regarding the number of combinations.[147] Last but not least, central to the entire work was the idea of universal harmony, which Leibniz expressed by referring to Bisterfeld's doctrine of "the universal *immeatio* and *perichōrēsis* of all things in all things . . . the similitude and dissimilitude of all things with all things, the principle of which is relations."[148] Twenty years later Leibniz had grown more cautious; but even while realising the limitations and even mistakes of his youthful work, its novelty, importance, and potential remained clear in his mind. When the *Dissertatio de Arte Combinatoria* was republished in Frankfurt without his knowledge in 1690, he publicly expressed his displeasure at this unauthorized edition in a note in the *Acta Eruditorum* of February 1691. While frankly acknowledging the shortcomings of a work composed when he was not yet twenty years old, he also defended the fact that it contained "many new and not unsatisfactory meditations through which the seeds of the *ars inveniendi* were spread . . . and, among the others, the one which deserved the palm was the meditation on the Analysis of human thoughts into something like an Alphabet of quasiprimitive notions."[149] As late as September 1712 he was still turning over in his mind the wonderful project conceived in his youth of an "Alphabet of human thoughts" ("Alphabetum cogitationum humanarum") which could have transformed the Lullian art of combinations into a much more perfect tool.[150]

To complete his education, Leibniz was lacking at this point only the highest degrees: the licence and the doctorate in law. According to the Leipzig statutes, after earning his Bachelor's degree in law in September 1665, he was technically required to study for at least another two years before earning the licence and a further year after that before the doctorate. In practice, however, it was not impossible to shorten the full duration of law studies, either by gaining the licence less than a year after the Bachelor's degree, or by obtaining the licence and the doctorate at the same time. Through such expedients Leibniz might well have become the youngest doctor of law ever produced in Leipzig but for the opposition of older students, which was upheld by the faculty. In order to secure for themselves the next available positions of assessors in the faculty of law, the older students set out to block the early graduation of younger colleagues, Leibniz amongst them.[151] When they seemed to have gained the support of the faculty, Leibniz, disgusted by their intrigues, changed his plans and decided to begin travelling and to devote himself to the study of mathematics. Making the best of a disagreeable situation, he recalled much later, he decided that it was unworthy "for a young man to be tied to the same place," especially since he had already "ardently desired" for some time "to earn more glory in the sciences and to get to know the world."[152] His subsequent curriculum would amply demonstrate how ardent this love of learning and travel was and also how tenuous were the ties which bound him to his birthplace. He left Leipzig at the end of September 1666 and was to return there in the course of his life only for a few brief visits. Yet even the unfortunate circumstances of his departure did not entirely sour his memories of his native city. When toward the end of his life a correspondent from Leipzig referred to the town as his "ingrate native land,"[153] Leibniz replied,

I am glad that our Leipzig is blossoming again after struggling through some very difficult times. I love it as a homeland and do not feel it as ungrateful . . . Nor, however, does this cause me to repent of my impatience; divine providence puts right the mistakes of human beings, so that often things which are thrown badly fall well[.][154]

Given the proliferation of universities in sixteenth- and seventeenth-century Germany, if regulations or other obstacles blocked one's path or pace of advancement in one institution, one had merely to transfer to another. On 4 October 1666, therefore, Leibniz enrolled in the faculty of law of one of the youngest of these institutions: the University of Altdorf, situated within the territories subject to the imperial free city of Nuremberg. There he submitted almost immediately a thesis (which he must have at least begun to compose before leaving Leipzig) for both the licence and the doctorate in law, defending it as early as 15 November. Once again the topic chosen – already mentioned in his dissertation for the Master's degree in philosophy – spanned the fields of philosophy and jurisprudence; and once again it dealt not with a particular issue or even branch of the law but with a second-order question: namely, how in general to solve particularly uncertain or difficult cases in law (*Disputatio de Casibus perplexis in Jure*).[155] According to Leibniz, cases which could not be solved on the basis of civil law should neither be declared irresolvable, as some jurists proposed, nor left to the arbitration of the judge. Rather, appeal should be made to the principles of natural justice and international law which had the power to limit and determine civil law.[156] In yet another respect, Leibniz was arguing that a particular discipline such as law could only be properly taught, learned, and practiced within a broader encyclopaedia of the arts and sciences.

Although presented by such a young candidate so soon after his matriculation in Altdorf, the disputation – Leibniz later recalled with pride – went brilliantly. Thanks to his extraordinary mastery of the matter and his exceptionally clear exposition, the other disputants declared themselves completely satisfied. Praise for his impressive performance soon arrived from various quarters, including his former professors in Leipzig. The dean of the Altdorf faculty, Johann Wolfang Textor, wrote to the official responsible for education in Nuremberg, Johann Michael Dilherr, with word that the newly created doctor had graduated with the highest honours.[157] The official graduation ceremony, held in Altdorf on 22 February 1667, provided a further opportunity to impress the learned community in the environs of Nuremberg when Leibniz delivered two speeches: one in prose, the other in verse. The Latin prose oration was so eloquent (its author recalled much later) that the audience naturally assumed that he was reading from the papers that he had with him; and it was only when he began to read the verses, holding those same papers close to his eyes due to his short-sightedness, that the audience realised that the prose speech had been impromptu. Dilherr lost no time in attempting to recruit the outstanding new doctor to an Altdorf professorship. But Leibniz declined: his thoughts were already moving in a wholly different direction.[158] His "ardent desire to earn more glory in the sciences" was too great to be satisfied by a doctorate in law, and his wanderlust had not been satiated by a trip to Altdorf. Literally and metaphorically, he wanted to travel far further afield.

By the time he had completed his formal education, Leibniz's vision had been born. He had decided what to do with his life. Born into a fragmented world lacerated by religious, political, and intellectual crises, "Wilhelmus Pacidius", alias Gottfried Wilhelm Leibniz, was going to put the pieces together to achieve a universal synthesis for the glory of God and the happiness of mankind.[159] This synthesis would be designed to restore unity in multiplicity, unveiling the universal harmony which, despite apparently unbridgeable divisions, governed reality at both the metaphysical and the epistemological level, and thereby bringing about the *emendatio rerum* on which recent generations of central European reformers, inspired by Francis Bacon and their own indigenous traditions, had been working. His vast reading of theological and polemical literature from all camps had already shown him that "not all opinions which are commonly advanced are certain, and often things which are not so important are contested with excessive vehemence".[160] Surely agreement could be found amongst the Christian confessions, provided that each camp was willing to listen with open mind to the reasons of the others. Settling religious divergences would have assisted the process of reaching a durable peace at the political level. As for the competing world-views of the 'ancients' and the 'moderns', they too could be reconciled. Not surprisingly, he saw that the way to realise this Promethean dream was not to follow in the footsteps of his father and relatives and quietly settle down as a professor in one of the traditionally oriented German universities. He needed first of all to travel the world and broaden his horizons. He needed to realise his ideal of universal reform by selling his concrete proposals to enlightened princes. In short, after his brilliant promotion it was time for him to try his hand at the challenge embraced by many young people – changing the world. If was not destined to succeed on the scale he had imagined, he was nevertheless to make an extraordinary contribution to this ever returning enterprise.

Notes

1. See the huge and lavishly illustrated proceedings of the major exhibition and conference marking the 350th anniversary of the Peace of Westphalia edited by Klaus Bussman and Heinz Schilling: *1648: War and Peace in Europe.* 3 vols. Munich: Bruckmann, 1998.
2. This domestic dimension of the conflict is emphasized in Ronald G. Asch, *The Thirty Years War: The Holy Roman Empire and Europe, 1618–1648.* Basingstoke: Macmillan, 1997.
3. The international ramifications of the conflict are brought out in Geoffrey Parker, ed., *The Thirty Years War.* 2nd ed. London: Routledge, 1997. Notable earlier accounts emphasizing this aspect include S. H. Steinberg, *The 'Thirty Years War' and the Conflict for European Hegemony, 1600–1660.* London: Edward Arnold, 1966, and H. G. Koenigsberger, *The Habsburgs and Europe, 1516–1660.* Ithaca: Cornell University Press, 1971, ch. on "Europe's Civil War."

4. R. A. Bireley, "The Thirty Years War as Germany's Religious War." In *Krieg und Politik 1618–1648*. Ed. by K. Repgen. München: R. Oldenbourg, 1988, pp. 85–106.

5. For a contextualised survey of efforts at confessional reconciliation during and immediately after the war, see Howard Hotson, "Irenicism in the Confessional Age: The Holy Roman Empire, 1563–1648." In *Conciliation and Confession: Struggling for Unity in the Age of Reform*. Edited by Howard Louthan and Randall Zachman. Notre Dame: University of Notre Dame Press, 2004, pp. 228–85.

6. The term 'Reformed' refers to the second main variety of magisterial Protestantism, commonly termed 'Calvinist', but also embracing related communities such as Zwinglianism and the German Reformed tradition defined by the Heidelberg Catechism.

7. The classic instance at the outbreak of the war is treated in Hans Knapp, *Matthias Hoe von Hoenegg und sein Eingreiffen in die Politik und Publizistik des dreissigjährigen Krieges*. Halle, 1902, and Hans-Dieter Hertrampf, "Höe von Höenegg – Sächsischer Oberhofprediger 1613–1645." *Herbergen der Christenheit. Jahrbuch für deutschen Kirchengeschichte*. [= Beiträge zur Kirchengeschichte Deutschlands, vol. 7] Berlin, 1969, pp. 129–48. For a survey see Bodo Nischan, "Reformed Irenicism and the Leipzig Colloquy of 1631." *Central European History* 9 (1976): 3–26, here esp. pp. 19–25.

8. On the political aspect cf. Axel Gotthard, " 'Politice seint wir bäpstisch': Kursachsen und der deutschen Protestantismus im frühen 17 Jahrhundert." *Zeitschrift für Historische Forschung* 20 (1993): 275–319.

9. See Detlef Döring, *Der junge Leibniz und Leipzig: Ausstellung zum 350. Geburtstag von Gottfried Wilhelm Leibniz im Leipziger Alten Rathaus*. Berlin: Akademie Verlag, 1996, p. 24.

10. See ibid., pp. 82–5.

11. Leibniz's claim to nobility might have originated from his conviction that his ancestors belonged to the Polish noble family Lubeniecz (Lubienicius). The only person in Leibniz's family elevated to the peerage seems to have been the childless Paul von Leubnitz, a distant relative ennobled in August 1600. Cf. chapter II. 7, note 42; Pertz I, 4, 165; Ernst Kroker, "Leibnizens Vorfahren." *Neues Archiv für Sächsische Geschichte* 19 (1898): 315–38 (here pp. 315, 337).

12. Cf. *Selbstschilderung* (Pertz I, 4, 165; this autobiographical recollection is also published under the title of *Vita Leibnitii a se ipso breviter delineata* in *Nouvelles lettres et opuscules inédits de Leibniz*. Edited by A. Foucher de Careil. Paris: Auguste Durand, 1857, pp. 379–386 and in Gottschalk Eduard Guhrauer, *Gottfried Wilhelm Freiherr von Leibnitz. Eine Biographie*. 2 vols. Breslau: Hirt, 1842. 2nd enlarged ed. Breslau: Hirt, 1846 (repr. Hildesheim: Olms, 1966), II, Anmerkungen, pp. 52–8); Kroker, "Leibnizens Vorfahren," pp. 315–38; Kurt Müller, "Gottfried Wilhelm Leibniz. Sein Leben und Wirken." In *Leibniz. Sein Leben, Sein Wirken, Seine Welt*. Ed. by Wilhelm Totok and Carl Haase. Hanover: Verlag für Literatur und Zeitgeschehen, 1966, pp. 8–10; Rudolph Fischer, "Der Name Leibniz." In *Leipziger Namenkundliche Beiträge II*. Berlin,

1968 (Sitzungsberichte der Sächsischen Akademie des Wiss. Vol. 113. Issue 4), pp. 7–18 (esp. pp. 10–11); Arndt Richter and Weert Meyer, "Gottfried Wilhelm Leibniz (1646–1716). Pedigree and Ancestors." *Knowledge Organization* 23 (1996): 103–6. Fischer challenges the thesis proposed by V. Davídek, "G. W. Leibniz oriundus Lipnicky." *Revue internationale d'onomastique* 17 (1965): 93–8, according to which the family name "Leibniz" originated from the Slavic river and place name "Lipnica" (or "Lipnice" in Czech).

13. The name form 'Leibniz' was used by the young Gottfried Wilhelm at least from May 1671 onward. See Müller, "Gottfried Wilhelm Leibniz," p. 7.

14. Otto Rudert, "Der Raid des Grafen Holck im Jahre 1633." In *Schriften des Vereins für die Geschichte Leipzigs*. Vol. 16. Leipzig: Selbstverlag des Vereins, 1933, p. 47.

15. Cf. Döring, *Der junge Leibniz und Leipzig*, pp. 50–51 and Wilhelm Stieda, *Professor Friedrich Leubnitz, der Vater des Philosophen*. Leipzig: Teubner, 1917.

16. *Selbstschilderung* (Pertz I, 4, 165–6).

17. Döring, *Der junge Leibniz und Leipzig*, pp. 51–3.

18. Pertz I, 4, 173.

19. See Willy Kabitz, "Die Bildungsgeschichte des jungen Leibniz." *Zeitschrift für Geschichte der Erziehung und des Unterrichts* 2 (1912), p. 166.

20. See A I, 1, N. 157.

21. See Döring, *Der junge Leibniz und Leipzig*, pp. 54–6 and Paul Schrecker, "G.-W. Leibniz. Lettres et fragments inédits," *Revue philosophique de la France et de l'Étranger* 118 (1934): 5–134 (see pp. 57–83 for the extensive notes of Simon Löffler on two letters of 1669 written by Leibniz to his half-brother Johann Friedrich).

22. See for instance Johann Friedrich Leibniz to Leibniz, 7 September 1680 (A I, 3, 601–2). Cf. Döring, *Der junge Leibniz und Leipzig*, pp. 53–4.

23. See Schrecker, "G.-W. Leibniz. Lettres et fragments inédits," pp. 57–8, 65–83.

24. See Johann Friedrich Leibniz to Leibniz, 3 May 1692 (A I, 8, 605–6) and 11 October 1692 (A I, 8, 616).

25. Schrecker, "G.-W. Leibniz. Lettres et fragments inédits," p. 82, quoting Matthew 7:1.

26. See Leibniz to Johann Friedrich Leibniz, 30 April 1669 and 5 October 1669 (in Schrecker, "G.-W. Leibniz. Lettres et fragments inédits," respectively pp. 57, 67).

27. On the tolerant attitude of the court of Mainz see Paul Wiedeburg, *Der Junge Leibniz. Das Reich und Europa*. I Part: Mainz. 2 vols. Wiesbaden: Steiner, 1962, vol. 1, pp. 69–71 and Ursula Goldenbaum, "Transubstantiation, Physics and Philosophy at the Time of the *Catholic Demonstrations*." In *The Young Leibniz and His Philosophy, 1646–1676*. Ed. by Stuart Brown. Dordrecht: Kluwer, 1999, pp. 88–9.

28. See in particular Pertz I, 4, 173; *Nouvelles lettres et opuscules inédits de Leibniz*, p. 389; *Wilhelmus Pacidius. Entwurf einer Einleitung* (A VI, 2, 510–11); A VI, 4, 264–5.

29. See Döring's concise overview of this historiographical tradition in *Der junge Leibniz und Leipzig*, pp. 15–17. Notable exceptions signalled by Döring are Kabitz, "Die Bildungsgeschichte des jungen Leibniz," p. 165; Heinz-L. Matzat, "Die Gedankenwelt des jungen Leibniz." In *Beiträge zur Leibniz-Forschung*. Ed. by G. Schischkoff. Reutlingen: Gryphius-Verlag, 1947, pp. 38–9; and Kurt Huber, *Leibniz*. München: Oldenbourg, 1951, pp. 15–16.

30. See especially Döring, *Der junge Leibniz und Leipzig*, pp. 15–17.

31. See in general Arno Siefert, "Das höhere Schulwesen: Universitäten und Gymnasien." In *Handbuch der deutschen Bildungsgeschichte*. Ed. by Christa Berg et al. Vol. 1: *15. bis 17. Jahrhundert*. Ed. by Notker Hammerstein. Munich, 1996, pp. 197–374, here esp. pp. 284–312.

32. See Georg Erler, *Die jüngere Matrikel der Universität Leipzig (1559–1809)*. 3 vols. Leipzig: Giesecke and Devrient, 1909, vol. 2, p. 255.

33. Cf. Emil Dohmke, "Die Nikolaischule zu Leipzig im siebzehnten Jahrhundert." In *Programm des Nicolaigymnasiums in Leipzig*. Leipzig: Edelmann, 1874, pp. 22–31; Kabitz, "Die Bildungsgeschichte des jungen Leibniz," pp. 168–9; Döring, *Der junge Leibniz und Leipzig*, pp. 57–9.

34. Luther's enormously influential *Kleiner Katechismus* (1529), written to remedy religious ignorance among the German populace, was assiduously studied in the Nikolaischule not only in its original German but also in Latin and Greek translations (cf. Dohmke, "Die Nikolaischule zu Leipzig im siebzehnten Jahrhundert," pp. 23, 26). Leonhard Hutter's *Compendium locorum theologicorum ex scripturis sacris et libro concordiae collectum* (1610) quickly established itself as a precise and effective exposition of strict Lutheran doctrines.

35. Cf. Kabitz, "Die Bildungsgeschichte des jungen Leibniz," p. 171; Dohmke, "Die Nikolaischule zu Leipzig im siebzehnten Jahrhundert," pp. 35–8.

36. *Selbstschilderung* (Pertz I, 4, 166–7).

37. Ibid., 165–6.

38. Ibid., 166. Cf. Kabitz, "Die Bildungsgeschichte des jungen Leibniz," pp. 169–70.

39. Pertz, I, 4, 173; A IV, 4, 16.

40. *Selbstschilderung* (Pertz I, 4, 166). Cf. Kabitz, "Die Bildungsgeschichte des jungen Leibniz," pp. 169–70.

41. Cf. *Selbstschilderung* (Pertz I, 4, 166–7).

42. Cf. E. François, "Géographie du livre et réseau urbain dans l'Allemagne moderne." In *La Ville et l'innovation*. Paris, 1987, pp. 59–74.

43. Cf. A I, 3, xlv; Sabine Knopf and Volker Titel, *Der Leipzig Gutenbergweg. Geschichte und Topographie einer Buchstadt*. Leipzig: Sax-Verlag Beucha, 2001, pp. 14–15.

44. *Wilhelmus Pacidius. Entwurf einer Einleitung* (A VI, 2, 510–11).

45. See *Selbstschilderung* (Pertz I, 4, 167); *Nouvelles lettres et opuscules inédits de Leibniz*, p. 381; *Wilhelmus Pacidius. Entwurf einer Einleitung* (A VI, 2, 510–11); Leibniz to Nicolas Rémond, 10 January 1714 (GP III, 606).

46. Leibniz to Nicolas Rémond, 10 January 1714 (GP III, 606).

47. See *Selbstschilderung* (Pertz I, 4, 167); "Die Bildungsgeschichte des jungen Leibniz," p. 171; Kurt Müller and Gisela Krönert, *Leben und Werk von Gottfried Wilhelm Leibniz. Eine Chronik.* Frankfurt am Main: Klostermann, 1969, p. 5.

48. See Leibniz to Gabriel Wagner, 1696 (GP VII, 514–27).

49. At the very least it is doubtful that Leibniz had a first-hand knowledge of Aristotle at this stage. It is more plausible that the teenager encountered Aristotle in the profusion of textbooks of varying degrees of accuracy produced by the Aristotelian tradition.

50. See Leibniz to Gabriel Wagner, 1696 (GP VII, 516–17) and *Selbstschilderung* (Pertz I, 4, 167–8).

51. Leibniz to Gabriel Wagner, 1696 (GP VII, 517). See also Leibniz to F. W. Bierling, 7 July 1711 (GP VII, 496).

52. Leibniz to Gabriel Wagner, 1696 (GP VII, 516, 517).

53. Cf. Wilhelm Risse, *Die Logik der Neuzeit*. 2 vols. Stuttgart–Bad Cannstatt. Frommann, 1964–70; Wilhelm Risse, *Bibliographia logica: Verzeichnis der Druckschriften zur Logik mit Angabe ihrer Fundorte*, vol. 1: 1472–1800. Hildesheim: Olms, 1965.

54. Leibniz to Gabriel Wagner, 1696 (GP VII, 517).

55. Cf. Ann Moss, *Printed Commonplace-Books and the Structuring of Renaissance Thought*. Oxford: Clarendon Press, 1996

56. Leibniz to F. W. Bierling, 7 July 1711 (GP VII, 496). See also Leibniz to Gabriel Wagner, 1696 (GP VII, 517).

57. On this tradition, see most recently and comprehensively Howard Hotson, *Commonplace Learning: Ramism and Its German Ramifications, 1543-1630*. Oxford: Oxford University Press, 2007.

58. Johann Heinrich Alsted, *Encyclopaedia septem tomis distincta.* 7 tomes in 2 vols. Herborn, 1630. Howard Hotson, *Johann Heinrich Alsted 1588–1638: Between Renaissance, Reformation, and Universal Reform.* Oxford: Clarendon Press, 2000, provides the first holistic account of the ideas, institutions, and individuals of the Central European Reformed academic community.

59. On the Herborn Academy see Gerhard Menk, *Die Hohe Schule Herborn in ihrer Frühzeit (1584–1660): Ein Beitrag zum Hochschulwesen des deutschen Kalvinismus im Zeitalter der Gegenreformation.* Wiesbaden: Selbstverlag der Historischen Kommission für Nassau, 1981. For the latter stages of this post-Ramist tradition, see Howard Hotson, *The Reformation of Common Learning: Post-Ramist-Method and the Reception of the New Philosophy, 1618–1670.* Oxford: Oxford University Press, forthcoming.

60. See Georg Voigt, "Über den Ramismus an der Universität Leipzig." *Berichte über der Verhandlungen der königlichen sächsischen Gesellschaft der Wissenschaften zu Leipzig, Philologisch-historische Klasse*, 40 (1888): 31–61.

61. S. J. Walter Ong, *Ramus and Talon Inventory: A Short-Title Inventory.* Cambridge, MA: Harvard University Press, 1958 lists only one Ramist work published in Leipzig: an edition of the *Rhetorica* 1668 (no. 173).

62. For the university, see the discussion of Thomasius's eclecticism later in this chapter.

63. See G. W. Leibniz to his half-brother, Johann Friedrich Leibniz, 26 December 1684 (A I, 4, 680–81). Bartholomäus Keckermann, *Opera omnia*. 2 vols. in folio. Geneva, 1614. Johannes Althusius (1557–1638), *Dicaeologicae libri tres, totum et universum jus . . . methodicè complectentes*. Herborn, 1617, 1618; Frankfurt am Main, 1649. For Bisterfeld see below. Also from this semi-Ramist tradition were the works of Anton Matthaeus (1564–1637), professor of law in Herborn from 1594 to 1605, and the philosopher Johann Rudolph Lavater (d. 1625), a friend and editor of Keckermann in Heidelberg and student of Timpler in Steinfurt. Matthaeus's *Collegia Juris* (Franekerae 1647) was Leibniz's own acquisition of November 1664 (cf. A VI, 2, 20). For further details see Hotson, *Commonplace Learning*, pp. 120, 163–4, 209.

64. The annotations are published in A VI, 2, N. 26/1, N. 26/3, N. 26/4, and A VI, 1, N. 7.

65. See A VI, 1, 74; A VI, 1, 275, 279, 290, 323; *Selbstschilderung* (Pertz I, 4, 171).

66. See A VI, 1, 74 and Gerda Utermöhler, "Die Literatur der Renaissance und des Humanismus in Leibniz' privater Büchersammlung." In *Leibniz et la renaissance*. Ed. by Albert Heinekamp. Wiesbaden: Franz Steiner Verlag, 1983, pp. 221–38; cf. also Nelly Bruyère, "Leibniz, lecteur de Ramus." In *Leibniz et la renaissance*. Ed. by Albert Heinekamp. Wiesbaden: Franz Steiner Verlag, 1983, pp. 157–73.

67. These are the authors listed in Leibniz's recollections (see note below).

68. See *Wilhelmus Pacidius. Entwurf einer Einleitung* (A VI, 2, 510–11); *Selbstschilderung* (Pertz I, 4, 167); *Nouvelles lettres et opuscules inédits de Leibniz*, p. 381; Leibniz to Nicolas Rémond, 10 January 1714 (GP III, 606).

69. See *Wilhelmus Pacidius. Entwurf einer Einleitung* (A VI, 2, 511).

70. See Leibniz to Gabriel Wagner, 1696, GP VII, 517.

71. See *De numeris characteristicis ad linguam universalem constituendam*, spring–summer 1679* (A VI, 4, 265). Guhrauer, *Leibnitz*, I, pp. 20 ff. places the origin of this project at the end of Leibniz's school years; according to Kabitz it should rather be postponed to the university years (see Kabitz, "Die Bildungsgeschichte des jungen Leibniz," p. 173).

72. See *Dissertatio de Arte Combinatoria*, 1666 (A VI, 1, 199). The importance of the tradition represented by Alsted and Bisterfeld is stressed, amongst others, by Catherine Wilson, *Leibniz's metaphysics. A historical and comparative study*, Princeton: Princeton University Press/Manchester: Manchester University Press, 1989, chap. 1. On the combinatorial dimension of Alsted's encyclopaedic plans, see Hotson, *Alsted*, esp. pp. 168-70, 172-6, 226.

73. Respectively, A VI, 1, 160 and A VI, 1, 151. Leibniz read both works in the posthumous editions which appeared in Leiden in 1657.

74. See *Dissertatio de Arte Combinatoria*, 1666 (A VI, 1, 199).

75. See Massimo Mugnai, "Der Begriff der Harmonie als metaphysische Grundlage der Logik und Kombinatorik bei Johann Heinrich Bisterfeld und Leibniz." *Studia Leibnitiana* 5 (1973): 43–73; Donald Rutherford, *Leibniz and the Rational Order*

of Nature. Cambridge: Cambridge University Press, 1995, pp. 36–40; Maria Rosa Antognazza, "*Debilissimae Entitates?* Bisterfeld and Leibniz's ontology of relations." *The Leibniz Review* 11 (2001): 1–22.

76. See Heikki Mikkeli, *An Aristotelian Response to Renaissance Humanism: Jacopo Zabarella on the Nature of Arts and Sciences*. Helsinki, 1992; Hotson, *Commonplace Learning*, esp. pp. 137–40.

77. *Selbstschilderung* (Pertz I, 4, 168, 171). See also Leibniz to Nicolas Rémond, 10 January 1714 (GP III, 606); and for background E. Lewalter, *Spanisch-jesuitische und deutsch-lutherische Metaphysik des 17. Jahrhunderts*. Hamburg, 1935.

78. See *Theodicy* (1710), "Preface" (GP VI, 43).

79. See Leibniz to Daniel Ernst Jablonski, 2 Feb. 1700 (A I, 18, 322). On this aspect of the colloquy see Otto Ritschl, *Dogmengeschichte des Protestantismus: Grundlagen und Grundzüge der theologischen Gedenken- und Lehrbildung in den protestantischen Kirchen*. 4 vols. Leipzig: J. C. Hinrichs, 1908–27, vol. 4, pp. 106–56; Hans Leube, *Kalvinismus und Luthertum im Zeitalter der Orthodoxie*. Leipzig. A. Deichert, 1928, pp. 107–10; and Hans E. Weber, *Reformation, Orthodoxie und Rationalismus*. Gütersloh: Bertelsmann, 1951, Part 2, pp. 98–175.

80. *Selbstschilderung* (Pertz I, 4, 170–71).

81. See A I, 18, N. 194 (*Vorausedition*).

82. See *Theodicy*, "Preface" (GP VI, 43).

83. For an excellent introduction to Calixt see Johannes Wallmann, "Zwischen Reformation und Humanismus: Eigenart und Wirkungen Helmstedter Theologie unter besondere Berücksichtung Georg Calixts." *Zeitschrift für Theologie und Kirche* 74 (1977): 344–70. On the contrast with Reformed irenicism, Hotson, "Irenicism in the Confessional Age," esp. pp. 210–11.

84. Cf. Heinz Staemmler, *Die Auseinandersetzung der kursächsischen Theologen mit dem Helmstedter Synkretismus. Eine Studie zum "Consensus repetitus fidei vere Lutheranae" 1655) und den Diskussionen um ihn*. Waltrop: Spenner, 2005; Döring, *Der junge Leibniz und Leipzig*, pp. 82–5.

85. Cf. Arno Seifert, *Der Rückzug der biblischen Prophetie von der neueren Geschichte. Studien zur Geschichte der Reichstheologie des frühneuzeitlichen Protestantismus*. Vienna and Cologne: Böhlau, 1990.

86. For comparative matriculation data see Franz Eulenburg, *Die Frequenz der deutschen Universitäten*. Leipzig, 1904; repr. Berlin, 1994. For the following see also Emil Friedberg, *Die Leipziger Juristenfakultät, ihre Doktoren und ihr Heim*. [= *Feschrift zur Feier des 500jährigen Bestehens der Universität Leipzig*, vol. 1] Leipzig, 1909, pp. 51–3; Lother Rathmann, ed., *Alma Mater Lipsiensis. Geschichte der Karl-Marx-Universität Leipzig*. Leipzig, 1984, pp. 72–5.

87. Christia Mercer insists on the importance for Leibniz's intellectual development of the "conciliatory eclecticism" of his teachers. See her "The Young Leibniz and His Teachers." In *The Young Leibniz and his Philosophy, 1646–1676*. Ed. by Stuart Brown. Dordrecht: Kluwer, 1999, pp. 19–40 and *Leibniz's Metaphysics*, esp. pp. 32–9. On Leibniz's teachers and their eclecticism see also Döring, *Der junge Leibniz und Leipzig*, pp. 73–6, 85; Ulrich G. Leinsle, *Reformversuche*

protestantischer Metaphysik im Zeitalter des Rationalismus. Augsburg: Maro Verlag, 1988, pp. 20–26, 63–87, 139–49; Henri Joly, "Thomasius et l'Université de Leipzig pendant la jeunesse de Leibniz." *Revue philosophique de la France et de l'étranger* 6 (1878): 482–500.

88. See Joly, "Thomasius," p. 484.

89. Cf. Mercer, "The Young Leibniz and his Teachers," especially pp. 27 and 35 and Christia Mercer, *Leibniz's Metaphysics: Its Origins and Development.* Cambridge: Cambridge University Press, 2001, pp. 203–4.

90. *Wilhelmus Pacidius. Entwurf einer Einleitung* (A VI, 2, 511) and Leibniz to Simon Foucher, 1675 (A II, 1, 247). See also Joachim Friedrich Feller, ed., *Otium Hanoveranum, sive, Miscellanea ex ore & schedis illustris viri, piae memoriae, Godofr. Guilielmi Leibnitii.* Lipsiae: Impensis Joann. Christiani Martini, 1718, p. 164 and Yvon Belaval, "Premières animadversions de Leibniz sur les *Principes de Descartes.*" In *Mélanges Alexandre Koyré t. II: L'aventure de l'esprit.* Paris: Hermann, 1964, pp. 29–56.

91. These are Daniel Stahl's *Compedium Metaphysicae in XXIV Tabellas redactum* and Thomasius's *Philosophia Practica* (A VI, 1, N. 2 and 3). Leibniz's early encounter with Gassendi and Hobbes has been detailed by Konrad Moll, *Der junge Leibniz.* 3 vols. Stuttgart–Bad Cannstatt: Frommann-Holzboog, 1978–96 (see esp. vols. II and III).

92. See Daniel Garber, "Motion and Metaphysics in the Young Leibniz." In *Leibniz: Critical and Interpretative Essays.* Ed. by Michael Hooker. Manchester: Manchester University Press, 1982, p. 160.

93. See A I, 14, 224 and GP III, 606. In both letters Leibniz placed this episode at the age of fifteen, that is, in the year in which he left school and began his university studies. This date has been questioned by a number of interpreters, who read his choice as a rejection of Aristotelianism as such. Against such an interpretation and in favour of taking at face value Leibniz's word regarding the time of his Rosental meditations argues convincingly Mercer, *Leibniz's Metaphysics*, pp. 24–49. In the letter to Thomas Burnett, Leibniz described his choice as between "Aristotle and Democritus," that is (as he explained in the *Confessio Naturae contra Atheistas* of 1669), "corpuscular philosophers, such as Galileo, Bacon, Gassendi, Descartes, Hobbes, and Digby" (A VI, 1, 490).

94. 1697, GP III, 205: "I began very young to meditate; and I was not quite fifteen years old when I strolled for whole days in a grove to choose between Aristotle and Democritus."

95. 1714, GP III, 606: "After finishing the *ecoles triviales* I fell upon the moderns, and I recall walking on my own in a grove on the outskirts of Leipzig called the Rosental, at the age of fifteen, to deliberate whether I should keep the substantial forms."

96. GP III, 606.

97. Cf. Garber, "Motion and Metaphysics in the Young Leibniz," p. 160.

98. GP IV, 478. Emphasis added. Cf. Mercer, *Leibniz's Metaphysics*, p. 25.

99. See text at note 111 below.

100. This interpretation thus coincides with the important work of Christia Mercer both in accepting Leibniz's original dating of this episode against the attempts to establish a later dating and, still more importantly, in concluding that the young Leibniz intended virtually from the outset to reconcile mechanism with crucial insights derived from Aristotle. It differs from Mercer's approach, however, primarily in the role to be assigned to Thomasius in this process.

101. Cf. Mercer, *Leibniz's Metaphysics*, pp. 27, 45.

102. *Confessio Naturae contra Atheistas*, 1669 (A VI, 1, 489–90) and Leibniz to Rémond, January 1714 (GP III, 606). See also *Discours de Métaphysique*, 1686 (A VI, 4, 1542–3); Leibniz to Antoine Arnauld, 14 July 1686 (GP II, 58); *Système nouveau de la nature*, 1695 (GP IV, 478).

103. Cf. Maria Rosa Antognazza, "Leibniz and the Post-Copernican Universe. Koyré Revisited." *Studies in History and Philosophy of Science.* 34 (2003): 309–27 (csp. pp. 312–15).

104. See Scherzer's celebrated polemical writings against the traditional enemies of the Lutheran confession: Catholics, Reformed, and Socinians (*Heptas Catholica, seu de Catholico, quatenus fidei et ecclesiae tribuitur, VII. dissertationes academicæ.* Lepzig: Typis Christiani Götzi, 1683; *Anti-Bellarminus.* Leipzig, 1703; *Collegium anti-Calvinianum.* Leipzig: Zschau, 1704; *Collegium anti-socinianum.* Leipzig: F. Lanckisius, 1672). Cf. Döring, *Der junge Leibniz und Leipzig*, pp. 75, 85.

105. On Comenius see most recently Werner Korthaase, Sigurd Hauff, and Andreas Fritsch, eds., *Comenius und der Weltfriede.* Berlin: Deutsche Comenius-Gesellschaft, 2005. On the German Reformed background see Hotson, "Irenicism"; Hotson, *Alsted*, pp. 125–6, 133–5, 197.

106. On the Platonism in Ramus himself, see for instance Nelly Bruyère, *Méthode et dialectique dans l'oeuvre de la Ramée.* Paris: J. Vrin, 1984. For later Ramist and semi-Ramist eclecticism cf. Hotson, *Commonplace Learning*, esp. pp. 107–8, 225–46, 284–6.

107. Cf. Mercer, *Leibniz's Metaphysics*, pp. 33, 37, 51.

108. Wilhelm Schmidt-Biggemann, *Topica Universalis: eine Modellgeschichte humanistischer und barocker Wissenschaft.* Hamburg: Meiner, 1983, pp. 107-13; Hotson, *Alsted*, esp. pp. 39–65, 82–109, 144–81.

109. Cf. Mercer, *Leibniz's Metaphysics*, pp. 32–8.

110. Cf. Jakob Thomasius, *De Sectarum Conciliationibus. Praemissa Disputationi, habitae Anno 1668. d. 20. Junii. De Quaestione: an Deus sit materia prima? Resp. Joh. Friderico Hekelio, Gerano.* In Jakob Thomasius, *Praefationes sub auspicia Disputationum suarum in Academiâ Lipsiensi, recitatae, Argumenti varii.* Lipsiae: Apud Johann. Fuhrmannum & Matthaeum Ritterum, 1681, pp. 413–17 (esp. p. 416). See also *Adversus Philosophos Novantiquos.* In Jakob Thomasius, *Dissertationes LXIII: argumenti magnam partem ad historiam philosophicam & ecclesiasticam pertinentes.* Halae Magdeburgicae: Impensis J. F. Zeitleri, 1693 and Döring, *Der junge Leibniz und Leipzig*, pp. 67–8.

111. On the Dutch tradition in general see C. Louise Thijssen-Schoute, *Nederlands cartesianisme*. Amsterdam: Noord-Hollandsche Uitg. Mij., 1954; Edward G. Ruestow, *Physics in 17th and 18th-Century Leiden*. The Hague: M. Nijhoff, 1973, esp. pp. 44–66; Theo Verbeek, "Dutch Cartesian Philosophy." In *A Companion to Early Modern Philosophy*. Ed. by Steven Nadler. Oxford: Blackwell, 2002, pp. 167–82. On Clauberg and Duisburg see esp. Francesco Trevisani, *Descartes in Germania. La ricezione del cartesianismo nella Facoltà filosofica e medica di Duisburg 1652–1703*. Milan, 1992; Theo Verbeek, ed., *Johannes Clauberg (1622–1665) and Cartesian Philosophy in the Seventeenth Century*. Dordrecht: Kluwer, 1999. On their relationship with Leibniz see for instance Jean-Christophe Bardout, "Johannes Clauberg." In *A Companion to Early Modern Philosophy*. Ed. by Steven Nadler. Oxford: Blackwell, 2002, p. 130; Christia Mercer, "The Seventeenth-Century Debate between the Moderns and the Aristotelians: Leibniz and Philosophia Reformata." *Studia Leibnitiana supplementa* 27 (1990): 18–29; Mercer, "Clauberg, Corporeal Substance, and the German Response." In *Johannes Clauberg*. Ed. by T. Verbeek. Dordrecht: Kluwer, 1999, pp. 147–59; Mercer, "Mechanizing Aristotle: Leibniz and Reformed Philosophy." In *Studies in Seventeenth-Century European Philosophy*. Ed. by M. A. Stewart. Oxford: Clarendon Press, 1997, pp. 117–52; Mercer, *Leibniz's Metaphysics*, p. 124 n. 83.

112. Leibniz's note (probably written during the 1660s) published in Alexandre Foucher de Careil, *Mémoire sur la philosophie de Leibniz*, Paris: F. R. de Rudeval, 1905, Part I, pp. 6–7. Cf. Mercer, *Leibniz's Metaphysics*, p. 43.

113. See A II, 1.

114. A VI, 1, 7.

115. See *Discours de Métaphysique*, 1686 (A VI, 4, 1541) and Leibniz to Ernst von Hessen-Rheinfels, undated (GP II, 131). Cf. Aiton, *Leibniz*, p. 14.

116. A VI, 1, 11. A detailed discussion of the *Disputatio Metaphysica de Principio Individui* is offered by J. A. Cover and John O'Leary-Hawthorne, *Substance and Individuation in Leibniz*. Cambridge: Cambridge University Press, 1999, pp. 26–50.

117. The importance of Weigel for the development of Leibniz's thought is expounded in detail by Moll, *Der junge Leibniz*, vol. I.

118. Cf. Mercer, "The Young Leibniz and His Teachers," especially pp. 27 and 35 and Mercer, *Leibniz's Metaphysics*, pp. 203–4.

119. See in particular Weigel's *Analysis Aristotelica ex Euclide Restituta* of 1658.

120. Cf. Guhrauer, *Leibnitz*, vol. 1, p. 33; Döring, *Der junge Leibniz und Leipzig*, pp. 40–41; A VI, 2, 4.

121. The extant draft is published in A VI, 2, N. 24.

122. For an introduction see Margreet Ahsmann, "Teaching in Collegia: The Organisation of Disputationes at Universities in the Netherlands and Germany during the 16th and 17th Centuries." In A. Romano, ed., *Università in Europa. Le istituzioni universitarie dal Medio Evo ai nostri giorni*. Soveria Mannelli: Rubbettino, 1995, pp. 99–114.

123. Such *collegia* may have been a fairly general feature of education in Alsted's circle. In Alsted's *Panacea philosophica*, Herborn, 1610, p. 40, they are attributed to Johannes Sturm, *Academicae Epistolae*. Strasbourg: Rihel, 1569 and Keckermann, *De modo discendi* (cf. *Opera omnia*, vol. 2). They are designated *collegia* (or *loci communes*) *Gelliana*, after the method of compilation employed by Aulus Gellius. See Hotson, *Commonplace Learning*, pp. 241-2.

124. Leibniz to Johann Friedrich Leibniz, 26 December 1684 (A I, 4, 681). Leibniz actually mentioned in his letter "Manuscripta ut Collegii quaerentium," probably conflating his memories of the Leipzig and the Jena *collegia*.

125. See Müller-Krönert, *Leben und Werk*, p. 7 and Döring, *Der junge Leibniz und Leipzig*, p. 87. Kabitz, "Die Bildungsgeschichte des jungen Leibniz," pp. 181–2 advances the hypothesis that Leibniz did not actually begin his jurisprudence studies until after his graduation as philosophy Magister (7 February 1664) on the ground that he earned his Bachelor's degree in law only in September 1665. However, since the statutes of the university prescribed two years of studies in the juridical faculty before the Bachelor's degree (cf. E. Friedberg, *Die Leipziger Juristenfakultät, ihre Doktoren und ihr Heim, 1409 1909*, Leipzig 1909, p. 142), the date of Leibniz's baccalaureate does on the contrary indicate a beginning of his juridical studies in the autumn of 1663.

126. See Döring, *Der junge Leibniz und Leipzig*, p. 88.

127. *Selbstschilderung* (Pertz I, 4, 168–9).

128. See A VI, 1, 362.

129. See A VI, 1, xiv and Kabitz, "Die Bildungsgeschichte des jungen Leibniz," p. 179.

130. See A VI, 1, N. 4 (esp. pp. 83 and 89) and Mercer, *Leibniz's Metaphysics*, p. 46.

131. See *Specimina Juris*, 1667–9 (A VI, 1, N. 11). It collects revised versions of A VI, 1, N. 4, N. 5, N. 6 and N. 9.

132. There are no extant sources which reveal how Leibniz reacted to this loss.

133. See A II, 1, N. 2.

134. This was the title under which the dissertation was republished in 1669 in the *Specimina Juris* (A VI, 1, N. 11).

135. See A VI, 1, N. 5 and N. 6.

136. See A VI, 1, N. 8.

137. See A VI, 1, 228.

138. Leibniz certainly knew the combinatorial works included in the edition of Lull's *Opera* published in Strasbourg in 1598 (see *De Arte Combinatoria*, A VI, 1, 196). Cf. also Ramon Lull, *Ars Magna generalis ultima*, Venice, 1480.

139. Lull's table is reproduced in Louis Couturat, *La logique de Leibniz*, Paris, 1901, p. 541. See also Couturat, *La logique de Leibniz*, pp. 36–9; E. W. Platzeck, "Gottfried Wilhelm Leibniz y Raimundo Llull." *Estudios Lulianos* 16, nos. 2–3 (1972): 1–193 (esp. pp. 130–42); Wolfgang Hübener, "Leibniz und der Renaissance-Lullismus." In *Leibniz et la Renaissance*. Ed. by Albert Heinekamp. Wiesbaden: Franz Steiner Verlag, 1983, pp. 103–12.

140. Cf. Schmidt-Biggemann, *Topica Universalis*, pp. 107-13; Hotson, *Alsted*, esp. pp. 39-50, 82-94, 150, 163-77.

141. Cf. Platzeck, "Gottfried Wilhelm Leibniz y Raimundo Llull," pp. 133–6; Couturat, *La logique de Leibniz*, esp. pp. 35, 49; A VI, 2, 548.

142. A II, 1, 5.

143. A II, 1, 160.

144. See for instance *Meditationes de Cognitione, Veritate, et Ideis*, November 1684 (A VI, 4, 585–92).

145. Cf. Couturat, *La logique de Leibniz*, pp. 48–50 and Massimo Mugnai, *Introduzione alla filosofia di Leibniz*, Turin: Einaudi, 2001, pp. 246–7.

146. Thomas Hobbes, *Elementorum philosophiae sectio prima de corpore*. London, 1655. Pars I: *Computatio sive Logica*, Caput I "De Philosophia," § 2.

147. I owe this list to Massimo Mugnai.

148. Leibniz, *Dissertatio de Arte Combinatoria* (A VI, 1, 199).

149. A VI, 2, 549.

150. See Leibniz to the Jesuit Ferdinand Orban, 24 September 1712 (LBr 699, Bl. 61–2; published in Hübener, "Leibniz und der Renaissance-Lullismus," pp. 111–12).

151. See Kabitz, "Die Bildungsgeschichte des jungen Leibniz," pp. 182–4 and Döring, *Der junge Leibniz und Leipzig*, pp. 90–93.

152. *Selbstschilderung* (Pertz, 4, 169).

153. Adam Rechenberg to Leibniz, 15 January 1708 (LBr 757).

154. Leibniz to Adam Rechenberg, end January 1708 (LBr 757, Bl. 2).

155. See A VI, 1, N. 9. Cf. also A VI, 2, 552.

156. See in particular A VI, 1, 236–40.

157. See *Selbstschilderung* (Pertz I, 4, 169–70); A IV, 4, 16 and 80.

158. *Selbstschilderung* (Pertz I, 4, 170).

159. See *Wilhelmus Pacidius. Entwurf einer Einleitung* (A VI, 2, N. 59).

160. *Selbstschilderung* (Pertz I, 4, 171).

2

The Vision Broadens: Nuremberg, Frankfurt, and Mainz (March 1667– March 1672)

I N THE EVENT, the travel plans of the eager young man did not take him very far. Leibniz spent the better part of his early to mid-twenties at the service of the Catholic archbishop and elector of Mainz, Johann Philipp von Schönborn. Yet sustained exposure to the intellectual, religious, and political circles revolving around the lively and tolerant court of Mainz broadened his horizons more than broader travels in narrower confessional circles could have done. In these years Leibniz realised the opportunity to contribute to an important programme of juridical reform commissioned by Schönborn, met prominent political and intellectual figures, and began corresponding with some of the key players of the European scientific, philosophical, and learned community. Most importantly, he gradually gave more definite form to his early philosophical and scientific aspirations, conceiving an all-embracing plan of reform and advancement of the whole encyclopaedia of the sciences intended to celebrate the glory of God through the improvement of the human condition. The realisation of this plan called first of all for the establishment of the "elements of philosophy," embracing metaphysics, logic, mathematics, physics, and practical philosophy. These principles would in turn lay the foundation of the catholic (or universal) theological demonstrations at the heart of the plan. Although this plan proved too ambitious to be realized either in Mainz or later on, it provided a philosophical, scientific, and practical programme which guided Leibniz for the duration of his life. Over the years, to be sure, it changed its shape and its tone, losing its emphasis on revealed theology and the mysteries of the Christian religion to become a more straightforward philosophical and scientific project within a theistic framework. But those parts of the project which were (at least to some significant extent) developed made up in their originality and fecundity for the lack of a more complete realisation.

Nuremberg, Frankfurt, and Mainz

Having renounced the economic security of a professorship in Altdorf, in April and July 1667 Leibniz was forced to ask the administrator of his family's estate, Christian Freiesleben, for additional loans above and beyond those already received during his studies from his sister Anna Catharina Löffler on 2 October 1666 and Freiesleben himself on 14 February 1667.[1] In the meantime, however, he had managed to secure at least a meagre income: his first paid job was that of secretary of a Nuremberg society devoted to secret alchemical experiments, including the search for the philosopher's stone.[2] Despite a number of discordant speculations, it is not certain when and how Leibniz became involved in the society, or even whether he actually moved to the imperial free city of Nuremberg which governed the nearby town of Altdorf. His participation in the meetings and activities of the society probably began as early as the winter of 1666–7;[3] but more important for his intellectual development than the precise dates was the very fact of his involvement. Again in contrast to his Leipzig teachers and in harmony with some of his bolder eclectic predecessors, the interests of the young philosopher and jurist evidently stretched to alchemy; and through the society he had the opportunity, at least for a short spell, to learn about it not only from books but from practice. Later in life he did not regret his youthful first-hand experience and the access it had given him to secret papers of some kind. Also valuable was the chance to observe how men he had "known very well" had "been carried along by the fair wind of the chemical dream,"[4] an experience which may have tempered his own interest with a salutary tincture of caution and circumspection.

Probably in the autumn of 1667, Leibniz left Nuremberg with the intention of undertaking a grand tour of the sort which capped the education of Europe's privileged young men in this period. His immediate objective was "a voyage down the Rhine to Holland,"[5] after which he hoped to travel still further to England, France, and Italy.[6] Given his ardent desire "to earn more glory in the sciences and to get to know the world,"[7] his initial destination was not surprising, since Holland's reputation as a centre of intellectual innovation was at its very apogee in these years. A European grand tour was no minor enterprise, especially for a young man lacking expert guidance, concrete contacts, solid finances, and immediate job prospects; but the first stage was clear: in order to board a

boat on the Rhine bound for Holland, Leibniz needed to reach Frankfurt
and then Mainz, where in 1666–7 the plague was still raging.[8] The date
of his arrival in the leading commercial city of Frankfurt is unknown, but
he was certainly there on 25 November 1667, when he visited a relative,
Friedrich Sigismund Deuerlein, to sign a fourth note promising to repay
further loans from Christian Freiesleben.[9]

Around this time Leibniz must also have first visited the nearby
Catholic court of Mainz, residence of the elector and prince-archbishop
Johann Philipp von Schönborn (1605–73). Schönborn's elaborate title
reflected a collection of responsibilities unique to the Holy Roman Empire:
as archbishop he exercised ecclesiastical authority over a huge swath of
central Germany from the mouths of the Weser and the Elbe in the north
to the Alps in the south; as a prince-archbishop he also exercised temporal
authority over a scattered archipelago of church lands within this vast
area, mostly around the confluence of the Rhine and the Main; and as
elector he was one of the seven (or, after 1648, eight) senior princes of the
Empire who elected the emperor himself and formed the highest and most
powerful college in the imperial diet or *Reichstag*. From such a position
he was well placed to exercise influence at the imperial and regional as
well as the territorial level. In the year after his appointment in 1647, in
fact, he had played an important role in the final stages of negotiating the
Peace of Westphalia signed in 1648; and having helped bring the Thirty
Years War to a close, he began to pursue major reforms aimed at restoring
to the Empire the kind of internal cohesion and external strength necessary to prevent a similar conflict in the future. Two such reforms were
to have an enormous impact on the impressionable young Saxon visitor.
Most novel to a young man raised in Saxony and of deepest eventual
impact on Leibniz was the ambitious plan to mend the rift at the heart of
German life resulting from the Reformation by reconciling Protestantism
and Catholicism – a plan conceived in Mainz and pursued with prudent
determination by the archbishop himself.[10] More immediately accessible and attractive to a promising, ambitious, and innovative young jurist
was the thorough reform and reorganisation of the *corpus juris* which the
elector had commissioned from his court jurist and counsellor, Hermann
Andreas Lasser.

Precisely how and when Leibniz caught wind of this legal project is
unknown; but when he did it appears to have captured his imagination
and changed his plans in an instant. Here was an opportunity to put

his newly acquired qualifications as doctor of law to the best possible use, to collaborate on a project leading toward a *jurisprudentia rationalis*, and in doing so to make a major contribution to that *emendatio rerum* so close to his heart.[11] Here also was a project the enormous theoretical significance of which was eclipsed only by its immense potential concrete benefit to the day-to-day lives of his countrymen and to the status of his country as a place in which the best of the political structures and juridical traditions developed over the ages were being used to foster the most up-to-date reforms necessary and potentially applicable across the whole of Europe. While the details of Leibniz's reaction are undocumented, such opportunities evidently proved too tempting to resist. Holland would have to wait.

Even as he travelled back from Mainz to Frankfurt the young jurist eagerly began to commit to paper the new method for learning and teaching jurisprudence on which he had probably already been working in Leipzig.[12] The work – hastily finished in a Frankfurt guesthouse and promptly passed to the Frankfurter printer Johann David Zunner[13] – appeared by the end of 1667 under the title of *Nova Methodus Discendae Docendaeque Jurisprudentiae*.[14] Dedicated to Johann Philipp von Schönborn, the pamphlet was designed to serve as a presentation of his credentials and abilities to the elector in the hope of being hired as Lasser's assistant for the work of juridical reform.[15] Written in haste and without access to books ("sine libris"),[16] it nevertheless incorporated such numerous citations and wide-ranging erudition that it must have been based on preparatory notes dating back to his legal studies.[17] Yet even if a far more leisurely gestation is granted, the *Nova Methodus* represented a striking accomplishment.

Like the *Dissertatio de Arte Combinatoria*, the *Nova Methodus* was a work very close in several crucial respects to the encyclopaedic and pansophical reform aspirations typical of the Herborn school.[18] Its basic purpose, first of all, was pedagogical: it sought to develop a *New Method for Learning and Teaching Jurisprudence*. The scope of this reform, second, was encyclopaedic: whereas the second part of the work outlined a reformed method of legal studies, the first part applied similar methods to the whole university curriculum. The justification for placing this reform of legal education in an encyclopaedic context, third, was essentially Ramist: as Leibniz recalled much later, his early methodology was "not much different from the Ramist one";[19] and the key rule of the *methodus naturalis* proposed in this work for organising knowledge in general (as opposed to the *methodus occasionalis* employed in specific disciplines) was little more than a restatement of the basic law of Ramist method: "if one thing can be known without a second, but the second cannot be known without the first, the first should be put before the second."[20] Since knowledge of law presupposed knowledge of many other disciplines, and indeed since legal principles were derived in no small measure from other disciplines, it followed that the reorganisation and rationalisation both of jurisprudence and of legal education needed to be situated within a reform of the entire cycle of the disciplines. In so arguing, the young jurist was furthering the leitmotiv of his dissertation for the Master's degree in philosophy: the thesis that jurisprudence must be grounded on universal philosophical principles.[21] Only in this context could jurisprudence find its proper place and be reorganised and rationalised on the basis of clear principles. From these principles an ordered system could then be deduced, superseding the confusing array of laws characterising the existing juridical *corpus*. Finally, in order to produce the most compact formulation, the most rigorous demonstration, and the most efficient education possible, this body of fundamental and derivative legal principles needed to be articulated in the form of geometrical demonstrations and manipulated in combinatorial fashion – yet another resemblance to the aspirations of Alsted and Bisterfeld. In effect, the *Nova Methodus* thus outlined a substantial portion of the universal combinatorial encyclopaedia of all the arts and sciences.

Something of the intrinsically encyclopaedic nature of this early project is also evident in its elaboration of the strong parallels with theology already proposed in the *Dissertatio de Arte Combinatoria*. In Leibniz's view, theology was almost a kind of jurisprudence since it could be regarded as the *jus* obtaining in the *respublica* or kingdom of God over mankind.[22] Both theology and jurisprudence rested on a twofold foundation: reason, from which natural theology and natural jurisprudence derived, and scripture, from which positive divine laws and positive human laws derived.[23] Regarding the natural jurisprudence of the *jus naturae*, Leibniz followed the tradition of Roman law expressed by Ulpian's three fundamental maxims,[24] and identified three degrees which were to remain a constant structure of his juridical thought. The first degree was expressed by the maxim "harm no one" (*neminem laedere*) and corresponded to Grotius's *jus strictum* or right of war and peace, which grounded the first kind of justice identified

by Aristotle: commutative justice. The second degree was expressed by
the maxim "give to everybody his own" (*suum cuique tribuere*) and corresponded to the *aequitas* which grounded the second kind of justice
identified by Aristotle: distributive justice. Finally, the third degree was
the *pietas* which grounded universal justice and was expressed by the
maxim "live honestly" (*honeste vivere*). This was the supreme degree of
justice which perfected and gave effect to the others.[25]

The *Nova Methodus*, although drafted hastily, remained in Leibniz's
thoughts thereafter.[26] In a letter to Christian Woldenberg of 12 March
1671 he mentioned the idea of a new edition including an index prepared by a Rostock jurist, I. B. Zinzerling.[27] Over twenty years later, in
his anonymous description for the *Acta Eruditorum* of August 1693 of
his collection of medieval legal documents entitled *Codex Juris Gentium
Diplomaticus*, he repeated his wish for a new edition of the youthful work.
Between 1695 and 1709 he prepared three different sets of notes for a
second edition,[28] but was once again forced to sideline his plans in order
to keep working at his main assignment, a history of the Guelf dynasty.[29]
In two letters of 1712 to Friedrich Wilhelm Bierling, professor of history,
eloquence, and politics at the University of Rinteln, Leibniz asked for an
opinion on the early juridical work, which he was still hoping to republish
in revised form.[30] In 1716, the very year of his death, he was still seeking
feedback on the *Nova Methodus*, this time from the Hanoverian jurist
Christian Ulrich Grupen.[31]

Unfortunately, like so many of Leibniz's *desiderata*, this relatively minor
one of a second, revised edition of the *Nova Methodus* remained unfulfilled; but meanwhile the first edition quickly achieved the main immediate
purpose for which it had been written: shortly after receiving a copy of the
work in early 1668, Schönborn employed Leibniz to work with Lasser on
the reform of the *corpus juris* for a weekly remuneration.[32] Their collaboration was close: Leibniz soon took up residence in Mainz in Lasser's house
and was still living there as late as February 1671.[33] And their progress
was swift: in June 1668 they published together a *Ratio Corporis Juris
Reconcinnandi*, outlining the principles that would guide their reform;
and they seem to have completed much of the *Corpus Juris Reconcinna-
tum* itself during a relatively brief collaboration, although the text has
unfortunately been lost.[34] An impression of their intentions is conveyed
in Leibniz's letter of July 1670 to Thomas Hobbes, full of praise for the
English philosopher – a classic case of an eager young man trying to attract

the attention of a senior figure in the hope of stimulating further epistolary exchange: "Four years ago, I started to work out a plan for compiling in the fewest words possible the elements of the law contained in the Roman Corpus . . . so that one could, so to speak, finally demonstrate from them its universal laws."[35] In a report of August 1671 to the Holy Roman Emperor, Leopold of Habsburg (1658–1705), Leibniz specified further (in a manner again reminiscent of the post-Ramist method of reworking established authorities) that this reform did not aim to modify the substance of the *corpus juris* but only to reorganise and rationalise its form to produce a clear, brief, comprehensive, and coherent summary of the principles of Roman law.[36] Something of the satisfaction of Archbishop Schönborn with this progress is evident in his promotion of Leibniz – proudly recalled twenty years later to Duke Ernst August of Hanover – to the prestigious position of *Revisionsrat* at the supreme court of appeal (*Oberappellationsgericht*) in Mainz – and this despite his young age and his Lutheranism.[37]

Yet this relationship with Schönborn and with Lasser, although initially important, was not ultimately the most crucial one which Leibniz developed in the inner circle of the Mainz court. Probably at some point after his arrival in Frankfurt in late 1667, he met the person who was to become his prime patron and estimator, and who played the central role in the next stage of the young German's life: Baron Johann Christian von Boineburg. Born in 1622 in Eisenach (Thuringia), Boineburg was educated at the Lutheran University of Helmstedt, where he studied under the famous jurist Hermann Conring (1606–81) and was exposed to the school of theological irenicism founded there by Georg Calixt. After a successful diplomatic career, serving first at the Hessen court and then for two years as Hessian envoy to the court of Queen Christina of Sweden, in the summer of 1652 he met Schönborn in Schwalbach. Despite his Lutheranism, Boineburg greatly impressed the archbishop, who offered him the position of prime minister, probably under the condition that he embrace the Catholic faith. In 1653 Boineburg underwent a seemingly genuine and certainly permanent conversion to Catholicism. His previous religious history and his formation in irenical and tolerant circles were clearly instrumental in fostering the strongly ecumenical views which helped shape Leibniz's similar inclinations into a lifelong pursuit of ecclesiastical reconciliation.

Boineburg's fortune, however, was soon to change. Due to disagreements with Schönborn's politics towards the superpower of the time, the France of Louis XIV, Boineburg was disgraced and even imprisoned until the charges against him proved unsubstantiated.[38] No longer *persona grata* at the Mainz court, he had moved to Frankfurt and then to Cologne, where he lived until about 1670. He had already left for the latter city when Leibniz arrived in Frankfurt,[39] but between 20 March and 16 April 1668 he was back in Mainz, where his reconciliation with Schönborn was sealed by the marriage of his daughter to the elector's nephew, Melchior Friedrich von Schönborn.[40] By that time he had already met and come to appreciate Leibniz. On 26 April 1668, once returned to his residence in Cologne, he sent his former teacher Hermann Conring a copy of the *Nova Methodus*, warmly recommending its author as a young man whom he knew "very well":

He is a twenty-two-year old doctor in law: very learned, a good philosopher, committed, able and prompt in speculative reasoning. . . . He is certainly a man of great knowledge, of disciplined judgement, and of great capacity for work. He lives now in Mainz, not without my support.[41]

On 5 July of the same year, Boineburg sent Conring three copies of the newly published *Ratio Corporis Juris Reconcinnandi*,[42] paving the way for the stimulating epistolary exchange on juridical and historical questions between Leibniz and the famous jurist.[43] When, two years later, Conring asked the Baron for further information on his protégé, Boineburg sketched a second, still more detailed and appreciative intellectual profile of the young Leibniz:

He is a young man, twenty-four years old, from Leipzig, a doctor of law, and a more learned one could scarcely be imagined. He understands the whole of philosophy thoroughly and is a productive thinker in both the old and the new. He is furnished above all with the ability to write. He is a mathematician, hard-working and ardent, who knows and loves natural philosophy, medicine, and mechanics. Of independent judgement in religion, he is a member of your [Lutheran] confession. He has mastered not only the philosophy of law but also, remarkably, legal practice[.][44]

Conring was not the only influential personage to whom Boineburg recommended his protégé. In May 1668, soon after the marriage of his daughter to the younger von Schönborn, he drew the attention of his newly acquired son-in-law to the able young Saxon, pointing out that the elector might secure Leibniz's valuable services for a modest annual remuneration.[45] Boineburg himself made Leibniz one of his closest and most trusted collaborators, introducing him to his learned circle, opening for him his channels of communication, and entrusting him with tasks ranging from the legal representation of his family to the cataloguing of his extensive library,[46] from collaboration on political and diplomatic schemes to the defence of the Christian religion.

Supported and guided by Boineburg, Leibniz had the opportunity to meet other prominent intellectuals at the court of Mainz, amongst whom three deserve special mention. Closest to the Mainz court was the leading Catholic theologian Peter van Walenburch (1610–75), with whom Leibniz spent hours discussing religious questions.[47] Peter had succeeded his older brother Adrian (1609–69) as auxiliary bishop of Cologne and co-authored with him a series of very influential treatises discussing the controverted points of doctrine separating Catholics and Protestants. One of the closest collaborators of Archbishop von Schönborn,[48] Peter van Walenburch also played a major role in shaping the religious and political direction of the court of Mainz. Like Boineburg and the archbishop, he was actively engaged in colloquia and negotiations dedicated to advancing the reunification of the Christian churches, and it was perhaps in the context of one of these colloquia in Cologne in 1670 that Leibniz met the irenical Reformed theologian from Heidelberg, Johann Ludwig Fabricius (1632–96).[49]

One step further removed from the Mainz court was one of the most prominent persons whom Adrian van Walenburch had converted from Lutheranism to Catholicism: Leibniz's future employer, Duke Johann Friedrich of Hanover (1625–79). The duke's attention was initially drawn to Leibniz, however, not in Mainz but in Frankfurt, in particular by Christian Habbeus von Lichtenstern, the Swedish resident in the city. Habbeus was evidently so impressed by the young Saxon that he had already recommended him to the Swedish Imperial chancellor, Magnus Gabriel de La Gardie, as a travelling companion for his son Gustav Adolph;[50] and his description of Leibniz to Johann Friedrich was so glowing that the duke asked the diplomat to urge the young jurist to depart immediately for Hanover. Habbeus, however, urged caution: he had some misgivings regarding the desirability of Hanover as a workplace and advised Leibniz not to commit himself until they could discuss this opportunity upon his return to Frankfurt the following February.[51] Not for the last time, Leibniz chose to keep his options open, tacitly declining to pack his bags at once, yet opening an important epistolary exchange with the duke in early 1671.[52] In this first letter he mentioned a "meditation," committed to paper not long before and circulated to Boineburg and the duke, in which he discussed for the first time issues which would be central to his *Theodicy* almost forty years later: the freedom of human beings, God's foreknowledge, and God's grace.[53] Leibniz's comment regarding the aim of this meditation reflected his general attitude towards theoretical work: "here, as always, my aim has been, not to pack the shops with books filled with nothing but hot air, but where possible to achieve something useful through them" – in this case the reunion of the Christian churches, deeply divided on issues such as grace and predestination.[54] Another text written about the same time stated this approach to the contemplative life even more forcefully: "the sole end of philosophising", he asserted, echoing once again his Ramist predecessors, was "for use in life and", adding a genuinely Baconian note, "to increase the power and happiness of mankind."[55] In other words, as he had already expressed in his youthful axiom of searching always for usefulness in things, theoretical reflection should be pursued in the last instance *ad usum vitae*.[56] In the series of important letters to the duke which followed, the young man revealed much of his aims and aspirations. Probably in October 1671, Leibniz and Johann Friedrich met for the first time face to face, as the duke passed by Frankfurt in the course of a trip to Italy.[57]

Although Johann Friedrich was to play the crucial role of patron and employer after Leibniz's return from Paris in 1676, a third figure performed the important function of introducing Leibniz into English philosophical circles before and during his two visits to London in 1673 and 1676: Heinrich Oldenburg (1615*–77). Born in Bremen and educated under Matthias Martinius in the Reformed academy there (a daughter school, in effect, of the Herborn academy), Oldenburg was a product of the post-Ramist tradition in northwestern Germany which had contributed so much to the establishment of Leibniz's youthful intellectual agenda. After several visits to England from around 1640 onward, Oldenburg eventually became integrated into a network knit together between 1630 and 1660 around three other foreigners: the displaced Anglo-German 'intelligencer', Samuel Hartlib (c. 1600–62), the expatriate Scottish irenicist, John Dury (1596–1680), and the exiled Moravian pedagogue and pansophist, Jan Amos Comenius. Comenius's dream was to progress beyond the eclectic encyclopaedism of his teacher, Alsted, to a more perfect and organic pansophic distillation of reality capable of being communicated through a universal education to every member of the Christian community and thereby of replacing an era of perpetual warfare with one of ecclesiastical and political peace. Dury complemented this visionary programme with a protracted series of indefatigable negotiations aimed at reconciling the Lutheran, Reformed, and English churches. Hartlib, for his part, not only networked incessantly to raise the financial and political capital needed to realise his comrades' dreams; he also added a more genuinely Baconian emphasis on the exploitation of technological and natural philosophical knowledge for the betterment of the human condition and sought to institutionalise his extraordinary efforts to disseminate useful knowledge in a permanent institution. As for Oldenburg himself, he and his main early patrons in England – Lady Ranelagh (1614–91), who entrusted him with the education of her son, and her brother, the pioneering chemist Robert Boyle (1627–96) – belonged to Hartlib's circle. Oldenburg eventually married Dury's daughter; and the Hartlib circle's contribution to the great English philosophical and scientific achievements of the Restoration era is nowhere more evident than in Oldenburg's long service as the most crucially important early secretary of the Royal Society of London, founded in 1660. Leibniz was therefore fortunate to find so centrally situated within the Royal Society a man whose formation and outlook so closely resembled his own and who was eager to introduce a countryman into the English scientific circles so recently grown prestigious, not least in the hope of fostering similar scientific activities in their native Germany.

Oldenburg's first contact with the young Saxon seems to have been established through Boineburg. Writing on 20 August 1670 to the baron, Oldenburg expressed his deep concern for the lamentable fragmentation of science and philosophy in their native Germany:

Would that those who excel in litigation and in the sciences in our Germany would make their contributions towards the restoration and perfection of philosophy with a better will than they have shown hitherto, and would eagerly imitate in this the example of England, France, and Italy herself in turning to experiments. What we are about is no task for one nation or another singly. It is needful that the resources, labors, and zeal of all regions, princes, and philosophers be united, so that this task of comprehending nature may be pressed forward by their care and industry.[58]

Boineburg would have been hard pressed to think of anyone more eager or able to respond to Oldenburg's exhortation than his young protégé; and it was he in all likelihood who encouraged Leibniz to make epistolary contact with the German secretary to the Royal Society in the summer of 1670.[59]

Leibniz's Great Plan: The *Demonstrationes Catholicae* and Their Prolegomena

One might suppose that the task of reducing the *corpus juris* to a methodical compendium would have posed a challenge sufficient for even the most able and intellectually ambitious young jurist. Yet Leibniz's papers from this period teem with other topics: logical, metaphysical, physical, ethical, political, and theological; and many of these can be related to a second and still vaster project, stimulated by the ecumenical atmosphere in Mainz and again undertaken in close consultation with Boineburg, which was destined to engage much of his energy and enthusiasm for the rest of his life. This great all-embracing plan, the *Demonstrationes Catholicae* (*Catholic Demonstrations*), although never realised in its entirety and shifting in shape and description in different periods, provides a kind of Ariadne's thread for those who wish to reconstruct the unity underlying Leibniz's labyrinthine intellectual odyssey. Organised into four main parts subdivided into individual chapters, Leibniz's plan was probably already drafted in the early months of 1668. It foresaw the "Demonstration of God's Existence" (part 1); the "Demonstration of the Immortality and Incorporeity of the Soul" (part 2); the "Demonstration of the Possibility of the Mysteries of the Christian Faith" (part 3); and the "Demonstration of the Authority of the Catholic Church" and "of the Authority of Scripture" (part 4). During the following year the twenty-two-year-old kept tinkering with it, amending, adding, or deleting one chapter or another.[60] The effort expended in shaping and reshaping his plan was easily explained by its breath-taking inclusiveness. As *prolegomena* to the catholic (that is, universal) demonstrations proper, the young Leibniz listed the "elements of philosophy", namely the first principles of metaphysics (*de Ente*), of logic (*de Mente*), of mathematics (*de Spatio*), of physics (*de Corpore*), and of ethics and politics or "practical philosophy" (*de Civitate*).[61] This plan as a whole, in other words, was a first draft of a systematic encyclopaedia of the sciences which found its unity both in the precise order of the disciplines and in its final aim of supporting the key tenets of Christian theology. At one and the same time it therefore also embodied a titanic theoretical project of reordering, developing, and reforming the sciences and an equally audacious practical scheme of political and ecclesiastical reconciliation and reunification based on universally agreeable rational grounds. In short, it represented the most rounded early version of Leibniz's life-long, all-encompassing intellectual programme.

In a brief text written between the autumn of 1669 and the beginning of 1671, the young Leibniz spelled out in detail how he proposed to conduct this reform of the encyclopaedia.[62] As the basic blueprint he took the most polished and comprehensive systematic work of its kind extant: the eponymous *Encyclopaedia* of Johann Heinrich Alsted, the first main work so called, which had been published in seven parts in 1630.[63] According to Leibniz, the first thing necessary in order to perfect Alsted's work was the accurate demonstration of "the elements of the true philosophy." To this effect he proposed to update Alsted's encyclopaedia with what he regarded as the best results of philosophical and scientific inquiry in the fields of the philosophy of mind (including logic), mathematics (taken primarily as geometry), physics, and practical philosophy (namely, jurisprudence and politics).

According to Leibniz's proposal to emend Alsted's encyclopaedia, the logical portion of the revised work would be based on his own *Ars Combinatoria* supplemented by material from the *Logica Hamburgensis* (Hamburg 1638) of Joachim Jungius, the brilliant, massive compendium of Aristotelian and late medieval logic written by one of the authors most admired by Leibniz in this field. In turn, these texts would be complemented by excepts from the *Logica vetus et nova quadripartita* (Amsterdam 1654) of the pioneering German Cartesian Johannes Clauberg, and the famous *Logique, ou l'art de penser* (Paris 1662) of Antoine Arnauld and Pierre Nicole. The key text in mathematics (geometry), Leibniz continued, would be the *Elements* of Euclid, supplemented with subsequent discoveries and demonstrations achieved through the application of the Euclidean method. In physics (broadly conceived as natural philosophy), the entire *De Corpore* of Thomas Hobbes was to be inserted into the Encyclopaedia, albeit somewhat amended.[64] As additions he recommended the doctrine of motion developed by Galileo Galilei, Christiaan Huygens, and himself, together with selected doctrines from the physics of Aristotle and of Kenelm Digby (1603–65), an eclectic English thinker who attempted to reconcile Aristotle with mechanistic physics. In the sphere of practical philosophy, alongside the *De Cive* of Hobbes, Leibniz regarded as fundamental his own "demonstrations on natural law", on the concept of "usefulness", and on the ideal of the best possible *civitas*. Finally, "in support of the true theology" he recommended his newly elaborated philosophy of mind, that is, his early response to Descartes's philosophy of mind and body based on a reinterpretation and expansion of the concept of conatus proposed in Hobbes's *De Corpore*.[65]

Having sketched out this all-embracing scheme, the young Leibniz was eager to present it to his patrons and other key intellectual players of the *république des lettres*, notably the prominent French philosopher and theologian Antoine Arnauld (1612–94). In two letters of the autumn of 1671 to Duke Johann Friedrich and Arnauld, Leibniz proudly presented his accomplishments and projects in a number of fields,[66] emphasizing precisely the disciplines conceived as *prolegomena* to the catholic demonstrations, together with his work towards the demonstrations themselves. To Arnauld Leibniz proposed an order of sciences in which geometry or *philosophia de loco* was presupposed by physics or *philosophia de motu seu corpore*, which in turn was presupposed by the "science of mind."[67] In all of these fields, Leibniz claimed, he had already reached results of the first importance in their own right. Consistent with his plan for the catholic demonstrations, however, these sciences were not to be pursued as ends in themselves but as preconditions for the demonstration of the existence of God and the defence of the Christian mysteries. From the new philosophy of mind (*elementa de mente*) which he was developing, Leibniz explained to Arnauld, he dared to promise "some considerable light" on the defence of the controversial mysteries of the Trinity, the Incarnation, predestination, and the Eucharist.[68]

Logic, the Characteristica Universalis, and Scientific Collaboration

Although at first sight seemingly miscellaneous, a great many of the young Leibniz's essays, drafts, and notes fall into a comprehensible pattern when viewed as preparatory sketches of the component parts of one titanic project: the *Demonstrationes Catholicae* and their encyclopaedic *prolegomena*. In the field of logic, he began work on the development of a *characteristica universalis* – the universal formal language designed to eliminate the ambiguity and fluctuation of natural language, reducing it to an "arithmetical calculation" and thereby allowing the peaceful resolution of all manner of controveries. Leibniz was following here in the footsteps of a

medieval ideal, embraced for instance by William Ockham, of constructing a "mental language" which could mend the confusion generated by
the Babel of natural, historical languages. In the early modern period this
ideal underwent an extraordinary rejuvenation. Thomas Hobbes advocated in his *Computatio sive Logica* of 1655 the idea that to think is to
calculate, and authors such as the Scot George Dalgarno (1626*–87), the
Englishmen John Wilkins (1614–72) and Cave Beck (1623–1706*), and
the Germans Athanasius Kircher (1602–80) and Johann Joachim Becher
(1635–82) attempted to create an artificial, universal language.[69] Following the teaching of Hobbes, Leibniz was convinced that human thought
always needed to be supported by sensible "signs" such as written or spoken words, figures drawn on paper or other material, and mental images.
Since signs were inevitably employed for the articulation of our thoughts,
most common thinking consisted of the combination of the signs themselves without reaching the ideas and thoughts beyond the signs. As
early as 1671 Leibniz called this sort of mental process "cogitationes cae-
cas" ("blind thoughts").[70] The problem is, Leibniz noted, that in many
instances we assume that proper concepts and ideas correspond to the
signs, when this is not necessarily the case. In his view, the best solution
to this problem was the creation of an artificial language in which a clear
and unambiguous correspondence between signs and concepts was established. Following the usage established by other authors intent in developing an artificial language, Leibniz used the term "characters" (*characteres*)
to refer to the written signs which supported thought and the term *characteristica* for the discipline devoted to developing the system of signs which
were to constitute the universal artificial language. As already sketched
in his *Dissertatio de Arte Combinatoria* (1666), this project required three
main phases: (1) the systematic identification of all simple concepts; (2)
the choice of signs or characters which designated these concepts and
constituted a sort of universal alphabet of the artificial language; and (3)
the development of a combinatorial method governing the combination
of these concepts. In short, Leibniz was reworking in a new perspective
the two classical procedures of analysis (phase one) and synthesis (phase
three) fundamental both to traditional Aristotelian–scholastic logic and
to the structure of the Euclidean demonstrative method. Moreover, he
was eager to stress that the artificial language would represent a powerful
expansion of both the *ars judicandi* (that is, the art of judgement or method

for drawing valid inferences from given concepts) and, more importantly, the *ars inveniendi* (that is, the art of discovery or method for the discovery of new concepts and truths).[71]

In Mainz he continued work towards the realisation of this huge project, discussing it in his letters with the author of one of the most famous attempts at a universal language and *ars combinatoria*, the mysterious, learned German Jesuit based in Rome, Athanasius Kircher.[72] Leibniz himself focused in particular on the analysis of concepts, drafting between the second half of 1671 and the early months of 1672 an extensive table of definitions modelled on the tables of concepts developed by another of his main predecessors in the quest for an artificial language, John Wilkins, who shared with Oldenburg the office of secretary to the Royal Society.[73]

Wilkins also shared with Oldenburg and other members of Hartlib's circle a keen interest in the development of an artificial language, an interest probably stimulated at least in part by the visit of Comenius to England in 1641.[74] In the first letter to Oldenburg on 23 July 1670, Leibniz foregrounded his efforts towards the *ars combinatoria* and the artificial language alongside his novel work in physics, advertising especially his early contribution to the creation of a combinatorial method in his *Dissertatio de Arte Combinatoria* and his interest in the work of Kircher and Wilkins on the artificial language. News of Wilkins's *Essay towards a Real Character and a Philosophical Language*, he explained to Oldenburg, had reached him through another correspondent of Hartlib, the Tübingen law professor and friend of Comenius, Magnus Hesenthaler (1621–81).[75] A few months later a copy of Wilkins's work was procured for Leibniz by Sir William Curtius, a German-born former student of Alsted and correspondent of Dury now serving as the English Resident in Frankfurt. On 9 May 1671 Leibniz wrote to Oldenburg that he had read Wilkins's *Essay* and wished it could be translated into Latin – clearly implying that in his mid-twenties he had already acquired at least a basic reading knowledge of English.[76] In a letter of the same year to Hesenthaler, which included an *epicedium* commemorating the death of Comenius on 15 November 1670, Leibniz stressed that his own conception of the perfect encyclopaedia, like that of Comenius, was indissolubility linked to the project of defining terms and perfecting language. No less apparent was the proximity of his conception to that of Alsted, a proximity evident in his definition of the encyclopaedia as a "System of all (as far as is feasible) true propositions and

useful things which have hitherto been thought."[77] Yet even these earliest
sketches also manifested his own intellectual fertility and originality. The
table of concepts modelled on Wilkins's *Essay* in 1671–2, for instance,
contained a number of striking definitions which already indicated his
distinctive doctrines on key epistemological and metaphysical issues –
for instance, the definitions of "nihil" ("nothing") as "whatever can be
named, but cannot be thought" ("quicquid nominari potest, cogitari non
potest"), of "notion, concept, idea" as "thought in so far as it is a thought
of something" ("cogitatio quatenus alicuius cogitatio est"), of relation
as "the thinking together of two [things]" ("duorum concogitabilitas"),
and of faith as "judging that the words of another are true" ("sententia de veritate verborum alterius").[78] These were the first of countless
preparatory notes scattered throughout Leibniz's life in which he tirelessly
inched his way towards the *characteristica universalis*; and already implicit
within them were many of the seeds which would grow into his mature
philosophy.

Another opportunity to reflect on the issue of language was presented
to Leibniz between 1669 and early 1670 in the form of one of his many
and varied commissions from Boineburg: in this case, the preparation of
a new edition of the work first published in Parma in 1553 by the Italian
humanist Mario Nizolio under the title *Antibarbarus seu de veris principiis et
vera ratione philosophandi contra pseudophilosophos* (*Antibarbarus, that is, on
the true principles and the true way of reasoning in philosophy against pseudo-
philosophers*).[79] In this work Nizolio criticised the doctrines of scholastic
logicians and advocated a reform of philosophical language which would
avoid obscure technicalities and barbarisms. Moreover, he embraced a
strictly nominalistic position, maintaining that words designated things
directly without any need of introducing universals as a medium between
words and things. Leibniz's edition, in print for the Frankfurt book fair of
Easter 1670,[80] included a long preliminary dissertation which presented
for the first time important aspects of his ontology of logic.[81] Leibniz's
position was an intermediate one: while he did not hesitate to disclose his
sympathies toward nominalism, he openly criticised the extreme version
embraced by some modern authors, notably Thomas Hobbes. In Leibniz's
view, nominalism was right to maintain, in accord with 'Ockham's razor',
that universals were names and not things.[82] This position was not to be
seen as a limitation to the fecundity and variety of God's creation but

as an expression of the supreme divine wisdom. The rule established by 'Ockham's razor' was essentially that the simplest hypothesis is the best:

The general rule is the one normally employed by the nominalists: *Entities should not be multiplied beyond necessity*. This rule is occasionally opposed by others as if it were an insult to the divine fecundity, which is generous rather than frugal and which rejoices in the variety and abundance of things. But those who thus object do not, in my view, sufficiently grasp the nominalists' intention, which (although obscurely expressed) is as follows: *an hypothesis is better in so far as it is simpler*[.][83]

Thomas Hobbes, however, went a step further and proposed a form of ultranominalism which made truth completely arbitrary.[84] Leibniz decisively rejected this reduction of truth to mere convention, as he rejected a strictly empiricist position which reduced generalisation to mere induction. In his view, induction alone was insufficient even to arrive at a proper generalisation, but required the "addition" or "support" of universal propositions which did not derive from experience.[85] From very early on, Leibniz was convinced that there could not be knowledge without the contribution on the part of the mind of universal propositions which depended on the "universal reason" and were the necessary precondition for the organisation of sense-data.[86] In the summer of 1669, for instance, the young Leibniz recorded with a firm hand the following principle in the margin of his extracts from the *Appendix practica* of Johann Joachim Becher's pansophical didactic: "nothing is in the intellect which was not previously in the senses, except the intellect itself"[87] – a claim which returned virtually *verbatim* many years later in the *Nouveaux Essais* in response to Locke's empiricism.[88]

Leibniz fully realized that the sort of titanic project envisaged by the creation of the *characteristica universalis*, and more generally, the reform and development of the whole encyclopaedia of sciences needed to be a collaborative enterprise. England and France had already established their academies of sciences – respectively the Royal Society of London, founded in December 1660, and the Parisian Académie Royale des Sciences, founded in 1666. To establish a similar enterprise in Germany was much more difficult due to the country's fragmentation into numerous semi-independent political entities, loosely united by the very limited authority of the Holy Roman Emperor and the imperial Diet. In a frank passage in his first letter to Oldenburg, Leibniz echoed the previous generation of German intellectual reformers in noting that "Remarkable experiments are not wanting among us, but, such is the state of politics now, on account of the open eagerness of one and hidden envy of another, that there can be no uniting into societies, nor is it easy for so many states to be combined into one nation."[89] Yet precisely this fragmentation, this lack of a natural national centre such as Paris or London, increased the urgency of deliberately coordinating efforts towards the advancement of science in the Empire. In attempting to address this problem, the obvious first place for the young Saxon to turn was to the emperor in Vienna, Leopold of Habsburg. Supported by Boineburg, as early as October 1668, and then again in November 1669, Leibniz wrote to the emperor asking for an imperial privilege for his plan to edit a semiannual journal reviewing the new publications which appeared at the two major book fairs of Frankfurt a. M. and of Leipzig.[90] This *Nucleus Librarius Semestralis* was meant to follow the example of the French *Journal des Sçavans*, first published only three years before, and would have constituted the first learned journal in Germany.[91] Christoph Gudenus, the Viennese resident of the court of Mainz, acted as intermediary, joining his efforts to those of Leibniz and Boineburg in trying to secure the key approval of the Emperor's librarian, Peter Lambeck.[92] Frustrated in these efforts, Leibniz turned to his employer, Johann Philipp von Schönborn, proposing to the elector's trusted friend, Johann von Saal, the transformation of the imperial *Bücherkommisariat* in Frankfurt into an office based in Mainz for the direction of German book production.[93] The creation of a "German Learned Society" was intended to follow, financed by a tax on paper and with a regular venue for its meetings (possibly in Frankfurt), the lack of which had stunted the German Academia Naturae Curiosorum, founded in 1652 by a group of physicians and specifically focused on the development of medicine. Remarkably, this institution had dedicated itself from its inception to the same general aim which was to inform Leibniz's lifelong intellectual programme: the exploration of nature for the benefit of humankind and the celebration thereby of the glory of God.[94] The purpose of the new foundation proposed by Leibniz would have been to join the efforts of the French, English, and Italian academies in fostering "the universal harmonious relationship of the learned" through its support of learning and of science, including medicine and mathematically based experimental sciences.[95] An astute awareness of one of the difficulties of organising scientific inquiry nationally in a country deeply divided confessionally is also evident in the explicit exclusion of theological questions

from the proposed society's remit – an echo perhaps of the declared intention of the Royal Society to restrict its business to cultivating "knowledge
of nature and useful arts by means of observation and experiment".[96]

This was the first of many Leibnizian proposals for the creation of
academies of sciences, within and outside his native Germany. Two rather
different sorts of proposals were drafted in 1671. In all likelihood Leibniz
intended to present them once again to Johann Philipp von Schönborn,
hoping that the elector, engaged at the time in a massive diplomatic and
political offensive aimed at uniting the German princes against the French
superpower, would be sympathetic to efforts to promote the intellectual
unification of the Empire.[97] Indeed, these presentations of Leibniz's plan
read more like heartfelt exhortations to the German nation than as practical proposals or draft regulations. Opening his *Bedenken von Aufrichtung
einer Akademie oder Societät in Deutschland zu Aufnehmen der Künste und
Wissenschaften* (*Reflections on the Establishment of an Academy or Society
in Germany for Fostering the Arts and Sciences*) Leibniz lamented: "It is
no honor at all to us Germans that we have been the first in discovering
large parts of the mechanical, natural, and other arts and sciences, but
are now the last in increasing and improving them." In order to change
this situation it was now time to create a proper German Academy or
Society of Sciences following above all the example of that in London.[98]
In the *Grundriß eines Bedenkens von aufrichtung einer Societät in Deutschland zu aufnehmen der Künste und Wissenschaften* (*Outline of Reflections for
Establishing an Academy or Society in Germany for Fostering the Arts and
Sciences*) Leibniz revealed the deepest underpinning of this project in theology, metaphysics, and ethics. In short, the advancement of science was
undertaken for the glory of God, which also coincided with the general
good. Advancement of our knowledge of nature enhanced our awareness
of the universal harmony at work in nature and celebrated in turn the
reflection in nature of the perfect harmony of power, wisdom, and love in
God's own nature. Our awareness of the perfect harmony of the divine
nature in turn grounded our love of God; and the love of God constituted our highest good. For this reason, "to love God above everything"
is "nothing else than to love the general good [*amare bonum publicum*]
and the universal harmony". This love must take the form of practical
activity: it had to be an "efficacious love" (*caritas efficax*) which found its
realisation in "good works" (*bona opera*).[99] Undertaken in this spirit, the
advancement of science celebrated God's power, wisdom, and love not

only through a theoretical contemplation of the beauty of His creation but also through the practical application of that knowledge to promote the general good. Towards the end of his life, writing on 16 January 1712 to the Russian chancellor, Gavriil Ivanovič Golovkin, Leibniz summarised these lifelong commitments, stating that from his youth onward he had aimed at contributing to the glory of God through the advancement of the sciences.[100]

This exhortation to the German nation was not intended to promote narrow nationalism. Evidence of a far wider design is contained in a remarkable text written around 1669 in which Leibniz envisaged a *Societas Philadelphica* the proposed aim of which was the "promotion of the utility of human kind (above all by means of medicine)".[101] In pursuing this end, the collaborative work of a society would bring infinitely more fruit than the isolated efforts of individuals or even individual nations, which Leibniz likened to "arena sine calce" ("sand without lime"). This society was meant to span religious and political divisions, embracing the emperor and the pope, the king of France, German principalities large and small, the English Royal Society, the Dutch East India Company, and learned religious orders.[102] The Society of Jesus in particular provided a model for an international society, with the crucial difference that the new foundation proposed by Leibniz would not be confessional in nature. On the contrary, it was designed to prepare for the reconciliation of the Christian churches in accordance with an idea further developed in a text from the same period outlining a *Societas Confessionum Conciliatrix*.[103]

Regarding the promotion of medicine as a direct means for improving the human condition, the years 1669 to 1671 were probably the most important in Leibniz's life. In 1671 or 1672 he penned a striking proposal, the guiding principles of which he was to repeat again and again.[104] His *Directiones ad rem Medicam pertinentes* could hardly have been more forceful in emphasising the importance of medicine:

Moral and medical matters [moralia et medicinaria]: these are the things which ought to be valued above all. For this reason I value microscopy far more than telescopy; and if someone were to find a certain and tested cure of any disease whatsoever, he would in my judgement have accomplished something greater than if he had discovered the quadrature of the circle.[105]

For a man who was to square the circle with his infinitesimal calculus,[106] this was a remarkable manifesto. For someone often characterised as a dreamer – with an outstanding capacity for logical, mathematical, and metaphysical abstraction, and a professional life restricted for the most part to court circles – Leibniz kept his feet firmly on the ground in clearly understanding that health and decent social conditions contributed more to the happiness of mankind than many elevated meditations. Once again, these youthful convictions remained with him for the rest of his life, as is suggested, for instance, by their echo in a letter of 1712 to the physician Konrad Burchard Vogther: "I have always been of the opinion that, after virtue, nothing is more excellent than health; but no art is more difficult and more in need of support than the art of restoring health."[107]

As early as the *Directiones ad rem Medicam pertinentes* Leibniz also saw clearly that the effective advancement of medicine required the support of the state and that the task of promoting the health of the population was one of the first duties of government. This conviction was repeated many years later in the *Nouveaux Essais* (1703–5): "Indeed, I believe that this aspect of public policy will become almost the chief concern of those who govern, second only to the concern for virtue; and that one of the greatest results of sound morality and sound politics will be our promoting an improved medical science."[108] In Leibniz's view, in order to discharge this duty, rulers should foster scientific collaboration between physicians, leading to the systematic collection of data and the establishment of effective therapies. Properly regulated state support would also help resolve endemic problems such as the persistent paucity of physicians and the corruption of health by avarice: since "human life is a sacred thing", Leibniz argued, "it should never be subject to the marketplace".[109]

Metaphysics and Physics

If the reform and development of logic was one fundamental *prolegomenon* to the catholic demonstrations, the reform and development of metaphysics was another. More explicitly than in any other period, during the Mainz years the driving force beyond Leibniz's work on metaphysics was clearly theological – not only the natural theology needed to defend theism in general but also the revealed theology needed to defend the doctrines and mysteries of the Christian religion. It was with Christian theology in mind that Leibniz eagerly worked to develop the "true notions" of substance, mind, and body. His aim was to build a metaphysics consistent with two sets of doctrines to which he was deeply committed: the mechanistic explanation of nature put forward by the "moderns" and the central tenets of the Christian religion. The result was the gradual development of notions of substance, mind, and body which contained the germ of his mature metaphysics. As one would expect, his doctrine on such complex issues did not spring from his head fully formed. In the space of a few years, between 1668 and 1672, he tried several different solutions to the problem of substance and changed his views on important points of his doctrines of mind and body, shifting from an initial position quite close in important respects to the Cartesian one to a radically novel 'mentalisation' of body.[110] But his aims and basic intuitions did not change. He remained convinced both that modern mechanistic physics was the best explanatory hypothesis of the phenomena of nature and that it required a theistic metaphysical foundation. This crucial addendum hinged on the intuition, already to be found in Aristotle, that an incorporeal principle of unity and activity was required in order to give reason, in the last instance, for our experience of the corporeal world. This was a meta-physical principle, that is, a principle which went beyond experience but which was necessary to postulate in order to give reason for experience itself. In his successive attempts to formulate a doctrine of substance, mind, and body coherent with the mysteries of the Christian religion, he struggled to define the nature of this incorporeal principle of unity and activity, proposing different solutions to the problems that confronted him at each turn.

The first articulated presentations of this metaphysical vision were to be found in an essay probably written in the spring of 1668 – the *Confessio Naturae contra Atheistas* – and in a long letter of April 1669 to his former teacher Jakob Thomasius.[111] As Leibniz explained to Thomasius, he drafted his essay "in a period of leisure, but working in the confusion of an inn", and its immediate publication was not foreseen. Yet Leibniz did share his anonymous and untitled draft with Boineburg; Boineburg passed it on to a friend of the Frankfurt pastor and leading early German pietist, Philipp Jakob Spener;[112] and Spener, in turn, communicated it to the Augsburg deacon Gottlieb Spitzel, who published the text without Leibniz's knowledge under the title *Confessio Naturae contra Atheistas*.[113] Despite Leibniz's complaint first to Thomasius and then, politely, to Spitzel himself that the printed version was strewn with inaccuracies,[114] the *Confessio Naturae* was a remarkable document in its own right and a landmark in the development of its author's early thought. The first part proposed a demonstration of the existence of God based on the argument that a full "explanation [ratio] of Corporeal Phenomena cannot be provided without an incorporeal Principle, that is God." The second part sought to demonstrate the immortality of the soul through a continuous sorites, that is, a chain of categorical syllogisms appropriately linked to one another.[115] In developing his arguments, the young Leibniz both sketched a pioneering (albeit still implicit) distinction between physics and metaphysics and employed for the first time one of the cardinal principles of his philosophy: the principle of sufficient reason. Thanks to the "admirable" progress of science recorded in his own century, he argued, it had "become apparent that mechanical explanations – reasons from the figure and motion of bodies, as it were – can be given for most of the things which the ancients referred only to the Creator or to some kind . . . of incorporeal forms."[116] As a result of this positive development which did not "unnecessarily resort to God" in the explanation of corporeal phenomena, "truly capable men" concluded that God could be eliminated from the world altogether. But this second step, Leibniz insisted, was unjustified. The key to avoiding the apparent atheistic consequences of modern science was to be found in the distinction between mechanical and metaphysical explanations of the universe, the latter of which began where "mechanism" left off and then dug deeper to arrive at "foundations and principles". Rather than rejecting mechanical explanations of phenomena altogether, as some conservative contemporaries urged, Leibniz proposed merely to reject the premature claim that bodies were self-sufficient and could exist without an incorporeal principle. This conclusion contained an implicit distinction between physics and metaphysics as two different kinds of knowledge concerning the same object. The task of metaphysics was to unearth the most universal principles, which were implicit in but not proper to physics itself:

we must agree with those contemporary philosophers who have revived Democritus and Epicurus and whom Robert Boyle aptly calls corpuscular philosophers, such as Galileo, Bacon, Gassendi, Descartes, Hobbes, and Digby, [who argue] that in explaining corporeal phenomena, we must not unnecessarily resort to God or to any other incorporeal thing, form, or quality . . . but that so far as can be done, everything should be derived from the nature of body and its primary qualities – magnitude, figure, and motion. But what if I should demonstrate that the origin of these very primary qualities themselves cannot be found in the essence of body? Then indeed, I hope, these naturalists will admit that body is not self-sufficient and cannot subsist without an incorporeal principle.[117]

In fact, Leibniz claimed, the origin of these "primary qualities" of bodies could not be found in the essence of body, defined in a Cartesian manner as "that which exists in space [spatio inexistere]". This conclusion was defended by bringing into play for the first time the principle central to Leibniz's later philosophy but not yet formally stated: the principle of sufficient reason. A reason (*ratio*), Leibniz insisted, must be given for every property of a being. This reason must be found either in the being in itself or in something else. Now, the reason for the fundamental properties ("primary qualities") of bodies – magnitude, figure, and motion – could not be derived from the definition of body because this consisted solely of the terms "space" and "existing in". If the *ratio* could not be found in body, then it had to be found in something which was not body, that is, in an incorporeal principle. "It readily becomes apparent," Leibniz concluded,

that this incorporeal being is one for all because of the harmony of things among themselves... But no reason can be given why this incorporeal being chooses one magnitude, figure, and motion rather than another, unless he is intelligent and wise with regard to the beauty of things and powerful with regard to their obedience to his command. Therefore such an incorporeal being will be a mind ruling the whole world, that is, God.[118]

The explicit mention of the principle of sufficient reason – stated as "nihil sine ratione" ("nothing is without a reason") – as the ground of a demonstration of the existence of God appeared only a few months later in the first chapter of the first part of the *Demonstrationum Catholicarum Conspectus*.[119] The principle itself – this time formulated in full as "Nihil est sine ratione, seu quicquid est habet rationem sufficientem" ("Nothing is without a reason; anything which is has a sufficient reason") – was more fully expounded in a text probably written between the autumn of 1671 and the beginning of 1672.[120]

In his letter of April 1669 to Jakob Thomasius, Leibniz reiterated the intuition of the *Confessio Naturae* that Aristotle was not incompatible with the "moderns", but could and ought to be reconciled with them. Indeed Leibniz initially went beyond emphasising the compatibility of

ancient and modern physics and proposed to Thomasius a "mechanisation" of Aristotelian physics itself.[121] In other words, in keeping with the
philosophia novantiqua recently espoused by Clauberg and some of the
early Dutch Cartesians, the former pupil tried to show to his Aristotelian
teacher that Aristotelian physics, properly interpreted, was quite compatible with mechanistic physics. This attempt to argue that Aristotle was, at
heart, a mechanist was soon abandoned. What was not abandoned was the
more important claim that mechanistic physics must be grounded in metaphysical principles already intuited by Aristotle. In his correspondence
with Thomasius, as in the *Confessio Naturae*, the passage from physics
to metaphysics hinged on the claim that the fundamental properties of
bodies (or primary qualities) identified by mechanistic physics did not
have their ultimate foundation in the nature of body. Unlike the *Confessio
Naturae*, however, Leibniz's correspondence with Thomasius restricted
the list of mechanical qualities which did not follow from the nature of
body to motion alone.[122] As he wrote in a previous letter to Thomasius
dated 6 October 1668,

> Since body is nothing other than matter and figure, and the cause of motion certainly
> cannot be understood either from matter or from figure, the cause of motion must be
> outside body. And since outside of body nothing is thinkable except a thinking being,
> or mind, mind will be the cause of motion. But the Mind which rules the universe is
> God.[123]

In his letter of April 1669 Leibniz explained further:

> The nature of body . . . is constituted by extension and antitypy . . . Therefore we can
> assume nothing in bodies which does not follow from the definition of extension and
> antitypy. But from these concepts are derived only magnitude, figure, situation, num-
> ber, mobility etc. Motion itself is not derived from them. Hence, properly speaking,
> there is no motion as a real thing [ens reale] in bodies.[124]

The fact that the origin of motion could not be found in bodies "left
to themselves" had important consequences not only for the demonstration of the existence of God but also for the ontological status of bodies.
From a quite Cartesian definition of the nature of body as constituted
by extension (that is, "to be" or "to exist in space"; *esse in spatio*; *spatio
inexistere*),[125] Leibniz drew the adamantly anti-Cartesian conclusion that
body (conceived as the Cartesian *res extensa*) was not a substance. This
conclusion followed from his contemporary efforts to elaborate a "true
notion" of substance compatible with the mysteries of transubstantiation

and the Incarnation. In this same period, in fact, Leibniz drafted a number of texts in which he tried to provide an explanation of Eucharistic transubstantiation.[126] In a note on transubstantiation probably written between 1668 and 1670, Leibniz moved from the definition of substance given in the *Dissertatio de Arte Combinatoria* of 1666 as "whatever moves or is moved" to the following definition: "a substance is a being that subsists in itself, that is, which has a principle of action within itself."[127] In this period he also maintained that "every action of body is motion".[128] Since motion, in his view, did not follow from the nature of body, bodies did not have in themselves the principle of (their) action. Therefore, following the definition of substance given above, body did not qualify as a substance. Since it was not a substance, it could only fall into the category of "accident" (defined as "whatever is not substance").[129] Moreover, if the principle of action (that is, motion) of bodies could not be found in themselves, it had to be found in something which was not body, that is, an incorporeal being or mind. A corporeal substance could therefore only be the union of body with mind: "the Substance of a body, therefore, is union with a sustaining mind."[130] In other words, in order to be a substance, body required an incorporeal principle of action.

This, however, led to a difficulty which, after Leibniz had struggled with it for some time, eventually produced one of the most remarkable features of his mature metaphysics. As originally formulated, the only physical beings endowed with their own individual, incorporeal, internal principles of activity or minds were human beings. For all nonrational creatures or inanimate bodies, the principle of activity had to be the universal mind or God: "Substance is union with mind. Thus the substance of the human body is union with the human mind, and the substance of bodies which lack reason is union with the universal mind, or God."[131] It was not long, however, before Leibniz came to regard this solution as problematic, not least because it came dangerously close to a pantheistic position in which God was the world soul.[132] This dissatisfaction was evident as early as an essay of 1669 or 1670 discussing the hypostatical union involved in the mystery of the Incarnation: in it Leibniz was at pains to distinguish the way in which the mind is united to the body (in rational beings) from the way in which God is united to bodies. Although the former qualifies as hypostatical union, he claimed, the latter does not.[133] Leibniz's uneasiness with the identification of God as the immediate principle of activity in inanimate bodies and nonrational creatures was even more evident a year after his letter of April 1669 to Thomasius. Upon publishing the first summary of his philosophy in his edition of Nizolio (in print by Easter 1670), he deleted or modified references which indicated God as the only and direct principle of activity (motion) in bodies.[134] A radical solution to this problem, and with it a significant evolution of Leibniz's notion of substance, took shape between 1670 and 1672. Since it proved unsatisfactory to ground the principle of action of "bodies which lack reason" – and therefore the condition of their substantiality – in an external being (that is, a universal mind or God), Leibniz postulated the existence of incorporeal or mind-like principles *internal* to bodies themselves. But to put an incorporeal, mind-like principle in all bodies (and not just in rational creatures) meant a radical transformation of the ontological status of body; and this led to a 'mentalisation' of body which was the direct ancestor of Leibniz's future monadology.[135] Given the fact that the notion of motion was central to Leibniz's inquiry into the nature of bodies, it is not surprising that this evolution should have taken place in the context of Leibniz's studies on physics.[136]

Leibniz's sustained interest in physics proper and in the discovery of the laws of motion in particular can be traced back at least to the summer of 1669. In August he accompanied Boineburg in one of his visits to Bad Schwalbach, a favourite spa town where learned men and politicians were accustomed to meet during the summer months. There a close friend of the baron, the professor of law at the University of Kiel, Erich Mauritius (1631–91), acquainted Leibniz with the discussion of the laws of motion currently agitating the scientific world, showing to him copies of the *Philosophical Transactions*, the official journal of the Royal Society, owned and edited by Heinrich Oldenburg.[137] The issue of motion and, especially, of the laws regulating the collision of bodies was one of the central points of debate in seventeenth-century physics. Since the middle of the century, Cartesian physics had established itself as the generally accepted framework of the inquiry into the laws of nature. Its explanatory paradigm was based on two principles: matter and movement. According to this model, matter was everywhere (with the consequent exclusion of the void), and movement (basically conceived as vortices) was propagated through the collision of bodies. In this context, the accurate formulation of the laws of impact was crucial;[138] and in 1668 the Royal Society therefore solicited accounts of these laws from three of its members best qualified to comment on the subject: the English mathematicians John Wallis

(1616–1703) and Christopher Wren (1632–1723), and the Dutch mathematician, physicist, and astronomer Christiaan Huygens (1629–95).[139]

Galvanised by this debate, Leibniz dashed off his own account of the laws of motion while still in Bad Schwalbach,[140] entrusting Mauritius with a copy to be forwarded to the Royal Society. Mauritius passed it on to Martin Fogel, a professor of mathematics in Hamburg, who disagreed with Leibniz's essay and therefore failed to pass it any further. By the time Leibniz became aware of this fact in early 1671, he did not regret Fogel's inaction: as appears from the critical annotations later added to his own text and from two incomplete attempts to demonstrate his theorems, in the meantime he had recognised the flaws in his first impulsive attempt to formulate the laws of motion.[141] A decisive new direction in his physical hypotheses – which also indicated the way toward a solution of the metaphysical difficulties in his philosophy of mind and body – was his study in depth of Thomas Hobbes's work *De Corpore* and his consequent adoption and reinterpretation of Hobbes's concept of *conatus* or "endeavour" (in the English philosopher's own translation). This study took place in all likelihood during the spring of 1670 and certainly before Leibniz's letter to Hobbes of 23 July 1670, in which the concept of *conatus* was employed.[142] This letter, sent as an enclosure within Leibniz's first letter to Oldenburg,[143] remained unanswered, possibly because Oldenburg, despite his assurances to the contrary,[144] failed to forward it to Hobbes. The experienced German intelligencer may well have thought that if his young protégé wanted to be in good terms with the Royal Society it would be best to steer him clear of the ageing English philosopher, who was currently engaged in a dispute with one of the Society's most prominent members, John Wallis.[145] Whatever the case, in Leibniz's hands Hobbes's concept of *conatus* proved extremely fecund. Its fruits were already apparent in Leibniz's fourth and fifth drafts of his physical theory, the latter of which constituted a first version of his *Theoria motus abstracti* or theory concerning the basic principles of abstract motion or motion in itself.[146]

While his thoughts on motion considered 'in abstract' were taking more precise and satisfactory shape, Leibniz also began no later than the summer of 1670 to reflect on the laws of motion considered 'in concrete', that is, on the laws which regulate the phenomenal world which we experience. These reflections eventually constituted a twin treatise complementary to the *Theoria motus abstracti*: his *Hypothesis physica nova* or "Theoria motus concreti" ("Theory of concrete motion"), in which he presented an explanatory model consistent with experimental discoveries of his time and with the world systems of both Nicolaus Copernicus and Tycho Brahe.[147] His first letter to Oldenburg of 23 July 1670 gave some hints regarding his physical studies on the laws of motion which applied to our world; but these brief remarks suggest that this part of his physical theory was still in its infancy.[148] Oldenburg's reply was very encouraging: Leibniz's scarce indications, he wrote on 20 August 1670, "whet my appetite (and that of others)";[149] and he therefore urged him to provide a more detailed summary of his hypotheses as soon as possible, probably with a view to reading it at one of the meetings of the Royal Society. Leibniz could not have asked for a better opportunity to have his views presented to one of the most prestigious fora of scientific discussion in Europe; and in the ensuing correspondence he worked hard to provide an overview of his theories. The bulk of his letter of 28 September 1670 summarised the *Theoria motus abstracti* and presented the gist of his *Hypothesis physica nova* in a "brief and crude form"[150] – another indication of the fact that the treatise on motion under abstract conditions was mature before its companion piece on the laws of motion contingent upon the concrete conditions of our world of experience. A couple of months later Leibniz had evidently made good progress. On 29 December 1670 he wrote to Jakob Thomasius that two sheets of the *Hypothesis physica nova* – corresponding to roughly two-thirds of the entire work – had just been printed.[151] By February a third sheet was in print.[152] In his letter to Oldenburg of 11 March 1671 he was able to satisfy the pressing invitation to provide more details on the whole theory: he not only expanded his account of abstract motion but also sent the first forty-nine paragraphs of the newly printed *Hypothesis physica nova* – regrettably not yet the whole work as he had intended, due to mistakes by the printer.[153] In his accompanying letter he was eager to point out that he had dedicated his *Hypothesis* to the Royal Society.[154]

Despite the incompleteness of the work as dispatched, Oldenburg presented it to the Royal Society at the first opportunity. At the meeting of 2 April 1671, Robert Boyle, Robert Hooke, John Wallis, and Christopher Wren were asked to examine Leibniz's *Hypothesis* and to report on it. Of the four, only Hooke and Wallis seem to have read the text: although Hooke's judgement was characteristically curt and dismissive, Wallis's was appreciative and substantially in agreement with Leibniz. At the end of April Leibniz sent the missing parts of the *Hypothesis physica nova* together with a copy of the *Theoria motus abstracti*, which was also finally in print.[155]

Having dedicated the *Hypothesis* to the Royal Society, Leibniz thought fit to dedicate its companion piece, the *Theoria motus abstracti*, to the other leading scientific academy of his day: the Parisian Académie Royale des Sciences, with which he had recently initiated contact. Through the mediation of the Parisian lawyer Louis Ferrand (d. 1699), he had written a letter discussing physical issues to the mathematician Pierre de Carcavy (c. 1600–1684), who served as Custodian of the Royal Library from 1663 to 1683 and had been a member of the Académie since its foundation in 1666. Carcavy's reply of 7 June 1671 reported on the encouraging first reception of Leibniz's ideas at the Académie.[156] A subsequent letter of 20 June 1671 from Carcavy contained the first known mention of Leibniz's calculating machine, which its young inventor had evidently described in his first letter to the French mathematician. Carcavy, while noting that his countryman Pascal had produced a machine capable of adding and subtracting many years earlier, did not hide his keen interest and urged Leibniz to send his machine to Paris so that it could be shown to Louis XIV's minister, the founder of the Académie, Jean-Baptiste Colbert (1619–83).[157]

Between these two main poles of the European scientific world, things seemed to be moving in Leibniz's favour. A few weeks later, Oldenburg wrote again with more good news: he copied to Leibniz the positive account given by John Wallis of the young German's physical theories and announced his decision to have them reprinted by John Martyn, the printer of the Royal Society.[158] Probably on the same day, Leibniz was answering Carcavy's letters expressing his hope that the copies of the *Theoria motus abstracti* and of the *Hypothesis physica nova* which he had sent to him had meanwhile arrived.[159] Oldenburg's active support and Wallis's positive reports were to prove crucial for the favourable reception which awaited Leibniz in London a year and a half later and for his early election as a fellow of the Royal Society on 19 April 1673.[160] The honeymoon with the Académie Royale des Sciences, however, was cut short: on 10 July 1671 a letter of barely two paragraphs from Carcavy explained in courteous but cool terms that the fellows of the Académie who had perused his two treatises had found them "difficult and obscure".[161]

Despite this mixed reception, Leibniz's early physical works were remarkable accomplishments. In them were presented some basic convictions which were permanently to remain distinctive features of his thought. His work in physics, to be sure, remained immature at this stage, especially since he still lacked the advanced mathematical training obtained during his trip to Paris. Yet the intuitions of these early years provided the germs of Leibniz's mature theories and discoveries, the guidelines which directed the development of his more precise and sophisticated explanations of fundamental characteristics of the universe from this early stage onwards. One of these intuitions was the conception of natural reality as the infinite 'repetition' of the same template. The discovery of the infinity of microcosms revealed by microscopists such as Robert Hooke, Pierre Borel, and Marcello Malpighi played an important part in the genesis of this explanatory model.[162] Another conviction, already found in the *Confessio Naturae*, was that the primary qualities of bodies identified by mechanistic physics – magnitude, figure, and motion – were insufficient to give reason, in the last instance, of our experience of the phenomena of the corporeal world. The very analysis of corporeal phenomena called for the postulation of an incorporeal, that is, spiritual or 'mental' principle.[163] But unlike previous writings of the years 1668–9, in the *Theoria motus abstracti* this spiritual or mind-like principle was placed in bodies themselves. The concept which allowed Leibniz to reach this result was the bewildering proto-force notion of *conatus* which Leibniz described as nothing less than the "Porta philosophiae", the "Gate of philosophy".[164] The labyrinthine path which led Leibniz to this gate was the analysis of the vexed problem of the continuum.[165]

The problem of the continuum had ancient origins. Zeno of Elea had graphically summarised it in the paradox of "Achilles and the tortoise" as early as the fifth century B.C. The fleet-footed Achilles could never catch up with the tortoise (which had been given a head start) because, no matter how fast he ran, he had first to reach the place previously occupied by the tortoise. But while he was doing this, the tortoise had advanced a bit farther, and so on for as long as the tortoise kept moving. For many centuries thereafter, the framework for further discussion of this paradox was provided by Aristotle's solution to it, which hinged on a distinction between actual division and divisibility. In this account, a body is never actually divided into an infinity of parts, even though it is potentially divisible to infinity.[166] In opposition to Aristotle, Galileo maintained that the continuum was in fact divided into an infinity of parts, called "infinitesimals," which had no determinate magnitude and were indivisible.[167] Galileo's follower, Bonaventura Cavalieri (1598*–1647), used the concept of "indivisible" throughout his *Geometria indivisibilibus continuorum nova quadam ratione promota* (1653).

In the *Theoria motus abstracti*, Leibniz admitted, in opposition to Aristotle and especially Descartes, the actual division of the continuum into an infinity of parts. In particular, he explicitly rejected the Cartesian thesis that continuous magnitudes, such as extension, were divisible indefinitely, but not into an actual infinity of parts.[168] Instead, following the teaching of Galileo and Cavalieri, Leibniz maintained the existence of nonextended "indivisibles."[169] Following Hobbes (who regarded himself as a Galilean on this point), Leibniz arrived at the conception of the indivisible parts of motion as "conatus". The most important feature of Hobbes's concept of conatus was that of infinitesimal motion or "motion made through the length of a point, and in an instant or point of time."[170] Leibniz's definition of conatus was borrowed directly from Hobbes: "Conatus is motion through a point in an instant."[171] In other words, conatus was for Leibniz an indivisible, nonextended part of motion, the beginning or end of motion.[172] Bodies in motion were conceived as bodies which at every instant had some conatus, so that the laws of motion were reduced to laws of persistence of conatus.[173] As for the laws of impact which were at the heart of the abstract theory of motion, the outcome of the collision of two bodies was explained by Leibniz through the combination of the conatus of the two bodies at the moment of collision.[174]

Moreover, the cohesion of bodies was explained in terms of "*bodies which push* or impel *each other*",[175] that is, in terms of the impact of two moving bodies; and from this thesis Leibniz drew momentous consequences. If cohesion depended upon the impact of moving bodies, then "there is no cohesion or consistency in bodies at rest, contrary to what Descartes thought."[176] Extending this proposition still further, Leibniz claimed that "there is no body at rest, for such a thing would not differ from empty space."[177] The essence of body, in other words, could not be extension, because extension was also a property of empty space. From this it followed that "the essence of body consists rather in motion",[178] which in turn was analysed in terms of conatus.[179] So the principle of the activity proper of bodies (and therefore the condition of their substantiality) – motion, which in turn is composed of conatus – was now placed in bodies themselves.[180] Bodies, which we perceive as extended things, were in reality grounded in the last instance in something which was not extended: conatus.

But here Leibniz's thinking took a still more extraordinary twist: for conatus, strictly speaking, is an action proper to the mind, as Leibniz wrote to Johann Friedrich on 21 May 1671: "for just as the actions of bodies consist of motion, so the actions of minds consist of conatus".[181] Leibniz thereby arrived at the stunning conclusion that "every body is a momentary mind, or one lacking recollection [*recordatio*]."[182] It is merely a momentary mind because conatus is "in a moment", that is, instantaneous, and body "does not retain its own conatus and the other contrary one together for longer than a moment."[183] On the other hand, "true" minds are endowed with memory, that is the ability to retain all the conatus which are compared and harmonised.[184] In order to have sensation, pleasure, or pain, it is necessary to have this ability of retaining, comparing, and harmonising conatus. Since body lacks this ability, "it lacks the perception of its own actions and passions; it lacks thought."[185] "This", Leibniz announced triumphantly, "opens the door to the true distinction between body and mind, which no one has explained heretofore."[186] It was indeed a striking position which self-consciously broke with the Cartesian's sharp distinction between mind and body, *res cogitans* and *res extensa*. No wonder that the French Académie, accustomed to the mechanism and dualism of the great French thinker, dismissed the *Theoria motus abstracti* as "obscure."

This new conception of corporeal substance as grounded in the last instance in an internal, mental-like principle which was unextended and indivisible was immediately put to work by Leibniz for the explanation of one of the most difficult mysteries of the Christian religion: the resurrection of bodies.[187] Writing on 21 May 1671 to Duke Johann Friedrich, Leibniz enclosed in his letter an essay *De Usu et Necessitate Demonstrationum Immortalitatis Animae* (*On the Use and Necessity of the Demonstrations of the Immortality of the Soul*) complete with an appendix *De Resurrectione Corporum* (*On the Resurrection of Bodies*).[188] In both the letter and the essay, Leibniz argued for the existence "in every thing" – that is, not only in human beings and animals, but also in plants and minerals – of a "kernel of substance" or a "seminal centre" which remained intact no matter how drastic the changes which bodies underwent. This kernel or seminal centre was "diffusivum sui" ("self-diffusing"), that is, a sort of metaphysical principle from which the body in its various stages of development resulted. Despite the fact that the material body could change completely during its lifetime and in death could be completely dispersed or changed into other chemical elements, the identity of that particular corporeal being remained indestructible because it was constituted by an unextended and indivisible spiritual "point" (*punctum*) of which the body was only a manifestation.[189] Leibniz seemed therefore to be interpreting the essence of bodies as consisting in a spiritual principle of which "flesh and bones" were mere phenomenical manifestations. Given this conception of bodies, their resurrection no longer posed a problem, since "the body must resurrect in a spiritual form." In other words, resurrected bodies would become what, metaphysically, all bodies really are beyond their changing physical appearance: beings which result from an indestructible spiritual principle. The young Leibniz was already inching his way toward the theory of monads of his mature metaphysics.[190]

Ethics and Politics

Alongside logic, metaphysics, and physics, the prolegomena to the *Demonstrationes Catholicae* included the first principles of "practical philosophy", that is, ethics and politics.[191] As Leibniz explained to Duke Johann Friedrich in his later presentation of the project, it was necessary to demonstrate "the true ethics and politics" in order to know what "justice, justification, freedom, pleasure, beatitude, beatifical vision" are and how to reach the "happiness of human kind also down here and in this life".[192] During the Mainz years the moral underpinning of Leibniz's conception of the universe began to take the distinctive shape which in its basic features was also to characterise his mature thought. The universe was conceived as a harmonious order created and governed by God, in whom the harmony of all things is grounded. From this conception derived an ethical vision which reduced to a minimum the ultimate 'ingredients' of morality, in tune with Leibniz's early 'minimalist' conviction that the best hypothesis is that which explains the most phenomena in the simplest way.[193] The basic moral virtue was that of justice, which was conceived as universal love or benevolence grounded in the basic dianoetic virtue, wisdom (*sapientia*).[194] Wisdom, in turn, was characteristically defined as the "science of happiness" (*scientia felicitatis*). So wisdom was both the foundation of true justice and the way to true happiness – justice and happiness which, although fulfilled only in the eternal life, must also be sought "down here" in the life of both the individual and the collectivity.[195]

Given Leibniz's background as a jurist, it is not surprising that the early reflections on the notion of justice which sowed the seeds of Leibniz's mature ethical thought should be found in his studies for the development of a "rational jurisprudence" and, in particular, in a series of texts of 1669 to 1671 sketching the *Elementa Juris Naturalis* ("Elements of natural law"). Moreover, his notion of jurisprudence itself assumed from early on a very broad meaning, incomparably more extended than that of a technical juridical doctrine. Rather, it came to embrace the very notion of the order given by God to creation and of the laws governing both the realm of nature and the realm of grace. In this context Leibniz laboured to outline his doctrine of justice, starting from a definition of "justice" and of "just" which tried to harmonise individual and collective good: "Justice is a constant striving [*conatus*] toward the common happiness which preserves at the same time one's own happiness"; "What is just is proportionate between love of self and love of the neighbour."[196] In the first mature draft of the *Elementa Juris Naturalis*, Leibniz critically evaluated his own definitions, asking how it was possible to reconcile one's own good with the good of others. Would perhaps justice be the "habit of willing others' good for the sake of one's own good"? "This is close to the truth", Leibniz replied to his own hypothesis, "but somewhat distorted."[197] True justice demands that the good of others is sought for its own sake and not merely in view of one's own good. But "how can it be that others' good be identical with our own and yet still be sought for its own sake"? The answer, Leibniz wrote, "depends on the nature of love":

The true definition of love [is as follows:] When we love . . . someone, their good is our delight. . . . Since then justice requires that the good of others is sought for its own sake, [and] since to seek the good of others for its own sake is to love others, it follows that love is of the nature of justice. *Justice* will therefore be the habit of loving others (or of seeking the good of others for its own sake, [or] of taking pleasure in the good of others).[198]

This definition of justice was basically reiterated in the second mature draft of the *Elementa Juris Naturalis* with an added emphasis on the inclusiveness of love: "Justice is the habit of loving all human beings."[199] From there it was a short step to the definition of justice as "caritas sapientis" ("charity of the wise"), characteristic of Leibniz's thought from 1677 onward.[200] By late 1671 or early 1672 the young Leibniz had already come very close to this formulation of the basic scheme of his ethical thought, as demonstrated by the link between wisdom, love, happiness, and harmony that he established in the *Demonstratio Propositionum Primarum*: "*Wisdom* is the science of happiness [scientia felicitatis]. . . . A *good man* is one who loves all human beings. *To love* is to find delight in the happiness of another. To find delight is to feel harmony."[201]

During the Mainz years Leibniz's political theory also began to take a definite shape. Indeed his determination to unite *theoria cum praxi* and to apply himself directly as well as indirectly to the betterment of human affairs led him to devote attention to concrete political questions as well as abstract theoretical ones. His undertakings in this area were chiefly stimulated by his relationship with his still influential and politically active patron, Boineburg. Among other things, the baron entrusted him with the important task of drafting political pamphlets in support of various diplomatic and political plans devised with or without the knowledge and approval of the elector. It was in the context of the first of these pamphlets, commissioned by Boineburg in support of his campaign for the election of Pfalzgraf Philipp Wilhelm von Neuburg (1615–90) to the Polish throne, that Leibniz proposed the distinction between the immediate goal (*scopus*) which leads to the constitution of the state and the ultimate aim (*finis*) for which the state is constituted. In accordance with Hobbes, Leibniz maintained that the immediate goal which leads to the constitution of the state is the need to guarantee security. However, reverting to an Aristotelian paradigm, he added that the ultimate aim (*finis*) for which the state is constituted is happiness.[202] In some preparatory notes to the *Elementa Juris Naturalis* dating back to 1669–70 he reiterated the distinction between *securitas* and *felicitas*, which was to remain a characteristic feature of his political thought.[203]

Leibniz's pamphlet for the election to the Polish throne (left vacant since September 1668 by the abdication of King Johann Kasimir) presented other striking features as well – above all the very method adopted by Leibniz in his argumentation. His case in support of Philipp Wilhelm von Neuburg was conducted in the form of a mathematical demonstration which was supposed to convince the electors on the basis of clearly stated, stringent reasons for favouring Boineburg's preferred candidate – no doubt the young German was being overoptimistic about the power of reason in determining political choices. Although he had worked "day and night" on the pamphlet over the winter,[204] due to the slowness of the Königsberg printer to whom the manuscript had been entrusted, the essay was not ready in time for the electoral assembly held in Warsaw between 2 May and 19 June 1669 and addressed by Boineburg on 12 June.[205] In any case a mathematical demonstration would hardly have been the rhetorical form most suited to dislodging the complex dynastic interests which resulted in the election of a member of the Polish nobility from the Piast house, Michael Wisniowiecki (1640–73). Leibniz, however, was not deterred from political and diplomatic involvement by this early defeat. In May 1669 he wrote a pamphlet advising the Duke of Württemberg to move his residence from Stuttgart to Cannstatt.[206] Around February 1670 he was busying himself with one of the problems left open by the peace of Westphalia. The ambiguous formulation of the third paragraph of the peace treaty signed by the emperor and the king of France did not make clear whether the emperor had relinquished the right to intervene in defence of the Burgundian circle of the Empire permanently or only as long as the war between France and Spain continued. After the death of Charles of Burgundy in 1477, this territory had become in fact a bone of contention between France and the Habsburg family. Controlled since the second half of the sixteenth century by the Spanish Habsburgs, it had been excluded from the Westphalian peace settlement on the ground that the war between France and Spain was still raging. When this conflict was ended with the Treaty of the Pyrenees (7 November 1659), the question returned with full force of whether the emperor had the right and duty to intervene in defence of the Burgundian circle. Against France's interpretation of the contentious paragraph, Leibniz upheld the emperor's right to protect this territory from French attacks.[207] Sometime in 1671 he argued once again against the French interpretation of another of the ambiguous settlements of the peace of Westphalia: the French claim that not only the cities of Metz, Toul, and Verdun had been assigned by the peace treatise to France, but also their considerable vassal territories.[208]

Meanwhile, the aggressive foreign politics of Louis XIV had prompted the duke of Lorraine to form an alliance with the archbishops of Mainz and Trier. In July 1670 the three allies agreed to send a diplomatic representation to Vienna to convince the emperor to join them in the anti-French 'Triple Alliance' formed by the Dutch Republic, England, and Sweden. Their hope was that other German princes would then follow their example. In Boineburg's view, however, this policy was dangerous. According to him, the interest of Mainz and of the other Rhine princes would have been best served by cultivating a friendly relationship with France. Forging closer links with the Habsburg emperor would have inevitably been regarded in Paris as a hostile move and might have undermined rather than enhanced the security of the Rhineland. Instead, Boineburg envisaged an alliance among the German princes which would have provided a neutral buffer zone between the two main powers in continental Europe, the Habsburgs and France.[209] Of course, the baron was no longer Prime Minister, and even after his reconciliation with the elector in 1668 he had not completely regained the trust of Schönborn. Nevertheless, he could still obtain a hearing from the elector, and for this purpose he enlisted once again the help of his able protégé. In August 1670 Leibniz wrote for him the first part of a heartfelt patriotic *Bedenken welchergestalt Securitas publica interna et externa . . . im Reich iezigen Umbständen nach auf festen Fuß zu stellen* (*A reflection regarding the form of internal and external public security . . . to establish in the Empire under current circumstances*).[210] During the same month France invaded Lorraine. This development prompted Boineburg to ask Leibniz to add a second part to his *Bedenken* with the aim of convincing the elector that the French design was to invade Holland, and not the Empire, during the following spring.[211] Both parts of Leibniz's work were sent to Schönborn, but they failed to change his strategy. The elector's efforts to bolster the Triple Alliance came to nothing, not because of Leibniz's inspired words, but because of a change of side by perfidious Albion: in the secret Treaty of Dover of 1 June 1670, the king of England, Charles II (1660–85), agreed to break with the Dutch in exchange for a consistent subsidy and military help from France in dealing with internal unrest. French money also oiled the disengagement of Sweden from the alliance, leaving Louis XIV free to prepare to wage war against the now skilfully isolated Dutch.[212]

Defeated once again, yet undiscouraged, the young Leibniz did what he could to preserve a fragile peace. This time he sought to appeal directly to the king of France and to convince Louis XIV that it was in his interest to invade Egypt instead of Holland.[213] Although traditionally disparaged as a lapse of judgement on Leibniz's part, in the political circumstances of the time this proposal had a certain logic to recommend it. If France had emerged as the Holy Roman Empire's most dangerous enemy to the west, the Ottoman Turks were well entrenched as the Empire's mortal enemy to the east; and Egypt was part of the Ottoman Empire. What better solution, from the German perspective, than for these two enemies to fight one another? If 'the most Christian king' was determined to cultivate his 'gloire' through feats of arms, then surely it was better to do so by checking the spread of Christian Europe's great adversary in the Mediterranean basin and alleviating Muslim pressure on Europe's borders, rather than by slaughtering their Dutch neighbours – a Christian people, albeit one predominantly of another Christian confession. Ambitious as it was, the plan won the immediate favour of Boineburg; and encouraged and supported by him, Leibniz began to develop his scheme in the autumn of 1671, without the knowledge of the elector. A first draft was sketched in December 1671;[214] but already Louis XIV's expansionistic policies were moving faster than Leibniz's pen. In December a French ambassador arrived in Mainz to announce the king's intention to invade Holland and to request the permission of the elector to allow the free passage of ships on the Rhine and the use of his influence to prevent the intervention of the emperor and of the other German princes.[215] Leibniz redoubled his efforts, producing in January four texts related to his and Boineburg's secret plan.[216] On 20 January 1672 Boineburg wrote to Louis XIV, announcing the plan in rather vague and general terms and including a memorandum drafted by Leibniz. A further memo, once again drafted by Leibniz, was sent to the king in February.[217] Time was running out, and in haste Leibniz tried to complete his most important and extended account of the plan, the *Justa Dissertatio*;[218] but by the time he departed for Paris on 19 March 1672 it was not quite ready and was about to be overtaken by events. When he arrived in Paris at the end of March, England had already started war with Holland, and France joined the conflict on 6 April 1672.

Theology

In his work towards the *Demonstrationes Catholicae* during the Mainz period, Leibniz did not confine himself to developing their encyclopaedic prolegomena or to advancing their practical consequences: he also worked intensely on the demonstrations themselves. The first part of these demonstrations was devoted to the existence of God, an enterprise which he continued to pursue throughout his life with the formulation and reformulation of a variety of arguments. In this period the most sustained attempt was made in the *Confessio Naturae contra Atheistas*,[219] but preparatory work for demonstrations based on the principles listed in the first part of the *Demonstrationum Catholicarum Conspectus* – "that nothing is without reason", "that there cannot be motion without continuous creation", "that in bodies there is no origin of motion", "that in bodies there is no origin of ceasing from motion", "that the beauty of the world originates from a mind"[220] – were scattered all over Leibniz's more philosophical correspondence and his work on the prolegomena, especially in the fields of physics and of the philosophy of mind and body. In turn, his reflection on the nature of the mind directly paved the way to the demonstration of the immortality and incorporeity of the soul planned for the second part of the *Demonstrationes Catholicae*, and specifically attempted in the second part of the *Confessio Naturae* as well as in the essay for Duke Johann Friedrich enclosed in the letter of 21 May 1671.[221] The third part of the plan, devoted to the "Demonstration of the Possibility of the Mysteries of the Christian Faith,"[222] was also tackled during the Mainz years in a variety of texts. Particularly remarkable was Leibniz's reflection on Eucharistic transubstantiation[223] and on the mysteries of the Trinity, the Incarnation, and the resurrection of bodies, for all of which his metaphysical work on the development of the "true" notion of substance was clearly of paramount importance. The fact that Leibniz – who never abandoned Lutheranism – should take such pains in developing a philosophical justification of the Roman Catholic doctrine of the transubstantiation of the sacramental bread and wine into the body and blood of Christ, instead of resting content with defending the Lutheran doctrine of the real presence of the body of Christ in the Eucharist, calls for an explanation. The Eucharist was one of the central theological issues involved in the reunification of the Christian churches. At least in this period, Leibniz was convinced that there was no essential philosophical difference between the doctrine of transubstantiation and that of the real presence.[224] At the Catholic court of Mainz and in his correspondence with Duke Johann Friedrich and Antoine Arnauld (both Catholics), he therefore undertook to defend transubstantiation straight away by elaborating a philosophical doctrine that, in his view, could accommodate the Catholic as well as the Lutheran doctrine of the Eucharist. In so doing he was hoping to provide a fundamental stepping stone towards reconciliation. Leibniz's justification of the Eucharist hinged on his newly developed conception of the substance of body as consisting not in extension but in a force or principle of action.[225]

Indeed, one of the first appearances of the fundamental link established by Leibniz between action and substance was in a text of 1668 devoted to the issue of Eucharistic transubstantiation.[226]

With his defence of the mysteries of the Trinity and of the Incarnation, Leibniz likewise plunged right into another great ongoing theological and philosophical controversy, in this case stirred by the spread of the antitrinitarian movement chiefly represented by the Socinians.[227] Following the teaching of the Italian heretic Faustus Socinus (1539–1604), the Socinians rejected the dogmas of the Trinity and the Incarnation on the basis of their alleged irrationality and insufficient biblical foundation. Persecuted for their heretical views, they found refuge in Poland, where a lively community was allowed to flourish until Socinianism was banned from that country as well in 1658, whereupon many of its leaders gravitated to the Dutch Republic. Throughout his life, Leibniz defended the mysteries of the Trinity and the Incarnation against the antitrinitarian charges. His anti-Socinian battle, announced in the *Demonstrationum Catholicarum Conspectus*,[228] began without delay thanks to yet another task assigned to him by Boineburg. In October 1665 the leading Polish Socinian, Andreas Wissowatius (1608–78), sent to Boineburg from his exile in Mannheim a letter containing a detailed refutation of the doctrine of the Trinity. In the spring of 1669, as the baron prepared to depart for Poland in order to attend the election of the new Polish king, Boineburg asked Leibniz not only to write in support of the candidacy of Philipp Wilhelm von Neuburg but also to rebut Wissowatius's antitrinitarian attack, probably with the intention of taking Leibniz's reply with him to Poland.[229] Leibniz obliged, engaging with Wissowatius in a close logical duel in which, on the basis of a sophisticated analysis of the nature of the copula ("est") in syllogistic propositions, he defended the doctrine of the Trinity against the charge of logical contradiction. In 1669–70 the objections against the Trinity and the Incarnation by another antitrinitarian, Daniel Zwicker (1612–78), received an equally sharp refutation.[230] His defence of the Incarnation against the charge of contradiction was followed up in this period by the attempt to formulate a positive explanation of the hypostatical union of two different natures implied by this mystery. The resulting essay on *De Incarnatione Dei seu de Unione hypostatica*, while searching for a solution to this theological problem, marked an important phase in Leibniz's reflection on the notion of substance and in his philosophy of mind and body. The same applied to another theologico-philosophical text of this period on a "difficult" mystery: the resurrection of bodies, discussed in the appendix to the essay on the immortality and incorporeal nature of the soul sent to Duke Johann Friedrich on 21 May 1671.[231]

The fourth and last part of the *Demonstrationes Catholicae* envisaged the demonstration of both "the authority of the Catholic Church" and "the authority of Scripture". By "Catholic Church" Leibniz meant the "multitude of Christians",[232] that is, the truly 'catholic' or universal community of Christians spanning the entire ecclesiastical tradition over and above the boundaries of particular churches. Already in the *Conspectus* he seemed, however, to assume that the ecclesiastical reunification of Christians could happen in the institutional framework of the Roman Catholic church[233] – a design which Leibniz would maintain at least until the mid-1690s.[234] During the Mainz years the most sustained piece of work related to this part of the catholic demonstrations was an essay discussing the issue, hotly debated at the time, of the last instance of judgement in controversial matters: should doctrinal differences be resolved by reference ultimately to the "balance of reason", the "norm of the text", or the authority of the Church? Leibniz's answer to this question needed to respond simultaneously on a number of fronts, notably to the position of the Roman Catholic church, powerfully represented by the polemical treatises of the Walenburch brothers,[235] to the radical theological rationalism of Cartesian inspiration advanced by Spinoza's friend, Lodewijk Meyer, in his *Philosophia S. Scripturae Interpres* (1666), and, last but certainly not least, to the *Tractatus Theologico-Politicus* (1670) of Spinoza himself.[236] Leibniz's adherence to the Augsburg Confession was evident in his clear inclination to favour the "norm of the text".[237] Regarding Spinoza's position, Leibniz, despite his critical stance towards the *Tractatus*, was impressed by the outstanding learning and penetration of the Jewish thinker.[238] On 5 October 1671 he approached him on the basis of their common interests in optics, including in his letter a tiny optical treatise he had written,[239] yet clearly hoping for more than a technical discussion of scientific matters. In his reply of 9 November Spinoza gave him exactly the opening he was angling for, offering to send a copy of the *Tractatus* and encouraging further correspondence.[240]

In a single overview, Leibniz's work towards the catholic demonstrations turned out to be truly encyclopaedic. But no matter how varied his theoretical reflections and practical activities – from logic to metaphysics and physics, from ethics and politics to theology – there was a constantly returning leitmotiv which emerged as a sort of regulative idea: the idea of universal harmony, defined as "unity in multiplicity" or *diversitas identitate compensata* ("diversity compensated by identity") and grounded in the last instance in God himself.[241] In a key letter of May 1671 to Magnus Wedderkopf, professor of jurisprudence in Kiel, the young Leibniz explained in a striking and compact way how the universal harmony governing the world played a pivotal role in the grand scheme of things. In so doing he painted a picture of Platonic inspiration, anticipating a number of his distinctive metaphysical and ethical doctrines. Most notable of these was the thesis that this is the best of all possible words, together with its corollary that the evil present in this world cannot be regarded as absolute evil but as a necessary ingredient of the best series of compossible things – that is to say, a combination which includes the maximum of goodness and perfection of things all connected to one another in an all-embracing universal harmony. In the letter to Wedderkopf, this best-of-all-possible-worlds thesis was ultimately grounded by Leibniz in his conception of God. The essences of things as mere logical possibilities are not created by God but are coeternal with God as ideas *in mente Dei*, that is as God's eternal thoughts. The divine intellect containing the ideas (or essences) of all possible beings constitutes in turn the basis of God's will. God's will to create a certain series of compossible things is based on his knowledge that this series is the best. God's choice, in other words, is grounded in his consideration of the nature of things. But the nature or essence of things does not depend on God's will, although it depends on God's intellect as its foundation: that a triangle has three sides follows from the nature of a triangle as eternally thought by God. God can chose to create a series of things which contains triangles and does so if that series of things is the best. But God cannot change the nature of a triangle intended as an eternal logical possibility. If, *per absurdum*, He were to think of the essence of a triangle in a different way (say, as a figure having four sides), He would not be thinking of a triangle but of something else. Moreover, possible things are thought by God not in isolation but in their relation to one another, that is, as combinations of compossible things or as possible worlds. The infinite possible worlds embraced by the infinite divine intellect cannot be modified by God's will because these combinations are simply expressions of the eternal nature of things as eternally thought by God. In Leibniz's striking phrase in the letter to Wedderkopf, nothing is the ultimate basis of the harmony of things. The harmony of things is just the way in which the nature of things is manifested. What

God can do and does is to will the existence of the best possible series, which inevitably includes a certain amount of evil:

What, therefore, is the ultimate basis of the divine will? The divine intellect. For God wills those things that he perceives to be the best and, likewise, the most harmonious; and he selects them, so to speak, from the infinite number of all the possibles. What, therefore, is the ultimate basis of the divine intellect? The harmony of things. And what is the ultimate basis of the harmony of things? Nothing. For example, no reason can be given for the fact that the ratio of 2 to 4 is that of 4 to 8, not even from the divine will. This depends on the essence itself, i.e., the idea of things. For essences of things are just like numbers,[242] and they contain the very possibility of entities, which God does not bring about, as he does existence, since these very possibilities – or ideas of things – coincide rather with God himself. However, since God is the most perfect mind, it is impossible that he is not affected by the most perfect harmony and thus must bring about the best by the very ideality of things. But this does not detract from freedom. For it is the highest form of freedom to be forced to the best by right reason. . . . From this it is evident that an absolute will, not dependent on the goodness of things, is monstrous. On the contrary, there is no permissive will in an omniscient being, except insofar as God conforms himself to the ideality itself of things, i.e., to what is best. Therefore, nothing is to be considered absolutely evil, otherwise either God will not be supremely wise with respect to its comprehension or God will not be supremely powerful with respect to its elimination.[243]

Moreover, as early as 1669–70 Leibniz had already come to the conclusion that "one mind is, in a certain sense, almost a world in a mirror," since it reflected the universal harmony linking everything to everything in God's creation.[244]

The Road to Paris

Having made epistolary contact with both the Royal Society and the Académie Royale des Sciences, Leibniz was eager to further these relationships in person.[245] On 13 July 1671 the theologian Johann Leyser wrote from Paris assuring him that Pierre de Carcavy and the mathematician Jean Gallois – editor of the prestigious *Journal des Sçavans*, member and secretary of the Académie Royale des Sciences since 1668[246] – desired nothing more than to benefit at the meetings of the Académie Royale from Leibniz's learning.[247] Even discounting a large measure of courtly flattery, the young German must have been delighted, and no later than the autumn of 1671 he began planning a trip to Paris to present his new discoveries and theories to the French learned world. With this trip in mind, Leibniz asked Duke Johann Friedrich for a letter of recommendation,

listing the encouraging contacts he had already made with Colbert, Carcavy, and Ferrand, and his desire to present (among other things) his new
theological demonstrations on the Eucharist to Antoine Arnauld. The one
material difficulty, he hinted, was that financial funding for such a visit
was still to be secured;[248] but by that time Leibniz was already busily
scheming with Boineburg, and it must have occurred to him that their
secret Egyptian plan could have been his ticket to Paris. In addition to the
noble cause of saving European peace, Boineburg also had more prosaic
reasons for sending his capable protégé and lawyer on a mission to Paris.
Since 1658, France had owed Boineburg a considerable amount of money
for an annual pension and the annual rent of a property in the Ardennes,
and the baron had so far been unsuccessful in his attempts to recover the
arrears.[249] The intrigued reaction of the French court to the vague presentation of the Egyptian plan contained in Boineburg's correspondence
addressed to Louis XIV in early 1672 prompted Boineburg to announce
to the king's foreign minister, Simon Arnauld de Pomponne (1618–99),
that the author of the plan himself was coming to Paris.[250] With such a
prospect opening, Leibniz had little difficulty declining the opportunity
arranged a few weeks earlier by Christian Habbeus to enter into Danish
service.[251] The last preparations for Paris were made in haste and without
fully disclosing to the elector which objectives Leibniz was to pursue in
Paris: assuming that it was a short visit for scientific purposes, Johann
Philipp von Schönborn gave his young employee permission to leave.[252]
On 18 March Boineburg provided Leibniz with full power of attorney
regarding his rent and pension, a modest advance of 100 talers for his
expenses (to be paid back from Leibniz's commission on the successful
recovery of the arrears), and a letter of presentation to Simon Arnauld de
Pomponne in which Leibniz was described as "a man who, his unpromising appearance notwithstanding, will certainly be able to deliver what he
promises."[253] On 19 March 1672, escorted by a servant, Leibniz departed
for Paris, where he arrived at the end of March.

Notes

1. See A I, 4, 672.
2. See Johann Georg Eckhart, *Lebensbeschreibung des Freyherrn von Leibnitz*. In *Journal zur Kunstgeschichte und zur allgemeinen Literatur*. Ed. by Chr. G. von Murr.
   Nürnberg 7 (1779): 123–321 (here p. 137) (repr. in J. A. Eberhard and J. G.
   Eckhart, *Leibniz-Biographien*. Hildesheim: Olms, 2003).

3. Cf. George M. Ross, "Leibniz and the Nuremberg Alchemical Society." *Studia Leibnitiana* 6 (1974): 222–48. Ross dispels a number of unwarranted speculations, including the myth that the Nuremberg society was Rosicrucian. On Leibniz and alchemy see also George M. Ross, "Alchemy and the Development of Leibniz's Metaphysics." In *Theoria cum Praxi, Akten des III. Internationaler Leibniz-Kongresses*. Vol. 4 (Naturwissenschaft, Technik, Medizin, Mathematik). Wiesbaden: Franz Steiner Verlag, 1982, pp. 40–45.

4. See Leibniz to Gottfried Thomasius, 17 December 1696 (quoted and translated from LBr 925, Bl. 13*r* by Ross, "Leibniz and the Nuremberg Alchemical Society," pp. 241–2) and Leibniz, *Oedipus Chymicus*, in *Miscellanea Berolinensia* I (Berlin 1710), p. 22. See also Bodemann, *Briefwechsel*, p. 337.

5. This was Leibniz's recollection in a manuscript of 1704 (LH XIII 27 Bl. 109*v*).

6. *Kürzere Fassung des Vortrags vor Kaiser Leopold I*, second half of September 1688 (A IV, 4, 80). See also A IV, 4, 16.

7. *Selbstschilderung* (Pertz I, 4, 169).

8. See A VI, 2, xviii.

9. See A I, 4, 672.

10. On Johann Philipp von Schönborn's skilful politics and ecumenical stance see Wiedeburg, *Der Junge Leibniz*, I. Teil: Mainz, pp. 59–79 (cf. esp. pp. 60, 64, 70–73, 75, 78) (Darstellungsband). Schönborn's tolerant attitude was reflected in his willingness to employ Protestants in prominent positions at his court without pressing for their conversion. The irenical atmosphere of the court was in turn instrumental in attracting a circle of converts keen to pursue, together with the archbishop, the reunification of Protestants and Catholics. Schönborn's relationship with Rome was predicated on the fine art of maintaining a degree of independence and critical reflection towards the conclusions of the Council of Trent while at the same time accepting its main doctrines. Among the reforms introduced in his diocese, most noteworthy was the use of a German translation of the Bible finished under his supervision in 1660 and published in 1661 – a clear signal that the Protestant Reformation had identified areas of Catholicism in genuine need of reform.

11. See Leibniz to Daniel Wülfer, 19 December 1669 (A I, 1, 79).

12. See *Nova Methodus Discendae Docendaeque Jurisprudentiae* (A VI, 1, 292) and Feder, *Commercium epistolicum*, p. 145.

13. See Leibniz to Friedrich Wilhelm Bierling, 16 March 1712 (GP VII, 504) and Leibniz to Duke Johann Friedrich, 21 May 1671 (A II, 1, 107).

14. Published in A VI, 1, N. 9.

15. Leibniz to Friedrich Wilhelm Bierling, 16 March 1712 (GP VII, 504).

16. *Nova Methodus* (A VI, 1, 292). See also Leibniz to Friedrich Wilhelm Bierling, 19 April 1712 (GP VII, 505).

17. See A VI, 2, xvii–xviii.

18. Cf. Cesare Vasoli, "Enciclopedia, Pansofismo e Riforma 'Metodica' del Diritto nella 'Nova Methodus' di Leibniz." *Quaderni fiorentini per la storia del pensiero giuridico moderno* 2 (1973): 37–109; Cesare Vasoli, *L'enciclopedismo del Seicento*.

Naples: Bibliopolis, 1978, pp. 74–88; Roberto Palaia, "Unità metodologica e molteplicità disciplinare nella *Nova Methodus Discendae Docendaeque Jurisprudentiae.*" In *Unità e Molteplicità nel Pensiero Filosofico e Scientifico di Leibniz.* Ed. by Antonio Lamarra and Roberto Palaia. Florence: Olschki, 2000, pp. 143–57.

19. Leibniz to Friedrich Wilhelm Bierling, 7 July 1711 (GP VII, 496).

20. *Nova Methodus*, I, § 26 (A VI, 1, 280).

21. Cf. *Specimen Quaestionum Philosophicarum ex Jure collectarum*, 1664 (A VI, 1, N. 4).

22. See *Nova Methodus*, II, § 5 (A VI, 1, 294) and *Dissertatio de Arte Combinatoria* (A VI, 1, 168, 190–91).

23. See *Nova Methodus*, II, § 4 (A VI, 1, 294).

24. Cf. Francesco Piro, "Jus – Justum – Justitia. Etica e Diritto nel giovane Leibniz." *Annali dell'Instituto Italiano per gli Studi Storici* 7 (1981/1982), p. 25; Hans-Peter Schneider, "Der Begriff der Gerechtigkeit bei Leibniz." In *Pensamiento jurídico y sociedad internacional.* Vol. 2. Madrid: Centro de Estudios Constitucionales, Univ. Complutense, 1986, p. 1090; Hubertus Busche, "Die drei Stufen des Naturrechts und die Ableitung materialer Gerechtigkeitsnormen beim frühen Leibniz. Zur Vorgeschichte der 'caritas sapientis'." In *Realität und Begriff.* Ed. by Peter Baumanns. Würzburg: Königshausen & Neumann, 1993, pp. 105–49.

25. See *Nova Methodus*, II, §§ 73–5 (A VI, 1, 343–5). Cf. also Leibniz to Hermann Conring, 23 January 1670 (A II, 1, N. 15).

26. See A VI, 2, xix–xx.

27. A I, 1, 127–8. See also Leibniz to Duke Johann Friedrich, 21 May 1671 (A II, 1, 107–18).

28. See A VI, 2, N. 28.

29. See Leibniz to H. E. Kestner, 9 October 1709 (in Bodemann, *Briefwechsel*, p. 111).

30. See GP VII, 504–5.

31. See Christian Ulrich Grupen to Leibniz, 13 September 1716 (LBr 337, Bl. 17–18).

32. Although in March 1669 he had to remind his employer that for some time his stipend had not been paid: see Leibniz to the Elector of Mainz, 27 March 1669 (A I, 1, 20–21).

33. See Johann Christian Boineburg to Hermann Conring, 22 April 1670 (in I. D. Gruber, *Commercii Epistolici Leibnitiani, ad omne genus eruditionis comparati, per partes publicandi, tomus podromus. Pars 1. 2.* Hanoverae et Gottingae: Apud Io. Wilhelm. Schmidium, 1745, p. 1285) and Leibniz to Joh. Georg Graevius, 28 February 1671 (A I, 1, 125).

34. The *Ratio Corporis Juris Reconcinnandi* is published in A VI, 2, N. 30.

35. Leibniz to Thomas Hobbes, 23 July 1670 (A II, 1, 57). Also in Thomas Hobbes, *The Correspondence.* Ed. by Noel Malcolm. Vol. II. Oxford: Clarendon Press, 1994, pp. 713–16 (here p. 714).

36. A I, 1, N. 26.

37. A I, 7, 60. See also A I, 7, 57.

38. See Wiedeburg, *Der Junge Leibniz*, I. Teil: Mainz, p. 96 (Darstellungsband).

39. See Hochstetter, "Zu Leibniz' Gedächtnis," pp. 4–5, 7.

40. See Müller – Krönert, *Leben und Werk*, p. 13 and A IV, 1, xxiii.

41. J. D. Gruber, ed., *Commercii Epistolici Leibnitiani, ad omne genus eruditionis comparati, per partes publicandi. Tomi prodromi pars altera*. Hanoverae et Gottingae: Apud Io. Wilhelm. Schmidium, 1745, pp. 1208–9.

42. See Gruber, *Commercii Epistolici*, p. 1221.

43. Leibniz's first letter to Conring dated from 23 January 1670, the last one from February 1679. The nineteen extant letters exchanged between them are published in A II, 1.

44. Boineburg to Conring, 22 April 1670 in Gruber, *Commercii Epistolici*, pp. 1286–7.

45. See *Kritischer Katalog der Leibniz-Handschriften*, prepared by Paul Ritter et al. (Berlin 1908), 1 N. 126.

46. See A I, 1, 13; A I, 1, 376; A I, 1, 380. On Leibniz's legal representation of the Boineburg family see for instance his trip to Düsseldorf in the summer of 1669 (*Kritischer Katalog der Leibniz-Handschriften*, 1, N. 245).

47. See Leibniz to Simon Löffler, 30 April 1669 (A I, 1, N. 34) and Leibniz to Ernst von Hessen-Rheinfels, early 1681* (A I, 3, 260–61).

48. On Peter van Walenburch see Wiedeburg, *Der Junge Leibniz*, I. Teil: Mainz, pp. 79–92 (Darstellungsband).

49. See *Theodicy*, "Preface" (GP VI, 43).

50. See *Kritischer Katalog der Leibniz-Handschriften*, 1, N. 216 and Leibniz to Earl de La Gardie, 28 May 1669 (A I, 1, N. 136).

51. See Christian Habbeus to Leibniz, 10 December 1669 (A I, 1, N. 137). Although Habbeus recommended Leibniz to the duke in the context of a discussion in which Johann Friedrich lamented the death of his chancellor Heinrich Langenbeck, there is no evidence that the duke intended to offer such a senior position to Leibniz, contrary to what is suggested by Müller-Krönert, *Leben und Werk*, p. 17.

52. See A II, 1, N. 42.

53. See A II, 1, 83. This "meditation" seems to correspond to two pieces written between 1669 and 1671: *De Possibilitate Gratiae Divinae* (A VI, 1, N. 19) and *Von der Allmacht und Allwissenheit Gottes und der Freiheit des Menschen* (A VI, 1, N. 20).

54. Leibniz to Duke Johann Friedrich, 13 February* 1671 (A II, 1, 83–4).

55. *Hypothesis physica nova*, winter 1670/71* (A VI, 2, 257).

56. Cf. above chap. I. 1; Leibniz to Duke Johann Friedrich, second half of October* 1671 (A II, 2, 160); Leibniz to Antoine Arnauld, early November 1671 (A II, 1, 180).

57. See Leibniz to Duke Johann Friedrich, February 1679 (A II, 1, 556).

58. *The Correspondence of Henry Oldenburg*. Ed. by A. Rupert Hall and M. Boas Hall. 13 vols. Madison and London: University of Wisconsin Press and Taylor and Francis, 1965–86, vol. VII, pp. 107–8:108–9. The first set of pages refers to the original text, the second set to the English translation.

59. Leibniz approached Oldenburg for the first time in a letter of 23 July 1670 (A II, 1, N. 26); *The Correspondence of Henry Oldenburg*, vol. VII, pp. 64–6:66–7. Oldenburg enclosed his reply to Leibniz in the letter to Boineburg of 20 August 1670 (cf. *The Correspondence of Henry Oldenburg*, vol. VII, pp. 107:108).

60. *Demonstrationum Catholicarum Conspectus*, 1668–9* (A VI, 1, N. 14).

61. *Demonstrationum Catholicarum Conspectus* (A VI, 1, 494).

62. *De ratione perficiendi et emendandi Encyclopaediam Alstedii* (A VI, 2, N. 53).

63. On the post-Ramist tradition of systematic encyclopaedism culminating in Alsted's eclectic work, see Hotson, *Commonplace Learning*. For his combinatorial reconception of the encyclopaedia see also Hotson, *Alsted*, esp. pp. 163–72.

64. Hobbes's *De Corpore* was part of the following trilogy: *Elementorum philosophiae sectio prima de corpore*. London, 1655; *Elementorum philosophiae sectio secunda de homine*. London, 1658; *Elementorum philosophiae sectio tertia de cive*. Paris, 1642.

65. See *De ratione perficiendi et emendandi Encyclopaediam Alstedii* (A VI, 2, 395). On Leibniz's early physics, philosophy of mind, and practical philosophy see below.

66. Leibniz to Duke Johann Friedrich, second half of October* 1671 (A II, 2, N. 84) and Leibniz to Antoine Arnauld, early November 1671 (A II, 1, N. 87). On the direct presentation of the Catholic Demonstrations plan in a letter of 1679 to Duke Johann Friedrich see chap. II. 4.

67. See A II, 1, 172.

68. See A II,1, 173.

69. Cf. in particular George Dalgarno, *Ars Signorum, vulgo character universalis et lingua philosophica*. London, 1661; John Wilkins, *Essay towards a Real Character and a Philosophical Language*. London, 1668; Athanasius Kircher, *Polygraphia nova et universalis ex combinatoria arte detecta*. Rome, 1663; Joh. Joachim Becher, *Character, pro notitia linguarum universali. Inventum steganographicum hactenus inauditum*. Frankfurt, 1661; Cave Beck, *The Universal Character, By which all the Nations in the World may understand one anothers Conceptions*. London, 1657. Leibniz certainly knew the work of Dalgarno, Wilkins, Kircher, and Becher. On artificial languages in the early modern period see Gerhard F. Strasser, *Lingua universalis: Kryptologie und Theorie der Universalsprachen im 16. und 17. Jahrhundert*. Wiesbaden: Harrassowitz, 1988 and Rhodri Lewis, *Language, Mind and Nature. Artificial Languages in England from Bacon to Locke*. Cambridge: Cambridge University Press, 2007.

70. See *Demonstratio Propositionum Primarum*, autumn 1671 – early 1672* (A VI, 2, 481).

71. See for instance Leibniz to Heinrich Oldenburg, 1673* (A II, 1, 239). Cf. Massimo Mugnai, "Leibniz: Vita di un genio tra logica, matematica e filosofia." *Le Scienze* 5, no. 29 (2002), p. 35, and Philip Beeley, "A Philosophical Apprenticeship: Leibniz's Correspondence with the Secretary of the Royal Society, Henry Oldenburg." In *Leibniz and His Correspondents*. Ed. by Paul Lodge. Cambridge: Cambridge University Press, p. 65.

72. See Athanius Kircher to Leibniz, 23 June 1670 (A II, 1, N. 23). See also A II, 1, N. 96. On Kircher see esp. Thomas Leinkauf, *Mundus combinatus: Studien zur Struktur der barocken Universalwissenschaft am Beispiel Athanasius Kirchers SJ (1602–1680)*. Berlin: Akademie Verlag, 1993 and Paula Findlen, ed., *Athanasius Kircher. The last man who knew everything*. New York and London: Routledge, 2004.

73. A VI, 2, N. 58. Cf. Wilkins, *Essay towards a Real Character and a Philosophical Language*, Part II, chap. I, pp. 26–33.

74. See Beeley, "A Philosophical Apprenticeship," p. 67. Cf. also C. Hill, *Intellectual Origins of the English Revolution*. Oxford: Oxford University Press, 1965, pp. 106–7; J. Přívratská and V. Přívratská, "Language as the Product and Mediator of Knowledge: The Concept of J. A. Comenius." In *Samuel Hartlib and Universal Reformation. Studies in Intellectual Communication*. Ed. by Mark Greengrass, M. Leslie, and T. Raylor. Cambridge: Cambridge University Press, 1994, pp. 171–2; Lewis, *Language, Mind and Nature*.

75. See Leibniz to Heinrich Oldenburg (A II, 1, N. 26); *The Correspondence of Henry Oldenburg*, vol. VII, pp. 65 6:67.

76. See William Curtius to Leibniz, 23 October 1670 (A II, 1, N. 31), and Leibniz to Heinrich Oldenburg, 9 May 1671 (A II, 1, 104).

77. See A II, 1, N. 97 and N. 98. On the importance of the term 'systema' to the post-Ramist tradition, see Hotson, *Commonplace Learning*, esp. pp. 148–52, 161–5, 182–6.

78. A VI, 2, 487–9, 493.

79. See Leibniz to Jakob Thomasius, September 1669 (A II, 1, 26–7) and Leibniz to Ph. J. Spener, 20 February 1670 (A I, 1, 88). On Leibniz and Nizolio see esp. Ignacio Angelelli, "Leibniz's Misunderstanding of Nizolius' Notion of 'multitudo'." *Notre Dame Journal of Formal Logic* 6, no. 4 (1965): 319–22.

80. See Jakob Thomasius to Leibniz, 21 October 1670 (A II, 1, 67).

81. A VI, 2, N. 54.

82. See A VI, 2, 450.

83. A VI, 2, 428.

84. See A VI, 2, 428–9.

85. A VI, 2, 431. Cf. Mugnai, *Introduzione*, p. 36.

86. A VI, 2, 432.

87. A VI, 2, 393. Cf. Johann Joachim Becher, *Appendix practica, über Seinen Methodum Didacticam*. Munich, 1669.

88. See *Nouveaux Essais*, book II, chap. 1, § 2 (A VI, 6, 111).

89. Leibniz to Heinrich Oldenburg, 23 July 1670 (A II, 1, 59); *The Correspondence of Henry Oldenburg*, VII, 64:66.

90. See A I, 1, N. 1, N. 2., N. 12, N. 13.

91. See A I, 1, 5.

92. See for instance Gudenus's letter to Leibniz of 9 December 1668 (A I, 1, N. 7) and Boineburg's letter to Lambeck of 18 November 1669, drafted by Leibniz himself (A I, 1, N. 15). See also A IV, 3, 776.

93. See Leibniz's two proposals of January 1670 (A I, 1, N. 23 and N. 24).

94. At its foundation, the purpose of the Academia was presented in the following preamble: "The glory of God, the enlightenment of the art of healing and the resulting benefit for our fellow men shall be the goal and the only guide of the Academy of Sciences." Quoted from the official website of the Academia, formerly renamed the Deutsche Akademie der Naturforscher Leopoldina and since 18 February 2008 known as Germany's National Academy of Sciences.

95. Leibniz for the *Dompropst* and *Statthalter* of Mainz (Johann von Saal), January 1670* (A I, 1, N. 25, esp. p. 54). On the early history of the Academia Naturae Curiosorum see Rolf Winae, "Zur Frühgeschichte der Academia Naturae Curiosorum." In *Der Akademiegedanke im 17. und 18. Jahrhundert*. Ed. by Fritz Hartmann and Rudolf Vierhaus. Bremen, 1977, pp. 117–37; Frances Mason Barnett, *Medical Authority and Princely Patronage: The Academia Naturae Curiosorum, 1652–1693*. University of North Carolina at Chapel Hill, 1995. (Unpubl. Ph.D. dissertation). On its shortcomings see A IV, 1, 548–9. An important step toward the effectiveness of the Academia was the foundation in 1670 of a journal (*Miscellanea curiosa medico-physica*). In 1687 the Academia was elevated by Emperor Leopold I to the status of an imperially protected institution with the name *Sacri Romani Imperii Academia Caesareo-Leopoldina Naturae Curiosorum*. Cf. Wieland Berg and Benno Parthier, "Die 'kaiserliche' *Leopoldina* im Heiligen Römischen Reich Deutscher Nation." In *Gelehrte Gesellschaften im mitteldeutschen Raum (1650–1820)*. Part I. Ed. by Detlef Döring and Kurt Nowak. Vol. 76, No. 2 of *Abhandlungen der Sächsischen Akademie der Wissenschaften zu Leipzig. Philologisch-historische Klasse*. Leipzig: S. Hirzel, 2000, pp. 39–52.

96. See Oldenburg to E. Leichner, 23 September 1663 (O.S.). In *The Correspondence of Henry Oldenburg*, vol. II, pp. 110:111.

97. *Grundriß eines Bedenkens von Aufrichtung einer Societät in Deutschland zu Aufnehmen der Künste und Wissenschaften* (A IV, 1, N. 43) and *Bedenken von Aufrichtung einer Akademie oder Societät in Deutschland zu Aufnehmen der Künste und Wissenschaften* (A IV, 1, N. 44).

98. See esp. *Bedenken* (A IV, 1, 548–9).

99. See *Grundriß*, esp. A IV, 1, 531–3. Cf. also *Societät Gottgefällig*, 1671* (A IV, 1, N. 48).

100. In FC, *Oeuvres*, VII, 502–3.

101. On the advancement of medicine see in particular some notes probably written between 1671 and the beginning of 1672 (A VI, 2, N. 42/6, N. 42/7, N. 43).

102. See A IV, 1, 553–5.

103. A IV, 1, N. 46.

104. *Directiones ad rem Medicam pertinentes* (LH III, 1 Bl. 1–8, 9). Leibniz's manuscript is published by Fritz Hartmann and Matthias Krüger in *Studia Leibnitiana* 8, no. 1 (1976): 50–68. The editors's illuminating introduction to the manuscript has been essential in locating the texts of Leibniz on medicine

quoted below. See also Fritz Hartmann and Wolfgang Hense, "Die Stellung der Medizin in Leibniz' Entwürfen für Sozietäten." In *Leibniz in Berlin*, pp. 243–244.

105. LH III, 1 Bl. 9. In Fritz Hartmann and Matthias Krüger, eds., *"Directiones ad rem Medicam pertinentes. Ein Manuskript G. W. Leibnizens aus den Jahren 1671/72 über die Medizin."* *Studia Leibnitiana* 8, no. 1 (1976), p. 67.

106. On Leibniz's successful solution to the mathematical problem of the quadrature of the circle see chap. I. 3.

107. Leibniz to Konrad Burchard Vogther, 1712 (Bodemann, *Briefwechsel*, p. 365). Cf. also Grua, 659 and *De eo quod Franciae interest* (*Consilium Aegyptiacum*), January 1672* (A IV, 1, 250).

108. *Nouveaux Essais*, book IV, chap. 3, § 20 (A VI, 6, 387). Trans. by Peter Remnant and Jonathan Bennett. Cambridge: Cambridge University Press, 1996.

109. *Bedenken von Aufrichtung einer Akademie oder Societät in Deutschland*, 1671 (A IV, 1, 552).

110. Cf. Daniel Garber, "Motion and Metaphysics in the Young Leibniz." In *Leibniz: Critical and Interpretative Essays*. Ed. by Michael Hooker. Manchester: Manchester University Press, 1982, pp. 160–84.

111. Respectively A VI, 1, N. 13 and A II, 1, N. 11.

112. Leibniz considered Spener one of his "special friends" during his stay in the Frankfurt area (see Leibniz to Ernst von Hessen-Rheinfels, early 1681*; A I, 3, 260).

113. In his *De atheismo eradicando . . . Epistola.* Augsburg, 1669, pp. 125–35. See A II, 1, 24. See also A VI, 2, 569–70.

114. A II, 1, 24 and Leibniz to Gottlieb Spitzel, 22 December 1669; A I, 1, 81.

115. See respectively A VI, 1, 489–92; A VI, 1, 492–3. This type of syllogistic argument should not be confused with the sorites paradox.

116. A VI, 1, 490 / L 109–10.

117. A VI, 1, 490 / L 110. Cf. Maria Rosa Antognazza, "Leibniz and the Post-Copernican Universe. Koyré Revisited." *Studies in History and Philosophy of Science* 34 (2003): 309–27 (esp. pp. 312–15).

118. A VI, 1, 490–92 / L 110–12.

119. A VI, 1, 494.

120. *Demonstratio Propositionum Primarum* (A VI, 2, 483).

121. Cf. Garber, "Motion and Metaphysics in the Young Leibniz," p. 162; Mercer, "Mechanizing Aristotle: Leibniz and Reformed Philosophy," pp. 117–52; Christia Mercer, "Leibniz and His Master. The Correspondence with Jakob Thomasius." In *Leibniz and His Correspondents*. Ed. by Paul Lodge. Cambridge: Cambridge University Press, 2004, pp. 10–46. See also R. Bodéüs, *Leibniz–Thomasius, Correspondance, 1663–1672*. Paris: J. Vrin, 1993.

122. See Garber, "Motion and Metaphysics in the Young Leibniz," p. 163.

123. A II, 1, 11.

124. A II, 1, 23 / L 101–2. I have modified Loemker's translation following Garber, "Motion and Metaphysics in the Young Leibniz," p. 164.
125. See respectively Leibniz to Thomasius, 30 April 1669 (A II, 1, 23) and *Confessio Naturae* (A VI, 1, 490). The definition of body as *esse in spatio* recurs in *De Transsubstantiatione*, 1668* (A VI, 1, 508).
126. See A VI, 1, N. 15/1–4 (esp. N. 15/2 *De Transsubstantiatione*, 1668*).
127. Respectively A VI, 1, 169 / L 73 and A VI, 1, 508 / L 115.
128. A VI, 1, 508. See also *Confessio Naturae* (A VI, 1, 493) and the preparatory notes for the *Theoria Motus Abstracti* (A VI, 2, 168).
129. A VI, 1, 509. Cf. also *De Incarnatione Dei seu de Unione hypostatica*, 1669–70* (A VI, 1, 533).
130. A VI, 1, 509. I follow Robert Adams's translation in Robert Merrihew Adams, *Leibniz: Determinist, Theist, Idealist*. New York and Oxford: Oxford University Press, 1994, p. 359.
131. A VI, 1, 509 / L 116.
132. See Garber, "Motion and Metaphysics in the Young Leibniz," p. 165.
133. On this text and its explanation of the hypostatical union see Maria Rosa Antognazza, *Leibniz on the Trinity and the Incarnation: Reason and Revelation in the Seventeenth Century*. New Haven, CT: Yale University Press, 2007, pp. 35–41.
134. The revised version is published in A VI, 2, 433–44. Cf. Garber, "Motion and Metaphysics in the Young Leibniz," p.171; Mercer, *Leibniz's Metaphysics*, pp. 137–44; Christia Mercer and R. C. Sleigh, Jr. "Metaphysics: The early period to the *Discourse on Metaphysics*." In *The Cambridge Companion to Leibniz*. Ed. by Nicholas Jolley. Cambridge: Cambridge University Press, 1995, p. 78.
135. Cf. Garber, "Motion and Metaphysics in the Young Leibniz," pp. 168–78. Adams suggests that Leibniz's early "mentalization of body" could be also interpreted as a "physicalization of mind" (see Adams, *Leibniz*, p. 218, footnote 3).
136. See especially A VI, 2, N. 38–41, N. 48. See also A VI, 2, N. 42/3–42/4, N. 45.
137. Cf. Leibniz to Heirinch Oldenburg, 28 September 1670 (A II, 1, 62).
138. See Mugnai, *Leibniz: Vita*, pp. 53, 60.
139. See M. Boas Hall, "The Royal Society's Role in the Diffusion of Information in the Seventeenth Century." *Notes and Records of the Royal Society of London* 29 (1975), p. 188. In the *Philosophical Transactions* of January 1669 Oldenburg published the papers sent by Wren and Wallis, but not that of Huygens, on the ground that it had arrived late and contained laws largely identical to those discovered by Wren. Huygens was understandably annoyed by this turn of events; and fearing that he would be accused of plagiarism, he published in March a French summary of his results in the *Journal des Sçavans*, vindicating the priority and originality of his discovery of the laws. As a consequence, a Latin translation of Huygens's summary appeared in the April issue of the *Philosophical Transactions*, accompanied by a note in which Oldenburg acknowledged the merits of Huygens and accounted for the delayed publication of his

results. Cf. Christiaan Huygens, "Extrait d'une lettre de M. Hugens à l'Auteur du Journal." *Journal des Sçavans* (18 March 1669): 22–24; Christiaan Huygens, "A Summary Account of the Laws of Motion, communicated by Mr. Christian Hugens in a Letter to the R. Society, and since printed in French in the Journal des Scavans of March 18, 1669. St. n." *Philosophical Transactions* 46 (12 April 1669) (O.S.): 925–8. See also Oldenburg to Huygens, 26 April 1669 (O.S.). In *The Correspondence of Henry Oldenburg*, vol. V, pp. 501:502–3. Cf. Beeley, "A Philosophical Apprenticeship," pp. 54–5 and Mugnai, *Leibniz: Vita*, p. 60.

140. *De Rationibus motus*, August–September* 1669 (A VI, 2, N. 38/1).

141. Cf. A VI, 2, xxxi–xxxii. See Heinrich Oldenburg to Leibniz, 18 December 1670 (A II, 1, 71); Leibniz to Martin Fogel, 13 February 1671 (A II, 1, 82); A VI, 2, 161; A VI, 2, N. 38/2; A VI, 2, N. 38/3.

142. See A II, 1, 57–8.

143. A II, 1, N. 26.

144. See Heinrich Oldenburg to Leibniz, 20 August 1670 (A II, 1, 62).

145. See Beeley, "A Philosophical Apprenticeship," pp. 61–2.

146. Cf. respectively A VI, 2, N. 38/4 and N. 38/5. These texts were probably written between the spring of 1670 and the winter of 1670–71.

147. See A VI, 2, 221, 223.

148. See Leibniz to Oldenburg (A II, 1, 59–60). On the genesis of Leibniz's *Hypothesis physica nova* traced through his correspondence with Oldenburg see the excellent account of Beeley, "A Philosophical Apprenticeship," pp. 52–9.

149. A II, 1, 61; *The Correspondence of Henry Oldenburg*, vol. VII, pp. 110:112.

150. A II, 1, N. 28 (here A II, 1, 65; *The Correspondence of Henry Oldenburg*, vol. VII, pp. 165:169).

151. A II, 1, 74.

152. See Leibniz to Hermann Conring, 8 February 1671 (A II, 1, 80) and Leibniz to Joh. Georg Graevius, 28 February 1671 (A I, 1, 124).

153. See Leibniz to Oldenburg (A II, 1, 88) and Beeley, "A Philosophical Apprenticeship," pp. 56, 58, quoting the version of Wallis's letter to Oldenburg of 17 April 1671 published in John Wallis, "Dr Wallis's opinion concerning the Hypothesis Physica Nova of Dr. Leibnitius, promised in Numb. 73. and here inserted in the same tongue, wherein it was written to the Publisher, April. 7. 1671." *Philosophical Transactions* 74 (14 August 1671) (O.S.): 2227–31.

154. A II, 1, 91. See the dedication in A VI, 2, 222.

155. See A VI, 2, 220 and Beeley, "A Philosophical Apprenticeship," p. 59. The *Hypothesis physica nova* and the *Theoria motus abstracti* were published, respectively, in A VI, 2, N. 40 and N. 41.

156. See A II, 1, N. 61. The letter written by Leibniz to Carcavy has not been found.

157. A II, 1, N. 65.

158. Oldenburg to Leibniz, 22 June 1671 (A II, 1, N. 68); *The Correspondence of Henry Oldenburg*, vol. VIII, pp. 99:103–4. John Wallis's report on the *Hypothesis physica nova* was also printed in the *Philosophical Transactions* 74 (14 August 1671). The edition by John Martyn appeared in London in 1671.

159. A II, 1, 125–6.
160. See Thomas Birch, *The History of the Royal Society of London*. 4 vols. London: A. Millar, 1756–7, vol. III, p. 82 and Beeley, "A Philosophical Apprenticeship," p. 69.
161. A II, 1, N. 70.
162. Cf. Mugnai, *Introduzione*, pp. 100–101; Beeley, "A Philosophical Apprenticeship," p. 58; and Antonio-Maria Nunziante, *Organismo come Armonia. La genesi del concetto di organismo vivente in G. W. Leibniz*. Trento: Verifiche, 2002, pp. 65–6. On the impact of the microscope on early modern philosophy see Catherine Wilson, *The Invisible World. Early Modern Philosophy and the Invention of the Microscope*. Princeton: Princeton University Press, 1995.
163. Cf. Mugnai, *Introduzione*, pp. 101–2, 125. On the fact that the analysis of the physical world itself brought Leibniz to postulate, at the metaphysical level, an incorporeal or mental principle which was required as the ultimate foundation of physical phenomena, see the fundamental and innovative work of Richard Arthur focusing on the problema of the continuum, notably his extensive introduction to G. W. Leibniz, *The Labyrinth of the continuum: writings on the continuum problem, 1672 – 1686*. New Haven and London: Yale University Press, 2001, pp. xxiii–lxxxviii; "Infinite Aggregates and Phenomenal Wholes: Leibniz's Theory of Substance as a Solution to the Continuum Problem." *Leibniz Society Review* 8 (1998): 25–45; "Russell's Conundrum: On the Relation of Leibniz's Monads to the Continuum." In *An Intimate Relation. Studies in the History and Philosophy of Science*. Ed. by J. R. Brown and J. Mittelstrass. Boston-Dordrecht-London: Reidel, 1989, pp. 171–201.
164. *Summa hypotheseos physicae novae*, second half of 1671* (A VI, 2, 332). The expression "bewildering proto-force" is used by Howard Bernstein in "*Conatus*, Hobbes, and the Young Leibniz." *Studies in History and Philosophy of Science* 11 (1980), p. 25.
165. In the "Preface" to the *Theodicy* (1710) Leibniz famously wrote of two "labyrinths": the labyrinth of freedom and the labyrinth of the continuum. On the problem of the continuum in the young Leibniz see in particular the work of Philip Beeley, *Kontinuität und Mechanismus. Zur Philosophie des jungen Leibniz in ihrem ideengeschichtlichen Kontext*. Stuttgard: Steiner, 1996. More generally, on the problem of the continuum see the work of Richard Arthur (cited above).
166. Cf. Beeley, *Kontinuität und Mechanismus*, chap. 1.
167. See Galileo Galilei, *Opere*. 20 vols. Florence: Barbera, 1968, vol. VIII, p. 80. Quoted by Mugnai, *Introduzione*, pp. 104–5.
168. See Garber, "Motion and Metaphysics," p. 168.
169. See the first four "Fundamenta praedemonstrabilia" ("pre-demonstrable principles") of the *Theoria motus abstracti* (A VI, 2, 264).
170. *The English Works of Thomas Hobbes of Malmesbury*. Ed. by Sir William Molesworth. 11 vols. London, 1839–45, vol. I, p. 206. Cf. Bernstein, "*Conatus*, Hobbes, and the Young Leibniz," pp. 26–7.
171. Leibniz to Heinrich Oldenburg, 9 May 1671 (A II, 1, 102). Quoted from Garber, "Motion and Metaphysics," p. 168. See also *Theoria motus abstracti* (A VI, 2,

265); Leibniz to Lambert van Velthuysen, May 1671 (A II, 1, 98); Leibniz to Antoine Arnauld, beginning of November 1671 (A II, 1, 173); Leibniz to Johann Friedrich, 21 May 1671 (A II, 1, 108).

172. See *Theoria motus abstracti* (A VI, 2, 264–5) and Daniel Garber, "Leibniz: Physics and Philosophy." In *The Cambridge Companion to Leibniz*. Ed. by Nicholas Jolley. Cambridge: Cambridge University Press, 1995, p. 274.

173. Garber, "Motion and Metaphysics," p. 168.

174. Garber, "Leibniz: Physics and Philosophy," p. 274.

175. A VI, 2, 266 / L 141.

176. Leibniz to Antoine Arnauld, beginning of November 1671 (A II, 1, 172 / L 148). See also *Theoria motus abstracti* (A VI, 2, 270).

177. Ibid. Later on, however, Leibniz rejected the existence of the void.

178. Ibid.

179. Garber, "Motion and Metaphysics," p. 170.

180. Cf. Leibniz to Antoine Arnauld, beginning of November 1671 (A II, 1, 175).

181. A II, 1, 108.

182. *Theoria motus abstracti* (A VI, 2, 266) / L 141. See also Leibniz to Antoine Arnauld, beginning of November 1671 (A II, 1, 173).

183. *Theoria motus abstracti* (A VI, 2, 266) / L 141.

184. Cf. *De conatu et motu, sensu et cogitatione*, spring–autumn 1671* (A VI, 2, 282 and 285).

185. *Theoria motus abstracti* (A VI, 2, 266) / L 141. See also the letters written by Leibniz to Heinrich Oldenburg on 11 March and 9 May 1671 (respectively A II, 1, 90 and A II, 1, 102).

186. *Theoria motus abstracti* (A VI, 2, 266).

187. See A II, 1, 115.

188. See A II, 1, N. 58 and N. 59.

189. A II, 1, 108–9, 115–16 (pp. 175, 183–5 of the new edition).

190. Cf. Ross, "Alchemy and the Development of Leibniz's Metaphysics," p. 44.

191. See *Demonstrationum Catholicarum Conspectus* (A VI, 1, 494).

192. See Leibniz to Duke Johann Friedrich, autumn 1679* (A I, 2, 226 and A II, 1, 489).

193. See for instance A VI, 2, 428 in Leibniz's preliminary dissertation to his edition of Nizolio. On Leibniz's methodological nominalism, inspired by Ockham's razor ("entities should not be multiplied beyond necessity"), and the ontological 'minimalism' derived from it see Mugnai, *Introduzione*, esp. pp. 152–63.

194. Cf. Francesco Piro, *Spontaneità e Ragion Sufficiente. Determinismo e Filosofia dell'Azione in Leibniz*. Roma: Edizioni di Storia e Letteratura, 2002, esp. pp. 169–170.

195. Cf. Albert Heinekamp, "Das Glück als höchstes Gut in Leibniz' Philosophie." In *The Leibniz Renaissance. International Workshop (Firenze 1986)*. Florence: Olschki, 1988, pp. 99–125 and Donald Rutherford, *Leibniz and the Rational Order of Nature*. Cambridge: Cambridge University Press, 1995.

196. *Elementa Juris Naturalis*: respectively *Untersuchungen*, 1669–70* (A VI, 1, 454) and *Untersuchungen*, 1670–71* (A VI, 1, 455).

197. *Elementa Juris Naturalis*, 1670–71* (A VI, 1, N. 12/4, here p. 463).

198. A VI, 1, 464–5.

199. *Elementa Juris Naturalis*, second half of 1671* (A VI, 1, N. 12/5, here p. 465).

200. Leibniz to Duke Johann Friedrich, May 1677 (A I, 2, 23). On Leibniz's conception of justice as *caritas sapientis* see especially Patrick Riley, *Leibniz's Universal Jurisprudence. Justice as the Charity of the Wise*. Cambridge (MA): Harvard University Press, 1996.

201. A VI, 2, 485.

202. See *Specimen Demonstrationum politicarum*, spring 1669 (A IV, 1, 7–8). In this work Leibniz adopted the pseudonym of Georgius Ulicovius Lithuanus.

203. See A VI, 1, 446. For later texts presenting the same doctrine see Piro, "Jus – Justum – Justitia," p. 30; Piro, *Spontaneità*, p. 74 (n. 147); and Maria Rosa Antognazza and Howard Hotson, eds., *Alsted and Leibniz on God, the Magistrate and the Millennium*. Texts edited with introduction and commentary. Wiesbaden: Harrassowitz Verlag, 1999, p. 110.

204. See two letters written by Leibniz around the end of December 1673, respectively to Jakob Münch (A I, 1, 376) and to Anna Christine von Boineburg (A I, 1, 380).

205. Previous speculations attributing to Leibniz the speech given by Boineburg on 12 June 1669 in support of Philipp Wilhelm von Pfalz-Neuburg (*Propositio Legati Serenissimi Ducis Neoburgici*) have proved to be mistaken (cf. A IV, 1, xx).

206. A IV, 1, N. 2.

207. See A IV, 1, N. 3 and N. 4.

208. See A IV, 1, N. 19. A second text relating to this diatribe was written in Paris in 1672 (A IV, 1, N. 20).

209. Cf. Kurt Müller, "Gottfried Wilhelm Leibniz. Sein Leben und Wirken." In *Leibniz. Sein Leben, sein Wirken, seine Welt*. Ed. by W. Totok and C. Haase. Hanover: Verlag für Literatur und Zeitgeschehen, 1966, p. 22.

210. A IV, 1, N. 5 and N. 6. On the insightful discussion in this text of the issue of sovereignty in the Holy Roman Empire see Peter Schröder, "Reich versus Territorien? Zum Problem der Souveränität im Heiligen Römischen Reich nach dem Westfälischen Frieden." In Olaf Asbach et al., eds., *Altes Reich, Frankreich und Europa*. Berlin: Duncker and Humblot, 2001, 123–43, esp. pp. 124, 134–43.

211. A IV, 1, N. 7 (21 November 1670), N. 8, N. 9.

212. See A IV, 1, xxiii and John A. Lynn, *The Wars of Louis XIV*. Harlow: Longman, 1999, pp. 109–10.

213. See *Consilium Aegyptiacum*, 1671–2 (A IV, 1, N. 10–18).

214. *Regi Christianissimo* (A IV, 1, N. 10).

215. See Guhrauer, *Leibnitz*, I, p. 98; Aiton, *Leibniz*, p. 38.

216. A IV, 1, N. 11–14.

217. See A I, 1, N. 170, N. 171, N. 172. Boineburg's letter as well was drafted by Leibniz. See also A I, 1, N. 173.

218. A IV, 1, N. 15.

219. See above.

220. A VI, 1, 494.
221. See A VI, 1, 494–5; A VI, 1, 492–3; A II, 1, N. 58 and N. 59. See above.
222. See A VI, 1, 495–9.
223. See the series of texts written between 1668 and 1671 on the *Demonstratio Possibilitatis Mysteriorum Eucharistiae* (A VI, 1, N. 15/1–4).
224. See *De Demonstratione Possibilitatis Mysteriorum Eucharistiae*, autumn 1671* (A VI, 1, 516). He later put some distance between himself and the doctrine of transubstantiation: see for instance his letters to Bartholomew Des Bosses of September 1709 and January 1710 (respectively GP II, 390 and 399).
225. See Adams, *Leibniz*, pp. 358–9.
226. See *De Transsubstantiatione* (A VI, 1, N. 15/2) and Michel Fichant, *"Actiones sunt suppositorum*. L'ontologie Leibnizienne de l'action." *Philosophie* 53 (1997): 135–48 (esp. p. 136).
227. See Antognazza, *Leibniz on the Trinity and the Incarnation.*
228. A VI, 1, 495.
229. See A VI, 1, 518.
230. See respectively *Defensio Trinitatis contra Wissowatium* (A VI, 1, N. 16) and *Refutatio Objectionum Dan. Zwickeri contra Trinitatem et Incarnationem Dei* (A VI, 1, N. 17). On Leibniz's argumentation see Maria Rosa Antognazza, "The Defence of the Mysteries of the Trinity and the Incarnation: An Example of Leibniz's 'Other' Reason." *British Journal for the History of Philosophy*, 9/2 (2001), pp. 295–302 and Antognazza, *Leibniz on the Trinity and the Incarnation*, pp. 22–33. For discussions of the nature of the copula in syllogistic propositions in seventeenth-century German philosophy, see the outstanding study by Gino Roncaglia, *Palaestra Rationis. Discussioni su natura della copula e modalità nella filosofia 'scolastica' tedesca del XVII secolo*. Florence: Olschki, 1996.
231. See A VI, 1, N. 18 and A II, 1, N. 59. On both texts see above.
232. See A VI, 1, 499.
233. See A VI, 1, 500.
234. See for instance the letter of the autumn of 1679 in which Leibniz presented his plan of the *Demonstrationes Catholicae* to Duke Johann Friedrich (A II, 1, 488; A I, 2, 225). On the cooling of Leibniz's sympathies towards the Roman Catholic Church from the mid-90s onward see chapter II. 6.
235. Cf. Adrian and Peter van Walenburch, *Tractatus Generales de Controversiis Fidei*. Coloniae Agrippinae: Apud Ioannem Wilhelmum Friessem juniorem, 1670; Adrian and Peter van Walenburch, *Tractatus Speciales, de Controversiis Fidei*. Coloniae Agrippinae: Apud Ioannem Wilhelmum Friessem juniorem, 1670.
236. A copy of the *Tractatus Theologico-Politicus* with Leibniz's annotations was recently found in Boineburg's library. Cf. Ursula Goldenbaum, "Die Commentatiuncula de judice als Leibnizens erste philosophische Auseinandersetzung mit Spinoza nebst der Mitteilung über ein neuaufgefundenes Leibnizstück." In *Labora Diligenter*. Ed. by M. Fontius et al. Stuttgart: Steiner, 1999, pp. 61–107.

237. Cf. *Commentatiuncula de Judice Controversiarum*, 1670–71* (A VI, 1, N. 22). The fact that Spinoza's *Tractatus* was published anonymously in 1670 seems to suggest that the *Commentatiuncula* do not date back as far as 1669, as suggested in the Akademie-Ausgabe. On the *Commentatiuncula* see Goldenbaum, "Die Commentatiuncula," and Antognazza, *Leibniz on the Trinity and the Incarnation*, pp. 50–59.
238. Leibniz commented negatively on Spinoza's *Tractatus Theologico-Politicus* in a letter of 5 May 1671 to Joh. Georg Graevius while recognising at the same time Spinoza's evident learning (A I, 1, 148). See also Leibniz to Jakob Thomasius, 3 October 1670 (A II, 1, 66); Leibniz to Antoine Arnauld, November 1671 (A II, 1, 171); Leibniz to Gottlieb Spitzel, 8 March 1672 (A I, 1, 193).
239. See A II, 1, N. 80 and *Notitia Opticae Promotae*. Francofurti: Apud Joh. David. Zunnerum, 1671 (Ravier 16).
240. See A II, 1, N. 89. Although these are the only two surviving letters, all evidence indicates that more must have been exchanged between the two great thinkers. See Georg Hermann Schuller to Spinoza, 14 November 1675 (in *Opera*. Ed. by Carl Gebhardt. 4 vols. Heidelberg: Carl Winters Universitätsbuchhandlung, 1925, vol. IV, p. 303); Spinoza to Georg Hermann Schuller, 18 November 1675 (in *Opera*, vol. IV, p. 305). Cf. G. Friedmann, *Leibniz et Spinoza*. 2nd ed. Paris: Gallimard, 1962, p. 65; G. H. R. Parkinson, "Leibniz's Paris Writings in Relation to Spinoza." In *Leibniz à Paris (1672–1676). Symposion de la G. W. Leibniz-Gesellschaft*. 2 vols. Wiesbaden: Steiner, 1978, vol. 2, pp. 74–5; Steven Nadler, *Spinoza: A Life*. Cambridge: Cambridge University Press, 1999, p. 299.
241. See for instance A VI, 1, 419; A VI, 1, 499; A VI, 2, 283; A II, 1, 174.
242. The comparison between the essences (or ideas) of things and numbers was already present in the *Dissertatio de Arte Combinatoria* of 1666. I am grateful to Massimo Mugnai for drawing my attention to this point.
243. A II, 1, 117–18. Trans. by Robert C. Sleigh, Jr. in G. W. Leibniz, *Confessio Philosophi: Papers Concerning the Problem of Evil, 1671–1678*. New Haven and London: Yale University Press, 2005, pp. 3–5.
244. *Elementa Juris Naturalis* (*Untersuchungen*) (A VI, 1, 438).
245. See for instance A II, 1, 164–5.
246. See A I, 1, 297.
247. See A I, 1, 159.
248. See A II, 1, N. 84.
249. See A I, 1, N. 174, N. 176.
250. See A I, 1, N. 170, N. 171, N. 172; Simon Arnauld de Pomponne to Boineburg, 12 February 1672 (Klopp II, pp. 115–16); Boineburg to Simon Arnauld de Pomponne, 4 March 1672 (Klopp II, pp. 124–5).
251. See Christian Habbeus to Leibniz, 7 February 1672 (A I, 1, N. 159).
252. See A I, 1, xxx.
253. See, respectively, A I, 1, N. 175; A I, 1, N. 255; and Klopp II, p. 125. The 'taler' was the currency commonly used in the states of the Holy Roman Empire.

3

Old Wine in New Bottles: Paris, London, and Holland (March 1672–December 1676)

W HEN LEIBNIZ ARRIVED in Paris at the end of March 1672, the French capital was the most sophisticated and advanced centre of European culture. As part of the splendour and power of Louis XIV's monarchy, the French scientific, philosophical, and learned community counted many of the most prominent savants of the time. The young German, who had come to Paris with grandiose plans embracing the reform and advancement of the entire encyclopaedia of sciences for the improvement of the human condition, felt more than a little overwhelmed. As one might expect, it was the blossoming scientific and learned Parisian life and its innovative infrastructure that made the most powerful impression on Leibniz. In a report of 20 December 1672 to Johann Philipp von Schönborn he wrote with undisguised admiration,

The fellows of the Academy are people extremely learned in various fields who could compose an Encyclopaedia of arts and sciences; they meet twice a week (on Wednesdays and on Saturdays) at the Royal Library where some of them also live. Their secretary is Gallois, who also edits the so-called *Journal des Sçavans*. The king, however, has also had an observatory constructed on the outskirts of the city, in faubourg S. Jacques, which commoners originally mistook for a citadel; and here some of them, especially the astronomers, are going to live. Near the Royal Library is the garden and laboratory of the Academy; for several years they have grown here almost all botanic specimens and analyzed chemical elements. The Royal Library has more than 35,000 printed volumes and around 10,000 manuscripts.[1]

In January 1675, nearly three years into his extended stay, he could still write to Duke Johann Friedrich in similar terms: "Paris is a place where one can achieve distinction only with difficulty. One finds there, in all branches of knowledge, the most knowledgeable men of the age, and one needs much work and a little determination to establish a reputation there."[2] His first steps toward this goal were not easy. To begin with, when Leibniz arrived in Paris his mastery of the French language needed improvement.[3] Moreover, far from being an accomplished courtier, he was conscious of his inability to make a good first impression. "Where one has to drink to impress," he confided to his old friend and supporter, Christian Habbeus, "you can well imagine that I am not in my element."[4] Finally and most importantly, in Paris and during his first visit to London (January–February 1673), Leibniz was made painfully aware of the limitations of his mathematical preparation and of his lack of up-to-date knowledge of work in the field; and this soon led to the further realisation that, in order to carry his plans forward, he would first need to forge himself new tools.[5] During the four years spent in the French capital he therefore worked with most intensity on mathematics, science, and technology.[6] As he explained to Duke Johann Friedrich, "I thought here neither of jurisprudence nor of literature nor of controversies – things which were my main concern in Germany. Instead I began a completely new study in order to deepen my knowledge of mathematics."[7] Thankfully, Leibniz was nothing if not a quick learner: by the end of his Parisian sojourn, in fact, the self-confessed mathematical apprentice had invented the infinitesimal calculus. But his general plan, although put on the back burner while he was in the process of "achieving a knowledge of mathematics a bit above average,"[8] continued to be in its essence the one formulated earlier. The new scientific and mathematical studies were intended to pave the way for a renewed assault on the catholic demonstrations.[9] Inverting the scriptural parable,[10] Leibniz set about putting old wine – the youthful projects derived in Leipzig and Mainz from a long and fertile central European tradition – into new bottles – the scientific and mathematical tools recently developed in western European centres such as Paris and London.

First Steps in Paris (March 1672–January 1673)

With the war against Holland already under way, one of Leibniz's main tasks in Paris – the presentation of the Egyptian plan to Louis XIV – was in need of radical revision. Yet Leibniz did not put any further work into it, aside from composing a *Breviarium* or summary of the project in the autumn of 1672 and sending it to Schönborn, who in the meantime had become aware of Leibniz and Boineburg's scheme.[11] Access to the French court was proving difficult in any case, as was the successful completion of the other main task assigned to him by Boineburg, the recovery of the French rent and pension. Leibniz's dealings with one of the French finance officers, Morel, met with the delays and slowness typical of a bureaucratic machine, and in May he considered returning to Germany over the summer.[12] On 12 June Morel explained that he could not look into Leibniz's claims on behalf of Boineburg until he (Morel) had spoken to the foreign minister, Simon Arnauld de Pomponne, who was away. In any case, nothing could be done until Morel's own return to Paris, hopefully by the end of July.[13] In September Leibniz was still trying to secure a meeting with Simon Arnauld de Pomponne through the intermediation of the uncle of the French foreign minister, Antoine Arnauld.[14]

Fortunately, Leibniz had better luck with Arnauld himself. By September he had already met with him on several occasions to discuss philosophical matters.[15] During the meetings of savants which were held in Arnauld's house, Leibniz was introduced (inter alia) to Arnauld's friend and collaborator Pierre Nicole (1625–95), co-author of the so-called *Port-Royal Logic*,[16] and to the mathematicians Jacques Buot (d. c. 1675) and Ignace Gaston Pardies (1636–73). He also met in person two of the key people with whom he had corresponded prior to his departure for Paris, Louis Ferrand and Pierre de Carcavy.[17] Probably for the latter, he wrote around July a report on the experiments on the vacuum by the leading German physicist, Otto von Guericke (1602–86), with whom he had been in epistolary contact between May 1671 and March 1672.[18] In due course Leibniz encountered also a number of other scientists, including the inventor and physicist Denis Papin (1647–c. 1712) and the astronomers Giovanni Cassini (1625–1712) and Ole Christensen Rømer (1644–1710).[19]

In the autumn he was finally able to meet Christiaan Huygens, who was effectively the director of the Académie Royale des Sciences, having been entrusted by Louis XIV's powerful minister of finance, Jean-Baptiste Colbert, with its planning and organisation. The relationship with the eminent Dutch mathematician and scientist played a decisive role in the development of Leibniz's mathematics and mechanics, despite the very different ways in which the young German and the Dutch scientist approached their scientific work. Huygens was cautious, inclined to take clear, measured, and directly relevant steps, rather than announcing grandiose schemes which spread far beyond the problem at hand. In this respect Leibniz was the opposite: whatever problem concerned him, he always saw it as a part of his all-embracing encyclopaedic plan. For Huygens's taste, he was far too keen to launch himself into insufficiently lucid presentations of his Promethean programme of reform instead of restricting his attention to the clear exposition and solution of a circumscribed and manageable problem. Despite these differences, the exceptional acuity and fertility of the young man's eager mind did not escape the Dutch scientist, who during the Parisian years acted as a sympathetic, generous, and sometimes also patient tutor in guiding Leibniz through cutting-edge research in mathematics and mechanics – a fact for which Leibniz remained deeply grateful.[20]

At their first meeting, which probably took place at Huygens's quarters at the Royal Library, Leibniz mentioned that he had discovered a method for summing infinite series – an important result which he had reached by reflecting on Euclid's axiom that the whole is always greater than the part.[21] When still in Mainz, Leibniz had considered this axiom to be in reality a provable theorem, that is, a statement which could be reduced to the only two types of unproved truths he proposed to admit, namely definitions and identities. In keeping with the 'austerity' of his later full-fledged system, which admitted only a minimum of 'ingredients', the only proper axiom turned out to be that of identity.[22] In a note composed between the autumn of 1671 and early 1672 on the demonstration of primary propositions (*Demonstratio Propositionum Primarum*), Leibniz endeavoured to prove the statement that the whole is always greater than the part. His demonstration took the form of a syllogism of which the major premise (1) was a definition, the minor premise (2) was an identical proposition, and the conclusion (3) was the given theorem:

| *c* | *d* | *e* |

[1] *Per definition* that of which a part is equal to the whole of the other, is greater (Major)

[2] The part (that is, *de*) of the whole *cde* is equal to the whole *de* (that is, to itself)

[3] Therefore *cde* is greater than *de*; the whole [is greater] than the part.[23]

By means of the axiom of identity Leibniz developed his main theorem on the summation of the consecutive terms of a sequence of differences and arrived eventually at the result reported in his first meeting with Huygens, namely that summation of a series could be carried out even over an infinite number of terms. This was the first major mathematical discovery of Leibniz in Paris.[24] Huygens, whose attention had been drawn to Leibniz by Oldenburg,[25] was intrigued. To put the promising mathematician to the test, he asked him to determine the sum of the infinite series of reciprocal triangular numbers. Taking up a tutorial role, he also directed the young German to relevant literature, in particular the *Arithmetica Infinitorum* (Oxford 1656) of John Wallis and the *Opus geometricum* (Antwerp 1647) of Grégoire de Saint-Vincent, in which geometrical progressions and the summation of infinitely many terms were treated.[26] Leibniz did not lose any time. He borrowed Saint-Vincent's book from the Royal Library[27] and began work on Huygens's problem. Although Leibniz found Saint-Vincent's way of writing unsatisfactory, his book indicated to him the path towards a novel and comprehensive general method which allowed him to provide an elegant solution to the problem proposed.[28] Given the numerical series of differences

$$b_1 = a_1 - a_2, b_2 = a_2 - a_3, b_3 = a_3 - a_4, \ldots,$$

he noted that it was possible to obtain the sum $b_1 + b_2 + \cdots + b_n$ as a difference, that is as $a_1 - a_n + 1$. Extrapolating this simple law to the infinite he was able to find, amongst other things, the sum of the series of reciprocals of triangular numbers.[29]

The young German was understandably delighted to return to Huygens with this result in his hands. Huygens was pleased and graciously reciprocated, demonstrating for him his own method of summation.[30] Encouraged by this success, Leibniz composed a small treatise, the *Accessio ad Arithmeticam Infinitorum*, containing his results.[31] His intention was to send it to the secretary of the Académie Royale des Sciences and editor of the *Journal des Sçavans*, Jean Gallois, for publication in the journal. But no new issues of the periodical were published between 12 December 1672 and the beginning of 1674, and during this interval Leibniz came to recognise that the only originality he could claim for himself was the method of summation rather than the results themselves.[32] Since the core of his paper was therefore superseded, he preferred to leave the *Accessio ad Arithmeticam Infinitorum* unpublished.

The summation of series was not the only mathematical activity which exercised Leibniz's enthusiasm in this first Parisian period. At the same time he was also energetically carrying forward his research on the calculating machine, supervising the production of an at least partially functioning wooden model which, completed by no later than the beginning of 1673, was judged by Huygens as "very ingenious".[33] Unlike Pascal's calculator, which could perform only addition and subtraction, Leibniz's machine was also designed to perform automatically multiplication, division, and even the extraction of square and cube roots.[34]

Although mathematics gradually emerged as the main focus of Leibniz's intellectual endeavours in Paris, philosophy was never far from his mind, especially during his first and his last year in the French capital. Between his arrival at the end of March 1672 and his departure for London in January 1673, Leibniz's philosophical investigations continued in the pattern established in Mainz: he continued to reflect on physics and the philosophy of mind and body (of which his twin theories of motion had been the most important outcome) and on theological-philosophical issues such as the rejection of atheism, the problem of evil, the universal harmony governing everything, and its relation to God's justice and freedom. Possibly as early as the first six months of his stay in Paris, Leibniz wrote an extensive series of notes on physics. In them his thesis that a merely corporeal world could not exist and that an incorporeal principle was necessary to justify motion was supported with new arguments which rejected his previous claims of the existence of void and of atoms or indivisibles (conceived now as minima as opposed to the unextended entities identified in the *Theoria motus abstracti*).[35] In one of these notes Leibniz extended to the world the thesis of the ancient Greek physician Hippocrates (fifth century B.C.) that in the human body everything 'breathes together' (*sympnoia panta*).[36] This metaphor would later reappear in some of Leibniz's most famous mature works, such as the *Nouveaux Essais* and the *Monadology*, to express Leibniz's doctrine of universal harmony.[37]

Probably between the autumn of 1672 and early 1673, when he was intensively reading Galileo's *Discorsi e dimostrazioni matematiche intorno a due nuove scienze* (Leiden, 1638),[38] Leibniz also composed one of the most important works of his youth, a sort of proto-theodicy entitled *Confessio Philosophi*[39] written in the form of a "petit dialogue" between a "Catechista Theologus" and a "Catechumenus Philosophus". It seems that Leibniz showed it around 1673 to Antoine Arnauld and Gilles Filleau Des Billettes (1634–1720), a technician whom he met in Arnauld's house;[40] but like all the philosophical works of the Paris period it remained unpublished during Leibniz's lifetime. Its subject matter was a cluster of concerns – namely the justice of God, divine and human freedom, and the nature of evil – eventually explored in the *Theodicy* of 1710 and already evident in various sketches from the Mainz years. In Mainz Leibniz had already written on the relationship between God's omnipotence and omniscience and human freedom;[41] and in its general inspiration the *Confessio Philosophi* was also characteristic of his earlier philosophico-theological reflections and constituted a continuation of the philosophical refutation of atheism in which Leibniz had recently been engaged. Indeed, many of its theses were schematically anticipated in the plan of the *Demonstrationes Catholicae*; and the similarity of the *Confessio* to his letter of May 1671 to Magnus Wedderkopf even suggests that Leibniz's dialogue might have had its origins during the Mainz years. [42] Despite these similarities, the dialogue certainly looked forward in a new way to a number of distinctive points of Leibniz's mature philosophy: among others, the issue of human freedom was discussed in relation to the principle of sufficient reason (of which the *Confessio Philosophi* offered two proofs),[43] the notion of universal harmony as implying the connection in the universe of everything with everything, the thesis that the world which actually exists is the most harmonious, and the claim that every soul is fully determined by the complete set of circumstances in which God has placed it (including its spatio-temporal circumstances).[44] The Platonic paradigm already employed in the letter of May 1671 to Wedderkopf also reappeared: the presence of evil in the world was ultimately explained as inevitably required by the maximum of positive compossibilities which made up the best possible world. Precisely because it was the best, this world had been selected for existence amongst the infinite possible worlds embraced by the divine intellect. The vexed question discussed in the *Confessio Philosophi* of who is the author of sin was revisited by Leibniz shortly afterward in a short text written around 1673. In it he challenged the thesis that "God is the author of everything that is real and positive in sin" but is not responsible for sin itself, since sin is "a pure privation without any reality, and . . . God is not the author of privations." Those embracing this view, Leibniz argued, made "God the author of sin" while claiming "to do just the opposite."[45]

In November, after attempting unsuccessfully for several months to carry out the two main missions of his Parisian trip, Leibniz received a letter from Boineburg announcing the arrival in Paris of his only son, Philipp Wilhelm (1656–1717), and asking Leibniz to supervise his education.[46] On 16 November the sixteen-year-old boy arrived, together with Boineburg's son-in-law, the archbishop's nephew, Melchior Friedrich von Schönborn, who had been sent with the task of convincing Louis XIV to agree on Cologne as the place for a general peace conference. Worried by the incipient advancement towards the Rhine of the troops of Brandenburg and the emperor hostile to the French, Johann Philipp von Schönborn was attempting to play a conciliatory role, offering his mediation in the ongoing Dutch war, which was opposing France and England to Holland, Brandenburg, and the Empire. While Melchior Friedrich von Schönborn was seeking an audience with Louis XIV, Leibniz drafted an agenda including points to be discussed and an exhortation for Melchior Friedrich to read to the king.[47] For this purpose, Leibniz and Peter Schick (the son of a Mainz merchant and travelling companion of a nobleman in Paris) accompanied Melchior Friedrich to Versailles on 24 November. Leibniz was not permitted to attend the audience, and Melchior Friedrich did not actually read the speech which he had prepared;[48] but the archbishop's nephew and Boineburg's protégé did develop a friendly and trusting relationship, as can be gleaned, for instance, from the series of notes on Mainz's policy toward France quickly jotted down by Leibniz in December 1672 after discussions with Melchior Friedrich.[49] Nor was Leibniz's allegiance to Johann Philipp von Schönborn forgotten: during his first year in Paris, in addition to briefing him properly on the Egyptian plan through the *Breviarium*, he composed a short text for the elector outlining policies designed to serve the best interest of both Mainz and the Empire.[50] Two notes probably written sometime before his departure for London in January 1673 also demonstrated Leibniz's increasing familiarisation with the political situation in France and represented his first of several notable attempts to turn the weapon of sarcasm against Louis XIV's aggressive and expansionistic foreign politics.[51]

On the morning of 22 December 1672, Philipp Wilhelm von Boineburg was informed of the sudden death of his father by a gentleman conveying Pomponne's condolences. The tragic news of the baron's decease on 15 December had just reached the French Foreign Minister via a French courier from Mainz.[52] At just fifty years of age, Boineburg had suffered a heart attack following the devastation of his estate by Brandenburg's troops.[53] Melchior Friedrich and Leibniz, who had written his last letter to the baron the day before,[54] were stunned by the news but tried to hide their distress from the young Philipp Wilhelm. Over dinner they received mail from Germany, including a letter of 9 December from Boineburg himself mentioning in passing the deterioration of his health, a letter of 16 December from the Mainz privy counsellor, Joh.

Christoph Jodoci, leaving little hope of recovery, and finally a letter from the French envoy in Mainz, the Abbé Jacques de Gravel, giving them "le coup fatal" and removing any doubt concerning this sudden tragic turn of events.[55]

Leibniz was shaken by the loss of his friend, mentor, and patron, not to mention his understandable worry for the meagre income which sustained him in Paris. As tutor of the young Boineburg he nevertheless tried to bring some consolation to the grief of a teenager who had just lost his father while far away in a foreign country. On the very day on which the sad news reached them, he wrote to the boy's maternal uncle, Joh. Friedrich Schütz von Holtzhausen:

The young Baron received such tragic news with the tenderness of a good son, which could not but move everyone to compassion. I had difficulty in restoring his spirits somewhat, fearing that he might fall ill. I explained to him that he should take consolation from the fact that his father left him his fame instead of himself; and that this fame would be his companion wherever he went and would grant him a favourable introduction to all the great men of Europe. He had only to follow the happy example of his father's life and he would never lack good servants or friends or happiness or esteem. And in fact, what I said to console him served as consolation for me as well, since after the loss of such a great man who had honoured me of his friendship, I look with pleasure at the fine disposition of this young nobleman, who will bring his father back to life. He will be serious and solid, and I recognise in him the traces of his father[.][56]

After asking Joh. Friedrich Schütz's reassurance for his own position as the young Boineburg's tutor, on the same day Leibniz wrote a letter of condolences to the late baron's widow, Anna Christine. In the heartfelt words of esteem for a man who had been his support and friend in decisive years, Leibniz also gave a glimpse of his views on the meaning of life, death, and immortality:

The death of those whose whole fame is buried with them may be inconsolable; but those who live on after death through their unforgettable renown can be regarded as fortunate: they can die whenever they wish. Because they do not die too early who have already achieved everything that a sensible human being can desire. For their good friends, however, and for the common good, they would always die too soon, even if they were to live another 1000 years. The immortal soul [of such people], now liberated from all that remains of temporal imperfection, triumphs twice over, thanks to a crown of glory gained in this life as well as the next.[57]

An echo of these thoughts resounded in a note written by Leibniz in Paris around 1673, probably not long after becoming aware of Boineburg's death. In it he hinted at the true way of 'expanding' one's life – a lesson which he put into practice better than most:

> The greatness of a life can only be estimated by the multitude of its actions. "We should not count the years: it is our actions which constitute our life" says Ronsard in his poem on the death of Charles IX. Time appears great only by virtue of the multitude of changes which transpire within it. And thus it is within our power to determine how long we live, if only we render perceptible even the smallest portions of our time. One could write a dissertation on the prolongation of life.[58]

The First Visit to London (End January–End February 1673)

To Leibniz's relief, Anna Christine von Boineburg confirmed the arrangements made by her late husband for the education of her son.[59] Meanwhile all hope of convincing Louis XIV to convene a peace conference in Cologne had evaporated. Melchior Friedrich was left with no choice but to resume his journey and travel to London in the hope of finding a better hearing at the court of Charles II. For Leibniz, who was allowed to accompany the delegation, this represented the long-awaited opportunity to be introduced in person to Oldenburg and the Royal Society. On 11 January he departed with the others for the English capital, arriving in Calais on the evening of 17 January. After being detained there for several days by bad weather, they were finally able to cross the channel, reaching Dover on 21 January. On the evening of 24 January 1673 the delegation arrived in London, where a German whom they met on the ship served them as an interpreter, since none of them spoke English.[60]

Huygens himself had announced Leibniz's imminent arrival to Oldenburg in a letter of 14 January, mentioning in particular that the young German was taking with him a model of his calculating machine for demonstration to the Royal Society.[61] Shortly after arriving in London, Leibniz visited Oldenburg.[62] On 1 February he was given the opportunity to demonstrate his calculating machine at a meeting of the Royal Society.[63] The fellows were intrigued by the ingenious invention, although it could not yet perform automatically the multiplication and division for which it had been designed. Robert Hooke, who had previously expressed a dismissive judgement on Leibniz's *Hypothesis physica nova* and was notoriously unwilling to give credit to the merits of others,[64] examined the machine, Leibniz recalled, "at close quarters ... removed the black plate which covered it, and absorbed every word" uttered by its inventor.[65] Unfortunately the young German soon discovered that Hooke had inspected his invention a bit too closely. Subsequently he was dismayed to learn that, in his absence, Hooke not only had harshly criticised his machine at the meeting of the Royal Society of 15 February, but had promised a new model. When this model appeared a month later, it proved suspiciously similar, Leibniz complained bitterly to Oldenburg, to the original machine.[66] Although Leibniz's relationship with Hooke was doomed to unpleasantness, other, more sympathetic members also conveyed the unnerving news that further competitors were inventing calculators. At the meeting of 8 February, the vice-president of the Society, Sir Robert Moray (c. 1608–73), mentioned to Leibniz that Charles II's salaried "Master of Mechanicks", Sir Samuel Morland (1625–95/96), had also invented an arithmetical machine.[67] During the same meeting Oldenburg read a letter of René François de Sluse (1622–85) in which the Belgian mathematician communicated his "method of drawing tangents to any geometrical curves"[68] – an event significant for the quarrel over priority in the invention of the infinitesimal calculus which broke out over three decades later between Leibniz and Newton. One day after the meeting, the expert networker Oldenburg had already arranged a meeting between Leibniz and Morland for the morning of 10 February in order to carry out a comparison of their machines.[69] As it turned out, Leibniz's calculator, although admittedly still imperfect, presented a superior technical conception because it was designed to perform multiplication and division automatically, whereas Morland's arithmetical machine relied for these operations on the so-called Napier's bones.[70]

On 12 February Leibniz met Robert Boyle (1627–91) at the house of his sister, Lady Ranelagh, where he lived. Boyle was the most eminent and influential representative of the experimental philosophy in the community surrounding the Royal Society, and the young Leibniz felt honoured by the kind way in which he was received by "a man to be counted among the greatest of the race."[71] Unfortunately, however, the meeting in Lady Ranelagh's house also proved a source of enduring embarrassment to Leibniz, thanks to the presence of John Pell (1611–85). Although regarded by contemporaries as second amongst established British mathematicians only to John Wallis, Pell had failed to realize his brilliant youthful potential, leaving in his wake a number of unfulfilled promises; yet this did not prevent him from correcting a promising junior colleague in a manner easily construed as a charge of plagiarism. When the discussion turned to mathematical topics, Leibniz proudly reported that he had a general method for the representation and interpolation of series by constructing a series of differences; and to this Pell replied pointedly that this supposed discovery "was already in print, reported by Mr. Mouton, canon of Lyon, as the discovery of the very noble François Regnaud of Lyon, formerly well known to the learned world, in the book of the meritorious Mouton, *De diameteris apparentibus solis et lunae*."[72] After the meeting Leibniz hastily borrowed from Oldenburg the book by Gabriel Mouton (1618–94), published in Lyon in 1670, and discovered to his chagrin the correctness of Pell's claim.[73] In a matter of hours he wrote a detailed letter of explanation to the Royal Society, addressed as customary to its secretary, Heinrich Oldenburg, passionately defending himself against any suspicion of plagiarism:

I believed I had to take trouble, lest any suspicion should be entertained that I sought (under an implicit title to originality) to gain for myself credit for the thoughts of others. And I hope it will appear that I am not so lacking in ideas of my own that I go around begging for those of other men. I will vindicate the honesty of my conduct by two arguments: first by displaying my actual disordered notes in which not only my discovery appears but the occasion and the manner of making it; and second by adding certain points of great importance not stated by Regnaud and Mouton, which it is not likely that I could have huddled together since yesterday evening, nor are they to be readily expected of a copyist.[74]

Whereas there is no doubt regarding the honesty of Leibniz in this instance, the letter itself unwittingly demonstrated once again his shaky knowledge of relevant mathematical literature, as he acknowledged himself many years later.[75] Worse still, the unfortunate episode permanently documented by it was to be redeployed against Leibniz during the quarrel on the calculus. Whether because of the embarrassing encounter with Pell or for some other reason, Oldenburg did not see fit to invite Leibniz to the meeting of the Royal Society held a couple of days later on 15 February – and perhaps this was as well, since the young German was at least spared the humiliation of hearing Hooke denigrating his calculating machine. Despite his sympathy with Oldenburg, Leibniz's relations with the Royal Society had got off to a troubled start. Sadly, this was a taste of things to come.

Yet although not an unqualified success, Leibniz's brief first trip to London marked another milestone in his intellectual development. It had provided him with precious personal contacts in the English world, and with "the best of England's books" which his "purse could afford."[76] Even the few unpleasant encounters had helped him obtain a surer, safer grip on the cutting-edge scientific and mathematical research which, if handled carelessly, could instantly eviscerate one's reputation for intellectual and moral probity: Leibniz's later caution in announcing his intellectual innovations was doubtless shaped in part by his clashes with Hooke and Pell. Best of all, the fellows of the Royal Society, whatever their reservations on specific points, were sufficiently impressed by the young German to admit him unanimously into the Society. After his formal letter requesting admission was read during the meeting held on 1 March, Moray proposed him as a candidate. At the Royal Society meeting of 19 April 1673, the twenty-six-year-old Leibniz was duly elected F.R.S.[77]

By that time, however, Leibniz had been forced to make a hasty departure from England. In mid-February the Mainz delegation had received the unexpected news of the serious illness of the Elector Johann Philipp von Schönborn.[78] Former plans to travel back to Mainz via Holland were abandoned, and their departure from London on 20 February was organised in such haste that Leibniz did not even have time to take personal leave from Oldenburg. Oldenburg was preoccupied with some urgent court business and could only leave a brief note for Leibniz, together with a short letter for Huygens and a copy of the *Philosophical Transactions*, including Sluse's paper on tangents, both to be delivered to the Dutch scientist.[79] In return Leibniz left for Oldenburg a letter of greeting, some books he had borrowed from him, and the request, which Oldenburg had encouraged, for election to the Royal Society. In Calais the delegation became aware of the archbishop's death on 12 February.[80] Coming so soon after the death of Boineburg, this was a further blow for Leibniz, who lost in Johann Philipp von Schönborn another congenial and understanding patron whom he regarded as "one of the most enlightened princes that Germany ever had. He was an elevated mind who cared above all for the general concerns of Christianity. Always well intentioned, he sought to ground his glory in assuring the peace of his native country, believing that he could accommodate his interest [as prince and archbishop] with that of the Empire [as a whole]."[81]

Paris: The Middle Period (March 1673–October 1675)

Back in Paris by the beginning of March, Leibniz resumed his duties as tutor of the young Philipp Wilhelm von Boineburg, while Melchior Friedrich von Schönborn travelled back to Mainz to put himself at the

service of the new elector, the bishop of Speier and Worms, Lothar
Friedrich von Metternich. The death of Johann Philipp von Schönborn,
who had granted Leibniz a leave of absence to undertake the Paris trip and
who was therefore nominally his employer, added to the uncertainty of
Leibniz's situation. Since he regarded the new elector as a prince who was
"interested in mechanics as well as in learned topics,"[82] Leibniz hoped to
be considered by him as engaged on a sort of scientific–political mission
in Paris. With a bit of luck the new prince-archbishop might therefore
agree to pay him the arrears on his salary for the past two years; and if
a salary was secured, Leibniz would have liked to continue to serve the
interests of the Mainz court from Paris, reporting on scientific progress,
maintaining contact with the French learned world and the court of Louis
XIV, and travelling back to Mainz at least once a year. This itinerant
existence between France and Germany would have suited him very well,
as he confided to Christian Habbeus from Paris three years later: "As
for me, I think I would like to be an amphibian, sometimes in Germany,
sometimes in France, having – thank God –what I need to live for the
time being in the one place and in the other."[83] Since Melchior Friedrich
von Schönborn was returning to Mainz, he entrusted these wishes to his
friend,[84] who reported on 5 May the mixed results of his petition: the
elector had granted Leibniz permission to remain in Paris "for some more
time . . . without danger for his post"; but neither a salary nor a position
as cultural and political resident in Paris was forthcoming.[85]

With these hopes of remaining in Paris on an income from Mainz frustrated, Leibniz needed to consider other possibilities even more urgently
than before. For the moment his only salaried job was the supervision of
the young Boineburg's education – a common form of employment for
young scholars of limited means in foreign cities during the seventeenth
century, but often a very problematic one as well. Perhaps with a view to
stabilizing his position, in March Leibniz drew up for Philipp Wilhelm an
extremely demanding daily schedule: after rising at 5.30 a.m., he would
follow a programme of lessons, study, and reading until 10 p.m., virtually uninterrupted apart from three one-hour slots for lunch, dinner, and
mass between 9 and 10 a.m.[86] Although the boy's mother responded to this
exemplary regime by formally confirming Leibniz's role in April 1673,[87]
the young baron proved less delighted with this punishing workload.
Writing in the autumn to the secretary of the Boineburg family, Jakob
Münch, Leibniz complained about his young charge's lack of interest

and diligence.[88] Toward the end of December, moreover, he found himself in the unpleasant position of having to ask Boineburg's widow to pay his outstanding salary not only as her son's tutor but also for the many tasks assigned him by the late baron for which additional remuneration had been promised in writing.[89] The chief of these tasks, however – the recovery of Boineburg's French rent and pension – had continued to meet with difficulties;[90] and in the end, instead of obtaining recompense for his efforts, on 13 September 1674 Leibniz received a cool note from Anna Christine dismissing him from her service.[91] Never before or thereafter was his financial and professional situation so perilous, and this experience of losing so many of his patrons, positions, and future prospects so suddenly may account in part for Leibniz's determination later in life to ensure that he always had firm support, official positions, and tangible income simultaneously arranged in a number of quarters.

Leibniz, in fact, had been seeking another position for some time and had already received at least two separate offers of employment. The first had been communicated to him very soon after his return to Paris by the very person who had first recommended Leibniz to the Hanoverian court: Christian Habbeus. Through Habbeus's mediation, Leibniz was offered a position as secretary to the Danish prime minister, Count Ulrik Frederik of Güldenlöw, for which he would receive an annual stipend of 400 talers together with free accommodation and dining rights.[92] Despite the attraction of such financial security, Leibniz was not yet prepared to jeopardise his freedom to pursue intellectual agendas in a major cultural capital in order to serve the needs of the mighty, as he politely tried to explain to Habbeus in his far from enthusiastic reply of 5 May 1673:

You know my inclination, which is neither to attempt to amass money, nor to indulge in the ordinary diversions, but to please the spirit by producing something real and useful for the public. If you believe therefore that Monsieur de Guldenlow is of a solid geniality, able to appreciate and prepared to support with his authority enterprises of manifest usefulness... and if I can hope of his complete trustworthiness – not being accustomed to subjecting myself to the political caprice characteristic of some great men, and preferring to keep my distance from all affairs of this kind rather than living in continuous unrest – all this being established, sir, I am ready to receive your orders[.][93]

Whether his Excellency the Count of Güldenlöw was not enough of a "genie solide", or whether he found Leibniz's requests to be granted the title of royal counsellor and the use of a copyist to help him with the more mechanical tasks a trifle excessive, nothing came of it.

About the same time, Leibniz received a renewed offer from a second figure to which he had originally been recommended by Habbeus: Duke Johann Friedrich of Hanover.[94] To a letter from Leibniz of 26 March 1673 reporting on his scientific, philosophical, and theological work in Paris and London,[95] the duke responded on 25 April renewing his expressed desire to attract Leibniz to his service and offering him the position of court counsellor with a "very decent" annual stipend of 400 talers.[96] The duke of Hanover struck Leibniz as a more congenial potential patron; but even so he did not accept the offer until 21 January 1675,[97] well after the termination of his employment with Boineburg had deepened his financial difficulties; and even then he took no immediate steps to depart from Paris. Instead he paid his bills by undertaking some legal work for the annulment of the second marriage of Duke Christian Louis von Mecklenburg-Schwerin, whom he had met in Paris.[98] Once again, Leibniz attempted to turn this limited commission into a more stable position of state counsellor to the duke, though without – as he wrote in March 1675 to Mecklenburg – being "forced to follow his Court, since if I had been willing to settle down so soon in a fixed place, I would long ago have been in employment as advantageous as I might wish."[99] He was evidently determined to find an enlightened German prince who would employ him as his adviser on scientific and learned matters, and allow him to serve his country while pursuing his studies outside it. Mecklenburg proved as reluctant as the other prospective employers to offer a salary while Leibniz remained in Paris.

In such straits, in the autumn of 1675 he could not avoid approaching the administrator of his family estate, Christian Freiesleben, and his half-brother, Johann Friedrich, to request more money.[100] A little negotiation produced the required sum, yet relations with his family were not without difficulties of their own. The year before, on 17 January 1674, Johann Friedrich had written complaining that his half-brother had not sent any news in a long time and reprimanding his failure to visit the place where his parents and sister were buried.[101] A letter of 16 May 1675 brought a similar rebuke: could Leibniz not even bother to acknowledge the death, communicated to him half a year before, of his brother-in-law, Simon Löffler?[102] Leibniz was surprised and saddened by his half-brother's assumptions. He had in fact sent detailed replies to the only two letters received from him during the past two years, without having any answer from his half-brother in return. As for the death of Simon Löffler, he had heard of it "with not a little sorrow" only in the most recent letter of 16 May,[103] and he expressed special affection for his late sister and brother-in-law's young son, Friedrich Simon Löffler (1669–1748),[104] with whom he later exchanged many letters between 1690 and the end of his life. Last but not least, Leibniz firmly defended his actions against the suspicion that he had sold out to a foreign country and an alien faith:

In the presence of Princes and Lords I have . . . often defended the truth of my faith with the utmost reasonable freedom. . . . I have not tried to harm anyone, from which it follows that I have never made an enemy. . . . I do not say this because I want to disguise my failings. I readily admit that through inexperience I have made many and large mistakes; but fortune – that is, providence – has corrected such things and has observed my good will and right intention, from which I also, God's willing, never wish to deviate.[105]

That Leibniz was so determined to stay in Paris is easily explained by the fact that his lack of monetary rewards there was easily offset by his intellectual ones.[106] When it came to the persistent paucity of his income, he was prepared to look at it on the bright side, "for I see and experience that those who have much often waste much, whereas those who have little gain. One who has less must work more; and the more he works, the more accomplished he becomes."[107] One thing Leibniz was certainly never short of was the willingness to work hard, especially when he set his mind on a particularly challenging intellectual task. Having been forced in London to confront the fact that his acquired knowledge of mathematical literature was incommensurate with his native mathematical talent, he energetically plunged back into the study of mathematics once back in Paris.

Immediately after returning to the city on the Seine, Leibniz met the French mathematician Jacques Ozanam (1640–1718), "a young man highly skilled in algebra" – as he described him on 8 March in his first letter from the French capital to Oldenburg – who had given an elegantly simple algebraic solution to several problems in number theory.[108] In the same letter Leibniz returned to the issue of the representation and interpolation of series discussed in Boyle's house, asking in particular about Pell's views on the accomplishments of the Italian mathematician Pietro Mengoli (1626–86).[109] Oldenburg's brief reply of 16 March was followed on 16 April with a fuller letter including a long but rather incoherent report on British mathematics prepared by his adviser on the subject, John Collins (1625–83).[110] Collins, who had not met Leibniz during his first visit to London, was originally an accountant and arithmetical practitioner who had become enthusiastically interested in the progress of research in higher mathematics by his fellow countrymen; but his grasp of it was rather limited and the mathematical newsletters he prepared for Oldenburg (who was no mathematician) to brief foreign correspondents were often prolix and rambling documents.[111] Collins's mathematical report for Leibniz was no exception, and it passed over with a brief reference a development which was to be of considerable importance to Leibniz: a general method for the "quadrature of all Curvilinear figures" being developed by a young mathematician at work in Cambridge, Isaac Newton (1642–1727).[112] This was the first hint that Leibniz had received of Newton's discoveries in higher analysis,[113] but there was little that he could have learned or used for his own mathematical investigations from Collins's superficial report, and all evidence indicates that he merely skimmed through it.[114] In the exchange of letters with Oldenburg that followed, Leibniz was forced to reduce drastically the extent of his claim to originality regarding the summation of the infinite series of reciprocal figurate numbers;[115] and this busy exchange was succeeded by a lofty silence between Oldenburg's last letter of 5 June 1673 and Leibniz's resumption of the correspondence on 15 July 1674.[116] This silence appears to express the young German's realisation that before making any more bold claims of discoveries and inventions, he needed to do some serious work; and the lapse in his correspondence with Oldenburg saw Leibniz refashioning himself under the vigilant tuition of Huygens from an exceptionally gifted but rather immature novice into an accomplished and original mathematician.[117]

The letter and enclosed copy of the *Philosophical Transactions* for Huygens, entrusted to Leibniz by Oldenburg at the eve of his departure from London, provided a convenient pretext for visiting the eminent Dutch scientist – an opportunity made the more welcome by Oldenburg's observation in the postscript: "Mr. Leibniz has gained a great deal of esteem here, as he assuredly deserves."[118] At the time Huygens was in the process of publishing the fruits of a decade of research on the frictionless motion of a body along an inverted cycloid's arc in his *Horologium oscillatorium* (Paris 1673), a copy of which he gave to Leibniz.[119] As Leibniz later candidly recalled, a conversation on a related topic betrayed his limited knowledge of geometry: when he remarked that "a straight line drawn through the centre of gravity always divides the figure into two equal parts. . . . Huygens laughed" and directed him to relevant literature, including Grégoire de Saint-Vincent, Sluse, Honoré Fabri, James Gregory, Descartes (whose *Geometry* Leibniz studied in Frans van Schooten's edition), and Pascal.[120]

While reading Pascal's *Lettres de A. Dettonville* (Paris 1659), Leibniz took a decisive step towards the invention of the calculus. Due to the Copernican revolution and the development of the new Galilean physics, the study of motion in general and the mathematical measurement of curves in particular became central to seventeenth-century scientific inquiry. Two problems were especially relevant: the "quadrature" of a curve – that is, the calculation of the area intercepted by a given curve – and the determination of a tangent to a given curve. To find the tangent meant to calculate the velocity of a body at a given instant.[121] Working on the quadrature of the circle, Pascal had associated a triangle with infinitesimal sides – what Leibniz called a "characteristic triangle" – with a point on a circumference. The French mathematician's method of calculation was based on the similarity between the "characteristic triangle" dx, dy, ds and the triangle y, $a - x$, a (figure 3.1).

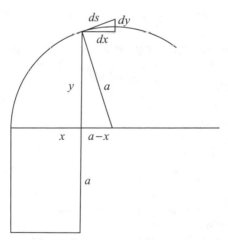

Figure 3.1. As in J. E. Hofmann, *Leibniz in Paris 1672–1676. His Growth to Mathematical Maturity*. Cambridge: Cambridge University Press, 1974, p. 49. Lettering slightly altered.

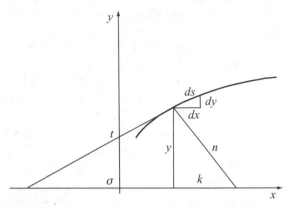

Figure 3.2. As in Niccolò Guicciardini, *Reading the Principia. The Debate on Newton's Mathematical Methods for Natural Philosophy from 1687 to 1736.* Cambridge: Cambridge University Press, 1999, p. 139. The characteristic triangle (*ds*, *dy*, *dx*).

Leibniz generalized this method and applied it to any curve (figure 3.2) by replacing the radius of the circle (*a* in figure 3.1) with the normal to the curve (*n* in figure 3.2).[122]

Huygens was quite delighted when presented with this result and noted that he had himself made use of the same method in specific cases.[123] This discovery – probably reached by the spring of 1673 – was Leibniz's first remarkable contribution to the geometry of infinitesimals. As he noted in a text written in 1673, the characteristic triangle represented a crucial step for the quadrature of curves:

from a simple diagram depicting nothing but a short arc and some straight lines intersecting one another, I have deduced over thirty wonderful propositions, through which many curves are either squared or transformed into other curves by means of a method as simple as that used to treat rectilinear figures in Euclid's *Elements*. The whole thing depends on a right-angled triangle with infinitely small sides, which I am accustomed to call 'characteristic', in similitude to which other triangles are constructed with assignable sides according to the properties of the figure. Then these similar triangles, when compared with the characteristic triangle, furnish many propositions for the study of the figure, through which curves of different kinds can be compared with one another. There are few things which are not deduced from this 'characteristic triangle'. But the combinatorial art can be brought to bear so that nothing escapes notice[.][124]

The second discovery followed a few months later. From the similarity of triangles (in figure 3.2, above, triangles (i) *ds*, *dy*, *dx*; (ii) *n*, *k*, *y*;

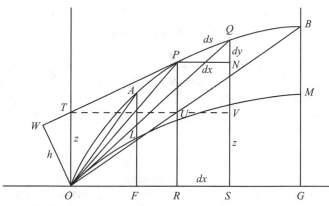

Figure 3.3. As in Hofmann, *Leibniz in Paris*, p. 55. Lettering slightly altered. See also Guicciardini, *Reading the Principia*, p. 140. Following Guicciardini's suggestion, I have added *dy* on one of the catheti of the characteristic triangle.

and (iii) *t*, *y*, *o*) Leibniz obtained several geometrical transformations which allowed him to transform a problem of quadrature into another problem.[125] The most important of these transformations was the fundamental "transmutation theorem" (figure 3.3) by which Leibniz was able to deduce in an elegant and economical way all results so far gained in the field of geometrical quadratures.[126] Relating tangents and quadratures to one another, the theorem showed that, in a certain sense, the problem of tangents was the inverse of that of quadratures. From Leibniz's general transmutation theorem immediately followed the arithmetical quadrature of the circle, which he achieved by the end of 1673 or early in 1674.[127]

With these results in hand, Leibniz resumed his correspondence with Oldenburg on 14 July 1674. First he reported on the long-awaited model of the improved calculating machine, which had "at last been successfully completed . . . after overcoming very great difficulties and at no slight cost." After trying "the patience of a few craftsmen," Leibniz had finally found "a man who preferred fame to fortune" – a French technician named Ollivier – who had built a model able to "produce a multiplication by making four turns of a particular wheel, without any mental effort."[128] Having thus, he hoped, placated Oldenburg with the fulfilment of the promise he had made to the Royal Society regarding the calculator,[129] Leibniz hinted at his discoveries in geometry, mentioning his quadrature of a particular segment of a cycloid and other theorems "of considerably greater importance, of which that especially is most wonderful by means of which the area of a circle or some given sector of it may be exactly expressed by a certain infinite series of rational numbers."[130]

Oldenburg, who had recently seen more than one of Leibniz's major discoveries dwindle in magnitude upon closer inspection, did not reply. On 16 October Leibniz wrote in still more triumphant tones to Oldenburg, claiming that

no one has given a progression of rational numbers whose sum continued to infinity is exactly equal to a circle. Truly, I have at last happily succeeded in this . . . Whoever has hitherto sought the exact quadrature of the circle has not so much opened a path by which one might hope to be able to arrive at it; I would dare to state that this has now first been done by me.[131]

When Oldenburg's reply of 18 December finally arrived, it was a cold shower:

What you relate about your success in the measurement of curves is very fine, but I would like you to know that the method and procedure for measuring curves has been extended by the praiseworthy Gregory, as also by Isaac Newton, to any curve whatever . . . As for what you truly say, that no one has up to the present given a series of rational numbers whose sum continued to infinity is *exactly* equal to a circle, while you yourself have at last succeeded in this, I congratulate you; but I must add [that] . . . the above-mentioned Gregory is now about to prove in writing that it is impossible to obtain this 'exactly'.[132]

The Scot James Gregory (1638–1675) – eight years older than Leibniz – was one of the two most original British mathematicians of the new generation, the other being Isaac Newton. Oldenburg, who was himself no expert, seems to have been inclined to take Gregory's word over Leibniz's, although the reference to the Scotsman's proof of the impossibility of squaring the circle was not in this case appropriate, since Leibniz and Gregory's claims were in fact not incompatible.[133]

Oldenburg's cool reply did not discourage Leibniz. On 9 January 1675 he pressed ahead with a demonstration of the much improved calculating machine to the Académie Royale des Sciences.[134] On 21 January he reported his success to the duke of Hanover, Johann Friedrich, mentioning that Colbert had ordered a copy of the calculator for the Royal Observatory and that others were destined for use in the financial offices.[135] Stimulated by Huygens's invention of the balance–spring watch, on 24 April Leibniz presented to the Académie another device: a chronometer the movement of which was regulated by springs.[136] As Leibniz remarked in the article for the *Journal des Sçavans* in which his invention was presented, the principle he "thought upon some years ago for making exact portable Watches" was "altogether different from that which consists in an Equal duration of Unequal vibrations of pendulums or Springs, applied to Watches by M. *Hugens*."[137] However ingenious, Leibniz's mechanism turned out to be impractical.

Meanwhile a letter of 22 April from Oldenburg was on its way to Paris. Responding to the claims of mathematical achievements reiterated in Leibniz's letter of 30 March,[138] it included Oldenburg's Latin translation of Collins's latest report on the progress of mathematics in Britain, confused and rambling as usual and marred in this case not only by Collins's limited grasp of higher mathematics but by errors in transcription and translation as well.[139] Moreover, although it contained details of James Gregory's and Newton's work, it only mentioned their results, not their methods. It is therefore extremely unlikely that Leibniz could have used it to reconstruct their achievements; yet it would later be deployed in precisely this manner as a key plank of the Newtonian's argument that Leibniz had not developed the calculus independently but merely copied Newton's findings and claimed them as his own.[140]

Another highly unlikely source from which Leibniz was later alleged to have received key information on the results obtained by the British mathematicians in analysis was Ehrenfried Walther von Tschirnhaus (1651–1708), a young nobleman from Saxony who arrived in Paris in the late summer of 1675 after spending several months in London.[141] Tschirnhaus had studied in Leiden, where he had devoted himself to extensive studies in philosophy and mathematics, developing remarkable skills in formal algebraic calculation and enthusiastically embracing Cartesianism. Between May and August 1675 he visited London, where he was warmly received, especially through the good offices of his fellow countryman, Oldenburg. With a letter of introduction from the secretary of the Royal Society in hand, he met Wallis and discussed his algebraic researches. On 9 August, shortly before leaving for Paris, he also met Collins, who was so impressed by the young German,[142] that he ranked him amongst the very best European algebraists, on a par with Gregory and Newton. After transferring to Paris, Tschirnhaus met Leibniz in early October 1675,[143] and over the following weeks the two men rapidly established a close friendship. But contrary to the chronologically scrambled statement of Newton's later champions, Tschirnhaus received from Wallis and Collins no news on British progress in analysis beyond the generalities already known to Leibniz.[144] Even once translated to Paris, the young nobleman did not appear to appreciate the novelty and importance of the new infinitesimal methods which were taking shape in Leibniz's mind, rendering all the more implausible that he could have fed crucial information without fully realising what he was dealing with.[145]

Notwithstanding his young friend's incomprehension of the exciting mathematical thoughts leading to the discovery of the calculus, Leibniz's great enjoyment of their common work in mathematics is testified by numerous notes and joint studies.[146] Among other things, they perused together some of the mathematical manuscripts of Pascal made available to Leibniz in June 1675 by Pascal's nephews, the Périer brothers.[147] During a visit to Paris one year earlier, the older of the brothers, Étienne, had promised to communicate the papers to the young mathematician whose calculating machine he had just admired.[148] Leibniz and Tschirnhaus found the manuscripts very interesting and upon returning them to Étienne Périer on 30 August 1676, Leibniz recommended the publication of the papers on conics, which he judged "sufficiently complete and polished to be published."[149] Unfortunately, the manuscripts subsequently went missing, and Leibniz's summary of the highlights of the lost papers in his covering letter to Périer thereby became a much more precious document than its author could have foreseen.[150]

During his middle period in Paris Leibniz was so engrossed in mathematics and technology that even his (by his standards) scarce philosophical notes were mainly stimulated by his mathematical work and related mostly to logic, with the exception of two pieces on philosophico-theological topics.[151] The most important philosophical by-product of his mathematical studies and discoveries was a more rigorous way of tackling his great perennial project: the *characteristica universalis*. A key component of the *characteristica* was the development of the *ars inveniendi* or method for discovering new concepts and truths; and between the spring of 1673 and 1675 Leibniz composed a number of studies related to the *ars inveniendi*, as well as carefully annotating the *Ars signorum* of the Scot George Dalgarno and the published correspondence on the *ars combinatoria* between Quirinus Kuhlmann and Athanasius Kircher.[152] During this period Leibniz also continued to encounter prominent philosophers and savants: probably between January and March 1675, for instance, he seized the opportunity to further his acquaintance with the Parisian Oratorian priest Nicolas Malebranche (1638–1715).[153] One of the leading philosophers of the time, Malebranche had branched out from Cartesianism to produce the most influential and systematic presentation of the so-called occasionalist doctrine. With him Leibniz was to carry out a stimulating philosophical conversation. They corresponded intermittently until 1712 and Leibniz gained an extensive knowledge of Malebranche's doctrines through careful reading of the main works of the French thinker.

The Last Year in Paris (October 1675–October 1676)

The last year in Paris was one of Leibniz's *anni mirabiles*. He discovered the infinitesimal calculus, which allowed the mathematical treatment of all kinds of known curves and variable quantities, and which was to exercise an enormous influence on the development of modern physics. Notably, with his calculus, Leibniz tackled not only the curves which Descartes had classified in the second book of the *Géométrie* as "geometrical" (or, in Leibniz's terminology, "algebraic") but also those called by Descartes "mechanical" (in Leibniz's terminology, "transcendental"). Perhaps the greatest achievement of Leibniz's calculus was the mathematical treatment of transcendental curves, that is, of the type of curves involved in most quadrature problems.[154] Meanwhile, philosophically, he pored over the work of key authors in contemporary and classical philosophy, including the unpublished manuscripts of Descartes; and he returned to metaphysics, as documented above all by the *De Summa Rerum*, a harvest of notes which represented Leibniz's most coherent body of metaphysical texts between the *Confessio Philosophi* of 1671 and the *Discours de Métaphysique* of 1686.

The crucial final steps which resulted in the invention of the two parts of the calculus – differential and integral – were taken in October 1675.[155] Reflecting on the characteristic triangle, Leibniz conceived the idea of connecting the study of numerical series, which had exercised him from his first months in Paris, with the geometrical analysis of curves for the determination of tangents and of quadratures.[156] As Leibniz explained some twenty years later in a letter to John Wallis, "consideration of the differences and of the sums in numerical series sparked my first flash of illumination when I realized that the differences corresponded to the tangents and the sums to the quadratures."[157] One of his most important discoveries consisted precisely in his recognition of the inverse relationship

existing between the determination of tangents and of quadratures.[158] As
he wrote to Tschirnhaus in 1679,

> Finding tangents to curves is reduced to the following problem: to find the differences
> of series; whereas, finding the areas of figures [i.e., quadratures] is reduced to this:
> given a series to find the sums, or (to explain this better) given a series to find another
> one, whose differences coincide with the terms of the given series.[159]

In proceeding first of all to the invention of the differential calculus (which
provided a general solution to the problem of finding tangents to curves),
Leibniz imagined dividing a given curve represented in a Cartesian co-
ordinate system into an infinite number of infinitesimal intervals s_1, s_2,
s_3. . . . As a consequence, both the x-axis and the y-axis of the Cartesian
coordinate system were divided into an infinite number of infinitesi-
mal intervals, respectively x_1, x_2, x_3, . . . ; y_1, y_2, y_3, ... The difference
between two successive values of each of the variables s, x, y was called
"differential" (indicated by the sign 'd', first employed by Leibniz in a
publication in 1684).[160] The differential dx was defined by Leibniz as x_{n+1}
$- x_n$. Likewise, the differentials dy and ds were equal, respectively, to y_{n+1}
$- y_n$ and $s_{n+1} - s_n$.[161] The characteristic triangle had sides dx, dy, ds (see
figure 3.4). As Leibniz later explained,

> to find the *tangent* means to draw a straight line connecting two points of the curve
> which have an infinitely small distance between them, that is to lengthen [one] side of

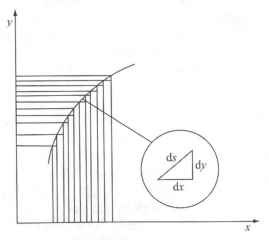

Figure 3.4. Differential representation of a curve.
As in Guicciardini, *Reading the Principia*, p. 143.

the polygon with infinite angles which for us is equivalent to the curve. This infinitely small distance, however, can always be expressed through a known differential, such as dy, or through a relation to it, that is through a known tangent.[162]

In other words, the key principle on which the differential calculus was based was the consideration of a curve as equivalent to a polygon with an infinite number of sides, as Leibniz in another text explicitly stated:

In my view, on the other hand, this and other methods which I have thus far used can all be deduced from a certain general principle of mine for measuring curvilinear figures, according to which *a curvilinear figure must be considered equipollent to a Polygon of infinite sides*. From this it follows that everything which can be demonstrated of such a Polygon can also be demonstrated of the curve, whether the number of sides is not taken into account at all, or whether it is made more true by assuming a greater number of sides, so that the error will always be less than any given error.[163]

In working toward the invention of the integral calculus (which provided a general solution to quadrature problems), Leibniz considered the area subtended by a given curve as equal to the sum of infinitely many strips ydx (see figure 3.4).[164] To indicate this sum he initially used the abbreviation 'omn.' (for *omnes*) following Cavalieri, Mengoli, and Fabri. In the middle of a paper of November 1675, however, he introduced his own symbol $\int$ – an elongated 's' for *summa*.[165] The first occurrence of the integral symbol $\int$ in a publication was in 1686.[166] The use of symbols allowed Leibniz to create a very efficient algorithm. In a sense, with the calculus he had managed to accomplish part of what he was planning to achieve in logic with regard to thought in general: the creation of a rigorous, symbolic language in which, thanks to the manipulation of symbols according to predetermined rules, thought was reduced to calculation and error in reasoning was minimised.[167] In this respect Leibniz's approach to the calculus was very different from Newton's. For the great Cambridge mathematician, his calculus or method of fluxions was basically a brilliant way to solve some difficult mathematical problems. For Leibniz, typically, it was part of a much broader project with implications reaching far beyond mathematics and physics to logic, philosophy, religion, ethics, and politics: the project of the *characteristica universalis*. As he explicitly wrote to Oldenburg on 28 December 1675,

This algebra (of which we deservedly make so much) is only part of that general system. It is an outstanding part, in that we cannot err even if we wish to, and in that truth is as it were delineated for us as though with the aid of a sketching-machine. But I am truly willing to recognise that whatever algebra furnishes to us of this sort is the fruit of a superior science which I am accustomed to call either Combinatory or Characteristic, a science very different from either of those which might at once spring to one's mind on hearing these words. . . . I cannot here describe its nature in a few words but I am emboldened to say that nothing can easily be imagined which is more effective for the perfection of the human mind[.][168]

Hints of Leibniz's great discovery of October 1675 were disseminated throughout his scientific correspondence during the following months. On 2 November he communicated to Gallois his intention to explain his discoveries in letters to well-known persons of repute.[169] At the same time he was preparing for the *Journal des Sçavans* a new summary of his arithmetical quadrature of the circle.[170] Similar topics were discussed further in a letter possibly addressed to Gallois.[171] After a silence of several months, he wrote again to Oldenburg at the end of December 1675 mentioning, among other things, his successful solution, by means of a new method he had invented, of a geometrical problem which had hitherto proved intractable, in all likelihood the problem of inverse tangents which Leibniz had recently solved employing his new calculus.[172]

In the spring of 1676 (probably between April and the beginning of May), Leibniz met the Danish mathematician Georg Mohr, who had recently arrived from London and reported to Leibniz on his recent discussions with Collins.[173] The mathematical portion of Leibniz's letter of 12 May 1676 to Oldenburg, together with Tschirnhaus's insistence on the overwhelming influence of Descartes on British mathematics, prompted Collins hastily to compose in May and June a long and incoherent document know, from 1712 onwards as the "Historiola."[174] This was a sort of collage of brief accounts of the preceding thirty to forty years of British mathematics, together with excerpts of letters sent to Collins by James Gregory (who had died prematurely in his late thirties in October 1675) and Newton. The prolixity of the "Historiola" stretched even the patience of Oldenburg, who asked his mathematical adviser to summarise it; and the resulting "Abridgement" was sent by Oldenburg to Leibniz on 5 August 1676. Also included was Newton's so-called *epistola prior*, in which the English mathematician, at Oldenburg's request, clearly summarised his achievements without providing either methods or proofs.[175] Leibniz received this material on 24 August and promptly drafted a reply which was dispatched in a revised form to Oldenburg on 27 August.[176] Once again this succession of events was to be distorted during the quarrel on the priority, with the Newtonian camp unjustly accusing Leibniz both of having received in Newton's *epistola prior* key information for the development of his own calculus and of having mulled over it for several weeks before replying. For the moment, however, the relationship between the two great mathematicians was not evidently poisoned by suspicion.[177] Newton replied to Leibniz's letter with the so-called *epistola posterior*, in itself a small treatise dated 24 October 1676 (O.S.; 3 November 1676 N.S.). By the time it was finished Leibniz had already left Paris: it eventually reached him in Hanover on 1 July 1677 (21 June O.S.), having been dispatched there on 12 May 1677 by Oldenburg, who had been waiting for a suitable opportunity to send securely such a precious and extensive communication. Despite their caution in not revealing too much and the part they played in the ensuing acrimonious priority dispute, the two *epistolae* were indeed gems. They constituted the fullest presentation yet composed of Newton's mathematical ideas directly addressed to a specific reader and closed his mathematical correspondence with anyone for several years.[178]

As if inventing the calculus was not enough of a challenge, during the last year in Paris Leibniz energetically returned to philosophy. Although he was obviously familiar with Descartes's philosophy, his knowledge of it up to this point had been basically second-hand.[179] During the winter of 1675–6 and the spring of 1676 he plunged into a careful reading of Descartes's *Principia Philosophiae* (Amsterdam 1644), leaving a trail of notes.[180] Further testimony to this direct encounter with Cartesianism was his notes on a publication regarding the relationship between Cartesianism and biblical theology by the Parisian lawyer Géraud de Cordemoy (1614–84), one of the first proponents of occasionalism whom Leibniz had the opportunity to meet in person, at the home of Colbert's son-in-law, the Duke of Chevreuse.[181] Probably around 24 February 1676, accompanied by Tschirnhaus, Leibniz called upon Claude Clerselier (1614–84), the editor and executor of Descartes's Nachlaß, obtaining permission to peruse many of Descartes's unpublished papers. The two friends made the best of this precious opportunity, making a number of excerpts from the manuscripts.[182] Coincidentally, the collection of Descartes's papers once held by Clerselier suffered the same fate as the manuscripts of Pascal inspected by Leibniz: at some point after Leibniz and Tschirnhaus's perusal they disappeared, and only Leibniz's extracts from these important Cartesian texts are now preserved.

Alongside Descartes, Leibniz's attention was also captured by another of the towering figures of early modern philosophy: Baruch Spinoza.

His close relationship with Tschirnhaus was certainly a major factor in Leibniz's renewed interest in Spinoza's thought. In Leiden Tschirnhaus had developed a friendship with a German medical student named Georg Hermann Schuller. During a stay in Amsterdam in 1674 he had met with some friends of Spinoza, notably Lodewijk Meyer, and made contact once again with Schuller, who had became in the meantime one of the members of Spinoza's circle. By January 1675 Tschirnhaus had met Spinoza himself at least once,[183] establishing with him a friendly and intellectually stimulating relationship continued through an exchange of letters. Between the winter of 1675–6 and the autumn of 1676 Leibniz returned to the *Tractatus Theologico-Politicus*, which he had already read in Mainz; but this time he did not focus on the parts in which Spinoza presented his philosophy, his disapproval of many aspects of which had elicited the negative opinions of the book forcefully expressed on previous occasions.[184] Instead, he concentrated on the more philological and exegetical aspects of the *Tractatus*, notably on Spinoza's treatment of the bible as history;[185] and this shift of focus lends some degree of plausibility to Tschirnhaus's claim, duly reported to Spinoza by Schuller, that Leibniz thought "very highly of the *Tractatus Theologico-Politicus*."[186] Yet Leibniz had also other reasons for signalling a positive reception of Spinoza's work. During his time in Holland Tschirnhaus had gained the trust of Spinoza and his circle to the point that he had been entrusted with a manuscript copy of the as yet unpublished *Ethica* under the strict condition that he not show it to anyone else without explicit permission. Leibniz was understandably eager for a glimpse at it: it would have never done to begin demolishing other writings of the *Ethica*'s author while hoping to have access to the carefully guarded manuscript. In any case Leibniz had always genuinely admired the learning and sharpness of Spinoza's thought and would continue to respect him as a person even as he disagreed with him as a philosopher.[187]

Tschirnhaus did his best to gain permission to show the precious manuscript to his German friend. Reporting the nobleman's plea, Schuller wrote to Spinoza in the autumn of 1675,

He relates . . . that he has met in Paris a man called Leibniz, of uncommon learning, well versed in many Sciences, and free from the common prejudices of Theology. He has formed an intimate friendship with him because it happens that like himself he is working at the problem of the continued perfecting of the understanding, than which, indeed, he thinks there is nothing better, and considers nothing more useful. In Morals, he says that he is perfectly disciplined, and speaks from the mere dictates of reason, uninfluenced by emotion. In Physics and especially in Metaphysical studies about God and the soul, he continues, he is very expert. Lastly, he concludes that he is most worthy of having communicated to him your writings, Sir, if consent has been first obtained, since he believes that thus great advantage will come to the Author, as he promises to show more fully if it please you, Sir. But if not, then let it cause no uneasiness lest he may not keep them secret conscientiously according to the promise he gave, as he has not made the slightest mention of them.[188]

Spinoza, however, would not have it. Although his previous epistolary contacts with Leibniz had given him the impression of "a man of liberal mind, and versed in every science," to entrust him a work which he knew to be highly controversial seemed to be premature. Apart from anything else he was also suspicious of what a German counsellor was up to in France, at the time still at war with Holland.[189] Tschirnhaus obliged, refraining from showing the manuscript, but not from speaking at some length of its content to his friend – at best a loose interpretation of Spinoza's instruction to keep the manuscript to himself. Leibniz, on his part, tried to take advantage of the next best thing offered to him by Tschirnhaus and wrote down what his fellow countryman had been willing to reveal.[190]

In addition to Descartes and Spinoza, Leibniz focused on the work of other prominent thinkers. Between December 1675 and the first half of February 1676 he made numerous extracts from four theological works by Robert Boyle, with whom he shared the deep conviction that there is no contradiction between the Christian religion and the results of modern science.[191] During the winter of 1675–6 he studied the massive work on natural law by the German political and moral philosopher Samuel Pufendorf (1632–94), *De jure naturae et gentium* (Lund 1672).[192] Judged from the external circumstances of their careers, Pufendorf and Leibniz had a great deal in common: both were Lutherans, both Saxons, both alumni of the universities of Leipzig and Jena, both philosophers of politics and law, both later court historians – respectively in Berlin and Hanover. The commonalities, however, ended more or less there: from a doctrinal standpoint there was very little that Leibniz approved in Pufendorf's voluntaristic political and juridical philosophy, and throughout his life he took a very critical stance toward his fellow countryman, starting from his first critical appraisal in Mainz of Pufendorf's *Disquisitio de Republica irregulari ad Severini Monzambano Cap. IV de Forma Imperii Germanici* (1669).[193] Although at some point during 1674 Leibniz wrote to Pufendorf and a few letters were exchanged in 1690–93, a substantial correspondence between the two never developed.[194]

In the spring of 1676 Leibniz summarised in Latin Plato's *Phaedo*, *Theaetetus*, and *Parmenides* and jotted down a series of notes on Simon Foucher's *Réponse pour la critique à la préface du second volume de la recherche de la vérité* (Paris 1676).[195] This was not the first time that Leibniz had taken a keen interest in the doctrines of the French Abbé. Foucher (1644–96) was an honorary canon of the Sainte Chapelle in Dijon (Burgundy) who had moved to Paris and served as chaplain on the Rue Saint-Denis. He promoted a revival of Academic scepticism – that is, the teaching of Plato's Academy in its last years – and was engaged in a lively polemic with Malebranche over the theory of ideas and Cartesian metaphysics. Having met in Paris, Leibniz and Foucher developed a stimulating and friendly philosophical correspondence which lasted until the year before Foucher's death in 1696.[196] Leibniz himself recounted later that he had once gone looking for Foucher's *Critique de la recherche de la vérité* (Paris 1675) in a Parisian bookshop; but when he referred to it as a work of metaphysics, the bookseller and his customers began to ridicule him, asking whether he knew the difference between logic and metaphysics.[197] At that moment, however, Foucher himself happened to enter into the bookshop and, recognising Leibniz, began to praise his outstanding intellectual qualities, at which point the attitude and demeanour of bookseller and company transformed completely, like some scene from a French farce. "I have never before noticed so clearly," Leibniz later recollected, "the power that prejudice and appearance have over human beings."[198]

Between May and July 1676 his attention turned to the manuscript of the still unpublished *Essay de Logique* of the mathematician and physicist Edme Mariotte (c. 1620–84), whom he had met in 1673 and with whom he corresponded from 1676 until the year of Mariotte's death.[199] During the last months of his stay in Paris he also began to devote more time to ethical topics and composed the only text on the philosophy of law of his Parisian years, possibly stimulated by the fact that he was finally getting ready to take up service at the Hanoverian court of Duke Johann Friedrich.[200] He studied the *Enchiridion* of the ancient stoic Epictetus (A.D. c. 55–c. 135) and the *Enchiridion Ethicum* (London 1668) of the Cambridge Platonist Henry More (1614–87).[201] He also conceived and began to draft a work, *De Vita Beata*, which argued for a conception of the "happy life" inspired by the Stoic ethical ideal; like so many others, it remained unfinished.[202] Meanwhile he continued to assemble materials and draft guidelines for the *characteristica*, the *ars inveniendi*, and the encyclopaedia,[203] collecting numerous passages for this purpose from the works of Comenius, Alsted, Clauberg, and Jungius.[204] His previous plans for the creation of academies of sciences devoted to organizing the huge collaborative effort required by his encyclopaedic project developed along the lines of a society or order the members of which, being relieved from other worries, could focus on research and study.[205]

But the most important and coherent body of philosophical texts written during this extremely fruitful last year in Paris was on metaphysics. Leibniz set out to compose a metaphysical system tentatively untitled *Elementa philosophiae arcanae, de summa rerum*.[206] This work too shared the fate of so many Leibnizian projects: it remained *in fieri*. As he wrote on 10 May 1676 with a touch of sadness to the Hamburg jurist Vincentius Placcius, "you will ask which of the things that I so liberally promised some time ago have been pushed forward since then: I answer, that I have pursued many but perfected and completed none."[207] But like many other unfinished Leibnizian works, the pile of notes for *De Summa Rerum* contained many gems. Despite its missing pieces and unsystematic discussions of various topics scattered across different sheets, this array of typically short texts and fragmentary essays succeeded in sketching a metaphysical system which adumbrated much of Leibniz's mature philosophy.[208] The first group of papers was written in Paris between December 1675 and April 1676.[209] From May to September 1676 Leibniz was probably too busy with his last desperate attempts to secure a position in Paris and then with the preparation of his return to Germany to complete it. If he wrote any philosophy in these months it was rather on ethics and jurisprudence – two fields closer to the heart of his new employer, the duke of Hanover.[210] But during his roundabout voyage back to Germany via London and Holland he returned his attention to the metaphysical thoughts of late winter and spring, writing a second group of papers which he probably continued until his first days in Hanover.[211]

By "de summa rerum" Leibniz meant two things. Sometime he intended to refer to the "totality of things," that is, to the universe. More often, in the context of the metaphysical papers of 1675–6, he intended to speak of the "highest of things," that is, of God and of His relation to His creatures.[212] His first series of reflections, possibly stimulated by his intensive reading of Descartes's *Principia* and by his conversations with Tschirnhaus on Spinoza's philosophy, tackled especially the nature of mind and matter and the relationship of soul and body.[213] Moreover, he discussed the problem of magnitude, of its infinity and continuity.[214] In a *Meditatio de principio individui* of 1 April 1676 he turned to the issue of causation.[215] Further reflections on motion and matter followed during the month of April, together with a cluster of notes on God as the subject of absolute attributes, on the mind, and on the origin of things.[216] In a paper probably written in early 1676 he sketched once again a plan for an all-embracing encyclopaedia.[217] After a break between May and September, Leibniz resumed his metaphysical reflections with the only complete, extensive essay included in the *De Summa Rerum* papers: the dialogue *Pacidius Philaleti* on philosophical problems concerning motion, notably the vexed issue of the continuum.[218] In connection with his visit in November 1676 to Spinoza in The Hague he prepared three papers on arguments for the existence of God and a note with questions concerning Spinoza's *Ethica*.[219] The last cluster of papers, written in December 1676, furthered the discussions of the distinction between spirit and body, of the possibility of the concept of God and of the world, and of the notion of harmony now boldly identified by Leibniz as his own distinctive principle ("principium meum").[220]

Already in the collection of papers written in Paris Leibniz employed this key idea of his metaphysics – the "principle of harmony" – in the sense of a general ontological principle, that is, a feature characterising all existing beings. "To exist," he wrote, "is nothing other than to be harmonious."[221] In the *Confessio Philosophi* of 1672–3 he had reiterated the definition of harmony embraced in the Mainz period: "What is . . . harmony? . . . similitude in variety, that is to say, diversity compensated by identity"; "Since [harmony and discordance] consist *in the relation* [*in ratione*] *of identity to diversity*, harmony is, in effect, unity in multiplicity; it is greater when it is the unity of the greatest number of apparently disorderly elements, which are resolved into . . . the greatest concordance [*concinnitatem*]."[222] In the light of these definitions, the identification of "to exist" with "to be harmonious" meant that "to exist" was to realise in a single individual that "unity in multiplicity" or "diversity compensated by identity" which constituted harmony. In turn, harmony was the criterion of God's choice in the creation of the world. Since not all possible beings were compossible – that is, not all of them could coexist in the unity of the same world – according to the "principle of harmony" God chose to create that series of compossible beings which contained the greatest quantity of essence. In the Platonic framework embraced by Leibniz, the degree of perfection enjoyed by a being was nothing else than the magnitude of its positive reality, that is, of what "is positive and absolute in essence."[223] In turn, the amount of positive reality of a being corresponded to the degree of its metaphysical goodness. To achieve the greatest metaphysical goodness meant to create the world which included the greatest perfection, that is, the greatest quantity of positive reality or essence to be found in beings which were in harmony with one other (that is, which were compossible).[224] In short, God created that world which was the best because it was the most harmonious in the sense that it contained the maximum of positive essence which could coexist, or the maximum of multiplicity which could be recalled to unity:

I take as a principle the harmony of things: that is, that the greatest amount of essence that can exist, does exist. It follows that there is more reason for the existing than for not existing, and that all things will exist, if that can come about. For since something exists, and all possibles cannot exist, it follows that those things exist which contain the most essence, since there is no other reason for choosing some and excluding the rest.[225]

A further key metaphysical idea to be found in the papers of *De Summa Rerum* was the thesis that every mind perceives everything that happens in the entire universe, albeit in a confused way. Each substance therefore expresses the entire universe – a core tenet of Leibniz's mature monadology.[226] Other theses characterising his mature philosophy were present as well. One instance was the momentous claims that no two things can be perfectly alike – a forerunner of his principle of the identity of indiscernibles. Another was the no less important doctrine that "all things are in a way contained in all things," which was justified on the basis of a forerunner of a further key tenet: namely, that there are no purely extrinsic denominations (that is, no properties of a thing which are purely 'external' to it and which therefore do not affect its ontological constitution).[227] Last but not least, from 1676 onward Leibniz proposed the fundamental metaphysical principle which paved the way to his new definition of force, namely the principle that the full cause is equipollent to the entire effect:

Just as in Geometry the principle of reasoning is usually taken from the equation between the whole and all the parts, so in mechanics everything depends on the equation between the full cause and the complete effect. Hence just as the first axiom of Geometry is that the whole is equal to the sum of the parts, so the first axiom of Mechanics is that the power of the full cause and of the entire effect is the same [causae plenae et effectus integri eadem potentia est].[228]

But far from being withdrawn into a pure world of high metaphysics and higher mathematics, Leibniz was simultaneously scrambling around trying to find a way to stay in Paris. On 27 October 1675, the death of the mathematician Gilles Personne de Roberval – one of the salaried members of the Académie Royale des Sciences – fuelled his hopes. Thanks especially to the support of Jean Gallois and of the duke of Chevreuse, Leibniz was proposed to the Prime Minister Colbert as Roberval's successor.[229] Unfortunately, due to a severe cold, Leibniz was forced to cancel a meeting with Gallois which would have served to further his candidacy;[230] the support of the self-centred and stubborn Gallois proved flimsy,[231] and Leibniz's hopes were rapidly dashed. His German birth had also put him at a disadvantage since it was felt that to have two prominent salaried positions already filled by foreigners – the Dutchman Huygens and the Italian director of the *Observatoire*, Giovanni Cassini – was quite enough. In a last desperate gambit, Leibniz addressed a plea directly to Colbert on 11 January 1676,[232] but he seems to have recognized that such tactics were doomed to failure: on the same day he resolved to confirm his acceptance of the position offered to him in Hanover.[233] Yet still he found one more avenue to pursue. A few days later, on 18 January, he wrote to the new archbishop of Mainz, Damian Hartard von der Leyen (1624–78), the successor to Lothar Friedrich von Metternich, in the hope of being employed by him in Paris;[234] but within a month this proposal had been declined.[235] On 24 January, Christian Freiesleben transferred to him 336 talers via the Parisian banker Nicolas Formont, momentarily relieving his financial situation;[236] but by the time those funds arrived, pressure to leave had begun to mount inexorably from another quarter.

On 27 January the chamberlain of Johann Friedrich, Johann Carl Kahm, wrote on behalf of the duke formalising his employment as counsellor at the Hanover court. As a sweetener, Leibniz's stipend was to be paid retroactively from 1 January. Less welcome was the fact that no promise could be given at this stage of an appointment as privy counsellor

(*Geheimer Rat*), a position vastly more prominent and well remunerated than that of simple court counsellor.[237] Leibniz did not stir, and on
12 April Kahm wrote again, communicating this time the duke's desire
for a prompt departure of Leibniz from Paris: should he wish to stay a
little longer, the duke was prepared to wait until Pentecost, which that
year felt on 24 May.[238] Still Leibniz did not take any action; and on 2 July
Kahm related the duke's ultimatum: either Leibniz packed his bags or
Johann Friedrich started looking for someone else to fill the vacant post.
Moreover, in addition to the counsellor position, for the first time the
duke was now envisaging for him the additional post of librarian, and was
perhaps prepared to supplement the agreed-upon annual remuneration of
400 talers with dining rights at court.[239] Although doubtless intended as
a further enhancement of Leibniz's position, this revised job description
may have had the opposite effect: the mundane duties of librarian were
a far cry from the position of sweeping cultural, scientific, and political
influence and ill-defined responsibilities he had imagined for himself. On
26 July the Hanoverian representative in Paris, Christophe Brosseau,
added his efforts to the campaign, accompanying his exhortations for
a swift departure with the concrete payment of 200 talers.[240] Leibniz
proposed to travel to Hanover via Brussels, the capital of the Spanish
Netherlands, but on 13 September Brosseau informed him that these
plans were unacceptable since the complex passport formalities required
could have delayed the trip for several months[241] – perhaps exactly what
Leibniz was angling for. On 26 September Brosseau again urged a speedy
departure.[242] Clearly the duke's patience could not stretch any further.
Nearly two years after his first acceptance of Johann Friedrich's offer,
Leibniz finally resigned himself to leaving the brilliant intellectual community of the French capital to take up residence in the relatively remote
and isolated northern German city of Hanover. At the beginning of October he took his leave from Brosseau and Antoine Arnauld. The latter
entrusted to him a letter for a Hanover Capuchin in which he remarked
that Leibniz was lacking only the true religion "to be truly one of the
great men of this age."[243] On the morning of Sunday 4 October 1676
Leibniz left Paris by postal coach. He was never to return to the great
European city where he had tried so hard to remain. The "amphibian"
way of life shuttling between France and Germany now joined the steadily
accumulating list of unfulfilled *desiderata*.[244]

Back to Germany via London and Holland

The postal coach which Leibniz boarded in Paris, however, was not bound east or northeast to Frankfurt or Cologne and then onward directly to Hanover: it was headed north via Abbeville to Calais. Despite the understandable eagerness of Johann Friedrich to see his employee in the flesh in Hanover, Leibniz had chosen a circuitous route to northern German via London and Holland. Arriving in Calais on the evening of 10 October, he was forced to wait there for five days due to bad weather conditions. On 15 October he was finally able to cross the Channel, and after spending the night in Dover he resumed his journey to London the following morning,[245] arriving in the late evening of the 18th, and remaining there until the 29th. His first call was naturally on Oldenburg, to whom he was eager to show the improved model of his calculator. One of the topics of their conversations seems to have been Spinoza, since Oldenburg let Leibniz copy three letters written to him by the philosopher between November 1675 and February 1676.[246] Unfortunately the Royal Society had not yet resumed its meetings, and Leibniz was unable to meet either Wallis or Newton, who were based, respectively, in Oxford and in Cambridge.[247] Having failed to encounter the two mathematical giants, he had to settle for a mathematician of incomparably lesser stature – John Collins – who allowed him to take notes from some manuscript papers of Gregory and Newton, notably the *De Analysi per aequationes numero terminorum infinitas* (1669) of the latter.[248] Strikingly, in his excerpts from Newton's *De Analysi*, Leibniz disregarded the sections relating to infinitesimals, probably because he was more than satisfied by his own solution to these problems.[249] In addition, he perused and made excerpts from Collins's "Historiola", which, although meant for him, had never been sent. From this text he copied in particular an example given by Newton in a letter to Collins of 20 December 1672 to illustrate his tangent-method. To the example Leibniz added the general rule which had already been communicated to him by Oldenburg in the letter of 5 August 1676.[250] Later on Newton was to claim that Leibniz had plagiarised his rule, to which the German mathematician retorted (truthfully but fruitlessly) that his source of inspiration had been Sluse's rule rather than Newton's.[251]

On 29 October Leibniz boarded a boat for the continent. The boat left London on 31 October and reached Gravesend on the same day; but there the vessel stalled: for four days it was anchored for the loading of cargo, and when it finally sailed, it was only to be stopped for almost a week at Sheerness, in the mouth of the Thames, due to adverse weather conditions.[252] Leibniz was growing restless:

The time passed very slowly, partly because of bad conditions on board the ship, partly because of the irksome waste of time [itself]; but for six days we had to be patient . . . More than once I was willing to be set on land and to go to Harwich, in order to pass over to Holland from there[.][253]

In truth, he was probably exaggerating his impatience for the benefit of his addressee, Johann Friedrich's chamberlain: when a philosopher has nothing else to do, he can always occupy his time with his own thoughts. Whatever his impatience, Leibniz found a profitable use for his time in writing the most extensive piece pertaining to *De Summa Rerum*, the impressive dialogue *Pacidius Philaleti*,[254] and, when tired of talking with the sailors, by keeping his mind busy with his "old plan for a rational language or script".[255] On the morning of Wednesday 11 November a strong northwest wind finally allowed a rapid passage to Rotterdam, where Leibniz spent Thursday night after arriving in the evening.[256] On 13 November he reached Amsterdam, where he met the mathematician and *burgemeester* Jan Hudde, the microscopist famous for his researches on insects Jan Swammerdam, and two members of Spinoza's circle: Georg Hermann Schuller and Jarig Jelles. Until 24 November he toured Haarlem, Leiden, Delft, and The Hague, sleeping on the boat taking him from one place to the other.[257] In Delft he met another famous microscopist, Antonie van Leeuwenhoek, who was revealing the existence of an entire microcosm of life in the tiniest parcel of matter – something which must have impressed Leibniz and given further inspiration to his metaphysical thoughts about nature.[258] In The Hague, where he seems to have stopped between 18 and 21 November, he conversed "several times and at great length" with Baruch Spinoza.[259] The topics discussed in their meetings ranged from Spinoza's *Ethica*, on which Leibniz had prepared a number of questions,[260] to the arguments for the existence of God, Descartes's theory of motion, Leibniz's plan for the *characteristica universalis*, and the political situation in the Dutch Republic.[261] Leibniz particularly recalled hearing from Spinoza of the savage lynching of the De Witt brothers, Cornelis (1623–72) and Johan (1625–72), which had transpired less than three months earlier. Johan De Witt had ruled the Dutch Republic between the death in 1650 of William II and the election of William III, Prince of Orange, as head of state on 28 June 1672. Two months later, the De Witt brothers had been assassinated by an Orangist mob in The Hague: Johan was shot and horrendously mutilated; his brother was disembowelled alive before his brains were knocked out and partially eaten; their naked bodies were then strung up in public; and their hearts were carved out for further exhibition. Leibniz's record of Spinoza's response to these events conveyed his own reaction as well:

I have spent several hours with Spinoza, after dinner. He told me that, on the day of the massacre of the De Witts, he wanted to go out at night and post a placard near the site of the massacre, reading *ultimi barbarorum*! [you are the worse of barbarians!]. But his host locked the house to prevent him from leaving, for he would have risked being torn into pieces.[262]

A particularly prominent place in their discussions was reserved for the arguments for the existence of God. Leibniz prepared several papers on the subject, one of which was written out in Spinoza's presence and discussed with him.[263] It reworked the classical ontological argument for the existence of God – the argument seeking to prove the existence of God through an analysis of the concept of God, independent of experience – which Spinoza himself had reformulated in part one of the *Ethica*.[264] Writing a year later to Gallois, Leibniz judged Spinoza's metaphysics "strange and full of paradoxes":

Among other things, he believes that the world and God are but a single substantial thing, that God is the substance of all things, and that creatures are only modes or accidents. But I noticed that some of his purported demonstrations, that he showed me, are not exactly right. It is not as easy as one thinks to provide true demonstrations in metaphysics.[265]

On 24 November Leibniz was back in Amsterdam, but not in good shape. The nights on the boat and the cold, humid air of a Dutch November had taken their toll.[266] Only at the end of November, after a few days of resting and keeping warm, was Leibniz able to resume his journey. At some point between 10 and 15 December 1676, over two months after leaving Paris, he arrived at last in Hanover – a final destination which turned out to be far more permanent than he had thought or wished.

Notes

1. A I, 1, 297–8.

2. A I, 1, 491–2. Trans. by G. H. R. Parkinson in G. W. Leibniz, *De Summa Rerum. Metaphysical Papers, 1675–1676.* New Haven and London: Yale University Press, 1992, p. xi.

3. See Hochstetter, "Zu Leibniz' Gedächtnis," p. 17.

4. See Leibniz to Christian Habbeus, 5 May 1673 (A I, 1, 416). In a letter of February 1679 to Duke Johann Friedrich, Leibniz still described himself as far from being a brilliant courtier (A II, 1, 553).

5. See Leibniz to Duke Johann Friedrich, autumn 1679* (A II, 1, 490).

6. See for instance A II, 1, 493.

7. 21 January 1675 (A I, 1, 492).

8. A II, 1, 490. See also A I, 1, 492.

9. See Yvon Belaval, "Introduction." In *Leibniz à Paris (1672–1676). Symposion de la G. W. Leibniz-Gesellschaft.* 2 vols. Wiesbaden: Steiner, 1978, vol. 1, p. 2.

10. Mark 2:22.

11. A IV, 1, N. 16.

12. See Leibniz to Joh. Heinrich Böckler, May* 1672 (A I, 1, N. 181).

13. A I, 1, N. 186.

14. Klopp II, 139.

15. Guhrauer, *Leibnitz*, pp. 118–19 reports of a meeting in Arnauld's house during which Leibniz proposed a prayer which did not mention Jesus Christ or the Trinity, incurring in so doing in the irate reaction of Arnauld. This anecdote, widely repeated in the literature and taken by some interpreters to indicate early deistic inclinations by Leibniz, is in fact the result of the mistaken attribution to Leibniz of a letter written in March 1685 by Ernst von Hessen-Rheinfels (published in A I, 4, N. 310). Indeed the protagonist of the whole episode was Landgraf Ernst and not Leibniz.

16. Antoine Arnauld and Pierre Nicole, *Logique, ou l'art de penser.* Paris, 1662.

17. See Müller–Krönert, *Leben und Werk*, p. 31.

18. See A II, 1, N. 108 and Otto von Guericke, *Experimenta nova (ut vocantur) Magdeburgica de vacuo spatio.* Amsterdam, 1672.

19. Further scientists and learned men met by Leibniz in Paris are listed in Erich Hochstetter, "Zu Leibniz' Gedächtnis: Eine Einleitung." In *Leibniz. Zu seinem 300. Geburtstage 1646–1946.* Ed. by Erich Hochstetter. Instalments 1–8. Berlin: W. de Gruyter, 1946–52, pp. 20–23; Müller-Krönert, *Leben und Werk*, pp. 44–5; Heinrich Schepers, "Leibniz." In *Neue Deutsche Biographie* (vol. 14, p. 122).

20. See for instance GM V, 257. Cf. H. J. M. Bos, "The influence of Huygens on the formation of Leibniz's ideas." In *Leibniz à Paris (1672–1676). Symposion de la G. W. Leibniz-Gesellschaft.* 2 vols. Wiesbaden: Steiner, 1978, vol. 1, pp. 59–68.

21. See Hofmann, *Leibniz in Paris 1672–1676*, pp. 12–15 and Aiton, *Leibniz*, pp. 41–2. Leibniz referred to this meeting with Huygens in two letters to Oldenburg

respectively of 26 April and 24 May 1673 (A III, 1, N. 17 and N. 20). See also
Michel Fichant, "Leibniz et l'exigence de démonstration des axiomes: 'La partie
est plus petite que le Tout'." In Michel Fichant, *Science et métaphysique dans
Descartes et Leibniz*. Paris: Presses Universitaires de France, 1998, pp. 329–73.

22. See Hofmann, *Leibniz in Paris*, p. 13. On Leibniz's 'austere' ontology and mini-
    malism see Adams, *Leibniz*, pp. 217 ff. and Mugnai, *Introduzione*.
23. A VI, 2, 482–3.
24. See Hofmann, *Leibniz in Paris*, pp. 14–15 and Aiton, *Leibniz*, p. 42. See also in A
    VII, 3 Leibniz's studies on differences, sequences, and series between 1672 and
    1676.
25. See Oldenburg to Huygens, 8 November 1670 (O.S.), in *The Correspondence of
    Henry Oldenburg*, vol. VII, pp. 240:241–2.
26. See Hofmann, *Leibniz in Paris*, p. 15 and Müller–Krönert, *Leben und Werk*,
    p. 29.
27. See Leibniz to Jakob Bernoulli, April 1703, postscript (GM III, 72).
28. See Hofmann, *Leibniz in Paris*, pp. 16–17 and Aiton, *Leibniz*, p. 43.
29. Niccolò Guicciardini, *Reading the Principia*, pp. 137–8.
30. See Hofmann, *Leibniz in Paris*, p. 19.
31. Leibniz for Jean Gallois, end of 1672 (A II, 1, N. 109).
32. See below (correspondence with Oldenburg). Cf. Hofmann, *Leibniz in Paris*,
    p. 22 and Aiton, *Leibniz*, p. 43.
33. See Huygens to Oldenburg, 14 January 1673, in *The Correspondence of Henry
    Oldenburg*, vol. IX, pp. 382:384.
34. Guhrauer, *Leibnitz*, I, 113. On the surprising reliability of Leibniz's calculating
    machine see Klaus Badur and Wolfgang Rottstedt, "Und sie rechnet doch richtig!
    Erfahrungen beim Nachbau einer Leibniz-Rechenmaschine." *Studia Leibnitiana*
    36, 2 (2004): 130–46.
35. See A VI, 3, N. 1–5 (esp. N. 3: *Demonstratio substantiarum incorporearum*; N. 4:
    De consistentia corporum; N. 5: *De minimo et maximo. De corporibus et mentibus*).
    Cf. A VI, 3, xxi. On *De minimo et maximo. De corporibus et mentibus* in its relation
    to the *Accessio ad Arithmetica Infinitorum* and to the Euclid axiom that the whole
    is always greater than the part see O. Bradley Bassler, "Towards Paris: The
    Growth of Leibniz's Paris Mathematics out of the Pre-Paris Metaphysics." *Studia
    Leibnitiana* 31, 2 (1999): 160–80, here 165–6.
36. See A VI, 3, 87 and A VI, 3, xxi.
37. See *Nouveaux Essais*, "Preface" (A VI, 6, 55) and *Monadology*, § 61. See also
    Rutherford, *Leibniz*, p. 38.
38. See A VI, 3, N. 11.
39. A VI, 3, N. 7. The *Confessio Philosophi* and related papers are translated and intro-
    duced by Robert C. Sleigh, Jr. in Leibniz, *Confessio Philosophi: Papers Concerning
    the Problem of Evil, 1671–1678*.
40. See Leibniz to Nicolas Malebranche, 2 July 1679 (A II, 1, 477–8) and *Theod-
    icy*, "Preface" (GP VI, 43). Cf. A VI, 3, xxiii and Sleigh, "Introduction" to
    Leibniz, *Confessio Philosophi: Papers Concerning the Problem of Evil, 1671–1678*,

p. xxiii. Müller–Krönert's identification of the "petit dialogue" with the *Dialogus de religione rustici* (November 1673; A VI, 3, N. 9) appears to be mistaken (cf. Müller–Krönert, *Leben und Werk*, p. 35).

41. See *Von der Allmacht und Allwissenheit Gottes und der Freiheit des Menschen*, 1670–71* (A VI, 1, N. 20).

42. See *Confessio Naturae contra Atheistas* (A VI, 1, N. 13); Leibniz to Magnus Wedderkopf, May 1671 (A II, 1, N. 60); *Demonstrationum Catholicarum Conspectus* (A VI, 1, N. 14). Cf. A VI, 3, xxii and Francesco Piro, "Postfazione." In G. W. Leibniz, *Confessio Philosophi e altri scritti*. Naples: Cronopio, 1992, esp. pp. 124–5, 128–9.

43. Cf. G. H. R. Parkinson, "Sufficient reason and human freedom in the *Confessio Philosophi*." In *The Young Leibniz and his Philosophy, 1646–1676*. Ed. by Stuart Brown. Dordrecht: Kluwer, 1999, pp. 199–222.

44. See Massimo Mugnai, "Leibniz on Individuation: From the Early Years to the 'Discourse' and Beyond." In *Studia Leibnitiana* 33 (2001), p. 38.

45. See *L'auteur du peché* (A VI, 3, 150–51). Trans. by Sleigh in Leibniz, *Confessio Philosophi. Papers Concerning the Problem of Evil, 1671–1678*, pp. 111–13.

46. See A I, 1, 282.

47. See A IV, 1, N. 35.

48. See A IV, 1, xxxii.

49. See A IV, 1, N. 36.

50. See A IV, 1, N. 37.

51. See respectively *Mala Franciae, 1672** (A IV, 1, N. 38) and *De Jure Belli Regis Christianissimi in Batavos*, early 1673* (A IV, 1, N. 39).

52. See A I, 1, 303 and A I, 1, 305.

53. See Guhrauer, *Leibnitz*, I, p. 121 and Müller–Krönert, *Leben und Werk*, p. 30.

54. See A I, 1, N. 205.

55. Leibniz to Joh. Friedrich Schütz von Holtzhausen, 22 December 1672 (A I, 1, 305). The letters mentioned by Leibniz have not been found. Regarding Jodoci's letter, either Leibniz did not remember its date correctly or Jodoci must have been unaware of Boineburg's death on 15 December. See also Johann Lincker to Leibniz, 19 December 1672 (A I, 1, N. 202).

56. A I, 1, 305.

57. Leibniz to Anna Christine von Boineburg, 22 December 1672 (A I, 1, 304). On Leibniz's esteem and gratitude towards the Baron see also *Biographische Aufzeichung über Johann Christian von Boineburg*, 1687–1688 (A IV, 3, N. 3).

58. *De propaganda vita* (A VI, 3, 378). Cf. Hochstetter, "Zu Leibniz' Gedächtnis," p. 1 and P. Ronsard, *Le tombeau du feu Roy Tres-Chrestien Charles IX* (1574): "L'âge ne sert de rien, les gestes font la vie."

59. See Joh. Friedrich Schütz von Holtzhausen to Leibniz, 6 January 1673 (A I, 1, N. 211), and Anna Christine von Boineburg to Leibniz, 16 January 1673 (A I, 1, N. 212).

60. See Müller–Krönert, *Leben und Werk*, p. 31 and Guhrauer, *Leibnitz*, p. 124.

61. See *The Correspondence of Henry Oldenburg*, vol. IX, 382:384.

62. See Hofmann, *Leibniz in Paris*, p. 23.

63. See Birch, *The History of the Royal Society of London*, vol. 3, p. 73.

64. See chap. I. 2; Hofmann, *Leibniz in Paris*, pp. 24–5; and Marie Boas Hall, "Leibniz and the Royal Society. 1670–76." In *Leibniz à Paris (1672–1676). Symposion de la G. W. Leibniz-Gesellschaft*. 2 vols. Wiesbaden: Steiner, 1978, vol. 1, pp. 173–5.

65. Leibniz to Oldenburg, 8 March 1673 (A III, 1, 40); *The Correspondence of Henry Oldenburg*, vol. IX, 489:493.

66. See Leibniz to Oldenburg, 8 March 1673 (A III, 1, 40–41); *The Correspondence of Henry Oldenburg*, vol. IX, pp. 489–90:493–4; Birch, *History of the Royal Society*, vol. 3, pp. 74–5. In fact Hooke's calculator, presented to the Royal Society on 15 March 1673 (Birch, *History of the Royal Society*, vol. 3, p. 77) was rather similar to Samuel Morland's arithmetical machine. See below and Hofmann, *Leibniz in Paris*, pp. 34–5.

67. See Oldenburg to Leibniz, 9 February 1673 (A III, 1, 21); *The Correspondence of Henry Oldenburg*, vol. IX, 431:432.

68. See Sluse to Oldenburg, 17 January 1673, *The Correspondence of Henry Oldenburg*, vol. IX, 386:392. The letter was published in the *Philosophical Transactions*, no. 90 (20 [30 N.S.] January 1673): 5143–7.

69. See Oldenburg to Leibniz, 9 February 1673 (A III, 1, 21); *The Correspondence of Henry Oldenburg*, vol. IX, 431:432.

70. See Leibniz to Jakob Bernoulli, 25 March 1697 and April 1703 (GM III, 57, 68); Leibniz to Johann Bernoulli, 25 June 1697 (GM III, 421); Leibniz to Guillaume François Antoine de L'Hôpital, 26 September 1701 (GM II, 343); Leibniz to Jacob Hermann, 6 September 1708 (GM IV, 335). Cited in Hofmann, *Leibniz in Paris*, p. 35 n. 16. Napier's bones consist of rods (originally often made of bone) on which digits are inscribed. They were invented by the Scottish mathematician John Napier (1550–1617), who devised a method for rendering the complex processes of multiplication and division into those of addition and subtraction by manipulating the rods.

71. Leibniz to Oldenburg, 8 March 1673 (A III, 1, 39); *The Correspondence of Henry Oldenburg*, vol. IX, 488:492.

72. Leibniz for the Royal Society, 13 February 1673 (A III, 1, 24); *The Correspondence of Henry Oldenburg*, vol. IX, 439:444. On this episode see the detailed account given by Hofmann, *Leibniz in Paris*, pp. 26–9. Cf. also Rupert Hall, "Leibniz and the British Mathematicians." In *Leibniz à Paris (1672–1676). Symposion de la G. W. Leibniz-Gesellschaft*. 2 vols. Wiesbaden: Steiner, 1978, vol. 1, pp. 133–4. On Pell see Noel Malcolm and Jacqueline Stedall, *John Pell (1611–1685) and His Correspondence with Sir Charles Cavendish. The Mental World of an Early Modern Mathematician*. Oxford: Oxford University Press, 2005 (for this encounter with Leibniz see pp. 221-2, 325).

73. See A III, 1, 24.

74. Leibniz for the Royal Society, 13 February 1673 (A III, 1, 24–5); *The Correspondence of Henry Oldenburg*, vol. IX, 440:444.

75. See Leibniz's marginal note on p. 32 of his own copy of the *Commercium epistolicum D. Joannis Collins et aliorum de analysi promota*, London, 1712, in which his letter to the Royal Society had been edited by Newton. Cf. Hofmann, *Leibniz in Paris*, p. 29, n. 28–9. On the *Commercium Epistolicum* see chapter II. 8.

76. See A I, 1, 418 and Boas Hall, "Leibniz and the Royal Society," p. 175.

77. See Birch, *History of the Royal Society*, vol. 3, pp. 76 and 82.

78. Hofmann, *Leibniz in Paris*, p. 30, n. 38.

79. See Oldenburg to Huygens, 9 February (O.S.) / 19 February 1673 and Oldenburg to Leibniz, 9 February (O.S.) / 19 February 1673, in *The Correspondence of Henry Oldenburg*, vol. IX, 456–8. Cf. *Philosophical Transactions*, no. 90 (20 [30 N.S.] January 1673): 5143–7.

80. Cf. Leibniz to the Royal Society, 20 February 1673 (A III, 1, N. 7) and Leibniz to Oldenburg, 8 March 1673 (A III, 1, 38–9); *The Correspondence of Henry Oldenburg*, vol. IX, 488:492.

81. Klopp I, "Einleitung," p. xviii. See also A II, 1, 39.

82. Leibniz to Oldenburg, 8 March 1673 (A III, 1, 9); *The Correspondence of Henry Oldenburg*, vol. IX, 488:492.

83. Leibniz to Christian Habbeus, 14 February 1676 (A I, 1, 445). See also A I, 1, 509.

84. See *Promemoria* for Melchior Friedrich von Schönborn, early March 1673 (A I, 1, N. 216) and Leibniz to Melchior Friedrich von Schönborn, 10 March 1673 (A I, 1, 315–16).

85. A I, 1, 349.

86. See A I, 1, N. 226.

87. Anna Christine von Boineburg for Leibniz. *Vollmacht*, 3 April 1673 (A I, 1, N. 228).

88. See A I, 1, 370–73.

89. See A I, 1, N. 255. See also Leibniz to Jakob Münch, end of December 1673* (A I, 1, N. 254).

90. See A I, 1, N. 246.

91. See A I, 1, N. 264.

92. See Count Ulrik Frederik of Güldenlöw to Christian Habbeus, 25 February 1673 (Klopp III, 224). On the scale employed at the court in Hanover around 1696, this was the pay of a middle-ranking court official. While the lord marshal, the master of the horse, the lord chamberlain, the majordomo, and the chief huntsman could expect around 1800–2000 talers per year, and the majordomo to the duchess and the chief cup-bearer received 1060 talers, the physician-in-chief earned 828 talers, the musician-in-chief 600, the head gardener 500 talers, and the court apothecary, the junior chamberlains, and the dancing master 400. The French chef, the court organist, and other gardeners and cupbearers were paid between 100 and 300 talers. Less than 100 talers was the stipend of lower employees such as the veterinarian, the lackeys, and the ratcatcher. Normally, all these positions included accommodation and dinner rights in addition to the annual stipend. See C. E. von Malortie, *Der Hannoversche Hof under dem Kurfürsten Ernst August*

und der Kurfürstin Sophie. Hanover: Hahn, 1847, pp. 37–41. Malortie's data are reproduced by Nicholas Rescher, "Leibniz Finds a Niche (Settling in at the Court of Hannover: 1676–77)." *Studia Leibnitiana* 24, 1 (1992): 25–48 (here pp. 33–4).

93. Leibniz to Christian Habbeus, 5 May 1673 (A I, 1, 416). Cf. also A I, 1, 418.
94. A I, 1, N. 327.
95. See A I, 1, N. 326.
96. See Johann Friedrich to Leibniz, 25 April 1673 (A I, 1, 491), and Leibniz to the Elector Damian Hartard of Mainz, 18 January 1676 (A I, 1, 399).
97. See A I, 1, 492–3.
98. See A IV, 1, N. 21–4.
99. A I, 1, N. 320. Cf. also A I, 1, 321.
100. See A I, 1, N. 287, N. 289, N. 292.
101. See A I, 1, N. 280.
102. See A I, 1. N. 284.
103. See Leibniz to Johann Friedrich Leibniz, 21 October 1675 (A I, 1, N. 288). Cf. also A I, 1, N. 287.
104. There are over 200 extant letters between Leibniz and Friedrich Simon Löffler (dating from 1690 to 1716), distinguishing him as the relative with whom Leibniz had the longest and most intense correspondence. He became Leibniz's sole heir. On Friedrich Simon Löffler cf. also chap. II. 6.
105. A I, 1, 431–2.
106. See for instance A I, 1, 479.
107. A I, 1, 432.
108. See Leibniz to Oldenburg, 8 March 1673 (A III, 1, 42); *The Correspondence of Henry Oldenburg*, vol. IX, pp. 490–91:494–5. Cf. Hofmann, *Leibniz in Paris*, p. 36.
109. A III, 1, 43; *The Correspondence of Henry Oldenburg*, vol. IX, pp. 491:495. Cf. Hofmann, *Leibniz in Paris*, p. 30.
110. See A III, 1, N. 13/1–6. Oldenburg's letter of 16 March is lost. See Hofmann, *Leibniz in Paris*, pp. 36–45.
111. See Hall, "Leibniz and the British Mathematicians," pp. 30–31.
112. A III, 1, 71; *The Correspondence of Henry Oldenburg*, vol. IX, p. 566.
113. Hofmann, *Leibniz in Paris*, p. 42, n. 54.
114. See Hall, "Leibniz and the British Mathematicians," p. 135.
115. See in particular A III, 1, N. 17, N. 20, N. 22. Cf. Aiton, *Leibniz*, p. 48.
116. See respectively A III, 1, N. 22 and N. 30.
117. See Hall, "Leibniz and the British Mathematicians," pp. 135–6 and Hofmann, *Leibniz in Paris*, 44–5.
118. *The Correspondence of Henry Oldenburg*, vol. IX, p. 457.
119. See Leibniz to Tschirnhaus, end of 1679* (GB, 407).
120. See Leibniz to Tschirnhaus, end of 1679* (GB, 407–13; here 407). Cf. Hofmann, *Leibniz in Paris*, p. 47 ff., and Hall, "Leibniz and the British Mathematicians,"

p. 13. Van Schooten produced two Latin editions of Descartes's *Géométrie* (1637): the first one was published in Leiden in 1649; a second, improved edition appeared in two volumes in Amsterdam in 1659–61.

121. See Mugnai, *Leibniz: Vita*, pp. 75–7.

122. See Guicciardini, *Reading the Principia*, p. 138 and Hofmann, *Leibniz in Paris*, pp. 48–9.

123. See Huygens, *Oeuvres complètes*, vol. 14, pp. 234, 314–46. Cf. Hofmann, *Leibniz in Paris*, p. 48.

124. LH 35 II 1, f. 256 (in Enrico Pasini, *Il reale e l'immaginario: La fondazione del calcolo infinitesimale nel pensiero di Leibniz*. Turin: Sonda, 1993, pp. 59–60). Cf. Mugnai, *Leibniz: Vita*, p. 80.

125. Guicciardini, *Reading the Principia*, p. 139.

126. Guicciardini, *Reading the Principia*, p. 141 and Hofmann, *Leibniz in Paris*, p. 54.

127. Hofmann, *Leibniz in Paris*, p. 59 and Hall, "Leibniz and the British Mathematicians," p. 135. According to Hofmann, *Leibniz in Paris*, p. 98, Leibniz possessed his own quadrature of the circle already in the autumn of 1673.

128. Leibniz to Oldenburg, 14 July 1674 (A III, 1, 119); *The Correspondence of Henry Oldenburg*, vol. XI, p. 42:45.

129. See Oldenburg to Leibniz, 18 December 1674 (A III, 1, 172).

130. Leibniz to Oldenburg, 14 July 1674 (A III, 1, 119–120); *The Correspondence of Henry Oldenburg*, vol. XI, pp. 43:45–6.

131. A III, 1, 131; *The Correspondence of Henry Oldenburg*, vol. XI, pp. 99:101–2.

132. A III, 1, 173–4; *The Correspondence of Henry Oldenburg*, vol. XI, pp. 139–40: 141.

133. See Leibniz to Oldenburg, 30 March 1675 (A III, 1, 210); Hofmann, *Leibniz in Paris*, p. 100; Aiton, *Leibniz*, p. 52.

134. See Leibniz for the Académie Royale des Sciences (A III, 1, N. 43).

135. See A I, 1, 492.

136. See Leibniz for the Académie Royale des Sciences (A III, 1, N. 50). See also Leibniz to Oldenburg, 30 March 1675 (A III, 1, N. 46/3). This letter was read at the meeting of the Royal Society of 25 April 1675 (Birch, *History of the Royal Society*, vol. 3, pp. 216–17). A detailed account of the disputes on clocks surrounding Leibniz's invention can be seen in Hofmann, *Leibniz in Paris*, chap. 9.

137. Cf. *Journal des Sçavans*, 7 (25 March 1675): 94–9. Trans. by Oldenburg for the *Philosophical Transactions* 10, 113 (26 April [6 May N.S.]) 1675: 285–8 (also in A III, 1, 193–201; here 194).

138. See A III, 1, N. 46.

139. See A III, 1, N. 49 and Hall "Leibniz and the British Mathematicians," pp. 143–4. For a detailed account see Hofmann, *Leibniz in Paris*, chap. 10.

140. See *Commercium Epistolicum*, pp. 39–41.

141. Cf. Hofmann, *Leibniz in Paris*, chap. 12, esp. pp. 164–6 and Hall, "Leibniz and the British Mathematicians," pp. 144–5.

142. See John Collins to James Gregory, 20 August 1675, in H. W. Turnbull, ed., *James Gregory Tercentenary Memorial Volume*. London: G. Bell & Sons, 1939, pp. 320–23.

143. See A III, 1, lxii.

144. See Hofmann, *Leibniz in Paris*, pp. 171–2. The letters from Oldenburg in which the English infinitesimal methods and Newton's tangent rule were communicated to Tschirnhaus dated from the early summer of 1676, not the early summer of 1675, as erroneously reported in the *Commercium Epistolicum*. By the summer of 1676 Leibniz had already invented the calculus (see below).

145. See Hall, "Leibniz and the British Mathematicians," p. 145 and Hofmann, *Leibniz in Paris*, pp. 184–6.

146. See A VII, 2, N. 54, N. 55, N. 59, N. 60, N. 61, N. 62, N. 63, N. 75, N. 76, N. 78. Cf. Leibniz to Oldenburg, 28 December 1675 (A III, 1, 327–8) and Leibniz to Christian Habbeus, 14 February 1676 (A I, 1, 446).

147. Leibniz acknowledged receipt of the papers on 4 June 1675 (A III, 1, N. 53). Further fragments on conics were probably communicated a few months later. See Hofmann, *Leibniz in Paris*, pp. 179–80 and Jean Mesnard, "Leibniz et les papiers de Pascal." *Leibniz à Paris (1672–1676). Symposion de la G. W. Leibniz-Gesellschaft.* 2 vols. Wiesbaden: Steiner, 1978, vol. 1, pp. 45–58.

148. See Étienne Périer to Leibniz, early June 1674 (A III, 1, N. 27); Nicolas Toinard to Leibniz, 20 June 1674 (A III, 1, N. 28); Leibniz to Oldenburg, 15 July 1674 (A III, 1, 121). Cf. Hofmann, *Leibniz in Paris*, p. 79.

149. Leibniz to Étienne Périer, 30 August 1676 (A III, 1, 588). Cf. also Leibniz to Johann Vagetius, 27 November 1686 (O.S.) (Dutens VI, 34 and Hofmann, *Leibniz in Paris*, p. 180).

150. See A III, 1, 588–91.

151. See *Dialogus de religione rustici*, November 1673 (A VI, 3, N. 9) and *De vera methodo philosophiae et theologiae ac de natura corporis*, 1673–5* (A VI, 3, N. 10). The *Dialogus* represents one of the very few occasions in which Leibniz described his feelings as moved by the beauty of nature. In it he remembered a return trip from Strasbourg on a Rhine boat in the summer of 1671.

152. See A VI, 3, N. 12, N. 14, N. 40–49. Cf. Antonio Lamarra, "The Development of the Theme of the 'Logica Inventiva' during the Stay of Leibniz in Paris." *Leibniz à Paris (1672–1676). Symposion de la G. W. Leibniz-Gesellschaft.* 2 vols. Wiesbaden: Steiner, 1978, vol. 2, pp. 55–71.

153. See André Robinet, *Malebranche et Leibniz. Relations personnelles*. Paris: Vrin, 1955, esp. pp. 10–21, 26.

154. I am grateful to Niccoló Guicciardini for advising me on this point.

155. For the genesis of the infinitesimal calculus I draw from the clear and concise reconstruction of Mugnai, *Leibniz: Vita*, pp. 73–83 and Guicciardini, *Reading the Principia*, pp. 136–45. For a classic detailed account of the invention of the calculus see Hofmann, *Leibniz in Paris*, esp. chap. 13. On the calculus see H. J. M. Bos, "Differentials, Higher-Order Differentials and the Derivative in the Leibnizian Calculus." *Archive for History of Exact Sciences* 14 (1974):

1–90. A rich discussion of historical, mathematical and philosophical issues surrounding Leibniz's calculus can be seen in Albert Heinekamp, ed., *300 Jahre "Nova Methodus" von G. W. Leibniz (1684–1984). Symposion der Leibniz-Gesellschaft . . . 28. bis 30. August 1984.* Stuttgart: Steiner, 1986 (see esp. the important contribution by Enrico Giusti, "Le Problème des tangentes de Descartes à Leibniz," pp. 26–37).

156. Mugnai, *Leibniz: Vita*, p. 78.

157. Leibniz to John Wallis, 28 May 1697 (O.S.) (GM IV, 25). Quoted by Mugnai, *Leibniz: Vita*, p. 77.

158. See Mugnai, *Leibniz: Vita*, p. 81–2 and Guicciardini, *Reading the Principia*, p. 145.

159. GM IV, 479. Trans. by Guicciardini in *Reading the Principia*, p. 145.

160. Cf. *Nova Methodus pro maximis et minimis, itemque tangentibus.* In *Acta Eruditorum* (October 1684): 467–73. The *Nova Methodus pro maximis et minimis* can also be seen in GM V, 220–26. In the margin of a manuscript of 21 November 1675 (*Methodi tangentium inversae exempla*) Leibniz noted (GB, 161) "∫ summa, d differentia."

161. Cf. Mugnai, *Leibniz: Vita*, p. 79 and Guicciardini, *Reading the Principia*, p. 142.

162. *Nova Methodus pro maximis et minimis* (GM V, 223).

163. *Additio ad Schedam . . . de dimensionibus Curvilineorum.* In *Acta Eruditorum* (December 1684): 585–7. Published also in GM V, 126–7 (here p. 126). Both texts (GM V, 223 and GM V, 126) are quoted by Mugnai, *Leibniz: Vita*, pp. 79–80.

164. See Guicciardini, *Reading the Principia*, p. 142.

165. See *Methodi tangentium inversae exempla* (GB, 161–7). Cf. Hofmann, *Leibniz in Paris*, p. 192.

166. See *De Geometria Recondita et Analysi Indivisibilium et Infinitorum.* In *Acta Eruditorum* (July 1686): 292–300. Published also in GM V, 226–33.

167. See Mugnai, *Leibniz: Vita*, p. 81.

168. A III, 1, 331. I follow the translation of this passage provided by Rupert Hall in *Philosophers at War. The Quarrel between Newton and Leibniz.* Cambridge: Cambridge University Press, 1980, pp. 61–2. A translation of the entire letter of Leibniz to Oldenburg (A III, 1, 327–34) can be seen in *The Correspondence of Henry Oldenburg*, vol. XII, pp. 97–8.

169. Leibniz to Jean Gallois (A III, 1, 304–7).

170. Leibniz to Jean Paul de La Roque, end of 1675 (A III, 1, N. 72).

171. End of 1675 (A III, 1, N. 73).

172. Leibniz to Oldenburg, 28 December 1675 (A III, 1, N. 70). Cf. Hall, "Leibniz and the British Mathematicians," pp. 145–6. The problem of inverse tangents is the following: given (the properties of) the tangent to a curve to determine the curve.

173. See Leibniz to Oldenburg, 12 May 1676 (A III, 1, 375).

174. See respectively A III, 1, N. 80 and A III, 1, N. 88/1.

175. See respectively Collins to Oldenburg for Leibniz and Tschirnhaus, 24 June 1676 (A III, 1, N. 88/3) and Newton to Oldenburg for Leibniz and Tschirnhaus, 23 June 1676 (A III, 1, N. 88/50).

176. See A III, 1, N. 89/1–2 and Müller-Krönert, *Leben und Werk*, p. 44.

177. Hall argues convincingly against the historiographical thesis (embraced, among others, by Aiton, *Leibniz*, p. 79) of the presence of hard feelings and suspicion in Newton towards Leibniz as early as 1676. See especially Hall, *Philosophers at War*, pp. 68–9.

178. See Hall, "Leibniz and the British Mathematicians," p. 148.

179. See Leibniz to Simon Foucher, 1675 (A II, 1, 247).

180. See A VI, 3, N. 15. Cf. Belaval, "Premières animadversions de Leibniz sur les *Principes* de Descartes."

181. See A VI, 3, N. 32 and Müller–Krönert, *Leben und Werk*, p. 44. These notes probably date back to 1675–6 and refers to Cordemoy's *Copie d'une Lettre Ecrite à un sçavant Religieux de la Compagnie de Jesus* [Gabriel Cossart]: *Pour montrer, 1. Que le Systeme de Monsieur Descartes, et son opinion touchant les bestes, n'ont rien de dangereux. II. Et que tout ce qu'il en a écrit, semble estre tiré du premier Chapitre de la Genese*, published anonymously in 1668. In Paris Leibniz met also the sharp critic of Descartes and Christian sceptic Pierre-Daniel Huet (1630–1721), with whom he corresponded between 1673 and 1692.

182. See A VI, 3, N. 34.

183. See Tschirnhaus to Spinoza, 5 January 1675 (Ep. 59 in Spinoza, *Opera*. Vol. IV, p. 268).

184. See above chap. I. 2.

185. See A VI, 3, N. 18.

186. Georg Hermann Schuller to Spinoza, 14 November 1675 (Ep. 70 in *Opera*, vol. IV, p. 303). See Parkinson, "Leibniz's Paris Writings in Relation to Spinoza," pp. 77–8.

187. Cf. *Nouveaux Essais*, Book IV, chap. 16, paragraph 4. Quoted by Nadler, *Spinoza*, pp. 302–3.

188. Schuller to Spinoza, 14 November 1675 (Ep. 70 in *Opera*, vol. IV, pp. 302–3). Trans. slightly adapted from *The Correspondence of Spinoza*. Trans. and ed. by A. Wolf. London: George Allen and Unwin, 1928, pp. 338–9.

189. See Spinoza to Schuller, 18 November 1675 (Ep. 72 in *Opera*, vol. IV, p. 305) and Nadler, *Spinoza*, pp. 300–302.

190. See A VI, 3, N. 33/4. For Leibniz's interest in Spinoza's thought, and in particular in the problem of the infinite, see also *Communicata ex literis Domini Schulleri*, February 1676* (A VI, 3, N. 19).

191. See A VI, 3, N. 16/1–4. The four works by Boyle are (1) *The Excellency of Theology, Compar'd with Natural Philosophy*. London: Printed by T. N. for Henry Herringman, 1674; (2) *Some Motives and Incentives to the Love of God*. 5th ed. London: Printed for H. Herringman, 1670; (3) *Some Considerations about the Reconcileableness of Reason and Religion*. London: Printed by T. N. for H. Herringman, 1675; (4) *Some Physico-Theological Considerations about the*

Possibility of the Resurrection. London: Printed by T. N. for Henry Herringman, 1675. Leibniz was also familiar with Boyle's account of the new physical science in *The Origine of Formes and Qualities (according to the Corpuscular Philosophy)*. Oxford: Printed by H. Hall ... for R. Davis, 1666. See E. Loemker, "Boyle and Leibniz." *Journal of the History of Ideas* 16, no. 1 (1955): 22–43.

192. See A VI, 3 N. 17.

193. Pufendorf's *Disquisitio* answered the objections raised against his pseudonymous Severinus de Monzambano, *De Statu imperii germanici* (Geneva 1667), in which the condition of the Holy Roman Empire was assessed and criticised. Cf. *In Severinum de Monzambano*, 1669–72 (A IV, 1, N. 32; see also A IV, 1, 672).

194. See A II, 1, N. 118; A I, 5, N. 355, N. 367, N. 392; A I, 9, N. 214, N. 233, N. 270; Bodemann, *Briefwechsel*, pp. 226–7.

195. See A VI, 3, N. 20/1–2 and N. 21. The text on Plato's *Parmenides* is lost.

196. On the correspondence between Leibniz and Foucher cf. Stuart Brown, "The Leibniz–Foucher Alliance and Its Philosophical Bases." In *Leibniz and His Correspondents*. Ed. by Paul Lodge. Cambridge: Cambridge University Press, 2004, pp. 74–96.

197. Both bookseller and customers seem to have assumed that Foucher's book was a work of logic in the classical sense of the study of the tools of valid reasoning, as opposed to the modern sense of an investigation into the nature of propositions and of truth.

198. Bodemann, *Handschriften*, p. 339.

199. See A VI, 3, N. 22. Mariotte's *Essay de Logique* was published in 1678.

200. *Definitionum juris specimen*, spring–summer 1676* (A VI, 3, N. 88). On jurisprudence cf. also *Remarques considérables sur la Jurisprudence*, 18 January 1676 (A IV, 1, N. 51). On the paucity of his juridical reflections in Paris (especially when compared to his activities in Leipzig and Mainz) see Leibniz to Vincentius Placcius, 10 May 1676 (A II, 1, N. 126).

201. See A VI, 3, N. 24 and N. 25. Leibniz saw Epictetus's *Enchiridion* in the 1670 edition published in Leiden and Antwerpen.

202. See A VI, 3, N. 89/1–6, esp. the fragment *De la vie heureuse* (A VI, 3, N. 89/5).

203. See A VI, 3, N. 23, N. 31, N. 50–56.

204. See A VI, 3, N. 23 and A VI, 3, xxv.

205. See A VI, 3, N. 56.

206. A VI, 3, 472.

207. A II, 1, 259.

208. See G. H. R. Parkinson, "Introduction." In Leibniz, *De Summa Rerum. Metaphysical Papers, 1675–1676*.

209. See A VI, 3, N. 57–77.

210. See the already mentioned *De Vita Beata* (A VI, 3, N. 89) and *Definitionum juris specimen* (A VI, 3, N. 88). *De Arcanis Motus et Mechanica ad puram Geometriam reducenda*, penned in the summer of 1676, contained, however, key metaphysical considerations (see below).

211. See A VI, 3, N. 78–87.

212. See Parkinson, "Introduction," pp. xiv–xv and A VI, 3, xxviii.
213. See A VI, 3, N. 57–8 and N. 61–2. For the following summary of the contents of the papers I am drawing from A VI, 3, xxviii–xxix.
214. See A VI, 3, N. 59, N. 63–66, N. 69.
215. See A VI, 3, N. 67. See also A VI, 3, N. 70.
216. See A VI, 3, N. 68, N. 71–75.
217. *Guilielmi Pacidii de rerum arcanis* (A VI, 3, N. 77).
218. A VI, 3, N. 78. Trans. by Arthur in Leibniz, *The Labyrinth of the continuum*, pp. 129–221. On the problem of the continuum see chap. I. 2.
219. See respectively A VI, 3, N. 79–81 and N. 82.
220. See A VI, 3, N. 83–87 (in particular p. 582).
221. See *De Arcanis Sublimium vel de Summa Rerum*, 11 February 1676 (A VI, 3, N. 60; here p. 474).
222. *Confessio Philosophi* (A VI, 3, 116, 122). Trans. of both passages by Fabrizio Mondadori in "A Harmony of One's Own and Universal Harmony." *Leibniz à Paris (1672–1676). Symposion de la G. W. Leibniz-Gesellschaft.* 2 vols. Wiesbaden: Steiner, 1978, vol. II, p. 152.
223. Grua, 324.
224. On the relation between perfection, quantity of essence, and harmony see Rutherford, *Leibniz and the rational order of nature*, pp. 22–45.
225. A VI, 3, 472. Trans. by Parkinson in Leibniz, *De Summa Rerum*, p. 21. See also *Confessio Philosophi* (A VI, 3, 146) and *Principium meum est, quicquid existere potest, et aliis compatibile est, id existere*, 12 December 1676 (A VI, 3, N. 83). Cf. Mondadori, "A Harmony of One's Own and Universal Harmony."
226. See *De Plenitudine Mundi*, spring* 1676 (A VI, 3, N. 76) and Parkinson, "Introduction," p. l. Cf. also Hans Poser, "Leibniz's Parisaufenthalt in seiner Bedeutung für die Monadenlehre." *Leibniz à Paris (1672–1676). Symposion de la G. W. Leibniz-Gesellschaft.* 2 vols. Wiesbaden: Steiner, 1978, vol. II, pp. 131–47 and Stuart Brown, "The Proto-monadology of the *De Summa Rerum*." In *The Young Leibniz and his Philosophy, 1646–1676*. Ed. by Stuart Brown. Dordrecht: Kluwer, 1999, pp. 263–88.
227. See A VI, 3, 491, 523; Parkinson, "Introduction," pp. xxxii, xli–xlii, l. There is a lively debate whether the *De Summa Rerum* contained pantheistic doctrines of a Spinozistic sort, which Leibniz later abandoned. Cf. in particular Mark Kulstad, "Exploring Middle Ground: Was Leibniz's Conception of God Ever Spinozistic?" *American Catholic Philosophical Quarterly* 76, no. 4 (2002): 671–90.
228. *De Arcanis Motus et Mechanica ad puram Geometriam reducenda*, summer 1676. Ed. by H. J. Hess in *Leibniz à Paris (1672–1676). Symposion de la G. W. Leibniz-Gesellschaft.* 2 vols. Wiesbaden: Steiner, 1978, vol. I, pp. 202–5 (here p. 203). See Michel Fichant, "Mécanisme et métaphysique: le rétablissement des formes substantielles. (1679)." In Michel Fichant, *Science et métaphysique dans Descartes et Leibniz*, Paris: Presses Universitaires de France, 1998, pp. 163–204 (esp. pp. 179–80, 197); Parkinson, "Introduction," p. xlii. On

the relevance of this principle to the Leibnizian concept of force see below, chap. II. 4.

229. See Leibniz to Duke Johann Friedrich, February 1679 (A II, 1, 556) and Müller–Krönert, *Leben und Werk*, p. 39.

230. See Leibniz to Gallois, 2 November 1675 (A III, 1, N. 67).

231. See Leibniz's appraisal of Gallois's personality in a letter to Johann Bernoulli of 24 June 1707 (GM III/2, 816).

232. See A I, 1, N. 313.

233. See A I, 1, N. 341 and N. 342.

234. See A I, 1, N. 267.

235. See Melchior Friedrich von Schönborn to Leibniz, 11 February 1676 (A I, 1 N. 269).

236. See Christian Freiesleben to Leibniz, 26 January 1676 (A I, 1, 441) and Müller–Krönert, *Leben und Werk*, p. 42.

237. See A I, 1, N. 345.

238. See A I, 1, N. 354.

239. See A I, 1, N. 355.

240. See A I, 1, N. 356.

241. See A I, 1, N. 357.

242. See A I, 1, N. 358.

243. *Deutsche Schriften* II, Appendix, pp. 66–7.

244. Writing on 14 February 1676 to Christian Habbeus, Leibniz confided that he wished to be like an "amphibian" (A I, 1, 445), a creature living in the two very different habitats of France and Germany.

245. See Leibniz to Johann Carl Kahm, 24* November 1676 (A I, 2, 3).

246. See *Epistolae tres D. B. de Spinoza ad D. Oldenburgium* (A VI, 3, N. 26).

247. See Hofmann, *Leibniz in Paris*, pp. 227, 292.

248. See A III, 3, N. 98. Cf. also A III, 3, N. 97 and N. 95.

249. See A III, 1, N. 98/1 and Hofmann, *Leibniz in Paris*, pp. 278–9.

250. See A III, 1, N. 88/2 and Hofmann, *Leibniz in Paris*, pp. 283–4.

251. See Aiton, *Leibniz*, p. 67.

252. See Müller–Krönert, *Leben und Werk*, p. 45.

253. Leibniz to Joh. Carl Kahm, 24* November 1676 (A I, 2, 3).

254. A VI, 3, N. 78.

255. See Leibniz to Gallois, September 1677 (A III, 2, 228–9).

256. See A I, 2, 3–4.

257. See Müller–Krönert, *Leben und Werk*, p. 46.

258. See Nunziante, *Organismo come armonia*, pp. 157–8.

259. See Leibniz to Gallois, September* 1677 (A II, 1, 379) and Leibniz to Ernst von Hessen-Rheinfels, 4 / 14 August 1683 (A II, 1, 535). Cf. also *Theodicy*, § 376 (GP VI, 339) and A II, 1, xxvii.

260. See A VI, 3, N. 82.

261. See A VI, 3, xxvii; Müller–Krönert, *Leben und Werk*, p. 46; Nadler, *Spinoza*, p. 341.

262. In A. Foucher de Careil, ed., *Réfutation inédite de Spinoza par Leibniz*. Paris, 1854, p. lxiv. Attention is drawn to this text (probably written in late 1676) by Nadler, *Spinoza*, p. 306. Trans. slightly adapted from Nadler, *Spinoza*, p. 306.

263. *Quod ens perfectissimum existit*, 18–21 November 1676* (A VI, 3, N. 81 and A II, 1, N. 131). See also A VI, 3, N. 79–80.

264. For an illuminating discussion of Leibniz's argumentation see Adams, *Leibniz*, esp. pp. 148–51.

265. A II, 1, 379–80. Trans. by Nadler in *Spinoza*, p. 341.

266. See Leibniz to Joh. Carl Kahm, 24* November 1676 (A I, 2, 4).

PART II

Dreams and Reality
(1676–1716)

4

A Universal Genius as Librarian, Historian, and Mining Engineer: Hanover and Lower Saxony (December 1676–October 1687)

HE TEN YEARS which followed Leibniz's return from Paris witnessed the clash between dreams and reality which was to characterise many aspects of his adult life. Upon his arrival in Hanover, he soon realised that what was expected from him primarily, albeit certainly not exclusively, was to act as keeper of a provincial private library. After his appointment to the supreme court of appeal (*Oberappellationsgericht*) in Mainz at a very young age, his experience of working on juridical reforms of the first importance, his recent years interacting with leading intellectuals in Paris and London, and his outstanding results in fields such as mathematics and technology, Leibniz quite rightly did not feel that his new position was commensurate with his credentials.[1] Notwithstanding his energetic and innovative work for the library, he always resisted being identified as the court librarian. In his mind, he had been appointed as a court counsellor who, among other things, saw to the improvement and rationalisation of the ducal library collections;[2] but who had projects infinitely grander for consideration by the duke. Despite the struggle to clarify his status and to be promoted, Leibniz found in Duke Johann Friedrich a supportive patron who gave a sympathetic hearing to his encyclopaedic plans for the reform and development of the sciences aimed at the defence and advancement of the Christian religion and at the promotion of the 'common good'. With Johann Friedrich's sudden demise in December 1679, this source of support and encouragement was lost. The new duke, Ernst August, did not have much time for Leibniz's Promethean efforts towards universal reform. What he wanted from him was to succeed in draining the water from the mines of the Harz, as Leibniz himself had proposed and promised, or (after the failure of this project) to get on with the writing of a history of the extended family from which the Hanoverian duke derived: the Guelf house. As the power and prestige of the Hanover court grew steadily under Ernst August, so did Leibniz's sense of intellectual isolation. His unease under the new patron was relieved only by his discovery in the duke's wife, Sophie von der Pfalz (1630–1714), of a kindred soul with whom he could discuss what really mattered to him. As he put it some twenty years after arriving in Hanover to his correspondent from England, the Scot Thomas Burnett of Kemney (or Kemnay):

All that bothers me is that I am not in a great city like Paris or London, where there are plenty of learned men from whom one can benefit and even receive assistance. For many things cannot be accomplished on one's own. But here one scarcely finds anyone to talk to; or rather, in this country it is not regarded as appropriate for a courtier to speak of learned matters, and without the Electress they would be spoken of even less.[3]

For a man who had wished an itinerant life pursuing the most up-to-date European research, the first ten years in the service of the dukes of Hanover, during which his travels were restricted to various places in northern Germany, must have felt very claustrophobic. But Leibniz had deep resources. His most exciting adventures were those in new uncharted territories of the mind, which he explored with the aid of all the best instruments devised by past and present generations. With typical enthusiasm he soon began presenting to the dukes a stream of ingenious (though often impractical) schemes for the betterment of their dominions and the generation of an income to be employed, above all, for scientific purposes. At the imperial level he continued to advocate a federal reform of the imperial constitution. At the territorial level he proposed a reorganisation of the legal system, an enhancement of economic and financial activities, the introduction of a greater range of state-supported schools and vocational training, and schemes aimed at the reduction of poverty, the improvement of health, and the provision of social security (including pensions and life insurance).[4] All of these were merely the more practical aspects of his all-embracing vision of universal reform for the improvement of the human condition. At the same time, he energetically resumed its more theoretical components by relaunching the plan of the Catholic Demonstrations conceived in Mainz. He assembled for this purpose vast amounts of preparatory material and developed a number of topics listed under the various chapter titles of the Mainz plan. This period, which in other respects or for other men could have been one of almost complete frustration, saw the refinement of Leibniz's philosophical system in the *Discours de Métaphysique* of 1686, the publication of his calculus (1684) and of other key essays in the *Acta Eruditorum*, the draft of an articulated theological system, and the development of striking innovations in logic, mathematics, and physics.[5]

Under Duke Johann Friedrich:
December 1676–December 1679

In Hanover Leibniz entered in 1676 the capital city of a still relatively unimportant imperial territory which had been elevated to a ducal residence only a generation earlier. In 1636, in the midst of the Thirty Years' War, Duke Georg of Calenberg (1582–1641) – the father of Leibniz's new employer, Duke Johann Friedrich of Hanover (1625–79) – had chosen Hanover as his residence in order to seek safety within the impressive fortifications which surrounded the city.[6] With the arrival of the court, Hanover lost the degree of political autonomy which it had previously enjoyed but gained in compensation importance as the principal residence of one of the Braunschweig-Lüneburg dukes, albeit by no means the most important. The duchy of Calenberg/Hanover was in these years the territory reserved for the junior members of the house of Braunschweig-Lüneburg: the elder sons of the family ruled over the richer and more prestigious neighbouring duchy of Celle. The house of Braunschweig-Lüneburg was, in turn, the cadet line of the Guelf family in Lower Saxony, junior in status to the duchy of Wolfenbüttel, which was ruled by members of the oldest branch of the family, the house of Braunschweig-Wolfenbüttel. Together these Guelf dukes shared descent from a dynasty of great importance in the earlier history of the Holy Roman Empire; collectively they ruled territories of considerable extent in the highly fragmented political geography of the Empire, but the practice of dividing their territory amongst a ruler's sons had fragmented these principalities, and with them the power, prestige, and influence of their rulers. As the sixth son of Duke Wilhelm of Lüneburg, Duke Georg of Calenberg/Hanover occupied a relatively humble official position within this extensive dynasty.

Within this complicated and constrained situation, Duke Georg's elder sons sought to advance themselves by the traditional means of working their way up the hierarchy of Guelf duchies. Georg's eldest son, Christian

Ludwig (1622–65), succeeded his father as duke of Hanover in 1641 and then graduated to the duchy of Celle seven years later after the duke of Celle, Friedrich, died without an heir. Georg's second son, Georg Wilhelm (1624–1705), succeeded his brother first as duke of Hanover in 1648 and then as duke of Celle after Christian Ludwig also died without an heir. It was therefore by something of a dynastic accident that the duchy of Hanover – with its attached territories of Göttingen and Grubenhagen to the southeast – unexpectedly passed to Georg's third son, Johann Friedrich, in 1665.[7]

Despite this unexpected inheritance, the forty-year-old duke proved a remarkably capable ruler, and under his leadership Hanover began its gradual but steady rise from its status as junior duchy of the Braunschweig-Lüneburg family to a prominent position within the Empire. From the outset, it appears, Johann Friedrich's ambitious political objective was higher still: the elevation of his dominions into the ranks of the Electorate – the eight senior princes of the Holy Roman Empire who elected the emperor himself and collectively constituted the college of electors, the highest chamber of the imperial assembly. As a first step towards this audacious goal, Johann Friedrich established in his duchy an absolutist form of government. Following the French model, he played a direct role in the government of all aspects of his domain, almost to a fault, insofar as he had a propensity to micromanage everything.[8] Well educated, he took a deep, personal interest in religious and philosophical questions, and the improvement of the artistic and cultural standing of his duchy featured high on his agenda. During his repeated trips to Italy as a young man, the splendour of Rome in particular had forcefully impressed upon him one of the central lessons of the baroque age, that the cultural splendour of a court was a measure of its power; and in subsequent years all of Europe had watched the evolution of Louis XIV's Paris and Versailles into the example *par excellence* of this marriage of culture and power. In his own comparatively small domains Johann Friedrich sought to replicate the same idea. He extended the Leineschloß – the palace on Hanover's river Leine, built by his father immediately after the transfer of his court. He transformed a modest grange on the outskirts of Hanover into a summer residence with extensive gardens, the palace of Herrenhausen. He employed French as the court language, introduced opera, created an art collection, and moved his private library from his former residence in

Celle to the Leineschloß. Last but not least, he sought to add intellectual lustre to his court by attracting brilliant minds to his service.

Small wonder, therefore, that the duke's attention had been attracted by the young Gottfried Wilhelm Leibniz as early as 1669.[9] Johann Friedrich's patience in waiting for the arrival of his new counsellor for nearly two years after the formal acceptance of his offer of employment is clear evidence of his appreciation of Leibniz's potential service to the court. Yet upon arrival in Hanover, Leibniz was initially disappointed by the terms of his employment. The duke's first approach to him in 1669 had taken place in the context of a cabinet reshuffle necessitated by the recent death of the chancellor in Hanover, Heinrich Langenbeck, a senior member of the duke's privy council. The young Leibniz – ambitious as well as optimistic – seems to have drawn the implication that he could expect an appointment to the privy council itself.[10] But despite his self-evident promise, the thirty-one-year-old peripatetic philosopher and jurist from Leipzig was still far too young and inexperienced to assume one of the central offices of state. The privy council or *Geheimer Rat* – led in the late 1670s by Otto Grote (1637–93) – constituted the highest administrative body of the duchy, charged with overall responsibility for its domestic and foreign affairs. Its members were the duke's highest officers, each responsible for managing an important section of the principality's administrative machinery. From 1665 the privy counsellor Hieronymus von Witzendorff (c. 1625–90) oversaw the *Kammer*, the cabinet office charged with the general administration of the duchy; the vice-chancellor Ludolf Hugo (1630–1704) directed the *Kanzlei*, the chancery or ministry of justice; from 1674 Gerhard Wolter Molanus (or van der Muelen, 1633–1722) supervised the *Konsistorium* or directorate of church affairs; and the nobleman Friedrich Casimir Freiherr von Eltz (c. 1620–82) served simultaneously as *Landdrost* (or governor) and *Berghauptmann* (or minister of mines) for the attached duchy of Grubenhagen.[11] With the smooth administration of the reorganised duchy at stake and the legitimate expectations of other loyal and longstanding senior servants to consider, it was no disparagement of Leibniz's potential for the duke to appoint him initially to a far more junior office. Leibniz was doubly distressed, to be sure, by the duke's decision at the outset to employ him primarily where he needed him most: in the direction of his library. Shortly after taking up his duties, Leibniz reminded the duke that he had been offered the position as a counsellor – if

not that of a privy counsellor or *Geheimer Rat*, at least that of a court
counsellor or *Hofrat* – and he therefore gently insisted that his remuneration as librarian should be in addition to the standard salary of a court
counsellor.[12] Such an arrangement eventually proved to be to Leibniz's
financial advantage, but as a junior *Hofrat* he nevertheless found himself
in a relatively humble position within the hierarchy of the Hanoverian
court: on the third lowest of ten rungs in the ladder of promotion.[13] As
a further index of his official status, the typical annual salary of a *Hofrat*
– some 400–500 talers – was scarcely one-quarter of the 1500–2000 talers
earned by a *Geheimer Rat*.[14]

As it turned out, the position of court librarian offered one very concrete
advantage which Leibniz proved very able to exploit. The library recently
transferred from Celle was rehoused within the Leineschloß, immediately
adjacent to the duke's private apartments and dining rooms. The library in
turn included quarters for the librarian, which were occupied by Leibniz
upon his arrival. Despite his position towards the bottom of the official
hierarchy, therefore, from his very arrival in Hanover Leibniz occupied a
physical position at the very heart of the court.[15] Although he was profes-
sionally excluded from the duke's formal privy council, physical proximity
to the duke's privy chambers facilitated frequent and relatively informal
direct interaction, through which Leibniz quickly came effectively to serve
as a personal adviser to the duke on a wide range of questions. Although
never entrusted by Johann Friedrich (or indeed Ernst August) with direct
responsibility for political decisions or diplomatic negotiations, Leibniz
was regularly consulted on questions of law and politics.[16] No less importantly, he noted in the duke a genuine interest in the intellectual, scientific,
and practical advancement of his principality which Leibniz was uniquely
equipped to shape and encourage. Last but not least, their personal closeness derived in significant measure from their shared commitments to
the advancement of the Christian religion and the reconciliation of its
churches.

To the great dismay of his Lutheran family and subjects, Johann
Friedrich, when he succeeded to the duchy of Hanover, had been a convert from Lutheranism to Catholicism for fourteen years. His marriage in
1668 to the sixteen-year-old Benedicta Henriette (1652–1730) – a Catholic
daughter of Eduard von Pfalz-Simmern (1625–63) and Anna Gonzaga
(1616–84), raised in France and carrying Paris in her heart for her whole
life – did nothing to reconcile the people of Hanover to their new prince.

Fortunately, like most of the German princely converts of his generation, having chosen his own religion, Johann Friedrich did not exercise his right to impose his new faith on his subjects.[17] Although he reserved the palace chapel for the Catholic cult, he allowed the building in Hanover of a major new Lutheran church, the St. Johannis Neustädter Kirche – raising in effect a permanent, concrete monument to his policy of religious toleration. More generally, Johann Friedrich respected the predominant Lutheranism of his subjects and family while promoting talks aimed at the reunification of the Catholic and Lutheran churches. For this purpose, he received favourably in Hanover in 1676 and 1679 one of the clergymen central to the emperor's entourage: the Franciscan Cristobal de Rojas y Spinola (c. 1626–95).[18] Born in the Netherlands to a Spanish noblewoman and an Italian officer, raised by the Franciscans in Cologne, and operating for his order in Spain and the Spanish Netherlands, Rojas had joined the imperial court in Vienna in 1660 as the confessor of the imperial minister, Prince Portia, before being nominated titular bishop of Tina in 1668. Although committed to the orthodoxy of Trent, his background in the Netherlands opened him to a tolerant attitude and to the search for ecumenical reconciliation. Entrusted by the Emperor with the task of sounding out the princes of German Protestant territories on the issue of church reunification, he toured the German courts at least four times, including visits to Johann Friedrich's Hanover in 1676 and 1679. However unsatisfactory such religious views may have been to the great majority of the duke's Lutheran subjects, Johann Friedrich's religious stance was in perfect harmony with Leibniz's irenical agenda – a harmony perhaps preestablished by their earlier frequentation of the irenical court of the prince-archbishop of Mainz.

On his arrival in Hanover in mid-December 1676 Leibniz was promptly summoned by the duke's librarian, Tobia Fleischer, who was impatiently waiting to hand over his responsibilities in order to move on to the position of cabinet secretary at the court of Denmark.[19] The receipt duly signed by Leibniz on 16 December 1676 documented that he had been entrusted "piece by piece" with the 3310 volumes and 158 manuscripts which constituted the ducal library[20] – meagre fare in comparison to the grandest Parisian libraries, but quite remarkable as a private collection. For all his misgivings about his status and remuneration, Leibniz took his new job to heart. As early as January 1677, he presented the Duke with a series of proposals for improving the library.[21] In his view the holdings of a general library should have been divided into two categories: books which were absolutely necessary (such as lexica, reference works, and textbooks) and books which were merely useful. After listing to the duke the many sources from which he could acquire material and information on the best current publications (notably his already vast network of correspondents), Leibniz pressed the necessity of a proper catalogue of the library holdings.

While settling into his new job, he began to meet the senior officers of the court, among them one of the people with whom he developed a close and trusting relationship stretching over four decades: the Lutheran Molanus, who presided over Hanover's ecclesiastical affairs as well as (after 1677) the Cistercian monastery of Loccum. Molanus had studied in the nearby university of Helmstedt under the leading irenical Lutheran theologian, Georg Calixt, before serving as professor of mathematics (1659) and of theology (1664) at the University of Rinteln (Hesse). As president of the *Konsistorium* and abbot of a prominent Lutheran monastery, he played a pivotal role in the Hanoverian talks on ecclesiastical reunification initiated by Leopold of Habsburg through Bishop Rojas. Although Leibniz was not directly involved in the first waves of negotiations, in due course he was to collaborate closely with both Molanus and Rojas. Not long after making Leibniz's acquaintance, Molanus facilitated the epistolary contact between him and one of his friends, the committed Cartesian and former professor of logic, physics, and mathematics in Rinteln, Arnold Eckhard (d. 1685).[22] The highlight of this philosophical and theological exchange was a debate on Cartesianism between the two thinkers arranged by Molanus in Loccum on 15 April 1677. In the presence of one of Molanus's friars, Leibniz and Eckhard discussed in particular the Cartesian argument for the existence of God hinging on the concept of *ens perfectissimum*.[23] The debate was followed by several letters on this issue, which grew into a rich and insightful philosophical exchange which stretched until the summer.[24]

At the beginning of November 1677 another prominent person joined the entourage of Johann Friedrich: the famous Danish physician, anatomist, and geologist Niels Stensen (or Nicolaus Steno) (1638–86). Stensen, who had converted from Lutheranism to Catholicism in 1667, had been sent to Hanover by Pope Innocent XI as apostolic vicar of the North on the suggestion of Johann Friedrich himself.[25] Leibniz had been anticipating his arrival since September, hoping to find a congenial conversation partner in the once very remarkable scientist and now keen theologian; but on both scores the encounter proved disappointing. Stensen had completely abandoned his scientific researches after his conversion to Catholicism, and refused even to speak of them. As Leibniz remarked later on in the *Theodicy*, "from a great Physician he became a mediocre Theologian. He almost did not want to hear talking of the marvels of nature, and it would have been necessary a direct order from the Pope *in virtute sanctae obedientiae*" to get any new scientific observation out of him.[26] Theologically, on the other hand, he proved sceptical (if not downright unsympathetic) towards the way in which, over the years, Leibniz sought to advance ecclesiastical reunification. Perhaps the most fecund area of their exchange proved to be philosophy. Leibniz passed on to him a fair copy of his *Confessio Philosophi*.[27] Stensen read Leibniz's work with attention, writing his objections in the margin of the manuscript; Leibniz, in turn, meticulously annotated the manuscript with his replies to Stensen's remarks.[28] A further direct confrontation between Leibniz and Stensen on topics related to the *Confessio Philosophi*, notably the issue of freedom, took place on 7 December 1677 and was recorded by Leibniz in a philosophically highly significant text.[29]

In addition to direct exchange on philosophical and theological issues with Molanus, Eckhard, Stensen, and the Duke himself, Leibniz kept up a lively intellectual debate with a variety of correspondents, notably the new friends and contacts he had gained during his Paris period. These included Tschirnhaus (who copied for him the beginning of Descartes's *Recherche de la Vérité*, one of the pieces in the French philosopher's Nachlaß which they had perused together in Paris);[30] Spinoza's friend, Georg Hermann Schuller; the historian Henri Justel; and the philosophers Simon Foucher, Pierre-Daniel Huet, and Nicolas Malebranche. In this period, epistolary correspondence was for Leibniz virtually his only direct contact with cutting-edge mathematical and scientific research. During his first year in Hanover alone Leibniz's correspondents in these fields included Oldenburg, Schuller, Tschirnhaus, Gallois, Mohr, Mercator, Mariotte, Ollivier, Cassini, Hudde, Fabri, La Roque (the new editor of the *Journal des Sçavans*), Charles-Honoré Duc de Chevreuse, and Boyle (although the latter appears not to have responded to Leibniz's short note of October 1677).[31] Amongst the many topics of discussion, particular attention was given to the Cartesian doctrine of motion as well as to another field of research at the centre of seventeenth-century natural philosophy: optics. Especially in the correspondence with Mariotte and Huygens, Leibniz tackled issues with far-reaching scientific and philosophical implications, such as the doctrine of colours and the employment of revolutionary optical instruments, such as the microscope and the telescope. In turn, the wealth of technical innovations concerning measuring instruments (notably watches, barometers, thermometers, and hygrometers) could not fail to capture the young man's interest or to stimulate his own scientific and technical creativity.[32]

In the pile of letters accumulating on his Hanoverian desk with welcome news from the scientific world, one in particular was of outstanding value. On 1 July (21 June O.S.) 1677 he finally received the second, long letter from Newton (the so-called *epistola posterior*), dated 24 October (3 November N.S.) 1676 but belatedly forwarded by Oldenburg on 12 May 1677.[33] In it Newton compactly described his results, in particular concealing under an anagram the basic principle of his calculus. The anagram (the solution to which Newton later revealed in a letter to Wallis)[34] stated: from an equation containing fluents to find the fluxions, and vice versa.[35] Leibniz replied on the same day on which the letter arrived, returning (as usual via Oldenburg) a long commentary in which he introduced the principles and notation of his differential calculus.[36] This was one of the last letters which passed between Leibniz and the secretary to the Royal Society. During his usual summer holiday in his farm in Kent, Oldenburg became ill and died suddenly in September 1677. Leibniz's ensuing attempts to establish a correspondence with other Fellows of the Royal Society did not meet with success. With Oldenburg died his direct link with the Royal Society and English scientific circles more generally at the very moment at which, due to his Hanoverian isolation, he would most have benefited from it.

In the midst of all this private correspondence, Leibniz was trying to find a way to prove beyond doubt that he could be invaluable to the duke outside the library as well as within it. He had barely set foot in Hanover when he produced the first of a series of proposals on improving the duchy's judicial system.[37] An even better opportunity to employ his legal and historical abilities came in relation to the peace conference held in Nijmegen with a view to ending Louis XIV's aggression against Holland. The house of Braunschweig-Lüneburg was greatly offended that the Guelf princes had been refused direct representation at the conference on the ground that the Empire was adequately represented by the emperor and electors. Probably prompted by the duke, Leibniz sprang into action.

Between June and October 1677 he prepared under the pseudonym of "Caesarinus Fürstenerius" a substantial work in which he argued on historical and legal grounds for the right to a proper international representation of the major German princes who did not enjoy electoral status. In so doing, he developed the idea that sovereignty over a certain territory should be intended in a functional way. Sovereignty, according to this doctrine, could be shared by different authorities depending on the function they performed within a given territory. In the Holy Roman Empire, Leibniz conceded, the ultimate *majestas* rested with the emperor; but this did not override the supremacy of princes over their own territories. In contrast to Jean Bodin's model of absolute, eternal, and indivisible sovereignty,[38] Leibniz thereby proposed a federal model according to which sovereignty admitted degrees and division.[39] Applying this doctrine to the case of Braunschweig-Lüneburg, Leibniz claimed that the major nonelectoral German princes (though not the lesser German rulers) were as 'sovereign' in their territories as the electors or the king of France in their respective states and therefore had rightful claims to direct representation.[40]

Leibniz's memorandum, however, rapidly grew into a dense, learned, book-length Latin treatise rather than the agile pamphlet originally intended. In the hope of influencing the great and the mighty busily negotiating in Nijmegen, he therefore recast his main arguments into a lively French dialogue entitled *Entretien de Philarete et d'Eugene* which was distributed to the Nijmegen delegates by Leibniz's trusted contact in the Netherlands, Georg Hermann Schuller.[41] Shortly thereafter, Johann Friedrich sought to use his marital relations with the English crown to enlist the active support of Charles II in the campaign.[42] Once again on the duke's behalf, in mid-December 1677 Leibniz outlined the Braunschweig-Lüneburg case in a "Memorial" for Joachim Heinrich von Bülow, the duke's official representative in London.[43] While such diplomatic pamphleteering might seem a regrettable distraction for a man known to posterity above all as a brilliant mathematician, metaphysician, and logician, this federal ideal was a central part of Leibniz's comprehensive reform programme, grounded in his deepest principles, both theoretical and practical. At the theoretical level, this vision of federal unity in diversity was merely the working out on the political plane of Leibniz's fundamental metaphysical convictions. At the practical level, this clear delineation of the shared sovereignty of imperial and territorial institutions was the key,

in Leibniz's mind, to restoring the strength to the German empire necessary both for its peace at home and its security from enemies abroad. The
firmness of Leibniz's commitment to these principles is demonstrated
over the following fourteen years by no less than sixteen subsequent editions of the dialogue between Philarete and Eugene, each successively
adapted to constantly changing political conditions.[44]

Alongside these major incursions into the territory of politics, Leibniz
was also developing an effervescent entrepreneurial side. Firmly convinced that scientific progress and economic prosperity could and should
reinforce one another, Leibniz found a kindred spirit in Johann Daniel
Crafft, a trusted friend from the Mainz years with whom he carried out
a voluminous correspondence on chemical, technological, and commercial issues until Crafft's death in 1697.[45] In March 1677 he discussed
with Crafft the production of phosphorus, which had been accidentally
discovered in 1669 by Hennig Brand of Hamburg while attempting to
transmute silver into gold through the use of a distillate from urine. The
distillate did not perform the wonder Brand (and a host of other people)
was after, but was nevertheless a substance with remarkable properties,
notably the emission of flashes of light. The discovery was communicated to Crafft (at the time a commercial adviser to the court of Saxony),
whose help was enlisted for the advertisement of the new substance and
its possible commercial exploitation. Assuming a self-made role of adviser
in applied technology, Leibniz drew the duke's attention to this wonderful new chemical element and its commercial prospects, while also
publishing an article on the subject in the *Journal des Sçavans*.[46] The duke
was intrigued. At his request Leibniz arranged a visit from Brand for a
practical demonstration; but despite promising beginnings no viable commercial application could be found.[47] Meanwhile, Leibniz recommended
to the duke another of Crafft's technical ventures, an innovative wool
manufacture.[48] There followed a flurry of proposals to explore further
technical innovations, including a cipher-machine, a new type of wagon,
the mechanisation of silk production, improved watches, a number of
pharmacological remedies, and Leibniz's own calculating machine (for
further work on which the inventor tried to have the Parisian construc-
tor Ollivier called to Hanover, though without success).[49] In Leibniz's
judgement, even seemingly improbable enterprises were worthy of critical attention, such as the attempts at the production of gold carried
forward by the Baron Wenzel von Rheinburg in Vienna[50] and by Johann

Joachim Becher in Holland.[51] Far more mundane, but destined to have a far greater significance for his life, was his suggestion for the first time in August 1677 to investigate a possible link between the Guelf house and the ancient Italian noble family of Este.[52] Even less philosophically inclined princes than Johann Friedrich could see the dynastic attraction of this archival research; and long after many of these other projects had been shelved forever, Leibniz would continue to struggle with the outcome of this fateful suggestion.

Despite his best efforts to demonstrate his capabilities, Leibniz's first year in Hanover continued to be plagued by difficulties regarding his status, the appropriate remuneration for it, and the timely payment of his salary. What pained Leibniz most of all was the fact that he had not yet been officially introduced as a *Hofrat*, reinforcing the perception that he was merely the duke's librarian. In January 1677 he asked for the payment of the second instalment of his 1676 annual stipend, specifying that the 200 talers paid to him in Paris were not to be deducted from it, since they had been intended as travel expenses (or at least he had taken them to be).[53] In February he asked the duke to introduce him officially as *Hofrat* and to raise his pay on the ground of his additional duties as librarian.[54] By June Leibniz must have had more than a few misgivings about his acceptance of the Hanover post, since he prudently explored the possibility of being employed by the emperor: probably through the mediation of his friend Crafft, he sought a recommendation to Leopold I via Cristobal de Rojas y Spinola.[55] In September Leibniz's pay was raised to 500 talers per annum in two instalments, but he had to wait until November 1678 for the actual disbursement.[56] On 2 October 1677 he asked again to be introduced as a *Hofrat*.[57] The importance of one's formal place in the court hierarchy was doubtless being brought home to Leibniz by a thousand niceties of court protocol. Following the Christmas service of 1677, for instance, the duke's self-important physician, Jakob Franz Kotzcbue, loudly remonstrated to Johann Friedrich that Leibniz had taken a place ahead of him in church, without respecting what the physician regarded as the correct order of precedence according to rank.[58] As it happened, the duke had finally obliged Leibniz's plea to introduce him officially as a *Hofrat* shortly before this unpleasant episode, thereby neatly turning the tables on the indignant doctor. No doubt Leibniz's satisfaction was further increased by the simultaneous enhancement of his salary to 600 talers per annum in two instalments.[59]

With his status and remuneration at least provisionally sorted out, from the end of 1677 onward Leibniz was able to employ an assistant factotum, Jobst Dietrich Brandshagen.[60] By late 1677 the new *Hofrat* felt reasonably content with his lot in life. Hanover was not Paris, but there were a number of notable advantages to his new position. Writing to Gallois, he acknowledged that his stipend was significantly higher than the one initially offered by the duke and was supplemented by additional benefits such as accommodation and dining rights. More importantly, in Hanover he had "the satisfaction of being really close to a Prince the extraordinary talents and great virtues of whom cause a stir in the world. I enjoy . . . an access to the Prince that gives me the opportunity of feeling often the effects of his goodness, and of becoming aware of the generous sentiments of which he has the soul full."[61] At the beginning of 1678 he even tried to convince his friend Tschirnhaus to join him in Hanover, painting for this purpose a rosy picture of Johann Friedrich's court.[62]

But no matter how positive and stimulating his relationship with Johann Friedrich, the desire for an escape from the confines of Hanover must have grown quickly in a man who liked travelling and meeting people as much as Leibniz. Shortly after the death of Spinoza on 21 February 1677, Leibniz proposed to visit Holland in order to study the great philosopher's unpublished papers, but this suggestion regrettably came to nothing.[63] Aside from accompanying the court on a hunting expedition to Johann Friedrich's rural residence in Linsburg near Nienburg in June 1677, it was not until the summer of 1678 that Leibniz was able to undertake a trip outside the duchy to nearby Hamburg. The pretext was provided, as it happened, by his duties as ducal librarian: his main assignment there was to negotiate the acquisition of the substantial library of the late Martin Fogel, a Hamburg savant with whom Leibniz had been in epistolary contact during the Mainz years. Since Fogel's death in 1675, Leibniz had urged his friends based in Hamburg, Habbeus and Placcius, to prevent the dispersion of his valuable collection of some 3600 volumes. Now he was able to secure the entire lot for Johann Friedrich, doubling at a stroke the holdings of the ducal library. As he boasted to the duke, he had managed to lower the price from 2400 to 2000 talers, despite the fact that the collection was worth at least twice the final price.[64] More revealing still of his deeper intentions was his summary in a few words for the duke of his conception of an ideal library: "My opinion has always been and still is that a Library should be an Encyclopaedia, that is to say, when needed, one could learn in it of all the matters of consequence and of practice."[65]

But in Hamburg Leibniz was seeking more than Fogel's library. Although Spinoza's papers remained beyond reach, another highlight of his visit was his attempt to stimulate a proper edition of the manuscript Nachlaß of the Hamburg logician and philosopher whom Leibniz greatly admired: the greatest German philosopher of the previous generation, Joachim Jungius (1587–1657), to whose circle Fogel had belonged. Sadly, Leibniz's efforts did not bear fruit, and the virtue of the project was tragically revealed fourteen years later when the most significant part of Jungius's Nachlaß was destroyed by a fire in the house of its keeper, Jungius's student, Johann Vagetius.[66] During his visit Leibniz also met the leading German chemist and expert in mechanics, Johann Joachim Becher, with whom he discussed in passing possible improvements to wagons. Unfortunately Becher was a dubious character, not above deceiving the gullible with his chemical skills; and after Leibniz foiled one of his frauds, Becher revenged himself by distorting and ridiculing the Hamburg conversation about wagons in his posthumously published book, *Närrische Weisheit und weise Narrheit* (1682).[67] On 2 September Leibniz left Hamburg for Celle, though not before borrowing eighty-six manuscripts from Fogel's Nachlaß,[68] perhaps knowing from his own experience that a thinker's most innovative writings sometimes remain unpublished. Further evidence of his keen interest in the preservation and study of the manuscript remains of recently deceased philosophers was his acquisition (possibly in 1678–9 via Schuller) of a manuscript copy of Descartes's still unpublished *Regulae ad directionem ingenii*.[69]

In the autumn of 1678 Leibniz's fertile mind conceived yet another series of ingenious and wide-ranging practical projects. To begin with, he presented the duke with a *promemoria* on the enlargement and rebuilding of the library space needed to accommodate the Fogel collection – an enterprise which brought him into collision with the construction manager, Geronimo Sartorio.[70] Thereafter he tabled a number of comprehensive proposals for the duke's consideration, outlining amongst other things the means of improving the public administration, reorganising the archives under a general director (a position which he envisaged for himself), and enhancing farming and agriculture. In them he indicated concrete measures for simplifying and rendering more efficient the machine of the state according to a golden rule which reflected his distinctive outlook on day-to-day practical activities as best tackled in the context of a global plan: "Everything should be administrated through as few officers as possible, especially Justice, the police and other similar things. Many secretaries, and few counsellors; what is needed is universal men. For one who can connect all things can do more than ten people."[71] Once again, it is not difficult to surmise the identity of at least one of these "universal men." A more efficient and less expensive public administration, he argued further, would benefit everyone. Moreover, the habit of saving should be encouraged in the private sphere as well, for instance, by means of a tax on luxury items. A number of social security measures should be introduced to provide a safety net for those in need (such as widows and orphans), and allowances should be made to provide workers with the necessary time for leisure activities (including dancing and enjoying a good beer).[72] Although well beyond the scope of the 'new philosophy' narrowly conceived, many of these practical proposals were highly reminiscent of those promoted a few decades earlier by universal reformers such as Comenius, and still more by his Anglo-German associate, Samuel Hartlib.

During the same period Leibniz conceived a further series of plans for the advancement of culture and science through the creation of various societies, notably a *Societas sive Ordo Caritatis* or a *Societas Theophilorum ad celebrandas Laudes Dei*.[73] Just as, decades later, he summarized the objectives of the Berlin Society of Sciences with the motto *theoria cum praxi*, likewise in these early plans he envisaged a society composed of two kinds of people: "the contemplative" and "the active". On the model of an international society such as the Jesuits, the "contemplative" members of the *Societas* or *Ordo Caritatis* would devote themselves to celebrating the glory of God through the advancement of science, including the development of metaphysics, logic, jurisprudence, and moral philosophy, the compilation of a *Thesaurus* of the whole of human knowledge, and the creation of a universal, formal language to serve as the key instrument of evangelisation. The calling of the "active" members of the society would rather be "to succour the poor" and care for the sick, especially through the promotion of a proper medical system.[74] As for Leibniz himself, he dreamed of becoming a sort of minister of culture with the task of coordinating the sciences, the arts, the university, and the charitable foundations of the duchy of Hanover.[75]

The practical project which was to have the most important impact on his life, however, was another one: the project of draining water from the ducal mines in the Harz, a range of mountains situated southeast of Hanover between Wolfenbüttel and Göttingen. The Harz mines had been a crucial source of revenue for the Guelf dynasty since the discovery of silver there in 968. After a combination of famine, disease, and destruction reduced the local population by one-quarter by the end of the Thirty Years War, production in the mines bounced back until between 1661 and 1720 Harz silver – the most valuable mineral extracted from the mines – fluctuated between 41 and 53 percent of the entire German production. Not all of this flowed into the Hanoverian treasury, of course: the Guelf dukes divided the proceeds from their mines via a formula as complicated as that through which they divided their lands and based largely on the same dynastic principles. But in his experiments in the Harz, the newly arrived Hanoverian court counsellor was immersing himself, not in tangential matters, but in concerns central to the prosperity of the Guelf house over centuries.[76]

Mining is nevertheless far removed from metaphysics; and Leibniz's protracted entanglements in the Harz are yet another source of frustration to later philosophers, who lament his distraction from theoretical questions, and also of confusion to later historians, who have misconstrued his motives. Yet in the mind of Leibniz – as in the philosophical worldview developing within it – everything was connected to everything. In fact, Leibniz became so engrossed in the Harz project from the autumn of 1678 onwards precisely because he saw it as a way to generate a steady stream of income adequate to finance the core of his perennial plan to reform the entire encyclopaedia of the sciences: the development of the *characteristica universalis*. Such an audacious project was beyond the abilities of even the most gifted individual and could only be successfully pursued collaboratively. The organisation of this collective effort would require the establishment of a learned foundation, which in turn could be sustained only by a generous and perennial source of funding. If his employer – however sympathetic in principle – could not or would not release the funding needed for such a speculative philanthropic endeavour, Leibniz's best hope of obtaining the necessary finance lay in finding a way of tapping into the chief source of income, not only of the duke of Hanover, but of the Guelf dynasty as a whole: the steady stream of silver and other metals issuing from the Harz mines. From this perspective, the intractable technical problems confronted by the Harz miners represented for Leibniz an irresistible opportunity: if he could apply his technical ingenuity and advanced knowledge of physics and mathematics to the solution of one or more of these longstanding problems and thereby increase the efficiency of the Harz mines, he could rightly claim royalties on the resulting inventions and cream off from the wealth flooding from the mines the income necessary to fund his epoch-making philosophical project from his own greatly enhanced personal resources, both before and after his death.[77] Leibniz's tenacious attempts to solve the practical problems of the Harz, in short, were sustained by his equally tenacious desire to provide the practical foundations of his key theoretical project: the development of the *characteristica universalis.*

The problem which he eventually isolated for scrutiny and the solution which he proposed for it were both perfectly simple in principle. In order to drain the water which constantly seeped into the depths of the Harz mines, the miners had previously harnessed a network of mountain streams to power a system of hydraulic pumps. In dry years, however, the supply of water was insufficient to keep the Harz pumps working continuously, and the result was a drastic fall in production. As it happens, 1678–9 was one of those unlucky years, and the decrease of almost 50 percent in their income from the mines prompted the dukes to take seriously the search for alternative technical solutions. Where water power failed, the alternative source of inanimate energy was wind power; and Leibniz's basic idea was to supplement water power with wind power. Originally, in fact, this idea stemmed from another court counsellor working in the mining centre of Clausthal: the Dutch engineer Peter Hartzingk. But Leibniz insisted that he could devise windmills and pumps far more efficient than those envisaged by Hartzingk, and his persistent proposals eventually gained the favour of the duke.[78]

The basic arrangement was hammered out during Leibniz's first stay in the Harz between mid-September and early October 1679. On 30 September he signed a contract with the Mining Office in Clausthal in which he undertook to test, for the duration of one year and at his own expense, the efficiency of its machines in keeping one of the mines – the "Dorothea Landeskron" – free of water. After the successful completion of this test, in his capacity of inventor of the new devices, he would have earned a life annuity of 1200 talers.[79] Two days later, however, Johann Friedrich's chamberlain, Johann Carl Kahm, wrote on the duke's behalf asking Leibniz to break off his preliminary work in the Harz and return to Hanover for further consultation.[80] New objections had been raised against Leibniz's project and the duke wanted a fresh look at the situation. It took Leibniz a stream of letters written in mid-October to convince the duke of the soundness of his project, but in the end he succeeded.[81] On 25 October 1679 Johann Friedrich finally ratified the contract between his new, self-appointed mining engineer and the Mining Office.[82]

Despite his fresh victory, Leibniz did not head straight back to the Harz. His next trip out of Hanover in the second half of December was to visit the seriously ill Abbess of Herford, that is, Elisabeth von der Pfalz (1618–1680), oldest daughter of the Palatine Elector and 'Winter King' of Bohemia, Friedrich V, and of Elisabeth Stuart.[83] He had met Princess Elisabeth roughly one year before on the occasion of her visit to Hanover. Not surprisingly, in this very remarkable woman, who had played a key role in Descartes's life from 1643 onwards,[84] Leibniz found one of the very few persons with whom he could share his philosophical interests during his first Hanover years. Elisabeth drew Leibniz's attention to the *Conversations chrétiennes* of Nicolas Malebranche, from which (probably in December 1678) Leibniz transcribed a series of excerpts.[85] At the abbess's bedside in Herford, Leibniz met an old acquaintance of the Mainz period, Franciscus Mercurius van Helmont, who served as Elisabeth's physician,[86] as well as Elisabeth's sister, Sophie von der Pfalz.[87] Leibniz could scarcely have imagined from this first brief encounter the important role Sophie was to play as duchess of Hanover in relieving his intellectual isolation. Still less could he have anticipated how soon her residence in Hanover would begin. Yet on 4 January 1680 this little group in Herford received news of the unexpected death of Duke Johann Friedrich. The duke, who had left Hanover for Italy in November, had become ill in Augsburg, where he died on 28 December 1679. Leibniz abandoned his plan to travel further to Osnabrück, Paderborn, and Neuhaus to meet the bishop of Münster and Paderborn, Ferdinand von Fürstenberg. Instead he returned to Hanover, where the body of the late duke was accompanied by his brother, Ernst August. After Boineburg and Johann Philipp von Schönborn, the loss of Johann Friedrich cost Leibniz – still only thirty-five years old – his last genuinely sympathetic and supportive main employer. The two successive dukes whom he served in Hanover, Ernst August and his son, Georg Ludwig, were to regard him with increasing detachment and annoyance.

Under Duke Ernst August: January 1680–October 1687

From the marriage of Johann Friedrich and Benedicta Henriette were born four daughters but no male heir. The duchy therefore passed to the late duke's youngest brother, the Lutheran prince-bishop of Osnabrück, Ernst August (1629–98).[88] Ernst August was a very different character than his predecessor. He had no deep personal interest in art or science, which he supported only insofar as they boosted the prestige of his court and indicated its power. Religion itself had for him a merely political meaning. Unlike his brother Johann Friedrich, who had converted to and maintained Catholicism despite the fact that doing so endangered his accession to power, Ernst August would have happily exchanged his Lutheranism for another confession if a palpable political advantage had followed from it.[89] Since a good relationship with the Habsburg emperor was a virtual precondition of becoming the ninth Elector, Ernst August followed the example of Johann Friedrich and gave a sympathetic reception to Rojas when the bishop visited Hanover on behalf of Leopold I in 1683 for further talks on ecclesiastical reunification. Generally, however, Ernst August had always been much closer to his older brother Georg Wilhelm, the duke of Celle, than to Johann Friedrich: in fact, when Georg Wilhelm broke off his engagement to Sophie von der Pfalz, Ernst August was quite happy to step in and marry her with the approval of her former fiancé in 1658.

One might have thought that, by any standard, Sophie made an ideal wife. Intelligent, witty, and good looking, perhaps more importantly to Ernst August she also had plenty of blue blood in her veins. The twelfth child born from the union of the elector Palatine, Friedrich V, and Elisabeth Stuart, Sophie was thus the daughter and granddaughter of two kings: the 'Winter King' of Bohemia, and James VI of Scotland and I of England. Born and raised first in exile at The Hague and then back in the restored Palatinate, she maintained her Reformed confession throughout her life. Crucially, while all of Ernst August's older brothers died without legitimate heirs, Sophie blessed him with six sons and one remarkable daughter (Sophie Charlotte), and their royal pedigree helped intertwine the House of Hanover with some of the leading ruling families of Europe, with epoch-making consequences for the future of the family. Yet despite these obvious virtues, Ernst August, like his eldest brother, pursued extra-marital interests as well. Georg Wilhelm had preferred to marriage the relationship with a mistress, Eleonore d'Olbreuse, who gave him his only surviving child, Sophie Dorothea (1666–1726). For his part, Ernst August maintained an open liaison with the wife of his Prime Minister, Franz Ernst von Platen, which Sophie chose to tolerate with good grace.

Like Johann Friedrich, Ernst August set his sights on the elevation of his duchy to the rank of a ninth electorate. Unlike his predecessor, he was also prepared to pursue this objective regardless of the personal or familial distress it entailed. In a bold move designed radically to expand his duchy into a major state within the Empire, he arranged the marriage of his eldest son and heir, Georg Ludwig (1660–1727), to the young man's cousin, Sophie Dorothea, the sixteen-year-old daughter of Duke Georg Wilhelm of Celle. Such a match was strongly opposed by his wife Sophie, who continued to regard her illegitimate niece with suspicious and dislike despite Georg Wilhelm's eventual marriage to his mistress in 1675. Nor did this marriage of cousins bode well for the future mental health of the Hanoverian dynasty. But for a hard-headed ruler with limited scruples, the virtue of this union was undeniable: the marriage of these cousins would unite the senior duchy of Celle-Lüneburg with the junior duchy of Hanover under Ernst August's heir, doubling his lands and enhancing his dynastic status at one stroke. The marriage, which took place in November 1682, evolved into a personal tragedy for Sophie Dorothea, who spent the last thirty years of her life as an estranged wife living in complete isolation in Ahlden, where she was prevented from seeing her two children ever again.[90] But for the house of Hanover it was a triumph: on the death of Georg Wilhelm in 1705, Celle passed to Georg Ludwig and the two branches of the Lüneburg line were permanently united.

In the very year of the fateful marriage of Georg Ludwig and Sophie Dorothea, Ernst August took another decisive step in consolidating his duchy. Overruling once again the opposition of his wife, he abandoned the tradition, well-established in the Braunschweig-Lüneburg duchies, of territorial subdivision amongst the male children of a duke, introducing in its place the rule of primogeniture, by which the duchy passed undivided to his oldest son. From Ernst August's point of view, these two dynastic policies were necessary complements of one another: there was little point in uniting the heirs to Hanover and Celle in marriage if the two territories were to be divided among his six sons. Yet other members of his family were bound to see things differently: this decision, ratified by the emperor in 1683, predictably caused tension inside the Guelf house, notably between Ernst August and his younger sons as well as with the dukes of Braunschweig-Wolfenbüttel, who immediately detected the intentions of the cadet line of the Guelf house to eclipse them in wealth, territory, power, and status. More felicitous for all parties was the marriage arranged on 8 October 1684 between Ernst August's daughter, Sophie Charlotte (1668–1705), and Friedrich III von Hohenzollern (1657–1713), heir to the powerful electorate of Brandenburg-Prussia. From a skilful but ruthless and pragmatic ruler such as Ernst August, Leibniz was to receive little support for his incessant practical proposals of reform aimed at the 'common good,' let alone for his philosophical and religious reflections. Gradually his direct correspondence with the duke became scarcer. After several years of strenuous attempts to recreate with the new duke the kind of trusting relationship he had enjoyed with Johann Friedrich, from around 1684 onward Leibniz retreated to businesslike communications mostly focused on the defence of his activities in the Harz.[91]

At the announcement of Johann Friedrich's death, Leibniz's first concern was to be confirmed by the new ruler in his post. It was not long before the new duke reshuffled his privy council. He took with him from Osnabrück Franz Ernst von Platen (1631–1709), who was installed as Prime Minister. Otto Grote served as *Landdrost* of Grubenhagen (Harz) until the end of 1682 and then, from 1683, as president of the *Kammer*. Hieronymous von Witzendorff was confirmed president of the *Kammer* until 1682, and then created *Landdrost* of Diepholz before succeeding Grote as *Landdrost* of Grubenhagen in 1683. Albrecht Philipp von dem Bussche (1639–98) was named privy counsellor in 1682. Ludolf Hugo alone remained unmoved in his place as vice-chancellor.[92] But virtually all the more junior court officials were simply confirmed in their posts; and with his fears of dismissal laid to rest Leibniz was able to decline the unattractive post of counsellor to Count Burchard von Ahlefeldt, *Oberlanddrost* in Oldenburg, who offered an annual stipend of 300 talers (half of Leibniz's annual pay), plus expenses and accommodation.[93]

Between February and the beginning of March Leibniz visited Osnabrück to present himself to Ernst August, who was preparing for his official entry into Hanover on 13 March 1680. Even in advance of this visit and the duke's official installation, Leibniz had begun a stream of memoranda addressed to Ernst August and his chief ministers. Besides renewing his plea to be named archive director and general administrator of the conventual estates, he proposed the enlargement of the library and the creation of a series of complementary cultural institutions, including an art collection or *Kunstkammer*, a museum or *Wunderkammer*, a laboratory, and a ducal press (together with a regime of censorship).[94] Other proposals continued to appear especially during the first years of Ernst August's reign, as Leibniz groped for a significant project which would capture the duke's imagination. These included a host of measures for the improvement of state administration, coinage and the monetary system, and military policy; the formalisation of a *Corpus Brunsvico-Luneburgicum* or *Ernestino-Augustum* containing all the laws and ordinances of the duchy; a handbook surveying the duchy's most important archival materials; a proper topographical description of the territory; the creation of an academy for noblemen in Göttingen modelled on the recent foundation in Turin; the establishment of a trade agreement with the Dutch East India Company; and experimentation with new methods for smelting iron, producing steel, cutting alabaster, and even transmuting gold.[95] The invention in England of the pressure cooker by Denis Papin in 1679 – allegedly allowing even bones to be cooked for human consumption – captured his attention; and in an attempt to convince the duke to acquire it, he wrote a humorous *Requeste des Chiens* (*Request of the Dogs*) in which the court's hounds officially protested the deprivation of their ancient right to bones.[96] What really concerned Leibniz, however, was rather the health of his fellow human beings. In 1680 he proposed the introduction of an official medical system (or *collegium sanitatis*) designed to ensure the proper instruction of a sufficient number of physicians, the provision of pharmacies, and even oversight of diet, because, Leibniz pointed out, health generally depended more upon "the kitchen and the cellar than upon the pharmacy." Amongst the anticipated benefits of this centralised scheme were contributions from public funds to the pay of the physicians and the compilation of medical statistics regarding the main causes of diseases and death.[97] A long memo of 1681 applied some of these ideas to combating the spread of the plague, which was currently menacing the duchy.[98] Even more innovative applications of his mathematical facility to the direct promotion of the common good followed. Between 1680 and 1683, advanced methods of calculation linked to probabilistic considerations of life expectancy and demographic statistics produced numerous studies of life insurance and other forms of protection against loss, pensions, and life annuities, spelling out in each case their advantages for both the state and its subjects.[99] In addition, he produced sophisticated juridical-mathematical essays on the discounting of bills and on simple and compound interest.[100] He even discussed the link between the mechanisation of productive processes and the increase in unemployment.[101] A further complementary *desideratum* was state provision of education: "for the welfare of the Country it is required not only the nourishment but also the virtue of the inhabitants. Which entails that they be properly educated. . . . Indeed everything is based on such education."[102] Many of the most innovative of these schemes – far in advance of contemporary practice – must have gone straight into the duke's waste paper basket; but one minor proposal aimed at dynastic advancement rather than the common good was destined eventually to awaken his keen interest: as early as January 1680, Leibniz proposed to write a "short but thorough" history of the Guelf house.[103]

On 1 May 1680, the very day of the official funeral of Johann Friedrich, Leibniz wrote for the first time to a man who, in many respects, was to take the place of the late duke as one of his closest and most trusted confidants, especially on religious and political questions: Landgraf Ernst von Hessen-Rheinfels (1623–93). The Landgraf had converted in 1652 from Calvinism to Catholicism. A friend of Boineburg, he was, like other converts, an active promoter of the reconciliation of the Christian churches. In his view, however, the only realistic way forward was reciprocal toleration. Indeed, short of miraculous divine intervention, the pursuit of full reunification seemed to him a futile enterprise.[104] Leibniz mentioned him as early as 1669 in a letter of 30 April to his brother-in-low, Simon Löffler.[105] Subsequently he saw the Landgraf in Frankfurt and Bad Schwalbach, probably during one of his visits to the spa town in the company of Boineburg, but did not have the opportunity to speak to him.[106] The perfect occasion to establish direct contact with the Landgraf was provided by Leibniz's office as librarian when Ernst von Hessen-Rheinfels wrote requesting the return of the late duke's copy of a book Ernst had written on the current state and potential reconciliation of the Christian churches – a book printed in few copies and privately circulated due to the sensitive nature of its subject matter.[107] The book, Leibniz assured the Landgraf, was not in the library and must therefore have been amongst the duke's possessions in his private chambers. Nevertheless, Leibniz continued,

I have seen and read this work twice, firstly in Mainz by the late Baron of Boineburg, of whom I had the honor of being an intimate friend; and then again by a good

Nobertin Father in Schwalbach.[108] Since then I have done what I could to recover a copy: because . . . I believe that there have been few works in which are found so many useful and considerable remarks over the present state of the Church in Europe[.][109]

Leibniz's words ushered in a friendship expressed in a staggering amount of correspondence, which continued until the death of the Landgraf in 1693.[110] In it Leibniz felt free to be more open on philosophical, religious, and political issues than with many other correspondents who could (and sometime did) misjudge or distort his thought and his motives. For instance, when in September 1683 the Landgraf tried his best to convert him to Catholicism, sending a "Wake-up call to my as dearest as most capable Mister Leibnitz,"[111] this latter was prepared to "unveil to him the depths of [his] heart" and reveal his reasons for refusing to join the Roman church. These reasons did not concern dogmas proposed by Rome as articles of faith. "It is true," Leibniz wrote, "that if I were born in the Roman Church I would not leave it." Rather, the problem lay for him in the practices of the Roman church as well as in certain philosophical tenets which he regarded as demonstrable and which were nevertheless opposed by some Roman Catholic theologians. His intellectual integrity did not allow the deception of dissimulating these important philosophical ideas.[112] Putting this position in the context of Leibniz's conviction that the truth of the Christian religion was not the monopoly of any particular church –whether the Roman Catholic or any other – but the common heritage of the truly Catholic or Universal church he was trying to piece back together, it did not make sense for him to leave the particular church in which he was born to join another particular church which had the additional momentous disadvantage of questioning his philosophical opinions as well as promoting religious practices in need of serious reform. In any case, Leibniz's refusal to convert affected neither his friendship with the Landgraf nor their common willingness to pursue over the years a close dialogue on the issue of ecclesiastical reconciliation.[113]

In returning from one of his visits to the Harz in March 1683, for instance, Leibniz promptly informed his friend of the presence in Hanover of Bishop Rojas, who was pursuing the series of talks which Leibniz came to see as the most important step towards reunification since the outbreak of the Protestant reformation.[114] Rojas was already an experienced ecclesiastical negotiator, who in his previous visits to the courts of Protestant German princes on behalf of the emperor had tried to lay the basis of an understanding with Rome. The Hanoverian talks of 1683 marked a key moment in this process. Although not directly involved in the negotiations, Leibniz regarded the reunion strategy broadly agreed upon between Rojas and Molanus as the most realistic and promising plan which could be devised – a plan which he continued to push forward in the following years until finally confronted with its failure. Its guidelines were set out by Rojas in the *Regulae circa christianorum omnium Ecclesiasticam Reunionem* (1682–3), a document which was answered in the *Methodus reducendae Unionis Ecclesiasticae inter Romanenses et Protestantes* (1683) by Molanus and the Hanoverian court preacher Hermann Barckhausen. Basically, their strategy was twofold: first they envisaged a preliminary reunion of the Protestants with the Roman church before full agreement had been reached on controversial issues, at which point, second, a truly ecumenical Council would be summoned. Having been recognised at the outset as truly ecumenical, the Council therefore would be endowed with the authority to settle controversial issues. Both Catholics and Protestants would agree in advance to abide by its decisions. In effect, this strategy amounted to the suspension of the decisions of the Council of Trent, which had never been acknowledged by the Protestants as ecumenical and which was therefore devoid in their view of binding doctrinal authority. Moreover, as Molanus adamantly required, the reunion should have taken place *salvis principiis utriusque partis*, that is, preserving the principles of both parties.

Despite Rojas and Molanus's agreement, however, the plan met with cool and cautious reactions from the very beginning. Even the other two Lutherans directly involved in the negotiations – the theologians of the University of Helmstedt, Friedrich Ulrich Calixt (son of Georg Calixt) and Gebhard Theodor Meier – preferred to sign a complex and ambiguous dossier documenting the proceedings of the talks rather than openly endorsing Molanus and Barckhausen's *Methodus*. No joint agreement was produced. However similar, the *Regulae* and *Methodus* continued to represent the still distinct points of view of irenicists in the Catholic and the Lutheran parties. Moreover, not a few Lutherans doubted the soundness of Rojas's papal mandate to conduct negotiations on this paramount question: although Pope Innocent XI seemed to regard the bishop's efforts sympathetically, it was unclear how firm his commitment to Rojas's strategy actually was.[115]

Within this grand scheme involving pope, emperor, German princes, and troops of authorized Catholic and Lutheran theologians, there was little that Leibniz could expect to contribute at this particular juncture. But he did contribute what he could: he wrote, networked, and disseminated good will towards the enterprise. He discussed in several texts the problem of the division of the Christian churches and the possibility of a reunification of Catholics, Greek Orthodox, and Evangelicals[116] and mediated a contact between Rojas and Jacques-Bénigne Bossuet (1627–1704), which resulted in the dispatch of Rojas's *Regulae* to the French theologian via Duchess Sophie.[117] This was not the first time that Leibniz approached the highly influential tutor of the Dauphin and Bishop of Meaux. Having missed him in Paris, in February 1679 Leibniz had taken the initiative of writing to Bossuet, praising the French theologian's conciliatory attitude in the *Exposition de la doctrine de l'Eglise catholique sur les matières de controverse* of 1671 and mentioning the recent visit of Rojas at the court of Johann Friedrich.[118] Indeed, Leibniz pinned great hope on the contribution which the French church and its most prominent theologian might have made to ecclesiastical reunification. Although part of the communion of the Roman church, the French church was to some extent autonomous. In particular, Bossuet was a leading proponent of 'Gallicanism', the French form of Catholicism which aimed to limit papal authority through appeal to the authority of the universal church.[119] Yet the dialogue between Leibniz and Bossuet, repeatedly interrupted and regularly resumed, never attained the degree of intimacy and trust achieved with some of Leibniz's other Catholic correspondents; and it ended on a bitter note, soured above all by the rigid and aggressive confessionalism of the French king. In 1685, Louis XIV's revocation of the Edict of Nantes sent streams of angry, persecuted Huguenot refugees to Germany, England, and the Dutch Republic and constituted perhaps the most serious single blow to the project of reconciling Protestants with Catholics suffered in Leibniz's lifetime.[120]

The revocation of the Edict of Nantes was, amongst other things, a paradigmatic example of the entanglement of religion with politics. The intense discussion of religious questions in the correspondence between Leibniz and Landgraf Ernst naturally also led to the fundamental question of the relationship between temporal and spiritual powers. The Landgraf – the modernist in this exchange, it would appear – advocated a complete separation between church and states. Leibniz, by contrast, inclined towards the medieval order already defended in *De Jure Suprematus*, which described the pope and the Holy Roman Emperor as the "two heads" of Christendom, both of whom retained supranational authority: the emperor as the "secular arm of the Universal Church" and "the born leader of Christians against the infidels"; the pope as the spiritual authority who nevertheless maintained the right to "curb the tyranny and ambition of the great."[121]

"The tyranny and ambition of the great" most in need of curbing in the early 1680s for the supranational good of the Christian world certainly included in Leibniz's mind both the traditional foe of medieval Christendom – the steadily expanding Islamic empire of the Ottoman Turks to the east of the Holy Roman Empire – and the imperialist foreign and intolerant domestic policies of Louis XIV to the west. In September 1681, Leibniz committed to paper, probably on Otto Grote's request, a *Deliberation sur l'Estat present de l'Empire* in which he discussed the quandary facing the Empire. Should it declare war on France to recover the territories already occupied by the French? Or should it seek an armistice and pacify its western front, in order to reorganize its forces and concentrate on countering the looming advance of the Ottoman Empire from the east?[122] Two or three weeks later the seizure of the leading imperial free city of Strasbourg by the armies of the Sun King prompted the shocked Leibniz to write a heartfelt *Aufforderung zum Widerstand gegen Frankreich* (*Exhortation to resistance against France*) marked by a new version of the old litany previously referring to the Turks: *a furore Gallorum libera nos Domine* (free us, Lord, from the wrath of the French).[123]

In subsequent years, the emperor was confronted simultaneously with the creeping expansionism of Louis XIV on the Rhine and the even greater immediate threat of the Turks on the Danube, who appeared in the summer of 1683 at the very walls of Vienna.[124] Needless to say, in the months surrounding the siege of Vienna, Leibniz's correspondence with Landgraf Ernst and others returned repeatedly to the perilous situation of the Empire.[125] The siege of Vienna was one of those turning points which had the potential to change the course of Western history dramatically: the shape of Europe would have been quite different if the capital of the Holy Roman Empire had fallen into Muslim hands during that critical summer of 1683.[126] Yet even in these weeks and months Leibniz's political passion was directed against France's expansionistic politics rather than to an extended direct discussion of the enormous danger posed to Christianity by the military offensive of the Ottoman Empire.[127] In fact, he saw in Louis XIV's aggressive policy towards other Christian nations the reason for the weakness of the Empire against the Turks. Since he had no direct diplomatic or political mandate from the Hanoverian court,[128] he concentrated on undermining French expansionism with the best weapon he had at his disposal: the pen. At the height of the siege, in the last weeks before the liberation of Vienna on 12 September 1683, Leibniz wrote the most acidic political satire of his career: the *Mars Christianissimus seu Apologia armorum Regis Christianissimi contra Christianos* (*The most Christian war-God or apology of the arms of the most Christian king against Christians*).[129] Rather than directly attacking the Sun King's unprovoked aggression, Leibniz adopted the mask of a "German Gallo-Greek" and bitterly satirized the misapplied scriptural premises and the tortuous reasoning from which Louis's propagandists sought to justify the relentless aggression of the ruler traditionally identified as 'the most Christian king'. In the masterfully poignant final paragraph of the work, for instance, Leibniz implied – not for the first time – that the most legitimate outlet for the French king's insatiable appetite for war would be a decisive campaign against the un-Christian Turks:

There will be some who will imagine that his Most Christian Majesty would do better to begin his beautiful designs by routing the Turks than by afflicting poor Christians: but these people do not reflect at all that it is the Germans and the Flemish who live on the frontiers of France, and not the Turks: that one must pass from one's neighbours to people far away, and move in these great matters by solid degrees, rather than by vain and perilous leaps. But, without looking for political reasons, here is one of conscience: which is that the king wishes to follow the rules of the New Testament, which commands that one begin with the Jews, and then orders that one turn *ad gentes*. The king, in imitation of this, will create for himself by the reduction of the Christians a sure passage to go one day to the infidels.[130]

The idea of producing such a pamphlet had been suggested to him in November 1682 by Landgraf Ernst himself, who regarded it as "a work as agreeable to God as to the fatherland *et omnibus rectis corde*." The Landgraf even offered to see to its anonymous publication.[131] Between this invitation and the time in which the pamphlet was finally ready, the political situation had deteriorated even further. On 14 August 1683, in the midst of the siege of Vienna, Leibniz wrote to the Landgraf with the same bitter sarcasm displayed in the *Mars Christianissimus*:

It is said that the most Christian King . . . is contented by so very little (that is to say, by some beautiful Provinces, and by one of the most remarkable Cities of the Empire [Strasbourg]) . . . It is said that he refuses to come to our aid before what he demands is surrended to him; as for me, I believe that we should try to do without his help since, in my view, this help is at the moment to be feared as much as his enterprises.[132]

No later than 29 September Leibniz's anti-French satire had been completed in both an original Latin version and a French translation. On that day Leibniz wrote again to his friend mentioning "a manuscript written in French under the title of *Mars Christianissimus*" which had been communicated to him and deserved in his view to be printed.[133] The exceeding circumspection of Leibniz, reluctant to acknowledge in writing the authorship of the pamphlet, revealed his awareness that his attack against Louis XIV's policies could hardly have been more virulent and would certainly frustrate any lingering aspirations he might have maintained eventually to transplant himself back to Paris. Landgraf Ernst was in any case more than happy to oblige and to see the manuscript through the press. The actual text was sent by Leibniz to the Landgraf in two instalments, respectively on 5 December 1683 and on 11 January 1684. Sometime after Pentecost 1684 the *Mars Christianissimus* was finally in print.[134] Meanwhile Leibniz had continued to reflect on the relationship between France and the Empire, writing around the second half of March another long essay in which he carefully weighed the reasons for and against an armistice with France, concluding that, all things considered, the best way forward was to agree to a cease-fire.[135] The essay, apparently written in consultation with Otto Grote and certainly foreseen for publication, did not actually reach the printer. In the mean time the emperor and the majority of German princes had agreed to seek an armistice with France. Superseded by events, Leibniz's work remained unpublished.[136]

Louis XIV's intolerance of Protestantism within his borders and his determination to expand them at the expense of Holland and Germany were not the only developments which tainted Leibniz's first years under Duke Ernst August with bitterness. Closer to home, he soon came to realise that his new employer did not have much time for the first main task that had been entrusted to him by Johann Friedrich: the care of the library. When the new duke planned the extension and rebuilding of the

Leineschloß necessary for the arrival of his family and court, he concluded that the palace could not continue to accommodate something of so little use to him as the library. Pending the identification of a suitable new location, the books were stored in the remotest corner of the castle.[137] It was no doubt with deep dismay that Leibniz saw the treasures which he and Johann Friedrich had so carefully accumulated treated with so little respect and his first memoranda on the enhancement of the ducal collections so comprehensively disregarded. Nor is it difficult to understand why, in July 1680, Leibniz attempted to put forward his candidacy for the post of imperial librarian vacated by the death in Vienna of Peter von Lambeck.[138] However, as he explained to Johann Lincker von Lutzenwick (the privy counsellor to the archbishop of Trier through whom he sought to advance his candidacy), he was prepared to accept the position only on the condition that he was also made a *Reichshofrat* or member of the Imperial Aulic Council, that is, the supreme court of appeal in Vienna. Ostensibly, this audacious condition was justified by the argument that exchanging a position as *Hofrat* for that of "a bare librarian and historiographer" would have represented a retreat "from the light of public business into the shadows" and as such a demotion.[139] Yet it must also already have been clear to Leibniz that, whatever his formal status in Hanover, he was unlikely to enjoy much limelight on any stage directed by Ernst August, and some deeper motivation must therefore have led Leibniz to insert this strict condition, which undermined at the outset his chances of securing a far more prestigious position in the chief city of the Empire. Just such a motivation, which could not have been revealed to a Catholic intermediary such as Lincker, was in fact confided to his trusted friend Crafft: Leibniz did not wish to convert to Catholicism. Since some of the positions on the Imperial Aulic Council were reserved for Protestants, Leibniz believed that his standing as a *Reichshofrat* would have helped him to resist pressure to change his confession, while the chance to fill one of these positions with a moderate Protestant already well-known in Vienna as an advocate of reconciliation with Rome might have appealed to the emperor.[140] But whatever Leibniz's reasoning, nothing came of these overtures.

In November 1680, Leibniz found himself pleading once again for the rescue of the Hanover library. In a letter to the duke he wrote:

Regarding the library, I beg Your Grace to instruct Monsieur Witzendorff or someone else to examine what remains [of it]. There are books which were paid for a long time ago but which have not yet been bound; I believe that Your Grace's intention is to have them bound. There are others [evidently published in installments] of which we are still lacking the continuation . . . I believe that Your Grace will not wish to leave these pieces incomplete.[141]

The duke, as always, was busy with other schemes and had no time whatsoever for Leibniz's "plan for assembling a Library" designed to provide "an encyclopaedia or *science universelle* enclosed in three or four rooms".[142] Despite Leibniz's regular appeals and complaints,[143] the library remained closed and completely unusable from 1680 to at least 1684.[144] Leibniz's early specification of the meagre sum of 300 talers per annum as a minimum acquisitions budget remained a dead letter.[145] Whereas between 1676 and 1679 Johann Friedrich had spent some 4500 talers on library acquisitions, in the following eight years (1680–1687) Ernst August disbursed in total a mere 700 talers, of which at least 440 talers went to pay bills left outstanding at Johann Friedrich's death.[146] The duke's recalcitrance in settling library bills even forced Leibniz in March 1681 to anticipate 30 talers from his private coffers – some five percent of his annual pay – in order to placate one of the duke's creditors.[147]

Without a useful library, Ernst August had little need for a librarian; but the duke found numerous ways of profiting from Leibniz's historical and legal expertise. One of the most important services rendered by Leibniz to the house of Braunschweig-Lüneburg was to furnish the key historical and legal arguments in support of the Guelf dukes's claim to inherit the duchy of Sachsen-Lauenburg.[148] Situated between the river Elbe south of Hamburg and the Baltic south of Lübeck, this duchy was an immediate neighbour of the Lüneburg principalities. Despite its relatively small size, it possessed the lucrative right to tax traffic on the Elbe. Luckily for the Guelf house, Duke Julius Franz of Sachsen-Lauenburg (1641–89) had no male heirs, opening up the opportunity for a claim on his land on the part of his neighbours, the Lüneburg dukes.[149] From 1681 onward Leibniz prepared for Ernst August and his ministers a harvest of historical and legal papers efficaciously supporting the Guelf case on the ground of the original supremacy over Sachsen-Lauenburg of the Guelf's distinguished ancestor, Heinrich der Löwe (1129 or 1130–95).[150] As a supplementary guarantee that these historic-juridical claims would be recognized, at the death of Duke Julius Franz of Sachsen-Lauenburg the Braunschweig-Lüneburg dukes prudently occupied the neighbouring duchy militarily and remained there until the emperor finally legally recognised their right to Sachsen-Lauenburg on 28 April 1716, a few months before Leibniz's death.[151] Far more momentous was Ernst August's pursuit of a prize which could not be obtained by *de facto* annexation backed up by scholarly argument: the elevation of his duchy into the ninth Electorate of the Empire. Here too Leibniz contributed in a decisive way to the formulation of historical and legal arguments in support of the duke of Hanover's claim, producing in the autumn of 1685 a first memorandum for Ernst August, which was followed by numerous other essays.[152]

All of this projecting, pamphleteering, networking, and researching notwithstanding, by far the most time-consuming and absorbing practical enterprise undertaken by Leibniz during these years turned out to be the Harz project. In fact, between 1680 and 1686 he made thirty-one separate trips to the Harz and spent at least 165 weeks there out of a total of 365.[153] The final result for so much effort was a complete failure. No doubt it would have been better for Leibniz to abandon the whole idea when, at the death of Johann Friedrich, the agreement reached only a few months earlier had been thrown into question. Instead, during his visit to Osnabrück in early 1680 to make the acquaintance of his new employer, Leibniz immediately sought Ernst August's endorsement of the contract ratified by Johann Friedrich on 25 October 1679.[154] To Leibniz's disappointment, the new duke had been urged by the president of the *Kammer*, Witzendorff, to reconsider the project carefully.[155] It was not until 24 April 1680 that Ernst August took his decision: Leibniz was to try three windmills at the mine named "Catharina" (instead of the "Dorothea Landeskron"); the costs of the test were to be equally divided amongst the duke, the Clausthal mine office, and Leibniz; and if the test proved successful, Leibniz would be entitled to the life annuity of 1200 talers previously agreed.[156] In the summer Leibniz began the commute back and forth from the Harz which was to become a fixture of the next six years. His first move there, however, did nothing to gain the sympathies of the miners themselves, who were already ill-disposed towards an inexperienced outsider imposed from above. After a closer inspection of the mines, Leibniz amended his plans, resurrecting a scheme which he had sharply criticised when it was first proposed by Hartzingk a couple of years before:[157] instead of simply using the windmills to drain the flood water from the mines, he now envisaged a more complex system of windmills and pumps by which the drained water was to be collected and reutilised to operate the water pumps in a continuous cycle. The proposed

change engendered a bitter dispute with the mining office, which refused
to humour Leibniz in his experimentation beyond what had already been
clearly agreed.[158] Following the intervention of Otto Grote, on 1 and 2
October a compromise was reached. Both systems were to be tested: the
windmill which was already under construction near the "Catharina" was
to be employed to raise the drained water from underground as envisaged
by the new scheme, while the other two windmills were to be used simply
to drain the water as previously foreseen. The costs were to be divided
into three equal parts as before.[159]

However unpleasant the process of reaching the new agreement may
have been, the worst for Leibniz was yet to come. From this point onwards
he encountered an interminable string of technical difficulties in the construction of the windmills and their maintenance in good working order.
Weather conditions proved adverse: either there was too much wind or,
typically, too little. Costs mounted precipitously: by mid-1683 the project
had already cost 2270 talers instead of the estimated expenditure of 300
talers per windmill. The miners of Clausthal, whose livelihoods were
jeopardised by all this disruptive experimentation, were joined in the
opposition to further testing by workers of the Zellerfeld mines, who had
been involved in the project since April 1682. On 14 October 1682 the
mining offices of the two towns released a joint report declaring once again
the failure of Leibniz's schemes. In November 1683 the lack of wind prevented a demonstration of the windmills to members of the privy council
inspecting the mines, whose visit provided the mining people with an
opportunity to voice their strong opposition directly to the duchy's most
senior officials.[160] The privy counsellors's negative report to the duke
undermined further an already precarious situation, and on 6 December
1683 Ernst August wrote to Leibniz announcing his decision to reconsider
the whole enterprise. Financial contributions by the duke himself and the
mine office were suspended until further notice.[161]

This was the last thing Leibniz needed. As a simple court counsellor making 600 talers per year, the disbursement of 760 talers to cover
one-third of the expenses already incurred would have stretched his
finances. The arrival in early 1682 of 761 talers due him from his mother's
inheritance eased his situation temporarily,[162] but at the same time the
debts incurred with the administrator of his family's estate, Christian
Freiesleben, were catching up with him. On 1 August 1680 his half-
brother, Johann Friedrich (whom he had seen on 10 July 1680 during

a short visit to Leipzig), informed him of the death of Freiesleben and
of the request of his widow, Clara Elisabeth, to repay 476 talers still
outstanding.[163] Moreover, Clara Elisabeth urged the prompt sale or
removal from her house of the vast library left by Leibniz's father, grandfather, and stepgrandfather. This gave rise to a pointed quarrel with
Freiesleben's widow over the exact amount Leibniz owed to her, a dispute exacerbated by Leibniz's reluctance to authorize the auction of the
library to settle the remaining debts.[164] Eventually Leibniz relented and
allowed the sale, which took place in September 1685; but the auction
raised a mere 238 talers –nowhere near enough to placate Freiesleben's
widow. Leibniz's last resort at this point was the attempt to recover the
portion of the Schmuck inheritance still due him, for which purpose he
enlisted the help of his nephew, Johann Friedrich Freiesleben, and of his
cousin, Aegidius Strauch.[165]

Astonishingly, despite this uncertain financial position, these intractable technical problems, the animosity of the miners in the Harz, and
his dwindling backing in Hanover, Leibniz informed Ernst August on 13
January 1684 of his intention to continue the Harz experiment until the end
of the year at his own expense.[166] Between 29 January and 18 March 1684,
during one of the periods in which Leibniz was absent from the Harz, a
series of tests were performed, but no agreement was reached on whether
the trial should be deemed satisfactory. In March Leibniz prepared a
memo for the duke defending his project and detailing the advantages of
an alternative kind of windmill, for the construction of which the duke had
recently granted 200 talers: a horizontal model promising lower building
costs, greater resistance to storms, and more efficient exploitation of even
mild winds.[167] Meanwhile the friction between Leibniz and the mining
community continued to escalate: Leibniz's genuine effort to understand
and enhance their cultural heritage – demonstrated *inter alia* by his studies
on the ancient language used by the Harz community[168] – did little to
placate these hard-headed mountain men. At Ernst August's instigation,
between late May and early June 1684 a five-day conference was held in
order to clarify and resolve the many points of disagreement between the
litigants, but the unbridgeable gulf of distrust and opposition between
the two parties is perhaps best revealed by their differing accounts of the
financial outcome of the experiments thus far: whereas the mine office
calculated that the project had cost the duchy some 128,100 talers of
potential income over twelve years, Leibniz opposed his own calculation

of a net gain of 115,509 talers and 12 *Groschen* over the same period.[169] This complete polarisation alone might well have convinced the duke that the whole enterprise was doomed to fail; but he too was evidently entranced by the potential financial benefits of the project. 1684 had been a dry year. In the autumn, rain was still to come, and the duke decided to give Leibniz a final chance. A second series of tests was performed, once again in Leibniz's absence, and again assessments of the nature and magnitude of the difficulties experienced were confused. Leibniz took care therefore personally to supervise the next set of tests, performed in January and February 1685; but this time, too, the experiment was only partially successful. On 15 March the ducal *Kammer* reiterated that financial support for the Harz project had been frozen,[170] and one month later, on 14 April, the *Kammer* notified Leibniz of the duke's resolution to stop any further work.[171]

Even in this seemingly hopeless situation, Leibniz – as tenacious as he was optimistic – did not abandon the Harz mines immediately. During the following months he produced yet another scheme, this time for a water-operated mechanism to take the place of the horses employed for lifting the ore from deep underground to the surface.[172] By this point, however, Ernst August had despaired of Leibniz's practical schemes – even those with clear potential to generate income – and had identified a very different way in which his idiosyncratic court counsellor could contribute to his all-important dynastic project: through the composition of a history of the Guelf house in general and of the dynasty of Braunschweig-Lüneburg in particular.

Leibniz was obviously not new to the investigation of the antiquity, genealogy, and grandeur of the Guelf house. Historical researches of this kind had substantiated the political and dynastic arguments which he had already advanced on behalf of the Hanoverian dukes. Ironically, the fateful suggestion to synthesize this material into a brief history of the house was his. As early as August 1677 he had started to investigate the link between the Italian noble house of Este and the Guelfs.[173] In 1680 he had twice suggested the composition of a history of the Guelfs, although on these occasions his proposal was to concentrate on the recent past.[174] In March 1685 he had been called upon by Duke Ernst August to referee the results of the genealogical researches of the Venetian abbot Teodoro Damaideno,[175] who had produced a genealogy of the Guelfs spanning over 2436 years and linking the Braunschweig-Lüneburg house to the

Este family. In his reports for the duke and the ensuing correspondence with the abbot, Leibniz exposed the flimsy historical and philological basis of Damaideno's *Opus Genealogicum* while outlining the standards for a methodologically sound historical investigation of the origins of the Guelf house.[176] And in doing so he had sealed his own fate. Although medieval history and philology were of no more intrinsic interest to Ernst August than metaphysics or mathematics, the duke needed a pedigree worthy of an elector; and in a political system still governed in large part by genealogy, systematic archival researches of the kind proposed by Leibniz might yield other concrete dividends as well. For once an aspect of Leibniz's intellectual interests – albeit a rather tangential one – intersected with the duke's ambitious strategy; and when the collapse of the Harz project in April 1685 was followed in May by word from Otto Grote that Leibniz was willing to undertake the Guelf history,[177] Ernst August acted with the decisiveness characteristic of his pursuit of dynastic advantage generally. The duke's rescript of June 1685 instructing Leibniz to undertake the project was formalized on 10 August 1685 in a "Resolution" addressed to Leibniz himself. Although he was not officially named court historiographer, the new task offered him financial advantages and consolidated his status at court: his salary was transformed into a life pension supplemented with travel expenses; his appointment as court counsellor was made permanent; a secretary was assigned to him at last;[178] and he was relieved from chancery work.[179]

Leibniz could scarcely have imagined that this relative security and apparent freedom would be purchased by binding himself to the Guelf history for the rest of his life. His initial plan was to complete a relatively brief work in a reasonably short time. For the two following years he set about his new task with notable energy, visiting a host of archives and libraries in Lower Saxony which held materials pertaining to the history of the Braunschweig-Lüneburg family, notably in Braunschweig, Wolfenbüttel, Lüneburg, and Celle.[180] He also perused the Nachlaß of the court archivist and *Kammermeister*, J. H. Hoffmann, who at his death in March 1680 had left unpublished the fruit of some twenty years of research on the Braunschweig-Lüneburg history.[181] His correspondence with European savants, which during the recent years dominated by the Harz project had significantly diminished, picked up again and extended to new correspondents specifically contacted in connexion with his new historical assignment.[182] Yet in Leibniz's omnivorous mind, everything was related to everything else; and as he ploughed his lonely furrow through virtually untilled archives, his collections of materials, ideas, and intentions directly and indirectly related to this historical project began to multiply in typical profusion. One of the first places in which this tendency manifested itself, remarkably but not uncharacteristically, was in the place one might least expect to find it: in his previous investigations in the Harz. For a year and a half after the formal demise of the Harz project and for over a year after the commencement of his new historiographical assignment, Leibniz continued to spend extended periods in the mountain region. Over half of 1686, in fact, was spent at the two main mining centres of Zellerfeld and Clausthal.[183] In part these visits were devoted to old business: regulating the accounts of the failed windmill project and promoting his new idea for the water-powered lifting machines.[184] But Leibniz was also carrying forward an entirely separate line of investigation. What began as a typically baroque collection of interesting minerals, fossils, and bones found during his excursions in the Harz evolved into a geological and paleontological inquiry. The historical assignment unexpectedly gave these investigations a new lease of life, and they would eventually produce the deepest stratum of a radically enlarged history of Lower Saxony and its leading dynasty.[185] Many of Leibniz's projects, to be sure, threatened to snowball into things of unmanageable proportions; but in this case there was a crucial, perhaps unique difference. The Guelf history was the pet project, not of Leibniz himself – who ordinarily preserved the liberty to pick up and put aside lines of inquiry as his muse dictated – but of his chief employer; and the Hanoverians dukes had no intention of letting him abandon this project before it was finished. Yet the longer they kept him on the task, the more unmanageable that task became.

By the time Leibniz succeeded in disengaging himself more fully from the Harz, in fact, the Guelf history promised to draw him still further afield. Within two years, his correspondence and archival researches in Lower Saxony had reached an impasse: he was still missing the crucial piece of the puzzle regarding the origins of the northern Italian margrave who was considered the common ancestor of the Guelf and Este families, Albert (or Adelbert) Azzo II.[186] No later than mid-May 1687 it had become clear to Leibniz that a visit to Munich and other archives in southern Germany would be necessary in order to fill this crucial gap, although at this point he had not anticipated that his trip would have taken him as far as Italy and extended well beyond the "entire summer" of 1687 as he had initially planned.[187] It was not until the end of October 1687 that Leibniz was able to depart, accompanied – ironically – by the mining superintendent, Friedrich Heyn, who served during the trip as his secretary.

Leibniz's Great Plan: From the *Demonstrationes Catholicae* to the *Scientia Generalis* and the Demonstrative Encyclopaedia

During the entire period just discussed, underneath the visible level of Leibniz's strikingly varied public activities, a more private level provided the deeper motivations and foundations of his praxis-oriented endeavours and of his search of enlightened patronage. This deeper dimension consisted of his all-embracing encyclopaedic plan of reform and advancement of the sciences for the promotion of the common good – a plan which he considered a celebration of the glory of God as expressed in the universal harmony governing His creation. As he wrote in 1678, "all these things are connected, and have to be directed to the same aim, which is the glory of God and the advancement of the public good by means of useful works and beautiful discoveries".[188] And again in 1699: "To contribute to the public good and to the glory of God is the same thing. It seems that the aim of all humankind should chiefly be nothing other than the knowledge and development of the wonders of God and that it is for this reason that God has given to humankind dominion over this globe."[189]

This more private level occasionally surfaced when Leibniz thought he had found a sympathetic patron who could provide the support necessary for carrying the plan forward, or when he reckoned that specific aspects of it were mature enough to be presented privately in correspondence with individual thinkers or publically within learned journals. The frosty reception that the most mature presentation of his metaphysics found in the philosopher he most wanted to convince – "the great Arnauld" – explains in large measure why Leibniz was so cautious in releasing the still evolving fruits of his thought. Of the staggering number of philosophical studies committed to paper between 1677 and 1690, including at least eighty substantial essays ripe for publication, only three (sharing the common characteristic of criticising various aspects of Cartesianism) actually appeared in learned journals,[190] against twenty-two articles on mathematical, scientific, and technical matters.

Three years into his service in Hanover, Leibniz felt sufficiently confident of his relationship with Duke Johann Friedrich to present to him
his great plan in the form in which he had conceived it back in Mainz: the
Demonstrationes Catholicae (Catholic Demonstrations). A letter to Johann
Friedrich of the autumn of 1679 constitutes the best direct presentation
of Leibniz's intentions in this period.[191] This plan, Leibniz explained,
was "of the greatest importance" and had enjoyed the complete approval
of the late Boineburg.[192] It embraced the whole of natural and revealed
theology, including the demonstrations of the existence of God and of
the immortality and incorporeity of the soul on the one hand,[193] and the
defence of the mysteries of the Christian religion against the charge of
absurdity and contradiction on the other.[194] Moreover, in a clear attempt
to bridge the chasm between Catholics and Protestants, the final part of the
plan was devoted to demonstrating the authority of what Leibniz regarded
as the two complementary sources of theological truth: the catholic (in
the sense of 'universal') church and Scripture.[195] Most importantly, in
his presentation to the duke, Leibniz also explained why these theological
demonstrations needed to be preceded by an inquiry into the foundations of the entire encyclopaedia of sciences, notably logic, metaphysics,
physics, ethics, politics, and mathematics. First of all, logic – intended as
the study and improvement of methods of valid reasoning – needed to
be developed. The kind of demonstrations which Leibniz was envisaging
in the part of his plan devoted to the defence of the Christian mysteries
required a new branch of logic capable of "weighing" probabilities.[196]
This was, in turn, a *pendant* to his broader project of developing a formal,
universal language or *characteristica universalis*. No better tool could be
found, Leibniz explained enthusiastically to the duke, for solving religious controversies and propagating the Christian religion through the
work of missionaries.[197] In turn, a development of metaphysics or *scientia
de ente* was required in order to reach true notions of "God, the soul, person, substance, and accident",[198] all of them fundamental for the planned
demonstrations of the existence of God and the immortality of the soul,
for the defence of mysteries such as the Trinity, the Incarnation, and the
resurrection, and for the explanation of the Eucharist.

This letter to Johann Friedrich recorded also Leibniz's first 'public' mention of a momentous development in the evolution of his
philosophical thought: his explicit rehabilitation of substantial forms.[199]
Not surprisingly, for the religiously oriented duke, Leibniz emphasised

especially the theological reasons which had always played an important role in his propensity to revive substantial forms: the rejection of substantial forms, he claimed, together with the Cartesian reduction of the nature of bodies to extension, had rendered mysteries such as transubstantiation impossible.[200] In a few lines he was therefore stating for Johann Friedrich his anti-Cartesian programme regarding the conception of the nature of substance, mind, and body. A new doctrine of mind – namely logic intended this time as philosophy of mind or *elementa de mente* – and an accompanying new doctrine of bodies – physics or *elementa de corpore* – were therefore needed by the *Demonstrationes Catholicae* (especially for the demonstrations of the existence of God, of the immortality and incorporeity of the soul, and of the possibility of the resurrection of bodies).[201] Finally, it was necessary to demonstrate "the true ethics and politics" in order to know what "justice, justification, freedom, pleasure, beatitude, beatifical vision" are and how to reach the "happiness of the human kind also down here and in this life."[202] To forge the rigorous way of thinking required by all these demonstrations, Leibniz concluded, the study of mathematics was essential, for which reason he had spent so much time studying it in Paris. His interest in mathematics was not in fact an end in itself: it was aimed in the last instance at the realisation of his grand plan.[203]

The years 1678–9 therefore marked a key moment in Leibniz's intellectual life. The 'public' relaunch of his encyclopaedic plan in the form of the *Demonstrationes Catholicae* was accompanied by exciting developments in the disciplines which were to constitute their Prolegomena, notably metaphysics (in which he rehabilitated the doctrine of substantial forms) and physics (in which around 1678 he produced a ground-breaking study on the notion of force). In addition, he conceived a 'qualitative' treatment of Euclidean geometry based on consideration of the congruence, similitude, and other relationships between geometrical figures (the *characteristica geometrica* or *analysis situs*), began to develop the idea of a dyadic or binary arithmetic, laid the foundations for an advanced philosophy of probability, and wrote a series of key logical papers which provided the basis of a logical calculus while presenting as the criterion of truth the inclusion of the predicate in the subject of a proposition.[204] Around the same period he also proposed to the duke the creation of new means of organising scientific research and new learned societies to collaborate on the titanic encyclopaedic task.[205] The sudden demise of Johann Friedrich in

December 1679 dramatically dashed Leibniz's hopes of finding in Hanover the support he once had expected from Boineburg. Leibniz's all-embracing plan, however, was far from abandoned. Once again around 1679, he began to refer to it as the *scientia generalis* ("general science") and the "demonstrative" and "inventive" encyclopaedia, and continued to accumulate a staggering amount of material towards its development.[206]

In a narrow sense Leibniz meant by *scientia generalis* a science of method embracing the *ars judicandi* (or *demonstrandi*) and the *ars inveniendi*, analysis and synthesis. In a word, according to this restrictive meaning, the *scientia generalis* was 'logic' itself in its classical sense of the study and development of the tools of valid reasoning. This meaning was apparent, for instance, in a text of 1679 where the *scientia generalis* was defined as the science which "teaches to all other sciences how to discover and demonstrate from sufficient data."[207] In a broader sense, however, the *scientia generalis* was for Leibniz the science of the principles or foundations of all the sciences, or the investigation of the elements of the whole encyclopaedia and of the highest good. In a word, according to this broader meaning, the *scientia generalis* was 'philosophy' itself in its classical sense of the search for 'wisdom' by means of the tools of a rational investigation:

By *scientia generalis* I mean the science which contains the principles of all the other sciences, and the method for using the principles, so that everyone endowed with ordinary abilities will quickly descend to any specific matters whatsoever by easy meditation and short experience, understanding even the most difficult things, and will be able to discover the most beautiful truths and the most useful applications, as far as is humanly possible from the principles given. The *scientia generalis* must therefore treat both the method of valid reasoning – that is of discovering, judging, governing the emotions [affectus], remembering, and recollecting – and also the elements of the whole encyclopaedia and the investigation of the Highest Good, which is the cause of the undertaking of any meditation, and wisdom is in fact nothing else than the science of happiness [scientia felicitatis].[208]

Compared with the plan of the *Demonstrationes Catholicae*, the *scientia generalis* seemed therefore to be the heir of their Prolegomena. As originally formulated, these were intended to embrace "the elements of philosophy", namely "the first principles of Metaphysics (de Ente), of Logic (de Mente), of Mathematics (de Spatio), of Physics (de Corpore), of Practical Philosophy (de Civitate)."[209] In keeping with the encyclopaedic aspirations of the previous generations epitomised by the works of Alsted and Comenius, Leibniz emphasised the philosophical advantages of the proposed reorganisation for the advancement of knowledge and its pedagogical advantages for the transmission of knowledge. No less importantly, and again in accord with past generations of post-Ramist and 'Baconian' reformers, he stressed its praxis-oriented aim of improving the human condition and of pursuing the true happiness of mankind which is grounded in wisdom. In a text of the winter of 1678–9 which presented this conception of the *scientia generalis* as the search for "wisdom" or *scientia felicitatis*, Leibniz spelled out in more detail the relationship between the *scientia generalis* and the encyclopaedia:

In my view, wisdom is nothing other than the science of happiness, and true learning, considered as a preparation for wisdom, is the habit of a soul most plentifully supplied with the knowledge of how to live well and happily. But since the most important of our affairs deal with the whole nature of things, many of which can help or harm us, we need a manifold knowledge of our mind and of those things which can act upon us or be acted upon by us. But above all the universal science or science of the causes of things should be sought in the first place from God, the author of all things, from whom our happiness, as well as anything else, depends; secondly from the nature and condition of other minds, and finally from corporeal nature and of the various qualities of bodies. In one way or another all these things can contribute to avoiding harm and procuring good. From this it follows that it is in the interest of the happiness of mankind that there be brought together a certain *encyclopaedia* or orderly collection of truths, sufficient (as far as possible) for the deduction of all useful things. And this will be like a public treasury to which could be added all remarkable [subsequent] discoveries and observations. But since [this Encyclopaedia] will be of the most massive bulk, especially regarding matters of civil and natural history, in the meantime a certain *Scientia Generalis* is needed containing the first principles of reason and experience[.]210

In short, the *scientia generalis* was intended as a compendium of the encyclopaedia in the sense that it contained the principles, elements, or foundations of all the sciences, out of which the whole encyclopaedia could be expounded. Accordingly, in several proposals sketched by Leibniz for a preliminary work containing the "Introduction to the Secret Encyclopaedia" or the "Initia et Specimena" ("Beginnings and Examples") of the *scientia generalis* proper, the *scientia generalis* was emblematically defined as pertaining to "the instauration and advancement of the sciences for the common happiness" ("de instauratione et augmentis scientiarum ad publicam felicitatem") – a definition resonant with Baconian echoes.211 As for the theological demonstrations which constituted the object proper of the *Demonstrationes Catholicae* themselves, they seemed to retain their central place as the "science . . . of God" which "should be sought above all" (*inprimis expetenda*).[212] Finally, in a later text written around the second half of 1688, Leibniz was explicit in equating the *scientia generalis seu princeps* ("general or first science") with Aristotle's science of first principles.[213] The *scientia generalis* therefore embraced metaphysics and logic (the latter intended in the modern sense of a theory about the nature of propositions and of truth) as a sort of Aristotelian "first philosophy" oriented towards the ethical aim of reaching the true happiness grounded in wisdom:

> for wisdom there is needed a *scientia generalis*, which treats the causes of things, the harmony of the universe, and the principles and orderly arrangement [*oeconomia*] of truths. . . . The general or first science, which we attempt to treat, is the theory of the wise; but wisdom is the application of [this] first science.[214]

In turn, the notion of encyclopaedia itself was employed by Leibniz in these years in two different senses, one more familiar, the other less so. In the former sense, Leibniz meant by encyclopaedia a sort of inventory of past and present knowledge compiled by means of a systematic survey of the best literature in every field by savants collaborating in the institutional framework of the proposed academies or societies of sciences. This survey was in his view the necessary precondition of the full development of the *scientia generalis* and of its key instrument or 'organon', the *characteristica universalis*.[215] On this familiar notion, however, Leibniz superimposed the notion of a "demonstrative" and "inventive" encyclopaedia. In this second sense, the encyclopaedia, rather than being a precondition of the *scientia generalis*, was its fruit. More precisely, it was the way in which the *scientia generalis* could be systematically expounded. The *scientia generalis* was intended to embrace the principles of all current knowledge as well as the methods both of its discovery in the past and of its future development. Once it had been established, it would provide the foundations and the tools for a systematic and rigorous reconception and development of all the disciplines of the encyclopaedia.

Between 1682 and 1686, from the ocean of Leibniz's private papers pursuing his encyclopaedic goal, a gem occasionally surfaced in the form of a published article. It was not by chance that the vehicle chosen by Leibniz for this sort of public communication was Germany's first learned journal, the recently established *Acta Eruditorum*. As early as October 1668, and then again in 1669 and in 1670, Leibniz himself had proposed the establishment of a similar journal, the *Nucleus Librarius Semestralis*, but nothing had come of it.[216] In the autumn of 1679 he tried again, this time conceiving an even more ambitious plan. In addition to systematically reviewing recent literature, the proposed *Semestria Literaria* would have included editions both of rare ancient and medieval codices and of texts by contemporary thinkers. It would also have collected significant excerpts from correspondence, diaries, and scientific notes, with the aim of building a *Bibliotheca Universalis*. Ultimately, all these publications were foreseen as providing material towards the compilation of an *Encyclopaedia Universalis* together with a complementary *Atlas Universalis*.[217] Unfortunately, Leibniz's plan remained once again a dead letter. In 1681 however, two former companions of his studies in Leipzig, Otto Mencke and Christoph Pfautz,[218] enlisted his support for the establishment of a German learned journal on the model of the *Journal des Sçavans*. Leibniz did not fail them. Between 1682 and 1686 he contributed to the new journal thirteen papers, mostly on mathematical and scientific topics.[219] Among them, three were jewels of outstanding value: the *Nova Methodus pro Maximis et Minimis* (October 1684), in which Leibniz finally revealed to the broader public the infinitesimal calculus invented in 1675;[220] the *Meditationes de Cognitione, Veritate, et Ideis* (November 1684), offering a key presentation of central elements of his epistemology against the backdrop of a critical confrontation with Descartes; and the *Brevis demonstratio erroris memorabilis Cartesii et aliorum circa legem naturae* (March 1686), a seminal paper publicly uncovering his opposition to Descartes's thesis of the conservation in the universe of the same quantity of motion (estimated by the product of mass times speed – mv) and proposing his alternative law of the conservation of force, estimated by mv^2.

The year in which the *Brevis Demonstratio* saw the light, 1686, was perhaps, from an intellectual point of view, Leibniz's *annus mirabilis* par excellence.[221] In the aftermath of the failed Harz project he seemed to find the peace of mind and intellectual energy necessary to bring to fruition thoughts which had exercised his mind over a number of years, condensing them into four milestone texts on physics, metaphysics, theology, and logic. It was probably in the isolation of the Harz, where he sojourned from the beginning of January to the beginning of April, that he wrote the *Brevis Demonstratio* and sent it for publication to Otto Mencke on 16 January 1686.[222] A few days of forced inactivity in this wintry mountain seclusion prompted Leibniz to compose "un petit discours de Metaphysique" ("a little discourse on Metaphysics") intended for Antoine Arnauld's perusal. On 11 February 1686 he wrote to his trusted friend, the Landgraf Ernst von Hessen-Rheinfels, asking him to act as an intermediary with Arnauld, who had fled the persecution of Jansenism by Louis XIV in June 1679 and was now living under cover in the Netherlands:

Being in a place where I had nothing to do for a few days, I recently wrote a little discourse on metaphysics, on which I would like Monsieur Arnauld's opinion. Because the issues of grace, God's concurrence with creatures, the nature of miracles, the cause of sin and the origin of evil, the immortality of the soul, ideas, etc. are touched upon within it in a way which seems to offer fresh approaches capable of clarifying some very great difficulties. I have added here the summary of the articles which it contains, since I have not yet been able to have a fair copy made. I beg therefore Your Grace to have this summary sent to him with the request that he give it some attention and communicate his opinion.[223]

This letter marked the beginning of a crucially important philosophical correspondence with Arnauld, which over the following couple of years revolved around the topics discussed in the *Discours de Métaphysique* (*Discourse on Metaphysics*). But Leibniz's productivity was not exhausted by these landmark studies in physics and metaphysics. Between April and October he composed the most voluminous of his philosophical and theological texts written between 1677 and 1690: an *Examination of the Christian Religion* of such breath as to merit the title of *Theological System* in the minds of its nineteenth-century editors.[224] Last but not least, during this amazingly fruitful year he wrote his most comprehensive work in the field of logic, the *Generales Inquisitiones de Analysi Notionum et Veritatum*, in which appeared the idea of interpreting contingent truths as propositions in which the inclusion of the predicate in the subject cannot be proven. According to this conception, the analysis of contingent propositions is an infinite process the end of which (that is, the proof) is never reached.[225] The *Generales Inquisitiones* also outlined the foundations of the enormously innovative logical calculus on which Leibniz had been working since 1679, which resembled the logical systems later developed by George Boole (1815–64) in many important respects. Two of these fundamental texts of 1686 surfaced from the abyssal depths of Leibniz's private papers into the light of the public. The first, the *Discours de Métaphysique*, was unveiled only partially in the form of the summary sent as a personal communication to Arnauld via Landgraf Ernst. The second, the *Brevis Demonstratio*, appeared as a proper publication in the

Acta Eruditorum. In both cases bitter polemics and misunderstandings awaited Leibniz's decision to share with others ideas that he had been privately developing; and these unpleasant experiences may ultimately account for the fact that the great majority of his papers did not reach the printer until after his death.

Logic and Mathematics

Amongst these private papers, a great number were devoted to preliminary work towards the *scientia generalis*, the *characteristica universalis*, and its deployment in the *calculus universalis*. In them Leibniz focused in particular on the relationship between 'things' and 'concepts', truth and knowledge; on the identification of the predicamental order of things through the painstaking compilation of tables of definitions and the listing of primitive concepts; and on the analysis of complex concepts and of natural language as a basis for the development of the *characteristica* and the *calculus universalis*.[226] In numerous papers bearing upon the relationship between logic and metaphysics and the logical-ontological foundations of truth and knowledge, Leibniz prepared the ground for the metaphysical conception of substance which found its mature formulation in the *Discours de Métaphysique* of 1686. More precisely, in the logical papers of April 1679 he explicitly formulated the doctrine of truth which constituted the bedrock of his theory of the complete concept corresponding to individual substances, namely his claim that a proposition is true if and only if the concept of its predicate is included in the concept of its subject: "every true categorical affirmative universal proposition signifies nothing other than some connection between predicate and subject . . . so that the predicate is said to be in the subject, or contained in the subject . . . That is to say that the concept of the subject, either in itself or with some addition, involves the concept of the predicate."[227] In the context of discussions of the classical methods of analysis and synthesis and of the *ars judicandi* and *ars inveniendi*, this same doctrine was reproposed in the claim that a true proposition is either an identical proposition or reducible to one.[228] Moreover, as he lucidly summarized in the *Meditationes de Cognitione, Veritate, et Ideis* published in the *Acta Eruditorum* of November 1684, the most perfect kind of knowledge – adequate knowledge – is reached when the analysis of all the concepts contained in a proposition "is carried through to the end," that is, when primitive concepts which cannot be further reduced to other concepts are reached.[229] This conception of truth and knowledge as involving an analytic reduction of complex propositions and concepts to identical propositions and primitive concepts explains why Leibniz pursued so energetically the identification of the primitive concepts out of which all truths are ultimately formed. Hence his tireless compilation of lists of such concepts and of chains of definitions which were intended to formulate that "alphabet of human thought" advocated as early as 1668 in the *Dissertatio de Arte Combinatoria*.[230]

The identification of these concepts was also the first step toward the development of the *characteristica universalis*. Once these concepts (or at least, as many of them as possible) had been found, the subsequent tasks would have been the identification of appropriate 'characters', 'signs', or 'symbols' to represent them and the formulation of the rules for their correct 'combination'. The development of the *characteristica universalis* had therefore both an analytic aspect (leading to the identification of primitive concepts) and a synthetic or 'combinatorial' aspect. In turn, its outcome would have been a dramatic advancement of both the *ars judicandi* and the *ars inveniendi*.[231] In a letter of 19 December 1678 to the mathematician Jean Gallois, Leibniz argued that his conception of the *characteristica* represented a considerable advance on previous attempts to create an artificial universal language as a means to promote universal communication. This advance consisted of its power of discovery and of sound judgement following the model of algebra and arithmetic:

I am more and more convinced of the usefulness and reality of this general science, and I see that few people have understood its scope. But to render it easier and, so to speak, sensible, I intend to employ the *characteristica* of which I once told you, and of which algebra and arithmetic are merely samples. This *characteristica* consists of a certain writing or language (since one who has one can have the other) which perfectly corresponds to the relations of our thoughts. This character will be completely different from those which have previously been projected. Because the most important thing has been overlooked, namely that the characters of this writing must assist discovery and judgement as in algebra and arithmetic ... [T]his writing is much more instructive than that of the Chinese, which requires that one be learned in order to be able to write.[232]

The reference to Chinese is easily explained by the fact that a month or so before Leibniz had started an interesting correspondence with Johann Sigismund Elsholz, the physician of the Elector of Brandenburg, on Chinese writing and language – a tradition that Leibniz found deeply intriguing in the context of his own studies towards the development of a symbolic formal language.[233] But perhaps the most revealing aspect of this letter to Gallois was the explicit mention of algebra and arithmetic both as the models to be followed for the development of the *characteristica* and as mere components of a broader project under which they should ultimately have been subsumed. Indeed, Leibniz's work towards the *characteristica* presented the development of a logical calculus modelled on algebra (or, more precisely, on François Viète's *logistica speciosa*) as one of its most striking and distinctive features.[234]

The basis of this logical calculus was laid in the cluster of essays written in April 1679.[235] In them Leibniz employed letters and numbers to indicate concepts and formulate propositions. In particular, since primitive concepts cannot be further divided into simpler elements, he proposed to designate them through prime numbers.[236] Accordingly, a complex concept (that is, a concept composed of primitive concepts) could be expressed as the product of prime numbers. Moreover, Leibniz expressed through algebraic equations the four standard categorical propositions graphically represented by the 'square of opposition'. It was in the context of these reflections on the relationship between propositions and their numerical expression that Leibniz formulated the criterion of truth of a logical argument, proudly announcing that with his new calculus it was possible to derive all the modes and figures of the syllogism simply by applying the rules which govern numbers. In the logical texts of 1678–84 he outlined a logical calculus – defined as *calculus universalis* – in which he focused on the form of the argumentation, that is to say, on the structure which remains valid independent of the different contents which can be assigned to the letters employed in the proposition to designate terms (for instance: a = 'animal', b = 'rational', etc.).

With the *Generales Inquisitiones de Analysi Notionum et Veritatum* of 1686 Leibniz felt he had reached an important breakthrough, as he noted near the title: "Hic egregie progressus sum" ("Here I made remarkable progress").[237] In this work Leibniz defined a notion of coincidence valid both for terms and for propositions: two terms (or two propositions) coincide (*coincidunt*) if they can be substituted for one another *salva veritate* ("preserving truth"), that is to say, if their substitution for one another does not alter the truth-value. He also distinguished in the calculus two fundamental relations: the relation of "being included in" (expressed through the copula 'is' (*est*)) and the relation of "coincidence" (expressed through the sign '='). Moreover, he proposed as an idea of the greatest importance the reduction of propositions to terms: for instance, the

reduction of the categorical proposition 'A is B' to 'the being B of A' or
'the B-ness of A'. This reduction was conceived by him as a process of
abstraction which gives rise to a new kind of abstracts ('notional abstracts'
or logical abstracts) of key importance for the introduction of the calculus
in philosophy. Through them Leibniz was able not only to reduce categorical propositions to terms, but also hypothetical propositions to categorical
propositions. An analogous procedure was to be adopted later on by algebraists of logic such as George Boole, Charles S. Peirce (1839–1914), and
Ernst Schröder (1841–1902):

> These abstracts are very suitable for my general plans of introducing calculation into
> philosophy; for just as I reduce categorical propositions to simple terms affected
> by '*est*', I also reduce hypothetical propositions to categorical ones into which these
> abstracts are introduced. For instance, I reduce this hypothetical proposition 'If Peter
> is wise, Peter is just' to this categorical proposition: 'to be wise Peter is to be just
> Peter'. This way the same rules are valid for hypothetical propositions as are valid for
> categorical propositions.[238]

A group of essays written around 1686–7 contained important developments of Leibniz's logical calculus, notably the introduction of the "real
addition" – a logical operation in which concepts rather than numbers
were added or (as Leibniz put it) "composed." To distinguish it from
arithmetical addition, Leibniz used the symbol $\oplus$ instead of $+$.[239] Unfortunately but not uncharacteristically, these developments remained buried
in Leibniz's Nachlaß until the twentieth century.

Leibniz also kept to himself the paper in which he proclaimed his
ideal of a peaceful solution of all disputes attainable on the only ground
on which true dialogue is possible: reason. Reformulated in terms of his
universal calculus, he proposed, in a word, *calculemus*:

> But to go back to the expression of thoughts through characters, this is my opinion:
> it will hardly be possible *to end controversies* and impose silence on the *sects*, unless we
> recall complex arguments to simple *calculations*, [and] terms of vague and uncertain
> significance to determinate *characters*. . . . Once this has been done, when controversies
> will arise, there will be no more need of a disputation between two philosophers than
> between two accountants. It will in fact suffice to take pen in hand, to sit at the abacus,
> and – having summoned, if one wishes, a friend – to say to one another: '*let us calculate*'
> [*calculemus*].[240]

Nor was Leibniz's famous *calculemus* an improbable manifesto of the
omnipotence of human reason. If Leibniz was overoptimistic regarding
something, this was not so much the power of human reason as the human
willingness to follow reason. He was in fact well aware of the limits of

the created intellect and of the fact that in everyday life, as well as in crucial fields such as medicine, jurisprudence, and religion, exact data on which to base his logical calculation were not (and often could not be) available. Nevertheless, he insisted, since reason had a role to play also in these fields, his *characteristica* would still be extremely useful insofar as it was nothing else than "a supreme exaltation, and *an extremely efficient [compendiosissimus] use of human reason by means of symbols and signs.*"[241] His point was not that everything would eventually be fully understood and subjected to an exact mathematical calculation. Rather, in the many fields in which strict demonstrations were and would remain impossible for us, we could nevertheless put our reason to best use through the employment of an unambigous formal language. In so doing we could agree on reasonable decisions also in uncertain situations. In other words, in the many circumstances in which we were forced to operate with conjectures rather than adequate data, we should aim at determining "not only what is more plausible [verisimilius] but also what is *more secure [tutius]*" through a novel and revolutionary part of logic at which Leibniz was working – "*a part of logic*, so far virtually untouched, devoted to the estimation of degrees of probability; a steelyard of proofs, presumptions, conjectures, and clues."[242]

In fact, some ten years before writing these words, Leibniz had penned a paper which constituted a turning point in the philosophy of probability. In *De incerti aestimatione*, written in September 1678, he argued that "probability is degree of possibility" – and in so doing indicated the idea fundamental to the classical theory of probability formulated over a century later by Pierre Simon de Laplace (1749–1827).[243] At the same time, he was acutely conscious of the fact that much more needed to be done to create a fully fledged logic of probability or, as he was fond of saying, a "balance of reason" able to weigh (rather than count) reasons on the two sides of an issue.[244] Once again he stressed his firm intention to work on it, bitterly regretting the fact that his many occupations were preventing him from devoting the necessary amount of time to the development of this novel part of logic. Such was in his view its importance that in 1697 – feeling that his life was entering its final phase – he expressed the wish of giving absolute priority to its development:

It is often justly said that reasons should not be counted but weighted; but no one has yet given us a balance able to weigh the strength of reasons. It is one of the greatest deficiencies of our logic, from which we suffer even in the most serious and important matters of life, which regard justice, the tranquillity and wellbeing of the state, the health of human beings, and religion itself. . . . If God gives me more life and health I will make of this my principal concern.[245]

Predictably but not therefore less astonishingly, in addition to drawing on mathematical models for the development of the *characteristica universalis* and of the logical calculus, Leibniz kept himself busy with mathematics itself, reaching once again striking new insights. A prime example of this effort was his work on the *analysis situs* (analysis of situation) or *characteristica geometrica*, which he conceived as a special form of the *characteristica universalis*. He mentioned this novel geometrical science as early as 1678 in the letter of 19 December to Gallois. In August 1679 he had ready a first essay entitled *Characteristica geometrica*.[246] On 18 September 1679, in the same packet to Christiaan Huygens which contained a sample of phosphorus and the invitation to experiment with its "perpetual light," Leibniz also included a paper outlining his new *Characteristica geometrica*.[247] As it was explained in the accompanying letter, he had come to the conclusion that the application of algebra to geometry was not the best way to deal with geometrical problems, since algebra "expresses magnitude" whereas geometry is essentially concerned with "situation" (*situs*). It was therefore necessary to develop a new kind of "properly geometrical or linear analysis which directly expresses *situs* to us, just as algebra expresses magnitude." This, as he proudly announced to Huygens, was precisely what he was trying to accomplish: "I believe I can see the means of doing it, and that it will be possible to represent figures and even machines and motions in characters, as algebra represents numbers or sizes."[248] In short, Leibniz's basic idea was to express situation, angles, and movements by symbols instead of figures and then to operate with them in an efficient and clear way.[249] In order to illustrate what he had in mind, he proceeded to give a sample of the symbolic expression of simple geometrical loci. For instance, the congruence between two triangles (Fig. 4.1) could be expressed as ABC ŏ DEF, where the relation of congruence was indicated by the symbol ŏ.[250] He concluded his paper with an example of demonstration conducted through this new kind of geometrical calculus.[251]

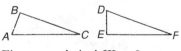

Figure 4.1. As in A III, 2, 854.

Huygens was not impressed. Unfortunately he failed to appreciate the enormous potential of what Leibniz's described not as an accomplished method but as "an overture that, in its field, should take us as far as algebra in its respective field".[252] Instead he objected that all the results given by Leibniz were already well known and that this wonderful new *characteristica* was in his view nothing more than "wishful thinking."[253] Although deeply discouraging, Huygens's dismissive words did not deter Leibniz completely. Probably around 1693 he wrote a further essay on his *Analysis situs* and continued (albeit occasionally) to refer to this project until as late as 1716.[254]

On the other hand, from 1679 onwards, yet another striking invention was beginning to take shape in his mind: a dyadic or binary arithmetic from which he anticipated remarkable discoveries.[255] Once again, Leibniz's intuition was far ahead of his time. Hampered as he was by technical difficulties, it did not have a chance to flourish, though Leibniz returned to the project repeatedly and eventually related it to some of his most basic objectives, as we shall see. More immediately successful was his invention in January 1684 of determinants and the discovery of their properties. Determinants are used to eliminate the unknowns and thereby to solve systems of linear equations (that is, finite sets of equations with the same unknowns, the common solutions of which have to be determined: for instance, $a_{10} + a_{11}x + a_{12}y = 0$ and $a_{20} + a_{21}x + a_{22}y = 0$, in which x and y are the unknowns). In a key manuscript of 22 January 1684, Leibniz arrived at the general rule for the solution of systems of linear equations through determinants, now known as 'Cramer's rule' after the Swiss mathematician Gabriel Cramer (1704–52), later accredited with the discovery. Despite the importance of this discovery, Leibniz published nothing on this new fundamental theory in linear algebra.[256] At some point before 1683, Leibniz also proved for the first time what is known as Fermat's little theorem.[257]

Metaphysics and Physics

Logic, in which such outstanding progress was made by Leibniz in this period, was for him a 'mirror' of reality. This explains why the intensive logical work of these years provided the direct underpinning for the metaphysics emblematically expressed in his *Discours de Métaphysique* in the doctrine of the complete concept which corresponds to an individual substance. In addition to logic, however, a cluster of equally important mathematical, physical, theological, and metaphysical reflections converged to reshape Leibniz's youthful intuitions via a fundamentally coherent process of evolution into his mature philosophical views. Indeed, as he emphatically stressed towards the end of his life, the principles of his system were "such that they [could] hardly be torn apart from one another. Whoever knows one well knows them all."[258]

Originating from a more strictly metaphysical strand of reflections, the rehabilitation of substantial forms announced to Duke Johann Friedrich in 1679 certainly constituted an essential element of the philosophical system proposed by Leibniz in the 1680s and beyond, and, in particular, of the notion of substance which took shape especially during the decade after 1679. The doctrine of substantial forms was a central Aristotelian and scholastic tenet which had been rejected by the 'moderns', notably the Cartesians. In his early thought Leibniz himself had regarded with suspicion if not with downright contempt the invocation of substantial forms in the explanation of the phenomena of nature which the 'moderns' rightly explained mechanistically.[259] He seems, however, to have always left the door open to a possible reinterpretation and reemployment of this doctrine in the correct metaphysical context. Around 1668, in particular, he defined "substantial form" in *De Transsubstantiatione* as the principle of action required for a being to qualify as a substance and corresponding to what Aristotle called "nature."[260] Although after 1671 the term "substantial form" tended to disappear from Leibniz's vocabulary, in a text composed between 1673 and 1675 he equated the principle of action or *conatus* which is internal to bodies and constitutes their principle of "substantiality" with what "the scholastics . . . called substantial form."[261] In 1673–5 he still evidently entertained the idea that the traditional doctrine of substantial forms, when correctly interpreted, could provide a powerful instrument of explanation in a metaphysical conception of the corporeal world which postulated an "incorporeal principle" – that is, the incorporeal principle envisaged as early as 1668 in the *Confessio Naturae*, further specified in texts of 1668–9 as a principle of activity required by beings in order to qualify as substances, and explicitly labelled with the scholastic term of "substantial form." One crucial departure is nevertheless apparent. Within the *Confessio Naturae* and in these texts of 1668–9, the "incorporeal principle" or "principle of activity" had been interpreted for nonrational beings in terms of a transcendent Mind (that is, God). Around 1670–72, however, Leibniz had come to the conclusion that to avoid pantheistic consequences this principle of activity (and therefore substantiality) needed to be immanent in bodies.[262] No later than 1679 Leibniz was prepared to state in an 'official' letter to his employer that this immanent principle of activity required by substances could be interpreted in terms of the traditional doctrine of substantial forms.

Meanwhile, under the stimulation of Leibniz's studies on physics, this principle was being reinterpreted in a strikingly new way in terms of the 'force' or 'power' of action internal to things.[263] In January 1678, in an unpublished paper on the laws of motion and on the collision of bodies (*De corporum concursu*), Leibniz quantified force for the first time as the product of mass (m) and the square of speed (v^2).[264] It is not the quantity of motion (mass times speed or mv) which is conserved in the universe, as Descartes maintained, but the quantity of force (mass times the square of speed or mv^2).[265] This result, reached as early as 1678–9, was divulged in March 1686 with the publication in the *Acta Eruditorum* of the *Brevis demonstratio erroris memorabilis Cartesii et aliorum circa legem naturae*. In it Leibniz struck at the core of Cartesian physics, namely the principle of the conservation of motion. He argued that the mistake of Descartes and the Cartesians lay in their identification of the quantity of motion with motive force. From this erroneous identification they concluded that the same quantity of motion is conserved in the universe. In contrast, Leibniz showed that motive force is not identical to the quantity of motion, and it is force and not motion which is conserved.[266] Leibniz's argument was ultimately grounded on the fundamental metaphysical principle of the equivalence between the full cause and the entire effect, recognised since 1676 as the foundation of the application of geometry to mechanics.[267] It followed from this principle that force must be estimated from the quantity of the effect that it can produce, as Leibniz already wrote between the summer of 1678 and early 1679:

Force or power should now be treated; when it is to be known, it must be estimated from the quantity of the effect. But the power of the effect and of the cause are equal to each other . . . Here it is worth showing that the same quantity of motion cannot be conserved, but that on the other hand the same quantity of power is conserved.[268]

A French translation of the *Brevis Demonstratio* was published in September 1686 in the *Nouvelles de la République des Lettres*, a learned journal edited in Holland by Pierre Bayle (1647–1706). Besides giving rise to a

correspondence with Bayle which was to continue until 1702, this publication fuelled a long polemic with the Cartesian Abbé Catelan, Nicolas
Malebranche, and Denis Papin.[269] In particular, in a letter of 9 January
1687 addressed to Bayle and published in the *Nouvelles de la République
des Lettres* of February 1687, Leibniz, responding to the objections of the
Abbé Catelan, proposed to substitute the Cartesian principle of the equivalence of motive force and quantity of motion with "another *Law of nature*"
which was, in his view, "the most universal and the most inviolable":

namely, that there is always a *perfect equation between the full cause and the entire effect.*
This law not only says that the effects are proportional to the causes, but also that
each entire effect is equivalent to its cause. And despite the fact that this axiom is
indeed metaphysical, it is nevertheless among the most useful which can be employed
in physics and provides the means to reduce forces to a geometrical calculation.[270]

From this fundamental principle and its consequence – namely that force
must be estimated by the quantity of the effect – Leibniz drew an important metaphysical conclusion:

I will add a remark of consequence for metaphysics. I have shown that force should
not be estimated by the composition of speed and mass [mv], but by the future
effect. Nevertheless it appears that force or power is something real from the present
[moment], and [that] the future effect it is not. Hence it follows *that it will be necessary
to admit in bodies something different from mass and speed, unless one wishes to deny to
bodies all power of acting.*[271]

Indeed, one of the main aims of Leibniz's metaphysical doctrine, corroborated by what could be observed in the physical word, was precisely to
ascribe an internal source of activity – an active force or power – to created
things. This was the point at which he disagreed fundamentally with the
occasionalism of Malebranche, who admitted genuine power or causal
efficacy in God alone.[272] Unsurprisingly, therefore, a few lines later Leibniz took issue with Malebranche. Thereby he began a sustained discussion
documented in the *Nouvelles de la République des Lettres* and in Leibniz's
private papers, and complementing the direct epistolary exchange of 1679
between the two thinkers on Cartesianism and related topics.[273]

The development of a new mechanics founded on the law of the conservation of force (mv^2) converged with other strands of reflection in
suggesting a metaphysics in which something, in order to qualify as "one"
being in a proper sense (*ens aliquod*), required an immaterial principle of
unity and activity, a "soul" or "form". As early as 1678–9 Leibniz came

to the conclusion that every being which was properly "one" (*hoc aliquid*, or *unum quiddam*) was "animated" in the sense of having a soul or form endowed with perception and appetite:

Now there follows the subject of incorporeals. There turn out to be certain things in body which cannot be explained by the necessity of matter alone. Such as the laws of motion, which depend on the metaphysical principle of the equality of cause and effect. Here therefore the soul must be treated, and it must be shown that all things are animated. Unless there were a soul, i.e., a kind of form, a body would not be an entity, since no part of it can be assigned which would not again consist of further parts, and so nothing could be assigned in body which could be called *this something* [*hoc aliquid*], or *some one thing* [*unum quiddam*]. It is the nature of a soul or form to have some perception and appetite, which are passions and actions of the soul... It is foolish to want to attribute perception to man alone; for all things can have some perception in proportion to the measure of their perfection[.][274]

In a text of 1685 explicitly conceived as a *specimen* of the *Demonstrationes Catholicae*, Leibniz vividly described his meandering intellectual journey in search of an explanation for those aspects of bodies which were irreducible to extension. His recognition of the "true notion of body" in the power of action (*vis agendi* or active force) and the power of passion or resistance (*vis patiendi* or passive force), corresponding respectively to the "substantial form" and the "matter" of the Aristotelian tradition, was like an unexpected emersion from a labyrinth at the very starting point from which the journey had begun. During this journey he was also confirmed in his early conviction, dating at least from the *Confessio Naturae*, that physics must be grounded on metaphysical principles, although these principles are beyond what physics proper investigates and should not enter into the mechanical explanation of phenomena:

the true notion of body is not known, for it does not consist in extention but in the power of acting and being acted upon, that is the power of moving and resisting movement [agendi patiendique, hoc est movendi resistendique vis]...I have shown...that the laws of mechanics themselves do not flow from geometric but from metaphysical principles, and if all things were not governed by a mind, they would be very different from what we experience. And neither can body be understood as something one per se: on the contrary it would be nothing but an aggregate of points, which is impossible unless it contains a substantial form which is in a certain way analogous to the soul, namely the first act or power of acting implanted by the will of the creator in any body whatever... In turn I have shown that matter no more consists in extention than force [vis] consists in action, so that force is therefore that from which action follows unless something obstructs it, just as matter is the power in whatever body of being acted upon or of resisting from which follows a determinate extention of the body . . . And so what occurred to me was like that which happens to someone who, having wandered for a long time in a forest, suddenly emerges into an open field and against all hope finds himself back in the same place from which he had first strayed to immerse himself in the forest.[275]

The Aristotelian polarity of form and matter from which substances are constituted played a key role in the doctrine of corporeal substances, which represented one of the most prominent hallmarks of Leibniz's metaphysics in this period.[276] Famously, it was discussed at length in the correspondence with Arnauld instigated by the *Discours de Métaphysique*. Corporeal substances originate from the union of a substantial form with a body, which is in turn an aggregate of other corporeal substances, each of which results from the union of a substantial form with a body, and so on. Following the scholastic tradition, Leibniz conceived as "secondary matter" the body to which a substantial form is united to form a corporeal substance and which in turn is made up of other corporeal substances. "Primary matter," on the other hand, was conceived by him as the "passive force" which complements the "active force" corresponding to the substantial form.[277] In short, Leibniz was trying to identify what sort of (created) thing qualified as a substance, that is, qualified as a being endowed with an internal principle of unity and activity. His conclusion was that for bodies to qualify as substances they needed an immanent incorporeal or immaterial principle – the substantial form or active force – which constituted their principle of unity and of activity. The ultimate 'ingredients', which were not further reducible and from which corporeal substances received whatever degree of reality or 'substantiality' they had, were the indivisible unities of substantial form and primary matter or, in more distinctively Leibnizian terms, of active force and passive force. In one text written at some point between 1683 and 1686 Leibniz went so far as to interpret primary matter and substantial form in terms of confused and distinct expression of something by a substance:

if there is something real [in bodies], it is only the power of acting or being acted upon; and in this therefore (rather like matter and form) the substance of body consists; but those bodies which do not have a substantial form are merely phenomena, or at least merely aggregates of the true bodies [verorum aggregata]. Substances have metaphysical matter or passive power insofar as they express something confusedly; [they have] active power insofar as [they express something] distinctly.[278]

At least in some passages of his correspondence with Arnauld, Leibniz seemed to indicate that only these indivisible unities, sometimes identified without qualification with substantial forms, qualified strictly speaking as substances:

The body is an aggregate of substances, and, properly speaking, it is not a substance. As a consequence, everywhere in the body there must be indivisible, ingenerable, and incorruptible substances which have something which corresponds to souls.

I maintain that one could not better reestablish philosophy and reduce it to something precise than by acknowledging the only substances or accomplished beings, endowed with a true unity with their different states which follow one another, everything else being nothing but phenomena, abstractions or relations.

Only indivisible substances and their different states are absolutely real.[279]

Together with the doctrine of corporeal substances, another hallmark of Leibniz's theory of substance in this period was the discussion of individual substances, of which the *Discours de Métaphysique* offered the most articulated account. From an account of truth according to which a proposition is true if and only if the concept of its predicate is contained in the concept of its subject, Leibniz arrived at the metaphysical doctrine of individual substances according to which the concept corresponding to an individual substance contains all the predicates which can be attributed to that individual substance with truth:

the term of the subject must always include the term of the predicate so that one who perfectly understands the notion of the subject, will also judge that the predicate belongs to it. This being the case, we can say that the nature of an individual substance, or of a complete being, is to have a notion so complete that it is sufficient to comprehend and to deduce from it all the predicates of the subject to which this notion is attributed.[280]

As Leibniz himself stressed, the doctrine of the complete concept corresponding to an individual substance had many momentous consequences. One notable implication was that each state of a substance was a consequence of its preceding state and that the present state of a substance contained "some remnants of all that has happened to it, and the marks of all that will happen to it, and even the traces of all which happens in the universe." Due to the interconnection of all things, each individual substance therefore expresses the entire universe. Other consequences included the identity of indiscernibles ("it is not true that two substances

resemble one another completely and differ only numerically"), the claim
that substances can only begin by creation and end by annihilation, and
the theses that each created substance is like a "world apart" and that no
created substance is a real cause of the state of another substance. From
this basic metaphysical doctrine also followed all the main elements of
what Leibniz would later call the doctrine of "pre-established harmony" –
that is, the thesis that there is a universal harmony pre-established by God
among the internal states of all substances so that each substance expresses
or mirrors the states of all other substances without there being real causation among them.[281] Alarmingly, however, the complete-concept theory
of substance also seemed to drag Leibniz down the slippery slope of necessitarianism, as Arnauld was quick to point out. If the complete concept
of an individual substance contained all its predicates – "the necessary as
well as the contingent, past, present, and future"[282] – there seemed to be
no space for freedom and genuine contingency. Worse, not only human
freedom seemed to be endangered, but God's freedom as well: if God,
being supremely good, could not but chose the best of all possible worlds,
which was, in turn, a fixed connection of things in which the concept
of every individual substance contained from the very beginning all that
would ever happen to it, how could there be genuine divine freedom?
Understandably, Leibniz was not prepared to accept these consequences.
Not only in his letters to Arnauld but also in many of his private papers,
he passionately defended his system from the charge of necessitarianism
and presented his account of how genuine contingency, and human and
divine freedom, were preserved.[283]

Basically he proposed two kinds of solution. The first one, firmly rooted
in the scholastic tradition and already outlined in the *Confessio Philosophi*
of 1672–3, hinged on the distinction between absolute and hypothetical
necessity. There is absolute necessity when the contrary of a proposition implies a contradiction. There is hypothetical necessity when the
contrary of a proposition does not imply a contradiction, that is, when
something is or happens in a certain way not because it could not have been
otherwise, but because it follows from a certain set of preconditions or
hypotheses:

Absolute necessity is when a thing cannot even be understood to be otherwise, but it
implies a contradiction in terms, e.g., three times three is ten. *Hypothetical necessity*
is when a thing can be understood to be *otherwise* in itself, but, *per accidens*, because
of other things already presupposed outside itself it is necessarily such and such. For

example: it was necessary for Judas to sin, supposing that God foresaw it, or supposing that Judas believed that it would be best.[284]

The second (and preferred) solution emerged around mid-1686 as an "unexpected light" suddenly shining from where Leibniz "least hoped" to receive it, "namely from mathematical considerations on the nature of the infinite."[285] It was recorded in his private papers but not employed either in the *Discours de Métaphysique* or in the correspondence with Arnauld, possibly because Leibniz – being aware of its novelty and of the need of a mathematical appreciation of the meaning of infinite analysis in order fully to comprehend the force of his new argument – did not want to complicate further an already difficult debate.[286] This solution hinged on the thesis that in the case of necessary truths the inclusion of the predicate in the subject of a proposition can be demonstrated in a finite number of steps, whereas in the case of contingent truths this is not possible. More precisely, although also in contingent truths the predicate is included in the subject, it is not possible to demonstrate this inclusion, since it implies an infinite analysis; that is to say, it implies an infinite process in which the end is never reached. Only God – who (as the tradition teaches) does not need the discursive or demonstrative reason typical of limited beings but knows everything by adequate intuitive knowledge – immediately sees the containment of the predicate in the subject in all kinds of propositions, including contingent ones:

And here is uncovered the hidden difference between necessary and contingent truths, which is not easy to understand if one does not have at least a smattering of mathematics. In necessary propositions, of course, one arrives at an identical equation by means of an analysis continued to a certain point; and this is precisely what it means to demonstrate truth with geometrical rigour. In contingent propositions, however, the analysis proceeds infinitely [in infinitum], through reasons of reasons [per rationes rationum], so that there is never a full demonstration; nevertheless, the reason [ratio] of the truth always subsists, although it can be perfectly understood only by God, who alone can go through the infinite series in a single mental thrust.[287]

This doctrine of infinite analysis marked a key development in Leibniz's thought. Although, on the one hand, it was introduced to account for the distinction between necessary and contingent truths, on the other hand, it pointed to their structural identity.[288] In the case of both necessary truths and contingent truths the predicate is included in the subject, but

whereas the demonstration of this inclusion is available to us in the case
of necessary truths, such a demonstration is not possible in the case of
contingent truths since they involve the infinite. This is why human beings
will never be able fully to grasp the complete concept corresponding to an
individual substance and the adequate knowledge of individual substances
is open only to the infinite mind of God.

Theology

In the letter of 1679 to Duke Johann Friedrich presenting his comprehensive plan of the *Demonstrationes Catholicae*, Leibniz promised to push
"metaphysics much further than has been done so far, in order to have true
notions of God and of the soul, of person, of substance, and of accidents."
It seems plausible that the *Discours de Métaphysique* was precisely meant
to provide the philosophical framework of his all-embracing project.[289]
Between April and October 1686, while his correspondence with Arnauld
was in full swing, Leibniz drafted a substantial work which, in some
respects, constituted a complement to the *Discours*: an extensive theological system of clearly Roman Catholic orientation, the *Examen Religionis
Christianae*.[290] Since both Landgraf Ernst and Arnauld were Catholics it
could well be that the *Examen* was written with at least one eye on them,
although in the end Leibniz did not even mention its actual composition
to either of them. At any rate, he had intended for a long time to gain the
official approval of Rome for his interpretations of certain points of the
Council of Trent which, in his view, would have implied contradiction
if not correctly understood. In the letter of 1679 outlining the plan of
the *Demonstrationes Catholicae* to Johann Friedrich, Leibniz had explicitly presented this endorsement from Rome – actively sought by him and
Boineburg, and for which they meant to enlist the help of Arnauld – as
the necessary precondition of going ahead with the Catholic Demonstrations.[291] Being now engaged in a full-scale philosophical correspondence
with Arnauld, Leibniz perhaps thought that this was his chance to show
to the illustrious French thinker that not only his philosophical doctrines
but also his theological views could agree with the standpoint of a Catholic
and that they might therefore advance ecclesiastical reunification in the
framework of the Roman church. It is possible that the unfavourable
reception of his metaphysics by Arnauld convinced him that, for the time

being, there was little point in passing on this further piece of work for his perusal.[292]

On the other hand, the *Examen Religionis Christianae* was far too inclined in favour of Roman Catholic doctrines to be considered a plausible platform for ecclesiastical reunification of the sort under discussion between Molanus and Rojas. Indeed, Protestants would hardly have regarded it as following Molanus's golden rule, approved by Leibniz, that reunion should take place *salvis principiis utriusque partis* ("preserving the principles of both parties").[293] Rather, the *Examen* seems to have been part of Leibniz's long-standing personal strategy of convincing his Catholic patrons, friends, and correspondents that his philosophy as well as his religious beliefs could in good conscience accommodate all the main doctrinal points of Roman Catholicism when these points where expounded in a proper way. If one recalls that, up to 1686, the clear majority of his actual or potential most important patrons and supporters had been Roman Catholics – Philipp von Schönborn, Boineburg, Duke Johann Friedrich, Landgraf Ernst, Emperor Leopold, Arnauld – it becomes clear why it was so important to Leibniz to gain the full trust of this party short of actually converting to Catholicism. The *Examen* seems therefore to have been an exercise in this sort of 'proper' exposition which, on the one hand, conceded as much as possible to the doctrines and even practices of the Roman church, and, on the other hand, coloured Roman Catholicism in distinctively Leibnizian tones. From a philosophical point of view, the *Examen* featured a number of clearly Leibnizian metaphysical doctrines strikingly similar to those of the *Discours de Métaphysique*. From a more strictly theological point of view, it proposed a distinctly Leibnizian theology of love in which the love of God above all things was regarded as the principle of true religion.[294] In short, the *Examen* does not seem to have been written in the hope of gaining the approval of all the main Christian confessions, but as an exposition of Leibniz's fundamental philosophical and theological beliefs which did not conflict with the core doctrines of Roman Catholicism.

All this being said, Leibniz did not convert to Catholicism despite the pressure exercised by his Catholic partners and the fact that he had just drafted an entire treatise of Roman Catholic systematic theology which, although not a personal confession of faith, would have been quite acceptable to him. A revealing marginal note to one of his private papers of 1680–84 discloses the extent to which Leibniz felt he could agree with Roman Catholic doctrines once the practices had been reformed:

However often I consider in my own mind which dogmas I would myself propose if I were granted the supreme power of deciding, all things considered I would be inclined to preserve the dogmas of the Roman Church, and I would correct merely certain practices which have been disapproved of by pious and prudent men of that [the Catholic] side for some time now, [but] which until now have generally been tolerated in the Roman Church due to the failings of times and men. If I had been born in the Roman Church I would certainly not have abandoned it, and yet I would believe all the things which I now believe.[295] The authority of the pope which frightens off many people above all, in fact deters me least of all, since I believe that nothing can be understood as more useful to the Church than its correct use.[296]

But, despite his good will, the problem was that the official Catholic *nihil obstat* for his philosophical and theological interpretations never materialized – not least because Leibniz, possibly discouraged by Arnauld's negative reactions to his philosophical views, kept his *Examen* to himself. As he confided to his Catholic friends, without this assurance that his views would not have been regarded by Rome as against the Christian doctrine, he could not have converted to Catholicism in good conscience.[297] Even more fundamentally, he seems to have regarded as ultimately unjustified the departure from the particular Christian church in which he was born and of which he shared the basic beliefs in order to join another particular Christian church of which he could also have shared the beliefs. If nothing else, such a move would certainly have sent the wrong signal regarding what was, in his view, the true church. Rather, the most consistent way forward was to work toward the reunification of these particular churches in the light of the truly catholic or universal Christian tradition. Against this backdrop one can understand Leibniz's repeated affirmation that if he had been born in the Roman Catholic church he would not have left it, but since he had not he could not in good conscience join it.[298] Likewise, some fifteen years earlier he had countered the accusation of his half-brother, Johann Friedrich, that he was one step from becoming a Calvinist with the claim that "it is foolish to flee from one fortress to the other" when "there is no difference regarding the foundation of salvation."[299]

Whatever the case, the *Examen Religionis Christianae* was certainly part of the broader plan of the Catholic Demonstrations. So were numerous shorter texts composed between 1677 and 1690 in which Leibniz discussed central doctrines of revealed Christian theology, notably the

Trinity and the Incarnation.[300] His general approach with respect to the mysteries of the Christian religion was that already adopted in his early writings and constantly maintained to the end of his life.[301] Mysteries are above human reason but cannot be against reason. Necessary truths such as the principle of noncontradiction hold in the divine as well as in the human sphere.[302] An authentic divine revelation must therefore conform to reason in the sense that it must not imply a proven contradiction. As long as no contradiction has been positively proven, mysteries which have been proclaimed by the age-old tradition of the universal church as divine revelation can legitimately be held to be true even though, by definition, it is not possible for limited human reason to prove their truth. As propositions above reason they are object of revelation and of belief, and not of demonstrative knowledge. Belief is nevertheless based on rational motives of credibility. In addition to the lack of a proven contradiction, historical and philological evidence of the trustworthiness of the source of an alleged revelation must be provided, and revealed propositions must have some intelligible meaning. Although it is not possible, by definition, to comprehend a mystery fully, it must be possible to understand to some extent what the propositions expressing it mean. Accordingly, through the employment of the classical instrument of reasoning from analogy Leibniz tried to provide an explanation of the central mysteries of the Christian revelation which, on the one hand, would help dispel fears of irrationality and, on the other hand, would offer some degree of understanding of their meaning.[303] As foreseen for the last part of his *Demonstrationes Catholicae*, he also discussed the vexed issue of the authority of Scripture and of the Church, together with the question (already tackled in the Mainz period) of who is the ultimate judge in the adjudication of controversial religious matters.[304]

Ethics and Jurisprudence

Leibniz's theology of love was probably inspired more by St. Paul, tinted by Stoicism, than by Martin Luther, who emphasised faith rather than love.[305] The ethical counterpart of this theology was to be found in the conception of justice as *caritas sapientis* (the charity of the wise) explicitly proposed by Leibniz from 1677 onward. Justice was defined in these terms for the first time in a letter to Johann Friedrich of May 1677. In it Leibniz telegraphically stated that the foundation of the whole of natural

jurisprudence rested upon this concept of justice: "Demonstrations concerning natural jurisprudence [derived] from this principle alone: that
justice is the charity of the wise."[306] In the following years Leibniz
returned to this definition many times, unpacking its far-reaching ethical, political, and juridical consequences.[307] The years between 1677 and
1687 witnessed in fact a rekindling of Leibniz's work on jurisprudence
which had lain dormant during the Paris period. Notably, in the context
of a cluster of papers clearly written with the *scientia generalis* in mind,
Leibniz presented an analysis of the concept of the "just" (*justus*) which
constituted one of the best early examples of how he intended to conduct
the conceptual analysis required by the *characteristica universalis*. Perhaps
already in the summer of 1678, he also stated in one of these juridical–
philosophical papers that "every ultimate subject is a complete being and
involves the whole nature of things" ("omne subjectum ultimatum esse
Ens completum, et involvere totam rerum naturam") and that "it is necessary for the predicate to be in the subject" ("necesse est predicatum
subjecto inesse").[308] At some point between August 1680 and February
1685 he committed to paper a *Praefatio novi codicis* which was intended to
serve as an introduction to the new *Codex Leopoldinus* he had proposed to
the emperor's *Hofkanzler*, Johann Paul Hocher, in July 1678.[309] Unlike
the sustained work on jurisprudence of the early years in Leipzig, Altdorf, and Mainz, however, none of the pieces on the philosophy of law
written between 1677 and 1688 was published – once again a measure of
the difficulty Leibniz was having in presenting even the parts of his great
plan which could have had a more direct juridical–political impact and
application.

However, justice (as well as the jurisprudence founded upon it) had for
Leibniz a very broad meaning and a direct bearing on metaphysics and
theology insofar as he conceived the community of God and humankind
in terms of a juridical–political analogy. As he wrote in both the *Discours de
Métaphysique* and the *Examen Religionis Christianae*, God is the monarch
and legislator governing the city of God or the republic of spirits. Revelation, in turn, is the law which God has explicitly given to this community
as expressing his will.[310] This is the point at which

it is necessary to join ethics to metaphysics, that is to say, it is necessary to consider
God not only as the principle and cause of all substances and of all beings, but also
as the chief of all persons or intelligent substances and as the absolute monarch of
the most perfect city or republic which is that of the universe, composed of all spirits
together[.][311]

According to Leibniz, "the whole nature, end, virtue, and function of substances" was nothing else than "to express God and the universe." Since no other substances could do so better than intelligent ones, it seemed undeniable to him that God cared about intelligent beings – with whom he could "so to speak, enter into conversation and even into society" – more than about anything else in the universe.[312] In short, the whole metaphysical and theological system that Leibniz had sketched on the basis of his reflections on a number of different fields, notably logic, mathematics, and physics, had for him a basically ethical and religious inspiration.[313] The final aim was the celebration of the glory of God in his creation by concurring at the realisation of God's "principal design": "the happiness of this city of God,"[314] or the common good of humankind, towards which Leibniz worked through all his kaleidoscopic theoretical and practical endeavours.

Finally, a staggering number of reading notes, excerpts, and translations accumulated during the first ten Hanover years bear witness to his voracious appetite for reading and his propensity to listen to the voices of others.[315] As one might expect, some of the chief representatives of the encyclopaedic, combinatorial, and universal language traditions were well represented – amongst others, Johann Heinrich Alsted, Theodor Zwinger, Erhard Weigel, J. B. Schupp, Ivo Capucinus, Athanasius Kircher, John Wilkins, George Dalgarno, Gerardus Joannes Vossius, Caspar Schoppe, Ph. Labbe, Caramuel de Lobkowitz, Adam Bruxius, and L. Th. Schenkel. Amongst ancient authors Augustine is notable as one to whom Leibniz repeatedly returned. Of his contemporaries, special attention was devoted to Joachim Jungius (whom he counted amongst the "greatest men", along with Pythagoras, Democritus, Plato, Aristotle, Copernicus, Galileo, Bacon, and Descartes),[316] Descartes himself,[317] Spinoza, and Malebranche. As soon as he had in his hands the newly published *Opera posthuma* of Spinoza (Amsterdam 1677), which included the first edition of the *Ethica*, Leibniz read it with great care.[318] Between mid-1684 and early 1686 his attention was drawn to Malebranche's *Traité de la Nature et de la Grace* and to the published polemical correspondence between Malebranche and Arnauld;[319] and probably around 1686 he also studied in depth the French thinker's *Recherche de la vérité*, which he had acquired in 1685 for the ducal library.[320]

Viewed synoptically through the prism of his private papers, Leibniz's first decade in the service of the Hanoverian dukes was extraordinarily fruitful with revolutionary new insights in a number of distinct intellectual fields. Observed from the public perspective of his more practical projects, however, it did not appear nearly so profitable to Leibniz's employer, Duke Ernst August. Leibniz's greatest innovations in logic, mathematics, and philosophy were so far ahead of his time, so anti-intuitive, or so inextricably linked to one another that few of his contemporaries could have properly appreciated them; but to a hard-headed ruler like Ernst August, the discovery of the exquisitely sophisticated system of theoretical clockwork articulated with such care and precision in the mound of papers rapidly accumulating in his *Hofrat*'s private study would only have increased his annoyance that the wooden wheels of his windmills in the Harz stubbornly refused to turn. Yet even without glimpsing more than a tiny fraction of Leibniz's ongoing theoretical endeavours, the duke had seen enough rightly to conclude that, although his court counsellor advocated the union of *theoria cum praxi*, his personal gifts lay more with the former than the latter. The duke therefore seized upon a seemingly academic project of great potential practical advantage to his dynastic aspirations and assigned as Leibniz's next official project a history of the Guelf dynasty. Far more than the Harz project, the history offered Leibniz a pretext to ramble far beyond the confines of Hanover – an excuse which he was happy to exploit to the fullest – and he also exhibited considerable ingenuity in grafting onto it a number of tangentially related philosophical projects far closer to his heart. But unlike the mining adventure, the historical assignment contained no escape clause, and the Guelf history would repeatedly drag its unwilling author back to the archives and back to Hanover, ultimately even after the chief of the Guelf rulers had departed the city for London.

Notes

1. See Leibniz to Duke Johann Friedrich, January 1677 (A I, 2, N. 6) and February* 1677 (A I, 2, N. 10).
2. See for instance Leibniz to Duke Anton Ulrich, second half of December 1690* (A I, 6, N. 16).
3. Leibniz to Thomas Burnett of Kemney, 17 March 1696 (A I, 12, 476).
4. See Hans-Peter Schneider, "Leibniz und der moderne Staat." In *Leibniz und Niedersachsen*. Ed. by Herbert Breger and Friedrich Niewöhner. Stuttgart: Steiner, 1999, pp. 23–34. For more detail on these schemes see below.
5. In his forthcoming book on the development of Leibniz's thinking on the physical world and its metaphysical grounding, Daniel Garber stresses the crucial importance for Leibniz's intellectual journey of the period covered by this and the

following two chapters (that is, in Garber's phrase, the "middle years that go from roughly the late 1670s to the mid- or late-1690s"). I am very grateful to him for sharing with me a penultimate version of this book, which represents a milestone contribution to the current debate on Leibniz's views on body and substance, force and individuality.

6. Cf. *Allgemeine Deutsche Biographie* vol. 8, pp. 629–634 and Günter Scheel, "Hannovers politisches, gesellschaftliches und geistiges Leben zur Leibnizzeit." In *Leibniz. Sein Leben, sein Wirken, seine Welt.* Ed. by W. Totok and C. Haase. Hanover: Verlag für Literatur und Zeitgeschehen, 1966, pp. 83–115. See also Georg Schnath, *Geschichte Hannovers im Zeitalter der neunten Kur und der englischen Sukzession. 1674–1714.* 4 vols. Hildesheim and Leipzig, 1938–82.

7. Cf. the Guelf genealogical tree from Henricus Superbus (d. 1139) to 1707 compiled by Leibniz (Wolfenbüttel, Herzog August Bibliothek, 193 Blankenburg, fol. 26ᵛ–27ʳ; printed in Herbert Breger and Friedrich Niewöhner, eds., *Leibniz und Niedersachsen.* Stuttgart: Steiner, 1999, fig. 15).

8. See Schnath, *Geschichte Hannovers*, I, pp. 33–4; Scheel, "Hannovers politisches, gesellschaftliches und geistiges Leben," pp. 91, 96–9; and Gerda Utermöhlen, "Leibniz im kulturellen Rahmen des hannoverschen Hofes." In *Leibniz und Niedersachsen*, p. 214.

9. See Christian Habbeus to Leibniz, 10 December 1669 (A I, 1, N. 137) and chap. I. 2.

10. Contrary to Aiton, *Leibniz*, pp. 71–2, Leibniz was never appointed privy counsellor (*Geheimer Rat*), a position confused by Aiton with that of court counsellor (*Hofrat*). The highest position reached by Leibniz in Hanover was that of *Geheimer Justizrat* or privy counsellor of justice (13 August 1696), which is the seventh highest of ten degrees of seniority and still far inferior in authority and prestige to a *Geheimer Rat* (cf. Schnath, *Geschichte Hannovers*, II, p. 384).

11. See Schnath, *Geschichte Hannovers*, I, pp. 32–3 and Rescher, "Leibniz finds a niche," pp. 30–31.

12. A I, 2, 13–14.

13. See Schnath, *Geschichte Hannovers*, II, p. 384. Quoted in Rescher, "Leibniz finds a niche," p. 31 and Utermöhlen, "Leibniz im kulturellen Rahmen des hannoverschen Hofes," p. 219.

14. See Rescher, "Leibniz finds a niche," pp. 30–32.

15. See Heinrich Lackmann, "Leibniz' Bibliothekarische Tätigkeit in Hannover." In *Leibniz. Sein Leben, sein Wirken, seine Welt.* Ed. by W. Totok and C. Haase. Hanover: Verlag für Literatur und Zeitgeschehen, 1966, p. 337 and Günter Scheel, "Leibniz als herzoglicher Bibliothekar in Leineschloß." In G. Schnath, *Das Leineschloß.* Hanover: Hahn, 1962, p. 250.

16. Günter Scheel, "Leibniz als politischer Ratgeber des Welfenhauses." In *Leibniz und Niedersachsen.* Ed. by Herbert Breger and Friedrich Niewöhner. Stuttgart: Steiner, 1999, pp. 35–52, esp. pp. 36–7.

17. See Leibniz to Thomas Burnett of Kemney, 3 September 1697 (A I, 14, 444–445).

18. Following Spanish custom, I refer to Cristobal de Rojas y Spinola as 'Rojas'. However, in much of the literature he is known as 'Spinola'. On Rojas and his

ecumenical efforts see especially Karin Masser, *Christóbal de Gentil de Rojas y Spinola O.F.M. und der lutherische Abt Gerardus Wolterius Molanus: Ein Beitrag zur Geschichte der Unionsbestrebungen der katholischen und evangelischen Kirche im 17. Jahrhundert.* Münster: Aschendorff, 2002.

19. See Rescher, "Leibniz finds a niche," p. 40.
20. See Lackmann, "Leibniz' Bibliothekarische Tätigkeit in Hannover," p. 325 and Müller–Krönert, *Leben und Werk*, p. 47.
21. See esp. A I, 2, 15–18.
22. A II, 1, N. 138, N. 139.
23. A II, 1, N. 140.
24. See A II, 1, N. 142, N. 143, N. 146, N. 148. See also the important letter of 1678 on Descartes and the demonstration of the existence of God, probably addressed to Elisabeth von der Pfalz (A II, 1, N. 191), a number of other letters in which Leibniz discussed Cartesianism, notably A II, 1, N. 133, esp. pp. 298–300 (Leibniz to Honorato Fabri, end of 1676), and A II, 1, N. 219 (1679*, unknown addressee). An illuminating commentary of the exchange between Leibniz and Eckhard on the issue of the *ens perfectissimum* is offered by Adams, *Leibniz*, esp. pp. 120–22.
25. Scheel, "Hannovers politisches, gesellschaftliches und geistiges Leben zur Leibnizzeit," p. 107.
26. *Theodicy*, § 100. See also Leibniz to Hermann Conring, 13 January 1678 (A II, 1, 385). Leibniz recorded a conversation with Stensen on the issue of freedom held on 7 December 1677 (A VI, 4, N. 262).
27. On the *Confessio Philosophi* (A VI, 3, N. 7), written in all likelihood between the autumn of 1672 and early 1673, see chap. I. 3.
28. See A VI, 3, 115 and Sleigh, "Introduction" to Leibniz, *Confessio Philosophi. Papers Concerning the Problem of Evil, 1671–1678*, pp. xxi–xxii.
29. *Conversatio cum Domino Episcopo Stenonio de Libertate*, 7 December 1677 (A VI, 4, 1377). Trans. by Sleigh in *Leibniz, Confessio Philosophi. Papers Concerning the Problem of Evil, 1671–1678*, pp. 112–30.
30. Tschirnhaus for Leibniz, 16 November 1676 (A II, 1, N. 132). Cf. A VI, 3, N. 34.
31. A III, 2, N. 91.
32. Cf. the scientific and technical correspondence published in A III, 2; see also A I, 2, N. 46. Some of Leibniz's texts on scientific instruments and related scientific research are published in G. W. Leibniz, *Nachgelassene Schriften physikalischen, mechanischen und technischen Inhalts.* Ed. by Ernst Gerland. Leipzig: Teubner, 1906.
33. See A III, 2, N. 38 and chap. I. 3.
34. Newton to Wallis, 27 August O.S. (6 September) 1692 (cf. John Wallis, *Opera mathematica*, vol. II, Oxford, 1693, p. 391).
35. See Hofmann's detailed presentation and commentary on the *epistola posterior*'s contents (*Leibniz in Paris*, chapter 19; here pp. 263, 273).
36. See Leibniz to Oldenburg, 21 June (1 July N.S.) 1677 (A III, 2, N. 54) and Aiton, *Leibniz*, pp. 80–81.

37. Leibniz for Duke Johann Friedrich, *Vorschlag wegen Aufrichtung eines Commissions-Gerichts*, 13 December 1676 (A I, 2, N. 2). Other proposals can be found in A I, 2, N. 33, N. 37, N. 139 (p. 177), N. 146.
38. The French thinker Jean Bodin (c. 1529–96) was one of the major political theorists of the sixteenth century. As a theorist of absolutism he conceived the sovereign as the lawgiver who is not bound (*absolutus*) by the positive laws he promulgates, though he remains bound by natural and divine law.
39. Schneider, "Leibniz und der moderne Staat," p. 26. See also Patrick Riley, "Introduction." In G. W. Leibniz, *The Political Writings of Leibniz*. Cambridge: Cambridge University Press, 1988, pp. 26–30.
40. *Caesarini Fürstenerii de Jure Suprematus ac Legationis Principum Germaniae*, A IV, 2, N. 1 and Riley, "Introduction," p. 27. See also A IV, 2, N. 2–4, N. 6, N. 8.
41. See A IV, 2, 282.
42. Johann Friedrich's father-in-law, Eduard von Pfalz-Simmern, was a grandson of James VI of Scotland and I of England. In 1658 Johann Friedrich's younger brother, Ernst August, had married Eduard's sister, Sophie von der Pfalz.
43. A IV, 2, N. 7.
44. A IV, 2, N. 5. See also A IV, 2, xx.
45. Müller-Krönert, *Leben und Werk*, pp. 23 and 49.
46. *Le phosphore de M. Krafft*, 2 August 1677. See Ravier 81.
47. See the *Historia inventionis Phosphori*. In *Miscellanea Berolinensia*. Berlin: Sumptibus Johann. Christ. Papenii, 1710, pp. 91–8. See also correspondence with Brand on the subject: A I, 2, N. 46 (p. 57), N. 52, N. 57 (p. 64 ff.), N. 64, N. 66, N. 69, N. 150.
48. See Leibniz for Duke Johann Friedrich, May* 1677 (A I, 2, N. 11) and Leibniz to Duke Johann Friedrich, May* 1677 (A I, 2, N. 12).
49. See A III, 2, xxix and A I, 2, xxx–xxxi.
50. Leibniz to Duke Johann Friedrich, end of December 1678 (A I, 2, N. 92).
51. Leibniz to Duke Johann Friedrich, mid-June 1679 (A I, 2, N. 139, p. 177); Leibniz to Christiaan Huygens, 18 September 1679 (A III, 2, 849). See also A I, 2, N. 170.
52. See Leibniz to Bonaventura Nardini, 18 August 1677 (Ms XXIII, 186, H. V, Bl. 76). This still unpublished letter will eventually appear in a *Nachtrag* to the first series of the Akademie-Ausgabe. Nardini was chaplain and *Pagengouverneur* in Hanover.
53. Leibniz to Duke Johann Friedrich, January 1677 (A I, 2, 11). The note accompanying the payment, penned on 26 July 1676 by Johann Friedrich's representative in Paris, Christophe Brosseau, did not directly mention travel expenses (see A I, 1, N. 356).
54. A I, 2, N. 10.
55. See Leibniz's letter of 3 June 1677, probably addressed to Joh. Daniel Crafft (A I, 2, N. 247).
56. Leibniz for Franz Kuckuck, Quittungen, November 1678 (A I, 2, N. 84).
57. Leibniz for Duke Johann Friedrich, Memorial, 2 October 1677 (A I, 2, N. 18).
58. A I, 2, N. 34.

59. By the time the bureaucratic machinery got around to paying his 1677 stipend in November 1678, Leibniz had to point out that meanwhile his pay had been increased: Leibniz to Duke Johann Friedrich, November 1678 (A I, 2, N. 85).
60. A I, 2, N. 533.
61. Leibniz to Jean Gallois, September* 1677 (A II, 1, 379).
62. Leibniz to Tschirnhaus, January/February 1678 (A III, 2, 340–41). See also Leibniz's report to Conring of June 1678 (A II, 1, 419–20) and the only letter to his godfather, Martin Geier, probably written in 1678 (A I, 2, N. 385).
63. Leibniz for Johann Friedrich, May* 1677 (A I, 2, 22).
64. Leibniz and Georg Held, Contract, 26 July 1678 (A I, 2, N. 51) and Leibniz to Johann Friedrich, end of July 1678 (A I, 2, N. 60).
65. Leibniz to Johann Friedrich, May 1679 (A I, 2, 175). I am grateful to Stephan Waldhoff for helping me to locate this text. See also A IV, 3, 350; A I, 3, 101–2 and Leibniz's comprehensive plan for a reference library drafted in 1689 for Theodor Althet Heinrich von Strattmann (A I, 5, N. 247).
66. See Guhrauer, *Leibnitz*, I, p. 199; *Allgemeine Deutsche Biographie*, vol. 14, pp. 721–6. It is surprising, after such an experience, that Leibniz did not take greater precautions to preserve his own papers from a similar fate.
67. See Ernst von Hessen-Rheinfels for Leibniz (A I, 3, N. 231; enclosure to the Landgraf's letter of 12 November 1682), and Leibniz to Ernst von Hessen-Rheinfels, 24 March 1683 (A I, 3, 278); also Guhrauer, *Leibnitz*, I, 200–202.
68. A I, 3, N. 312.
69. Niedersächsische Landesbibliothek, Ms. IV, 308, Bl. 1–67. The manuscript is entitled *Ren. Cartesii Regulae de inquirenda veritate* and is in the hand of an unknown copyist with limited knowledge of Latin. Leibniz's marginal notes are published in A VI, 4, N. 221. It is possible that the manuscript was instead received in 1683 via Tschirnhaus. See Lackmann, "Leibniz' Bibliothekarische Tätigkeit in Hannover," pp. 331, 345 and A VI, 4, 1031.
70. A I, 2, N. 80–81; Rescher, "Leibniz finds a niche," pp. 40–41.
71. *Epargne d'un Prince*, autumn 1678* (A IV, 3, 329).
72. See A I, 2, N. 70, N. 71, N. 72, N. 73, N. 94; A IV, 3, N. 26, N. 27, N. 40 (see especially A I, 2, 75, 79; A IV, 3, 329). Similar proposals were presented in the following years (see especially A IV, 3, N. 28–39). A helpful survey of Leibniz's wealth of suggestions for reforms and improvements in virtually all aspects of state administration is provided by Schneider, "Leibniz und der moderne Staat."
73. See two proposals of the autumn of 1678* (A IV, 3, N. 130 and N. 131 resp.). The first mention of an *Ordo Caritatis* or *Societas Theophilorum* is to be found in Leibniz's memorandum of September 1678 for Duke Johann Friedrich (A I, 2, 76–7). This memorandum proposed also the establishment of a *Collegium Combinatorium*, conceived as a "working place for the learned" (A I, 2, 76).
74. A IV, 3, 847–8. Further proposals related to the advancement of science followed in 1679 (see *Consilium de Scribenda Historia Naturali*, A IV, 3, N. 132; and *Consultatio de Naturae Cognitione*, A IV, 3, N. 133).

75. Leibniz to Duke Johann Friedrich, December 1678* (A I, 2, 111). The Guelf dukes were the patrons of the Lutheran University of Helmstedt, near Wolfenbüttel.

76. Jürgen Gottschalk, "Der Oberharzer Bergbau und Leibniz' Tätigkeit für Verbesserungen." In *Leibniz und Niedersachsen*. Ed. by Herbert Breger and Friedrich Niewöhner. Stuttgart: Steiner, 1999, pp. 173–86, esp. pp. 173–83 and A I, *Supplementband Harzbergbau 1692–1696*, xxxi.

77. See in particular Leibniz to Duke Johann Friedrich, 8 April 1679 (A I, 2, N. 127, esp. pp. 155–8); also A II, 1, N. 197a and N. 204a.

78. A I, 3, xxxiii.

79. Leibniz and the Mining Office in Clausthal, Contract, 30 September 1679 (A I, 2, N. 169).

80. A I, 2, N. 171.

81. See A I, 2, N. 173–9.

82. A I, 2, N. 181.

83. Christof Pratisius to Leibniz, 13 December 1679 (A III, 2, 910) and Günter Scheel, "Fürstbistum und Stadt Osnabrück im Leben und Werk von G. W. Leibniz." In *Osnabrücker Mitteilungen* 74 (1967), pp. 146–90.

84. See Stephen Gaukroger, *Descartes: An Intellectual Biography*. Oxford: Clarendon Press, 1995, esp. pp. 385 ff. and Desmond Clarke, *Descartes: A Biography*. Cambridge: Cambridge University Press, 2006, esp. 248–75.

85. See Leibniz's annotated excerpts in A II, 1, N. 196 and Leibniz's letter to Malebranche of 23 January 1679 (A II, 1, N. 197). See also A II, 1, N. 191.

86. Christof Pratisius to Leibniz, 13 December 1679 (A III, 2, 910).

87. Scheel, "Fürstbistum und Stadt Osnabrück," pp. 154–5.

88. See Scheel, "Hannovers politisches, gesellschaftliches und geistiges Leben zur Leibnizzeit," pp. 99–102 and *Allgemeine Deutsche Biographie*, vol. 6, pp. 261–3.

89. See Schnath, *Geschichte Hannovers*, I, pp. 488–91 and A I, 3, xxxi.

90. Schnath, *Geschichte Hannovers*, II, pp. 121–220. On Sophie Dorothea's tragic story see chap. II. 6.

91. A I, 4, xxxv.

92. A I, 3, xxvii.

93. See Burchard von Ahlefeldt to Leibniz, 22 January 1680 (A I, 3, N. 263) and Leibniz to Burchard von Ahlefeldt, 6 February 1680 (A I, 3, N. 270).

94. See Leibniz's *Repraesentanda*, probably addressed to Franz Ernst von Platen towards the end of January 1680 (A I, 3, N. 17); cf. also A I, 3, N. 21, N. 27, N. 28, N. 40.

95. See A IV, 3, N. 26–48; A IV, 2, 24–6; A I, 3, N. 17, N. 21, N. 27, N. 28, N. 40, N. 42, N.69, N. 74, N. 75, N. 89, N. 90, N. 99, N. 100; also A IV, 3, N. 113–114. A number of these proposals are listed in A I, 3, xxx–xxxi, from which I draw here.

96. A I, 3, N. 67 (November* 1680); Utermöhlen, "Leibniz im kulturellen Rahmen des hannoverschen Hofes," pp. 221–2. See also A I, 3, N. 66.

97. A IV, 3, N. 34 (esp. p. 373).

98. A I, 3, N. 108.

99. See A IV, 3, N. 49–57, N. 61–62; A IV, 4, N. 140–147. An illuminating commentary on these texts is offered by Jean-Marc Rohrbasser and Jacques Véron, "Leibniz et la mortalité. Mesure des 'apparences' et calcul de la vie moyenne." *Population* 53, 1–2 (1998): 29–44. I am grateful to René Leboutte for drawing my attention to this paper.

100. See A IV, 4, N. 124–138 and A IV, 3, N. 58–60. See in particular in A IV, 4, N. 138, the essay published in 1683 in the *Acta Eruditorum*.

101. *Discussion d'une Question utile*, 1687* (A IV, 4, N. 83).

102. *Erfordernisse einer Guten Landesregierung*, 1680* (A IV, 3, 366).

103. See A I, 3, 20 and 57.

104. Eisenkoft, *Leibniz und die Einigung der Christenheit*, pp. 62–5.

105. A I, 1, N. 34.

106. Leibniz to Landgraft Ernst, 14 August 1683 (A I, 3, 317).

107. Ernst von Hessen-Rheinfels, *Der so warhaffte als gantz auffrichtig- und discret-gesinnte Catholischer*. N. pl., 1666. On the work see H. Raab, "Der 'Discrete Catholische' des Landgrafen Ernst von Hessen-Rheinfels (1623–1693)." *Archiv f. mittelrhein. Kirchengeschichte* 12 (1960): 175–98.

108. Order founded by St Norbert (c. 1080–1134).

109. Leibniz to Landgraf Ernst, 1 May 1680 (A I, 3, 243).

110. Bodemann, *Briefwechsel*, p. 408 records 1783 folios.

111. See A I, 2, N. 250.

112. Leibniz to Landgraf Ernst, 11 January 1684 (A I, 4, 321). In a letter of 3 November 1682 to Landgraf Ernst (A I, 3, 272) Leibniz had written, "Most of the objections which can be raised against Rome are rather against the practices of people than against dogmas. Were those practices to be publicly disavowed, these objections would cease." See also A I, 3, 246–7; A I, 3, 272; A I, 6, 165–6; A I, 6, 148 and A VI, 4, 2286–7.

113. See for instance Leibniz for Landgraf Ernst, second half of October* 1685 (A I, 4, N. 324).

114. See Leibniz to Landgraf Ernst, 24 March 1683 (A I, 3, 280).

115. See Leibniz to Landgraf Ernst, November 1687 (A I, 5, 19–21); Heinz Weidemann, *Gerard Wolter Molanus, Abt zu Loccum: Eine Biographie*. 2 vols. Göttingen: Vandenhoeck & Ruprecht, 1925 and 1929, vol. 2, pp. 30–88; Paul Eisenkopf, *Leibniz und die Einigung der Christenheit. Überlegungen zur Reunion der evangelischen und katholischen Kirche*. München-Paderborn-Wien: Schöningh, 1975, pp. 59–61; Robert Merrihew Adams, "Leibniz's Examination of the Christian Religion." *Faith and Philosophy* 11, 4 (1994): 518–26. Rojas and Molanus's negotiations are examined in detail by Masser, *Rojas y Spinola und Molanus*, esp. pp. 235–80. Two copies of the *Methodus* are found among Leibniz's manuscripts (LH I, 12, 1 Bl. 112–19 and LH I, 7, 2 Bl. 1–8). On the disputed authorship of the *Regulae* see Wolfgang Hübener, "Negotium Irenicum. Leibniz' Bemühungen um die brandenburgische Union." In *Leibniz in Berlin*. Ed. by Hans Poser and Albert Heinekamp. Stuttgart: Steiner, 1990, p. 122.

116. See four texts written in the second half of 1683 (A IV, 3, N. 16–19): *De unitate Ecclesiae*; *Apologia fidei Catholicae ex recta ratione*; *De Schismate*; *Reunion der Kirchen*. Leibniz disapproved of the word "Lutheran" and preferred to refer to his own confession as "Evangelical."

117. See Leibniz to Rojas, Mid* April 1683 (A I, 3, 567); Leibniz to von Eyben, 6 September 1692 (A I, 8, 409); Bossuet to Rojas, 22 August 1683 (in Bossuet, *Correspondence*, vol. II, pp. 391–2); Sophie to Louise Hollandine, 20 September 1691 (A I, 7, N. 94); Bossuet to Marie de Brinon, 29 September 1691 (A I, 7, N. 96).

118. A I, 2, N. 412.

119. See the fourth article of the *Declaratio cleri Gallicani de ecclesiastica potestate* of 19 March 1682. The text of the *Declaratio* was written by Bossuet.

120. The Edict of Nantes, emanated on 13 April 1598 by the French king, Henry IV, granted toleration to the French Calvinists, the Huguenots.

121. *Caesarini Fürstenerii de Jure Suprematus ac Legationis Principum Germaniae*, A IV, 2, 15–17. Trans. by Riley in Leibniz, *Political Writings*, pp. 31–2 ("Introduction.")

122. A IV, 2, N. 20.

123. Autumn 1681; A IV, 2, N. 21, here p. 442. See also A IV, 2, 437.

124. On Leibniz's reaction to the great danger represented by the military pressure of the Ottoman Empire against the Holy Romane Empire in this period see esp. A IV, 2, N. 24–25.

125. A I, 3, xxxix.

126. For detail see John Stoye, *The Siege of Vienna*. London, 1964, esp. pp. 132 ff.

127. A IV, 2, xxv.

128. Even the opportunity he was given in August 1681 to accompany Otto Grote on an official diplomatic mission – the conference on Louis XIV's 'reunions' held in Frankfurt am Main – had come to nothing due to his commitments in the Harz. See A I, 3, N. 93, N. 96, N. 99, N. 100, N. 102, N. 106, N. 420.

129. A IV, 2, N. 22. See also Leibniz to Landgraf Ernst, 5 December 1683 (A I, 3, 334).

130. A IV, 2, 502. Trans. adapted from Riley in Leibniz, *Political Writings*, p. 36.

131. A I, 3, 275. Ernst mentioned that also Johann Lincker von Lutzenwick, privy counsellor to the elector-archbishop of Trier, was keen to see Leibniz's pen put to good use in an attack to Louis XIV's expansionism.

132. A I, 3, 320.

133. A I, 3, 329.

134. See A I, 3, 334; A I, 4, 321; A I, 4, 323. The German translation which appeared in 1685 was not by Leibniz.

135. *Raisons touchant la guerre ou l'accommodement avec la France* (A IV, 2, N. 23).

136. A IV, 2, 504.

137. Lackmann, "Leibniz' Bibliothekarische Tätigkeit in Hannover," p. 338.

138. A I, 3, N. 334.

139. A I, 3, 413.

140. A I, 3, xlv.

141. A I, 3, 101.

142. *Einrichtung einer Bibliothek*, November 1680 (A IV, 3, 350). See also A I, 3, 101–2.

143. See A I, 3, N. 80, N. 82–84, N. 86, N. 88, N. 90 (p. 119), N. 99 (p. 125), N. 113.

144. Lackmann, "Leibniz' Bibliothekarische Tätigkeit in Hannover," p. 339.

145. Leibniz to Duke Ernst August, May 1680 (A I, 3, 57–8).

146. A I, 3, xxxi.

147. Gottfried Schultze für Leibniz, 24 March 1681 (A I, 3, N. 389).

148. Rüdiger Otto, "Leibniz' Aktivitäten für die sachsen-lauenburgische Erbfolge." In *Leibniz und Niedersachsen*. Ed. by Herbert Breger and Friedrich Niewöhner. Stuttgart: Steiner, 1999, pp. 53–75; Scheel, "Leibniz als politischer Ratgeber des Welfenhauses," pp. 41–2; A IV, 4, xxix–xxxvi.

149. Scheel, "Leibniz als politischer Ratgeber des Welfenhauses," p. 41.

150. See A IV, 4, N. 18–69.

151. Scheel, "Leibniz als politischer Ratgeber des Welfenhauses," p. 42.

152. A I, 4, N. 173. See also A I, 7, N. 46 and A IV, 4, N. 70–77.

153. A I, 3, xxvii–xxviii.

154. A I, 3, xxxiii–xxxvii and A I, 4, xxxviii–xliv contain an excellent survey of the vicissitudes of the Harz project, on which I draw here.

155. A I, 3, N. 21, N. 27.

156. Ernst August for Leibniz, Resolution (A I, 3, N. 35). See also A I, 3, N. 29–32.

157. Leibniz for Duke Johann Friedrich, 9 December 1678 (A I, 2, N. 87).

158. See A I, 3, N. 47–54.

159. See A I, 3, N. 56–60.

160. A I, 3, xxxvi–xxxvii.

161. A I, 3, N. 216.

162. A I, 3, N. 558.

163. A I, 3, N. 544–545.

164. See A I, 3, N. 546; A I, 4, N. 564; A I, 3, xlv.

165. A I, 4, lv–lvi.

166. A I, 4, N. 4.

167. See A I, 4, N. 26 and xliii.

168. A I, 3, xxxvii.

169. Leibniz for the mine office in Clausthal, beginning of August* 1684 (A I, 4, N. 56).

170. A I, 4, xl–xli.

171. A I, 4, N. 147.

172. See A I, 4, xliv and A I, 4, N. 165–167, N. 172, N. 185, N. 207–220, N. 227–232.

173. See Leibniz to Bonaventura Nardini, 18 August 1677 (Ms XXIII, 186, H. V, Bl. 76).

174. See A I, 3, 20 and A I, 3, 57.

175. Hortensio Mauro for Leibniz, 21 March 1685 (A I, 4, N. 415 and N. 416).

176. See respectively A I, 4, N. 149 and N. 158; A I, 4, N. 454 ff. Cf. also A I, 4, xlvi–xlvii and G. W. Leibniz, *Schriften und Briefe zur Geschichte*. Ed.

with introduction and commentary by Malte-Ludolf Babin and Gerd van den Heuvel. Hanover: Verlag Hahnsche Buchhandlung, 2004, pp. 86–93.

177. See Niedersächsische Staatarchiv Cal. Br. 23 IV Nr. 25 Bl. 142. Quoted in Günter Scheel, "Leibniz als Historiker des Welfenhauses." In *Leibniz. Sein Leben, sein Wirken, seine Welt*. Ed. by W. Totok and C. Haase. Hanover: Verlag für Literatur und Zeitgeschehen, 1966, p. 244.

178. See Duke Ernst August for Leibniz. "Resolution" (A I, 4, N. 159); A I, 4, xliv; Müller–Krönert, *Leben und Werk*, p. 75; Scheel, "Leibniz als Historiker des Welfenhauses," p. 245.

179. *Sitzungsberichte Akademie Wien, phil. hist. Kl.* 22 (1856), p. 272. Quoted in Scheel, "Leibniz als Historiker des Welfenhauses," p. 245.

180. Leibniz to Iustus von Dransfeld, 18 July 1687 (A I, 4, N. 537). See also A I, 4, N. 354 and N. 356.

181. Scheel, "Leibniz als Historiker des Welfenhauses," p. 243; A I, 4, xlvii; Müller– Krönert, *Leben und Werk*, pp. 60–61.

182. A I, 4, l; Scheel, "Leibniz als Historiker des Welfenhauses," p. 245.

183. Müller–Krönert, *Leben und Werk*, pp. 78–9.

184. Leibniz for Joh. Arend Hentze, 6 July 1686 (A I, 4, N. 237).

185. See the description of a *Harzreise* between the end of October and the beginning of November 1685 in a manuscript held in Kassel, Universitätsbibliothek 4° Ms hist 40 [8].

186. Scheel, "Leibniz als Historiker des Welfenhauses," pp. 245–6.

187. Leibniz to Landgraf Ernst von Hessen-Rheinfels, mid-May* 1687 (A I, 3, 432); Scheel, "Leibniz als Historiker des Welfenhauses," p. 247.

188. Leibniz to Duke Johann Friedrich (A I, 2, 111).

189. Draft of a letter to Thomas Burnett (A I, 18, 377). See also a text of 1671 (A IV, 1, 532): "To love the public good and the universal harmony, or (what is in a sense the same thing) to understand and, as far as one can, to augment the glory of God."

190. A VI, 4, 1. The Academy edition of Leibniz's philosophical texts written between 1677 and June 1690 records 522 pieces totalling over 3000 pages. Only three texts, some twenty pages in total, were published by Leibniz: *Meditationes De Cognitione, Veritate, et Ideis* (*Acta Eruditorum* of November 1684; A VI, 4, N. 141); *Brevis demonstratio erroris memorabilis Cartesii* (*Acta Eruditorum* of March 1686; A VI, 4, N. 369); *Notata quaedam G. G. L. circa vitam et doctrinam Cartesii*, 1689*, published in Chr. Thomasius, *Historia sapientiae et stultitiae*. Vol. 2. Halae Magdeburgicae: Typis & Sumptibus Christophori Salfeldii, 1693, pp. 113–22 (A VI, 4, N. 376). Although the time span of this chapter is December 1676–October 1687, I will cover also some papers composed during Leibniz's trip to southern Germany, Austria, and Italy (November 1687–June 1690) due to their intellectual proximity to the philosophical texts of the decade 1677–87.

191. See the two versions of the letter in A II, 1, N. 213 and A I, 2, N. 187.

192. A II, 1, 488 and A I, 2, 225. Boineburg died on 15 December 1672.

193. See A II, 1, 488; A I, 2, 225; and parts I and II of the *Demonstrationum Catholicarum Conspectus* (A VI, 1, 494–5).

194. See A II, 1, 488; A I, 2, 225 and part III of the *Demonstrationum Catholicarum Conspectus* (A VI, 1, 495–9).
195. See part IV of the *Demonstrationum Catholicarum Conspectus* (A VI, 1, 499–500) and A II, 1, 488–9; A I, 2, 225.
196. A I, 2, 225 and A II, 1, 489.
197. A II, 1, 490–91 and A I, 2, 226–7.
198. A II, 1, 489 and A I, 2, 225.
199. Michel Fichant, "Mécanisme et métaphysique: Le rétablissement des formes substantielles. (1679)," p. 163. See also André Robinet, *Architectonique disjonctive, automates systémiques, et idéalité dans l'oeuvre de G. W. Leibniz*. Paris: Vrin, 1986, chap. 5 and Adams, *Leibniz*, p. 262.
200. A I, 2, 225 and A II, 1, 490.
201. See the *Prolegomena* to the *Demonstrationum Catholicarum Conspectus* (A VI, 1, 494) and the presentation of the plan to the duke (A II, 1, 226 and A I, 2, 489).
202. A I, 2, 226; A II, 1, 489.
203. A II, 1, 490; A I, 2, 226. See also Leibniz's *Selbstschilderung* for Duke Johann Friedrich, autumn 1679* (A II, 1, 492–3).
204. For a more detailed discussion of this series of striking insights in metaphysics, physics, mathematics, and logic gained around 1678–9 see below.
205. See especially the proposals of the autumn of 1678 (*Societas sive Ordo Caritatis*, A IV, 3, N. 130; *Societas Theophilorum ad celebrandas Laudes Dei*, A IV, 3, N. 131) and of 1679 (*Semestria Literaria*, A IV, 3, N. 116; *Consilium de Scribenda Historia Naturali*, A IV, 3, N. 132; *Consultatio de Naturae Cognitione*, A IV, 3, N. 133). This cluster of proposals is briefly expounded in the first part of this chapter. In particular the proposal for a *Societas sive Ordo Caritatis* clearly reflected the encyclopaedic task envisaged by the *Demonstrationes Catholicae*.
206. See Heinrich Schepers's "Einleitung," p. liii in A VI, 4 and his entry on Leibniz for the *Neue Deutsche Biographie* vol. 14, p. 125. François Duchesneau discusses encyclopaedia and *scientia generalis* in the first part of his *Leibniz et la méthode de la science*. Paris: PUF, 1993. He concludes (p. 101) that the project of the encyclopaedia forms the backdrop to Leibniz's whole methodological programme.
207. *Introductio ad Scientiam Generalem Modum Inveniendi Demonstrandique Docentem*, summer–autumn 1679* (A VI, 4, 370).
208. *Definitio Brevis Scientiae Generalis*, summer 1683–beginning 1685* (A VI, 4, 532).
209. *Demonstrationum Catholicarum Conspectus*, 1668–9* (A VI, 1, 494).
210. *Studia ad Felicitatem Dirigenda*, winter 1678/79* (A VI, 4, 137–8).
211. See especially *Introductio ad Encyclopaediam arcanam; Sive Initia et Specimina Scientiae Generalis, de Instauratione et augmentis scientiarum, deque perficienda mente, et rerum inventionibus, ad publicam felicitatem*, summer 1683–beginning of 1685* (A VI, 4, N. 126). See also A VI, 4, N. 85–86, N. 110, N. 115, N. 158–159. Francis Bacon's *De dignitate et augmentis scientiarum* (London: I. Haviland, 1623) constituted the first part of the comprehensive plan for reconstructing the entire edifice of knowledge envisioned in his *Instauratio Magna* (London: Apud Joannem Billium, 1620).

212. A VI, 4, 138.
213. See *Paraenesis de Scientia Generali*, August–December 1688* (A VI, 4, 980) and Aristotle, *Metaphysics* A 2, 982a4–983a23.
214. *Paraenesis de Scientia Generali* (A VI, 4, 979–80). Cf. A VI, 4, lvii.
215. *Fundamenta calculi ratiocinatoris*, summer 1688* (A VI, 4, 920).
216. See chap. I. 2 above.
217. *Semestria Literaria*, A IV, 3, N. 116, esp. pp. 789–95 ("Consilium de Literis instaurandi condendaque Encyclopaedia.")
218. Döring, *Der junge Leibniz und Leipzig*, p. 80.
219. Ravier 84–96. See for instance the paper on optics published in the *Acta Eruditorum* of June 1682 (Ravier 85), in which Leibniz deduced the laws of reflection and refraction from a single principle.
220. See also the complementary paper published in the *Acta Eruditorum* of July 1686, in which Leibniz presented his integral calculus: *De Geometria Recondita et Analysi Indivisibilium et infinitorum, Addenda his quae dicta sunt in Actis a. 1684.*
221. Mugnai, *Leibniz: Vita*, p. 102.
222. Cf. *Brevis Demonstratio* (A VI, 4, N. 369, here p. 2027) and Otto Mencke to Leibniz, 27 February 1686 (A I, 4, 564).
223. Leibniz to Landgraf Ernst, 11 February 1686 (A I, 4, 399). The definitive edition of the *Discours de Métaphysique* is A VI, 4, N. 306.
224. See *Examen Religionis Christianae* (A VI, 4, N. 420).
225. A VI, 4, N. 165. This doctrine is presented also in another text most probably written in early 1686: *De natura veritatis, contingentiae et indifferentiae atque de libertate et praedeterminatione* (A VI, N. 303). See Mugnai, *Leibniz: Vita*, pp. 42, 44. On Leibniz's doctrine of infinite analysis cf. R. C. Sleigh, *Leibniz and Arnauld. A Commentary on Their Correspondence.* New Haven: Yale University Press, 1990, pp. 83–9 and Mugnai, *Introduzione*, pp. 193–5.
226. A VI, 4, liv.
227. *Elementa calculi*, April 1679 (A VI, 4, 197). Trans. by G. H. R. Parkinson in *Leibniz: Logical Papers*. Oxford: Clarendon Press, 1966, pp. 18–19. The doctrine of the inclusion of the predicate in the subject had already appeared in a juridical paper probably written between the summer of 1678 and the winter of 1678–9 (*De legum interpretatione, rationibus, applicatione, systemate*, A VI, 4, 2789).
228. *De Synthesi et Analysi universali seu Arte inveniendi et judicandi*, summer 1683–beginning of 1685* (A VI, 4, N. 129; here p. 543).
229. A VI, 4, 587.
230. See *Paraenesis de Scientia Generali*, August–December 1688* (A VI, 4, 974). Attention to these texts is drawn by G. H. R. Parkinson, Review of Leibniz, *Sämtliche Schriften und Briefe*, vol. VI, 4. In *Studia Leibnitiana* 31, 1 (1999), p. 110.
231. See Mugnai, *Leibniz: Vita*, p. 35. On Leibniz's *characteristica* between 1677 and 1690 cf. Martin Schneider, "Leibniz' Konzeption der *Characteristica Universalis* zwischen 1677 und 1690." *Revue Internationale de Philosophie* 48, 2 = 188 (1994): 213–36.
232. A III, 2, 570–71. An abstract from the letter is published in A II, 1, N. 189.

233. See in A I, 2 their correspondence between 6 November 1678 and 17 September 1679.
234. François Viète (1540–1603) is considered the father of symbolic algebra. Between 1591 and 1593 he introduced the *logistica speciosa* or art of calculating with species, that is, general quantities. The *speciosa* combined logical and mathematical operations and employed letters of the alphabet to denote known and unknown quantities (respectively, consonants and vowels).
235. See A VI, 4, N. 56–64; Parkinson, Review of Leibniz, *Sämtliche Schriften und Briefe*, vol. VI, 4, pp. 112–13; Mugnai, *Leibniz: Vita*, p. 37. The following remarks regarding Leibniz's papers on the logical calculus between 1678 and 1687 draw on the outstanding exposition of Mugnai, *Leibniz: Vita*, pp. 37–52.
236. A prime number is a whole number greater than 1 that is exactly divisible only by 1 and itself: 2, 3, 5, 7, 11, etc.
237. A VI, 4, 739. Quoted in Mugnai, *Leibniz: Vita*, p. 44.
238. *De abstracto et concreto*, 1688* (A VI, 4, 992). Quoted in Mugnai, *Leibniz: Vita*, p. 45. On Leibniz's logical abstracts see also Mugnai, *Introduzione*, pp. 54–64.
239. See *Specimen calculi coincidentium*, April–October 1686* (A VI, 4, N. 173); *Specimen calculi coincidentium et inexistentium*, spring 1686–beginning 1687* (A VI, 4, N. 177); *Non inelegans specimen demonstrandi in abstractis*, February–April 1687* (A VI, 4, N. 178). On the "real addition" introduced in these texts and the complex question of the relationship between Leibniz's logical calculus and the logical systems developed by the father of modern logic, George Boole, see Karl Dürr, *Neue Beleuchtung einer Theorie von Leibniz. Grundzüge des Logikkalküls.* Darmstadt: Reichl, 1930; R. Kauppi, *Über die Leibnizsche Logik.* Helsinki: Societas philosophica, 1960; H. Burkhardt, *Logik and Semiotik in der Philosophie von Leibniz.* München: Philosophia Verlag, 1980; Franz Schupp's introductions to G. W. Leibniz, *Generales inquisitiones de analysi notionum et veritatum.* Hamburg: Meiner, 1982 and G. W. Leibniz, *Die Grundlagen des logischen Kalküls.* Hamburg: Meiner, 2000; Chris Swoyer, "Leibniz's calculus of real addition." *Studia Leibnitiana* 26, 1 (1994): 1–30; Mugnai, *Leibniz: Vita*, pp. 48–52; Wolfgang Lenzen, *Calculus Universalis: Studien zur Logik von G. W. Leibniz.* Paderborn: Mentis, 2004; Massimo Mugnai, "Review of Lenzen, *Calculus Universalis*, 2004." *The Leibniz Review* 15 (2005): 169–81
240. *De arte characteristica ad perficiendas scientias ratione nitentes*, summer 1688* (A VI, 4, 912–13).
241. Ibid., 913.
242. Ibid., 914.
243. See A VI, 4, N. 34 and Wolfgang David Cirilo De Melo and James Cussens, "Leibniz on Estimating the Uncertain: An English Translation of *De incerti aestimatione* with Commentary." *The Leibniz Review* 14 (2004): 31–53 (here pp. 31–2).
244. See for instance A II, 1, 489.

245. Leibniz to Thomas Burnett of Kemney, 11 February 1697 (A I, 13, 555).
246. See GM V, 141–68.
247. See A III, 2, N. 346 and N. 347.
248. A III, 2, 846.
249. See A III, 2, 851–3.
250. See A III, 2, 854.
251. See A III, 2, 858–9.
252. Leibniz to Christiaan Huygens, 20 October 1679 (A III, 2, 875).
253. See Christiaan Huygens to Leibniz, 22 November 1679 (A III, 2, 888–9).
254. See GM V, 178–83 and Müller-Krönert, *Leben und Werk*, pp. 58, 126, 151. See also GM V, 172–8, 183–211. On the *analysis situs* between 1712 and 1716 see Vincenzo De Risi's doctoral thesis *The Analysis Situs 1712–1716. Geometry and Philosophy of Space in the Late Leibniz* (Pisa 2005; revised version: *Geometry and Monadology: Leibniz's Analysis Situs and Philosophy of Space.* Basel, Boston, and Berlin: Birkhäuser, 2007) including an appendix in which numerous unpublished texts by Leibniz are collected.
255. See *De progressione dyadica*, 25 March 1679 (Couturat, 574); *De organo sive arte magna cogitandi*, March–April 1679* (A VI, 4, N. 50, esp. p. 158); *Summum Calculi Analytici Fastigium*, December 1679 (in Hans J. Zacher, *Die Hauptschriften zur Dyadik von G. W. Leibniz*. Frankfurt a. M.: Klostermann, 1973, pp. 218–24); Leibniz to Tschirnhaus, end of June 1682 (A III, 3, 655–6). For later writings on the dyadic see Zacher, *Die Hauptschriften zur Dyadik von G. W. Leibniz*, pp. 225–356. On the relationship between Leibniz's dyadic and computer science see Gregory Chaitin, "Leibniz, Information, Math and Physics." In *Wissen und Glauben/Knowledge and Belief. Akten des 26. Internationalen Wittgenstein-Symposiums 2003.* Ed. by Winfried Löffler and Paul Weingartner. Vienna: ÖBV & HPT, 2004, pp. 277–86 and "Leibniz, Randomness and the Halting Probability." *Mathematics Today* 40 (2004): 138–9.
256. For details see Aiton, *Biography*, pp. 125–7, referring to the following studies of E. Knobloch: "Die Entscheidende Abhandlung von Leibniz zur Theoric linearer Gleichungssysteme." *Studia Leibnitiana* 4 (1972): 163–80; "Studien von Leibniz zum Determinanten Kalkül." *Studia Leibnitiana Supplementa* 13 (1974): 37–45; *Der Beginn der Determinantentheorie.* Hildesheim: Gerstenberg, 1980; "Zur Vorgeschichte der Determinantentheorie." *Studia Leibnitiana Supplementa* 22 (1982): 96–118.
257. Pierre de Fermat (1601–65) was a French mathematician especially important for his work in number theory. He announced his 'little theorem' (if the integer x is not divisible by the prime number p, $x^{p-1}-1$ is divisible by p) without providing a proof. On Leibniz's discovery see Couturat, *La logique de Leibniz*, pp. 499–500.
258. Leibniz to Des Bosses, 7 November 1710 (GP II, 412).
259. See in particular the *Confessio Naturae contra Atheistas*, 1668 (A VI, 1, 489–90).
260. See A VI, 1, 511.

261. See *De vera methodo philosophiae et theologiae ac de natura corporis* (A VI, 3, 155–9; here p. 158). Attention is drawn to this and other pre-1679 texts in which the notion of substantial form occurs by the lucid analysis of Fichant, "Mécanisme et métaphysique," pp. 168, 172–8.

262. See chap. I, 2.

263. In a much later text, the *Système nouveau de la nature et de la communication des substances* (1695), the interpretation of "substantial form" as "force" is explicitly stated as follows (GP IV, 478–9): "It was therefore necessary to recall and, in a sense, rehabilitate the substantial forms so much disparaged nowadays, but in a way which would make them intelligible . . . So I found that their nature consists in force."

264. Published in Michel Fichant, *G. W. Leibniz. La réforme de la dynamique. De Corporum concursu (1678), et autres texts inédits.* Paris: Vrin, 1994.

265. See *Conspectus Libelli Elementorum Physicae*, summer 1678–winter 1678/79* (A VI, 4, 1989). Trans. by Arthur in *The Labyrinth of the Continuum*, pp. 231–5.

266. See A VI, 4, N. 369 and chapter 17 of the *Discours de Métaphysique*, where the same argument is summarized (A VI, 4, 1556–8).

267. See Fichant, "Mécanisme et métaphysique," pp. 179–80. Fichant points out that the text in which this metaphysical principle appears for the first time is *De Arcanis Motus et Mechanica ad puram Geometriam reducenda*, edited by H. J. Hess in *Leibniz à Paris*, vol. I, pp. 202–5. See above, chap. I. 3.

268. *Conspectus Libelli Elementorum Physicae* (A VI, 4, 1989). Trans. by Arthur in Leibniz, *The Labyrinth of the Continuum*, p. 235. Cf. Fichant, "Mécanisme et métaphysique," p. 197. In the *Brevis demonstratio erroris memorabilis Cartesii* Leibniz repeated that force must be estimated by the quantity of the effect (GM VI, 118).

269. On this controversy see in particular C. Iltis, "Leibniz and the Vis Viva Controversy." *Isis* 62, no. 1 (1971): 21–35 and David Papineau, "The Vis Viva Controversy." In *Leibniz: Metaphysics and Philosophy of Science.* Ed. by R. S. Woolhouse. Oxford: Oxford University Press, 1981, pp. 139–56.

270. GP III, 45–6. Catelan's objections were published in the *Nouvelles de la République des Lettres*, September 1686, pp. 999–1003. They can also be found in GP III, 40–42.

271. Leibniz to Bayle, 9 January 1687 (GP III, 48).

272. See Adams, *Leibniz*, p. 312 and Daniel Garber, "Leibniz and the Foundations of Physics: The Middle Years." In *The Natural Philosophy of Leibniz.* Ed. by Kathleen Okruhlik and James Robert Brown. Dordrecht: Reidel, 1985, pp. 122–3 (n. 166).

273. See in particular *Nouvelles de la République des Lettres*, April 1687, pp. 448–50 and July 1687, pp. 744–53; A VI, 4, N. 371; and the Leibniz–Malebranche correspondence published in A II, 1, N. 197, N. 204, N. 207, N. 208, N. 210.

274. *Conspectus Libelli Elementorum Physicae*, summer 1678–winter 1678/79* (A VI, 4, 1988–9). Trans. by Arthur in Leibniz, *The Labyrinth of the Continuum*, pp. 233–5.

275. *Specimen Demonstrationum Catholicarum* (A VI, 4, 2326). Attention is drawn to this and the previous text by Fichant, "Mécanisme et métaphysique," pp. 196–7, 204. Cf. also A VI, 4, 1465 and A VI, 4, 1504.

276. One of the most debated issues in contemporary literature is whether the doctrine of corporeal substances characteristic of Leibniz's 'middle years' is significantly different from the later monadological theory of substance or can be reduced to it. For the first position see especially Garber, "Leibniz and the Foundations of Physics: The Middle Years," pp. 27–130; for the second position see especially Adams, *Leibniz*, chapters 10–11. On Garber's position and the debate arising from it see Paul Lodge, "Garber's Interpretation of Leibniz on Corporeal Substance in the 'Middle Years'." *The Leibniz Review* 15 (2005): 1–26. In his forthcoming book (note 5 above), Garber revisits this debate, arguing that in the middle years (that is, roughly, the late 1670s to the mid- or late-1690s) Leibniz had not yet come upon the monadological metaphysics characteristic of his later years. In his view, reading texts of this period in the later light of the *Monadology* prematurely dissolves the world of bodies from which Leibniz began his philosophical investigation into the immaterial world of spiritual substances of his most idealistic later phase. On the issue of corporeal substances see also chap. II. 7.

277. See Adams, *Leibniz*, p. 324.

278. *De modo distinguendi phaenomena realia ab imaginariis* (A VI, 4, 1504). Attention is drawn to this text by Adams, *Leibniz*, p. 325 and Schepers, "Einleitung," A VI, 4, lxvi.

279. Quotations from, respectively, the letters of Leibniz to Arnauld of 23 March 1690 (GP II, 135–6), 30 April 1687 (GP II, 101), and 9 October 1687 (GP II, 119); highlighted in Mugnai, *Introduzione*, pp. 134–5. For an outstanding discussion of the nuances and tensions of Leibniz's doctrine of substance and substantial forms in the correspondence with Arnauld see Sleigh, *Leibniz and Arnauld*, chapters 6–7.

280. *Discours de Métaphysique* (A VI, 4, 1540).

281. See *Discours de Métaphysique*, esp. §§ viii, ix, and xiv (A VI, 4, 1541–2, 1549–51) and *Remarques sur la lettre de M. Arnauld, touchant ma proposition: Que la notion individuelle de chaque personne enferme une fois pour toutes ce qui luy arrivera à jamais* (GP II, 41) (draft for Leibniz's letter to Arnauld of 14 July 1686). Cf. Sleigh, *Leibniz and Arnauld*, pp. 10–11. A clear discussion of the derivation of these theses from the doctrine of the complete concept is offered by Nicholas Jolley, *Leibniz*. London and New York: Routledge, 2005, pp. 49–55. On the first occurrence of the expression "pre-established harmony" see chap. II. 6.

282. A VI, 4, 1618.

283. See for instance A VI, 4, N. 168, N. 270–274, N. 303. These papers were written between 1678 and mid-1686.

284. *Conversatio cum Domino Episcopo Stenonio de Libertate*, 7 December 1677 (A VI, 4, 1377). Trans. by Sleigh in *Leibniz, Confessio Philosophi. Papers*

Concerning the Problem of Evil, 1671–1678, pp. 119. Cf. Mugnai, Introduzione,
p. 195.

285. De libertate, contingentia et serie causarum, providentia, summer 1689* (A VI, 4,
1654).

286. Sleigh proposes the hypothesis that Leibniz actually arrived at this solution
after July 1686 as a result of his debate with Arnauld (Leibniz and Arnauld,
p. 88). Although, according to the editors of A VI, 4, the first paper in which
this solution appears (De natura veritatis, contingentiae et indifferentiae atque
de libertate et praedeterminatione, N. 303) was probably written between the
end of 1685 and mid-1686, it seems very plausible that the Leibniz–Arnauld
exchange played an important role in the development of Leibniz's doctrine of
infinite analysis. Another fundamental text for the genesis of this doctrine is the
Generales Inquisitiones of 1686. Cf. also Mugnai, Introduzione, pp. 197–8.

287. De contingentia, 1689* (A VI, 4, 1650). Attention to this text is drawn by Mugnai,
Introduzione, p. 194.

288. See Heinrich Schepers, "Non alter, sed etiam Leibnitius." The Leibniz Review
14 (2004), pp. 126–7.

289. See Leibniz to Johann Friedrich (A II, 1, 489), and Sleigh, Leibniz and Arnauld,
p. 10 and chap. 2.

290. A VI, 4, N. 420.

291. See A II, 1, 488. Cf. also A I, 2, 224–5.

292. See Sleigh, Leibniz and Arnauld, p. 23.

293. See Leibniz for Landgraf Ernst, second half of October* 1685 (A I, 4, N. 324)
and Adams, "Leibniz's Examination of the Christian Religion," esp. pp. 518–26.

294. See Adams, "Leibniz's Examination of the Christian Religion," pp. 526–36.

295. Although this and similar affirmations have sometimes been interpreted as
indications of Leibniz's basic indifference towards the specific doctrines of
the Christian revelation or the theological disagreements among the Christian
churches, such an interpretation is difficult to sustain in the light of the extensive body of texts in which Leibniz discussed issues of Christian theology in
great depth and took a stand for or against specific doctrines. In Leibniz's
view, theological disagreements amongst Christian confessions did not prevent
reunification, not because he cared little about the fine points of theology, but
because he believed that close investigation could reveal a degree of agreement
sufficient for reunification. Moreover, especially until the late 90s, Leibniz was
particularly convinced of the theological proximity between the Lutheran and
Catholic confessions on fundamental issues.

296. De Scriptura, Ecclesia, Trinitate, 1680–84* (A VI, 4, 2286–7). Leibniz did not
specify in this text which practices he wished to see reformed, but he was
probably referring to Protestant criticisms of such practices as the cult of saints
and images, especially in their extreme forms. As Leibniz himself indicated in
the text, by the time De Scriptura, Ecclesia, Trinitate was written many in the
Catholic church had themselves denounced the abuses related to such practices.

297. See for instance Leibniz to Landgraf Ernst, 11 January 1684 (A I, 4, 321).

298. See A VI, 4, 2286 and A I, 4, 321.
299. Leibniz to Johann Friedrich Leibniz, 5 October 1669 (in Schrecker, "G.-W. Leibniz. Lettres et fragments inédits," p. 67).
300. In addition to the one-hundred-page long *Examen*, A VI, 4 contains 35 pieces covering some 250 pages.
301. I have detailed Leibniz's views on the relationship between faith and reason, revelation and knowledge in *Leibniz on the Trinity and the Incarnation*.
302. See for instance *Dialogus inter Theologum and Misosophum*, second half 1678– first half 1679* (A VI, 4, N. 397) and *De non violando principio contradictionis in divinis*, February–October 1685* (A VI, 4, N. 414).
303. See for instance *De Deo Trino*, 1680–84* (A VI, 4, N. 404) and *De Persona Christi*, 1680–84* (A VI, 4, N. 405).
304. See for instance *De Scriptura, Ecclesia, Trinitate*, 1680–84* (A VI, 4, N. 403); *Sententia de natura et potestate Ecclesiae Catholicae*, February–October 1685* (A VI, 4, N. 413); *De Judice Controversiarum*, first half of 1677* (A VI, 4, N. 388).
305. Cf. 1 Corinthians 13, 13.
306. A I, 2, 23.
307. See for instance A VI, 4, 2767, 2773, 2777, 2792, 2798, 2803, 2809, 2871, 2890. Cf. Schneider, "Der Begriff der Gerechtigkeit bei Leibniz," pp. 1097–1101; Riley, *Leibniz's Universal Jurisprudence*.
308. See respectively *De cogitationum analysi*, summer 1678–winter 1680/81* (A VI, 4, 2773–4) and *De legum interpretatione, rationibus, applicatione, systemate*, summer–winter 1678–9* (A VI, 4, 2789). Cf. also *De legum rationibus inquirendis*, summer–winter 1678–9 (A VI, 4, N. 494).
309. See respectively A VI, 4, N. 508 and A I, 2, N. 332. As with most of Leibniz's proposals to the great and mighty, nothing came of it.
310. See *Discours de Métaphysique*, chapters XXXV–XXXVII and *Examen Religionis Christianae*, A VI, 4, 2357, 2361.
311. *Discours de Métaphysique*, chap. XXXV (A VI, 4, 1584–5).
312. See *Discours de Métaphysique*, chap. XXXV (A VI, 4, 1585).
313. See Fichant, *Science et métaphysique dans Descartes et Leibniz*, p. ix.
314. *Discours de Métaphysique*, chap. XXXVI (A VI, 4, 1586).
315. Cf. the overview of the most significant reading in A VI, 4, lxxxvi–lxxxix.
316. See *Notata quaedam G. G. L. circa vitam et doctrinam Cartesii*, spring–autumn 1689* (A VI, 4, 2064–5). See also GM VII, 357.
317. See Leibniz's annotations in his own copy of Descartes's *Opera Philosophica. Editio Secunda ab Auctore recognita*. Amsterdam, 1650 (A VI, 4, N. 335).
318. Leibniz's extensive comments, marginal notes, and excerpts of 1678 are published in A VI, 4, N. 336–338. Cf. Georg Hermann Schuller to Leibniz, 25 January 1678 (A III, 2, N. 133).
319. See A VI, 4, N. 444, N. 447 and N. 448, collecting excerpts and marginal notes from, respectively, Nicolas Malebranche, *Traité de la Nature et de la Grace*. Rotterdam, 1684; Nicolas Malebranche, *Trois lettres de l'auteur de la Recherche de la verité, touchant la défense de Mr. Arnauld contre la réponse au livre des vrayes*

et fausses idées. Rotterdam, 1685; Antoine Arnauld, *Lettres de Monsieur Arnauld, Docteur de Sorbonne, au R. P. Malebranche, Prêtre de l'Oratoire.* N. pl., 1685.

320. Leibniz's exceptionally extensive underlinings, marginal notes, and excerpts originating from at least three different readings are published in A VI, 4, N. 348. Cf. A I, 4, N. 128.

5

In the Footsteps of the Guelfs: Southern Germany, Austria, and Italy (November 1687– June 1690)

T HE RESEARCH TRIP in the footsteps of the Guelfs was supposed to take no more than a few months and to be limited to southern Germany. In the event, it stretched over almost two years and eight months and took Leibniz as far south as Naples. Its original official aim was to visit some archival collections in southern Germany, notably in Munich, in order to verify the origins of a northern Italian margrave, Albert Azzo II (996–1097). Azzo II was regarded as the common ancestor of both the Braunschweig-Lüneburg house and the prestigious Italian family of Este, which ruled Modena and Reggio with their surrounding territories in north-central Italy.[1] Doubts about this connection, however, had been raised by French and German historians: in particular, the famous historian Johannes Turmair, known as Aventin, in his printed Latin *Annals of Bavaria* had mentioned Azzo II as *Astenses* rather than *Estenses*. This designation traced back the origins of Azzo to the marquises of Asti, a town in the northern Italian region of Piemonte, rather than the far more prestigious house of Este. Since Aventin's original manuscripts were held in Munich, Leibniz decided to check them directly in the hope of tracing the historian's sources and finding further evidence which would decide the vexed question.[2] From the outset, however, it was quite apparent that Leibniz's agenda – as usual – was much broader than it seemed. Although he had not actually planned to travel as far as Italy and to stay away for so long, this research trip was for him a welcome opportunity to visit people and places which held for him great significance for his scientific, philosophical, theological, and political plans. Regarding his departure from Leipzig, he had long since written that a young man should not be tied to the same place and that he most ardently desired to promote the sciences and to get to know the world.[3] Now, having just turned forty-one, he was no longer all that young; but he was still unattached and as full as ever of the ardent desire to advance knowledge and to know the world. After the long periods of isolation in the narrow Harz valleys and the scarcely broader confines of Hanover, he was craving new horizons.[4]

The trip south quickly began to assume a familiar pattern. Boineburg's commissions had been Leibniz's ticket to Paris and London many years before, and Ernst August's historiographical assignment likewise became the pretext for a tour of the European *république des lettres* flourishing in southern Germany, Austria, and eventually even Italy. Once in Paris, he had sought every conceivable way to delay his return to Germany and had taken the most circuitous route back; now likewise his detours and month-long visits to places of at best tangential relevance to his historical researches fuelled the suspicion in Hanover that their *Hofrat* was wasting his time, as well as the genuine concern of Duchess Sophie regarding his whereabouts.[5] After intensive archival work and important discoveries in Munich and Augsburg, Leibniz realised that his historical researches must take him to the archives of the Este family in Modena. Permission to consult the Modena collection proved to be very long in coming; but the resourceful Leibniz found no shortage of ways to pass the intervening time with pleasure and profit. Nine months from May 1688 to February 1689 were spent in Vienna, happily engaged in a flurry of plans to present to the emperor and in long colloquia with Rojas y Spinola in his nearby bishopric in Wiener-Neustadt. In March he removed suddenly to Venice – moving in haste (he said) lest the spring thaw make the Alpine roads impassable. A month later, still awaiting access to the Este archives, he decided to take "a tour of Rome in order to profit from the weather and the proximity."[6] Having settled in the pontifical city, he left for a quick excursion to Naples before the summer heat became uncomfortable for a northerner like himself. Rome was scarcely on the outskirts of Venice, nor was Naples in the suburbs of Rome, especially if one had to travel by horse-carriage; but once Leibniz had escaped from Hanover and regained his freedom to travel, space, it would appear, became relative in practice as well as theory.

In his defence, the Hanoverian *Hofrat* could claim with complete conviction that he had not been idle. In fact, he had more than fulfilled his original historiographical mission, proving beyond doubt the connection between the Braunschweig-Lüneburg house and the Este family while locating, collecting, and studying crucial documentation on the Guelf descent in a half-dozen major archives. He had not, it is true, devoted every waking moment to examining medieval manuscripts. At odd intervals in his travels he studied Newton's *Principia Mathematica*, which had appeared in 1687, published an alternative cosmological theory to Newton's account of the motion of heavenly bodies in 1689, started work at a new branch of physics devoted to the study of forces, which he christened "dynamics," further developed his logical calculus in a series of important papers, refined his metaphysical theories, and continued to make progress on the *scientia generalis*.[7] As he travelled south, he also tried to mend the torn fabric of Europe, especially through extensive discussions with Landgraf Ernst and Bishop Rojas regarding ecclesiastical reunification. But no matter how ecumenical his views on religion or how great his thirst for a more stimulating and varied intellectual community, Leibniz was not prepared to compromise his principles. He declined both the prospect of becoming chancellor of the bishopric of Hildesheim and the curatorship of the fabulous Vatican library, because both positions would have required his conversion to Catholicism.

In Vienna, he finally realized a wish that he had been nurturing for twenty years: he obtained an audience with the Holy Roman Emperor. For him this encounter with Leopold I represented a golden opportunity to obtain the support of central Europe's senior ruler for his all-embracing perennial plan: the improvement and development of the whole encyclopaedia of sciences for the common good. At the beginning of the paper which he painstakingly composed between August and September 1688, in preparation for his audience with the Emperor, he noted, "from my earliest youth onward, as if by a mysterious instinct of nature, I have directed my mind toward the common good and in particular toward the general perfection [*ad perfectionem Generalem*] of humanity's sciences[.]"[8] From the very outset of his intellectual career, he explained in other words, he had directed his efforts "to the Encyclopaedia and to the general perfection of humankind's sciences" in order to bring "utility to the commonwealth."[9] For these efforts to have a significant impact on the concrete conditions of his fellow human beings, however, he needed political and financial backing for ambitious scientific research and wide ranging institutional reforms. In early modern terms, he needed the support of an enlightened prince.

All in all, this was a happy period for Leibniz. He thrived in the intellectual stimulation of places and people of vast cultural riches, became part of

the circle of the Accademia Fisico-Matematica in Rome, was approached
for tempting positions (including that of imperial historiographer), and
was described in the Italian learned community as "the first man of learning of our century . . . deeply versed in all sciences" and second to no one
in his "supreme erudition, the depth in philosophy and mathematics, in
addition to all his other good qualities."[10] Shortly before leaving Italy, on
23 March 1690 he wrote to Arnauld from Venice summarising in a few
lines what this trip had meant to him:

Since this journey also helped me to relax from ordinary occupations, I had the
satisfaction of conversing with many able people on matters of science and learning,
and I have communicated to some of them my more unusual thoughts . . . and there
have been people who, being dissatisfied with the standard doctrines, have found
extraordinary satisfaction in some of my opinions[.][11]

Indeed, travelling and meeting people seems to have been Leibniz's idea of
la dolce vita. Yet even a visit to Italy at the height of the baroque era failed
to awaken in him an appreciation of the visual arts: not a line appears to
have been written by him celebrating the architectural wonders of Venice,
Florence or Rome.[12] This silence is probably explained by the simple
fact that he could not observe his surroundings properly, having being
very short-sighted at least since he was twenty years old.[13] In any case,
his love of travelling was clearly grounded in the opportunity of making
new acquaintances and meeting old friends, rather than in the joys of
sightseeing. On his scale of the pleasures of life, intellectual exchange and
conversation came second to nothing.

Central and Southern Germany (November 1687–May 1688)

Leibniz and his secretary, Friedrich Heyn, recorded in a travel diary the
main stages of their journey until their arrival in Vienna.[14] After departing
from Hanover at the end of October 1687, on 1 November Leibniz visited
in Hildesheim the Capuchin father Dionysius Werlensis, who related to
him his discussions on church reunification with Bishop Rojas. The stop
in Hildesheim was also the occasion for seeing the collection on natural
history of the late physician Dr. Friedrich Lachmund, followed (probably
one day later) by the perusal of the cabinet of natural curiosities of the
Landgraf of Hesse-Kassel. Especially the fossils of plants and animals in
Hildesheim captured the interest stimulated in Leibniz by his geological

researches in the Harz and connected to his theoretical work on the origin of the earth.[15]

From 3 to 5 November Leibniz was in Frankenberg (Hesse) waiting in vain for his hyperactive friend, Johann Daniel Crafft – a man who could stand comparison even with Leibniz in his ability to conceive technical and commercial projects and who, perhaps precisely for this reason, had made such a lasting impression on the German genius. Crafft failed to materialize, but Leibniz always had something handy to occupying his mind in idle moments. In this case, the reading of Paracelsian literature (notably Valentin Weigel), as well as reflections on the works of Robert Barclay (1648–90), Henry More, and van Helmont, kept him busy.[16] After a visit to Marburg (where he entertained himself with talks on various experiments with the physician Dr. Johann Jacob Waldschmidt), around 12 November Leibniz arrived at his first main halting place: the residence in Rheinfels of his trusted friend and correspondent, Landgraf Ernst. Among the highlights of Leibniz's two-week-long stay were naturally discussions on the issue of Church reunification, its political implications, and Leibniz's own religious stand with an eye on the absent third man of the triad, Antoine Arnauld.[17] In particular, during his visit Leibniz prepared a long memo outlining his position on ecclesiastical reunification.[18] Basically he summarized and fully endorsed the method for the reunion of Catholics and Protestants (intended primarily as the followers of the Augsburg Confession of 1530) which had emerged in the Hanover talks of 1683 on the basis of Rojas's proposal.[19] In his presentation to Landgraf Ernst his consciously pragmatic approach to the problem emerged.[20] Whereas the Landgraf pinned his greatest hopes for peace on toleration, according to Leibniz toleration was a starting point rather than the ultimate solution to the conflict amongst the Christian confessions. Toleration was like a cure which tackled "the most pressing symptoms" of the illness but not its cause. Brushing aside the "way of rigour" as of dubious legitimacy and uncertain results, Leibniz granted that even "the way of dispute or discussion," in which controversial points were examined in detail by the opposing parties, had proven of "little effect" in these matters.[21] For all his indefatigable efforts towards the development of a *characteristica universalis* which would have settled all controversies including religious ones,[22] Leibniz was realistic enough to see that the solution of the endemic religious conflicts which constantly threatened and upset European peace could not wait for the creation and universal acceptance of his wonderful formal language. Instead a bold pragmatic move was needed – a move which Leibniz was also to regard later on as the basic way forward. As Rojas had proposed in his *Regulae circa christianorum omnium Ecclesiasticam Reunionem* (1682/1683) and the Lutheran counterpart represented by Molanus and Barckhausen had endorsed in their *Methodus reducendae Unionis Ecclesiasticae inter Romanenses et Protestantes* (1683), the reunion strategy hinged on two complementary steps: a preliminary reunion between Protestants and Catholics before agreement had been reached on controversial issues, and the convocation of a truly ecumenical council endowed as such with the authority to settle controversial issues, the decisions of which both Catholics and Protestants agreed in advance to respect. According to Leibniz, the "nodal point of the business" was precisely to reach agreement not upon specific doctrines but upon the convocation of this "free and ecumenical Council", which would have decided on the main controversial issues.[23]

While Leibniz was at Rheinfels, Ernst and the court counsellor of the archbishop and elector of Cologne, Karl Paul von Zimmermann, entertained the idea of proposing him for the position of chancellor of the Catholic bishopric of Hildesheim. Not without a certain regret, the Hanoverian *Hofrat* declined to pursue this opening any further due to his allegiance to the Augsburg confession.[24] On 2 December he was once again on his way carrying with him a letter of recommendation penned by Landgraf Ernst and addressed to the Palatine elector, Philipp Wilhelm von der Pfalz – a glowing reference which in the end remained unused because the opportunity for a detour to Heidelberg did not arise.[25] Between 17 and 20 December Leibniz was back in one of the cities of his youth, Frankfurt am Main. Here he met once again with the orientalist Hiob Ludolf and discussed the plan of Fr. Chr. Paullini and W. E. Tentzel to found a *Collegium Imperiale Historicum* to publish chronicles of German history, to edit medieval documents, and to create a journal on historical sources. Great hope was invested in Leibniz's ability to convince the emperor to establish the *Collegium*; but despite quite detailed preparatory work, the plan fell victim to the war declared by Louis XIV against the Empire on 24 September 1688: with a new major conflict on his doorstep, the emperor had other priorities than providing financial support for the enhancement of German scholarship.

While in Frankfurt, the possibility was apparently suggested to Leibniz of marrying there the wealthy niece of Hermann Barckhausen, court

preacher in Hanover and co-author with Molanus of the *Methodus*.[26]
Whether or not this was a firm prospect, Leibniz must not have pursued
it too strenuously. Instead of pondering matrimony, on 21 December
he had already left Frankfurt for Aschaffenburg to examine the extensive collection of historical manuscripts of an old acquaintance, the late
Johann Gamans, S. J., who had been preparing a history of the dioceses
presided over by the archbishop of Mainz.[27] From 25 to 28 December
Leibniz was in Würzburg visiting the rich archives and libraries of the
various religious orders based in the prominent Catholic episcopal city.
On 31 December he arrived in Nuremberg. After a week of visits to old
friends from his university years, on 7 January 1688 Leibniz resumed
his journey, reaching Sulzbach two days later as the guest of Christian
Knorr von Rosenroth (1636–89). Rosenroth, together with Leibniz's earlier acquaintance, Franciscus Mercurius van Helmont, was amongst the
most prominent exponents of the so-called Christian Kabbalah, that is,
the tradition which aimed at reexamining the Jewish Kabbalah in a Christian light. Regarded by Leibniz as "perhaps the most accomplished man
in Europe in the knowledge of the most mysterious things of the Jews,"[28]
Rosenroth had provided in his monumental *Kabbala denudata* the most
important source of non-Judaic kabbalistic literature in the early modern
period.[29] With him Leibniz spent several days in sustained discussion,
emerging deeply impressed by Rosenroth's insight into the kabbalistic
tradition.[30] The Kabbalah was not, however, the only highlight of his
Sulzbach sojourn: he also found time to discuss fossils and minerals with
a keen collector, Elias Wolfgang Talientschger de Glänegg, as well as
visiting some lead mines near Freyung and Erbendorf.[31]

Probably around 11 January, Leibniz left Sulzbach for a detour into
the nearby regions of Northern Bohemia, trying once again to track down
his friend Crafft, who for several years had been at the service of the Freiherr von Lammingen at Choden castle (Thranov). After passing through
Pilsen, on 20 January Leibniz arrived at the castle only to discover that
Crafft was much further north, in the town of Graupen, almost on the
frontier with Saxony.[32] Despite the raging winter, Leibniz made his way
north, finally managing to meet Crafft in Graupen toward the end of
January. The two reunited friends busily schemed at various innovative
technical projects, including the extraction of ore, gold washing, dye
manufacture, and the reform of coinage. Last but not least, they planned
a common visit to Vienna for the presentation of their schemes to the

emperor.[33] Leibniz's return trip to Sulzbach during the first half of February demonstrated that the lack of success of the Harz project had failed to extinguish his interest in mining: he stopped to visit a number of sites, gaining up-dated impressions of new mining techniques.[34] On 21 February he travelled from Sulzbach to Amberg, where he sojourned for some twenty days in the town and its neighbourhood before resuming his journey on 11 March. The following day he reached Regensburg, site of the sittings of the permanent imperial diet, where he spent a fortnight striking up a close relationship with the imperial secretary, Philipp Wilhelm von Hörnigk. Toward the end of March Leibniz was finally ready to leave for Munich. The letter he wrote on 25 March to Ernst von Hessen-Rheinfels suggested that he intended to make his way back to Hanover, possibly via Augsburg and Ulm, immediately after his key work in the Bavarian capital ("I proceed from here to Munich, from there I could go to Augsburg and to Ulm, and I have not yet determined which route I will take for my return.")[35] The trip to Vienna recently planned with his accomplice Crafft suggests rather different intentions. On 26 March 1688 he left Regensburg, entrusting to Hörnigk part of his luggage, and four days later – five months after his departure from Hanover – he arrived around noon at his original main destination: Munich.

Until this point Leibniz had sent no news to Hanover. The only sign of life from the long gone court counsellor had been a note of 24 January 1688 to the government secretary in Osterode (Harz), Friedrich Wilhelm Leidenfrost, and even that communication had been far from informative as to Leibniz's whereabouts.[36] Although it was written from Bohemia, probably during the visit to Choden castle, Leibniz had pretended to be in Nuremberg, no doubt to disguise his considerable deviation from the high road south to Munich. Once his intended destination was finally reached, it was safe to make contact with Hanover again. Even so, Leibniz did not communicate directly with his employer or with the Hanoverian ministers, but with Duchess Sophie's secretary, Bartolomeo Ortensio Mauro, since it was from those quarters that he could expect the most sympathetic hearing after taking such a long time to reach his destination.[37] Sophie was in fact above all relieved to hear from him, although there was no mistaking the gentle reproach hidden beneath her light teasing:

I cannot refrain, Monsieur, to express my joy that you have not in fact gone to the other world in search of the origin of the House of Brunswick, as was supposed here, since after your departure we had heard nothing to reassure us that you were still alive – until now, when Mr Hortance has delighted me with your letter from Munich, which made me realise that you have been so busy researching the things of the past that you have forgotten those of the present and to send us your news; I had already begun to mourn you as a dead man, by which you can judge of the affection and perfect esteem that I have for you[.][38]

With sharpened awareness that he needed to produce results, Leibniz approached the *Kapellmeister* (the court director of music), Agostino Steffani, to gain access to the library of the Bavarian dukes. On 5 and 6 April he visited the library twice, studying the German manuscript of Aventin from which the historian's printed Latin *Annals of Bavaria* had been prepared. Unlike the printed work, the German manuscript recorded the sources from which information had been drawn. In particular, Leibniz discovered that the source for Aventin's mention of Azzo II was a manuscript codex held at the Benedictine monastery of St. Ulrich and Afra in Augsburg.[39] Galvanized by this discovery, Leibniz was eager to further his research in the Electoral manuscript collections before travelling to Augsburg to check the codex. But the initial permission granted by the duke was unexpectedly withdrawn due to the intervention of some suspicious court counsellors: although the ostensible reason was a formal mistake made by Leibniz in his request for permission, the underlying cause may have been fears of espionage on the part of the Hanoverian *Hofrat*.[40] Despite Steffani's efforts on his behalf, nothing could be done for the moment to obtain readmission to the library. Pending a final decision, on 11 April Leibniz left Munich for Augsburg, where he arrived the following day at noon. Not without some difficulty, he eventually located the manuscript *Historia de Guelfis principibus*, which contained the solution of the riddle.[41] As he wrote jubilantly in his long overdue reports on his activities for his employers

I found not *Astensis*, but *Estensis* in old but readily legible characters, and from this I recognised that Aventin had corrupted it in his published work, due to a false affectation of Latinity, as he often does . . . And so in an instant the difficulty is removed and the common origin of Brunswick and Este established better than by everything that has previously been seen.[42]

Leibniz's pride was justified. For the history of the Guelf descent, this was a very significant discovery, which prompted him to further his researches in Italian territory. After finding proof of the dynastical connection

between the Este family and the Braunschweig-Lüneburg house, on 15
April Leibniz wrote to the latter's representative in Venice, Francesco de
Floramonti, asking him to act as an intermediary in establishing a contact with the Este court in Modena.[43] On the same day he left Augsburg
for Munich, where he was hoping that a decision in his favour would
reopen the doors of the ducal library. His journey, falling during the
Easter triduum, afforded him the opportunity to glimpse the more san-
guine and emotional religiosity of Catholic southern Germany, expressed
in the processions on Good Friday. Whether or not such piety was at
odds with his austere Protestant sensibility, the sermon of a Jesuit who
"lowered [the emphasis on] mortifications and elevated love to its proper
height" seemed to strike a chord with the Leibnizian theology of love,
characterized by rather un-Lutheran tones.[44]

On 16 April, however, he found in Munich that permission to work in
the library was still lacking. Normally cool and measured in his reactions
to large and small setbacks, this time Leibniz was enraged.[45] On 24 and
27 April he wrote detailed reports on his trip addressed, respectively,
to the Hanoverian minister Albrecht Philipp von dem Bussche and to
Ernst August himself, hinting to the latter that a perusal of the documents
relating to the ancestors of the Este and Monselice houses and a visit to
the Este archives in Modena were now quite necessary.[46] Without waiting
for replies from Hanover, on 29 April he left Munich for Vienna where
he arrived by Danube boat on the afternoon of 8 May 1688.[47]

Vienna (May 1688–February 1689)

Leibniz was to remain in the Imperial capital for nine months. The practical reason for such a long stay in a city which did not feature at all in
his original historiographical remit was that he awaited word from Floramonti regarding permission to visit the Este archives. In fact, Leibniz was
more than happy to take this opportunity for an extended sojourn in the
Habsburg capital. Apart from the generic attraction of being at the heart of
central European political affairs, there were more specific motives which
recommended Vienna as a stimulating and interesting place. First of all,
it was home to Leopold I. Since October 1668,[48] and regularly thereafter,
Leibniz had tried to attract the emperor's attention either in support of
his plans or as a prospective employer. Now was his chance to press his

case in person.[49] In addition to the emperor, another prominent personality justified Leibniz's desire to reside in Vienna for a while: Cristobal Rojas y Spinola, the architect of the reunification between Rome and the Protestants, who since 1686 had been nominated Bishop of nearby Wiener-Neustadt.

Although Leibniz was keen to pursue his contacts with both Leopold and Rojas, he did not forget his duties and allegiance to Hanover. Shortly after his arrival he called upon the Braunschweig-Lüneburg representative, Christoph von Weselow, whom he knew from Hanover. Weselow was happy to see his colleague *Hofrat*, especially since he had on his hands a difficult legal-dynastical case – the claim of the Braunschweig-Lüneburg house to the duchy of East Frisia – for the prosecution of which Leibniz's legal-historical advice was an asset. Leibniz obligingly prepared for Weselow a document which could serve as a basis for the formal presentation of the Guelf claim to the emperor.[50] Next in line to request his assistance was Duchess Sophie herself, who asked Leibniz to plead for the promotion from colonel to general of her second son, Friedrich August (1661–90), who, together with his younger brother, Karl Philipp (1669–90), served as an officer of the imperial army in the ongoing war against the Turks.[51] To Sophie's great distress, both were to die during the war only a couple of years later.

Beside representing Braunschweig-Lüneburg's interests at court, Leibniz also continued to unearth its historical and dynastical connections both through his work in the rich imperial library and through his correspondence.[52] This time he found in the successor of Peter Lambeck as the emperor's librarian, Daniel von Nessel, a very supportive colleague with whom he developed a learned friendship.[53] While he was immersed in the extensive Viennese collections, discomforting news came from another library – the one of which he was supposed to have direct oversight: the ducal library in Hanover. On 30 June, the vice-archivist Georg Michael Backmeister informed Leibniz that, in his absence, the entire library and his personal belongings had been removed from the Leineschloß to make space for the new opera house under construction.[54] Although Backmeister was at pains to assure him that the move had been closely supervised and that both his possessions and the library collections were safely stored in the house of Maria Elisabeth von Anderten in the Leinstraße, the way in which library and librarian had been unceremoniously removed from their quarters without giving so much as a word of forewarning spoke volumes about Ernst August's attitude towards the ducal collections and their curator.

Leibniz cannot have been pleased, and the lack of consideration shown for him might well have sharpened his desire to find a new patron. In any case he gave serious consideration to the possibility of being employed as historiographer of the emperor, advanced in the autumn of 1688 by the court chancellor, Theod. Althet Heinrich von Strattmann.[55] Although Leibniz's official motive for momentarily declining the offer was his previous commitment to writing the history of the Guelf house,[56] it seems that the real reason was the persistent lack of clarity regarding the status being offered him at the Viennese court.[57] From his memo of late October 1688 for the emperor, and his further inquiry at the beginning of May 1690 during his briefer sojourn in Vienna after the Italian tour, it is clear that the offer was very alluring to him and contained many advantages. However, as in the occasion of his application of July 1680 to be appointed imperial librarian after Peter Lambeck's death,[58] in this case too the sticking point appears to have been his desire to be nominated simultaneously as a member of the Imperial Aulic Council in Vienna (*Reichshofrat*).[59] Whatever the case, nothing came of it.

The same applied, unfortunately, to the many proposals that he had prepared for the emperor, despite the tide of moderate optimism which pervaded the imperial city upon his arrival in May 1688. After its dramatic rescue from the Turkish siege during the summer of 1683, the Empire's season of good fortune during the liberation of Hungary in 1686 seemed to be sealed by the conquest of Belgrade on 6 September 1688.[60] Although the pressure of unending troop movements continued to weigh heavily on Vienna, the perspective of the long-awaited armistice with the Ottoman Empire justified the expectation that some financial resources could be snatched from the jaws of the omnivorous war machine to be invested in worthy scientific, technical, and scholarly activities. Alas, the hope of relatively peaceful times to come was short-lived. While the Habsburg victory at Belgrade was greeted with joy and relief by other Catholic powers, Louis XIV felt menaced by it. Now that Leopold had finally won his war against the Ottoman Empire, he could have turned his armies against France and demand the restitution of occupied territories – including Strasbourg and Luxembourg – which remained in French hands after the truce signed at Ratisbon on 15 August 1684. Louis XIV decided that swift action was called for before Leopold had time to recover from the exhausting Turkish war. On 24 September 1688 a *Mémoire* was released in Versailles demanding that the decisions of the treaty of Ratisbon become permanent and that France's protégé, Cardinal Wilhelm Egon von Fürstenberg, be elected archbishop and elector of Cologne.[61] The *Mémoire* was tantamount to a declaration of war, which confronted Leibniz and the other inhabitants of Vienna with the gloomy reality of a second front flaring up again to the west even before the danger to the east had been eliminated.[62] On 18 October the emperor's answer to Louis XIV's declaration was published in Latin and in German translation.[63] Although the attribution of this text to Leibniz has not been supported by appropriate findings in his Nachlaß,[64] another much more extensive work documents his passionate engagement with the issue. During the autumn and winter of 1688–9 Leibniz composed a substantial political pamphlet which – bearing for the second time the title of *Mars Christianissimus* – embraced again the weapon of sarcasm against Louis XIV's unashamed aggressive politics.[65] Foreseen for publication, an abstract of the work was sent in November to court chancellor Strattmann,[66] followed on 30 December by the dispatch of the first part to both Strattmann and the imperial vice-chancellor, Leopold Wilhelm von Königsegg.[67]

Despite the drastic deterioration of the political situation, with the assistance of Daniel Crafft (who had joined him in Vienna during the first half of August) Leibniz pressed ahead with his proposals, asking for an audience with the emperor. His longstanding wish was finally fulfilled toward the end of October 1688, when he was granted a hearing from Leopold of Habsburg.[68] Leibniz prepared for the meeting with great care,[69] drafting before and after the audience a number of memos outlining a variety of proposals to be presented to the emperor and his ministers – from ideas regarding the historiography of the Empire and the establishment of the *Collegium Imperiale Historicum* to the reform of coinage and of the monetary system;[70] from the creation of a factory for the production of dyes from minerals (intended as first building block of an Imperial *Bergkollegium* deemed to co-ordinate all technical issues linked to mining) to the improvement of trade and linen manufacture;[71] from a voluntary Turk-tax to finance the costs of the war against the Ottoman Empire and the introduction of a tax on luxury items of clothing to the reform of the archives and the creation of a universal reference library;[72] from the establishment of an insurance system to the illumination of the streets of Vienna with oil lamps.[73] Finally, this array of proposals could not lack a fairly detailed plan for ecclesiastical reunification.[74]

This plan was conceived in close communication with Bishop Rojas[75] whom Leibniz met repeatedly during his Viennese sojourn. After the return of Rojas from a year-long stay in Rome (September 1683–August 1684) and his installation in 1686 in Wiener-Neustadt, rumours circulated that the bishop's hopes for ecclesiastical reunification had cooled down and that he was enjoying his rich bishopric instead. Leibniz was glad to discover that these rumours were unjustified and that Rojas continued to share his commitment to ecclesiastical reunification.[76] In June and September 1688 he paid extended visits to Wiener-Neustadt, where he and his friend Crafft were received with great warmth.[77] Galvanized by his talks with Rojas, on 17 June 1688 Leibniz wrote to Duchess Sophie trying to convince her that – given the support of the emperor, of Pope Innocent XI, and of Ernst August for Rojas's plan – the next step toward church reunification was to gain the approval of the Brandenburg court.[78] Sophie was in fact preparing to travel to Berlin towards the end of June to assist her daughter Sophie Charlotte, due to give birth in August;[79] but on 24 August Sophie replied from Berlin with discouraging news. The recent death of the Brandenburg elector, Friedrich Wilhelm, and the subsequent passage of power to Sophie Charlotte's husband, Friedrich III, had left the principality in a state of chaos. Even worse, for all the assurances given by Leibniz and Rojas that the king of France was not against the reunification proposal,[80] Louis XIV's revocation of the Edict of Nantes in 1685 certainly did not aid reconciliation. On the contrary, Berlin was filled with Huguenot refugees forced to flee France and shouting "Anathema!" against Catholicism, whereas in the city's churches God was expressly thanked for the liberation from "the Papist blindness" – not the ideal climate for pursuing the reunion of the Protestants with Rome, despite Sophie's own efforts on behalf of Rojas and her protégé.[81]

Busy as he was with his reunification plans, his torrent of schemes for the emperor, and his historiographical researches, Leibniz also found time to concentrate on important logical, philosophical, and scientific issues as well.[82] In a remarkable private paper probably written during the Viennese period, for instance, he explicitly formulated his distinctive thesis of the nonexistence of purely extrinsic denominations, that is, of properties which are completely 'external' to the thing of which they are predicated. On this issue, the standard scholastic view was that extrinsic denominations (for instance, James's property of being heavier than Mark) were founded in intrinsic properties of the subjects (in the example: James and Mark's respective weights). However, it was normally held that a change in the intrinsic properties of only one of the subjects would have as a result a change of relation without necessarily implying also a change in the properties of the other subject. Following the above example, if James were to lose weight and become lighter than Mark, it was thought that the change in the intrinsic properties of James would imply a change in the relation between James and Mark, but would not affect the intrinsic properties of Mark. Leibniz departed from this view in maintaining that a change in relation between two subjects was necessarily accompanied by a change in the intrinsic properties, not only of the two related subjects, but of all the individuals in the world: Mark as heavier than James would be intrinsically different from Mark as lighter than James even if Mark's weight had not changed at all; and by extension of this reasoning all the individuals of the world would be intrinsically different if James were to become lighter than Mark. The reason for this fact was, according to Leibniz, the universal connection of everything with everything:[83]

what Hippocrates said about the human body is true of the whole universe: namely, that all things conspire and are sympathetic, i.e. that nothing happens in one creature of which some exactly corresponding effect does not reach all others. Nor, again, are there any absolutely extrinsic denominations in things.[84]

In a marginal note to the same text he also specified that "multiple finite substances are simply different expressions of the same universe in accordance with different relations and the limitations proper to each."[85]

But it was in the fields of physics and cosmology that Leibniz's philosophical work in Vienna intersected most directly with the latest developments within the international scientific community at large. In the issue of the *Acta Eruditorum* of June 1688 he came across the review by Christoph Pfautz – a professor of mathematics in Leipzig with whom he had been in epistolary contact since 1679 – of Isaac Newton's epoch-making *Philosophiae Naturalis Principia Mathematica* of 1687. According to Leibniz's own account, even before he had read Newton's *magnum opus* itself this review prompted him to publish his own theories on the matters discussed in the *Principia*, some of which had been germinating since his years in Paris.[86] The result was the hasty publication of three essays in the *Acta Eruditorum*. The first and shortest, *De Lineis opticis et alia* (January 1689), set the scene for the more substantial pair which followed. The second, on motion in a resisting medium (*Schediasma de Resistentia Medii et Motu projectorum gravium in medio resistante*, January 1689), tackled a topic treated in the second book of the *Principia*; while the third, on the causes of planetary motion (*Tentamen de Motuum caelestium Causis*, February 1689), took issue with important aspects of the world system articulated in Newton's third book.

The mountain of his unpublished papers suggests, however, that Leibniz was not being candid in his account of the origin of these papers. In the case of the *Schediasma de Resistentia Medii*, his sustained reflection on this problem is richly documented in a series of notes dating back to his visit to Paris. The cosmological theories discussed in the *Tentamen de Motuum caelestium Causis*, however, lack this paper trail: within his extant papers, they first emerge in an important series of notes responding to the *Principia* itself and evidently written in Vienna in the autumn of 1688, contrary to his claim that he read Newton's *Principia* for the first time during his sojourn in Rome (that is, at some point after 14 April 1689, the date of his arrival there, and therefore after the publication of the *Tentamen de Motuum caelestium Causis* in February 1689).[87] For a court historiographer, Leibniz's reconstruction of events tellingly lacks chronological precision. He was presumably drawn into overstating his independence from Newton in an attempt to avoid an equal and opposite understatement. His thinking on the issues discussed in these papers genuinely derived at least in part from ideas which began evolving before he had read either the *Principia* itself or Pfautz's review of it; and he therefore wished to present his theories as more than mere elaborations of Newton's work.[88] Yet given his subsequent entanglement in a priority dispute with the English mathematician regarding discoveries even more significant and enduring than the speculations offered in the *Tentamen*, this was a dangerous strategy. And as far as Newton himself was concerned, at any rate, Leibniz might just as well not have bothered: the Cambridge professor was openly contemptuous many years later when, commenting on the three papers of 1689, he claimed that "the Propositions contained in them (Errors and Trifles excepted) are Mr Newton's (or easy Corollaries from them)".[89]

If Leibniz was unwise to pretend that he had not read the *Principia* before writing these three essays, Newton was also unfair in dismissing them as unoriginal. In the *Tentamen* Leibniz in fact attempted to provide a mechanical explanation of the force of gravity entirely unlike anything postulated by Newton. From a philosophical point of view, the lack of some such account in the work of the eminent English mathematician was unacceptable not only to Leibniz but to a great many of his contemporaries. Without it, Newton's work appeared to rely by default on a mysterious or occult attraction operating throughout the universe which lacked a physical explanation.[90] Leibniz, on the other hand, elaborated a theory of Cartesian inspiration, proposing a mechanical explanation based on vortices and an imbalance between opposite tendencies or *conatus*.[91] According to this account, planetary motion was the result of three forces: a harmonic vortex of fluid matter swirling about the sun and sweeping the planets around in their orbits like boats in a whirlpool; and two contrary forces: a centrifugal force, derived from the circulation of the planets together with the vortex, and a gravitational force towards the sun, also derived (in a less satisfactory fashion) from the impulsions of fluids.[92] This picture was the final outcome of a series of tentative cosmological studies in the autumn of 1688 which, although stimulated by a direct reading of the *Principia*, nevertheless contained original conceptions nowhere implied or suggested by Newton.[93] The Lucasian professor, in fact, had famously refused to frame hypotheses to explain gravitational attraction; and Leibniz, in confronting the problem neatly sidestepped by Newton, was addressing an exceptionally difficult conundrum which, three centuries later, remains without a satisfactory explanation. In struggling with this intractable problem, he did nevertheless produce one interesting ray of light: in paragraph ten of the *Tentamen* Leibniz mentioned for the first time in print the important distinction (inspired by Galileo and by Lorenzo Magalotti's *Saggi di Naturali Esperienze Fatte nell'Accademia del Cimento* of 1666) between 'dead' and 'living' force – a distinction which he had already 'privately' introduced during the Parisian period in a letter to Mariotte and in his *De Arcanis Motus* (1676), albeit probably without the technical meaning assumed by these notions from the late 1670s onward.[94] According to him dead force was mass times an infinitesimal speed, whereas living force or *vis viva* was mass times the square of speed (mv^2).

In November 1688 the rigours of the winter took their toll. Leibniz was ill for several weeks, lamenting the symptoms of a severe flu.[95] At the end of the year he was still trying to recover. Writing on 30 December to Otto Grote, he described his predicament with a touch of humour:

For three weeks I have not put one foot outside the house, having been attacked by the worse catarrh I ever had in my life. To be sure, I have never been as old as I am now. I lost my appetite, something which weakened me a lot; and I still have a cough which worsens as soon as I enter cold air. So I will remain in my room a little longer.[96]

Despite being seriously unwell, Leibniz had continued to work. Thanks to the cordial relationship established with the emperor's librarian, Daniel von Nessel, books, manuscripts, and even the catalogue had been brought from the library to his lodgings. The period of forced confinement had been used for intensive study of the sources of the Guelf history, and Leibniz had not hesitated to burn his candle, sometimes working through the night. As he forcefully stated in his letter to Grote: "It is not necessary to live, but it is necessary to work and to do one's duty. It would do me a great injustice to suppose that I have wasted my time." His plan to visit some mines in Hungary had been jeopardized by his illness and now he thought only of his return.[97]

This declared intention to rush back to Hanover the moment his health was restored turned out to be another overstatement, although perhaps one only fully discernable in retrospect. On 16 January, Leibniz finally received something which he had been seeking for nine months and had now virtually despaired of ever obtaining: the long-awaited letter from Floramonti informing him that the duke of Modena, Francesco II (1662–94), had granted him permission to use the Este archives.[98] This unexpected good news did wonders for his recuperation, and his missives to Grote modulated abruptly from a minor to a major key.[99] Another week's rest and he would be on his feet and ready to brave the Alpine passes, even in the middle of the winter. Indeed, he must depart at once, because the spring thaw would soon make the mountain roads impassable. The urgency with which Leibniz apologized that he must set out immediately, before they had time to reply, suggests that his haste was driven by fear that his Italian adventure might be not merely delayed by the melting of the snow but frozen altogether by a frosty reception from Hanover.[100] Better to be gone before his employers had a chance to qualify Leibniz's confident assumption that they would be delighted with his decision to follow their ancestors' footsteps across the Alps.[101] At any rate, he assured Grote, "I will not stay there longer than is needed to obtain the clarifications I need";[102] yet as a prudent precaution he dropped by Bishop Rojas before setting out and departed with numerous reference letters, including one addressed to Cardinal Azzolini in Rome.[103] Clearly a lonely traveller far from home needed to be prepared for every eventuality. Despite his haste, preparations for departure took a good three weeks; but on 11 February 1689 he was safely on his way, having left his own carriage, horses, and coachman in the care of Rojas and part of his luggage at the "Steyner Hof" in Vienna awaiting his return.[104]

Italy (March 1689–March 1690)

Travelling by post-coach or shared carriages, Leibniz arrived in Trieste at the beginning of March 1689 – but not without stopping on the way to see the quicksilver mines of Idria.[105] From Trieste, probably by boat, he reached Venice on 4 March where he stayed until the end of the month *en attendant* Dragoni.[106] Earl Francesco Dragoni was in fact supposed to let him know by post the final arrangements for his visit to the archives in Modena, but neither Dragoni's letters nor Leibniz's go-between, Floramonti, were anywhere to be found.[107] Little is known of Leibniz's activities in Venice apart from his work on a detailed plan for a reference library (promised to Strattmann)[108] and his meeting with the third son of Duchess Sophie, Maximilian Wilhelm (1666–1726), engaged like his brothers Friedrich August and Karl Philipp in the war against the Turks.[109]

After four weeks, having lost his patience with the fruitless waiting for Dragoni's letters – and, perhaps, having exhausted the things he wanted to do in Venice – he left the doges' city. The fact that in Venice, as in Vienna, he appears to have left no clear instructions for forwarding his correspondence seems to suggest that, after all, he was not overly concerned about receiving news from Dragoni or, for that matter, from Hanover.[110] *En route* to Ferrara, he embarked on a small boat for Mesola; and – as his first biographer, Johann Georg Eckhart, tells the tale – a storm rapidly engulfed the boat. The sailors, believing that the foreign traveller could not understand their language, agreed to throw him overboard, lighten their boat, and divide his belongings amongst them. Leibniz, however, had an ace up his sleeve – or rather a rosary in his pocket. Upon seeing the learned northern evidently imploring celestial protection for their endangered vessel in good Catholic fashion, one of the sailors repented and managed to convince the others that the stranger was no heretic and that therefore they would endanger themselves further by killing a good Christian.[111] This curious anecdote – which Leibniz allegedly repeated with a certain pride – reveals both his cunning in providing himself with a rosary while travelling towards the centre of the Catholic world stronghold, and, perhaps more interestingly, the fact that after only a month or so in Italy he had already picked up enough passive knowledge of the local idiom to understand what was happening.

On 1 April he arrived in Ferrara, where he spent a week.[112] From Ferrara he wrote to Duchess Sophie, announcing his intention to take "a tour of Rome in order to profit from the weather and the proximity." For Leibniz one of the attractions of travelling to the eternal city was the possibility of seeing Queen Christina of Sweden (1626–89), the former patroness of Descartes who, after her conversion to Catholicism and abdication of her throne in 1654, had settled in Rome. Perhaps to sweeten the pill for Sophie, who was clearly eager to have him back in Hanover, he added his hope of meeting the duchess's two youngest sons, Christian (1671–1703) and Ernst August (1674–1728), who were also making a Roman tour.[113] On 7 April he left Ferrara by post-coach, reaching Rome on 14 April after passing through Bologna and Loreto. In Rome Leibniz was unable to see either the two young princes, who had already left by the time of his arrival, or Queen Christina, who died unexpectedly on 19 April. The demise on 8 June of her close friend and heir Cardinal Azzolini blocked access to the Queen's rich manuscript collections, which Leibniz was hoping to peruse.[114] Yet he met other interesting savants and scientists, including the mathematician, astronomer, and founding member of the Parisian Académie Royale des Sciences Adrien Auzout. At Auzout's villa he read for the first time Ralph Cudworth's *True intellectual system of the universe* (London 1678),[115] and drafted for Auzout the *Notata quaedam circa vitam et doctrinam Cartesii*, foreseen as a contribution to the biography of Descartes being prepared by Adrien Baillet.[116]

While Leibniz's *De Linea Isochrona* appeared in Leipzig, closing the controversy on Cartesian physics with the Abbé Catelan,[117] the Hanover court counsellor decided to make "a tour to Naples" before the weather became too hot.[118] The beginning of May found him touring the beautiful Italian city and its stunning neighbourhood, including Pozzuoli, the Solfatara, and Mount Vesuvius.[119] As intoxicating as it might have been to plunge into the natural beauty surrounding Naples, Leibniz did not forget the Guelf history, seeking and obtaining access to the library, where he studied manuscripts pertaining to Duke Otto of Braunschweig-Grubenhagen, the forth husband of Queen Giovanna I of Naples (d. 1382).[120] In mid-May he returned to Rome.[121] This time he was in no hurry to go (or, more to the point, go back) anywhere: his second sojourn in Rome stretched over six months.

Although such a long stay was hard to sell to his patrons, Leibniz was not eager to leave the eternal city to resume his isolated life in Hanover. Too much was going on in Rome for him to resist the temptation of prolonging the visit. To begin with, Innocent XI – who had reigned over the Roman church since 21 September 1676 – was ill, something that Leibniz regarded with concern since the pope had been supportive towards Rojas's efforts at reunification between Catholics and Protestants and had, according to Leibniz, high moral standards.[122] As he wrote to Landgraf Ernst on 23 March 1690:

the Ecclesiastics accustomed to worldliness spoke ill of him; and it was amusing to hear German Protestants and French Huguenots take the side of the Pope in Rome even against monks and priests . . . Nevertheless, since nobody could criticize his habits and his intentions which appeared to be holy and good, he retained the veneration of the people . . . In the end, one might say that he did well in major things and perhaps lacked sometimes in minor ones[.][123]

Unfortunately Leibniz's wishes for Innocent XI's recovery remained unfulfilled:[124] the pope died on 12 August 1689.[125] The ensuing conclave, held in the autumn and followed with great interest by Leibniz,[126] brought to Rome a crowd of high-ranking prelates. On 16 October the almost eighty-year-old Cardinal Ottoboni from Venice became Pope Alexander VIII. The election was greeted by Leibniz with a long *Carmen Gratulatorium*[127] and with the hope that the reputation of Ottoboni as an "enlightened man" would make of Alexander VIII a supporter of science and learning.[128]

As if to put this reputation to the test, Leibniz discussed with his new savant friends in Rome the possibility of convincing the Vatican to lift the ban against Copernicanism.[129] A certain optimism seemed to be justified by the fact that the new pope had in the past "judged with moderation" the Copernican issue.[130] Moreover, shortly after his election he had promoted to high rank a young member of the Roman Accademia Fisico-Matematica, Francesco Bianchini, favourably disposed toward the new Galilean–Copernican astronomy and close to Leibniz. Other highly placed participants at the meetings of the Accademia also displayed an open attitude towards the Copernican system, notably the Jesuit Antonio Baldigiani, who held the chair of mathematics at the Collegio Romano. These circumstances prompted Leibniz to commit to paper a number of texts, at least one of which was probably destined for Baldigiani, pressing for the abolition of the censure against the Copernican system.[131] Writing in 1699 to Antonio Magliabechi, he remembered,

When I was in Rome I exhorted certain distinguished men endowed with authority to promote intellectual freedom in a subject that is not in the least dangerous and to allow to be lifted or abolished by disuse the prohibitions regarding the system of the earth's motion; and I showed that it was in the interest of the Roman Church itself that it not appear to the ignorant to afford protection to ignorance and error. Nor indeed did these men recoil from this advice of mine, so that I hope . . . that the ancient liberty might be recovered, the suppression of which greatly harms the lively genius of the Italians[.][132]

Despite the reluctance of the Vatican to review its official position on Galileo and Copernicus, Leibniz found (no doubt to his surprise) that the enlightenment had spread also to the Roman Curia. In fact, an open discussion was taking place in Rome amongst scholars and scientists convened by Cardinal Gregorio Barbarigo, himself favourable to the Copernican system:[133]

In my recent journey I became aware that light is dawning in Italy and a contagion (so to speak) is spreading gradually in the study of the purer [traditions of] antiquity. Even in Rome, at the instigation of the admirable Cardinal Barbarigo, groups of learned men meet regularly in the Congregation for the Propagation of the Faith itself. I was present myself several times with the friends who invited me, and if this continues I expect a not inconsiderable harvest from this sowing[.][134]

Through such means Leibniz became fully engaged in the Roman learned circles, eagerly participating in the daily evening meetings of the Accademia Fisico-Matematica, founded and animated by Giovanni Giustino Ciampini (1633–98).[135] Through the Accademia he was personally introduced to Jesuits who had returned from the mission in China and were preparing for a new departure for the Orient. In particular, Leibniz developed an interesting correspondence with the mathematician Claudio Filippo Grimaldi (1639–1712), which brought to him precious first-hand news of the intellectual heritage of Chinese civilisation.[136] But perhaps the most outstanding fruit of Leibniz's assiduous frequentation of the Accademia Fisico-Matematica was its stimulation of his creativity in physics: during this interval he started developing a new part of physics which studied motion in relation to force. This novel science was christened by him *Dynamica* ("dynamics," from the Greek word *dynamis*, force).[137] Although, strictly speaking, Leibniz's *Dynamica* was born in Rome in 1689, his new creature had been in gestation for over a decade. Indeed its beginnings dated back to 1676–8, when Leibniz had first introduced the principle of equivalence between full cause and entire effect (*De Arcanis Motus*, summer 1676) and had composed in January 1678 the breakthrough paper *De corporum concursu*, in which the force conserved when bodies interact was characterized for the first time as mv^2.[138] The immediate precursor of his new science was a transition piece which paved the way to the *Dynamica*: the *Phoranomus seu de potentia et legibus naturae*, probably written in the second half of July 1689 and left incomplete.[139] The *Phoranomus* was cast in the form of two dialogues on physics starring some of the key actors of the Roman scientific scene and elaborating on discussions which Leibniz was having with his new friends of the Accademia Fisico-Matematica. Although the word *dynamica* did not yet appear in this piece, in it Leibniz spoke (albeit tentatively) of "a new science of force and effect."[140] The challenge was for him to show that his new science was superior not only to Cartesian physics (against which he defended his principle of conservation of force measured by mv^2) but also to Galilean science. According to Leibniz, the latter was limited by its construction a posteriori. It therefore applied only to a specific and empirically grounded system of phenomena. His intention was to develop a system of a priori arguments which were corroborated by experience and could account for all phenomena involving motion. In short, in the *Phoranomus* he attempted to develop a theory of force built a priori on principles such as the equivalence between full cause and entire effect.[141]

Probably perceiving the shortcomings of his first attempt, Leibniz abandoned the *Phoranomus* rather abruptly to start work in August and September 1689 on a substantial treatise which he was to call *Dynamica de Potentia et Legibus Naturae Corporeae*. The bulk of this treatise, expounding in technical detail Leibniz's new science, was finished in 1689–90. Although foreseen for publication, it never reached the press during Leibniz's lifetime.[142] Following the example of his early twin treatises on physics, the *Theoria motus abstracti* and the *Hypothesis physica nova*, the work was divided into two parts, discussing abstract and concrete dynamics. Like the *Phoranomus*, the *Dynamica* elaborated his distinction between dead and living force (*vis mortua* and *vis viva*),[143] reiterating his opposition to the Cartesian principle of the conservation of motion based on the demonstration of Descartes's confusion between the concept of quantity of motion and the concept of quantity of live force. On the other hand, the *Dynamica* surpassed the *Phoranomus* in recasting and developing arguments tentatively introduced in the previous text, and in so doing achieved the first accomplished, formal expression of Leibniz's new theory of force. Whereas the *Phoranomus* spoke of "a new science of force (power) and effect," for instance, the *Dynamica* was described as "a new science of force (power) and action" which expounded demonstratively "the genuine laws of nature in place of imaginary ones."[144] The shift from the concept of "effect" to that of "action" indicated a change of focus pointing to the central ingredient of the new theory: the novel concept of "formal action" introduced by Leibniz, where "formal" designated the "essential" features of action as opposed to features depending on the contingent *situs* of bodies in a certain physical system.[145] In the *Dynamica* Leibniz distinguished between "formal effect" and "formal action":

The quantity of formal effect in motion is that whose measure consists in a certain quantity of matter (motion being equidistributed) being moved through a certain length.

The quantity of formal action in motion is that whose measure consists in a certain quantity of matter being moved through a certain length (motion being uniformly equidistributed) within a certain time.[146]

Formal action was considered from two points of view: its *extensio*, that is, its formal effect in spatial displacement; and its *intensio*, that is, "the quantity of speed by which the effect is produced or the matter is carried through length."[147] As a result of considering the extensive and intensive aspects of action, Leibniz arrived at a conception of action as a power to act both in the sense of a propensity to act and as the actualisation of that propensity in the motive effect.

During the fruitful months spent in Rome, Leibniz also continued his cosmological studies, writing a *Tentamen de Physicis Motuum Coelestium Rationibus* and working at a second version of the *Tentamen de Motuum caelestium Causis.*[148] One reason for going through his recently published *Tentamen* with a red pen was the desire, related to his contemporary efforts to have the censure of Copernicanism abolished, to recast his theory in a light more readily acceptable to the Catholic church. From a more technical point of view, he also wanted to improve his definitions and calculations (including the correction of some mistakes) and to propose a new model of gravity. The new theory no longer located the cause of gravity in the same fluid which carried the planets but in a fluid emitted from a centre and 'pushing' bodies towards the centre itself.[149]

The fertility of the Roman interval for Leibniz's scientific thought could not but stimulate his more strictly philosophical reflections as well. In a series of papers probably written between the spring of 1689 and March 1690, he returned to many of the epistemological and metaphysical issues which had exercised his mind, especially during his long Hanover years. For instance, in a remarkable text of the summer of 1689, he wrote of the two "labyrinths" made famous by the *Theodicy.*[150] Many of his metaphysical and ethical ruminations represented his struggle to find a way out of them. "There are undoubtedly two labyrinths of the human mind – one regarding the composition of the continuum, the other regarding the nature of freedom – which originate from the same source of the infinite."[151] In another key text of mid-1689 he lucidly summarized the logical–metaphysical principles of his philosophy, starting from the principle of identity/noncontradiction and the consequent thesis of the inclusion of the predicate in the subject of any true proposition, and working his way from there through the other characteristic tenets of his philosophy, including the principle of sufficient reason, the identity of indiscernibles, the thesis that there are no purely extrinsic denominations and that every individual substance involves in its complete notion the whole universe, the thesis that every particle of the universe contains a world of infinite creatures, and, finally, the thesis that the "substantiality" of bodies must be grounded in an unextended principle, since extension, motion, and bodies themselves "in so far as they consist of these alone, are not substances but true appearances."[152]

Beside enjoying the intellectual stimulation of the Roman savants, for the explication of his main historiographical duty Leibniz took advantage of the enormous wealth of printed and manuscript material held by the numerous libraries and archives in Rome, including the fascinating

Vatican archives and also, in the end, the collections of the late Queen Christina, to which he briefly gained access shortly before leaving. The outstanding erudition of the German visitor did not fail to attract the attention of influential prelates. Indeed, at some point between his Roman sojourn and February 1695, Leibniz's candidacy was mooted for the prestigious office of custodian of the Vatican library.[153] In a letter of 5 February 1695, Antonio Alberti (alias Amable de Tourreil, a French Jansenist based in Rome) reported that a prominent cardinal of the Roman Curia "assured that if he [Leibniz] was disposed to rejoin the Church, he could count not only on the post of *primus custos* of the Vatican Library but also on many other advantages. This way he could employ the rest of his life usefully and honourably in the service of the public."[154] Informed of the offer, Leibniz was obliged to decline, since conversion to the Roman church was part of the package.[155] For all his little subterfuges and equivocations in prolonging his travels to the south, Leibniz was not prepared to bend his principles and convert to Catholicism, despite the great attraction of settling in such an intellectually stimulating environment. What he wrote of Pope Innocent XI could perhaps have applied also to himself: "he did well in major things and perhaps lacked sometimes in minor ones[.]"[156] In any event, in Rome he had finally received two letters of April from Dragoni, clearing his way into the Este archives.[157] This being the case, around 20 November 1689, he finally packed his bags and left the eternal city.

The next stop was Florence, where he arrived a couple of days later.[158] There he met the librarian of the Grand Duke, Antonio Magliabechi, with whom, from Hanover, he had previously tried without success to establish an epistolary contact. On Grand Duke Cosimo III's orders, Magliabechi introduced the German visitor not only into the rich archives and libraries of the splendid Tuscan city but also into the Florentine learned circles which included Galileo's last student, Vincenzo Viviani, the physician Francesco Redi, and the counsellor of state Lorenzo Magalotti.[159] The German nobleman Rudolf Christian von Bodenhausen (Bodenus), who served as tutor to the sons of the Grand Duke and acquainted Leibniz with them, was definitely impressed by his fellow countryman. A close friendship developed between the two men based on their common interests in mathematics. Leibniz took Bodenhausen through his differential and integral calculus, and Bodenhausen undertook to copy and see through the press the first part of the *Dynamica* composed by Leibniz in Rome – a worthy enterprise which unfortunately was not taken to completion.[160] It was in Leibniz's written and oral exchanges with the Baron von Bodenhausen that the word *dynamica* made its first appearance to designate the treatise which Bodenhausen intended to prepare for publication: on 31 December 1689, writing to Leibniz shortly after his departure from Florence, Bodenhausen referred to "other things from our *Dynamica*, of which I am making a fair copy." This first appearance of the word *dynamica* seemed therefore to indicate that the two friends had already started to use this term in their Florentine discussions.[161] Another significant acquaintance in Florence, the archivist Cosimo della Rena, passed on to Leibniz an important piece of information gained through a Pisan monk, Teofilo Macchetti: the tombs of the ancient Este family resided in the monastery of Vangadizza at Badia Polesine, near Rovigo – something which was unknown even in Modena.[162] For once the northerner's leisurely networking in the Mediterranean sunshine bore fruit directly related to his historiographical mission.

On 22 December, Leibniz left Florence for Bologna, where he was introduced by Magliabechi's contact, the mathematician Domenico Guglielmini, to the famous anatomist Marcello Malpighi. With Malpighi he spent whatever time he had during his short visit discussing the genesis of the earth along the lines on which he was to treat it in the *Protogaea*. From this discussion Leibniz emerged deeply impressed by the Italian scientist.[163] On the 28th he was again on his way, this time finally directed to the principal official destination of his Italian trip: the Este court in Modena. A couple of days after his arrival he was granted an audience by Duke Francesco II. Although the Italian letter written by Leibniz to the duke shortly after their meeting suggests that Francesco II's reaction had not been particularly enthusiastic, Leibniz was allowed to use the Este archives for his historical research.[164] Presented with such a wealth of unstudied material, he immersed himself in it completely, studying printed and manuscript documents with such intensity that he was soon complaining of a noticeable deterioration of his eyesight.[165]

In addition to writing their history, Leibniz found in Modena another way of advancing the interests of the Braunschweig-Lüneburg dukes: he tactfully presented the possibility of a marriage alliance between the Este and Guelf houses through the union of one of the late Johann Friedrich's daughters to the heir of the Este duchy, Rinaldo.[166] Steps in that direction had already been taken on behalf of the Hanover court by Earl Dragoni, but his somewhat maladroit attempt had been rebuffed. Informed by Leibniz of his intention of discretely sounding out the Este court regarding the marriage plan, Duchess Sophie immediately endorsed the idea.[167] For once, one of Leibniz's schemes was eventually crowned by success, and in 1696 Charlotte Felicitas of Hanover became Duchess of Modena through her marriage to Rinaldo III (1655–1737).[168]

Apart from a brief visit to Bologna, Leibniz remained in Modena for five weeks, departing on 2 February 1690 for Parma (3 February) and Brescello, where he spent three days with Earl Dragoni. After visiting Ferrara a second time (7–9 February), he headed to the monastery of Vangadizza (10 February).[169] There the value of his detour to Florence proved its full worth: visiting the tombs of the ancient Este he found the funerary monuments of Azzo II and his wife, Kunigunde (Cunizza) von Altdorf (c. 1020–55), the epitaphs of which unveiled the mystery of the exact connection between the Este and Guelf houses. Azzo, whose place within the Este family had been confirmed by the Augsburg manuscript, had married Kunigunde, an heiress of the Bavarian line of the Guelf house. From their union was born Welf IV (c. 1040–1101), elevated to duke of Bavaria as Welf I in 1070 and the direct ancestor of the Guelf line of the Braunschweig-Lüneburg dukes.[170] Jubilantly Leibniz left Vangadizza for Venice, from which he promptly reported his discovery to Otto Grote.[171] Having accomplished the task of unearthing the Este–Guelf connection, he rewarded himself with over a month basking in the lively intellectual community of the *Repubblica Serenissima*. In particular, Leibniz met the Franciscan priest and professor Michel Angelo Fardella, with whom he enjoyed fruitful philosophical conversations and was to develop a stimulating philosophical correspondence. It was reflecting on his talks with Fardella while still in Venice in March 1690 that he penned an important memo elaborating more fully his conception of the structure of corporeal substance.[172] Even in these final weeks of his southern voyage his main assignment was not altogether forgotten. On 6–11 March he interrupted his Venetian sojourn to travel to the ancestral homelands of the Este family, the small cities of Este and Monselice, taking this opportunity to visit Padua and the monastery of Carceri along the way.[173] The day before taking his final leave of Venice, he wrote his last known letter to Arnauld.[174]

On 24 March he headed for the Italian borders via Mestre and Trent, crossing the Alps at the Brenner Pass.

Return to Hanover (March–June 1690)

On 30 March, Leibniz was in Innsbruck.[175] He next stopped in Augsburg to visit Gottlieb Spitzel, delivering parcels of books from Magliabechi. In Passau he called on his friend Philipp Wilhelm von Hörnigk, who in the meantime had become archivist to the local prince-bishop.[176] In Augsburg orders from Ernst August apparently caught up with Leibniz, instructing him to make a detour to Vienna, where some sort of court business needed his attention. Needless to say, Leibniz responded with exemplary devotion to duty, not least because he had left there part of his papers and luggage. As he explained jokingly to Sophie, he was particularly anxious personally to see his papers safely home: "if I carried as much coins as I carried papers, I would have more cash than the Emperor's Chamber".[177] During his briefer second visit to the imperial city from the end of April to the middle of May, he was prompted by the objections of Denis Papin to his physical theories to write a paper on the cause of gravity and in defence of his anti-Cartesian demonstrations.[178] The paper was published in the *Acta Eruditorum* in the same issue of May 1690 in which the mathematician Jakob Bernoulli used the differential notation and introduced the term "integral" – this latter only reluctantly adopted by Leibniz because it seemed to him to obscure the sense of the operation.[179] In Vienna he also explored the possibility of reviving the offer of the office of historiographer, provided that a clarification could be given regarding his status at the Imperial court.[180] Alas, no such clarification came. After a last visit to Bishop Rojas during which the next steps to be taken in the negotiation of ecclesiastical reunification were discussed,[181] Leibniz departed from Vienna. Having discarded the initial plan of travelling back via Karlsbad where Ernst August was staying in that period, he took the route passing through Prague and Dresden.[182] The route skirted also Leipzig, but Leibniz (who had missed no opportunity to see his friends and acquaintances everywhere else) did not see fit this time to stop to visit his relatives[183] – a fact in itself very telling of the lack of real closeness to his extended family under the veneer of polite letters of circumstance. Around mid-June 1690 the peripatetic *Hofrat* was finally back in Hanover.

Notes

1. The Estensis were named after Este (near Padua, Northern Italy), where Albert Azzo II built a castle. They were Dukes of Ferrara, Modena, and Reggio until 1597, when they were forced to give up Ferrara to the Papal States. Their capital was transferred to Modena and they continued to rule the duchy of Modena and Reggio until 1796.

2. See Leibniz to Albrecht Philipp von dem Bussche, 24 April 1688 (A I, 5, 98–100), and J. Turmair, *Annalium Boiorum lib. VIII*. Basel, 1580, pp. 437, 483. Cf. Scheel, "Leibniz als Historiker des Welfenhauses," p. 247 and André Robinet, *G. W. Leibniz. Iter Italicum*. Florence: Olschki, 1988, pp. 5–6.

3. *Selbstschilderung*, Pertz I, 4, 169.

4. See GP II, 135.

5. See A I, 5, N. 38, N. 39.

6. Leibniz to Duchess Sophie, beginning of April 1689 (A I, 5, 410).

7. Some of the philosophical texts written during this trip have already been mentioned in the previous chapter due to their closeness in topic and inspiration to the philosophical reflections of the Hanover years.

8. *Kürzere Fassung des Vortrags vor Kaiser Leopold I*, second half of September 1688 (A IV, 4, 79).

9. *Ausführliche Aufzeichnung für den Vortrag bei Kaiser Leopold I*, second half of September 1688 (A IV, 4, 52). See also A IV, 4, 15 and 40.

10. See respectively Bernardino Ramazzini to Antonio Magliabechi, 4 February 1690 (A I, 5, N. 296ª), and Domenico Guglielmini to Antonio Magliabechi, 8 January 1690 (A I, 5, N. 286ᵇ).

11. GP II, 135.

12. See Robinet, *Iter Italicum*, p. 2.

13. See *Selbstschilderung*, Pertz I, 4, 169–70 and chap. I. 1. One of the few occasions on which Leibniz seemed to be touched by the beauty of nature was a trip by boat to Strasbourg in August–September 1671. See *Dialogus de religione rustici*, November 1673 (A VI, 3, N. 9) and chap. I. 3, note 151.

14. Cf. the facsimile of the manuscript published by Olms: G. W. Leibniz, *Reise-Journal. 1687–1688*. Hildesheim: Olms, 1966. My reconstruction of the first part of Leibniz's itinerary is based on the *Reise-Journal* (including the "Vorwort"); Müller – Krönert, *Leben und Werk*; and A I, 5, xxix–xxxix.

15. On Leibniz's main work in this field, the *Protogaea*, see chap. II. 6.

16. See his extensive reading notes in A VI, 4, N. 451 (*Aus and zu Schriften von Valentin Weigel, Paracelsus, Sebastian Franck und Paul Lautensack*); Leibniz to Johann Daniel Crafft, 6 November 1687 (A III, 4, N. 197); and Müller–Krönert, *Leben und Werk*, p. 83.

17. See Leibniz for Landgraf Ernst (*Bemerkungen zu einer Charakterisierung von Leibniz' religiösem Standpunkt durch Landgraf Ernst*), late November 1687 (A I, 5, N. 5), and Arnauld to Landgraf Ernst, 29 December 1687 (A I, 5, 9–10).

18. A I, 5, N. 6.

19. See chap. II. 4.

20. On Leibniz's pragmatism in theology see Adams, "Leibniz's Examination," pp. 536–41.
21. A I, 5, 11. Cf. also I, 4, 380. Landgraf Ernst's views of Rojas's efforts towards ecclesiastical reunification are expounded in Heribert Raab, " 'De Negotio Hannoveriano Religionis'. Die Reunionsbemühungen des Bischofs Christoph de Rojas y Spinola im Urteil des Landgrafen Ernst von Hessen-Rheinfels." In *Volk Gottes*. Ed. by Remigius Bäumer and Heimo Dolch. Herder: Freiburg, 1967, pp. 395–417.
22. See for instance A II, 1, 490–91 and A I, 2, 226–7.
23. See A I, 5, 19. For an example of Leibniz's political pragmatism regarding ecclesiastical reunification see also Leibniz to Duchess Sophie, 26 September 1688 (A I, 5, N. 128).
24. See A I, 4, N. 2 and N. 4.
25. See A I, 5, N. 8 and N. 62.
26. See Leibniz to Christof Pratisius, 20* December 1687 (A III, 4, 364).
27. See Leibniz to Otto Grote, end of November 1688 (A I, 5, 306).
28. Leibniz to Simon de la Loubère, 4 February 1692 (A I, 7, 554).
29. Christian Knorr von Rosenroth, *Kabbala denudata, seu doctrina Hebraeorum transcendentalis et metaphysica atque theologica*. Sulzbaci: Typis Abrahami Lichtenthaleri, 1677, *Kabbalae Denudatae Tomus Secundus: Id est Liber Sohar Restitutus* [. . .] *cui adjecta Adumbratio Cabbalae Christianae ad captum Judaeorum*. Francofurti: Sumptibus Joannis Davidis Zunneri, 1684.
30. See Leibniz's notes on his discussions with Rosenroth in A. Foucher de Careil, *Leibniz, la philosophie juive et la Cabale*. Paris: Auguste Durand, 1861; and Leibniz to Ernst von Hessen-Rheinfels, 20 January 1688 (A I, 5, 43). See also A I, 5, 109, 235.
31. See A I, 5, 103 and 121.
32. See A I, 5, xxx and N. 15.
33. See A I, 5, 55 and Müller–Krönert, *Leben und Werk*, p. 86. On the reform of coinage see A I, 5, N. 18 and N. 43 (pp. 103–4).
34. For details of this itinerary see Müller–Krönert, *Leben und Werk*, p. 86.
35. A I, 5, 79.
36. See A I, 5, N. 20.
37. See A I, 5, N. 34.
38. Duchess Sophie to Leibniz, 14 April 1688 (A I, 5, N. 38). Cf. also N. 39.
39. See Leibniz to Albrecht Philipp von dem Bussche, 24 April 1688 (A I, 5, 100).
40. See A I, 5, 99–100. Cf. also Leibniz to the Elector Max Emanuel von Bayern, 6* April 1688 (A I, 5, N. 36), and Agostino Steffani to Leibniz, 7* April 1688 (A I, 5, N. 7).
41. See A I, 5, 100.
42. A I, 5, 100. See also Leibniz for Duke Ernst August, 27* April 1688 (A I, 5, 119).
43. See A I, 5, N. 50.
44. See Leibniz to Duchess Sophie, 24* April 1688 (A I, 5, N. 43).
45. See A I, 5, N. 42, N. 43, N. 47, N. 48.

46. See A I, 5, N. 42, N. 49 (especially p. 119). Cf. also A I, 5, N. 43, N. 44, N. 56, N. 57.

47. For details of the itinerary from Munich to Vienna see Müller–Krönert, *Leben und Werk*, p. 89.

48. See A I, 1, N. 1, N. 2, N. 12, N. 13; A IV, 4, 15, 40, 50, 79. See chap. I. 2.

49. Between August and September 1688 Leibniz prepared with great care for his introduction to Leopold I, producing four versions of a text detailing his past achievements (from childhood onward) and future plans (A IV, 4, N. 6–9, pp. 15–90). One of his most detailed autobiographical recollections, this text represents a precious record of his own self-image, though not one, of course, unaffected by its political purpose. I am grateful to Stephan Waldhoff for drawing my attention to this source.

50. See A I, 5, N. 58, N. 59.

51. See A I, 5, N. 155, N. 167.

52. See in particular the correspondence with Christoph Joachim Nicolai von Greiffencrantz (A I, 5, N. 87–89, N. 129–131, N. 213) and Philipp Jakob Spener (A I, 5, N. 161). See also A I, 5, N. 107, N. 173, N. 185.

53. See A I, 5, xxxviii.

54. See A I, 5, N. 76 and Lackmann, "Leibniz' Bibliothekarische Tätigkeit in Hannover," p. 338. A first laconic announcement that the library had been moved, even though appropriate new premises for it had not yet been found, was contained in a short letter of 1 June 1688 written by Otto Grote to Leibniz (A I, 5, N. 66).

55. See A IV, 4, xxii.

56. See in particular Leibniz's letters of 5 December 1691 and January 1692 to his former charge, Philipp Wilhelm von Boineburg (respectively A I, 5, N. 246 and N. 308). Back in Hanover, Leibniz tried to revive Strattmann's offer through the intermediation of Boineburg, who was at the time in Vienna. See also Leibniz to Jo. Friedrich von Linsingen, 30 December 1689 (A I, 5, N. 274).

57. See in particular A I, 5, 574.

58. See chap. II. 4.

59. See A I, 5, N. 150 (esp. p. 274) and A I, 5, N. 331. Cf. also A I, 5, 496. In his letter of 5 December 1691 to Philipp Wilhelm von Boineburg Leibniz wrote generically of the offer to become the emperor's "Conseiller" (A I, 7, 453). The subsequent job-description is, however, consistent with the office of historiographer (see A I, 5, 574).

60. See Leibniz to the emperor, mid-September 1688 (A I, 5, N. 122) and A I, 5, xxxvi.

61. Cf. Lynn, *The Wars of Louis XIV*, pp. 169, 191–3.

62. Cf. Louis XIV's *Mémoire des raisons, qui ont obligé le Roy de France à reprendre les armes*. The *Mémoire* was circulated in a number of editions. See Leibniz's letters of 15 October 1688 to Duchess Sophie (A I, 5, 256) and to the Jesuit Friedrich Ladislaus Wolf von Lüdinghausen (A I, 5, 258).

63. *Responsio Sacr. Caesareae Majestatis ad Manifestum Gallicum*. Cf. A IV, 3, 73.

64. See A I, 5, xxxvii and A IV, 3, 73–4.

65. *Mars christianissimus ou Reflexions sur la declaration de la guerre, que la France fait à l'Empire* (A IV, 3, N. 10).

66. See A I, 5, N. 154.

67. See respectively A I, 5, N. 187 and N. 186. The copy addressed to Stattmann also included the table of contents of the entire work (cf. A I, 5, 327). The *Réflexions sur la déclaration de la guerre* do not seem to have been published in Leibniz's lifetime.

68. A I, 5, N. 149.

69. See A IV, 4, N. 1, N. 6–9.

70. See A I, 5, N. 150, N. 153, N. 18; A IV, 4, N. 10, N. 16.

71. See A III, 4, N. 204 (p. 379), A IV, 4, N. 9 (p. 86), N. 11. See also A I, 5, N. 222.

72. See A IV, 4, N. 2; A I, 5, N. 192, N. 221.

73. See A IV, 4, N. 3, N. 17.

74. See A I, 5, N. 191 (December 1688*).

75. See for instance Christoph de Rojas y Spinola for the emperor, December 1688–January 1689 (A I, 5, N. 190).

76. Cf. Leibniz to Duchess Sophie, 17 June 1688 (A I, 5, 162). See also A I, 5, xxxv and Eisenkopf, *Leibniz und die Einigung der Christenheit*, p. 61.

77. See A I, 5, 161, 189, 212, 307.

78. See A I, 5, 162–3.

79. Sophie's planned departure for Berlin had been announced to Leibniz by Otto Grote on 1 June 1688 (A I, 5, 156). At the end of August Leibniz wrote for the first time to Sophie Charlotte to congratulate her on the birth of her son – the new heir of the Brandenburg electorate, Friedrich Wilhelm – on 15 August (A I, 5, N. 115). See also A I, 5, N. 114.

80. See A I, 5, 162–3.

81. See A I, 5, N. 112.

82. Regarding Leibniz's logical and philosophical work, the following texts (including some important papers of 1688 already mentioned in chapter II. 4) appear to have been written during the Vienna sojourn: A IV, 4, N. 189–200, N. 206–209, N. 312–313, N. 370–371.

83. Cf. Mugnai, *Leibniz' Theory of Relations*, pp. 50–55 and 133–4; Antognazza, "*Debilissimae Entitates?* Bisterfeld and Leibniz's Ontology of Relations," p. 11.

84. *Specimen inventorum de admirandis naturae generalis* (A VI, 4, 1618). Trans. by Mary Morris and G. H. R. Parkinson in G. W. Leibniz, *Philosophical Writings*. London: J M Dent & Sons, 1973, p. 78. Although Parkinson dates this text around 1686, watermarks and internal features indicate a later date of composition, most probably during the Vienna visit (cf. A VI, 4, 1615).

85. A VI, 4, 1618. Trans. by Morris and Parkinson in Leibniz, *Philosophical Writings*, p. 77.

86. See Leibniz's account in his *De Lineis opticis, et alia*. In *Acta Eruditorum* (January 1689): 36–8. Also in GM VII, 329–31. In a letter to Christiaan Huygens of early

October 1690 (A III, 4, 610), Leibniz likewise claimed to have read the *Principia* for the first time while in Rome. Cf. Domenico Bertoloni Meli, *Equivalence and Priority: Newton versus Leibniz*. Oxford: Clarendon Press, 1993, pp. 7–8.

87. These conclusions have been reached by Bertoloni Meli in his impressive *Equivalence and Priority*. Leibniz's notes on the *Principia* and other relevant manuscripts documenting Leibniz's intellectual itinerary towards the *Tentamen* are published in Appendix 1 of Bertoloni Meli's study.

88. See Bertoloni Meli, *Equivalence and Priority*, p. 11.

89. Newton's extensive account of the *Commercium Epistolicum* was published in the *Philosophical Transactions* of January and February 1715 (vol. 29, no. 342, pp. 173–224, here p. 209).

90. See Bertoloni Meli, *Equivalence and Priority*, p. 2 and Garber, "Leibniz: Physics and Philosophy," p. 282.

91. Cf. Bertoloni Meli, *Equivalence and Priority*, pp. 2, 106, 116–17. Despite his opposition to Descartes on other points, Leibniz's conception of matter as initially fluid and moving in vortices was of clearly Cartesian inspiration. This conception was presented as early as the *Hypothesis physica nova* of 1670–71 and was also retained later (see for instance *Nouveaux Essais*, A VI, 59–60). See Mugnai, *Introduzione*, p. 102.

92. See Aiton, *Leibniz*, pp. 154–5 and Mugnai, *Leibniz: Vita*, p. 66. Leibniz summarized his theory in his last known letter to Arnauld (23 March 1690; GP II, 137).

93. Cf. Bertoloni Meli, *Equivalence and Priority*, chap. 5 (esp. pp. 116, 124–5).

94. Cf. Bertoloni Meli, *Equivalence and Priority*, pp. 86–7; André Robinet, "Dynamique et Fondements Métaphysiques." *Studia Leibnitiana Sonderheft* 13 (1984): 1–25 (here p. 18); Leibniz to Edme Mariotte, July 1673 (A III, 1, 107, 109–10: distinction between a "force morte" and a "force violente ou animée"); and *De Arcanis Motus*, in *Leibniz à Paris*, vol. I, p. 202 (distinction between "vis tantum mortua gravium" and "impetus ille vivus"). See also Leibniz to Arnauld, 8 December 1686 (GP II, 80). As Michel Fichant notes in *La réforme de la dynamique*, p. 64, from 1678 onward Leibniz substituted the quantity of force defined by mv^2 in the principle of conservation but did not yet call it *vis viva* ("living force").

95. See A I, 5, N. 170, N. 177.

96. A I, 5, 325.

97. A I, 5, 325.

98. See Francesco de Floramonti to Leibniz, 1 January 1689 (A I, 5, N. 194) and Leibniz to Heinrich Avemann, 16 January 1689 (A I, 5, 359).

99. See Leibniz to Otto Grote, 20 January 1689 (A I, 5, N. 207).

100. See A I, 5, N. 207, N. 211, N. 224 (esp. p. 392).

101. See Leibniz to Otto Grote, 20 January 1689 (A I, 5, 361). Cf. also Leibniz to Duchess Sophie, 23 January 1689 (A I, 5, 366).

102. Leibniz to Otto Grote, 20 January 1689 (A I, 5, 361).

103. See A I, 5, N. 264ª and A I, 5, xxxix.

104. See A I, 5, 465; Müller–Krönert, *Leben und Werk*, pp. 94–5; Robinet, *Iter Italicum*, p. 13. Robinet has meticulously detailed Leibniz's Italian journey, collecting and editing numerous unpublished texts.

105. See Leibniz to Duchess Sophie, beginning of April 1689 (A I, 5, 410).

106. Robinet, *Iter Italicum*, pp. 13–14; cf. also Müller–Krönert, *Leben und Werk*, p. 95.

107. See Leibniz to Duchess Sophie, beginning of April 1689 (A I, 5, 410).

108. See Leibniz for Theodor Althet Heinrich von Strattmann (draft of a *Bibliotheca Universalis Selecta*), May–autumn 1689 (A I, 5, N. 247). Leibniz's work, began in Venice, was continued throughout the summer and autumn (cf. A I, 5, xlii).

109. See A I, 5, 410. Cf. also A I, 5, N. 155 and N. 167.

110. See A I, 5, xxxix.

111. Eckhart, *Lebensbeschreibung*, 123–303 (here p. 159). Amongst others, the tale is endorsed by Müller–Krönert, *Leben und Werk*, p. 95; Aiton, *Leibniz*, p. 158; and Robinet, *Iter Italicum*, p. 17.

112. Robinet, *Iter Italicum*, p. 19.

113. A I, 5, 410–11.

114. Cf. Müller–Krönert, *Leben und Werk*, pp. 95–6; Robinet, *Iter Italicum*, p. 182.

115. See *Excerpta ex Cudworthii Systemate Intellectuali*, spring–summer 1689 (A VI, 4, N. 351) and Leibniz to Lady Damaris Masham, end 1703–beginning 1704 (GP III, 336–7).

116. See A VI, 4, N. 376. Auzout had been asked by Claude Nicaise to enlist the help of other savants for the preparation of the biography. Cf. Leibniz to Gerhard Meier, 26 October 1690 (A I, 6, 272); Leibniz to Adrien Auzout, April–November 1689 (A III, 4, 429); Adrien Baillet, *La Vie de Monsieur Descartes*. 2 vols. Paris: Horthemels, 1691, "Preface," p. xxvi.

117. *De Linea Isochrona, in qua grave sine acceleratione descendit, et de Controversia cum Dn. Abbate D. C [atelan]*. In *Acta Eruditorum* (April 1689): 195–8. On the controversy see chap. II. 4.

118. See Leibniz to Melchisédech Thévenot, 24 April 1689 (A I, 5, 680). Cf. also A I, 5, 421 and 464.

119. See Robinet, *Iter Italicum*, pp. 24–5.

120. See A I, 5, xlii and A I, 5, 601, 648, 665 (cited by Robinet, *Iter Italicum*, p. 26).

121. See Müller–Krönert, *Leben und Werk*, p. 96 and Robinet, *Iter Italicum*, p. 41.

122. See Leibniz to Landgraf Ernst, 23 March 1690 (A I, 5, 556). Cf. also Leibniz to Duchess Sophie, beginning of April 1689 (A I, 5, 411).

123. A I, 5, 556.

124. See Leibniz's poem of June 1689 (A I, 5, N. 246).

125. Leibniz's Nachlaß contains several texts relating to Innocent XI's death (LH XI, 4, Bl. 252, 259, 260–261).

126. See LH XI, 4, Bl. 253–4, 255–6, 257–8, 260–61, 263. Cf. also A I, 5, 472–3. Some of the pieces in LH XI, 4, Bl. 252–63 are in Italian. During the trip Leibniz began to write occasionally in this language.

127. A I, 5, N. 262.

128. See Leibniz to Melchisédech Thévenot, 3 September 1691 (A I, 7, 352–3). Cf. also Leibniz to Francesco Bianchini, 18 March 1690 (in J. G. H. Feder, ed., *Commercii Epistolici Leibnitiani Typis nondum vulgati Selecta specimena*. Hanover, 1805, p. 297; quoted by Robinet, *Iter Italicum*, p. 97). In the letter of 23 March 1690 to Landgraf Ernst, Leibniz took a dimmer view of Alexander VIII as being, unlike his predecessor, *maximus in minimis* and of rather relaxed morals (A I, 5, 556).

129. Cf. Robinet, *Iter Italicum*, pp. 96–118.

130. See A I, 7, 352–3.

131. These texts are listed in Robinet, *Iter Italicum*, p. 102. They include *Praeclarum Ciceronis dictum est* (LH I, III, 8, d, Bl. 7–8) and *Cum Geometricis demonstrationibus* (LH XXXV, IX, 1, Bl. 57–8), published at pp. 107–14 of *Iter Italicum*. Couturat erroneously considered *Cum Geometricis demonstrationibus* as the preface of the *Phoranomus* (cf. Couturat, 590–93 and Robinet, *Iter Italicum*, p. 85n). For the identification of Baldigiani as the intended recipient of at least one of the pro-Copernican pieces see Robinet, *Iter Italicum*, pp. 114–16.

132. Leibniz to Antonio Magliabechi, 30 October 1699 (LBr 595, Bl. 211v). Published in Robinet, *Iter Italicum*, p. 99.

133. See Antonio Alberti to Leibniz, 11 March 1690 (LBr 8, Bl. 2–3). Quoted by Robinet, *Iter Italicum*, p. 100.

134. Leibniz to Veit Ludwig von Seckendorff, 6 January 1692 (A I, 7, 497).

135. See Leibniz to Francesco Bianchini, 22 September 1690 (Feder, *Commercii Epistolici Leibnitiani Typis nondum vulgati Selecta specimena*, p. 45) and Robinet, *Iter Italicum*, esp. pp. 42–5.

136. See Robinet, *Iter Italicum*, pp. 121–36; Franklin Perkins, *Leibniz and China. A Commerce of Light*. Cambridge: Cambridge University Press, 2004, esp. pp. 125–7, 131; and A I, 5, xliii–xliv.

137. On the invention of the word *Dynamica* by Leibniz see Michel Fichant, "De la puissance à l'action: La singularité stylistique de la dynamique." In Michel Fichant, *Science et métaphysique dans Descartes et Leibniz*. Paris: Presses Universitaires de France, 1998, pp. 205–43, Fichant notes that the first occurences of the word *dynamica* (or *tractatum dynamicum*) are to be found in the correspondence with Baron Rudolf Christian von Bodenhausen (p. 206). See also François Duchesneau, "Leibniz's Theoretical Shift in the *Phoranomus* and *Dynamica de Potentia*." *Perspectives on Science* 6, 1–2 (1998): 77–109 (here p. 77) and André Robinet's presentation of the *Phoranomus*, in *Physis* 28, 2 (1991), 432. For a monographic study of Leibniz's dynamics see François Duchesneau, *La dynamique de Leibniz*. Paris: Vrin, 1994. On Leibniz and Bodenhausen see below.

138. See Duchesneau, "Leibniz's Theoretical Shift," pp. 78–9 and Fichant, *La réforme de la dynamique*, p. 9.

139. The first complete edition of the *Phoranomus* was published by André Robinet in *Physis* (Florence) 28, 2 (1991): 429–541 and 28, 3 (1991): 797–885. Extracts were

previously published by C. I. Gerhardt in *Archiv für Geschichte der Philosophie* 1 (1888): 575–81.

140. *Phoranomus.* In *Physis* 28, 3 (1991), 826: "nova de potentia et effectu scientia."

141. Cf. Robinet's presentation of the *Phoranomus*, in *Physis* 28, 2 (1991), esp. pp. 429–32 and 28, 3 (1991), esp. pp. 884–5, and Duchesneau, "Leibniz's Theoretical Shift," esp. pp. 83–5. Duchesneau challenges Robinet's account of a drastic shift of theoretical approach between *Phoranomus* and *Dynamica*, seeing instead a "relatively continuous methodological transition" between the two works (p. 107).

142. On Leibniz's plans for publication see Robinet, *Architectonique disjonctive*, pp. 261 ff. The *Dynamica* can be found in GM VI, 281–514.

143. See the passage from the *Phoranomus* quoted by Robinet in *Iter Italicum*, p. 95 and the *Dynamica*, II, I, prop. 28–33 (GM VI, 451–5).

144. *Specimen praeliminare* of the *Dynamica* (GM VI, 287); quoted by Duchesneau, "Leibniz's Theoretical Shift," p. 84.

145. This interpretation is proposed by Duchesneau, "Leibniz's Theoretical Shift," pp. 78, 84. On the concept of formal action see esp. pp. 101–6, from which this discussion is drawn. On the shift between the concepts of "effect" and of "action" see also Robinet's presentation of the *Phoranomus*, in *Physis* 28, 2 (1991), 432. Aiton, *Leibniz*, pp. 162–3 summarizes the contents of the *Dynamica*.

146. GP VI, 345–6. Trans. by Duchesneau in "Leibniz's Theoretical Shift," p. 102.

147. GP VI, 355. Trans. by Duchesneau in "Leibniz's Theoretical Shift," p. 103.

148. See respectively A VI, 4, N. 372 and GM VI, 161–87.

149. See Bertoloni Meli, *Equivalence and Priority*, p. 156 and Mugnai, *Leibniz: Vita*, p. 66.

150. GP VI, 29.

151. *De libertate, contingentia et serie causarum, providentia*, summer 1689* (A VI, 4, 1654).

152. See *Principia Logico–Metaphysica* (A VI, 4, N. 324). The text was first published in Couturat, pp. 518–23 and is also known under the title of *Primae Veritates*. Trans. by Morris–Parkinson in Leibniz, *Philosophical Writings*, pp. 87–92 (here p. 92).

153. I have found no primary sources supporting the received view that this offer was made in the autumn of 1689 by Cardinal Casanata (cf. A I, 16, 306 (footnote); Müller–Krönert, *Leben und Werk*, p. 97; Aiton, *Leibniz*, p. 159). All evidence available seems rather to indicate that the offer came in early 1695, around the time at which the encumbent, Noris, was about to leave this position to became a cardinal (cf. Robinet, *Iter Italicum*, pp. 179–81).

154. LBr 8, Bl. 14–15. Partially published in Bodemann, *Briefwechsel*, p. 4. Quoted by Robinet, *Iter Italicum*, p. 180. This letter of Alberti was addressed to Rudolf Christian von Bodenhausen. In turn, Bodenhausen forwarded it to Leibniz as an eclosure to his letter of 26 May 1695 (A III, 6, N. 119, cf. pp. 369, 373; see also Robinet, *Iter Italicum*, p. 180). The date of Alberti's letter given by

Bodemann, *Briefwechsel*, p. 4 and endorsed by A I, 16, 306 (i. e., 4 February 1694) is erroneous.

155. See Leibniz to Spanheim, end of July 1695 (A I, 9, 598); Leibniz to Bodenhausen (FC, *Oeuvres*, II, p. 79; quoted by Robinet, *Iter Italicum*, p. 180); Leibniz to Le Thorel, 5 December 1698 (A I, 16, 306).

156. A I, 5, 556.

157. See A I, 5, N. 234 and N. 235.

158. See Robinet, *Iter Italicum*, p. 195. For a detailed presentation of Leibniz's month in Florence see ibid., pp. 193–294.

159. See A I, 5, xlv.

160. At the death of Bodenhausen on 9 April 1698, Leibniz requested that his papers be sent back to him, and his Nachlaß includes the fair copy of the *Dynamica* prepared by Bodenhausen (LH XXXV, 9, 16). See Bodemann, *Handschriften*, p. 304. Leibniz's correspondence with Bodenhausen, which started in Florence in 1689 and ended in 1698 with the death of the Baron, is published in A III.

161. A III, 4, 436. Cf. Fichant, "De la puissance à l'action," p. 206.

162. See A I, 5, 649 (LBr 771) and A I, 5, 665–6. On the basis of LBr 771, Robinet, *Iter Italicum*, p. 223, has corrected the spelling 'Marchetti,' used by the Akademie-Ausgabe and Müller–Krönert, *Leben und Werk*, p. 99, into "Macchetti," already proposed by Bodemann, *Briefwechsel*, p. 239.

163. See A I, 7, 353–4 and Müller–Krönert, *Leben und Werk*, p. 99.

164. See Leibniz to Francesco II of Modena, 1 January 1690 (A I, 5, N. 276). Cf. also A I, 5, N. 271 and N. 301[a].

165. See Leibniz for Duke Ernst August, autumn 1690 (A I, 5, 666) and November–December 1691 (A I, 7, 59). Cf. also Leibniz to Duchess Eleonore of Celle, 13 January 1699 (A I, 16, 70).

166. See Leibniz to Duchess Sophie, 30 December 1689 (A I, 5, N. 271).

167. See Duchess Sophie to Leibniz, 30 January 1690 (A I, 5, N. 287).

168. See Robinet, *Iter Italicum*, pp. 340–45.

169. See Robinet, *Iter Italicum*, pp. 363–78.

170. See A I, 5, 525–6, 533, 534, 636–7, 666–7; A I, 6, 266; A I, 7, 473; *Scriptores rerum Brunsvicensium*, in Leibniz, *Schriften und Briefe zur Geschichte*, pp. 252–3; *Brevis synopsis historiae Guelficae*, in Leibniz, *Schriften und Briefe zur Geschichte*, pp. 810–11. Cf. Robinet, *Iter Italicum*, pp. 378–88 and Alois Schmid, "Die Herkunft der Welfen in der bayerischen Landeshistoriographie des 17. Jahrhunderts und bei Gottfried Wilhelm Leibniz." In *Leibniz und Niedersachsen*. Ed. by Herbert Breger and Friedrich Niewöhner. Stuttgart: Steiner, 1999, pp. 126–47.

171. A I, 5, N. 295.

172. See *Communicata ex disputationibus cum Fardella* (A VI, 4, N. 329; esp. pp. 1670–71). For a critical discussion of this text see Adams, *Leibniz*, pp. 274–7 and Daniel Garber, "Leibniz and Fardella. Body, Substance, and Idealism." In *Leibniz and his correspondents*. Ed. by Paul Lodge. Cambridge: Cambridge University Press, pp. 123–40.

173. See A I, 5, 551–2. In particular on Carceri see A I, 5, 556–7. Cf. Robinet, *Iter Italicum*, pp. 429–49 and Müller–Krönert, *Leben und Werk*, p. 102.

174. Leibniz to Antoine Arnauld, 23 March 1690 (GP II, 134–8).

175. See A I, 5, N. 321.

176. See A I, 5, N. 328 and A I, 5, xlviii.

177. See A I, 5, xlviii and Leibniz to Duchess Sophie, 11 May 1690 (A I, 5, N. 332).

178. *De Causa Gravitatis, et Defensio Sententiae Autoris de Veris Naturae Legibus contra Cartesianos* (GM VI, 193–203).

179. See J. E. Hofmann, "Vom öffentlichen Bekanntwerden der Leibnizschen Infinitesimalmathematik." *Sitzungsberichte d. Österr. Akad. d. Wiss. Mathem.-naturw. Kl.*, section II, 175, 8–9 (1966), 226. Quoted by Müller–Krönert, *Leben und Werk*, p. 103.

180. Leibniz for the emperor, beginning of May 1690 (A I, 5, N. 223). See also Leibniz to Joh. Friedrich von Linsingen, 30 December 1689 (A I, 5, N. 274).

181. See Leibniz to Duke Ernst August, mid-May 1690 (A I, 5, N. 335).

182. See Leibniz to Duchess Sophie, 11 May 1690 (A I, 5, N. 332).

183. See Müller–Krönert, *Leben und Werk*, p. 103. Leibniz's half-brother, Johann Friedrich, died on 19 March 1696.

6

Back under the Guelf Dukes: Hanover and Wolfenbüttel (June 1690–February 1698)

BACK IN HANOVER, it was not long before Leibniz felt a claustrophobic uneasiness closing in on him in the absence of the sustained intellectual conversation he had so much enjoyed during his trip south. The burden of many different occupations relating to his offices as historiographer and court counsellor weighed heavily on his shoulders. In October 1690 he confided to Huygens,

If I had the age and leisure which I had in Paris, I would hope it would serve to make the progress in physics which your first gift helped me make in geometry. But that mental vigour is quite diminished and in addition I am distracted by completely different studies which seem to require my complete attention. From time to time I manage to escape from this prison where I find myself, and the trip as far as Italy which I have just undertaken has cheered me up a bit; but now I must return more than ever to my ordinary duties, and in particular to a far-reaching historical work, laden with facts, which requires great precision.[1]

Writing on 29 November 1691 to one of his new correspondents on religious and philosophical issues, Paul Pellisson-Fontanier, he lamented, "Here, if I think about these things, it is as on the sly. One can hardly speak to anyone."[2] Intellectually, Leibniz was in fact a very gregarious spirit who thrived in his treasured exchanges with other minds. He always seemed to have time for a chat and apparently had the common touch as well – the gift of conversing with uneducated people. Although he never showed a romantic attachment to women,[3] he found in women very congenial conversation partners – not only in learned ones such as Sophie and her daughter, Sophie Charlotte, but also in the most simple women.[4] At any rate, many of his texts explicitly originated from his continuous listening, discussing, and reacting to theories, comments, and objections of others. As he wrote to Bossuet in 1694, "so one gradually advances, responding to the demands of the moment."[5] In Hanoverian isolation he supplemented the meagre direct conversation available with other savants with a gigantic epistolary correspondence which grew to proportions almost unmanageable for Leibniz himself.[6] Writing on 21 May 1697 to Andreas Morell, a famous antiquarian and numismatist, he confided, "The multitude of my papers and the division of my concerns amongst too many things sometimes result in unanswered letters going astray."[7] Two years earlier, in September 1695 he had complained in a letter to Vincentius Placcius,

I cannot say how extraordinarily distracted I am. I dig out various things from archives, inspect ancient documents, collect unpublished manuscripts. From these I try to shed light on Brunswick history. I receive and send a huge number of letters. Yet at the same time I have so much that is new in mathematics, so many philosophical plans, so many other literary investigations which I do not want to abandon, that I often don't know what to do next[.][8]

To be fair, no small amount of this hyperactivity was of his own doing. In 1691 Leibniz assumed additional duties (duly remunerated) at the court of Wolfenbüttel as director of the impressive library founded by Duke August (1579–1666), the father of the two co-rulers of the duchy, Rudolf August and Anton Ulrich. Wolfenbüttel became his second regular place of residence, where he had permanent quarters, thanks to the financial support of the local *Ritterakademie*.[9] Between 1692 and 1696, undeterred by his previous lack of success, he resumed his mining activities in the Harz.[10] A host of new technical schemes and commercial ventures were once again conceived in collaboration with his friend Crafft. The recurrent plan of creating societies and academies of sciences was energetically represented to new prospective patrons and patronesses such as the electress of Brandenburg, Sophie Charlotte, and the tsar of Russia, Peter the Great. He continued his philosophical, scientific, mathematical, and technical work, expanding his interests to the sustained study of other languages and cultures, notably those of China, and reaching important new insights and results.

In particular, the year 1695 marked an important moment for his public intellectual profile as well as in the establishment of his distinctive philosophical vocabulary. In April he published in the *Acta Eruditorum* the first part of a *Specimen Dynamicum* detailing for the broader scientific community the key ideas of his *Dynamica*.[11] In the summer there appeared in the prestigious *Journal des Sçavans* the first presentation in print of his mature philosophical system: the *Système nouveau de la nature et de la communication des substances, aussi bien que l'union qu'il y a entre l' âme et le corps*.[12] Moreover, both the expression "pre-established harmony" and the term "monad" used to indicate "real unities" or "simple substances" made their first appearance during this year.[13]

Yet, around this time, he seems also to have undergone a mid-life crisis characterized by hypochondriac and psychosomatic symptoms which lasted for a couple of years at least. Between 1693 and the spring of 1696 he became preoccupied with self-diagnoses of his state of health, fearing that some mortal illness could be lurking to rob him of the time he needed to complete his half-finished schemes.[14] Overwhelmed perhaps by his flurry of activities and by a recurrent dissatisfaction with his position in Hanover, approaching the age of fifty Leibniz was definitely aware that time was passing and that he had still too many unfinished projects on his hands. In March 1696, reacting to the rumour of his death reported by his correspondent from England, the Scot Thomas Burnett of Kemney, he remarked in one of his not infrequent displays of wit:

If death wants to give me all the time I need to finish the projects which I have already conceived, I will promise it in exchange not to start any new ones and to work with great diligence on those which I already have, though even with this deal I shall be seriously late. But death cares nothing for our plans or the advancement of the sciences.[15]

The general plan disregarded by such an unwelcome visitor was, as ever, the reform and advancement of the entire encyclopaedia of sciences for the improvement of the human condition. The theoretical reflections on logic, mathematics, metaphysics, physics, ethics, and theology were always, ultimately, at the service of this broader plan and *ad usum vitae*. The aim of the happiness of humankind grounded in wisdom was pursued through such diverse means as, for instance, the search for a better understanding of the concept of substance, the political negotiation of church reunification, and the development of a proper medical system. Although after 1688 Leibniz virtually ceased to refer to his great plan in terms of a *scientia generalis* embracing the principles or foundations of all the sciences or as "the investigation of the elements of the whole encyclopaedia, and of the highest good,"[16] the plan itself was far from abandoned. One of the main obstacles to even its partial realization was the lack of a prince able and willing to provide him with the firm institutional support that such a plan required. Leibniz never abandoned the hope of finding such a patron. Indeed, in the mid-1690s, in a *Mémoire pour des Personnes éclairées et de bonne intention* (*Memoir for Enlightened Persons of Good Intention*), he gave one of the most rounded summaries of the vision guiding his entire intellectual life. The survey of the various sciences and disciplines to be cultivated with the general aim of contributing "to the glory of God, or (what is the same thing) to the common good," read like a catalogue of his own endeavours and of his search for enlightened patronage especially (but certainly not only) in this period.[17]

At the Service of the Guelf Dukes

Nearly two years and eight months of absence were not easy to explain. During the first months back in Hanover, Leibniz was at pains to justify in the eyes of his employers his wanderings down south, not to speak of the need to recover the substantial travel expenses which he had met by supplementing with his own funds the money received from the Hanover court before and during his trip. A number of detailed reports were written highlighting not only his remarkable historiographical discoveries but also the many contacts, visits, and activities which had been his creative way to serve the interests of the Hanover duke over and above his immediate remit.[18] As for the expenses, Leibniz calculated that in two and a half years he had spent some 2300 talers, an average of 2.5 talers per day. Since his current salary was still 600 talers per year, he was understandably anxious to have this disbursement acknowledged as genuine travel expenses to be reimbursed rather than deducted from his wages.[19] In any case, it did not escape Leibniz's acute mind that the best way to present a convincing plea was simply to get on with writing the Guelf history. Between the autumn of 1690 and 1692 he sketched several outlines, notably a *Brevis synopsis historiae Guelficae*.[20] In mid-January 1691 he was granted an audience with Ernst August in order to report on his progress on the already long-awaited work. Unfortunately, Leibniz explained to the duke, he was still unable to present His Most Serene Highness with the history of his family, but estimated that he could finish it in a couple of years if appropriate help could be provided. Leibniz's rigorous historical methodology was in fact firmly based on direct consultation of the sources – a very time-consuming endeavour for the efficient fulfilment of which the help of able research assistants was needed.[21] Although there is no doubt that the

Hanoverian court counsellor had put in long hours poring over scarcely legible documents, he conveniently omitted to mention that, on the side, he had also engaged in a thousand other time-consuming endeavours which were at best loosely related to his core historiographical task. For his part, the duke did not hesitate to make further onerous calls on Leibniz's time when his expertise was needed in other court matters, such as the issue of the Sachsen-Lauenburg inheritance or the claim to electoral status.[22]

Amongst the distractions most germane to Leibniz's main historiographical task were his additional duties at the Guelf court of Wolfenbüttel. In October 1690 he had asked permission from Ernst August to accept the offer of Dukes Rudolf August and Anton Ulrich to become the director of the Wolfenbüttel library. By way of justification, he explained that he needed to travel there to consult its rich holdings in any case, and the position of director would make this work easier.[23] Whether Ernst August did not wish to cross his Wolfenbüttel relatives (with whom relations were already somewhat strained) or took at face value Leibniz's assurance that the new office would accelerate rather than delay the Guelf history, permission was granted and on 14 January 1691 Leibniz was named director of the outstanding library.[24] His task there was one of general supervision rather than of day-to-day care, which was entrusted instead to a library secretary.[25] Amongst other things, during the second half of 1691 Leibniz supervised the creation of a new general alphabetic catalogue of authors complemented by a general index of subjects (*index materiarum*). The catalogue was completed by 1699 and is still occasionally used at the Wolfenbüttel library.[26] How much this work might have contributed to the Guelf history is impossible to say; but regular extended visits to Wolfenbüttel certainly gave Leibniz ready access to encyclopaedic collections far richer than anything available in Hanover, as well as support from patrons in many ways far more sympathetic than his chief employer. Not to be entirely outdone, Ernst August eventually honoured Leibniz's pressing requests for assistance at least in part by granting him the additional annual sum of 150 talers from the beginning of 1691 with which to employ a copyist.[27]

An even more tenuous link with Leibniz's immediate historiographical remit was his investigations into prehistory, geology, and even cosmology. Any really thoroughgoing history, he managed to persuade the duke, needed to begin at the beginning; and the beginning, to someone of Leibniz's scientific as well as historical perspective, was marked not by the foundation of the Braunschweig dynasty, nor even by that of the Holy Roman Empire, but by the foundations of the world itself. Leibniz therefore proposed a plan to preface the Guelf history with two preliminary treatises. One of these, eventually entitled *Protogaea*, was to trace on essentially geological grounds the origin of the earth in general and of the region of Lower Saxony in particular. The second was to bridge this geological prehistory with the medieval past by means of an account of the prehistoric and ancient inhabitants of Lower Saxony and their roots in the great migrations of peoples traceable above all through the comparative study of languages – or, as he put it in April 1691 to Huldreich von Eyben, through a genetic study of "the harmony of languages."[28] What we appear to have here is further evidence of the incapacity of an encyclopaedic mind to resist connecting everything with everything else and the consequent tendency of all of his projects ultimately to snowball into unmanageable proportions. Yet although this holistic approach was undeniably part of his basic intellectual perspective, Leibniz's strategy in this case can also be construed in another, more respectable way.

One root of this idea to prefix a prehistory of Lower Saxony to his history of the Guelfs derived in all probability from reading the Helmstedt professor Hermann Conring's *De antiquissimo statu Helmestadii et vicinae conjecturae* (1665). On the basis of some paleontological samples, Conring had advanced the hypothesis that in prehistoric times Lower Saxony was inhabited by giants.[29] A second related stimulus for adding a geological as well as paleontological stratum to the work was provided by Leibniz's own collection of minerals and fossils, which gradually accumulated from 1682 onward during his long period in the mining communities in the Harz. A third and deeper philosophical motivation, expressed as early as a letter of July 1684 to Bernard Le Bovier de Fontenelle, was Leibniz's declared intention to improve upon the theories of Georgius Agricola, Descartes, and Niels Stensen.[30] At the time, investigations aimed at explaining the origin of the earth were far from uncontroversial, due to the difficult task of reconciling the biblical narrative with the scientific evidence which was progressively being accumulated. Much as the Copernican astronomical revolution had destabilized the accepted worldview regarding the relation between 'earth' and 'heaven', writing a natural history of the earth on new scientific premises required a reevaluation of the relationship between God and his creation. This was clearly a major aspect of any full programme of reform and development of the sciences and Leibniz, typically, met the challenge head on by developing his own theory.

Predictably, the key figure here was again Descartes, whose discussion of the origins of the universe in his *Principia Philosophiae* of 1644 had become the starting point for a flourishing period of geological and geogonical studies.[31] In it, the French philosopher had advanced a bold account of the origin and prehistory of the earth congruent with his mechanistic physics and then retreated behind a description of his theory as a mere hypothesis, put forward for purely explicative purposes and not intended to compete with the biblical account of creation.[32] Even for those who shared Descartes's mechanistic principles, such a formulation was unsatisfactory; and the result was to pose a twofold challenge which set the stage for a fresh wave of geological research and speculation. On the one hand, early modern natural philosophers were prompted to provide a more adequate and empirically grounded account of the origin and history of the earth coherent with the new mechanistic physics. One of the first to respond to this challenge had been Leibniz's fellow resident of Hanover, the Dane Niels Stensen, during his earlier period as an outstanding physician, anatomist, and geologist.[33] Especially in his influential and authoritative *De solido intra solidum naturaliter contento* (*On the solid naturally contained in a solid*) (Florence 1669) he had reached important geological conclusions which, together with his other works, formed the bedrock of Leibniz's own theories in the *Protogaea*.[34] On the other hand, theologically informed philosophers also felt compelled to square a fresh mechanistic explanation with a new reading of the biblical account of creation. The result was 'physico-theology', the speculative cosmology of the late seventeenth and early eighteen centuries, the analogue of late twentieth- and early twenty-first-century inquiries into the 'big bang', only bolder and more perilous insofar as it sought not merely to extend the scientific paradigms of the day but to reconcile the very different evidence of the books of nature and scripture. A landmark work in this tradition appeared in London in 1681: the *Telluris theoria sacra* by Thomas Burnet (1635*–1715), an English divine educated in Cambridge who was briefly clerk of the closet to King William III. Burnet's book attracted much attention and an English translation in two volumes was published in London in 1684–90. According to Burnet's *Sacred Theory of the Earth*, the world as we know it was not the terrestrial paradise created by God in the first chapter of Genesis but a mighty ruin left after the great flood narrated in the sixth through eighth chapters of that book.[35] Further works in the same vein flooded from the English scientific press in the following years, including the *Miscellaneous Discourses, Concerning the Dissolution and Changes of the World* produced by the leading Fellow of the Royal Society, John Ray, in 1692; John Woodward's *Essay towards a Natural History of the Earth* in 1695; and the *New Theory of the Earth* by Newton's protégé, William Whiston, in 1696. Far from being a Leibnizian eccentricity, physico-theology was an irresistible challenge to those who sought to harmonize faith and reason, scripture and natural philosophy; and Leibniz's *Protogaea* was intended to make an important early contribution to a lively debate carried out in subsequent years by some of the finest theoretical minds in Europe.

According to Leibniz's account, the origin of the earth was similar to that of all the other planets. The earth had begun as an incandescent, fluid mass the surface of which had gradually cooled and solidified, forming the terrestrial crust on which we live around a global core which remains incandescent, as volcanic eruptions periodically demonstrate. In the course of the solidification of the earth's crust, the fire "pushed" humidity into the air, which condensed and returned to the earth as water, gradually inundating the surface and filling the larger cavities to form lakes, seas, and oceans. Although Leibniz criticized Burnet for adopting a speculative approach insufficiently based on empirical evidence, he accepted to some extent the idea that "we live on ruins" created by the collapse of the earth's crust at the points at which vast cavities had formed beneath the surface. But his theory was notably more gradualist than Burnet's cataclysmic account: the current state of the earth, Leibniz maintained, was not the result of a single universal deluge but of a series of local inundations. Yet he too found the outlines of his account reflected in a few, plastic words from the book of Genesis: "the separation of light from darkness indicates the fusion caused by fire; and the separation of wet from dry signifies the effects of inundations."[36]

Returning the *Protogaea* to its historical context thus necessitates a reassessment of its relationship to the Guelf history. Rather than simply as an absurd, theoretical expansion of a provincial work on medieval history to cosmological dimensions, it can also be viewed as a successful, pragmatic attempt to transform at least part of a historical assignment into a scientific-philosophical one. Leibniz had not so much extended the historical project *ad infinitum* as turned it into the pretext for pursuing a

major missing piece of his own intellectual synthesis, which would complement his cosmological investigations stimulated around the same time by
Newton's *Principia*. The advantage of this strategy was obvious: Leibniz
incorporated into his official historical commission a number of virtually
independent, essentially philosophical elements of his grand intellectual
synthesis, thereby skilfully turning the duke's willing patronage of a limited, essentially dynastic project into the (doubtless less enthusiastic)
funding of a far broader programme of research on theoretical cosmology
and historical linguistics. The corresponding disadvantage was perhaps
less evident to an optimist prone to underestimate the difficulty of completing ambitious intellectual enterprises of this kind: with these additions
the history mushroomed into a massive enterprise, preventing Leibniz
from undertaking further official projects and eventually leaving a huge
mass of unpublished material in its wake. Already by 1693 – the year
which he had recently set for the completion of the entire history – he
had privately begun to describe it as an unending labour, a Sisyphean
stone.[37] By the end of 1694 he had managed to complete only the *Protogaea*; and since this was now conceived as the first of two main preambles
to a work which was never finished, the *Protogaea* remained unpublished
in Leibniz's lifetime, a casualty of his strategy of annexing essentially
philosophical projects to the Guelf history.[38] All that his contemporaries
could know about its contents was found in the brief summary which
advertised the forthcoming work in the *Acta Eruditorum* of January 1693,
supplemented later by a couple of paragraphs in the *Theodicy* of 1710.
Rather than establishing a new paradigm, the work became a paradigm
case of an innovative contribution to a topic at the forefront of intellectual
debate in the years in which it was written which rapidly became dated
thereafter until the whole project was abandoned altogether.

A very similar pattern was manifest in the history of the migrations of
peoples and the harmony of languages and in the more immediately historical work into which Leibniz threw himself in the 1690s. Once again,
he could not help but take the most holistic approach conceivable. As
lucidly conceptualised in one of his outlines of the Guelf history, Leibniz
consciously avoided the parochial minutiae of dynastic history and sought
instead to insert the local history of Braunschweig-Lüneburg into the context most significant for a broader public.[39] The principal affairs of the
Guelf family, he was certain, were comprehensible and significant chiefly
within the history of the Holy Roman Empire at large; and the history of

the Empire was inextricably interwoven in turn with broader European events and developments. Leibniz therefore chose to start his history in 768, with Charlemagne and the events leading up to the foundation of the Empire, and to proceed from there year by year in the form of *Annales Imperii Occidentis Brunsvicenses* (*Brunswick Annals of the Western Empire*) until 1235. As his material multiplied, this terminal date was reduced to 1024 – the year of death of the last emperor of the Saxon dynasty and the first of Braunschweig descent, Heinrich II – which would also have left space for the beginning of the new Braunschweig line coming from Azzo II (996–1097), since the common ancestor of the Este and Guelf families was born before the death of Heinrich II.[40] His dynastic history thus took on enormous chronological and geographical scope; and at the same time the project began to expand in another dimension as well. In 1693 Leibniz obtained the duke's approval for his plan to publish facsimiles of key coins and documents,[41] and this opened up a further research stream which produced by far the most voluminous historical works which Leibniz actually saw through to publication. Already in 1693 a thick volume of some five hundred pages appeared under the title of *Codex Juris Gentium Diplomaticus*, publishing – mostly for the first time – a collection of medieval legal documents of remarkable importance for the internal and external relations of European states. Although the planned second part extending the *Codex* to the fifteenth and sixteenth centuries never appeared, he published in 1700 a *Mantissa Codicis Juris Gentium Diplomatici*, which collected another five hundred pages of medieval documents especially significant for the understanding of the relationship between worldly and spiritual authority in the Middle Age.[42] The discovery of an interesting manuscript in Wolfenbüttel on the life of Pope Alexander VI also resulted in its publication in 1696 and 1697.[43] Meanwhile, only a few adumbrations of his more limited historical findings reached the press, notably a thirteen-page *Lettre sur la connexion des maisons de Brunsvic et d'Este*, published in 1695 to celebrate the marriage of Duke Rinaldo III of Modena to the oldest daughter of the late Duke Johann Friedrich, Charlotte Felicitas; and the nine-page *Dissertatio de Origine Germanorum* in 1697.[44]

Once again, Leibniz encouraged his employer to conceive of these volumes as the unshakeable foundations upon which the crowning glory of the Guelf history would eventually sit. Once again we see here also his tendencies towards universalisation and perfectionism: on the one hand the tendency to connect everything with everything else and therefore to set limited problems within an almost limitless context; on the other, the determination to pursue even the most ambitious project with the most uncompromising methodological rigour. Yet once again Leibniz's agenda was more subtle and clear-headed than any of these partial perspectives suggested. Combing through the principal archives of northern and southern Germany, Austria, and Italy, he had repeatedly encountered neglected documents far more relevant to his central practical and intellectual concerns than any narrow dynastic history could ever be; and it was this relevance, rather than their merely antiquarian value, which led him to publish these collections. The documentation of medieval international relations collected in the *Codex Juris Gentium Diplomaticus* addressed the most acute international issue of Leibniz's day: the defence of the rights of the Empire against constant incursions by the French. The "Preface" to the *Codex* drew out the implications of this material for his theory of justice as the charity of the wise, which related to international as well as national, local, and domestic affairs. The *Mantissa* of 1700 was likewise richly furnished with illustrations of the relationship between worldly and spiritual authority in the Middle Age – another aspect of the history of Europe and the Empire which Leibniz was eager to reform and restore.[45] A more broadminded prince might have been delighted to see the definitive history of his own dynasty put at the centre of a wider body of work of such wide-ranging significance and immediate contemporary relevance.

Above and beyond his historical work Leibniz was engaged in many other time-consuming activities related to his office as court counsellor. The years 1690–98 marked for the Hanoverian court a period of mixed fortune. To begin with, 1690 brought deep sorrow to Sophie with the death of two of her children, Karl Philipp and Friedrich August, during their imperial service in the war against the Turks. On 14 May 1691 she wrote bitterly to Leibniz,

if it had pleased God to take the trouble to create all the honourable people all at once and to spare mankind the trouble of generation, it seems to me that his work would have been more perfect and one would have less trouble believing that we are made in his image[;] but it appears that everything is in flux and that there is nothing but him who always subsists and that we endure much less than inanimate things[.][46]

More pain was to follow. In December 1691 her third son, Maximilian Wilhelm (1666–1726), now second in line to inherit the duchy, conspired against the controversial rule of primogeniture, introduced by his father nine years earlier. His father had decreed that the undivided duchy of Hanover, and eventually that of Celle, would pass to Georg Ludwig.[47] Maximilian Wilhelm sought instead to acquire Hanover for himself, leaving the senior duchy of Celle to his older brother; and this plan was supported by the dukes of Wolfenbüttel, who regarded the consolidation of Celle and Hanover into a single duchy as a threat to their status as senior branch of the Guelf family. The conspiracy, of which Sophie was aware, was discovered. Maximilian Wilhelm was arrested and imprisoned, and regained his freedom several years later, only after having renounced all his claims. He removed to Vienna, sustained by a generous allowance from Hanover but living in exile.[48]

Moreover, Rudolf August and Anton Ulrich did not welcome the fact that the claim to electoral status of the Guelf princes in Lower Saxony was advancing through the cadet line of Hanover rather than through the oldest branch of the family, their own line of Braunschweig-Wolfenbüttel. Leibniz therefore found his allegiances uncomfortably divided between his main employer, Ernst August, and his new patrons, the Wolfenbüttel dukes. Ever the conciliator, he seized the opportunity to mediate between the two branches of the family in the hope of avoiding an escalation of the conflict. During 1692 he carried out a number of talks with Duke Anton Ulrich on the two thorny issues of Prince Maximilian's conspiracy and of the electorate, reporting their contents to Ernst August.[49] As for his own opinion, on both issues his principles lead him to side firmly with Ernst August. The fragmentation of German territories into countless tiny and impotent principalities was largely responsible for throwing the Empire into a state of disorder and weakness. A reestablishment of primogeniture, as practised throughout the Empire until Emperor Friedrich II (1215–50), was a crucial plank in his programme of political reform.[50] As for the electorate, it was a crucial measure to help regain a more equitable balance between the three existing Protestant electors (the Palatinate, Saxony, and Brandenburg) and the five Catholic ones (the elector-archbishops of Mainz, Cologne, and Trier, the king of Bohemia, and the duke of Bavaria).[51] Leibniz therefore worked with alacrity to provide Ernst August with juridical, political, and historical paraphernalia in support of his case.[52] On 23 March 1692 the efforts of the Hanoverian court were crowned by success with the promulgation of a decree by Emperor Leopold granting the status of a ninth electorate to the territories of Calenberg (Hanover) and Celle.[53] The official investiture of the duke of Hanover as the ninth elector followed on 19 December 1692 in Vienna, where Otto Grote received (on behalf of Ernst August) the electoral insignia. On this occasion, Grote read a speech the historical part of which had been drafted by Leibniz – another clear indication of the direct political stakes of Leibniz's historical researches. The further task given to him by Grote of designing a medal commemorating the elevation to electorate was transformed into the opportunity for yet another minor reform – this time of the duchy's coat of arms with the symbolic representation of the traditional leopard of Braunschweig and lion of Lüneburg. During the next years Leibniz's historical and political learning was called upon to counter the opposition of Saxony and Württemberg against the *Reichserzamt* foreseen for Hanover. Like all other electorates, Hanover was now entrusted with an imperial office – the *Erzbanneramt*, or the task of guarding the banner of the Empire – and despite the essentially symbolic nature of this office, the controversy surrounding it raged until 1710.[54]

During the year of Hanover's great political success, around April Leibniz received via Jacob Auguste Barnabas Comte Des Viviers an invitation to join the service of Louis XIV at the splendid court of the Sun King.[55] The attraction of returning to the brilliant scientific and learned community of Paris was strong, as appears from Leibniz's answering words of May 1692 to Des Viviers:

What inclines me most are two great reasons. The first is the advantage I would have . . . of communicating with many able people, something that would give me the greatest pleasure, and of which I am currently quite deprived. The second is that I could perhaps contribute by this means to the public good, and put myself in a position to execute the vows in philosophical matters which seem to me most important, whereas otherwise many other occupations distract me.[56]

Notwithstanding this attraction, Leibniz turned down the offer with what must have been genuine regret. Behind the allusion to the first reason for his decision was in all probability the expectation of a conversion to Catholicism. The second reason lay in Leibniz's allegiance to the German nation against the bellicose politics of Louis XIV, which had brought so much loss and destruction to the Empire and to the Protestant cause. The third reason was his commitment to writing the history of the Guelfs, although at this point Leibniz regarded it as merely a "a temporal hindrance . . . of short duration". Finally, a fourth consideration was his doubt that the concrete conditions of employment offered at the French court would have been as good as those that he was currently enjoying in Hanover.[57]

The allusion to the Franco-German conflict in his letter to Des Viviers was not an isolated reference. Around the time in which Leibniz saw himself compelled to turn down the Parisian opportunity, he was following with increasing concern the events of what came to be called Nine Years War.[58] After the declaration of war on 24 September 1688, he had hoped that the Glorious Revolution of 1688–9 in England would lead to a rapid end of the conflict. The events which precipitated the British dynastic upheaval were rooted once again in religion as well as politics. In 1685 James II (1633–1701) had succeed his brother Charles II (1630–1685) on the English throne. Yet raised as he was in France during the Interregnum, the new monarch had converted to Catholicism and actively pursued philo-Catholic and philo-French policies. Worse still, on 10 June 1688 his second marriage to a Catholic princess was blessed by the birth of a son, James Francis Edward Stuart. A Catholic succession therefore seemed inevitable, since the rights of the newborn Prince of Wales clearly superseded those of the two Protestant daughters from James II's first marriage, Mary (1662–1694) and Anne (1665–1714). The fear of a reimposition of papal supremacy, combined with the kind of political absolutism personified by Louis XIV, prompted the English king's subjects into radical action for the second time in little more than a generation. William of Orange – the fierce enemy of Louis XIV, the husband of Mary Stuart, and the Dutch stadholder – was called to the rescue of the Protestant cause. The Glorious Revolution culminated in April 1689 with the crowning of William and Mary as joint sovereigns. The move from the philo-French policy of James II to the anti-French stand of the new monarchs did not, however, resolve the war between France and the Empire, as Leibniz had hoped. The conflict continued as badly as ever, bringing in the summer months of 1692 a number of setbacks to the anti-French alliance, the League of Augsburg. Alarmed by the dangers faced by the Empire, Leibniz resumed an old idea conceived in Vienna shortly after the onset of the conflict, namely the publication of a number of edicts issued in 1636 by the chief minister to Louis XIII, the famous Cardinal Richelieu (1585–1642), during the initial stages of direct French involvement in the Thirty Years War.[59] These edicts – which he had collected in the course of his Paris sojourn in 1672–6 – represented an excellent example of successful military strategy which, in his view, the German nation ought to learn from its own enemy. A draft of the introduction for this publication was prepared in the autumn of 1692, while the actual volume containing the edits (in both French and German translation) appeared anonymously in Amsterdam in 1694 under the title of *Fas est et ab hoste doceri* (*What Should Be Learned from One's Own Enemy*).[60] Copies of the book were sent to prominent people, including the *Reichsvizekanzler*, G. von Windischgrätz;[61] but Leibniz's efforts exercised little influence over the course of a devastating war which ended only in 1697 with the Treaty of Ryswick.[62] Moreover, the peace signed at the end of October between Louis XIV and Leopold I carried the seeds of further unrest between Catholics and Protestants. Its fourth article stipulated that those territories relinquished by Louis XIV at the end of the war in which the Catholic religion had been introduced during the French occupation were to maintain their new confession, whereas no religious concession was made to Protestant territories which remained under Louis XIV. As Leibniz bitterly commented in a letter of 15 November 1697 to the duke of Wolfenbüttel, Anton Ulrich,

it is easy to see that throughout this Treaty there reigns a spirit of animosity against the Protestants. . . . By virtue of the fourth article, the Roman religion which France has introduced during its usurpations will be preserved after the restitution of these places, without the Protestant religion being preserved in the territories which are ceded to the French, not even in those territories where this religion was established before their usurpation. What inequality and injustice![63]

Not for the first time, the need for a balance between Catholic and Protestant parties at all levels of the imperial government was evident.

Meanwhile, in the spring of 1693 Leibniz had started toying with the idea of having another go at the Harz mines. The way he saw it, his experiments had been only temporarily interrupted and, given the opportunity, he was prepared to try his hand again. Since his return from the long trip south, his preoccupation with the Guelf history and the political memos required by the duke's claims on Sachsen-Lauenburg and the ninth electorate had allowed only two visits to the Harz in September 1690 and November 1692.[64] But developments in March 1693 goaded him back into action. He became aware, probably via the Hanover *Kammer*, that the masters of the mints of Hanover and Celle (Rudolf Bornemann and his cousin, Justus Jacob Jenisch) claimed to possess an invention

which would reduce by half the number of horses and the quantity of
water currently employed in bringing the ore extracted from the mines
to the surface. Since Bornemann and Jenisch gave no details of their
alleged invention, Leibniz concluded that they were simply trying to
plagiarise his own technical innovations of 1686, notably his introduction of an endless cable. In a *promemoria* to the *Kammer* of Hanover of
1 April 1693, Leibniz therefore reasserted his priority in the invention
and requested permission to resume his experiments.[65] Understandably,
Ernst August was not keen to see his employee disappear once again in
the Harz mountains for months at a time instead of working at his historical assignment. It required a series of petitions to the elector during
the month of May, in which Leibniz committed himself to give priority
to the history of the Guelfs and to entrust the supervision of the Harz
experimentations to his deputies, before Ernst August finally relented in
July and granted Leibniz permission to resume his Harz attempts until
December.[66]

Once again, the *Hofrat*'s experiments did not proceed in practice as
they were designed in theory. A number of difficulties conspired to frustrate Leibniz's December 1693 deadline. Despite his assurances to the
elector, his presence was often needed on the Harz site in 1693 and 1694.
Abandoning the discredited idea of employing wind power for the operation of pumps, Leibniz now concentrated instead on the retrieval of
the extracted minerals, on the improvement of the pumps themselves,
and on the fresh idea of a better exploitation of the iron and steel fumes
in the smelting furnaces. As during the previous phase, in this second
period of experiments stretching over the years 1693–6 he encountered
the opposition of the local mining community reluctant to invest time
and resources in complex machinery of doubtful effectiveness. While
Leibniz was trying to build functioning machines employing technical
innovations which would eventually bear an economic return, they were
interested above all in immediate results. On the other hand, the court
counsellor, philosopher, librarian, and historiographer doubtless lacked
sufficient knowledge of all the technicalities involved in his experiments
and possibly underestimated the amount of practical expertise needed
by the machine builders and operators themselves. The sum of all these
factors, once again, was a failure to produce immediately applicable positive results. Ironically, future generations were to find some of Leibniz's
inventions highly useful, such as the endless cable still in use today.[67]

True to form, Leibniz's difficulties in the Harz did not deter him from advancing a wide variety of further technical, scientific, and administrative proposals. Writing on 16 May 1693 to the Electress Sophie, Leibniz returned to a topic close to his heart: the introduction of a proper medical system financially supported by the government and coordinated by a permanent "Health Council" in which political counsellors would join representatives of the medical profession. In particular, he pressed the importance of systematically recording the course of diseases in order to build on past experience and prevent epidemics.[68] He followed up his idea with a number of interventions aimed at the introduction of annual medical statistics on the model of those produced (with his own encouragement) by Bernardino Ramazzini, the able physician of the court of Modena, whom he had met during his Italian trip. Notably, on his advice, Ramazzini's statistics for 1690 were reproduced in the appendix to the *Ephemerides* of 1691 published by the German physicians of the Academia Naturae Curiosorum (founded in 1652 and known since 1687 as the Imperial Academia Leopoldina).[69] Having become aware of a new remedy against dysentery, he also endeavoured to disseminate it through private correspondence and a published report of 1696 to the Academia Leopoldina.[70] Meanwhile Leibniz continued to conceive new commercial schemes, together with Crafft. After trying unsuccessfully in December 1692 and June 1693 to secure a position for his friend in either Hanover or Wolfenbüttel,[71] he met Crafft in Hamburg at the end of September 1693 and discussed, amongst other things, the establishment of a brandy distillery in the Netherlands. This led Leibniz to undertake in November 1694 the last of his escapades with his adventurous friend before Crafft's death in Amsterdam three years later. Apparently without the knowledge of the Hanover court, he travelled to Amsterdam and The Hague to further their discussions on the brandy distillery, for which they sought the support of the Prince of Orange, since 1689 William III of England.[72]

The year 1694 was a sad one for the Hanoverian court due to tragic developments in the marriage between the electoral heir, Georg Ludwig, and Sophie Dorothea, the only daughter of the duke of Celle. Having had enough of their unhappy relationship and of her husband's affairs, in July the princess planned to elope with Count Philipp Christoph von Königsmarck. The discovery of the plan claimed the life of the count, who was murdered in mysterious circumstances, and caused the lifelong forced confinement of Sophie Dorothea in the castle of Ahlden, where she was denied any contact with her two children for the rest of her life. In the divorce proceedings which followed the arrest of the princess, Sophie Dorothea was declared the culprit in the failed marriage because of her elopement plan – notwithstanding her husband's serial infidelities. Leibniz's involvement in these events seems to have been limited to commenting briefly on an inaccurate account of the facts sent by Sophie's niece, Elisabeth Charlotte von der Pfalz, Duchess of Orléans.[73]

While Ernst August's court was troubled by the unhappy affair, the death in October 1694 of the court historiographer in Berlin, Samuel Pufendorf, rekindled Leibniz's hope of leaving Hanover for what appeared to be a better destination. Yet nothing came of his discrete approaches via his learned correspondent, the state counsellor of Brandenburg, Ezechiel Spanheim (1629–1710), in late 1694 and early 1695, due amongst other things to Leibniz's own hesitation regarding a definitive move from Hanover to Berlin.[74] In 1695 and early 1696, the combination of Leibniz's interest in the post and the publication of some posthumous works by the late historiographer and philosopher resulted in a sustained engagement on Leibniz's part with Pufendorf's thought. Aside from the occasions in which he was moderating his judgement for the benefit of his intended audience, Leibniz's general attitude towards Pufendorf continued to be sharply critical, as of somebody who wrote "with as much negligence as audacity."[75]

Elevation in July 1696 to *Geheimer Justizrat* (privy counsellor of justice) went a long way towards consoling Leibniz for his failure to succeed Pufendorf at the Berlin court. His new rank – the seventh highest in a hierarchy of ten[76] – was still well below the coveted position of *Geheimer Rat* (privy counsellor), but the cumulative pay of the newly created *Geheimer Justizrat* began to compare to the roughly 1800 talers per annum of a Hanoverian privy counsellor in the same period. Following his elevation, Leibniz's annual pay at the Hanover court was increased to 1000 talers. Added to the annual recompense of 400 talers from the Wolfenbüttel dukes for his directorship of their library and the 200 talers per annum received since 1691 from the Celle court (at the recommendation of Sophie) as contribution towards his writing of the Guelf history, it made for a handsome stipend.[77] For all the endless postponements of the Guelf history and the frustration of his Harz designs, Leibniz had proven himself a very useful person to have around. The Guelf claim to the Sachsen-Lauenburg duchy was worth a fortune in purely financial terms; the claim to electoral status was of inestimable value in political ones; and Ernst August aimed to transform the prince-bishopric of Osnabrück from a dominion *pro tempore* into a permanent acquisition of the house of Hanover.[78] A court official capable of making crucial contributions to all of these vital affairs of state – however eccentric and unreliable in other respects – had proved a profitable investment for Ernst August and one which he succeeded in preserving through timely promotion.

Orthodoxy and Heresy

The years between 1690 and 1698 also confronted Leibniz with many aspects of the perennial debate between orthodoxy and heresy, and with the related twin problems of church reunification and religious toleration. Inevitably, the question of who was the bearer of the orthodox doctrine and who was the heretic continued to receive diametrically opposite answers. The deeper problem, as Leibniz had long recognized, was to determine not only what the true doctrine was but also, first and foremost, what was the criterion for deciding whether a doctrine was true or not. In a letter of 30 January 1692 to his Catholic friend, Landgraf Ernst, Leibniz lucidly summarized the positions of the main parties – the Roman Catholic and the Greek Orthodox churches, the Protestants, and the more radical Christian movements emblematically represented by the theological rationalism of the Socinians – giving in a nutshell his own view on the matter:

One might say that the parties have three principles: 1.) the authority of traditions, 2.) Scripture [and] 3.) philosophy. Authority leads principally the Greeks and the Romans, Scripture the Protestants, and philosophy the Socinians. All three principles are good, but one can abuse them, and this [abuse] causes errors.[79]

In a typically conciliatory way Leibniz was acknowledging the merits of all three approaches. In so doing, however, he was also taking a precise stand. First of all, from his own Protestant starting point, he was admitting the legitimacy of a recourse to "the authority of the Traditions" against a rigid application of the Protestant rule of "Scripture alone." Moreover, he was rejecting, on the one hand, irrationalistic positions which sought to bar all 'philosophy' or rational motives from the realm of faith and castigating, on the other hand, the Socinian abuse of reason as the sole, ultimate criterion of religious truth. As for the identification of heretics condemned to eternal damnation, Leibniz adamantly refused to single out anyone for the flames of hell. In his view, although there existed an objective religious orthodoxy which needed to be discovered, agreed upon, and defended against heresies, the subjective salvation of people who might in good faith believe false doctrines (or not believe true ones) was in the hands of God alone. Only God was able to see the secrets of human hearts and to discern whether individuals were ultimately guided by a sincere love of Him; and this was the only thing, in Leibniz's view, which really counted when it came to eternal salvation. Both church reunification and religious toleration could only be built on this premise.[80]

The occasion for plunging into the thick of these debates presented itself to Leibniz in the summer of 1690 straight after his return from the long southern trip. Duchess Sophie inquired after his opinion of a book which had provoked quite a stir since its publication in Paris in 1686: the *Reflexions sur les differends de la religion* by Paul Pellisson-Fontanier (1624–93). Pellisson was a prominent fellow of the Parisian Académie Royale des Sciences who in 1670 had abandoned his Huguenot faith to convert to Catholicism. Like many other converts, he was keen for a restoration of communion between Catholics and Protestants; but in his view the only real way of achieving reunification was for Protestants to realize their errors and return to the Roman church. Following Sophie's request, Leibniz pursued a close, sometime pointed, but generally friendly and respectful epistolary debate with Pellisson. Intermediary in this exchange was Marie de Brinon, the secretary of Louise Hollandine von der Pfalz, one of Sophie's sisters who had converted to Catholicism in 1658 and been named abbess of the convent of Maubuisson (near Paris) by Louis XIV.

In 1691 Pellisson published his epistolary exchange with Leibniz as the fourth part of his *Reflexions sur les differends de la religion*, though without informing his correspondent.[81] A second edition appeared in 1692 under the title *De la tolerance des religions* following Leibniz's request to insert some later letters which clarified his position and avoided possible misunderstandings, notably the unjust charge that, in defending toleration, he was advocating some kind of religious indifference. Leibniz did not reject the necessity of appealing in certain controversial cases to the authority of the truly universal or 'catholic' church, and even accepted its infallibility in matters pertaining salvation. However, contrary to Pellisson, he did not equate the Roman church with this universal or catholic church.

According to him, the Roman church was only one of the particular Christian churches which possess fragments of a truth to be traced through a respectful examination of their doctrines in the light of the entire ecclesiastical tradition. If no particular Christian church had a monopoly on truth, then no particular church could have the right to exclude from salvation those who did not follow all of its doctrines.[82] Moreover, appealing to the teaching of Catholic theologians themselves,[83] Leibniz forcefully reproposed his theology of love according to which "*it is possible to be saved in every Religion, provided that one truly loves God above all things.*"[84] Regarding the subjective salvation of individuals, Leibniz pointed out, it is necessary to distinguish (once again following the Roman Catholic tradition itself) between material and formal heretics. Material heretics are those who believe in a doctrine which is objectively erroneous and against the teaching of the universal or catholic church but are not aware that this is the case. Formal heretics are those who not only believe in an objectively erroneous doctrine but are also conscious of their opposition to the teaching of the universal church. In his view and – he claimed – according to many Catholic theologians, only formal heretics were excluded from salvation. As long as a material heretic sincerely loved God, his or her objective error was not cause of damnation.[85]

In the midst of this debate, the Bishop of Meaux, Jacques-Bénigne Bossuet, made his reappearance.[86] In July 1691 Leibniz had sent to Marie de Brinon his own French translation of the official document of 20 March 1691 empowering Bishop Rojas to conduct negotiations towards church reunification with the Protestant princes in Germany on behalf of the emperor. Leibniz's hope was to involve France in mediating these discussions through the intervention of prominent personalities close to Louis XIV, such as Pellisson and Bossuet.[87] Bossuet (who had followed with attention the published epistolary exchange between Leibniz and Pellisson) asked Marie de Brinon to obtain from Hanover a new copy of the writings which had provided the basis of discussion in the negotiations toward church reunification of 1683, notably Rojas's *Regulae circa christianorum omnium Ecclesiasticam Reunionem*. Duchess Sophie had in fact sent him a copy back in 1683, but since the negotiations had apparently reached an impasse, Bossuet had misplaced the document and could not find it again.[88] Molanus took it upon himself to oblige Bossuet's request; but instead of sending the official documents of 1683, he composed a fresh one under the title of *Cogitationes privatae de Methodo Reunionis Ecclesiae*

protestantium cum Ecclesia Romano-Catholica (1691).[89] In December this
text was sent by Leibniz to Bossuet.[90] By June 1692 the bishop of Meaux
had penned a reply, which he submitted for Pellisson's perusal before
sending it to Hanover on 26 August.[91] Although Molanus and Leibniz
were initially encouraged by Bossuet's answer and planned to write a
reply,[92] things did not develop as they had hoped. First of all, Leibniz
resented the personal way in which Bossuet, in the conclusion of his reply,
had intimated that he was not excused "from the obstinacy which makes
the heretic" – a charge which was tantamount to declaring Leibniz a formal heretic.[93] Having complained to Pellisson about this treatment, he
received from the latter the firm assurance of Bossuet's "estimation and
friendship" towards him.[94] More significant from a general point of view
was the fact that, whatever Bossuet's personal opinion of Leibniz, the
status of the Council of Trent proved to be an insurmountable impasse.
Whereas Molanus and Leibniz called for a suspension of its decisions
until a new council acknowledged as truly ecumenical by all the parties
could be called, Bossuet from the outset of his renewed contact with
Hanover refused any concession on dogmatic matters decided at Trent.[95]
In defence of this stand he denied that the revision of some aspects of the
Council of Constance (1414–18) by that of Basel (1431–7) constituted a
pertinent precedent.[96] Confronted with Bossuet's rigidity, Molanus withdrew from any further discussion, leaving Leibniz alone in his campaign to
convince the bishop. Their correspondence continued until April 1694,[97]
until Bossuet failed to reply to Leibniz's letter of 12 July 1694 despite the
latter's desire to continue their debate.[98]

As it happens, in this last letter before the break in communication,
Leibniz wrote about his philosophical work, encouraged by the fact that
Bossuet in the previous correspondence had seemed interested in knowing more. In particular he mentioned a piece he was composing on the
issue of the union of mind and body – the *Système nouveau de la nature
et de la communication des substances* – and he also joined to his letter
two other philosophical writings: his *Réflexions sur l'avancement de la
Métaphysique réelle* (an enlarged French version of his article *De Primae
Philosophiae Emendatione, et de Notione Substantiae* which had recently
appeared in the *Acta Eruditorum* of March 1694) and his reply to some
objections raised by Jacques L'Enfant (1661–1728), one of the ministers
of the French refugee church in Berlin.[99] "If you think it appropriate,"
Leibniz prompted Bossuet, "the two enclosed pieces could be put into

the *Journal des savants*, in order to give some indication of my plan."[100]
Unfortunately this time he met with stony silence.

Meanwhile Pellisson had suddenly died on 7 February 1693, followed
on 12 May 1693 by Leibniz's trusted confident on religious issues, Landgraf Ernst. Finally, on 12 March 1695 Leibniz lost the Catholic partner
on the reunification issue who was closest to his own views, Bishop Rojas.
With Pellisson, Landgraf Ernst, and Bishop Rojas dead and the correspondence with Bossuet brusquely interrupted, from 1695 onward Leibniz's
efforts towards church reunification lost their focus on the reconciliation
of Protestantism with Rome and concentrated instead on the reunification
of the Protestant confessions with one another. At the same time, his
sympathy for the Roman Catholic church had cooled down considerably.
He had pinned a great deal of hope on a favourable reception of his philosophical and theological views from the two Roman Catholic theologians
whom he regarded as the greatest of his time, Arnauld and Bossuet. In
both cases he had been bitterly disappointed, meeting with rigidity and
discouragement. While his fundamental principles remained unchanged,
circumstances appeared to dictate that he seek new means of applying
them, at least for the time being.

Leibniz's attention, however, was not directed only towards the main
Christian confessions. In this period as well as throughout his life he also
engaged in a debate with radical religious movements the theology of
which, more often than not, he rejected. His constant conviction of the
necessity to distinguish between the errant and the error was reflected in
his own attitude towards these movements. Although he did not hesitate
to engage in sophisticated argumentative duels to counter views that he
regarded as heretical, he rejected the use of violence and persecution
against people embracing these views. Moreover, when some theological
doctrines appeared to be incorrect but not necessarily heretical or were
in any case quite harmless, his own pragmatic opinion was that the best
course of action was simply to leave them alone. As he explained to
Duchess Sophie in a letter of 26 October 1691,

under the pretext of preventing heresies, they have been engendered. Normally these
things fade away on their own when they lose the attraction of novelty; but when
one wants to suppress them with noisy denunciations, persecutions, and refutations,
it is like wanting to extinguish a fire with a pair of bellows.... For fear of being
short of heretics Messieurs the theologians sometimes do everything they can to find
some[.][101]

Leibniz was referring in particular to a case which was agitating the Guelf courts in 1691 and 1692: the alleged visions of Christ by a young noblewoman, Rosamunde Juliane von der Asseburg. Amongst other things, Rosamunde's visions seemed to support the millenarian doctrines of her protector, the superintendent of the churches of Lüneburg, Johann Wilhelm Petersen – doctrines which the Hanover *Konsistorium* had prohibited Petersen from teaching publicly. Distancing himself from the contemptuous reaction of some contemporaries, Leibniz concluded from a careful study of the evidence that Rosamunde's visions could be explained in natural terms as an extraordinary example of the still poorly understood powers of the human mind. As for Petersen, he regarded both him and his doctrine as basically benign.[102] Since Rosamunde's visions could be explained in a naturalistic way and Petersen's brand of millenarianism was in itself quite innocuous, there was no reason for concern about either of them. Moreover, in his view, there were even cases in which a dubious theology could positively enhance the moral stand of a person. An excellent example of this was Leibniz's old acquaintance, Baron Franciscus Mercurius van Helmont. Not only was van Helmont a millenarian, he also held a number of kabbalist ideas which could hardly be squared with Christian orthodoxy, notably the central role attributed by him to human volition in the redemptive process.[103] And yet Leibniz, while taking issue with the strange and dubious elements which peppered van Helmont's thought,[104] was deeply intrigued by both the theoretical and the practical dimensions of the baron's outlook. Between March and September 1696, during a prolonged stay of van Helmont in Hanover, Leibniz met him regularly, often in the presence of Sophie, for long discussions on a variety of topics which he recorded in a diary kept around this time.[105] In particular, Leibniz was impressed by the baron's commitment to the general good, which stimulated the promotion of a number of practical schemes for the concrete improvement of the human condition. As he wrote on 20 December 1696 to Andreas Morell, "the touchstone of true illumination is a great eagerness for contributing to the general good." This was what really distinguished van Helmont from other millenarians and promoters of controversial religious movements generally, such as Jean de Labadie, Antoinette de Bourignon, and William Penn. "Among those who had extraordinary ideas," Leibniz concluded, "I have hardly found anyone beside van Helmont who shared this great principle of charity with me and who had a true eagerness for the general good, although in other respects we often had very different opinions about different matters."[106] In short, van Helmont's belief in universal salvation, combined with a radically optimistic eschatology expecting a future millennium and a final restoration of all things, although supported by shaky arguments, had played an important role in inspiring his love of God and his commitment to the common good.[107] Leibniz did not fail to acknowledge and admire this aspect of van Helmont's thought despite his distance from many of the baron's "extraordinary ideas."

A much more severe attitude was adopted towards the various species of antitrinitarians, notably the Socinians. At stake in this case were some of the core teachings of Christian revelation, such as the divinity of Christ and the very nature of God. The error therefore needed to be refuted, although as always without confusing the defence of orthodoxy with the persecution of the erroneous.[108] In this period Leibniz's attention was especially drawn to the Trinitarian polemics which raged across the English Channel and on which Thomas Burnett of Kemney kept him posted. In particular, in 1693 he found in the newly printed pamphlet of one of the champions of the "Socinians of England,"[109] the antitrinitarian Stephen Nye, an excellent opportunity for gaining an up-to-date overview of the English debate on the doctrine of the Trinity from the point of view of the 'enemy'.[110] True to the Ovidian motto "Fas est et ab hoste doceri,"[111] Leibniz studied the pamphlet carefully, taking extensive notes and penning a series of *Remarques* in which he finally passed his own verdict on the Trinitarian doctrines criticised by Nye, namely the controversial interpretations of the Trinity given, respectively, by the famous mathematician John Wallis, by the Dean of St Paul's, William Sherlock (1641–1707), by his irrepressible opponent, Robert South (1634–1716), by the Cambridge Platonist, Ralph Cudworth, and by the celebrated author of *The Lawes of Ecclesiasticall Politie*, Richard Hooker (c. 1554–1600).[112] In his comment, Leibniz took great care to avoid sliding inadvertently into one of the opposite extremes of tritheism or modalism with which those authors had variously been charged by their opponents. Keeping his eye on the age-old ecclesiastical teaching into which, in his view, one should be wary of introducing new terms, he proposed a reinterpretation of the traditional *analogia Trinitatis* – which found the best image of the Trinity in the mind reflecting upon itself – while proposing at the same time an ontologically 'robust' conception of the Trinitarian persons as "relative substances" in an "absolute substance."[113]

In 1694 and 1695 another English antitrinitarian, William Freke, occasioned further reflections on the Trinity in particular and on the use of the mathematical method in theology more generally.[114] In an anonymous pamphlet secretly distributed to the members of the English Parliament in December 1693, Freke had launched a virulent attack on the dogma of the Trinity, allegedly based on a direct reading of Scripture.[115] In March 1694, reporting to the Electress Sophie on the content of the pamphlet, Leibniz explained that its author was a follower of Arianism, that is, of the brand of antitrinitarianism which took its name from the ancient heresy of Arius (256–336).[116] Although the style and quality of Freke's argumentation was judged by Leibniz to be very low,[117] the scandal produced by the booklet seemed to demand an answer. When his nephew, Friedrich Simon Löffler, requested his guidance in choosing a topic for the final dissertation required for his theological studies in Leipzig, Leibniz suggested a refutation of Freke's pamphlet.[118] Löffler was happy to oblige, and even proposed to formulate his refutation using a mathematical method.[119] Despite his uncle's warnings regarding the difficulties and dangers of applying mathematics to theology,[120] Löffler sent to him for comment an outline of his demonstration.[121] Leibniz regarded his nephew's efforts as irreparably flawed; and together with a number of remarks highlighting these mistakes, he sent in reply a fresh outline offering a striking sample of biblical exegesis conducted by means of mathematical method.[122] For his part, Leibniz did not try to prove the Trinitarian nature of God (something which, in his view, could not and should not be attempted, given the epistemological status of the doctrine of the Trinity as a truth above reason); but he did endeavour to demonstrate that the doctrine of the Trinity is contained in Scripture and supported by the teaching of the ancient Church.

Physics, Metaphysics, and Mathematics

Force, Monads, and Pre-established Harmony: The Public Offensive of the Mid-90s

In a letter of March 1696 to Vincentius Placcius, Leibniz famously remarked that "he who knows me only from my publications does not know me."[123] Yet the two previous years had witnessed some of his boldest attempts at the public presentation of his philosophy. In March 1694

Leibniz had taken an important step: for the first time he explicitly expounded his metaphysics of substance for the broader community of savants by publishing in the *Acta Eruditorum* a short article, *De Primae Philosophiae Emendatione, et de Notione Substantiae* (*On the Emendation of First Philosophy, and on the Notion of Substance*).[124] Perhaps the most striking aspect of Leibniz's brief account was the central role given to a notion which linked physics and metaphysics, the notion of force.

I will say for the present that the concept of *forces* or *powers*, which the Germans call *Kraft* and the French *la force*, and for whose explanation I have set up a distinct science of *dynamics*, brings the strongest light to bear on our understanding of the true concept of *substance*.[125]

More was to follow. Having mulled for almost three decades over the concept of substance and in more recent years over the notion of force, Leibniz published in short order during 1695 both the first public account of his *Dynamica* – the *Specimen Dynamicum* (first part), which appeared in the April issue of the *Acta Eruditorum* – and the first public account of his mature metaphysics – the *Système nouveau de la nature et de la communication des substances, aussi bien que l'union qu'il y a entre l'âme et le corps*, within the *Journal des Sçavans* for June and July.[126] In both cases his decision to go public had been stimulated by the reaction of other savants to the communication of his ideas through conversation or correspondence. In his last letter to Bossuet of 12 July 1694, he described the complex network of contacts, requests, and responses which had helped to steer his intellectual journey – a description which transcended the case at hand and described his habit of advancing his theories not in isolation but in a continuous conversation with others. The long list of people mentioned to Bossuet included Antoine Arnauld, François Catelan, Nicolas Malebranche, Denis Papin, Jean-Paul Bignon and Melchisédech Thévenot (both fellows of the French Académie Royale des Sciences), Paul Pellisson-Fontanier, Simon Foucher, the Italian Franciscan priest Michel Angelo Fardella and the Jansenist Antonio Alberti (alias Amable de Tourreil) (both met in Italy), and Jacques L'Enfant. Dozens of important exchanges with these savants – whether in personal conversation, private correspondence, or printed articles – had paved the way to the key publications of 1695.[127] In particular, he recalled sending to Pellisson a sample of his dynamics intended for Malebranche's perusal and for further circulation amongst the fellows of the Académie Royale des Sciences.[128] Although this essay does not seem to have ever reached Malebranche, it was eventually read at a meeting of the Académie of 28 June 1692, apparently without making much of an impact.[129] In the absence of a more explicit reaction by the members of the Académie, Pellisson agreed that Leibniz should turn "to public opinion by publishing in the *Journal des savants* a general rule for the composition of movements" which was in conformity with his *Dynamica*.[130] As for his metaphysical thought, Leibniz recounted to Bossuet, many years earlier he had written a letter to Simon Foucher summarising the reasons for his opposition to occasionalism. In fact, in a letter of 1686 to the Canon of Dijon, he had basically outlined the future *Système nouveau*, further elaborating on it in a subsequent letter probably dating back to 1687 or 1688.[131] Pressed (among others) by Foucher, Fardella, and De Tourreil to provide a fuller explanation of his metaphysical hypothesis,[132] Leibniz arrived around July 1694 at a first formulation of his *Système nouveau*. After toying with the idea of sending it directly to the editor of the *Journal des Sçavans*, Louis Cousin,[133] he must eventually have decided that it was not ripe enough to be presented to the European community of savants. The *Journal des Sçavans* – the official organ of the Académie Royale des Sciences published since 1665 – was the best established and most widely read learned journal of the period. Leibniz's intention to use it as the outlet for his metaphysical system indicated that, having decided to divulge his views, he intended to do so in the most high-profile way. But the broader the audience, the more careful he needed to be: even in the new version dispatched for publication some ten months later he chose to hide his authorship under the initials "M. D. L." (Monsieur de Leibniz), being acutely aware that this sort of meditations were "by no means popular in style, nor such as can be appreciated by all types of mind."[134] As intermediary for the submission to the *Journal des Sçavans* he used one of the people who had closely witnessed the development of his thought on the matter, Simon Foucher, to whom between late May and early June 1695 he sent his manuscript.[135] By that time the first part of the *Specimen Dynamicum* had appeared in the *Acta Eruditorum*, inaugurating Leibniz's major public offensive of year 1695.[136]

In this *Specimen* of his *Dynamica* Leibniz offered a lucid analysis of the concept of force announced in the brief article of March 1694 as a notion which would shed the strongest light on humankind's understanding of the true concept of substance. In so doing he also sought to lay the metaphysical foundations of physics proper. As he had maintained for many years, the phenomena studied by physics required a further level of explanation, a level which strictly speaking was not physical but metaphysical, that is, was postulated by physics but lay beyond its proper remit.[137] The notion of force was situated by Leibniz at the interface between physics and metaphysics as the concept which allowed these two levels of explanation to be welded together into a coherent outlook on reality. The forces measured by physics and treated by it in mathematical terms were the phenomenal expression of something ultimately real. This real entity lay beyond that which appears to us in experience but needed to be admitted in order to give reason in the last instance of this same experience. In short, it was the very condition of possibility of our phenomenal experience of the corporeal world studied by physics.[138] As Leibniz put it in the *Specimen Dynamicum*,

we cannot derive all truths concerning corporeal things from logical and geometrical axioms alone . . . we must admit something metaphysical, something perceptible by the mind alone and above that which is purely mathematical and subject to the imagination, and we must add to material mass a certain superior and, so to speak, formal principle. Whether we call this principle form or entelechy or force does not matter, as long as we remember that it can only be explained through the notion of forces.[139]

This being the case, Leibniz proposed a classification of forces which afforded an elegantly economical reinterpretation of both physical and metaphysical levels of reality. This classification was based on two distinctions: the distinction between active and passive forces, and the distinction between primitive and derivative forces. Active force, according to Leibniz, was the force manifested in motion and was, in turn, of two kinds: dead force, that is, the force expressed in the possibility of motion (such as, for instance, "a stone in a sling being held in by a rope" or the "centrifugal force itself"), and living force, that is, the force expressed in actual motion.[140] Whereas active force is connected with motion, passive force is connected with resistance to motion and accounts for the impenetrability of bodies and their inertia.[141] As for the second main distinction, between primitive and derivative forces, the terminology adopted by Leibniz immediately indicated that the latter 'derive' from the former. More precisely, derivative forces were conceived as modifications of primitive forces.[142] As a result of this pair of distinctions Leibniz arrived at four principal varieties of force: (1) primitive active force and (2) primitive passive force; (3) derivative active force and (4) derivative passive force. Primitive active force is "nothing but the first entelechy" and corresponds to "the soul or substantial form." Primitive passive force "constitutes that which is called primary matter in the schools, if correctly interpreted."[143] Primitive active force and primitive passive force constituted therefore, at the metaphysical level, the essence of substance in a reinterpretation of the Aristotelic polarity of form and matter in which an active principle (or substantial form) and a passive principle (or primary matter) come together. On the other hand, the forces studied by physics were conceived as derivative forces (both active and passive). They are "that by which bodies actually act on one another or are acted upon by one another" and it is to their notions "that the laws of action apply, laws which are understood not only through reason, but are also corroborated by sense itself through the phenomena."[144]

The second milestone piece of 1695, the *Système nouveau*, revisited the issue of force in the context of a specifically metaphysical analysis devoted to the investigation of the "nature of substances and their communication" and of "the union of mind and body." In the opening paragraph Leibniz referred to his exchange with "one of the greatest theologians and philosophers of our time," Antoine Arnauld, as the highlight of the philosophical discussion with other savants which had eventually encouraged him to offer the following "meditations" to the public.[145] The way he saw it, the philosophical account he was about to give in the *Système nouveau* was therefore basically in continuity with the account he had presented in 1686 in the *Discours de Métaphysique* and defended in his correspondence with Arnauld – and this despite the fact that in the *Système nouveau* there was little trace of the "complete concept" theory central to the explanation of the concept of substance in the *Discours*. If, on the one hand, the sustained study of physics and the development of the *Dynamica* had led Leibniz to present his concept of substance in a new light, on the other hand this account seemed to complement, rather than compete with, the "complete concept" theory of substance more directly linked to his logical investigations.[146]

Immediately before unveiling his system to a broad audience, Leibniz saw fit to summarise in a few, precious lines the intellectual itinerary which had brought him there, starting from his youthful study of scholastic philosophy and his first encounters with the mechanism of the moderns:

I had gone far into the country of the scholastics, when mathematics and modern authors drew me out again, while I was still quite young. Their beautiful way of explaining nature mechanically charmed me, and I rightly scorned the method of those who make use only of forms and faculties, from which we learn nothing. But afterwards, having tried to go more deeply into the principles of mechanics themselves in order to explain the laws of nature which are known through experience, I realized that the consideration of mere *extended mass* is insufficient, and that use must also be made of the notion of *force*, which is perfectly intelligible, though it belongs to the sphere of metaphysics.[147]

The true notion of substance required a principle of real unity and activity which could only be found, Leibniz continued, in something similar to substantial form once this much despised notion had been restored to its proper significance:

I found, then, that the nature of substantial forms consists in force, and that from this there follows something analogous to feeling and desire [au sentiment et à l'appetit]; and that they must therefore be understood along the lines of our notion of *souls*. But just as the soul ought not to be used to explain in detail the workings of an animal's body, I decided that similarly these forms must not be used to solve particular problems of nature, although they are necessary for grounding true general principles. Aristotle calls them *first entelechies*. I call them, perhaps more intelligibly, *primary forces*, which contain not only *actuality*, or the mere fulfilment of a possibility, but also an originating *activity*. . . . It is only *atoms of substance*, that is to say real unities absolutely devoid of parts, that can be the sources of actions, and the absolute first principles of the composition of things, and as it were the ultimate elements in the analysis of substances. . . . It is only metaphysical or substantial points (constituted by forms or souls) which are both indivisible and real, and without them there would be nothing real, since without true unities there would be no multiplicity.[148]

Once he had established these real unities endowed with an internal principle of activity as the ultimate elements of reality from which everything else results, Leibniz proceeded in the second part of his essay (published a week after the first part in the *Journal des Sçavans* of 4 July 1695) to tackle the issue of the "communication" amongst substances and, more specifically, of the union of mind and body. This part revealed the full extent of his opposition to the brand of Cartesianism known as occasionalism. Although at a first glance Leibniz seemed to agree with the so–called "system of occasional causes" in that he also rejected a "real influence" of one substance upon another, in fact he struck at the very core of occasionalism by putting forward a concept of substance in which substances were endowed with an immanent principle of activity. In Cartesianism and, even more explicitly, in its occasionalistic interpretation, God was the sole source of activity, the sole causal power in the corporeal world. By contrast, Leibniz's substance had been created by God in such a way that it included an immanent principle of action, or, as it were, an internal "law" regulating once and for ever the series of all the operations and changes occurring to this substance independent of any other substance but in perfect harmony or conformity with every other substance. The union of mind and body was simply a corollary of this concept of substance.[149] As Leibniz had pointed out, the only ultimately real elements from which everything else results are the "real unities" endowed with an internal principle of activity (that is, as he would call them from late July 1695 onward, the monads).[150] Both mind and body are therefore ultimately made (so to speak) of the same metaphysical 'stuff'. Their union is a special case of the universal harmony existing amongst all "real unities."

As Leibniz had hoped, the *Système nouveau* caused quite a stir. The first to answer in print was Foucher himself. Two months after the publication of Leibniz's essay, Foucher's reply appeared in the issue of 12 September of the *Journal des Sçavans*.[151] Leibniz's answer – in which he introduced for the first time the expression "pre-established harmony" (*Harmonie pre-établie*) as a way to characterize his theory[152] – was ready within days and was sent to another of his French correspondents, the Marquis Guillaume François Antoine de L'Hôpital, to be passed on to the *Journal des Sçavans*.[153] Due to the delay in forwarding it to the editor of the journal, however, Leibniz's reply was not published until April of 1696, the very month in which Foucher died.[154] Meanwhile, towards the end of 1695, Leibniz had written to Henri Basnage de Beauval, the editor of a learned journal published in Rotterdam since 1687 under the title of *Histoire des ouvrages des savans*, summarising some of his main tenets.[155] On 13 January 1696 he added some further explanations evidently replying to Basnage's own comments.[156] With Leibniz's permission, Basnage published in the *Histoire des ouvrages des savans* of February 1696 an edited excerpt from the postscript of the January letter (now known as the "second explanation" of the *Système nouveau*). Interestingly, in his edited version Basnage omitted the characterisation "pre-established" (*pré-établie*) used by Leibniz in the original.[157] The full expression "the way of pre-established harmony" appeared, however, in print a few months later, when the *Journal des Sçavans* of 19 November 1696 published the so-called "third explanation" of the *Système nouveau*, that is, an excerpt from an explanatory letter of Leibniz sent in September to the journal.[158]

Alongside the expression "pre-established harmony", 1695 saw also the introduction of perhaps the most famous term in Leibniz's distinctive philosophical vocabulary: "monad". The use of the term "monad" (from the Greek *monas*, that is, unity or that which is one) in a philosophical context was far from new.[159] As early as 1663, in the preface to the very first of Leibniz's philosophical works, the *Disputatio Metaphysica de Principio Individui*, his teacher Jakob Thomasius used the term "monadic" to indicate an individual which constituted a species on its own.[160] Leibniz himself employed the term "monadic" in *De Dissertatio de Arte Combinatoria* of 1666.[161] Famously, Giordano Bruno (1548–1600) wrote in 1591 a work *De Monade* in which many elements of the neoplatonic, kabbalistic, and magical traditions converged. Although as late as the mid-90s Leibniz appears not to have read Bruno's *De monade* and his use of the term monad was not directly influenced by Bruno,[162] he certainly had an extensive knowledge of the work of other authors in the neoplatonic and kabbalistic tradition who employed the term of "monad" in various ways, notably Ralph Cudworth, Henry More, Christian Knorr von Rosenroth, Anne Viscountess Conway, and Franciscus Mercurius van Helmont, with the last of whom, as noted above, Leibniz spent long hours of discussion in the mid-1690s.[163] More than the term itself, what is interesting was its distinctive use by Leibniz to indicate his "real unities" or "simple substances." Indeed, 1695 also marked the point at which Leibniz started to speak increasingly of "simple" substances. In a series of posthumously published remarks penned shortly after the publication of Foucher's objections against his *Système nouveau* in the *Journal des Sçavans* of 12 September of 1695, Leibniz noted that "in actual substantial things, the whole is a result, or assembly, of simple substances, or indeed of a multiplicity of real unities."[164] A few months earlier, in an unfinished letter of 22 July 1695 to the Marquis de L'Hôpital, Leibniz used (apparently for the first time) the term *monas* to indicate "une unité reelle" ("a real unity").[165] Keeping in mind what Leibniz had just written in the *Système nouveau* about "les unités reelles" ("the real unities") which are the only ultimate real elements from which all things result, and his remarks on Foucher's objections in which the expression "simple substances" appeared to be equivalent to "real unities," it seems that at this point his mature monadology was well under way.[166]

The first actually to read about Leibniz's monads appears to have been Michel Angelo Fardella. In a letter of 13 September 1696 to the Italian savant, Leibniz explained, "the chief point seems to me to consist in the true notion of substance, which is the same as the notion of monad or of real unity [quae eadem est cum notione monadis sive realis unitatis]." He then proceeded to relate his doctrine of substance to considerations on the nature of the mathematical continuum,[167] another strand of reflection which, together with his logical investigations and his researches on physics, converged to shape Leibniz's mature theory of substance. According to Leibniz, one should distinguish between a mathematical continuum and a physical continuum. The latter appears to us as a continuum due to our way of perceiving the physical world. In reality (that is, without our imagination producing a perception of continuity), what we perceive as a physical continuum is an aggregate of an infinity of contiguous parts. The physical continuum (or, more precisely, the physical 'contiguous') has the character of actuality because the physical world is actually divided into an infinity of parts. The mathematical continuum, on the other hand, has the character of ideality because it is an abstraction based on our perception of the physical 'contiguous'. Its division is potential: that is, the mathematical continuum is divisible to infinity but not actually divided. According to Leibniz, the analysis of a mathematical continuum (for instance, an ideal segment) opened the door to the correct conception of substance. In short, the points of an ideal segments should not be conceived as the last components or 'parts' of the segment but as the 'conditions of possibility' from which that segment 'results'. In other words, without points there would be no segment, although the points are not 'parts' of the segment. Analogously, bodies 'result' from simple substances or monads although the latter are not 'parts' of bodies but the 'conditions of possibility' of bodies.[168] In his remarks on Foucher's objections, immediately after introducing the notion of "simple substances" from which "actual substantial things . . . result," Leibniz in fact added, "it is this confusion of the ideal and the actual which has quite obscured, and made a labyrinth of, 'the composition of the continuum'." Those who have erroneously conceived the points of a line as 'parts' of the line of which this latter is made up have also confused the mathematical continuum (in which division is potential) with the physical continuum (in which division is actual). Consequently they have "looked for primary elements in ideal things or relations in a way totally contrary to what should be done." On the other hand, "those who realized that relations like number, or space . . . could never be formed by the putting together of points, have for the most part then gone wrong by saying that substantial realities have no basic elements, as if they have no primary unities, and there are no simple substances." The latter, although rightly rejecting the conception of points as 'parts' making up a line, have mistakenly concluded that there are no basic elements or primary unities in real substantial things. In fact, although these basic elements or primary unities are not 'parts' of which a real substantial thing is made up, the real substantial thing results from them as a line results from points: "all in all, everything comes down to these unities, all the rest, or the resultants, being only well-founded phenomena."[169] The 'real things' of the physical world as they appear to us are therefore well-founded phenomena which result from ultimate "real unities" or simple substances.

Further important metaphysical ideas continued in this period to be elaborated by Leibniz in his private papers. For instance, in a striking paper dated 23 November 1697 on the ultimate origination of things (*De rerum originatione radicali*) he carried forward reflections on the existence of the maximum of com-possibilities begun over twenty years earlier. These reflections were based on the principle that "all things which are possible, or express essence or possible reality, tend by equal right towards existence in proportion to the quantity of essence or reality which they include, or in proportion to the degree of perfection which belongs to them." "Hence," Leibniz concluded, "it is seen to be most evident that out of the infinite combinations of possibles, and the infinite possible series, that one exists by whose means the greatest possible amount of essence or possibility is brought into existence."[170] In plainer words, this is the best of all possible worlds. In turn, in a paper on the search for the supreme cause of things written at some point after 1696 (*Tentamen Anagogicum. Essay Anagogique dans la recherche des causes*), Leibniz sketched one of the best pictures of the general 'architecture' of his philosophical and scientific research, stating that "in corporeal nature itself, there are, so to speak, two reigns which penetrate one another without confusing themselves and hindering one another: the reign of power, according to which everything can be explained *mechanically* by efficient causes . . . ; and also the reign of wisdom, according to which everything can be explained, so to speak, *architectonically* by final causes[.]"[171]

Dark Clouds on the Mathematical Horizon

In the letter to Fardella of 13 September 1696 in which he had introduced the term "monad" to indicate his notion of substance, Leibniz was also delighted to report that his calculus was catching on. In particular the Bernoulli brothers, Jakob and Johann, and the Marquis de L'Hôpital were promoting it enthusiastically.[172] Between 1691 and 1697, in fact, a series of articles appeared in learned journals applying the new infinitesimal analysis to the solution of problems such as that of the catenary proposed in 1690 by Jakob Bernoulli, and that of the curve of quickest descent (brachistochrone) proposed by his brother Johann Bernoulli in 1696.[173] In 1692 and 1694 Leibniz himself, from the pages of the prestigious *Journal des Sçavans*, explained that his analysis was more powerful than that of Descartes because it allowed the treatment of transcendentals, which were excluded by Descartes and yet very important in the application of mathematics to physics.[174] Problems such as the inverse method of tangents were discussed in correspondence with other mathematicians, including Huygens, L'Hôpital, and Newton himself, to whom Leibniz addressed his first direct letter on 17 March 1693 and from whom he received in October a courteous answer.[175] Moreover, L'Hôpital reworked the lectures of Johann Bernoulli, who had taught him in 1691–2, into the first textbook on the calculus, which he published in 1696.[176] The preface (written perhaps by Fontenelle) explained in a clear way the great significance of this discovery for the mathematical treatment of curves and therefore for the application of mathematics to physics:

An Analysis of this kind could by itself lead us to the true principles of curves. Since curves are nothing else than polygons with an infinity of sides and differ amongst themselves only in the difference of the angles which these infinitely small sides form between them, it is the task of the Analysis of infinitesimals to determine the position of these sides in order to have the curvature that they form, that is to say [in order to determine] the tangents of these curves, their perpendiculars, their flex points . . . The polygons inscribed in or circumscribed to the curves, which by the infinite multiplication of their sides are ultimately indistinguishable from them, have always been taken for the curves themselves. But people have stopped there: it is only since the discovery of the Analysis presented here that the extension and fecundity of this idea has been properly recognized.[177]

With the success of L'Hôpital's textbook the calculus was definitely becoming established. At the same time, however, dark clouds announcing the tempestuous controversy over the priority of its discovery began to gather on the horizon. The Swiss mathematician Nicolas Fatio de Duillier (1664–1753), to whom Newton had shown his letters to Leibniz of 1676 (the so-called *epistola prior* and *epistola posterior*), wrote to Huygens on 15 February 1692 overtly claiming that Leibniz had derived his method from Newton without acknowledging his debt to the great English mathematician. Moreover, according to him, Newton's method was much more advanced than Leibniz's.[178] In his correspondence with Leibniz, Huygens did not report Fatio's accusation, limiting himself to noting the Swiss mathematician's assurance that Newton knew "on this matter everything that he, and everything that you have ever discovered, and much more in addition," and that some publication on the matter was forthcoming.[179] Newton, however, was still reluctant to expound his method publicly, despite the urging of English friends worried about the spread of Leibniz's analysis. National pride being at stake, the doyen of English mathematicians, John Wallis, intervened, publishing in the second volume of his own *Opera mathematica* (1693) excerpts from Newton's letters to Leibniz of 1676.[180] Moreover, in the Preface to the first volume (which actually appeared after the second one in 1695), Wallis referred to the two *Epistolae* of Newton as writings in which the English mathematician "had exposed this method to Leibniz," thereby undermining Leibniz's claim to independent discovery.[181]

In the same year in which Wallis's first volume appeared in print, Leibniz replied from the pages of the July issue of the *Acta Eruditorum* to the criticism of the Dutch mathematician Bernard Nieuwentijt (1654–1718) against some aspects of his calculus.[182] Toward the end of the month he received news of the death of Huygens – the man who for over twenty years had been first his mentor and then one of his closest colleagues and correspondents on mathematical and scientific matters. This further loss added to his grief for the recent deaths of Pellisson, Landgraf Ernst, and Bishop Rojas. On 26 July 1695 he confided to Basnage,

I have just become aware, sir, of Huygens's death. It is my fate to write letters to friends who could no longer answer. Prince Ernst, Landgraf of Hessen, and [Veit Ludwig] von Seckendorff[183] could not read my [last] letters, and M. Pellisson in fact read my letter, but death prevented him from writing the answer which he had already promised. The loss of the illustrious Huygens is inestimable. Few people know this as I do. In my view his standing is equal to that of Galileo and Descartes; and aided by what they did, he has surpassed their discoveries. In a word he constituted one of the principal ornaments of this century.[184]

Unus ex nihilo omnia fecit

Apart from the promotion and application of the calculus, Leibniz continued to develop other aspects of mathematics, carrying forward ideas conceived during the previous years, notably his binary arithmetic or dyadic and the *analysis situs* or *characteristica geometrica*.[185] Amongst other things, in one of the papers devoted to the latter he explained the meaning of the sign he employed to indicate the relation of congruence ($\simeq$): "Figures are *congruent* which can be substituted for one another in the same place . . . which I designate as follows: ABC $\simeq$ CDA. For $\sim$ is for me the sign of similarity, and $=$ is the sign of equality, from which I compose the sign of congruence, since figures which are both similar and equal are congruent."[186] As for the dyadic, he found in Duke Rudolf August of Wolfenbüttel a fascinated listener, who imaginatively compared the generation of numbers out of 0 and 1 with the Biblical creation *ex nihilo* by God. In a memo for the duke of 18 May 1696 following their conversations on the matter, Leibniz elaborated on the idea that "everything originates from God and otherwise out of nothing" and that (referring to Luke 10:42) "Unum necessarium" ("only one thing is necessary").[187] In the same memo he also provided examples of the four operations performed according to the binary system.[188] Writing at the beginning of 1697 to Rudolf August to convey his best wishes for the New Year, Leibniz described a medal representing creation *ex nihilo* through the dyadic. As motto to be engraved on the medal he proposed "To produce all things *ex nihilo* [out of nothing]. One is enough" with the addition of a symbolic representation of the dyadic by means of a 0 with a 1 through it.[189] It is possible that a sketch of the medal was appended to the letter. Leibniz certainly tried his hand at it, drawing with the help of his assistants at least three examples of the medal with different inscriptions on them, although none of them exactly matched the final proposal for the Duke.[190]

Rudolf August found the idea enticing but possibly thought that to coin a medal following Leibniz's complex design would have been too difficult and expensive. Instead he issued a simplified seal with the motto *unus ex*

Figure 6.1. As in A I,
13, 128.

nihilo omnia fecit (one made all things ex nihilo) with the symbol proposed by Leibniz at the centre (see Figure 6.1).[191]

Further descriptions of the dyadic, with accounts of its potential and significance, reached as far afield as China. In a letter of early 1697 directed to the Jesuit Claudio Filippo Grimaldi (since 1694 superior of the Chinese mission and president of the 'mathematical tribunal' in Peking) Leibniz reported, among other things, on his progress in mathematics and related fields, including the successful construction of a new model of his calculator. In this account of his achievements a very special place was reserved for the dyadic, which Leibniz saw as a powerful means for the propagation of the Christian faith in that it so beautifully symbolized a concept alien to the Chinese, namely the creation *ex nihilo* through the only one God.[192] As usual, however, this central doctrine of the Christian faith took a distinctive Leibnizian flavour insofar as the dyadic was characterized for Grimaldi also as "Symbol of all things created by the unity [per unitatem] ex nihilo."[193] The idea that the variety and multiplicity of all things can and ought to be reduced to unity was one of the earliest and most constant guidelines of Leibniz's philosophical thought. Moreover, it had not been long since the concept of "real unities" endowed with an active and a passive principle or force had been presented to the broader public as the ultimate elements from which all things resulted,[194] and had even been designated in private letters with the technical word of monad. It seems that in Leibniz's mind the link between his metaphysical doctrine of monads and the dyadic was clear. It was undoubtedly also for its powerful metaphysical symbolism that he favoured the development of a binary arithmetical system over other possible systems he had considered. Back in the spring of 1679, in one of his very first texts mentioning the idea of a binary system, he had written,

It may be that there is only one thing which is conceived through itself, namely God himself, and besides this there is nothing, or privation. This is made clear by an admirable simile. When we count, we commonly use the decimal system, so that when we arrive at ten, we start again from unity. That this is convenient, I do not now dispute; meanwhile, I will show that it is possible to use in its place a binary system... The immense advantages of this system I do not touch on at present; it is enough to have noted in what a wonderful way all numbers are thus expressed by unity and by nothing.[195]

Nearly two decades later, he wrote in a letter of 14 May 1698 to Andreas Morell,

Since all spirits are unities, one can say that God is the primitive unity expressed [exprimée] by all the others according to their capabilities. His goodness moved him to act, and there are in him three primacies [primautés], power, knowledge, and will; from this results the operation or the creature, which is varied according to the different combinations of unity with zero, that is of the positive with the privative, since the privative is nothing but limits and there are limits everywhere in the creature just as there are points everywhere in a line.[196]

Leibniz's Multiculturalism: China, Russia, and Linguistic Studies

Leibniz's rich letter to Grimaldi of early 1697 was not an isolated one. On the contrary, it was part of a wide-ranging and sustained interest in natural, cultural, and religious aspects of China shown by Leibniz, especially since his first meetings in Rome with the Jesuits of the Chinese mission. In 1697, in fact, Leibniz published a collection of documents and writings communicated to him during his correspondence with the Jesuit missionaries, which he presented to the public with a preface of his own.[197] The encounter with China of which these *Novissima Sinica* ("latest news from China") were a fruit was intended by him as a "commerce of light":

I judge that this mission is the greatest affair of our time, as much for the glory of God and the propagation of the Christian religion as for the general good of men and the growth of the arts and sciences, among us as well as among the Chinese. For this is a commerce of light, which could give to us at once their work of thousands of years and render ours to them, and double so to speak our true wealth for one and the other. This is something greater than one imagines.[198]

In Leibniz's great plan – the advancement of all arts and sciences for the common good and the glory of God – China represented an enormous opportunity. Its ancient civilisation had reached independent results in a number of fields (notably the practical arts) comparable in richness and importance to those of Western civilisation.[199] If Europe was still superior in theoretical disciplines such as logic, metaphysics, and mathematics, in Leibniz's view the Chinese excelled in practical philosophy and "a more perfect manner of living" to the point that "if someone expert . . . in the excellence of peoples, were selected as judge, the golden apple would be awarded to the Chinese," were it not for "the divine gift of the Christian religion."[200] In short, Leibniz's "Preface" to the *Novissima Sinica* was a hymn to a multiculturalism in which the international community learns and profits from the treasures of different cultures – a view which placed him at the very forefront of a non-Eurocentric interest in other civilisations. Whereas even the most open of his contemporaries tended to measure other cultures against the standard of a presupposed European superiority, Leibniz genuinely seemed to regard different civilisations as the expression of the same universe from different perspectives.[201] Some things were simply seen better from the perspective of one culture, some things from the perspective of another, as in the case of the same city regarded from different viewpoints. Leibniz's multiculturalism was yet another manifestation of his outlook on reality as an ordered system ultimately governed by a universal harmony in which diversity was not to be feared or denied but celebrated as richness and fecundity.[202]

Leibniz's interest in China, over and above the other civilisations which were progressively being unveiled to the European mind, was apparently derived from his discovery within it of key aspects of his own theoretical and practical vision. Chinese symbolism was powerfully evocative in the context of his own search for a *characteristica universalis* or a universal formal language based on symbols expressing the alphabet of human thoughts. Moreover, from a moral and political point of view, Leibniz regarded China and its enlightened emperor as outstanding examples of a spirit of toleration and respect which had its practical outcome in the avoidance (or at least minimisation) of wars and of other violent means of settling controversies. Whereas in Europe the *Mars Christianissimus*, Louis XIV, had rekindled religious intolerance by abolishing the Edict of Nantes and continued an aggressive policy based on military supremacy, the 'pagan' emperor of China had negotiated a solid peace with Russia (despite China's clear military superiority) and had promulgated an Edict of Toleration in which Buddhism, Christianity, and Islam were granted equal rights.[203] Christianity, for its part, needed to cultivate a similar openness of mind which both recognized in distinctive Chinese traditions the basic truths of natural religion expressed through different names and customs, and tolerated those cultural practices which did not endanger the sincere profession of the Christian faith. In advocating this position, Leibniz was taking a stand on the two main theological controversies dividing accomodationist missionaries (mainly Jesuits) and antiaccomo- dationist missionaries (mainly Franciscans and Dominicans): namely, on the one hand, the issue of the existence in the Chinese language of a lexical equivalent to 'God' and, on the other hand, the so-called 'rites contro- versy'. On both issues Leibniz sided with the Jesuits who, following the conciliatory approach of their pioneer missionary in China, Matteo Ricci (1552–1610), allowed traditional Chinese terms as denoting 'God' and interpreted traditional rites honouring the ancestors and Confucius as basically civic and secular practices devoid of idolatry.[204] In the context of this flexible approach, Leibniz pressed for a missionary effort which pursued the propagation of faith through science (*propagatio fidei per scientiam*) as well as for a Protestant mission.[205]

Within Leibniz's international and multicultural outlook, Russia also came to play a key intermediary role, not only between Europe and China, but between the 'Latin' and 'Germanic' Christian traditions as well. In the first place, Leibniz campaigned for the opening of a land route to China through Russia. Since the sea lanes to China were controlled by Portugal and Spain, among other things, this route constituted the precondition for a Protestant mission.[206] In the second place, he saw in the continuous tradition of the Eastern (or Greek) Christian church reaching back to the apostolic times an invaluable means of correcting unwarranted innovations introduced by the Latin church.[207] In his view, it was only through the union of the three main Christian traditions – the Greek, the Latin, and the Germanic one – that the true teaching of the catholic or universal church could be restored in a truly ecumenical general council:

Nowadays one can divide Christians who acknowledge the ancient councils into three nations: the Greek nation (within which I would like to include some other eastern nations and the Muscovites); the Latin nation, within which I include the Italians, French, and Spaniards; and the German nation which includes the Germans, English, Danes, and Swedes. And I believe that all three are needed to form a General Council, which could make the views of the Church known to us.[208]

Further reasons for cultivating the relationship with Russia included the advancement of science and knowledge through contact with the Slavonic world and the patronage of the new tsar, Peter the Great (1672–1725). The opportunity to approach, if not the tsar himself (as Leibniz had hoped), at least people in his entourage presented itself in August 1697 when Peter the Great sojourned incognito in Coppenbrügge while travelling from Berlin to the Netherlands during his so-called Grand Embassy to western Europe of 1697 and 1698. The extraordinary outlook expressed in this embassy was the product of the young tsar's extraordinary upbringing. Proclaimed joint tsar with his half-brother Ivan in 1682 while still a child, Peter's age and Ivan's precarious health left real power in the hands of their elder sister, Sophia. Sensing the promise of leadership in her half-brother, Sophia made sure that Peter was excluded from government. As a result, Peter grew up away from the confining atmosphere of the palace, trying his hand at occupations such as carpentry, joinery, blacksmithing, and printing, and being exposed to the Western world through frequentation of the colony of foreigners near the village where he lived with his mother. In 1689 he succeeded in removing Sophia from power; at the death of Ivan in 1696 he became sole tsar; and the following year he began a grand tour of western Europe, travelling incognito within the Grand Embassy led by Franz Lefort, Fedor Alekseyevich Golovin, and Prokopy B. Voznitsyn. Although the ostensible objective of the embassy was to enhance the coalition against the Ottoman empire which continued to menace Russia, Peter's broader purposes were to explore western European relations more generally and to enlist foreign advisers for the full range of reforms which he envisaged. The latter aim was obviously music to Leibniz's ears.[209] Although his attempt to contact General Franz Lefort (and through him the tsar) did not meet with success, he gained access to the general's nephew, Peter Lefort, with whom he developed a correspondence centred on Leibniz's researches on Russian and Siberian languages.[210]

Gradually from the mid-1680s and more strikingly in the mid-1690s, Leibniz's interest in the study of national languages had significantly increased. Already in the mid-1680s he was studying the ancient form of German used in the Harz.[211] In subsequent correspondence with Huldreich von Eyben, Hiob Ludolf, and Gerhard Meier, he pursued the study of German language history, actively contributing to Meier's work towards a lexicon of the language of Lower Saxony.[212] Working on the regional level towards national goals, in the winter of 1696–7 he integrated these studies of Germanic linguistics into a far-reaching cultural programme for Wolfenbüttel, proposing to complement an enhanced library and the *Ritterakademie* with a third institution: a linguistic society dedicated to promoting, developing, and supporting the German language.[213] Around the same time he wrote his most important essay on German linguistics, the *Unvorgreiffliche Gedancken betreffend die Ausübung und Verbesserung der Teutschen Sprache* (*Thoughts on the Use and Improvement of the German Language*).[214] In it he claimed that "language is a mirror of thinking [*ein Spiegel des Verstandes*], and that when nations raise this ability of thinking to a high level, at the same time they fully exercise language as well." This thesis reflected Leibniz's conviction that our thought always needs to be supported by "signs," including (but not restricted to) the words of a language. In his view, words – intended as signs (*Zeichen*) both of our thoughts and of things – were necessary not only for communication amongst people but also for the articulation of our own thoughts.[215] That is to say, actual human thoughts always have a linguistic expression. Exercising and improving the German language (or, *mutando mutandis*, any other individual language) therefore meant refining and developing the nation's ability to think. According to Leibniz, German was particularly in need of developing a vocabulary for the expression of metaphysical and moral objects matching its already impressive terminology for concrete, sensible things and practical activities such as mining. On the other hand, this ability of the German language to express sensible things revealed in Leibniz's view its closeness to the *res*, that is, its preservation of the primitive and original relation of language to things on which the development of natural languages was based.[216] Finally, as mentioned above, from 1691 onwards he planned to integrate into his official history of the Guelfs a second main preliminary dissertation devoted to tracing the migration of peoples primarily through the harmony of languages.

These researches into linguistics and etymology seem a regrettable distraction to those approaching Leibniz primarily as a brilliant metaphysician and mathematician. His more particular advocacy of the German language likewise seems out of keeping both with his own practice of writing philosophy in Latin and French and with his international, ecumenical outlook. And his insistence on prefacing his Guelf history with a survey of tribal migrations and linguistic harmony appears yet again to demonstrate his ability to make the worst of a bad assignment. But a more holistic approach finds that these linguistic researches, like virtually all his major endeavours, were not conceived as ends in themselves but were undertaken as means of pursuing Leibniz's most fundamental objectives. His observations on the necessity of improving German, for instance, were related theoretically to his ongoing reflections on the philosophy of language and practically to his desire to promote the institutions of the Holy Roman Empire of the German Nation to a level capable of competing with and counterbalancing the ascendancy of France. His still more ambitious search for the *harmonia linguarum* (well established by predecessors such as Comenius, Bisterfeld, and Alsted) likewise promised to advance both his theological and his philosophical projects. According to Leibniz, the study of the different linguistic groups provided the means to reconstruct the origin and movements of the main ethnic groups[217] and thereby to confirm "the truth of Sacred Scripture."[218] The Bible implied not only that the human race shared a single, common origin but also that it had subsequently branched into three main families, corresponding to the three sons of Noah (Shem, Ham, and Japheth).[219] Japheth was regarded as the ultimate ancestor of the European peoples which, in Leibniz's view, had their origins in the migration of the Japhetic descent from anterior Asia to Scythia, the "vagina gentium".[220] His main (although not exclusive) focus of linguistic investigation therefore became the study of the languages of Anterior Asia, Scythia, and Europe. For this purpose he sent a questionnaire (*Desiderata circa linguas quorundam populorum*) to those of his correspondents who were best placed to obtain relevant language samples and conceived the idea of an "atlas of languages" which would have shown the spread of different tongues and their relations.[221]

From a metaphysical point of view, the *harmonia linguarum* which these painstaking etymological researches progressively unveiled complemented his conception of universal harmony, according to which multiplicity and variety can be ultimately traced back to unity and identity. The harmony of languages was, in a sense, the semiotic equivalent of the monadic expression of the same universe from different perspectives.[222] Viewed from an ethnic standpoint, the universal harmony revealed by the harmony of languages was that of blood and kinship: all branches of the human family derived from a common origin and were interrelated. Viewed from a cultural standpoint, the comprehensive map of linguistic similarities and differences promised to map out the network of distinct but interrelated linguistic systems through which the human race expressed itself. The *harmonia linguarum* thus ultimately revealed the unity in diversity of the human race as an organic and a cultural entity and therefore promised to foster mutual understanding and toleration while confirming the truth of Scripture.

On the other hand, in Leibniz's view, natural languages needed to be complemented by the artificial language, the *characteristica universalis*. Whereas natural languages were the vehicle for expressing human emotions and our aesthetic appreciation of the world, the artificial language (once developed) would have served for the expression of scientific thought, thanks to its fixed and unambiguous correlation between a determinate sign and a determinate concept. In other words, natural language and artificial language corresponded to the two complementary attributes of rational monads – respectively, *appetitus* and *intellectus*. As such they played different roles both with respect to society and with respect to our ability to grasp the world. In the same way in which poetry afforded an understanding of the world for which science could not be substituted, so the *characteristica universalis* was not meant to supersede natural languages.[223]

Alongside the idea of a linguistic society presented to the Wolfenbüttel dukes, in 1697 Leibniz perceived in the electress of Brandenburg, Sophie Charlotte, another opportunity to pursue his project of a German academy of sciences. A letter of 12 October 1697 from the privy cabinet archivist at the Brandenburg court, Johann Jacob Julius Chuno, brought to his attention Sophie Charlotte's wish to establish in Berlin an observatory modelled on the celebrated Parisian *Observatoire*.[224] Writing toward the end of November to Sophie Charlotte, Leibniz enthusiastically endorsed the plan, seeing it as an important step towards the creation in Berlin of a society of sciences.[225]

The Events of 1697 and the Protestant Cause

On the evening of 24 December 1697 further news arrived from Berlin: the Brandenburg diplomat, Ezechiel Spanheim, had been dispatched to Hanover to present to Ernst August a memorandum on the points of agreement and disagreement between the Reformed and Lutheran churches prepared by the Brandenburg court chaplain, Comenius's grandson, Daniel Ernst Jablonski (1660–1741).[226]

The ongoing discussions between Hanover and Brandenburg, in which Leibniz was directly involved, aimed at the reunion of the Protestant churches. These irenical negotiations had been given added impetus by two momentous events of 1697. In June 1697 the duke of Saxony, Friedrich August I, had converted to Catholicism – a move which conveniently gave him access to the Polish crown, to which he was elected as Augustus II later that year. Although the newly Catholic duke of Saxony, like Johann Friedrich in Hanover, chose not to exercise his right to dictate the religion of his subjects, his conversion represented an immense symbolic blow to Lutheranism, which had originated in Saxony 180 years earlier and which had since regarded the Saxon dukes as its most powerful and prestigious protectors within the empire. Worse still, the defection of the Saxon elector to the Catholic camp once again unbalanced the near parity of Catholic and Protestant electors within the imperial Diet so recently established with the elevation of Hanover. Moreover, in October 1697 the treaty of Ryswick, which ended the Nine Years War, included conditions clearly unfavourable for the Protestants: as noted above, it precluded the restoration of Protestantism in territories Catholicised by the French occupation.[227] Faced with both the clear erosion of the Protestant influence and such tangible evidence of its potential effects, the two neighbouring Protestant electorates remaining in northern Germany – Brandenburg and Hanover – felt compelled to reconsider their own religious differences to join forces in defence of the broader Protestant cause. Whereas Hanover was Lutheran territory under a Lutheran Prince, Ernst August (who was in turn married to a follower of the Reformed confession, Sophie), Brandenburg had been ruled since the beginning of the century by a Reformed dynasty despite the fact that the majority of the population still adhered to Lutheranism.[228] The arrival of Sophie Charlotte from Hanover and the flow towards Berlin of Reformed refugees – notably the Huguenots fleeing France after the revocation of the Edict of Nantes in 1685 – further exacerbated a complex religious situation. No wonder that Ernst August and Friedrich III were politically best advised to try to reconcile Lutheran and Reformed churches – an enterprise in which Leibniz eagerly enlisted his help.

For Leibniz as well, the mid-1690s marked a turning point. By 1695 his most trusted Catholic patrons and discussion partners – Boineburg, Schönborn, Johann Friedrich, Pellisson, Ernst von Hessen-Rheinfels, and Bishop Rojas – were all dead. The events of 1697 greatly alarmed him. With the prospects of a comprehensive ecclesiastical reunion temporarily diminished and the threat of a serious erosion of Protestantism in the empire worryingly heightened, Leibniz's focus shifted from his long-standing search for the reconciliation of Catholicism and Protestantism to the narrower project of the reunion of Lutherans and Calvinists, Evangelicals and Reformed, together with the political project of ensuring a Protestant (and indeed Hanoverian) succession to the English throne.[229]

Christmas of 1697 was not, however, the best time for trying to secure Duke Ernst August's support for the church reunion project. Since August he had been seriously ill; and assisted by the wonderful "steadfastness" and "greatest loyal tenderness" of his wife, he died in Herrenhausen on 2 February 1698.[230] The death of another princely employer marked another clear watershed in Leibniz's Hanoverian career; and another development, less dramatic but scarcely less important for the next phase of Leibniz's life, coincided with it very closely in time. Spanheim had brought from Brandenburg not only the invitation to Hanover to discuss church reunion but also an invitation to Leibniz to come to Berlin for an audience with Sophie Charlotte.[231] The next stage of Leibniz's career would be marked in no small part by the complementary activities of bridging Lutherans and Reformed, and shuttling between Hanover and Berlin.

Notes

1. A III, 4, 599. See also another version of the letter (A III, 4, 609 and Huygens, *Oeuvres complètes*, 9, 1901, p. 522), in which Leibniz wrote, "I am distracted by very different occupations which seem to demand my complete attention. And it is only through some escapades that I manage to get away from them from time to time."
2. A I, 7, 199.
3. Around 1696, at the green age of fifty, he seems to have proposed marriage; but since his intended demanded time to think it over, he lost interest until he realized that he had left the whole business of settling down till too late. The source of this tale is Leibniz's secretary and biographer, Johann Georg Eckhart (see *Lebensbeschreibung*, p. 198).
4. See Eckhart, *Lebensbeschreibung*, pp. 198–9. Cf. also Gerda Utermöhlen, "Die Rolle fürstlicher Frauen im Leben und Wirken von Leibniz," and George MacDonald Ross, "Leibniz's Exposition of His System to Queen Sophie Charlotte and Other Ladies." In *Leibniz in Berlin*. Ed. by Hans Poser and Albert Heinekamp. Stuttgart: Steiner, 1990, respectively pp. 44–60 and 61–9.
5. A I, 10, 143. Trans. WF, 30.
6. Between the summer of 1690 and the end of 1697 his general correspondence alone fills fifteen thick volumes of the on-going Akademie-Ausgabe (cf. A I, 6–14

and the *Harzbergbau 1692–1696 Supplement Band*). To this correspondence must be added Leibniz's more specifically philosophical, mathematical, scientific, and technical letters only partially published to date by the Akademie-Ausgabe.

7. A I, 14, 202.

8. Dutens VI, 1, 59.

9. See Müller–Krönert, *Leben und Werk*, p. 106.

10. See the *Harzbergbau Supplement Band* in A I.

11. *Specimen Dynamicum, Pro Admirandi Naturae legibus circa Corporum vires et mutuas actiones detegendis, et ad suas causas revocandis*. In *Acta Eruditorum* (April 1695): 145–157.

12. *Journal des Sçavans* of Monday 27 June 1695, pp. 294–300, and of Monday 4 July 1695, pp. 301–6.

13. See below.

14. This psychosomatic crisis is documented in Ekkehard Görlich, *Leibniz als Mensch und Kranker*. Hanover, 1987 (Dissertation for the Doctorate in Medicine), chap. 8 (see esp. pp. 117–18).

15. A I, 12, 476.

16. *Definitio Brevis Scientiae Generalis*, summer 1683–beginning 1685* (A VI, 4, 532). After 1688, the only text in which Leibniz spoke explicitly of *scientia generalis* appears to be a letter to Andreas Ludwig Königsmann of 30 October 1712 (LBr 491, Bl. 4; published by Antonio Lamarra in *Studia Leibnitiana* 24 (1992), 144): "Moreover natural theology especially needs metaphysics or *scientia generalis* which if properly treated would be of great importance but which remains little known." I owe this information and this quotation to Arnaud Pelletier, who has patiently combed Leibniz's Nachlaß searching for the *scientia generalis* after 1688. Although it is certainly possible that Leibniz mentioned the *scientia generalis* elsewhere in the mountain of his papers, there can be little doubt that, compared with the mass of writings devoted to it in the decade between 1678 and 1688, his work on this subject declined dramatically after his preparations to depart for Italy in early 1689. On the various meanings in which Leibniz spoke of *scientia generalis* between 1678 and 1688 see chap. II. 4.

17. See Klopp X, 7–21 (esp. pp. 9–21); trans. by Riley in Leibniz, *Political Writings*, pp. 103–10 (see esp. pp. 105–10). Cf. also *La Félicité*, 1694–8* (Grua, 579–84; pp. 581–4 are translated by Riley in Leibniz, *Political Writings*, pp. 83–4).

18. See esp. Leibniz for Duke Ernst August (*Reisebericht*), autumn 1690 (A I, 5, N. 396).

19. See Leibniz to Otto Grote, end of June 1690 (A I, 5, 599).

20. See Pertz I, 4, 227–39 and Leibniz, *Schriften und Briefe zur Geschichte*, pp. 800–837. The *Synopsis*, revised by Leibniz a number of times, reached its final form around 1695 (see Scheel, "Leibniz als Historiker des Welfenhauses," p. 250 and Leibniz, *Schriften und Briefe zur Geschichte*, pp. 800–801). Cf. also Pertz I, 4, pp. 240–55; A I, 6, N. 21; Eduard Bodemann, ed., "Leibnizens Entwürfe zu seinen Annalen von 1691 und 1692." *Zeitschrift des Historischen Vereins für Niedersachsen* (1885): 1–58; and the unpublished Ms XXIII 170 Bl. 15–30 (Hanover, Niedersächsische Landesbibliothek).

21. See A I, 6, N. 20–21.

22. See esp. A IV, 4, N. 29–77. On the Sachsen-Lauenburg claim see chap. II. 4.

23. See Leibniz to Duke Ernst August, 11 October 1690 (A I, 6, N. 3).

24. See Müller–Krönert, *Leben und Werk*, p. 107, correcting A I, 6, N. 17.

25. The first library secretary, Johann Thiele Reinerding, was helped from 1692 onwards by a second secretary, Johann Georg Sieverds. After 1705 Lorenz Hertel served as librarian under Leibniz, eventually succeding him as director in 1716.

26. See Leibniz to Johann Thiele Reinerding, beginning of July 1691, A I, 6, N. 48. See also O. von Heinemann, *Die Herzogliche Bibliothek zu Wolfenbüttel*. 2nd ed. Wolfenbüttel: Zwissler, 1894, pp. 114–15. Several texts on the structure and organisation of a library are collected in A IV, 5 and A IV, 6.

27. T. H. Ohnsorge, "Leibniz als Staatsbediensteter." In *Leibniz. Sein Leben, sein Wirken, seine Welt.* Ed. by W. Totok and C. Haase. Hanover: Verlag für Literatur und Zeitgeschehen, 1966, p. 177.

28. See Leibniz to Duke Ernst August, mid-January 1691 (*Entwurf der Welfengeschichte*) (A I, 6, 23–4) and A I, 6, 442. See also Pertz I, 4, 240–41 and A I, 11, lv–lvi.

29. See Hans-Joachim Waschkies, "Leibniz' geologische Forschungen im Harz." In *Leibniz und Niedersachsen.* Ed. by Herbert Breger and Friedrich Niewöhner. Stuttgart: Steiner, 1999, pp. 203–4.

30. See Leibniz to Jean Gallois, mid-October 1682 (A III, 3, 724–6) and Leibniz to Bernard Le Bovier de Fontenelle, in G. W. Leibniz, *Lettres et opuscules inédits.* Ed. by Louis Alexander Foucher de Careil. Paris, 1854, p. 197. Attention to both letters is drawn by Hans-Joachim Waschkies, "Leibniz' geologische Forschungen im Harz," pp. 199–201. On the early modern inquiry into the history of the earth see Paolo Rossi, *The Dark Abyss of Time: The History of the Earth and the History of Nations from Hooke to Vico.* Trans. by Lydia G. Cochrane. Chicago: University of Chicago Press, 1984.

31. See Descartes, *Principia*, III. 45– IV. 44.

32. See Descartes, *Principia*, III. 45. Quoted by Mugnai, *Leibniz: Vita*, pp. 91–2.

33. On Stensen see chap. II. 4.

34. See Waschkies, "Leibniz' geologische Forschungen im Harz," pp. 197–8 and Mugnai, *Leibniz: Vita*, p. 93.

35. See Basil Willey, "Introduction," in Thomas Burnet, *The Sacred Theory of the Earth.* London: Centaur Press, 1965, p. 5.

36. See Leibniz's summary of the *Protogaea* in the *Theodicy*, §§ 244–5 (here § 245, GP VI, 263). See also Mugnai, *Leibniz: Vita*, pp. 94–101.

37. Leibniz to Adamus Adamandus Kochanski, beginning of 1693 in E. Bodemann and S. Dickstein, eds., "Korespondencya Kochańskiego i Leibniza." *Prace Matematyczno-fizyczne* 12 (1901): 226–73 (here p. 262).

38. See *Acta Eruditorum* (January 1693): 40–42; Leibniz to Ludolf Hugo, 14 October 1694 (A I, 10, 74) and Leibniz to Ernst August, beginning of November* 1694 (A I, 10, 79). See also *Theodicy*, §§ 244–5. The *Protogaea* was published posthumously in 1749 by Ch. L. Scheidt. A modern edition (Latin text with French

translation) appeared in 1993 (Toulouse: Presses Universitaire du Mirail; introduction by Jean-Marie Barrande, pp. i–xxxi).

39. See Pertz I, 4, 240.
40. See Leibniz to Bernstorff, 8 December 1714 (Klopp XI, 22–3). On Azzo II see chap. II. 5.
41. See Niedersächsiche Landesbibliothek, LH XXIII vol. VII Bl. 33.
42. See Riley in Leibniz, *Political Writings*, p. 165; Scheel, "Leibniz als Historiker des Welfenhauses," pp. 262–3; Leibniz, *Schriften und Briefe zur Geschichte*, pp. 131–217.
43. See Ravier 37–8.
44. The *Lettre sur la Connexion des Maisons de Brunsvic et d'Este* was published in Hanover by the court printer in very few copies. It is reproduced in G. W. Leibniz, *Epistolae ad diversos*. Ed. by Chr. Kortholt. 4 vols. Leipzig, 1734–42, vol. 3, p. 214 ff. and in Leibniz, *Schriften und Briefe zur Geschichte*, pp. 896–906. Now also in A IV, 6. On the *Dissertatio de Origine Germanorum*, see Ravier 40.
45. See Riley in Leibniz, *Political Writings*, p. 165; Scheel, "Leibniz als Historiker des Welfenhauses," pp. 262–3; Leibniz, *Schriften und Briefe zur Geschichte*, pp. 131–217.
46. A I, 6, 40–41.
47. On the conspiracy see Schnath, *Geschichte Hannovers*, vol. I, pp. 575–91. On the dynastic situation underlying Maximilian Wilhelm's claims see chap. II. 4.
48. See Leibniz's reports to Landgraf Ernst in letters of 13 and 30 January 1692 (A I, 7, 243 and A I, 7, 260).
49. See A I, 7, N. 77, N. 78; A I, 8, N. 64.
50. See A I, 7, 260. Cf. also Klopp V, 115–17, 117–48.
51. The estates of Bohemia had consistently elected Habsburgs as kings of Bohemia since the battle of Mohac (1526), with the notable exception of Friedrich V of the Palatinate in 1619–20.
52. See esp. A IV, 4, N. 70–77. Further texts are published in A IV, 5. Cf. also A I, 4, N. 173; A I, 7, N. 46, N. 60; A I, 8, N. 47, N. 59, N. 65, N. 71.
53. See A I, 7, xxix.
54. See in particular Leibniz to Otto Grote, "Promemoria über Reichserzämter," end of December 1691 (A I, 7, N. 46, esp. p. 66) and Scheel, "Leibniz als Historiker des Welfenhauses," pp. 268–9. On Hanover's long battle between 1692 and 1714 to have its electoral status fully recognised, see Schnath, *Geschichte Hannovers*, vol. II, pp. 12–31; vol. III, pp. 398–448.
55. In late 1698 a rumour reached Leibniz that the Jesuit Antoine Verjus was trying to procure for him the position of librarian to Louis XIV. See Leibniz to Le Thorel, 5 December 1698 (A I, 16, 306).
56. A I, 8, 269.
57. See Leibniz to Jacob Auguste Barnabas Comte Des Viviers, May 1692 (A I, 8, N. 158).
58. On the onset of this conflict while Leibniz was in Vienna cf. chap. II. 5.

59. See the texts published in A IV, 4, N. 13–15, dating back to the end of October 1688–January 1689.

60. The title is a quotation from Ovid, *Metamorphoses*, IV, 28. The draft of the introduction and the book itself are published in A IV, 5, N. 67–68. For the history of this work see the very helpful introductory note to the Academy edition of *Fas est et ab hoste doceri*.

61. See A I, 10, N. 186.

62. On Leibniz's efforts in relation to the Nine Years War see also *Considerations sur les moyens de faire une paix juste et raisonnable,* 1694-mid-1695 (published in A IV, 5).

63. A I, 14, 113. See also Leibniz to James Cressett, 16 November 1697 (A I, 14, 689–90).

64. See A I, *Supplementband Harzbergbau*, xxix; A I, 6, N. 1; A I, 8 N. 305.

65. See A I, *Supplementband Harzbergbau*, xxix–xxx and N. 6.

66. See A I, *Supplementband Harzbergbau*, xxxi, N. 21 ff., N. 244.

67. See A I, *Supplementband Harzbergbau*, xxxi–xlv (esp. pp. xxxi, xliv–xlv).

68. See A I, 9, N. 33.

69. See Ravier 263; Bodemann, *Briefwechsel*, p. 366 (N. 966); *Project d'une histoire annale de médecine,* February 1694 (A IV, 5, N. 83). See also *Entwurff eines Artikels so in die Hanoverische Medicinalische Verordnungen kommen köndte,* beginning of 1694 (A IV, 5, N. 82); Leibniz to Chilian Schrader, respectively, 14 January and 19 February 1694 (A I, 10, N. 116, N. 155; Leibniz to Germain Brice, February 1694 (A I, 10, N. 163); Germain Brice to Leibniz, 21 May 1694 (A I, 10, N. 262); Ravier 135 (published in Dutens II, ii, 162–3).

70. Cf. texts published in A IV, 6.

71. See Leibniz to Ernst August, end of December 1692 (A I, 8, N. 80); Leibniz to Duke Rudolf August, mid-December 1692 (A I, 8, N. 73) and 30 June 1693 (A I, 9, N. 39).

72. See Müller-Krönert, *Leben und Werk*, pp. 124, 129; Aiton, *Leibniz*, p. 172. Crafft died on 6 April 1697.

73. See A I, 11, N. 40. On the Sophie Dorothea affair cf. Schnath, *Geschichte Hannovers*, vol. II, pp. 121–220 (esp. pp. 161–2 and 194 ff.). Further critical literature is cited in A I, 11, 51.

74. See A I, 10, N. 439 and N. 444; A I, 11, xxxii–xxxiii; Gerd van den Heuvel, "Leibniz zwischen Hannover und Berlin." In *Leibniz in Berlin*. Ed. by Hans Poser and Albert Heinekamp. Stuttgart: Steiner, 1990, p. 272.

75. Cf. texts published in A IV, 6 (quotation from *Sur le livre intitulé Jus Feciale Divinum de Pufendorf*). On Leibniz and Pufendorf see also chap. I. 3. For a later, still negative judgement of Pufendorf's work see Guhrauer, *Leibnitz*, II, *Anmerkungen*, pp. 15–16.

76. See Schnath, *Geschichte Hannovers*, vol. II, p. 384. Reproduced by Rescher, "Leibniz finds a Niche," p. 31.

77. See Müller-Krönert, *Leben und Werk*, pp. 105, 108, 140; Ohnsorge, "Leibniz als Staatsbediensteter," p. 181; A I, 6, xxv.

78. Scheel, "Leibniz als Historiker des Welfenhauses," p. 269.

79. A I, 7, 261.

80. Cf. Maria Rosa Antognazza, "Leibniz and Religious Toleration: The Correspondence with Paul Pellisson-Fontanier." *American Catholic Philosophical Quarterly* 76, 4 (2002): 601–22.

81. Paul Pellisson-Fontanier, *Reflexions sur les differens de la religion. Quatrième partie. Ou Réponse aux Objections envoyées d'Allemagne, sur l'unité de l'Eglise, et sur la question, si elle peut tolérer les Sectes.* Paris: chez la Veuve de Gabriel Martin, 1691.

82. Paul Pellisson-Fontanier, *De la tolerance des religions, Lettres de M. de Leibniz et Réponses de M. Pellisson, Ou quatrième partie des Reflexions sur les differends de la Religion.* Paris: Jean Anisson, 1692. See Antognazza, "Leibniz and Religious Toleration," esp. pp. 604–12.

83. Leibniz referred repeatedly to the Jesuits and, in particular, to Jacobus Pavya de Andrade. Other theologians (including L. Molina) are mentioned in A I, 6, 82–3.

84. Leibniz to Duchess Sophie for Paul Pellisson-Fontanier, beginning of August* 1690 (A I, 6, 78–9).

85. See for instance Leibniz for Paul Pellisson-Fontanier, end of October 1690 (A I, 6, 117 and 119) and Leibniz's marginal note on his copy of the fourth part of the *Reflexions* (A I, 6, 94). See also A I, 6, 80; A I, 6, 164.

86. This further phase of the correspondence between Bossuet and Leibniz is summarized by Eisenkopf, *Leibniz und die Einigung der Christenheit*, pp. 69–72.

87. See Leibniz to Marie de Brinon, 26 July 1691 (A I, 6, N. 102). The Imperial document and its translation are published in A I, 6, N. 102[a].

88. See Marie de Brinon to Leibniz, 31 August 1691 (A I, 7, N. 90) and Jacques-Bénigne Bossuet to Marie de Brinon, 29 September 1691 (A I, 7, N. 96). On the Hanover negotiations of 1683 see chap. II. 4.

89. Published in Jacques-Bénigne Bossuet, *Oeuvres complètes*. Ed. by F. Lachat. 31 vols. Paris, 1862–79, vol. 17, Paris, 1864, pp. 294–431.

90. See A I, 7, N. 115, N. 117, N. 119.

91. See Jacques-Bénigne Bossuet, *De scripto qui titulus: Cogitationes privatae… Episcopi Meldensis sententia* (published in Bossuet, *Oeuvres complètes*, vol. 17, pp. 458–99); Paul Pellisson-Fontanier to Leibniz, 29 June 1692 (A I, 8, 119–20); Jacques-Bénigne Bossuet to Leibniz, 26 August 1692 (A I, 8, N. 97). See also Bossuet's longer letter to Leibniz of 28 August (A I, 8, N. 98) which accompanied a French translation of the *Sententia* intended for Duchess Sophie and her sister, Louise Hollandine.

92. See for instance Leibniz to Huldreich von Eyben, October 1692 (A I, 8, 489).

93. The conclusion of the *Sententia* in both the original Latin and Bossuet's French translation is published in Klopp VII, 216–7.

94. See Leibniz to Pellisson, 8 December 1692 (A I, 8, 207) and Pellisson to Leibniz, 1 January 1693 (A I, 9, N. 61).

95. See A I, 7, 156–8.

96. On the Basel case cf. Eisenkopf, *Leibniz und die Einigung der Christenheit*, pp. 71, 187–91.

97. See Bossuet to Leibniz, 12 April 1694 (A I, 10, N. 80).

98. See Leibniz to Bossuet, 12 July 1694 (A I, 10, N. 90).

99. Published in *Correspondance de Bossuet*. Ed. by C. Urbain and E. Levesque. 15 vols. New Edition Paris, 1909, vol. 6, pp. 523–8. English trans. in WF, 31–5.

100. A I, 10, 143. English trans. WF, 30. See also the unsent letter to Bossuet of 3 July 1694 (A I, 10 N. 88) indicating that Leibniz was about to send some "Meditations Philosophiques." Whereas the editors of Bossuet's *Correspondance*, Urbain and Levesque, identified these "Meditations Philosophiques" with the *Système nouveau*, according to the Akademie-Ausgabe it is more probable that Leibniz was referring to the *Réflexions sur l'avancement de la Métaphysique réelle* sent as an enclosure to Leibniz's letter to Bossuet of 12 July 1694 (A I, 10, 143).

101. A I, 7, 38.

102. See Howard Hotson, "Leibniz and Millenarianism." In Antognazza and Hotson, eds., *Alsted and Leibniz on God, the Magistrate and the Millennium*, esp. pp. 170–77.

103. Cf. Allison P. Coudert, *Leibniz and the Kabbalah*, Dordrecht: Kluwer, 1995, chap. 5 and Hotson, "Leibniz and Millenarianism," pp. 187–92.

104. See for instance Leibniz's entries in his *Tagesbuch* of August 1696 (Pertz I, 4, 193, 198).

105. *Tagesbuch* (3 August 1696–21 April 1697). Published in Pertz I, 4, 183–224. On the meetings with van Helmont in Sophie's presence see Leibniz to Thomas Burnett of Kemney, 17 March 1696 (A I, 12, 478).

106. A I, 13, 399–400. Trans. by Hotson in "Leibniz and Millenarianism," pp. 187–8.

107. See Hotson in "Leibniz and Millenarianism," pp. 189, 192. The importance of the relationship between van Helmont and Leibniz for the adoption by Leibniz of the term "monad" has been investigated by a number of authors. See for instance Anne Becco, "Leibniz et François-Mercure van Helmont: Bagatelle pour des monades." In *Magia Naturalis und die Entstehung der Modernen Naturwissenschaften. Symposion der Leibniz-Gesellschaft: Hannover, 14. und 15. November 1975*. Wiesbaden: Steiner, 1978, pp. 119–41 (Studia Leibnitiana Sonderheft, vol. 7). On the appearance of the term "monad" in Leibniz's philosophical vocabulary see below.

108. See for instance A I, 4, 433; A I, 15, 489; Dutens V, 483.

109. See A I, 12, 367.

110. Stephen Nye, *Considerations on the Explications of the Doctrine of the Trinity, By Dr. Wallis, Dr. Sherlock, Dr. S-th, Dr. Cudworth, and Mr. Hooker*. London, 1693.

111. Cf. above.

112. See *Extrait*, 1693*, and *Remarques sur le livre d'un Antitrinitaire Anglois*, 1693*, in Maria Rosa Antognazza, "Inediti leibniziani sulle polemiche trinitarie," *Rivista di Filosofia neo-scolastica* 83, 4 (1991), pp. 539–45, 546–50. The definitive edition is now published in A IV, 5, N. 60–61.

113. A detailed commentary can be found in Antognazza, *Leibniz on the Trinity and the Incarnation*, pp. 91–110.

114. See Antognazza, *Leibniz on the Trinity and the Incarnation*, pp. 111–19.

115. William Freke, *A Dialogue By Way of Question and Answer, Concerning the Deity. All the Responses Being Taken Verbatim out of the Scriptures. – A Brief, but Clear Confutation of the Doctrine of the Trinity*. London, 1693.

116. See A I, 10, 18.

117. See A I, 10, 19.

118. See Friedrich Simon Löffler to Leibniz, 14 January 1694 (A I, 10, N. 469) and Leibniz to Friedrich Simon Löffler, 17 March 1694 (A I, 10, 681–2).

119. See Friedrich Simon Löffler to Leibniz, 22 December 1694 (A I, 10, N. 489).

120. See Leibniz to Friedrich Simon Löffler, 2 January 1695 (A I, 11, 122).

121. See Friedrich Simon Löffler to Leibniz, 26 January 1695 (A I, 11, 195).

122. See Leibniz for Friedrich Simon Löffler, *Sceleton Demonstrationis* (A I, 11, N. 163). Enclosed in Leibniz's letter to Löffler of 5 February 1695 (A I, 11, N. 160). See also A I, 11, N. 161–162.

123. Dutens VI, 65.

124. I say "explicitly" because hints of his metaphysics of substance were contained in other previously published texts.

125. *De Primae Philosophiae Emendatione, et de Notione Substantiae* (GP IV, 469). Trans. L 433.

126. See respectively Ravier 139 and 141.

127. More details can be found in the extensive and very helpful editorial notes in A I, 10, N. 90 and WF, 27–30. See also the opening paragraphs of the *Système nouveau* (GP IV, 477).

128. See Pellisson to Leibniz, 23 October 1691 (A I, 7, 172); *Essai de dynamique*, in FC, *Oeuvres*, I, 470–83 (first version of January 1692); Leibniz to Pellisson, 18 January 1692 (A I, 7, 247); Pellisson to Leibniz, 19 February 1692 (A I, 7, 272–3); Pellisson to Leibniz, 10 April 1692 (A I, 7, 305–6). A later version of the *Essai de dynamique* probably written around 1693 is published in GM VI, 215–31.

129. See Aiton, *Leibniz*, p. 191.

130. A I, 141–2; WF, 28. Cf. Aiton, *Leibniz*, p. 191. Leibniz is referring to his *Règle générale de la composition des mouvemens* published in the *Journal des Sçavans* of 7 September 1693, pp. 417–19.

131. See respectively GP I, 380–85, 390–94. See also WF, 37–8, 52–5.

132. See in particular Leibniz to Bossuet, 12 July 1694 (A I, 10, 142); Michel Angelo Fardella to Leibniz, LBr 258, Bl. 234–7; Amable de Tourreil to Leibniz, 16 December 1690 (GP VII, 443); Leibniz to Amable de Tourreil, April 1691 (GP VII, 446–9; excerpt published on pages 259–61 of the *Journal des Sçavans* of 18 June 1691); Simon Foucher to Leibniz, 26 May 1689 (trans. from the manuscript in WF, 38).

133. See Leibniz to Louis Cousin, 7 July 1694 (LBr 437, Bl. 114) (unsent).

134. *Système nouveau* (WF, 11).

135. Cf. WF, 39 (see especially the very informative n. 13).

136. Published in GM VI, 234–54 (both first and second part); trans. in AG, 117–38. Critical edition by Hans Günter Dosch, Glenn W. Most, and Enno Rudolph (Hamburg: Meiner, 1982). G. W. Most, "Zur Entwicklung von Leibniz' *Specimen Dynamicum*." In *Leibniz' Dynamica*. Ed. by Albert Heinekamp. Studia Leibnitiana Sonderheft, vol. 13. Wiesbaden: Steiner, pp. 148–63 offers an account of the composition of the *Specimen Dynamicum* with particular regard to the differences between the final text and an earlier draft originally entitled *Admirandae Naturae Leges*. Only part one of the *Specimen* was published in the *Acta Eruditorum*; part two remained unpublished in Leibniz's lifetime. Some of the most philosophically interesting ideas of the *Specimen* are expounded in a further important essay on dynamics dated May 1702 which also remained unpublished during Leibniz's life; see GM VI, 98–106 or GP IV, 393–400; AG, 250–56.

137. The genesis of this conception can be traced back as far as the *Confessio Naturae contra Atheistas* of 1668. Cf. chap. I. 2.

138. Cf. Adams, *Leibniz*, p. 339 and Mugnai, *Leibniz: Vita*, p. 57. For an in-depth discussion of the complex relationship between Leibnizian physics and metaphysics see in particular Adams, *Leibniz*, pp. 378–99, and Garber, "Leibniz and the Foundations of Physics" and "Leibniz: Physics and Philosophy."

139. GM VI, 241; AG, 124–5.

140. See *Specimen Dynamicum* (GM VI, 238; AG, 121–2).

141. See Garber, "Leibniz: Physics and Philosophy," p. 290 and "Leibniz and the Foundations of Physics," p. 80.

142. See Adams, *Leibniz*, p. 378.

143. See *Specimen Dynamicum* (GM VI, 236–7; AG, 119–20).

144. *Specimen Dynamicum* (GM VI, 237; AG, 120). Attention to this passage is drawn by Garber, "Leibniz: Physics and Philosophy," p. 292.

145. See *Système nouveau* (GP IV, 477; WF, 10). It should be noted that GP presents two different versions of the *Système nouveau*, namely the first draft (GP IV, 471–7), possibly corresponding to the version ready in July 1694, and the fifth extant manuscript (GP IV, 477–87) in which are recorded emendations which appear to postdate the version printed in the *Journal des Sçavans*. WF, 10–20 is a translation from the *Journal des Sçavans*. Cf. WF, 9–10.

146. The issue of continuity–discontinuity in Leibniz's treatment of substance in the writings of the 1680s and in the *Système nouveau* is debated in recent literature. For a view advocating discontinuity see in particular Wilson, *Leibniz's metaphysics*, chap. 5; for a view favouring basic continuity (notwithstanding certain changes) see Donald Rutherford, "Metaphysics: The Late Period." In *The Cambridge Companion to Leibniz*. Ed. by Nicholas Jolley. New York and Cambridge: Cambridge University Press, 1995, pp. 124–32.

147. *Système nouveau* (GP IV, 478; WF, 11).

148. *Système nouveau* (GP IV, 479, 482–3; WF, 12, 16).

149. See *Système nouveau* (GP IV, 483–7; WF, 17–20).

150. On the introduction of the term 'monad' see below.

151. Published in GP I, 424–7 and GP IV, 487–90.

152. See GP IV, 496; WF, 51.

153. See Leibniz to L'Hôpital, 30 September 1695 (GM II, 297). In this letter as well Leibniz uses the expression "pre-established harmony."

154. See Ravier 147; GP IV, 493–8; WF, 40, 47–52. Leibniz's reply to Foucher is also known as the "first explanation" of the *Système nouveau*.

155. See GP III, 121–2; WF, 61, 64–5.

156. See GP IV, 498–500.

157. See Ravier 145. On Basnage's omission and the first use of the expression "pre-established harmony" see the extensive note in WF, 137.

158. See Ravier 148; GP IV, 500–503; WF, 65–7.

159. See esp. the very helpful study of Anne Becco, "Aux sources de la monade: Paléographie et lexicographie leibniziennes." *Les Études Philosophiques* 3 (1975): 279–94.

160. A VI, 1, 7.

161. A VI, 1, 173, 185, 220, 222.

162. See Ludwig Stein, *Leibniz und Spinoza. Ein Beitrag zur Entwicklungsgeschichte der Leibnizschen Philosophie*. Berlin: Georg Reimer, 1890, pp. 197–206; J. Lewis McIntyre, *Giordano Bruno*. London: Macmillan, 1903, pp. 345–7; Becco, "Aux sources de la monade," p. 293.

163. See Becco, "Aux sources de la monade," pp. 285–94.

164. GP IV, 491; WF, 45. The paleographical studies of Becco document that the qualification of substances as "simples" found in the title of section XXXV of the *Discours de Métaphysique* (1686) is an addition by Leibniz probably dating as late as 1708–9. Moreover, she argues that the manuscript in which the expression "substantiae simplices" appears (LH IV 3, 2a, Bl. 3v), dated 1690 by Bodemann, *Handschriften*, p. 67 on the basis of the watermark, was actually written later. Finally, in her view, the occurrence "substance simple" in the fifth extant version of the *Système nouveau* should be dated 1695. See Becco, "Aux sources de la monade," pp. 280–83.

165. See GM II, 295. Attention is drawn to this letter by Müller–Krönert, *Leben und Werk*, p. 133.

166. Daniel Garber has argued that an important strand of Leibniz's thought in the middle years (that is, roughly until the mid- or late 1690s) proposed "a world of corporeal substances" which is "different from the world of the *Monadology*." See esp. Garber, "Leibniz and the Foundations of Physics," p. 75.

167. In *Nouvelles lettres et opuscules inédits de Leibniz*. Ed. by A. Foucher de Careil. Paris: Auguste Durand, 1857, p. 326.

168. On the relationship between Leibniz's analysis of the mathematical continuum and his concept of substance see the outstanding explanation by Mugnai, *Introduzione*, pp. 96–121, upon which I draw.

169. These quotations are from Leibniz's first remarks on Foucher's objections (1695) (GP IV 491–2; WF, 45–6; I have modified the WF translation on what seems to me one important point). Similar considerations are to be found, for instance, in Leibniz's letter to Sophie of 31 October 1705 (see GP VII, 558–65).

170. GP VII, 303; trans. by Morris and Parkinson in Leibniz, *Philosophical Writings*, pp. 137–8. Cf. also *Principium meum est, quicquid existere potest, et aliis compatibile est, id existere*, 12 December 1676 (A VI, 3, 582). Attention to this text is drawn by Massimo Mugnai and Enrico Pasini in their Italian translation of Leibniz's philosophical writings (G. W. Leibniz, *Scritti filosofici*. 3 vols. Turin: Utet, 2000, vol. I, p. 118).

171. GP VII, 273. Attention to this text is drawn by Mugnai and Pasini in Leibniz, *Scritti filosofici*, vol. I.

172. See *Nouvelles lettres et opuscules inédits de Leibniz*, p. 327. See also A I, 13, N. 248, N. 270, N. 299, N. 321.

173. For Leibniz's own solution of problems through the application of his infinitesimal analysis see for instance Ravier 110, 111, 114, 115, 149.

174. See Ravier 119, 136. Cf. also Ravier 125, 134. Cf. Aiton, *Leibniz*, pp. 202–3, 206.

175. See GM I, 168–9; *The Correspondence of Isaac Newton*, vol. 3, pp. 257–8, 285–6, and Aiton, *Leibniz*, pp. 203–5.

176. Guillaume François Antoine de L'Hôpital, *Analyse des infiniment petits, pour l'intelligence des lignes courbes*. Paris: de l'imprimerie royale, 1696. See Mugnai, *Leibniz: Vita*, pp. 80–81.

177. L'Hôpital, *Analyse des infinement petits* [pp. 2–3].

178. See Fatio de Duillier to Huygens, 15 February 1692 (in Huygens, *Oeuvres complètes*, vol. 10, pp. 257–8).

179. See Huygens to Leibniz, 15 March 1692 (A III, 5, 280 and Huygens, *Oeuvres complètes*, vol. 10, p. 270).

180. Wallis's *Algebra*, published in 1685, already included some more limited passages from Newton's letters.

181. See "Praefatio" in John Wallis, *Opera Mathematica*. vol. 1. Oxoniae: E Theatro Sheldoniano, 1695, [p. 3] and A III, 1, xxxvi.

182. See Ravier 142. Cf. also the *Addenda* published in the August issue of the *Acta Eruditorum* in which the death of Huygens is mentioned (Ravier 143). On the important controversy on the calculus started by Nieuwentijt's criticism in 1694 see Bernhard Vermeulen, "The Metaphysical Presuppositions of Nieuwentijt's Criticism of Leibniz's Higher-Order Differentials." In *300 Jahre "Nova Methodus" von G. W. Leibniz (1684–1984). Symposon der Leibniz-Gesellschaft . . . 28. bis 30. August 1984.* Ed. by Albert Heinekamp. Stuttgart: Steiner, 1986, pp. 178–84; Pasini, *Il reale e l'immaginario*, pp. 101–12.

183. Veit Ludwig von Seckendorff (1626–92), a German statesman and scholar, died a few weeks after his appointment as chancellor of the University of Halle. Leibniz had corresponded with him since February 1682.

184. GP III, 118.

185. On the dyadic see in particular A I, 12, N. 66, N. 67; A I, 13, N. 75, N. 321. On the *analysis situs* see in particular the papers published in GM V, 172–83 and De Risi, *Geometry and Monadology*.

186. GM V, 172.

187. Cf. the work by J. A. Comenius, *Unum necessarium*. 1668. In *Johannis Amos Comenii Opera omnia*. Vol. 18. Prague: Academia, 1974.

188. See A I, 12, N. 67 (esp. pp. 66, 70–71). Cf. also A I, 12, N. 66.

189. See Leibniz to Duke Rudolf August, 12 January (2 January O.S.) 1697 (A I, 13, N. 75).

190. See A I, 13, N. 76. Three further examples of medal were printed respectively by J. B. Wideburg, [Praes.] *Diss. math. De Praestantia arithmeticae binariae.* Jena, 1718 (title-page), J. Chr. Schulenburg, *Unvorgreiflicher Vorschlag zur Vereinigung d. Fest-Zeit.* Frankfurt and Leipzig, 1724 (title-page), and R. A. Nolte, *Mathematischer Beweis Der Erschaffung und Ordnung der Welt In einem Medallion.* Leipzig: Langenheim, 1734 (title-page) (reproduced in A I, 13, 124–5). The basis of Wideburg's illustration was the description of the medal by Rudolf Christian Wagner, who served as Leibniz's secretary between 1697 and 1699. Nolte seems to have reconstructed his illustration from Leibniz's description to the duke in A I, 13, N. 75. Cf. A I, 13, 122. See also Zacher, *Die Hauptschriften zur Dyadik*, pp. 34–41.

191. See A I, 13, N. 78, N. 79.

192. See A I, 13, 518–22.

193. A I, 13, 519.

194. Cf. *Système nouveau* and *Specimen Dynamicum.*

195. *De organo sive arte magna cogitandi* (A VI, 4, 158). Trans. by Mary Morris and G. H. R. Parkinson in Leibniz, *Philosophical Writings*, pp. 2–3. I am grateful to Massimo Mugnai for drawing my attention to this text.

196. Grua, 126.

197. *Novissima Sinica.* [Hanover], 1697 (2nd ed. [Hanover], 1699). See Ravier 39 for the extensive complete title. Modern edition: *Das neueste von China. Novissima Sinica.* Ed. by Heinz-Günther Nesselrath and Hermann Reinbothe. Cologne: Deutsche China-Gesellschaft, 1679. Leibniz's preface is translated in G. W. Leibniz, *Writings on China.* Ed. by Daniel J. Cook and Henry Rosemont, Jr. Chicago and La Salle, Illinois: Open Court, 1994.

198. Leibniz to the Jesuit missionary Antoine Verjus, 2 December 1697 (in *Leibniz korrespondiert mit China. Der Briefwechsel mit den Jesuitenmissionaren (1689–1714).* Ed. by Rita Widmaier. Frankfurt a. M., 1990, p. 55. Passage translated by Franklin Perkins at the outset of his illuminating essay on "Leibniz's Exchange with the Jesuits in China." In *Leibniz and His Correspondents.* Ed. by Paul Lodge. Cambridge: Cambridge University Press, 2004, pp. 141–61. See also Perkins, *Leibniz and China*, esp. chap. 3. For a possible context and source of this terminology, see J. A. Comenius, *Via Lucis.* 1641. In *Johannis Amos Comenii Opera omnia.* Vol. 14. Prague: Academia, 1974.

199. See *Novissima Sinica*, "Preface," § 2.

200. See *Novissima Sinica*, "Preface," §§ 2 and 10 in Leibniz, *Writings on China*, pp. 46, 50–51.

201. See Franklin Perkins, "The Theoretical Basis of Comparative Philosophy in Leibniz' Writings on China." In *Das Neueste über China.* Ed. by Wenchao Li and Hans Poser. Stuttgart: Steiner, 2000, pp. 275–93, Perkins, *Leibniz and China*, esp. chap. 2, and Perkins, "Leibniz's Exchange with the Jesuits in China," esp. pp. 142–3, 158–60.

202. See Hans Poser, "Leibnizens *Novissima Sinica* und das europäische Interesse an China." In *Das Neueste über China*, pp. 11–28.

203. See Poser, "Leibnizens *Novissima Sinica*," pp. 26–7.

204. On the so-called 'rites controversy' see the text appended by Leibniz to a letter of January 1700 to the Jesuit Antoine Verjus, in which he argued that the honors rendered by the Chinese to Confucius should be regarded as "a civil ceremony rather than religious cult" (*De cultu Confucii civili*; published in Widmaier, *Leibniz korrespondiert mit China*, pp. 112–14; trans. in Leibniz, *Writings on China*, pp. 61–5, here p. 61).

205. See "Introduction" in Leibniz, *Writings on China*, pp. 3–4 and Perkins, "Leibniz's Exchange with the Jesuits in China," pp. 143–4. On Leibniz's idea of the *propagatio fidei per scientiam* see his *Bedencken* of 1701 in connection with the newly founded Society of Sciences of Berlin (Klopp X, 353–61; 361–6).

206. On the role envisaged by Leibniz for Russia in respect to the evangelization of China see F. R. Merkel, *G. W. Leibniz und die China-Mission*. Leipzig: Hinrichs, 1920, pp. 151–6 and D. Lach, *The Preface to Leibniz' Novissima Sinica*. Honolulu: University of Hawaii Press, 1957, pp. 5–20.

207. See *Réponse de Leibniz au mémoire de l'Abbé Pirot* 16 (in *Oeuvres de Leibniz*. Ed. by L. A. Foucher de Careil. 2 vols. 2nd ed. Paris 1867–9, vol. 1, Nr. CXXXII, p. 470); Leibniz to Landgraf Ernst, 14 March 1685 (A I, 4, N. 308, p. 356); Leibniz to Bossuet, 14 May 1700 (A I, 18, N. 368, esp. pp. 636, 638–9, 646).

208. Leibniz to Landgraf Ernst, first half of December 1692 (A I, 8, 210).

209. See Woldemar Guerrier, *Leibniz in seinen Beziehungen zu Russland und Peter dem Grossen*. St. Petersburg and Leipzig, 1873, p. 14.

210. See Müller–Krönert, *Leben und Werk*, p. 147; A I, 14, N. 236 and lvii–lviii; Guerrier, *Leibniz*, pp. 12–14.

211. A I, 3, xxxvii.

212. See A I, 11, lviii; A I, 12, lxiii–lxiv; A I, 13, lviii; A I, 14, lix.

213. See A I, 13, xl–xli; *Unvorgreifliche Gedancken wegen ergäntzung und fortsetzung der weitberühmten Wolfenbütelischen Bibliothec* (Leibniz for Dukes Rudolf August and Anton Ulrich, January-beginning of April 1697; A I, 13, N. 87).

214. Published in the second part, pp. 255–314, of the posthumous *Collectanea Etymologica* (Hanover 1717), in which Leibniz's secretary, Johann Georg Eckhart, edited a number of etymological and linguistic studies by Leibniz. The original title, *Unvorgreifliche Gedancken betreffend die aufrichtung eines Teutschgesinneten Ordens*, indicates the close relation of this text to Leibniz's project of a linguistic society for the promotion of the German language. Cf. also Leibniz to Friedrich Wilhelm von Görtz, 12 January 1697 (A I, 13, N. 77) and Gerhard Meier to Leibniz, 1 November 1697 (A I, 14, N. 381, p. 657). Meier seems to have been the first to receive Leibniz's essay in manuscript.

215. *Unvorgreiffliche Gedancken*, pp. 255–7.

216. *Unvorgreiffliche Gedancken*, pp. 259–62. On the *Unvorgreiffliche Gedancken* see Massimo Mugnai, *Astrazione e realtà. Saggio su Leibniz*. Milan: Feltrinelli, 1976, esp. pp. 101–8.

217. See for instance A I, 11, N. 125, N. 493. It should be noted, however, that for Leibniz the inverse relation also obtained, namely that the study of the migrations of peoples could account for linguistic changes.

218. See A I, 11, N. 482.

219. See Genesis 9, 18–19.

220. A I, 8, 262. See also A I, 11, N. 334.

221. See A I, 11, N. 125 and lvi–lvii; A I, 12, N. 407 and lx.

222. See Stefano Gensini, "Leibniz Linguist and Philosopher of Language: Between 'Primitive' and 'Natural'." In *Leibniz and Adam*. Ed. by Marcelo Dascal and Elhanan Yakira. Tel Aviv: University Publishing Projects Ltd., 1993, p. 130.

223. Cf. Albert Heinekamp, "Ars characteristica und Natürliche Sprache bei Leibniz." *Tijdschrift voor Filosofie* 34, 3 (1972): 446–88 and Mugnai, *Astrazione e realtà*, pp. 99–112.

224. See A I, 14, N. 346.

225. See A I, 14, N. 440.

226. See Daniel Ernst Jablonski, *Kurtze Vorstellung der Einigkeit und des Unterscheides, im Glauben beyder Evangelischen so genandten Lutherischen und Reformirten Kirchen* (published by Hartmut Rudolph in *Labora diligenter*. Ed. by Martin Fontius, Hartmut Rudolph, and Gary Smith. Stuttgart: Steiner, 1999, pp. 128–64). Cf. Müller–Krönert, *Leben und Werk*, p. 150.

227. See above.

228. For background on Brandenburg see Bodo Nischan, *Prince, People, and Confession: The Second Reformation in Brandenburg*. Philadelphia: University of Pennsylvania Press, 1994. For the complex situation in Leibniz's day see also Kurt-Victor Selge, "Das Konfessionsproblem in Brandenburg im 17. Jahrhundert und Leibniz' Bedeutung für die Unionsverhandlungen in Berlin." In *Leibniz in Berlin*. Ed. by Hans Poser and Albert Heinekamp. Stuttgart: Steiner, 1990, pp. 170–85.

229. On Leibniz's reaction to the peace of Ryswick see this chapter above; on his work for the Protestant succession in England see chapters II. 7 and II. 8.

230. See Leibniz to Sophie Charlotte, 12 February 1698 (A I, 15, 21). The date of Ernst August's death is often reported according to the old style calendar (23 January 1698).

231. See Leibniz to Sophie Charlotte, 24 December 1697 (A I, 14, 868).

7

Between Brother and Sister: Hanover and Berlin (February 1698–February 1705)

I N THE FOLLOWING seven years, Leibniz's life was illuminated by a rising star: the electress of Brandenburg and (from 1701) queen of Prussia, Sophie Charlotte. The demise of Ernst August coincided with a steady increase in the importance of the late duke's daughter for Leibniz's personal and intellectual life. Over a relatively short period of time, an exceptionally close bond was established between him and Sophie Charlotte. The electress and queen continuously implored Leibniz to visit her in Berlin and Lützenburg, her summer residence, because she did not "have a living soul with whom to converse" and considered herself as "one of your disciples".[1] As for Leibniz, he wrote that his visits to Sophie Charlotte gave him "a leisure which I do not have at all elsewhere."[2] Back in Hanover, however, the great esteem and affection of the electress of Brandenburg was neatly counterbalanced by the attitude of her brother, the new elector, Georg Ludwig, who manifested not the least appreciation of his employee's kaleidoscopic activities and interests: in his considered opinion Leibniz was wasting his time fluttering from one place to another at the service of too many patrons instead of concentrating on the main assignment, for which he was handsomely paid, the history of the Guelfs. He complained sarcastically on one occasion: "Leibniz, for whom the Queen [Sophie Charlotte] pines so much, is not here . . . If one asks why he is never seen, he always has the excuse that he is working on his invisible book, the existence of which, it seems to me, will require as much trouble to prove as Jaquelot has taken with the [lost] book of Moses."[3]

To be sure, Leibniz was often away. Between February 1698 and February 1705 he was in Berlin for some twenty-four months, not to speak of his other travels, including regular visits to Wolfenbüttel, Braunschweig, and Celle, and a trip to Vienna. But a number of these visits were undertaken in the interest of the Hanover court as well – notably to support the

Hanoverian succession to the English throne, to discuss the reunification of the Protestant churches, and to negotiate with the Catholics following a direct summons from the emperor. Moreover, despite being named president in 1700 of the newly founded Society of Sciences of Berlin, he never rescinded his employment at the Hanover court and remained committed to writing the Guelf history. Despite his difficult relationship with Georg Ludwig, he had come to enjoy in Hanover a combination of freedom and job security difficult to replicate elsewhere, not least thanks to the unyielding protection of the dowager electress, Sophie.

The year 1700 brought him some particular satisfactions, with the foundation of the Berlin Society of Sciences under his presidency and his election as a foreign member of the Parisian Académie Royale des Sciences. His *Système nouveau* continued to attract widespread interest, and he entered in a lively debate about it with a number of thinkers, notably Pierre Bayle, François Lamy, Isaac Jaquelot, and Lady Damaris Masham. From the mid-1690s to 1704 he progressively focused on the philosophy of John Locke, following with great interest the controversy which opposed the English thinker to the bishop of Worcester, Edward Stillingfleet, and painstakingly commenting on Locke's *Essay Concerning Human Understanding* in his own famous *Nouveaux Essais sur l'Entendement Humain*. Interwoven with his reflection on Locke's epistemological doctrines was his discussion of their interpretation by Locke's self-appointed disciple, John Toland (1670–1722) – the controversial freethinker who found a hearing at the courts of Hanover and Berlin, and especially with Sophie Charlotte herself.[4] Important metaphysical reflections were developed in essays such as *De ipsa natura* (1698) and in his private correspondence with other savants, notably the Dutch professor of philosophy, physics, and mathematics Burchard de Volder. During the summer of 1702 the seeds of the *Theodicy* of 1710 were sown during conversations with Sophie Charlotte in the gardens of Lützenburg regarding the second edition of Bayle's *Dictionaire historique et critique*. Leibniz's interest in China remained high, especially after he entered an epistolary exchange with the French Jesuit missionary Joachim Bouvet, who claimed to have found a correspondence between Leibniz's dyadic and the hexagrams of the ancient Chinese *Book of Changes*, the *I Ching*. Less gratifying was the continual unfolding of the priority dispute regarding the invention of the calculus, which escalated in these years into the explicit charge of plagiarism. A still greater shock, which closed this period in Leibniz's life, was the sudden and unexpected death of Sophie Charlotte on 1 February 1705 – a loss which distressed Leibniz profoundly and touched him more personally than the loss of any other of his friends or relatives.

The Tie of Hanover and the Pull of Berlin

Leibniz greeted the advent of Georg Ludwig's rule over the Hanover Electorate with dutiful words of welcome to the "best son whom [Ernst August] could have desired to take his place."[5] Alas, Ernst August might well have been satisfied by the succession, but Leibniz soon discovered that he had personally little to rejoice in it. To start with, Georg Ludwig repeatedly withheld permission for Leibniz to call on his sister, Sophie Charlotte, in Berlin. Even Sophie Charlotte's renewed personal invitation on the occasion of her visit to Hanover during the first half of August 1698 did not succeed in mollifying Georg Ludwig's attitude.[6]

In September of the same year, a decade after their move from the Leineschloß to the Leinstraße, the library and its librarian were once again relocated, this time to the house of the widowed Sophie Elisabeth von Lüden in Schmiedestraße 10. The apartments, for which Leibniz paid an annual rent of 150 talers, were more spacious than those in the Leinstraße and were to remain his residence in Hanover until his death.[7] While trying to gain permission to visit Sophie Charlotte in Berlin, Leibniz continued to work at the Guelf history, assisted since the end of 1698 by a new secretary, Johann Georg Eckhart. To Eckhart, whom he described as "a rather learned young man,"[8] he also entrusted the editing of a new German language review journal which he had initiated and which appeared in Hanover between 1700 and 1702 – the *Monatlicher Auszug, Aus allerhand neu-herausgegeben, nützlichen und artigen Büchern.*[9] In 1698 and 1700 there appeared the two thick volumes of the *Accessiones Historicae* announced in the Leipzig book fair of 1694. In them Leibniz edited a number of manuscript sources on medieval history, which he had initially conceived of as part of a multivolume grand edition of German historical sources under the title of *Monumenta Historiam Brunsvicensem illustrantia.*[10] Despite this remarkable editorial achievement, the dukes of both Hanover and Celle continued to complain that the history of the Guelfs proper was nowhere to be seen. As a consequence, the annual supplement of 400 talers for hiring assistants, jointly granted by Hanover and Celle in the occasion of his promotion to *Geheimer Justizrat* on 12 July

1696, was cancelled.[11] Leibniz found himself in the unpleasant position of having to plead his cause with a number of people, notably the duchess of Celle, Eleonore d'Olbreuse, defending the high scholarly standards set for his history and his right to retain time for his own interests, especially for "the advancement of the sciences", which added its own lustre to the Guelf courts.[12]

Leibniz could claim with some justice that the interests of the Braunschweig-Lüneburg family were never far from his mind. According to his own account many years later to Caroline, princess of Wales, during the visit of King William III of England to Celle in the autumn of 1698, Leibniz pressed Duchess Eleonore to broach the subject of the succession to the English throne through the Protestant line of the Stuart descent.[13] At the accession of William and Mary in 1689, the Act of Settlement by Parliament had in fact excluded Catholic members of the royal family from succession to the English throne. Since neither of the two Protestant daughters of the deposed Catholic king, James II (r. 1685–1688) – Mary and Anne[14] – had surviving children, William III and the Parliament turned to the Protestant descendents of James I, that is, to the offspring of his daughter, Elisabeth Stuart. Of the many children of Elisabeth and Friedrich V von der Pfalz, only one child of Protestant faith still survived: Sophie, the dowager electress of Hanover. Sophie, however, showed little enthusiasm for the English crown; and her circumspection, although puzzling in hindsight, was explicable given the experiences of her blood relatives there in the seventeenth century. After ruling Scotland for centuries, the early Stuarts, arriving in England from the north in 1603, and the later Stuarts, returning from exile in France in 1660, had found the three kingdoms of England, Scotland, and Ireland virtually ungovernable. Sophie's father had likewise nearly ruined his house by leaving the Palatinate to accept the crown of Bohemia in 1619. What reason was there to suppose that a German offshoot of the Stuart line, with some fifty Roman Catholic relatives with stronger claims to the succession, would fare better in the intractable island kingdoms? Ambitious as he was, her son, Georg Ludwig, originally saw eye to eye with his mother on this issue: accustomed to the absolutist regime of his duchy, he did not relish the idea of haggling with the fractious parliament of a constitutional monarchy. So cool were the Hanoverians initially towards the idea of acquiring the British crowns that Sophie saw fit to remind the English Ambassador, George Stepney, of the rights of the young Prince of Wales, the Catholic son of James II living in exile under the protection of Louis XIV.[15] In light of this cautious response from Hanover, other possibilities were considered, such as succession through the house of Savoy.[16] Yet despite Sophie and Georg Ludwig's ambivalence, Leibniz was adamantly in favour of the Hanoverian succession from the outset and remained so during the protracted negotiations between 1689 and 1701; for he regarded the question not from a personal or dynastic standpoint but from a broader perspective. The absolute political priority remained, for him, the containment of the French hegemony which continued to destabilise Europe and posed a specific treat to the Protestant world. His longstanding opposition to the aggressive policy of Louis XIV had been sharpened by the events of 1697, in which he saw an imminent danger for Protestant territories – the conversion to Catholicism of the elector of Saxony and article IV of the peace of Ryswick.[17] England had emerged as the most powerful Protestant state in Europe; but the accession of a son of James VII and II, raised in the court at Versailles, would have only served to extend French hegemony over the entire British Isles. A Protestant succession to the throne was therefore for Leibniz an absolute imperative.

Given these commitments, the able English ambassadors, George Stepney and James Cressett, happily availed themselves of Leibniz's help in gently pushing the electress to reconsider her misgivings.[18] In numerous memos Leibniz assembled the juridical, political, and historical arguments justifying the precedence of the house of Hanover over other claimants.[19] Eventually Sophie relented,[20] encouraging William III to pursue with Parliament the matter of a Protestant succession.[21] In June 1701 the succession of the Hanoverian line to the English crown was officially sanctioned; and on 14 August 1701 an imposing delegation led by Lord Macclesfield brought to Sophie the Act of Settlement, naming her and her descendants as legitimate heirs after the deaths of William III and Princess Anne. In March 1702 King William died and Anne was crowned queen, bringing the Hanoverian succession one key step closer.

Meanwhile, important events gradually increased the significance of the Brandenburg court in Leibniz's life. A short first visit to Berlin took place on 10–12 November 1698. Leibniz's aim on this occasion was not to pay his respects to Sophie Charlotte but to advance talks on the reunification of the Protestant churches with Daniel E. Jablonski, who had visited Hanover the previous summer to discuss the issue with Leibniz and Molanus.[22] At the beginning of 1699 Leibniz was still struggling to obtain permission from Georg Ludwig to visit Sophie Charlotte. In his carefully worded letter to the elector of January 1699 he implicitly pointed out that the whole business was becoming somewhat embarrassing. Apart from resorting to the excuse of unfavourable weather conditions during the winter, he did not see how one could politely decline the invitation of such an important princess yet again.[23] But Georg Ludwig was as unmoved by his counsellor's embarrassment as by his sister's pleas. A new invitation related by Jablonski in a letter of 29 September again fell upon the elector's deaf ears.[24]

In February 1700 the welcome news lifted Leibniz's spirits that he had been elected foreign member of the French Académie Royale des Sciences.[25] His elevation was officially recorded in a diploma dated 13 March and signed by the president of the Académie, the Abbé Jean Paul Bignon, and its secretary, Fontenelle.[26] Shortly thereafter another of his long-nursed dreams was fulfilled: on 19 March Sophie Charlotte's husband, the Elector Friedrich III of Brandenburg, approved the establishment in Berlin of an astronomical observatory and a Society of Sciences, indicating Leibniz as its first president. Behind the elector's decision lay the work of a number of people who over the years had discretely but effectively advanced the cause of science and reform in Brandenburg.[27] Since his return in 1689 from almost a decade of diplomatic service in France, the high-ranking state counsellor, Ezechiel Spanheim, had convened a circle of Berlin intelligentsia. Amongst these were members of the Huguenot refuge in Berlin (which thrived thanks in part to the active protection of Spanheim) and other prominent representatives of central Europe's Reformed communities, notably Jablonski.[28] As the direct heir of Comenius's aspirations for the advancement of the sciences for the improvement of the human condition and the promotion of universal harmony through the reconciliation of the Christian churches, Jablonski was a natural partner for Leibniz's scientific and ecclesiastical projects. Close to Jablonski, a further handful of people conceived the plan of establishing a society of sciences in Berlin in consultation with Leibniz, especially the Brandenburg archive director, J. J. J. Chuno, and the court counsellor, Johann Gebhard Rabener. Last but not least, Sophie Charlotte herself lent her support to the enterprise. After the fall in 1697 of the powerful prime minister of Brandenburg, Eberhard von Danckelmann, Sophie Charlotte used her increased political influence on her husband to promote the cause of science, in which her protégé, Leibniz, played a key role. Her suggestion in 1697 to create an observatory which would have the task of overseeing the production of calendars set minds working.

Discussions were afoot on implementing in the German Protestant states the calendar introduced into Catholic countries by Pope Gregory XIII over a century earlier. In particular, Erhard Weigel, Leibniz's former teacher in Jena, had pressed the case for switching to the new Gregorian style of dating, suggesting the establishment of an imperial monopoly on the production of calendars, the proceedings of which would have been used to support the arts and sciences. Whereas Leibniz judged the establishment of an imperial monopoly unrealistic due to Germany's political fragmentation, he incorporated the idea into the unfolding plans for a Berlin observatory and society of sciences. In February 1700 the Gregorian style was introduced into the Protestant states of Germany, and Leibniz took this opportunity to propose the introduction into Brandenburg of a calendar monopoly, which would have served to finance the Berlin society and observatory.[29] The prospect of a firm financial basis did wonders in convincing Friedrich III to approve, on 19 March, the plan for these scientific institutions, which had been prepared by Jablonski with the help of Chuno, Rabener, and others.[30] On 23 March, writing on behalf of the elector, Jablonski invited Leibniz to Berlin to assist in the foundation of the Society.[31]

In the meantime Leibniz prepared for Friedrich III two memos outlining the aim and objectives of the Society and offering guidelines for its establishment.[32] In Leibniz's view, the hallmark distinguishing the Berlin Society from the illustrious academies in Paris, London, and Florence should have been the union of *theoria cum praxi*. Following in the footsteps of previous generations of central European universal reformers such as Comenius, Leibniz stressed that the advancement of knowledge promoted by the Society should be aimed at the improvement of the human condition for the glory of God, and not be pursued as a sterile aim in itself:

Such a princely society must not be directed at mere curiosity or lust for knowledge and fruitless experiments . . . more or less as occurs in Paris, London, and Florence . . . [O]n the contrary, one must orientate the entire enterprise from the very beginning toward utility and must think of such examples from which the princely founder will have reason to expect glory and the commonwealth abundance. The aim should thus be to unite *theoria cum praxi*, and to improve not only the sciences and the arts but also the country and its people, agriculture, manufacture and trade, and, in a word, the food supply[.][33]

With the firm invitation of the elector of Brandenburg in hand, on 28 March Leibniz pressed Georg Ludwig to let him go:

My lord. It appears that the honour done me in France of offering me membership of the now reorganized Académie Royale des Sciences[34] has attracted another one in turn. This is that the Elector of Brandenburg, having decided to establish a similar society and to have an observatory built, has invited me to make a brief trip to Berlin to give my advice; and he even wishes to entrust me with its direction, but from a distance, and without need of taking residence, supposing that such a thing could not displease Your Electoral Highness.[35]

This time Georg Ludwig could hardly refuse without offending the Brandenburg court, with which relations were already strained; yet the grounds of his reluctance to let Leibniz escape his oversight were soon made apparent. The "petit tour" to Berlin begun in early May gradually stretched into an eight-month absence from Hanover – four months spent in Berlin and another four wandering between Braunschweig, Wolfenbüttel, and as far afield as Prague and Vienna. As Leibniz pointed out in his own defence, travelling was his way to enjoy himself and remedied the health problems of an otherwise very sedentary life. And in any case he could always carry forward his historiographical work while away from Hanover.[36]

Once in Berlin, Leibniz was warmly welcomed by Sophie Charlotte, who put at his disposal accommodation in Lützenburg, her palace outside Berlin. There he was caught up in a series of court festivities marked by a whirl of demanding engagements and entertainments. Despite mildly complaining in a letter to Sophie of the lack of sleep that all these courtly activities caused, he deeply enjoyed himself, basking in the conversation and company of the variegated humanity which populated Berlin and Lützenburg.[37] Eventually Leibniz managed to extricate himself from these diversions and began in earnest the work of establishing the Society with the other founding members. Together they drafted the Society's statutes, which outlined its structure of government, pivoting around the office of a president and a council, and including a vice-president and a secretary.[38] Special care was taken to identify possible sources of income which could secure the financial viability of the whole enterprise. In addition to the calendar monopoly, Leibniz's fertile mind produced a wealth of other (perhaps a touch too inventive) suggestions: from the introduction of improved fire-pumps to the institution of a lottery, from the revenue gained by the checking of standards of weights and measures (facilitated by the adoption of a decimal system) to the creation of a series of new taxes – on trips abroad, on print, even on missions: since faith had to be propagated through science, why not to tax the clergy to finance the scientific institutions which provided them with the most up-to-date tools of evangelisation?[39]

On 11 July 1700, Friedrich III signed the *Stiftungbrief*, founding the Society "for promoting the glory of God, spreading His truth, and cultivating all the virtues and practices useful to the common-wealth . . . through which the treasury of already available but dispersed human knowledge might not only be rendered more orderly and concise, but also increased and properly applied."[40] In other words, the Society was conceived as the institutional blueprint for carrying forward the encyclopaedic aspirations for the betterment of humankind shared by Leibniz and his Berlin friends. The decision to call it a "Society" rather than an "Academy" was justified by the fact that in Germany the title of "Academy" tended to refer to teaching institutions.[41] The following day, 12 July, Leibniz was named president. Interestingly, in the letter of nomination his name appeared for the first time as "Gottfried Wilhelm von Leibniz", despite the fact that no other official document attested his elevation into the nobility.[42] It also mentioned the provision of an emolument for the president, which was fixed the following August at 600 talers per annum. This sum was intended to cover travel and correspondence expenses incurred by Leibniz in the exercise of his office.[43]

The presidency of the newly founded Society was not the only title bestowed on Leibniz during his first extended stay in Berlin. The same letter of nomination also appointed him privy counsellor of justice (*Geheimer Justizrat*) in Brandenburg.[44] In this capacity, he prepared two memos in August regarding the reforms of the principality's juridical system which were currently under discussion.[45] Shortly thereafter, on 22 August 1700, he left Berlin, to which he was not to return until October 1701. From the outset it had been agreed that Leibniz would direct the Society from Hanover, aside from a single annual visit to Berlin;[46] but this arrangement proved inadequate. His prolonged absence delayed the effective establishment of the Society despite the commitment and efforts of the members of the council, notably Jablonski, who served as vice-president; his elder brother, Johann Theodor, who was chosen as

secretary in October 1700; and Chuno.[47] The lack of funds and of dedicated buildings also conspired to make the Society little more than a paper
institution for the first decade of its existence: the Society's only serious
capital was 1000 talers provided by Jablonski out of his own pocket, and
the council meetings were held in the private lodgings of its members,
where the Society's records were also stored. To make matters worse,
Leibniz's habit of continuously conceiving and promoting new schemes
instead of concentrating on seeing a few to completion seriously jeopardised his ability to act effectively as a president, until he eventually found
himself marginalized, as we shall see.[48]

   After leaving Berlin, Leibniz did not go back to Hanover for another
four months. Instead he headed to Braunschweig and Wolfenbüttel. While
there, in September he received an invitation from Sophie and Sophie
Charlotte to join them on a trip to Aachen, a renowned international
spa where the ruling elite often convened. There they intended to campaign for the elevation of Friedrich III to the status of king in Prussia.
To Leibniz's great regret, the invitation reached him too late for him to
join the expedition.[49] Having missed this opportunity, he visited another
spa town instead, Töplitz in northern Bohemia, seeking treatment of an
annoying rheumatic and respiratory condition which had plagued him
during the previous spring.[50] From Töplitz he travelled at the end of
September via Prague, Kolin, Iglau, and Znaim to Vienna.[51] The decision to visit the imperial city followed a summons from the emperor
himself, who on 17 May had written to Georg Ludwig requesting the
dispatch of his "highly experienced, discreet, and qualified" *Geheimer
Justizrat* for further talks on the reunification of the Catholic and Protestant churches with Franz Anton von Buchhaim, the successor of Rojas
as bishop of Wiener-Neustadt.[52] In Vienna, where he remained from
the end of October to mid-December 1700, Leibniz met repeatedly with
Buchhaim and the apostolic nuncio in Vienna, discussing the issue of
reunification. He also availed himself of the opportunity to study Rojas's
Nachlaß, which included papers relevant to the ongoing negotiations.[53]
Before leaving, Leibniz obtained from the emperor a letter addressed to
the duke expressing his thanks for allowing the visit of his employee,
whose activities in Vienna were reported in glowing terms. "His well
grounded ideas, unsparing industry, and extraordinary knowledge" had
pleased Leopold greatly[54] – an especially gratifying message for Leibniz since he could anticipate receiving a less flattering description of his

eight-month absence from his chief employer the moment he returned to Hanover.

Upon arriving home on 30 December,[55] Leibniz was immediately immersed in two major unfolding political events, both triggered by dynastic complexities: the long-standing issue of the English succession, and the new crisis caused by the death of the king of Spain, Charles II, in November 1700. The blood of Europe's two most inimical dynasties – Habsburg and Bourbon – mingled in Charles' veins, relating him to the era's two arch-enemies, the Emperor Leopold I and the Sun King Louis XIV. Without direct heirs of his own, Charles II negotiated a partition of the territories controlled by Spain between the claimants to the succession. Pressured by Spanish forces contrary to the partition, however, the king had left a will which contravened the diplomatic solution and left the undivided succession to the Bourbon candidate, a grandson of Louis XIV, Philip, Duke of Anjou. The rights of the Habsburgs, embodied in the person of the second son of Leopold I, Charles, were completely disregarded. When the Duke of Anjou was installed on the Spanish throne as Philip V, the emperor prepared for war by signing a secret treaty with England and the Dutch Republic which represented the first nucleus of a broad anti-French coalition, the so-called Grand Alliance. In a number of texts devoted to the Spanish crisis, Leibniz predictably took the side of the Empire, observing with great concern this further expansion of Louis XIV's sphere of influence in Europe and beyond. In an anonymous pamphlet published in 1701 he attacked the Bourbon succession, disguising himself as a Hollander writing on 1 February 1701 from Amsterdam.[56] In 1703 he again took up his pen in defence of the rights of the Habsburg pretender, Charles III, penning an extensive *Manifeste* upholding the latter's claim to the Spanish succession.[57]

While the Bourbons and Habsburgs were building toward another bloody confrontation, a third leading European dynasty – the Hohenzollerns – was greatly enhancing its standing amongst the rulers of the *ancien régime*. On 18 January 1701, the Brandenburg elector was crowned Friedrich I, King in Prussia – the particular form of the title being dictated by the fact that part of Prussia was held as a fief to the king of Poland. Leibniz greeted with joy the elevation of Friedrich and Sophie Charlotte to royal dignity, designing a medal to commemorate the occasion and in all probability composing the *Gratulatio* offered to the new king by the Society of Sciences of Berlin.[58] At this point the pull of Berlin was

particularly strong; but pressure from the courts of Hanover and Celle to
produce the history of the Guelfs had also increased since Leibniz's return
in December 1700. On 12 July 1701 Leibniz wrote to Sophie Charlotte:

> I have not yet been able to present my regards to Your Majesty, as I ardently desire,
> since I have been placed under extreme pressure to push forward a task with which I
> am charged. But I do hope that I shall be allowed to breathe a bit and not to pass this
> summer without performing a duty which constitutes a good deal of my happiness.[59]

Leibniz's hope proved to be overoptimistic. On 22 August his service
"to such various princes" was castigated at the regular *Hauskonferenz*
held in Engensen by the dukes of Hanover and Celle. On that occasion
a copyist was assigned to him, but with the additional duty of reporting
on his progress with the Guelf history.[60] On 31 August, Leibniz wrote
again to Sophie Charlotte, apologizing for his inability to accompany
John Toland to Berlin.[61] The controversial English thinker had come
to Hanover shortly before the arrival of Lord Macclesfield's delegation
and Leibniz hoped to follow him to the court of the Queen in Prussia
as soon as the rest of the English party departed from Hanover.[62] In the
second half of September, instead of simply issuing another invitation,
Sophie Charlotte took matters into her own hands and sent him a *Fuhr-
Zeddel* – that is, a travel pass authorizing the use of carriage and horses
at the various travel stations along the journey to Lützenburg. On the
23rd Leibniz wrote from Wolfenbüttel to Sophie, announcing that he was
going to Berlin while reassuring her with the following words: "I shall
certainly not stay for long, and firmly intend to withdraw into my shell
during this winter in order to finish certain tasks."[63] In the event, he was
gone for almost four months. Informed by Sophie of Leibniz's departure,
Georg Ludwig was understandably displeased, commenting bitterly, "at
the very least he should tell me where he is going when he takes off. I
never know where to find him."[64]

In Berlin, Leibniz devoted much of his time to several memos designed
to consolidate the Society of Sciences.[65] Among the enterprises which
the Society was to promote were the epidemiological studies long since
proposed in Hanover, in which the systematic observation and recording
of illnesses would eventually produce valuable medical statistics identifying the relationship between weather, seasons, life-style, and specific
diseases.[66] More unusual was his role as a secret diplomat mediating
between Hanover and Brandenburg in a local crisis precipitated by the

Spanish succession that involved the dukes of Wolfenbüttel.[67] The latter pursued a pro-French policy and had assembled a remarkable army, funded in part by Louis XIV himself. In the mounting European crisis surrounding the Spanish succession, the troops in Wolfenbüttel were perceived as a direct danger to the Empire in general and to the two leading northern German states, Brandenburg-Prussia and Hanover, in particular. When reliable intelligence indicated that France was planning to attack Hanover and Hildesheim from Wolfenbüttel in the spring of 1702, Hanover and Celle resolved to launch a preventive strike against their Guelf relatives. Brandenburg-Prussia was also keen to eliminate the danger from Wolfenbüttel, but Hanover and Celle preferred to exclude Brandenburg's armies from Guelf soil. Leibniz this time was caught between three patrons, and in early December 1701 convinced Sophie Charlotte to grant him authority to represent Brandenburg in a secret mission to his own chief employer, the duke of Hanover.[68] On 5 or 6 December he presented the privy counsellors in Hanover with a *Vollmacht* signed by Sophie Charlotte and a stack of memos outlining Brandenburg's position. In the discussions which ensued, however, the Hanover privy counsellors eventually realized that neither King Friedrich I nor his ministers were behind Leibniz and Sophie Charlotte's move; and apart from returning to Berlin with a memorandum from Georg Ludwig, little came of Leibniz's attempt at semiofficial diplomacy. On 20 March 1702, at the beginning of the war for the Spanish succession, Celle and Hanover overpowered Wolfenbüttel – a Blitzkrieg mercifully conducted without bloodshed. While Leibniz's history of the Guelf house inched its way forward, relations between the living members of that family had reached their lowest ebb.

By the time this little war broke out, Leibniz had returned to Hanover, together with Sophie Charlotte and her entourage, in the second half of January 1702.[69] As soon as the Queen in Prussia was back in her kingdom, however, she started pressing Leibniz to rejoin her. A note of 15 March from Berlin read urgently, "I send you this letter, Sir, and hope that it will find you on the verge of departing. I shall wait for you impatiently at Lützenburg, where I shall go for Easter. This is all I have time to tell you right now."[70] A few days later she followed up her hasty note with a longer letter characterized by the same urgency to see Leibniz again as soon as possible: "You will see by means of this card, Sir, how impatient I am to see you here, and how much I treasure your conversation, seeking it with all imaginable urgency."[71] For good measure she added that her lady-in-waiting, Henriette Charlotte von Pöllnitz, was growing dizzy in her attempt to master a book of mathematics she had bought. Christian charity demanded that he come to her rescue.[72]

Despite his personal preferences, Leibniz could not come; but a month or so later he sent to the mathematical apprentice, Mlle de Pöllnitz, a sample of his dyadic.[73] She replied by pleading the cause of Sophie Charlotte once again. "Her Majesty the Queen invites you," she wrote on 8 April,

> and I beg you this very instant to come to Lützenburg. In truth you could do no better than to come immediately. For we find ourselves in the situation described in the German proverb: 'when the cat's away, the mice can play'. In addition Her Majesty is at the moment without any company. It is true that her taste is such that she prefers to be alone than in bad company, but it is also for this reason that she desires the pleasure of your conversation.[74]

On 2 May Mlle de Pöllnitz resumed the campaign:

> All that I ask of you is to come soon. In addition to the pleasure of seeing you, which for me is very great, I have the duty to press you as a zealous servant of Her Majesty. I assure you that it would be an act of charity to come here, since the Queen has no living soul with whom to talk. I believe you a zealous enough servant to come to our aid in such a pressing need.[75]

Obliging as ever, Leibniz eventually managed to extricate himself from Hanover: on 11 June 1702 he arrived in Lützenburg for a visit which lasted an entire year. He divided his time between philosophical conversations with Sophie Charlotte and other thinkers visiting or living in Berlin (notably John Toland and the French court preacher, Isaac Jaquelot), his own studies and correspondence, the pursuit of church reunification, and the Berlin Society of Sciences.

In order to provide a steady income for the latter he concocted yet another scheme – and another which failed to prosper despite efforts repeated until the end of his life. Instead of windmills in the Harz, he pinned his hopes this time on the silkworms which he had started farming experimentally on an allotment in Hanover.[76] Once a plantation of mulberry trees had been established – he argued in numerous memos to figures from the king on down – farming the worms, collecting the silk, and weaving the cloth could provide work for the unemployed, revenue for the principality, and profits with which to finance the Society.[77] Leibniz was not new to this kind of analysis of unemployment. When the invention of threshing machines and other mechanical devises provoked a sort of Luddism *ante litteram* on the grounds that their introduction would deprive the poor of work, Leibniz replied that these innovations could relieve human beings without endangering their livelihood. In his view, there were always opportunities for other kinds of work, although at the beginning these new occupations would be unfamiliar.[78] On 8 January 1703, Sophie Charlotte granted him a patent for silk-culture in Prussia, which was followed by a similar patent for Saxony granted on 11 May 1703 to Leibniz and the Saxon general, Jakob Heinrich von Flemming, by the elector of Saxony and king of Poland, Augustus II.[79] But despite a sympathetic hearing from Friedrich I of Prussia and his privy counsellor, Friedrich von Hamrath, in early February 1703, the proposed mulberry plantation was delayed, since the season was already too far advanced. Instead, Leibniz was politely but firmly invited to suspend his plans for the time being and return to Hanover, as he had announced he intended to do.[80]

So long had he loitered in Brandenburg, in fact, that suspicions of espionage on behalf of Hanover had begun to circulate in Berlin. Towards the end of February 1703, in a bitter letter to the dowager Electress Sophie in which he reported these charges, Leibniz crisply stated, "I will not stay in this country."[81] Yet in May he was still in Berlin, a prisoner, it would appear, of Sophie Charlotte, to whom he wrote on 8 May lamenting the contradictory suspicions of Berlin and Hanover, which plagued him whichever way he turned:

I hope that the King will not be prejudiced against me because I come from Hanover, and that the Royal Society [the Berlin Society of Sciences] will [not] suffer on this account. In that case I would be doubly unfortunate, having been suspected in Hanover of too great an attachment to Berlin. But I care for the common good, which is the true interest of both courts.[82]

Sophie Charlotte took up her pen in his defence, writing on 22 May to the Braunschweig-Lüneburg diplomat, Hans Caspar von Bothmer: "Monsieur Leibniz is still here. I could not bring myself to see him go. He is unhappy that in Hanover people believe he would like to quit his service there to be here. He says on the matter that he loves his freedom too much to become a slave."[83] Whatever this "slavery" was meant to refer to, it appears that at this point the lure of Berlin did not overturn the comfortable balance of privileges and duties that Leibniz had arranged in Hanover.[84] Despite the fulminations of the supposedly absolute ruler of Hanover, his peripatetic privy counsellor of justice had enough freedom to be absent without leave for twelve months at a time. "It is true that Hanover when it is most frequented is a solitude after Berlin," Leibniz wrote to Sophie Charlotte on 17 November 1703, "but it is a solitude that has its pleasant aspects, and after which magnificence will feel more agreeable, as one has more appetite after having been a while on a diet."[85]

At the beginning of June 1703, in fact, Leibniz was finally back in his Hanoverian "solitude." It was not long, however, before he again became restless. In August he wished to accompany Sophie to Lützenburg to visit her daughter, but "some small difficulties" from Georg Ludwig – as he put it delicately to Sophie Charlotte – prevented him from going. Instead he was able to work in the quiet of Herrenhausen in an apartment provided by the dowager electress.[86] It was not until January 1704 that he escaped to Berlin for a short stay. From there he departed in all probability in the company of Sophie Charlotte who, as usual, headed to Hanover to attend the festivities of the annual carnival.[87] Leibniz, however, did not return all the way, stopping in Braunschweig and Wolfenbüttel, where he conferred with Duke Anton Ulrich. A few days later, with the death on 26 January of his brother, Rudolf August, Anton Ulrich became the sole ruler of the duchy.[88]

Between 30 January and 2 February 1704 Leibniz was in Dresden "almost *incognito*" to promote amongst the elector's ministers the idea of founding a Society of Sciences in Saxony modelled in detail – from the calendar monopoly and silk manufacture to the presidency (envisaged for himself) – on that in Berlin.[89] As an additional source of income he proposed a tax on the consumption of tobacco – a product of which men had begun to make "excessive use at the expense of health" and which deserved "to be taxed even more", since it was mostly imported.[90] The Society project, which he had first discussed in correspondence with Carlo Maurizio Vota, the Jesuit confessor of the Saxon elector,[91] was well received and led to a draft constitution (and nomination of a president) prepared by Leibniz himself in August for the approval of Augustus II.[92] On the 18th he sent his secretary, Eckhart, to Poland with detailed instructions for negotiating the Society's establishment.[93] He himself, having received permission to travel to Berlin, arrived on 27 August 1704 at Lützenburg, commencing a visit extended this time over almost six months. During this period he met Princess Wilhelmine Caroline von Ansbach – the future wife of Georg Ludwig's son, Georg August, destined therefore to become Princess of Wales – who resided in Lützenburg from the end of August to December.[94]

In September, Leibniz's perennial ambitions for career advancement resurfaced once again. In 1698 and 1701 he had dismissed rumours of librarianships offered to him in Paris and Vienna on the grounds that conversion to Catholicism would have been expected, for which reason he had already declined the equally prestigious position of curator of the Vatican library.[95] In 1699 he had reopened the prospect of filling the position of historiographer at the Brandenburg court left vacant by Pufendorf; but his candidature was doubtless not enhanced by the well-known saga of the Guelf history, and nothing came of this overture.[96] On 24 August 1704, the death of the vice-chancellor in Hanover, Ludolf Hugo, seemed to open the flattering prospect of nearing the apex of the hierarchy of court officials in Hanover. Since it was no secret that Georg Ludwig did not particularly care for him, Leibniz asked both Sophie Charlotte and Sophie to recommend him as the new vice-chancellor. Meanwhile, he wrote to the elector on his own account asking to be given oversight of the Abbey of Ilefeld (Harz), also vacated by Hugo's death.[97] These high-born referees both approached their task with reservations, albeit for different reasons. Sophie Charlotte recognised that the elevation of Leibniz to vice-chancellor would deprive her of still more of his company, although as a good friend she was prepared to put his interest before hers and obligingly wrote to her brother as requested. Her mother – more perceptive and familiar with Leibniz's basic character – doubted that he would tolerate the tedious burdens which went with the job.[98] Whatever the views of the man's two great female protectors, Georg Ludwig himself responded to this revelation of Leibniz's ambitions with predictable sarcasm. As Sophie reported in a letter of 20 September, he

seems to complain that your abilities, which he esteems infinitely, do him no good since he rarely sees you and sees the history which you have undertaken to write not at all. . . . As for the position of vice-chancellor, he does not believe that it would suit your nature to assume such heavy duties instead of corresponding as far as the Indies.[99]

These hopes dashed, Leibniz turned to other plans. Between 8 and 26 December he was in Dresden, where he discussed the proposed Saxon Society of Sciences with several people, including his longstanding friend, Ehrenfried Walter von Tschirnhaus, whose direct involvement in the project was foreseen. An opportunity was procured to outline his proposal in an audience with the elector, Augustus II, who reacted favourably.[100] But once again the exigencies of warfare overcame the luxuries of science: the Great Northern War with Sweden, which threatened to deprive the elector of his Polish kingdom, left him insufficient revenue for founding a Society of Sciences. Returning empty-handed to Berlin, Leibniz drafted a memo in January 1705 for Friedrich I listing his services and expenses for Brandenburg-Prussia over the past years and requesting a payment of 2000 talers. He also sounded out the possibility of being employed at the Brandenburg court in a position which would have allowed him maximum freedom to pursue his agenda of advancing the sciences and reunifying the churches.[101] Nothing came of it, but thanks to the intervention of Sophie Charlotte, on 1 February 1705 the king sent him a present of 1000 talers.[102] Leibniz could not have imagined that this was to be the queen's last gift to him.

Negotium Irenicum

In addition to the increasingly close relationship with Sophie Charlotte and the task of building the Society of Sciences, since 1697 Berlin represented for Leibniz a pole of attraction for a third reason very close to his heart: the reconciliation of the Christian churches, or, more specifically, the reunification of the Lutheran and Reformed confessions. Not surprisingly, given their common dream of universal reform based on a metaphysical vision of universal harmony, Leibniz's main partner in this irenical endeavour in Berlin was Comenius's grandson, Daniel Ernst Jablonski. In response to the setbacks of 1697 for the Protestant party,[103] Jablonski had been instructed to prepare the groundwork for a possible reunification of Lutheran and Reformed confessions under the common denomination "Evangelical" – a terminology which Leibniz strongly preferred to any talk of "Lutheranism" in order to avoid any impression of sectarianism.[104]

Jablonski's anonymous treatise, brought to Hanover for discussion on 24 December 1697 by Ezechiel Spanheim, encapsulated in its very title the irenical aim of the entire enterprise dedicated to minimising and then overcoming inter-Protestant theological differences: *Kurtze Vorstellung der Einigkeit und des Unterscheides, im Glauben beyder Evangelischen so genandten Lutherischen und Reformirten Kirchen: woraus zugleich erhellet, daß sothaner Untersheid den Grund Christl[ichen] Glaubens keinesweges anfechte* (*A Short Exposition of the Unity and Difference in Faith of the Two Evangelical Churches (Commonly Called Lutheran and Reformed) Which Also Makes Clear That Such Difference in No Way Disturbs the Foundation of Christian Faith*). In short, on the basis of an open discussion of the *Confessio Augustana* of 1530, three main areas of surmountable differences were identified: the communication of specifically divine attributes (such as omnipresence, omnipotence, and omniscience) to the human nature of Christ; the issue of the real presence of the body and blood of Christ in the Eucharist; and the doctrine of election and predestination.[105] The document was communicated by Leibniz to Johann Fabricius and Johann Andreas Schmidt,[106] two moderate theologians of Helmstedt – the university founded and supported by the Guelf dukes – whose appointment Leibniz had supported in the hope of consolidating at Helmstedt the irenical Lutheran tradition of which Georg Calixt had been the champion. While Fabricius and Schmidt were busy composing their *judicium*, Leibniz started working on another answer to Jablonski, in close collaboration with Molanus. Their painstaking analysis stretched over a year, during which several drafts were produced. It was not until the beginning of 1699 that a substantial text – the *Unvorgreiffliches Bedencken über eine Schrift genandt "Kurtze Vorstellung"* – was ready to be sent to Berlin.[107] In it, of the many points under discussion, the issues of election and the Eucharistic real presence emerged as the two stumbling blocks with the most far-reaching philosophical and theological consequences. In the first case, the controversy between Lutherans and Calvinists bore upon the crucial points of any theodicy: the problem of human freedom and responsibility, the cause of sin, the justice and goodness of God. What balance should be found between the Protestant emphasis on the role of grace in salvation and the need to warrant human freedom and responsibility for sin? If election depends on God alone, how does this square with his justice and goodness? In the case of the Eucharist and of the real presence in it of the body and blood of Christ defended by the Lutherans, the problem for Leibniz was twofold: to present a philosophical conception of body which could accommodate the possibility that Christ's body could be simultaneously really present in all the places in which the Eucharist was being celebrated; and to fashion a theological interpretation of Reformed teaching which would not exclude the doctrine of real presence. In correspondence with Molanus and in the parts of the *Unvorgreiffliches Bedencken* which he drafted,[108] Leibniz tackled these two clusters of problems in a manner clearly preliminary to the *Theodicy* and in typical opposition to the Cartesian reduction of body to extension.

Although Molanus and Leibniz's preparation of a final answer to the *Kurtze Vorstellung* took over one year, in the meantime Jablonski had plenty of occasions to sound out their views. In particular, in early September and early October 1698 he conferred with them in Hanover[109] – visits which Leibniz reciprocated in November, responding for the first time to a summons to Berlin specifically for the purpose of discussing church reunification. On that occasion he presented the court chaplain with a *Tentamen Expositionis Irenicae*, composed in September, in which he summarized his views on the three major controversies amongst Protestants, namely the communication of Christ's attributes, the real presence, and the issue of election.[110] The text was forwarded by Jablonski to the leading Pietist, Philipp Jakob Spener (who received it "with applause"),[111] and to the Reformed theologians Samuel Strimesius and Barthold Holzfuss, who answered it with some *Annotata placida*.[112] Leibniz, in turn, replied to the Calvinist objections, reiterating that none of these three major controversies was such as to hinder unity at least in the form of reciprocal toleration.[113]

Despite Leibniz and Jablonski's irenical efforts, however, by March 1699 the Lutheran and Reformed discussants had still not found agreement.[114] The negotiations were stagnating when in the autumn an independent irenical initiative sent discussions moving in a direction which Leibniz neither anticipated nor approved of. Thanks to the mediation of Philipp Jakob Spener, two Swiss Reformed theologians, Jeremias Sterky and Benedict Pictet, had discussed inter-Protestant controversies with the Lutheran theologian of Hamburg, Daniel Severin Scultetus. In their view, the time was ripe to call a broad Protestant theological conference involving England, Scotland, Brandenburg, Braunschweig-Lüneburg, and possibly Denmark and Sweden.[115] The Helmstedt theologian Johann Fabricius was proposed as theological representative of the Braunschweig-Lüneburg duchies and Brandenburg seemed ready to favour the initiative as well.[116] In Leibniz's view, however, this initiative was more likely to exacerbate divisions than to mend them. In his view, reunification needed to be prepared in advance through the careful negotiation of agreement on controversial points by a small, select, but representative group of theologians working in private. To plunge straight into a large, international conference without a fairly firm platform in which theological differences had already been mediated was only likely to provoke intransigent confrontation. Especially in correspondence with Jablonski, Molanus, and the English ambassador, James Cressett, Leibniz summarized the status of the inter-Protestant controversies and the reason for his opposition to the proposed theological conference.[117] For once things developed in the direction favoured by Leibniz, although this would have provided meagre consolation. On 27 December 1699 Jablonski reported that the enthusiasm of the Brandenburg ministers for the conference had waned and that plans of holding it had been "put to one side."[118]

Towards the end of 1702 the Prussian king decided to take matters in his own hands and to pursue union between Lutheran and Reformed churches within his own dominions. Orders were given to his Evangelical bishop, Benjamin Ursinus, to convene a *Collegium Irenicum* in which the Reformed confession was represented by Jablonski and Strimesius, and the Lutherans by the Magdeburg Pietist deacon, Johann Joseph Winckler, and the Berlin provost, Franz Julius Lütke.[119] Even before the work of the *Collegium Irenicum* could begin in 1703, however, the book published by Winckler under the title *Arcanum Regium* (Frankfurt, 1703) caused a storm of polemics,[120] followed by a second tempest provoked by Lütke's printed protest against the way in which the *Collegium Irenicum* had been organised.[121] The whole affair might almost have been designed to illustrate Leibniz's reiterated warning that union needed to be carefully prepared by discussions behind closed doors, in order to prevent the otherwise inevitable cross-fire of polemical pamphlets.[122] On the Hanoverian side Molanus and Leibniz were also greatly displeased with the unilateral manner in which Friedrich I was pursuing the union, giving rise as it did to the age-old Lutheran suspicion that Reformed irenicism was merely a foil designed to achieve "not so much peace . . . between the two Churches as the introduction of Calvinism into the Brandenburg territories."[123] On 18 December 1703, on orders from the king, Ursinus wrote a conciliatory letter to Molanus which the abbot forwarded to Leibniz.[124] The two of them agreed on an answer, sent on 15 January 1704 to Berlin, which

pressed the case for general Protestant reunification as opposed to partic-
ularistic solutions of the sort attempted in Brandenburg. The outcome of
a territorial approach, Molanus and Leibniz warned, could in fact be "a
new division between Evangelicals."[125]

Confronted by this series of obstacles on the road to the ecclesiastical
reconciliation of Hanover and Berlin, Leibniz continued to hope that help
would come from across the Channel. England and the English ambassador, James Cressett, were by no means new entries into Leibniz's great
scheme of Protestant reunification: he regarded the Church of England as
potentially playing a decisive role of mediation between the Lutheran and
Reformed denominations.[126] From the first signs of movement on this
front following the worrying Treaty of Ryswick, Leibniz had written to
Cressett pointing out the leading role which the English king could play as
ruler of the greatest Protestant state in Europe.[127] Reminding the English
ambassador of the exemplary irenical efforts made during the previous
generation in Germany by a native of the British Isles – Comenius's close
associate, the itinerant Scotsman, John Dury (1596–1680) – Leibniz urged
that the time was now ripe for carrying these earlier attempts forward to
a successful conclusion. In his view, the task of reestablishing Protestant
unity comprised three different degrees of increasing difficulty: political
unity or "a good civic understanding", ecclesiastical toleration, and finally
theological agreement or "concord of views". "The first and the second
degrees," Leibniz continued,

seem to me necessary and achievable, and sufficient. The first degree is necessary on
political grounds for the conservation of both parties. The second degree is necessitated
by the principle of Christian charity, and in consequence is more than feasible. The
third degree does not seem attainable, but it is also not necessary. It would nevertheless
be good if some able theologians were to work at it at least as regards certain points
where, I believe, the disputes consist in fact more in formulations than in realities.[128]

Cressett responded eagerly that he would do his best to enlist the king's
support for the cause.[129] By 15 January 1698 he could report that the archbishop of Canterbury, Th. Tenison, and the bishop of Salisbury, Gilbert
Burnet, together with William III himself had been informed of Leibniz's
"good intentions" and that "the two prelates display much satisfaction in
such a design."[130] In preparation for the visit of William III to Celle in the
autumn of 1698, Leibniz therefore prepared a memo for Cressett in which
the political and religious pressure facing the Protestants was explained

for the king's benefit.[131] He also enlisted the help of the duchess of Celle in impressing upon the king the necessity of ensuring a Protestant succession in Britain through the Electress Sophie and her descent.[132] On 8 January 1699, Leibniz wrote on the matter of ecclesiastical reunification to Gilbert Burnet, a leading supporter of theological latitudinarianism – the position embraced by the majority of the English church's divines advocating the necessity of theological agreement only on a few fundamental articles of faith and leaving the rest to free opinion and interpretation.[133] Burnet's answer was warm and forthcoming in indicating the flexible attitude towards controversial doctrines adopted by the Church of England as the only realistic way out of the endless dissentions amongst Protestants. With a few strokes of a pen, Burnet spelled out how the two major stumbling blocks on the road to Protestant unity – the Eucharistic doctrine and the issue of election and predestation – could be removed on the Continent in similar fashion:

The only way in my poor opinion to establish a good correspondence among you is to follow the method that we have followed so happily in England. As to the manner of the Presence we doe only reject Transsubstantiation but leave the rest free to Divines to explain or illustrate it as they please. Some contend for a reall others for a figurative presence but this makes no quarrell among us. And as for the point of Predestination our Articles doe indeed favour S. Austins [Augustine's] doctrine yet not so formally but that men of other persuasions may with a good Conscience signe them so[,] tho the greater number among us receives that doctrine commonly called Arminian[,] yet some there are both Bishops and others who are for absolute decrees: but we doe all not only hold one communion but live in great love and friendship together notwithstanding that diversity of Opinion. Some method of this kind is that which must heal the breach among you or it must be given over as desperate and incurable.[134]

During the same year Burnet published his influential *Exposition of the Thirty-Nine Articles of the Church of England*: a detailed commentary on the official doctrine of the English church summarised in the Thirty-Nine Articles promulgated in 1571 by the Archbishop of Canterbury, Matthew Parker, and by Queen Elisabeth I. Since both Leibniz and Jablonski found that the formulations of the Church of England provided a useful theological mediation in the ongoing discussions, especially of election and predestination, Jablonski undertook a Latin translation of Burnet's exposition of article 17, devoted to "Predestination and Election", and Leibniz set out in turn to expound upon it. The result was a lengthy commentary on Burnet's exposition which, after evolving through three different drafts, was finally completed in 1705. It was ready for publication when the deterioration of the relationship between Hanover and Brandenburg in 1706 caused the manuscript to be shelved, together with the whole idea of inter-Protestant church unity.[135]

Leibniz had put considerable effort into this careful discussion of the views on election which divided the Protestants. In particular, he examined the issue regarded by Burnet as the "head and source" of the controversy: the doctrine of unconditional Election (or "absolute decree") defended by strict Calvinists. According to this doctrine, God's decree of election took place without any consideration of the actions and responses of creatures. Against this view had arisen the Dutch Reformed theologian, Jacobus Arminius (1560–1609), who, following in the footsteps of the humanistic tradition of Erasmus, argued that election does take into consideration the response of individuals to grace. Two of his followers, Simon Episcopius and Jan Uytenbogaert, systematised Arminius's teaching into five "articles of remonstrance" in 1610, articles which were condemned in turn by the international gathering of Reformed divines at the Synod of Dort in 1618–19. On the issues separating Calvinists and Arminians, Leibniz's sympathies definitely extended towards the latter, although in his commentary to Burnet he tried to provide a way of harmonizing the positions of the two parties, insisting on the simultaneity and interconnection of the totality of God's decrees at the moment of creation. In other words, God's creative decree entails from the very beginning a simultaneous consideration of all the factors which enter into the best possible world, including that of who are going to be the elect and how they will respond to His grace.[136]

Despite the cooling of his sympathy for Roman Catholicism, Leibniz also continued to pursue the reconciliation of Catholics and Protestants during the period in which he was primarily interested in Protestant reunification. Back in October 1696 he had received news via the general vicar of Wiener-Neustadt, Reiner von Vlostorff, that the emperor had instructed the successor of Bishop Rojas, Franz Anton von Buchhaim, to resume negotiations with Molanus and Leibniz on church reunification.[137] Many months passed without further developments before Leibniz inquired circumspectly in May 1698 whether there had been a change of plan.[138] The answer from Vienna was reassuring: Buchhaim was hoping to resume contacts with Molanus and Leibniz very soon, and was planning a visit to Hanover.[139] In early September secret talks were held in Loccum between

Buchhaim, Molanus, and Leibniz. On the basis of these talks, Leibniz and Molanus produced a document – the *Declaratio Luccensis* – which went a long way towards meeting Roman Catholic concerns. The Latin text was translated by Leibniz into French, and the two versions were presented to Georg Ludwig. For his part, Buchhaim sent a positive report about the discussions to Rome.[140] Despite the cautious optimism of Buchhaim, however, no concrete results were reached.[141] Further discussions along the lines set by the *Declaratio Luccensis* were pursued in Vienna during the last months of 1700 between Leibniz, Buchhaim, and the apostolic nuncio Da Via.

The report sent by the latter to Rome stressed how open the Protestant party – and Leibniz in particular – had been.[142] The strategy proposed by Leibniz and Molanus was in its key features the same agreed upon almost two decades before with Rojas: a preliminary reunification between Lutherans and the Roman church followed by the convocation of a council, acknowledged by both parties as truly ecumenical, with the task of settling controversial matters definitively. As Da Via pointed out, Leibniz was prepared to make significant concessions to the Roman church: provided that, following the models of the Greek churches and the Gallican church, a degree of autonomy of rites and practices could be granted to the churches of the Augsburg Confession – including the marriage of clergy and communion in both kinds – they would be prepared to accept the Catholic doctrines on justification, the sacraments, and papal authority. Once correctly interpreted, Leibniz maintained, these doctrines were not in fact incompatible with those of the *Confessio Augustana*.[143] Unfortunately, the very remarkable openings of the Lutheran party met with the rigidity of Cardinal Paolucci. Answering to Da Via, Paolucci castigated the "exorbitance of the conditions sought" and denied that the example of the Greek churches could be followed in introducing into the Latin church "diversity of rites or dogmas."[144]

While doors in Rome seemed to close, Leibniz had managed to reopen his channel of communication with Bossuet. Despite the silence from the bishop which ended their previous exchange in July 1694, on 16 October 1698 Leibniz took the initiative in writing to the French theologian.[145] One month later, probably sensing that the bishop needed more than this letter to break his silence, he enlisted the help of Duke Anton Ulrich. Writing to him on 17 November, Leibniz summarized the past exchange on religion between himself, Molanus, Pellisson, and Bossuet, asking the duke to use his influence and good relations with France to help reopen the interrupted negotiation.[146] Anton Ulrich forwarded Leibniz's letter to Louis XIV and Bossuet via the French ambassador at the Wolfenbüttel court, Charles-François de Caradas du Héron.[147] This time the bishop of Meaux obliged, replying to Leibniz on 11 January 1699.[148] Their renewed exchange on church reunification, however, was no more successful than the previous one. Rather it ended in a sharp polemic on the decree of the Council of Trent concerning the canon of the Sacred Scripture.[149] The death of Bossuet on 12 April 1704 sealed their troubled relationship. The following year, writing to Thomas Burnett of Kemney, Leibniz commented bitterly on his failed dialogue with the eminent French theologian:

the Bishop of Meaux . . . assumed too decisive a tone, and wanted to push things too far, advancing doctrines which I could not at all let pass without betraying my conscience and the truth. For these reasons I answered him vigorously and firmly, and adopted a tone as lofty as his to show him that, however great a controversialist he might be, I knew his subtleties too well to be taken by surprise. Our debates could fill an entire book.[150]

Leibniz's heartfelt appeal to Christian charity and evangelical love of peace as a basis for ending the division amongst Christians seemed to fall on deaf ears:

Charity (which is the highest of virtues), the love of peace, so recommended by Jesus-Christ, and the proofs of Christian moderation given for such a long time by this side, demand that we omit nothing now which is in our power and which could serve to remove or diminish the unfortunate schism which is so harmful to souls and which has rent the West for over a century and a half[.][151]

Philosophy and Mathematics

Reading Locke

Leibniz's commute between Hanover and Berlin and his indefatigable efforts on a variety of political, religious, and practical fronts might well have slowed down his progress on the Guelf history; but they did not prevent him from engaging in an amazing range of philosophical and mathematical exchanges.

From the mid-1690s to 1704 and beyond, for instance, his attention was drawn to one of the most important and influential works of seventeenth-century philosophy: John Locke's *Essay Concerning Human Understanding* of 1690. The year in which Locke's *magnum opus* appeared, Leibniz received a notice from Magliabechi listing it among recent publications.[152] At some point between 1690 and June 1695 he acquired and read the work in its first edition, mentioning it and its author for the first time in a letter to Thomas Burnett of Kemney of 21 June 1695.[153] From about this time until the death of Locke on 8 November 1704 (28 October O.S.), the Hanoverian court counsellor tried repeatedly to open a channel of communication with the English thinker, but, unfortunately, the opportunity for direct correspondence between these two key contemporaries was missed.[154] Locke politely but consistently declined to engage in an epistolary exchange, limiting himself to acknowledging Leibniz's efforts through the intermediation of Thomas Burnett of Kemney and, later on, of Lady Damaris Masham. Amongst the reasons for such reservation was probably the fact that from the very beginning Locke did not seem impressed by the sort of comments penned on his work by the German savant. Around 1695 Leibniz prepared a series of remarks on Locke's *Essay* which he sent on 17 March 1696 to his trusted correspondent from England, Thomas Burnett.[155] Burnett asked Leibniz's permission to forward these remarks "to Mister Lock himself, or some other able people",[156] obtaining Leibniz's ready agreement.[157] The Scotsman wasted no time. Availing himself of the mediation of the jurist Alexander Cunningham (1655*–1730), whom Leibniz had met in Florence in 1689, he lodged Leibniz's texts in Locke's hands.[158] Locke read and discussed them with Cunningham in the summer of 1696[159] but, regrettably, refrained from passing his reactions to Burnett.[160] On 11 February 1697 Leibniz gently pressed his correspondent to find out what Locke thought;[161] but Locke politely replied via Burnett merely that for the time being he did not have the leisure for the reflections which Leibniz's paper deserved and limited himself to sending the eager German thinker copies of his recent pamphlets.[162]

On 19 April 1697, an amended version of Leibniz's remarks was sent to Locke by his friend Jean Le Clerc; but the circuitous route by which they arrived frustrated Leibniz's intentions and succeeded only in putting him in a bad light in Locke's eyes. In July 1696 Leibniz had announced to Basnage de Beauval the composition of his remarks. Upon requesting and receiving a copy, Basnage's proposal was to use Leibniz's comments as an introduction to the French translation of Locke's *Essay* which Pierre Coste was preparing in Amsterdam.[163] Leibniz declined, judging it inappropriate to preface critical remarks to the work of another author without this latter's permission; but he did prepare a fresh version of his remarks which he sent to Holland in the hope of seeing them published in the *Histoire des ouvrages des savans* edited by Basnage.[164] Disregarding or misunderstanding Leibniz's intention, Basnage sent the remarks to Le Clerc who, in turn, passed them on to Locke. Le Clerc, who never had much sympathy for Leibniz, presented Basnage's scheme to Locke as if it were Leibniz's own, adding for good measure, "I have been told a thousand good things about this mathematician; for a long time now he threatens us with great and wonderful things [*magna et praeclara minatur*][165] without producing anything apart from a few loose demonstrations. In any event, I think he does not understand you, and (between you and me) I doubt that he fully understands himself"[166] – not the best overture to a direct exchange between the author of the remarks and the already reluctant author of the *Essay*.

Leibniz had to wait until 1708 to have a glimpse at Locke's unflattering reaction to his first comments. In *Some Familiar Letters between Mr Locke and Several of His Friends*, published posthumously in London in 1708, there appeared two letters of Locke to William Molyneux (1656–98) written respectively in April and May 1697. In the first one, referring to his careful reading of Leibniz's remarks in the company of Cunningham, Locke concluded,

> Mr. Leibnitz's opinion would not hold . . . I must confess . . . that Mr. Leibnitz's great name had raised in me an expectation which the sight of his paper did not answer, nor that discourse of his in the acta eruditorum,[167] which he quotes, and I have since read. . . . From whence I only draw this inference, That even great parts will not master any subject without great thinking, and even the largest minds have but narrow swallows.[168]

In the second letter, Locke quoted and endorsed the scathing opinion of Leibniz expressed by Le Clerc in his letter of 30 March (O.S.) / 9 April (N.S.) 1697, concluding, "I see you and I, and this gentleman [Le Clerc], agree pretty well concerning the man; and this sort of fiddling makes me hardly avoid thinking that he is not that very great man as has been talked of him."[169] It was perhaps no mere coincidence that after 1708 Leibniz's regard for Locke cooled noticeably. Writing on 24 October 1709 to Friedrich Wilhelm Bierling, a professor at the University of Rinteln, he stated dryly that "Locke's book on human understanding is unsatisfactory [parum satisfacit]".[170] Prompted by Bierling, in the following letter he elaborated further on the reasons for his negative judgement, this time implicating Le Clerc as well.[171] Even more cuttingly, in a letter to Malebranche of 1711 he declared to have tried "to fight in passing certain lax philosophers, such as Mr. Locke, Mr. le Clerc and the like, who have false and base ideas of humanity, the soul, the understanding, and even of the Divinity."[172] Later on, in a letter to Nicolas Rémond of 14 March 1714, Leibniz pointed out that Locke had seen his remarks but

spoke of them with distain in a letter to M. Molineux which can be found amongst other posthumous letters of Mr. Locke. I did not learn of his opinion until after this publication. I am not surprised by it: we were a bit too different in our principles, and what I proposed appeared paradoxical to him. . . . Mr Locke did have some subtlety and ability, and some kind of superficial metaphysics which he knew how to make appealing; but he was ignorant of the method of mathematicians.[173]

Leibniz felt stung especially because Locke had communicated his misgivings to a third party after having declined the opportunity of discussing them directly with him: "It appears from a letter of Mr Locke to Mr Molineux, included in Locke's posthumous letters, that this able English man did not take kindly to objections. Since his response to my work was never communicated to me, I was deprived of the possibility of replying."[174] At any rate, it was perhaps for the best that Leibniz did not encounter Locke's scathing comment until he had long finished his intensive study of the *Essay* and penned his extensive commentary upon it between 1703 and 1705.[175] At least up to that point his tone toward the English thinker continued to be very respectful, genuinely seeking to nudge him into a fruitful comparison of their philosophical systems.

Indeed this respectful attitude was very apparent in Leibniz's remarks about the dispute between Locke to the Bishop of Worcester, Edward Stillingfleet (1635–99), in the last years of the latter's life. In December 1696 Thomas Burnett wrote to Leibniz announcing the publication of the bishop's *Vindication of the Doctrine of the Trinity*.[176] In it Stillingfleet claimed that the epistemological theses of Locke's *Essay* presented serious dangers for the doctrine of the Trinity, as had been shown by the use made of them in a highly controversial book published in London in 1696: John Toland's *Christianity Not Mysterious*.[177] During the following few years, until at least February 1700, the unfolding debate peppered the correspondence between Leibniz and Burnett, with Burnett sending Leibniz the various *Answers* and *Replies* exchanged by Stillingfleet and Locke, and Leibniz commenting upon them in a renewed attempt to reach out to Locke and elicit a direct reaction from him.[178] In particular, to Burnett's assurance that Locke "would have been very keen to know your view of this controversy between him and the Bishop of Worchester,"[179] Leibniz responded in January 1699 with a long letter, which Burnett copied to Locke.[180] This was followed by a series of remarks on Locke's second *Reply* to Stillingfleet, which Burnett once again duly transmitted to Locke with the accompanying letter.[181] In these pieces Leibniz readily acknowledged that the dangerous consequences for the Christian mysteries were due to an abuse of Locke's epistemological theses by Toland rather than to their intrinsic perniciousness; and although Leibniz's sympathetic stand did not succeed in prodding Locke into a direct correspondence, the sustained study of the Locke–Stillingfleet dispute provoked a number of the reflections amplified later in the *Nouveaux Essais*.

In 1700, the French translation by Pierre Coste of the fourth edition of Locke's *Essay* appeared in Amsterdam and was promptly reviewed in the September issue of the Hanoverian *Monatlicher Auszug*.[182] Translation from the still obscure language of the island to the most widely read modern language of the continent opened the book to many European readers, amongst whom Leibniz candidly numbered himself: as he confessed to Thomas Burnett in a letter of 1696, the most he could manage in English was "a tolerable understanding of books written in that language" and he occasionally had some trouble in grappling with the proper meaning of the text.[183] According to his own account, the availability of the French translation stimulated his intensive study of Locke's work, which was further advanced by some "conversations on the book of Mr Locke" by the Marquis d'Ausson (the Chief Esquire of Sophie Charlotte), with whom he would have had many opportunities to meet during his year in Berlin between June 1702 and June 1703.[184] Uniquely, Leibniz proceeded to comment passage by passage on the entire text of Locke's voluminous *Essay*, composing in so doing his *Nouveaux Essais*.

This unique attention does not imply, however, that Leibniz regarded Locke's *Essay* as uniquely important, valuable, or difficult. On the contrary, he stated repeatedly that his commentary on it had been written, not in leisurely circumstances permitting extended periods of intense reflection, but in haste during a period constantly interrupted by court engagements and long journeys by coach.[185] His capacity to undertake this task in such disrupted circumstances was boldly explained in a letter to Jaquelot: having "resolved all these matters of general philosophy a long time ago in a manner which I regard as demonstrative or nearly so . . . I have almost no need of new reflections on these issues." He therefore regarded commenting upon Locke's masterpiece as a light-weight task, to be undertaken "during the time wasted during travelling, or at Herrenhausen" when "inquiries demanding more application" were not possible.[186] Indeed, the work had probably been begun in the summer of 1703, while Leibniz was staying with the court at Herrenhausen, or even during his usual commute between Hanover, Braunschweig, and Wolfenbüttel: as he remarked later to the Marquis d'Ausson, Locke's essay was "suitable for reading in a coach and for providing matter for comment in the solitude of a inn."[187] "Nevertheless," he concluded to Jaquelot, "the work could not fail to increase under my hands, since I found things to object to in almost every chapter, and many more than I had expected."[188]

On 17 November 1703 Leibniz mentioned to Sophie Charlotte his engagement with the French version of Locke's *Essay*, remarking in particular that, "since his philosophy does not agree with mine, such as when he believes that the soul is not imperishable, and [since] he does not lack a good deal of penetration[,] I made some remarks on it while going through a part of his work as I was travelling to Braunschweig and Wolfenbüttel. And when I will have the time, I will finish the rest."[189] On 3 December 1703 he informed Thomas Burnett of Kemney of his renewed critical reading of Locke's work, emphasizing some of his major points of disagreement with it.[190] Burnett replied on 25 January 1704, suggesting that he enter into "an amicable dispute" with Locke sooner rather than later. The health of the English philosopher was in fact in serious decline and since the early 1690s he had lived at Oates in the house of Lady Damaris Masham, the daughter of Ralph Cudworth.[191] Having failed to engage Locke in piecemeal discussion, Leibniz recognized that only speedy action stood a chance of provoking a substantive reply.[192] He therefore wasted no time. On 9 February he wrote to Isaac Jaquelot that he had read "with care the Essay of Mr Locke on the human understanding," composing "*currente calamo* [with a flying pen] some remarks which I will finish as soon as I have some free time."[193] Towards the end of April 1704 his remarks were "almost finished", and at that point Leibniz had already settled for the title of *Nouveaux Essais sur l'Entendement* rather than the former provisional title of *Sur l'Essay concerning l'entendement*.[194] The first complete draft of the *Nouveaux Essais* was in all probability ready by the end of May 1704; but the task of putting it in a fair copy (begun in February or March 1704), amending bits and pieces (including the transformation of the first two books from excerpts and critical notes into dialogue form), checking the language, and preparing the text for publication stretched over more than one year. A number of helpers – amongst them Leibniz's secretary, Konrad Johann Dannenberg, and the Berlin mathematicians Philippe Naudé senior and Philippe Naudé junior – worked to produce fair copies, which were checked linguistically by eight different people.[195] The first of these was Isaac Jaquelot, to whom Leibniz explained that the choice of French rather than Latin was dictated by the desire to give his work the broader readership being enjoyed by the French translation of Locke's *Essay* itself, which "was promenading in the great world outside England."[196]

Meanwhile Leibniz was trying once again to elicit a response from Locke through the good offices of his hostess, Lady Masham. In June 1704 Lady Masham explicitly informed him that, in her guest's own words, his "want of health . . . and the little remains he counts he has of life, has put an end to his enquiries into philosophical speculations."[197] This mention of Locke's life dwindling away, rather than deterring Leibniz, seemed to add urgency to his longstanding desire to know what Locke really thought of his doctrines before it was too late, and his subsequent letters continued to hammer away on Locke's philosophy.[198] Even Lady Masham's reiteration in August that Locke's health was in serious decline failed to discourage him:[199] Leibniz replied by suggesting that she discuss with her dying guest the issue of nonextended substance.[200] Leibniz, whose thought had so often been stimulated by exchanges with leading contemporaries of contrary viewpoints, could not resist the temptation to probe the thinking of one of his greatest philosophical contemporaries on a key issue, especially since there was a serious danger that the latter would enter eternal life without giving him an answer. Nor, evidently, could a man who would continue to discuss philosophy on his deathbed imagine the state of mind of a major philosopher for whom such queries were no longer welcome. Finally, just a few weeks after Naudé senior announced that everything was ready for the publication of the *Nouveaux Essais*,[201] the news of Locke's death on 8 November (28 October O.S.) arrived.

Leibniz repeatedly affirmed in the following years that Locke's death caused him to abandon the plan of publishing his own work. His aim had been "rather to clarify things, than to refute the views of someone else"; and the death of the author of the *Essay* had taken away the possibility of "benefiting from his clarifications."[202] Yet this decision was not made straightaway. That he was still envisaging publication in mid-January is apparent from a letter to Alphonse Des Vignoles, to whom he entrusted the manuscript for comment and revision. On 2 February 1705, the very day on which the manuscript was returned to him, he also received the news of the death of Sophie Charlotte; and the loss of his close friend, which disrupted for several months his interest in intellectual work and correspondence, may also have sapped the energy needed for the tedious work of preparing such a lengthy work for publication. Despite the affirmation of Naudé, it seems, the final polishing of the manuscript was still lacking. Leibniz tinkered with it at least as late as May 1705, but did not finish the work;[203] and by 10 July of that year he had resolved to withhold publication.[204] Just as one death in November 1704 may have deprived his contemporaries of Locke's response to Leibniz, another three months later deprived them of Leibniz's response to Locke. Readers had to await the appearance of Rudolf Erich Raspe's *editio princeps* of the *Nouveaux Essais* in 1765 to have access to one of Leibniz's two most voluminous philosophical writings.[205] As on numerous previous occasions, one cannot but be astonished at Leibniz's ability to turn his back on even his most polished and significant manuscripts.

The hasty and interrupted way in which the *Nouveaux Essais* had been written goes a long way towards explaining the somewhat rambling and fragmentary quality of significant portions of the final dialogue between Locke's spokesman (Philalethes, profusely quoting from Coste's translation) and Leibniz's own representative, Theophilus. Moreover, despite its length, Leibniz did not attempt to provided a rounded account either of his own philosophy or of Locke's. Yet for all these limitations, the *Nouveaux*

Essais were undoubtedly a masterpiece of philosophical thinking of exceptional depth and seemingly inexhaustible fertility.[206] As Leibniz saw it, by the time he turned to the study of Locke's *Essay*, his own philosophical doctrines on the issues discussed by the English philosopher had already been fixed for a long time.[207] Rather than pushing his own thought to new conclusions, he regarded his task as that of refining – through the application of his well-oiled philosophical tools – the materials which Locke had left somewhat rough after a rather "superficial" and "cavalier" handling. Following the blueprint of Locke's *Essay*, Leibniz's *Nouveaux Essais* were organized in four books discussing "innate notions", "ideas", "words", and "knowledge". In them he passed judgment on Locke's doctrines and presented his own on the same issues. While acknowledging the merits of the *Essay*, he summarized for Thomas Burnett some of the main points of his disagreement, namely the related issues of necessary truths, innate knowledge, and the role of experience; the theory of substance; Locke's account of personal identity and his denial of the natural immortality of the soul; and Locke's account of freedom. Interestingly, Leibniz located the root of Locke's shortcomings in the English philosopher's lack of a proper understanding of the nature of mathematics:

I am in favour of innate lights, against his *tabula rasa*. In our mind there is not only a faculty, but also a disposition to knowledge, from which innate notions can be drawn. For all necessary truths draw their proof from this internal light and not from the experiences of the senses, which merely give occasion of thinking about these necessary truths and could never prove a universal necessity, since they only give knowledge from the induction from some examples and of the probability of other sense-experiences which have not yet been tested. Mr Locke is not sufficiently aware of the nature of demonstrations; and I also note that he speaks of substance in a cavalier fashion because he has not examined what it is in sufficient depth, and that he does not distinguish true and false ideas well enough. He says good things about freedom but does not sufficiently clarify his views; and what he says about [personal] identity – as if it merely consisted in self-consciousness – is not at all correct. Above all I wish that he had not upheld [the idea] that it is only by grace, that is to say by a miracle, that the soul is immortal, since this dogma does not have good consequences. Finally there are an infinity of points where I would wish to explain myself in a completely different fashion than Mr Locke. I find these reflections quite often a bit superficial. . . . Yet one must also admit that there is an infinity of beautiful reflections in Mr Locke and that when he upholds truthful views, he presents them in a great and beautiful light. So that this is without doubt one of the most beautiful philosophical books of our time.[208]

Whether or not Leibniz misinterpreted or overinterpreted Locke on many points, the close confrontation with the masterwork of an outstanding

contemporary typically became for him the occasion for a sharper formulation or reformulation of a wealth of striking insights, especially into
the nature of knowledge and of language. Locke's famous diatribe on
innatism and the origin of ideas sparked some of Leibniz most sustained
explanations of his theory of ideas. Rejecting Locke's conflation of 'idea'
with 'image', and, consequently, his tendency to assimilate the sensory
to the intellectual,[209] Leibniz proposed a sophisticated doctrine of ideas
and signs, distinguishing ideas as they are in the mind of God (that is,
as a sort of Platonic archetypes of possible things) and as they are in the
human mind (that is, as objects of human thought and reflection). On the
bedrock of this key distinction, six main levels could be identified: (i) ideas
in themselves (present in human minds as dispositions, in God's mind
as thought in act); (ii) representations and images (associated with ideas
when these are conceived); (iii) concepts (ideas grasped by the human
mind); (iv) terms (single linguistic expressions with which human beings
indicate ideas and concepts); (v) propositions in themselves (or possible
thoughts); (vi) propositions which are actually grasped by a psychologi-
cal act of thought (actual thoughts). These last always have a linguistic
'covering'.[210]

The foundation of any reality both of ideas in themselves (that is, as
archetypes or essences of possible things) and of the necessary (or eternal)
truths which are predicated of them was to be found, according to Leibniz,
in God's intellect. Embracing an argument proposed by Augustine to
demonstrate the existence of God (the so-called argument *ex aeternis
veritatibus*)[211] Leibniz wrote in the *Nouveaux Essais*,

it will be asked where these ideas would be if there were no mind, and what would then
become of the real foundation of this certainty of eternal truths. This question brings
us at last to the ultimate foundation of truth, namely to that Supreme and Universal
Mind who cannot fail to exist and whose understanding is indeed the domain of
eternal truths. St Augustine knew this and expresses it pretty forcefully. . . . it should
be borne in mind that these necessary truths contain the determining reason and
regulating principle of existent things – the laws of the universe, in short. Therefore,
since these necessary truths are prior to the existence of contingent beings, they must
be grounded in the existence of a necessary substance. That is where I find the pattern
for the ideas and truths which are engraved in our souls. They are engraved there
not in the form of propositions, but rather as sources which, by being employed in
particular circumstances, will give rise to actual assertions.[212]

That is to say, ideas in themselves are in turn present in human minds
as natural dispositions. Here is the point at which Leibniz's conception

of innatism came into play. Its background was precisely the distinction between ideas in themselves and actual thoughts (propositions actually grasped by the human mind and constituted by concepts, which are always indicated by some sort of 'sign'). According to Leibniz, it was not the actual thoughts which were innate, but the natural dispositions which under the stimulus of experience allowed the formulation of actual thoughts: "Knowledge, ideas and truths can be in our minds without our ever having actually thought about them. They are merely natural tendencies, that is dispositions and attitudes, active or passive, and more than a *tabula rasa*."[213] To describe this transition from innate "dispositions and attitudes" to ideas actually conceived by the human mind, Leibniz proposed in the *Nouveaux Essais* two famous similes: a block of marble in which the veins already marked out the statue of Hercules, or, perhaps even more fittingly, a screen ("une toile") that is "not uniform but is diversified by folds representing items of innate knowledge" and on which images are projected.[214] To ideas and truths which are innate in us but not actually conceived correspond concepts and actual thoughts (truths as actually thought by someone), in which what was potential is actualized under the stimulus of experience. So experience is indeed essential to our actual knowledge, but not in the sense that our mind is a *tabula rasa* on which experience writes. Rather, experience brings to life what would be otherwise dormant.[215] On the other hand, experience is a necessary but not sufficient condition of all our knowledge: "Although the senses are necessary for all our actual knowledge, they are not sufficient to provide it all, since they never give us anything but instances, that is particular or singular truths. But however many instances confirm a general truth, they do not suffice to establish its universal necessity; for it does not follow that what has happened will always happen the same way."[216] In other words, we learn necessary truths on the occasion of experience but their epistemological status as 'necessary' cannot come from experience. It seemed obvious to Leibniz that "we contribute something from our side"[217] and that this "contribution" preceded experience and was the foundation of any demonstrative force of our reasoning. As he wrote (shortly before the composition of the *Nouveaux Essais*) in a key letter of 1702 to Sophie Charlotte regarding "that which is independent of the senses and matter," "it is by this *natural light* that the *axioms* of mathematics are also recognised. . . . And it is on such foundations that arithmetic, geometry, mechanics and the other demonstrative sciences are established, where, to be sure, the senses are certainly needed to obtain certain ideas of sensible things, and experiences are necessary in order to establish certain facts and even useful for verifying reasoning as if by a proof of sorts. But the force of demonstrations depends on intelligible notions and truths – the only ones capable of making us judge of that which is necessary."[218] Hence Leibniz's suggestion to Thomas Burnett that the shortcomings of Locke's epistemology were rooted in his insufficient understanding of mathematics and of the nature of its demonstrations.[219] Repeating *verbatim* a motto formulated as early as the summer of 1669,[220] Leibniz could therefore embrace the claim that *nihil est in intellectu quod non fuerit in sensu* but with a key emendation: *nisi ipse intellectus* ("there is nothing in the intellect that was not in the senses, except the intellect itself").[221]

Moreover, since (as the *Nouveaux Essais* reiterated) human beings cannot think without the support of some sort of sensible signs (characters), such as, for instance, sounds or written letters,[222] Leibniz had much to say about language.[223] In the third book of the *Nouveaux Essais* he devoted illuminating pages to the origin of natural languages, identifying in onomatopoeia (that is, the formation of a word by imitating the natural sound produced by or associated with the object or action involved) the basis on which natural languages were formed. According to Leibniz, onomatopoeic words are the result of the primitive emotional reaction (*affectus*) of human beings to things which they experience. In turn, the names which are attributed to things always refer originally to a plurality of individuals designated by the same term. In other words, a distinctive property of language is its generality, which reflects the distinctive property of thought in referring simultaneously to a plurality of things by abstracting from their individual features. On the basis of onomatopoeia, root words (*mots radicaux*) constituting the kernel of a language are formed. A language achieves an initial structure once a certain number of words designating concrete things have been developed, together with terms expressing relation (such as conjunctions and prepositions). The next step is the extension of the meaning of terms from the designation of concrete objects to the designation of abstract objects. In Leibniz's view, this transition was possible due to the employment of rhetorical tropes such as metaphors, synecdoches, and analogies.

Alongside these discussions on the nature of knowledge and of language, however, a strong metaphysical strand ran through the *Nouveaux Essais*,

revolving around Leibniz's doctrine of substance and the related issues of
the immateriality and immortality of the soul.[224] Indeed one of the aspects
of Locke's thought which bothered Leibniz most was his agnosticism
regarding the immaterial nature of the mind and his denial (as Leibniz saw
it) of the natural immortality of the soul.[225] It was this kind of metaphysical
problems which lay at the root of Leibniz's later suspicion (expressed in the
letters to Bierling of the autumn of 1709 and in the letter to Malebranche of
1711) of Locke's leanings towards a materialistic metaphysics of Socinian
inspiration.[226]

Clashes with Toland and Bayle

It was not until August 1701 that Leibniz had the opportunity to gain a
first-hand knowledge of the controversial work by Toland responsible for
stirring up much of the trouble between Locke and Stillingfleet. Toland
had come to Hanover shortly before the arrival of the delegation of Lord
Macclesfield, which brought to the Electress Sophie the Act of Settlement
on 14 August 1701. Considering his reputation as a freethinker and atheist,
his presence on such an occasion is rather surprising, and probably owed
more to the fact that he represented the radical faction of Whigs than
to the work he had written in support of the Protestant succession to
the English crown.[227] Whatever the explanation, he was treated with
regard by the court and favourably received by the Electress Sophie, who
judged his intentions "always . . . upright and good, despite the wrath
of his enemies."[228] For his part, Leibniz, having read Toland's *Life of
Milton*,[229] had formed the opinion that he "seemed an acute and learned
man" and was only in need "of a little more moderation."[230] Moreover, as
Leibniz wrote once again to Thomas Burnett, "I can readily believe that
people have been unfair to him, and that the liberty which he has taken
(sometimes perhaps a little excessive) has produced his bad reputation.
For it is the bad habit of ignorant people to label as atheists all those who
do not bend to all prejudices."[231]

When Toland arrived in Hanover, Leibniz was therefore reasonably
well disposed toward him and eager to meet.[232] Upon closer scrutiny
of Toland's philosophical, theological, and political ideas, however, his
benign view of the controversial freethinker darkened and became tinged
by suspicion. To begin with, Leibniz was finally able to acquire – probably from Toland himself – a copy of *Christianity Not Mysterious*. Upon

receiving it, he immediately penned on 8 August 1701 a series of remarks which he then communicated to Toland.[233] Behind Leibniz's polite tones, there was no mistaking his substantial disagreement with Toland's theses. Far from allowing a Christianity with no mysteries, Leibniz deployed his full arsenal in defending the presence of mysteries in both the natural and supernatural domain. In his view, human beings were able to provide a perfect explanation only of natural phenomena and not of things in themselves. This was because the comprehension of individual substances "involves the infinite" and therefore escapes the finite intellect. If this was the case in the natural domain, concluded Leibniz, "nothing prevents certain divinely revealed dogmas" from being above (human) reason.[234] Reporting to Thomas Burnett of Kemney on Toland's Hanoverian visit, Leibniz accordingly decreed, "He is very acute and even does not lack learning, but his views go too far."[235] The dowager electress, however, "took pleasure in listening to Mr Toland's discussions and in strolling with him in the garden of Herrenhausen" with Leibniz often in attendance[236] – until Sophie herself was warned against the Irishman by numerous people and chose to amend her ways. Leibniz also advised prudence regarding Toland's political motivations,[237] and in June 1702, in a letter to Ezechiel Spanheim, remarked that Toland had rendered himself odious to numerous people due to his controversial writings.[238]

Such growing caution in Hanover did not prevent Toland from being sympathetically received in Berlin, whence he transferred toward the end of August 1701 in order to call upon Sophie Charlotte.[239] When Leibniz eventually managed to follow a month or so later, Toland had probably left.[240] Further occasions for discussion arose the following year when Toland, to Leibniz's dismay,[241] arrived once again in Berlin in July 1702 and enjoyed the continuing willingness of Sophie Charlotte to engage in conversation despite the fact that she found him "very imprudent and bold."[242] Leibniz, who had arrived in Lützenburg on 11 June 1702 to remain for an entire year, was summoned by the queen to discuss philosophy and politics with Toland and other learned men of her entourage, notably the Lutheran theologian Isaac Beausobre.[243] Sophie Charlotte was particularly keen to learn what Leibniz thought of two questions which had been raised by Toland in correspondence with her mother, namely "whether there is something in our thoughts which does not come from the senses, and whether there is something in nature which is not material."[244] This proved the occasion for a debate involving Leibniz and Toland, with

Sophie Charlotte acting as mediator. In important letters addressed to the queen, Leibniz presented the key tenets of his theory of knowledge and his views on the physiology of perception, countering Toland's account.[245] The controversial freethinker, true to his reputation, proposed in fact a basically materialistic conception of the soul, which Leibniz regarded as grounded in "the doctrine of Lucretius, that is to say, on the concourse of corpuscles." Needless to say, the German philosopher was deeply displeased by such a materialistic conception, which in his view lacked a proper explanation of how matter came to have movement and order and of "how there is sentience in the world." Leibniz's caustic conclusion was that "instead of playing at philosophising, which is not all his forte, [Toland] would do better to concern himself with establishing facts."[246] As for Leibniz's own views, amongst other things, he treated Sophie Charlotte to one of his most lucid expositions of his doctrine regarding the fundamental epistemological role played by the faculty of imagination. Imagination, Leibniz explained to the Prussian queen, is an internal sense in which the perceptions of the external senses are united.[247] It constitutes a middle stage (shared with some species of animals) between the sensory side of the animal condition and the distinctively human intellectual faculty. By unifying the data provided by individual senses (for instance, the visual and tactile data of our perception of a table), imagination plays a fundamental role in our perception of the world. In fact, Leibniz regarded the objects of our experience as mental constructions or "well founded" phenomena (appearances) resulting from the unification of sense data by the imagination and the intellect.[248]

Besides gracing Sophie Charlotte and company with his own philosophical doctrines, Toland apparently brought to Berlin the second edition of Bayle's *Dictionaire historique and critique*, freshly published in Rotterdam.[249] Leibniz too had personal reasons for eagerly awaiting its publication and had in fact already received the three-volume work in Hanover, shortly before leaving for Berlin.[250] The footnotes of Bayle's masterpiece were famously evolving into a cornucopia of critical remarks on every conceivable subject; and his objections to Leibniz's *Système nouveau* had been inserted into an article on Jerome Rorarius (1485–1566) in the first edition of the *Dictionaire* in 1697. Leibniz had responded to these objections with an "explanation of the difficulties which M. Bayle found with the New System" which was published in the *Histoire des ouvrages des savans* in July 1698.[251] As Bayle himself had announced,[252] a new note to the article on Rorarius in the second edition replied to Leibniz's "explanation";[253] and from Berlin, on 19 August 1702 Leibniz responded in his turn to the latest remarks from Bayle.[254] Even more important than these direct published exchanges between the two men were the ongoing, informal conversations of Sophie Charlotte's entourage, which returned repeatedly to Bayle's work during the summer of 1702.[255] As Leibniz recounted later on, it was during these discussions that bits and pieces of the *Essais de Théodicée* published in 1710 took shape:

> the late Queen of Prussia gave occasion to this work. For on several occasions I was with her during the summer months at Lützenburg (a country house near Berlin which is now called Charlottenburg), and in my presence she had read to her some pungent passages from the works of Mr Bayle, passages in which – along with thousands of curious and agreeable things – he raises objections against providence and other articles of natural theology. I attempted to reply to them; and since my answers did not displease Her Majesty, she desired me from time to time to put them in writing. The result was numerous scraps which, on the urging of friends who knew about all of this, I stitched together to make a single work.[256]

Debating Metaphysics and the Foundations of Ethics

During the years of his increasing engrossment in the thought of Locke, Leibniz also continued to expound his own metaphysical doctrines in the context of the lively philosophical debate stimulated across the *république des lettres* by the publication in 1695 of both the *Specimen Dynamicum* and the *Système nouveau*. In September 1698 there appeared in the *Acta Eruditorum* an important paper – *De ipsa natura* – written with the intention of supporting and explaining one of the most fundamental metaphysical doctrines of his philosophical system in general, and of his dynamics in particular, namely the thesis that there is in created things an internal force which constitutes their own principle of action.[257] The occasion for the paper was the dispute ongoing since 1692 between the Cartesian philosopher and physicist Johann Christoph Sturm (1635–1703) and Günther Christoph Schelhammer. Sturm had already crossed Leibniz's path and corresponded indirectly with him in 1694 and 1695 on issues of philosophy, mathematics, and physics.[258] Following the doctrine of "occasional causes" proposed by certain Cartesians – La Forge, Cordemoy, Geulincx – and made famous by Malebranche, Sturm maintained the intrinsic passivity of created things.[259] According to this view, the

sole principle of activity is found in God. He is the only one who properly acts, whereas created things are merely the 'occasion' and not the
'cause' of action.[260] Taking issue with the claim that in this way the glory
of God was properly established, Leibniz pointed out that occasionalism
was headed down the slippery slope of Spinozism, no matter how pious
the intentions of its defenders.[261] If there is not a principle of activity in
things themselves and God does everything, then one should conclude
that God is everything and that created things are merely modifications
of the one divine substance, as maintained by Spinoza. According to a
fundamental philosophical principle embraced by Leibniz since his early
years and summarized in the traditional formula "*actiones sunt suppositorum*" ("*actions are proper to supposita*"),[262] the key criterion for qualifying
as a substance was in fact, in his view, to have in itself an internal principle
of action.

De ipsa natura, in summarising Leibniz's own doctrine of corporeal
substance, employed the term of "monad" for the first time in print,
which Leibniz had introduced in his private correspondence three years
earlier:[263]

it can be concluded that there must be found in corporeal substance a *primary entelechy*
or first recipient of activity, that is, a primitive motive force which, superadded to
extension, or what is merely geometrical, and mass, or what is merely material, always
acts . . . it is this substantial principle itself which is called *soul* in living beings and
substantial form in other beings, and inasmuch as it truly constitutes one substance
with matter, or a unit in itself, it makes up what I call a monad[.][264]

From the late 1690s onwards the term of "monad" became a regular
fixture of Leibniz's distinctive philosophical vocabulary. Whether in private correspondence or in print he resorted to it to encapsulate in one
word his doctrine of substance. At the same time he was often at pains to
explain to the public or to his correspondents what he meant by "monad."
For instance, in an important philosophical exchange of the late summer
and autumn of 1698 with his long-standing friend and fellow mathematician, Johann Bernoulli (1667–1748), Leibniz explained that "By a Monad
I understand a substance truly one, that is, which is not an aggregate
of substances," and then proceeded to summarize his conception of the
nature of body.[265] But it was in the correspondence with a colleague and
friend of Bernoulli, the Dutch professor Burchard de Volder, that Leibniz

offered his most rounded statement regarding the structure of corporeal substance in relation to his concept of monad.[266] Writing on 20 June 1703 to De Volder, he stated,

> I distinguish therefore (1) the primitive Entelechy or Soul, (2) Matter, i. e. primary matter, or primitive passive power, (3) the Monad completed by these two, (4) the Mass [Massa] or secondary matter, or organic machine, for which countless subordinate Monads come together [ad quam . . . concurrunt], (5) the Animal or corporeal substance, which is made One by the Monad dominating the Machine.[267]

This was arguably Leibniz's favourite definition of monad, where the monad was conceived as the basic metaphysical entity out of which everything else results and which is in turn constituted by two inseparable principles: a soul or substantial form or entelechy (also conceived as primitive active force) and primary matter (also conceived as primitive passive force).[268] In Leibniz's view, the only exception was God, in Whom there is no passivity and therefore no matter. The perhaps more notorious definition of monad as (*tout court*) a soul or soul-like immaterial entity, if correctly interpreted, was not inconsistent with the above definition: it may have been employed by Leibniz especially to win over Cartesian readers keen to preserve Descartes's sharp distinction between immaterial mind and material body and therefore more likely to be resistant to any talk of matter (primary or otherwise) as one of the two constituents of the basic metaphysical elements of reality. According to the neat ontological picture painted for De Volder in the text quoted above, corporeal substances were not competing metaphysical entities ultimately incompatible with Leibniz's mature doctrine of monads and therefore removed from the central stage of Leibniz's metaphysics (albeit never completely dismissed). Rather, they appeared to fit quite nicely into a monadological framework insofar as corporeal substances were conceived as aggregates of the indissoluble unities of soul and primary matter which Leibniz called monads. The difference between corporeal substances and the mere "Mass [Massa] or secondary matter, or organic machine" (also ultimately resulting from an aggregate of monads) lay in the fact that in corporeal substances a dominating monad provided the principle of unity required by anything in order properly to qualify as a substance – in this case a *corporeal* substance, that is, a substance with an organic body (the organic machine or secondary matter "for which countless subordinate Monads come together"). In other words, "the animal" – a microscopic organism, a worm, a cat, a human being – is a corporeal substance, that is, an entity which is properly "one" thanks to a perceiving soul-like form which dominates a piece of secondary matter (the body or organic machine of the animal). In the summary of his ontology presented to De Volder, substances were therefore clearly reminiscent of the Aristotelian polarity of form and matter – both at the level of the basic elements of reality (the simple substances or monads constituted by a primitive entelechy or soul and by primary matter) and at the level of corporeal substances (constituted by a soul-like form and by secondary matter). In the Leibnizian account, however, there was only one type of ontological 'ingredient' from which, in the last instance, the animal or corporeal substance resulted: the monads. Organic bodies as they appear to us were in his view the phenomenal expression of corporeal substances and, ultimately, of monads, that is, of indissoluble unities of form and matter conceived as primitive active and passive powers.

De Volder, however, was himself a proponent of Cartesianism. As such, he was committed to the robust substantiality of bodies conceived as *res extensa*, that is, as *substances* of which extension is the essence or principal attribute. On the other hand, the brand of Cartesianism favoured by De Volder was opposed to occasionalism.[269] Through the intermediation of Bernoulli, he had turned to Leibniz with great expectations for an account of the corporeal world which avoided resort to the infamous 'occasional causes'. Between December 1698 and January 1706 Leibniz and De Volder devoted a great deal of time and effort to an extensive philosophical correspondence in which the Dutch professor pressed Leibniz to clarify his metaphysics.[270] Alas, De Volder was ultimately disappointed. Despite his genuine desire to understand what Leibniz was proposing, he became increasingly baffled by his correspondent's theories, not least because Leibniz had a tendency to proceeded with characteristic circumspection when it came to revealing the most counterintuitive aspects of his metaphysics. They were over five years into their correspondence before Leibniz finally revealed in clear terms the extent of his metaphysical idealism. On 30 June 1704 he wrote to his correspondent,

It should be said that there is nothing in things except simple substances, and in them perception and appetite. Matter and motion, however, are not so much substances or things as phenomena of perceivers, the reality of which is situated in the harmony of the perceivers with themselves (at different times) and with other perceivers.[271]

When De Volder read this letter, he could scarcely believe his eyes. On 14 November he replied bewildered,

You now clearly seem to me to eliminate bodies completely, inasmuch as you consider them merely appearances, and substitute mere forces for things, and not even corporeal forces but *perception* and *appetite* – claims which truly envelope my mind in such darkness that even now, after I have read and re-read your letters many times over, I would not dare to claim that I properly understand what you are saying.[272]

Gradually it became patent that they were divided by radically different views on key issues such as the methodology to be employed in metaphysics, the nature of substance and extension, and Leibniz's conception of body as phenomenal or mind-dependent. Yet once again their correspondence bore fruit in forcing Leibniz to one of the most detailed and profound expositions of his metaphysics in the context of his critique of Cartesian philosophy of nature.

Other important philosophical exchanges in this period included Leibniz's correspondence with Isaac Jaquelot and Lady Damaris Masham, and François Lamy's discussion of the *Système nouveau*. Jaquelot, a French refugee who had fled France after the revocation of the Edict of Nantes and served as Reformed Court Chaplain in Berlin, had met Leibniz in 1702 during one of the latter's extended stays at the Brandenburg court. Between the two men there soon developed a close philosophical debate – first on the Cartesian argument for the existence of God,[273] and then on a variety of other topics, notably in 1704 and 1705 on Leibniz's doctrine of pre-established harmony.[274] Despite the fact that Leibniz's theory struck at the very core of occasionalism by asserting the presence of an internal principle of activity in things, to Jaquelot it appeared close to the doctrine of "occasional causes." In his view, it differed from the latter only in that all the soul's ideas were "put into it in advance, whereas in the system of occasional causes ideas are produced only when they are occasioned by the physical traces."[275] Leibniz was not impressed. Not only had Jaquelot missed the main ground of his disagreement with occasionalism; he also charged Leibniz's doctrine with destroying free will entirely.[276] In the ensuing correspondence, a lengthy debate unfolded on the issue of human freedom and its compatibility with the pre-established order of things and God's foreknowledge, culminating with the publication in 1705 of Jaquelot's *Système abregé de l'âme et de la liberté*, which Leibniz answered in a *Remarque*.[277]

In turn, by 1699 the French Benedictine François Lamy (1636–1711) had already published his contribution to the discussion of "the way of pre-established harmony."[278] In the second edition of his six-volume work *De la Connoissance de soi-même* (Paris 1699/1701), Lamy had discussed Leibniz's *Système nouveau*, referring also to Leibniz's so-called "third explanation" of it (published in the *Journal des Sçavans* of 19 November 1696) and to Leibniz's further "Eclaircissement des difficultez que Monsieur Bayle a trouvées dans le système nouveau de l'Union de l'âme et du corps [Clarification of the difficulties that Mr. Bayle has found in the new system of the union of soul and body]" (published in the *Histoire des ouvrages des savans* of July 1698).[279] Leibniz replied to Lamy's objections first in a series of remarks of 30 November 1702,[280] and then in a piece which was sent to the *Journal des Sçavans* in 1704 but had to wait until 1709 to see the light in one of the *Suppléments* to the journal.[281]

As for Lady Damaris Masham, this learned and intelligent woman was ideally placed to provide Leibniz with an opportunity to discuss the philosophies of both her distinguished guest, John Locke, and her famous father, the Cambridge Platonist Ralph Cudworth. Their correspondence began around the end of December 1703, when Leibniz became aware that Lady Masham had sent him a copy of her father's massive *True Intellectual System of the Universe* (London 1678) and wrote to her with his thanks for this gift.[282] With the gallant turn of phrase of a consummate courtier, Leibniz remarked that he would not have dared to enter into philosophical intricacies when he had "the honour of writing to a Lady" had he "not known the insight of which English ladies were capable," a sample of which he "had seen in the work of the late Viscountess Conway."[283] With this flourish another stimulating philosophical correspondence was under way, driven in this specific case by Leibniz's desire to mould his philosophical views into a shape which would appeal to those familiar, as Lady Masham was, with the thought of both Locke and Cudworth. In particular, in his second letter to Lady Masham, written in early May 1704, he introduced the principle that "everywhere and at all the time, everything is the same as here" – that is, the principle that there is in nature a uniformity which allows us to draw from our own experience a model which can be applied to the rest of the universe.[284] In the same letter, after thanking Lady Masham once again for sending a copy of her father's *System*, Leibniz confided his eagerness to reread this work, especially since he had been planning for some time to review his own "meditations on related subjects."[285] Further reasons for finally taking up the pen to write on the matter came from the invitations to clarify his views on Cudworth issued in print by Pierre Bayle and Jean Le Clerc (respectively in the *Histoire des ouvrages des savans* of August 1704 and in the *Bibliothèque Choisie* of 1705, tome 5).[286] Leibniz's *Considérations sur les Principes de Vie, et sur les Natures Plastiques*, addressing Cudworth's doctrine of plastic natures in the light of Leibniz's own system, were written at some point between May 1704 and May 1705, the date on which they where published in the *Histoire des ouvrages des savans* in the form of a letter to its editor, Basnage de Beauval.[287]

The favours of the philosophical muse were not, however, reserved for the ladies of England, such as Lady Masham and Viscountess Conway. A strong philosophical disposition ran no less clearly through the female descent of the Palatine family. Indeed, Sophie Charlotte had inherited this intellectual acumen from her mother, whose philosophical conversations also gave rise to remarkable texts by Leibniz. In a letter addressed to Sophie Charlotte from Hanover on 5 August 1703, Leibniz wrote,

Having had . . . a conversation with the Elector in the presence of the Electress on the nature of goodness and justice – whether it is an arbitrary thing, or whether it is grounded in eternal reasons, as numbers and figures are – I wrote a little discourse about it, and I do not know whether I will dare someday to show these bagatelles to Your Majesty.[288]

Since Georg Ludwig was no philosopher, the real convener of this discussion was in all likelihood Sophie. Its fruit was the *Méditation sur la notion commune de la justice*, perhaps Leibniz's most important and extensive writing on the notion of justice as charity of the wise and universal benevolence.[289] Organized in two parts of strongly Platonic inspiration, the *Méditation* was left unpublished. In it Leibniz took a firm stand against the voluntarism defended in various ways by some of his favourite critical targets – Descartes, Pufendorf, and Hobbes. Repeating almost verbatim Plato's celebrated 'Euthyphro dilemma', he opened the *Méditation* with the vexed question of whether there is an objective standard of goodness and justice:

It is agreed that whatever God wills is good and just. But there remains the question whether it is good and just because God wills it or whether God wills it because it is good and just: in other words, whether justice and goodness are arbitrary or whether they belong to the necessary and eternal truths about the nature of things, as do numbers and proportions.[290]

Following Plato, Leibniz's answer seized the second horn of this dilemma: justice and goodness belong to "eternal truths about the nature of things", which as such have the same kind of absolute necessity as the truths of logic and mathematics. Divine justice and human justice must therefore be of the same kind, differing from one another only in degree of perfection. As for the notion of justice itself, Leibniz claimed, "justice is nothing else than the charity of the wise, that is to say goodness toward others which is conformed to wisdom." In turn, wisdom "is nothing else than the science of felicity."[291]

The Escalation of the Calculus War

While Leibniz was busy with all his court duties, public enterprises, and multifaceted philosophical exchanges, the priority dispute on the invention of the calculus continued to unfold.[292] In April 1699 there appeared the third volume of John Wallis's *Opera mathematica*, which included a collection of Leibniz's mathematical letters to Newton, Oldenburg, and Wallis himself, together with the Newtonian *epistola prior* and *epistola posterior*. In the summer the volume came to the notice of the Marquis de L'Hôpital, who wrote with alarm to his German friend,

Wallis has published a third volume of his mathematical works in which he has inserted some of your letters to Mr Newton and others, and this, I believe, with the intention of attributing to the latter the invention of your differential calculus, which Newton calls 'fluxions'. It seems to me that the English are using every means possible to attribute the glory of this invention to their nation.[293]

Leibniz was not surprised by the publication of his letters in Wallis's volume because the eminent English mathematician had contacted him in advance, asking for permission and offering him the opportunity of revising the texts in question. Leibniz, however, was at the time too busy and in any case feared that he would be unable to retrieve the drafts of the original letters from the mountain of his papers. Trusting Wallis's good faith as a scholar, he granted permission without perusing the selection.[294] Presented with a fait accompli, Leibniz reacted calmly to L'Hôpital's worried words: "Mr Wallis asked my permission to publish my old letters and he even added that I could delete what I judged appropriate; but since I have nothing to fear from the naked truth, I replied that he could publish what he judged worthy."[295] When Johann Bernoulli reiterated L'Hôpital's observation that Wallis was behaving as a "valient champion of English glory,"[296] Leibniz (knowing that Wallis was not really interested in denigrating him) answered magnanimously, advocating a healthy patriotism which encouraged new discoveries for the universal benefit:

That Wallis, as you have said, is a valiant champion of English glory is grounds for praise rather than blame. I sometimes reproach my fellow countrymen that they are not sufficiently valiant champions of German glory. Competition amongst nations, while it should not lead us to speak ill of others, will nevertheless have the virtue of making us strive to equal or surpass others. The fruit of such competition comes to everyone; its praise to those who deserve it.[297]

The worst, however, was still to come, and this time Leibniz could not keep silent. About the same time Wallis's third volume was published, there appeared a treatise on the brachistochrone (that is, the curve of quickest descent) by the Swiss mathematician Nicolas Fatio de Duillier. In it Fatio suggested none too subtly that Leibniz might well have plagiarized Newton, while openly calling the German mathematician the second inventor of the calculus.[298] To add salt to the wound, Fatio's work was published with the imprimatur of the Royal Society, thereby suggesting that the Society approved of its charges. On 6 August 1699, Leibniz wrote to Wallis, venting his displeasure. Wallis replied on 29 August (O.S.), assuring Leibniz that Fatio's attack neither had his approval nor that of the Royal Society: the imprimatur had been granted by the vice-president, J. Hoskins, who had been quite unaware of the specific content of what he took to be a straightforward mathematical treatise.[299] The Secretary of the Royal Society, Hans Sloane, informed by Wallis of Leibniz's complaints, apologized in writing.[300] For his part, Leibniz replied in print to Fatio with a paper published in the *Acta Eruditorum* of May 1700.[301]

Further attacks against Leibniz's calculus, albeit of a different kind, came in 1700 and 1701. In the first half of 1700, one of the salaried mathematicians of the Académie Royale des Sciences of Paris, Michel Rolle, criticised Leibniz's differential calculus for lack of clarity, rejecting the concept of infinities and infinitesimals of higher orders.[302] Due to the absence of the recognised French authority on the calculus, the Marquis de L'Hôpital, the onus of answering Rolle's objections fell upon Pierre

Varignon, another salaried mathematician of the Académie. In a meeting in early August 1700, Varignon ably defended the calculus and demonstrated Rolle's ignorance on the matter. He then sent a letter to Johann Bernoulli in order to inform both Bernoulli and Leibniz of the dispute.[303] A few months later, in the May–June 1701 issue of the *Mémoires de Trévoux* (the journal of the French Jesuits), a new attack against the calculus appeared, this time asserting that it lacked the kind of evidence to be expected in geometrical demonstrations. Leibniz answered with a short reply published in the November issue of the journal.[304] Upon reading it, Pierre Varignon wrote directly to Leibniz, inviting him to provide a more exhaustive explanation which could serve to silence once and for all enemies of the calculus such as Rolle, as well as the people who had attacked it from the pages of the *Mémoires de Trévoux*.[305] Leibniz obliged, writing on 2 February 1702 a letter of explanation to Varignon which he passed on for publication in the *Journal des Sçavans* of 20 March 1702. In his letter Leibniz explained that mathematical infinitesimals were not to be taken as "real things" but as "ideal notions which shorten the process of reasoning, and are similar to what is called imaginary roots in the common analysis".[306] The same idea was reiterated in response to a letter of Varignon of 23 May 1702 in which the French mathematician informed Leibniz that the secretary of the Académie, Fontenelle, intended to write a piece outlining "the metaphysical elements of your calculus."[307] "Between the two of us," Leibniz replied, "I believe that Monsieur de Fontenelle, who has a gallant and beautiful mind, meant to joke when he said that he wanted to provide the metaphysical elements of our calculus. To speak the truth, I am not very convinced myself that our infinites and infinitesimals should be considered otherwise than as ideal things or well founded fictions."[308]

A new chapter in the unending calculus controversy was opened in the summer of 1703 by the publication by George Cheyne of an exposition of integration based on Newton's method of fluxions.[309] Apart from peppering his work with errors, Cheyne's claims regarding Newton's priority in his mathematical discoveries induced Johann Bernoulli to write to Leibniz that in Cheyne's view "the rest of us are nothing but Newton's apes, pointlessly repeating what he had already accomplished long before us."[310] If nothing else, Cheyne's inaccurate exposition of the method of fluxions at least seemed to convince Newton of the necessity of publishing his own account. To the first edition of his *Opticks*, published in

London in 1704, Newton therefore appended two mathematical treatises: *De quadratura curvarum*, revealing his method of fluxions, and the *Enumeratio linearum tertii ordinis*, devoted to the classification of cubic curves. Leibniz published an anonymous review in the *Acta Eruditorum* of January 1705, which served only to enrage Newton, once it was belatedly brought to his attention in 1711.[311] As Newton saw it, this was the true beginning of the priority controversy and Leibniz was nothing else than the aggressor.[312] Above all, the English mathematician took issue with the use by Leibniz of the word "substituit" (substituted): in his view this gave the impression that he had, so to speak, started from Leibniz's notation and then modified it in his fluxions.[313] Leibniz protested that this was a clear misunderstanding of what he had meant: he had clearly stated a few lines earlier that Newton "employs, and has always employed, *fluxions*"; and the verb "substituit" referred not to Leibniz and Newton but to what H. Fabri had done in availing himself of Cavalicri's method.[314] But such grammatical clarification did not placate the English mathematician, who castigated Leibniz's explanation as a mere excuse.[315] In short, Leibniz's review of January 1705, although not intentionally incendiary, turned out to be an explosive device with a six-year fuse. Despite their courteous dealings in the past, after 1711 Newton counted Leibniz amongst his enemies.

Mathematical Facets of the Characteristica Universalis

Leibniz's mathematical mind could not be satisfied merely by revisiting the calculus, and still less by dwelling on the polemics surrounding it. Other discoveries – although less celebrated by his contemporaries – continued to provoke his enthusiasm, namely his *characteristica geometrica* or *analysis situs* and his binary arithmetic or dyadic. Like the calculus, both the *characteristica geometrica* and the dyadic were conceived as components in his most ambitious philosophical project: the development of the *characteristica universalis*.[316] This in turn formed part of his plan for the *propagatio fidei per scientiam* (propagation of faith through science), to which the dyadic in particular offered its symbolism of the creation ex nihilo and its powerful link with the metaphysics of monads or "real unities." When, after his election as a foreign member of the Paris Académie Royale des Sciences, the secretary of the Académie, Fontenelle, wrote to him on 8 December 1700 inviting a contribution to the new official annual publication of the Académie – the *Histoire de l'Académie Royale des Sciences*[317] – Leibniz thought none of his discoveries more worthy of this distinguished venue than the dyadic. Between January and February 1701 he therefore worked up his *Essay d'une nouvelle Science des Nombres*, which was sent to Fontenelle on 26 February from Wolfenbüttel.[318] The *Essay*'s introductory explanation of the significance of this contribution linked it at the same time to his project of the *analysis situs*:

It might appear strange to propose to innovate in a science as well known and long cultivated as that of numbers. Yet it will be shown that this has not been proposed without reason. Moreover, a new geometry remains to be developed, which I call *Analysis situs*, that depicts situations without figures and that provides a means of calculating completely different from algebra or from the calculation of magnitude. This analysis does not presuppose any other element, and will have a great many uses; but for the moment let us consider only arithmetic. Everyone agrees that the decimal progression is arbitrary, so that sometimes other numbering systems are employed. This fact caused me to think of the dyadic, or of the double geometrical progression, which is the simplest and most natural. I decided at the outset that it would have no more than two characters: 0 and 1 . . . This way [of calculating] should not be employed for the practice of ordinary calculation; but it could contribute a great deal to the perfection of science . . . Some people have admired in it the surprising analogy between the origin of all numbers out of 1 and 0 and the origin of all things from God and Nothing: from God as the principle of perfections, and from Nothing as the principle of privations or of the voids of essence, without need of any matter independent of God in addition to that.[319]

In the accompanying letter to Fontenelle, however, Leibniz expressed his desire to defer publication until his "new science of numbers" could be further developed, perhaps with the help of some promising mathematician whom the Académie could steer toward this worthy enterprise.[320] Two months went by without further news from Fontenelle on the essay, until the Secretary of the Académie wrote again on 30 April 1701. Leibniz's work had been presented at the meeting of the Académie of 23 April and the fellows now awaited "its applications with impatience." Meanwhile, Fontenelle continued, the essay was going to be published in the 1701 issue of the *Histoire*. Faced with the disappointing expectation of immediate applications rather than an appreciation of the deeper significance of his discovery, Leibniz specifically asked Fontenelle to withhold publication. Fontenelle obliged, but not without reiterating that Leibniz should provide the public with an indication of the kind of important advantages which were to be expected from the dyadic.[321] On 6 January 1703 Leibniz thanked Fontenelle with a touch of bitterness: "I thank you, sir, for withdrawing at my request my binary essay from the *Histoire de l'Académie Royale*. One must accommodate public taste, which wants to see palpable benefits."[322]

The satisfaction he did not receive from the Académie arrived shortly thereafter from other quarters. Since 1697 Leibniz had corresponded with Joachim Bouvet (1656–1730), one of the French Jesuits of the Chinese mission, who had been sent by Louis XIV to the imperial court of Peking to teach mathematics and science to the emperor in the expectation of preparing for a conversion to Christianity.[323] On 18 October 1697, Bouvet took the initiative of writing to Leibniz to congratulate him on the publication of the *Novissima Sinica*. Included with his letter was Bouvet's recent biography of the Chinese emperor, which Leibniz republished in Latin translation in the second edition of the *Novissima Sinica* (Hanover 1699).[324] In the ensuing correspondence with the learned Jesuit, plenty of things were bound to attract Leibniz's keen attention, given their shared commitment to the *propagatio fidei per scientiam*. In particular, in a letter of 28 February 1698 sent shortly before returning to China, Bouvet mentioned for the first time his studies on the ancient Chinese *Book of Changes* or *I Ching*. Bouvet believed he had found the explanatory key which could unlock the sixty-four hexagrams which formed the basis of the *I Ching*. These hexagrams were all formed by the combination of two symbols: a broken line (- -), representing the *yin* or female principle of passivity, receptivity, and descent, and a solid line (–), representing the *yang* or male principle of activity and ascent. According to the *I Ching*, all changes in the universe were a consequence of the interaction between these two fundamental and complementary principles. Following the Chinese tradition, Bouvet identified the mythological emperor Fuxi or Fu-Hsi (c. 2900 B.C.) as the creator of the principal forms of these hexagrams and of the so-called Fuxi order of the hexagrams (although in fact they were developed much later by the Chinese philosopher, Shao Yung (1011–77)). Moreover, he saw the original trigrams on which the hexagrams in turn were supposed to be based as the oldest form of Chinese writing:[325]

If I had had a bit of free time I would have written a Chinese Oedipus, or the Analysis of the first characters of that nation composed of small broken and unbroken horizontal lines, the invention of which they attribute to Fo-hii, and of which I believe I have found the true key. These characters . . . represent in a very simple and natural way the principles of all sciences; or to put it better, this is the complete system of a perfect metaphysics, the knowledge of which the Chinese seem to have lost a long time before Confucius. Moreover, the true understanding of this system or of these characters . . . could be very useful not only for re-establishing the principles of the true and legitimate philosophy of the ancient Chinese, and perhaps for returning this whole nation to the knowledge of the true God, but also for establishing the natural method to be followed in all sciences[.][326]

The parallel with Leibniz's own project of the *characteristica universalis* – a universal formal language expressing the principles of all sciences – was obvious. Writing toward the end of 1698 to Antoine Verjus (1632–1706), the Parisian procurator of the Jesuit's mission, Leibniz explicitly commented on the connection between his lifelong project and the news filtering out of China:

Since my youth I have planned a new characteristic which would provide the means not only of signifying, as the characters of the Chinese do, but also of calculating exactly regarding many things about which people have previously reasoned only in a vague manner. I achieved a little of this in my new infinitesimal calculus, in order to join geometry better with physics, and in another method not yet published which I call the *calculus situs*. But I aim to advance much further, if God gives me enough life and enough leisure and assistance for this; and I believe that there is nothing which would be more useful to human reason than to achieve this characteristic. Now since the Reverend Father Bouvet hopes (judging from what he has written to me) to decipher certain ancient characters which are venerated by the Chinese and which he believes are related to philosophy (which by this means could be insinuated to them in order to serve our Theology) I thought that one could perhaps eventually make these characters suitable (if one was well informed about them) not only for representing things (as characters ordinarily do) but even for calculating and for aiding imagination and philosophical reflection[.][327]

Leibniz pinpointed the difference between the Chinese symbolic language and his own *characteristica* in the fact that the latter aimed not simply at the universal communication of thoughts but at their "calculation." This calculation would be made possible through three further features of the *characteristica*: the identification of concepts which are primitive (at least for us); the development of a fixed and unambiguous correlation between a determined sign and a determined concept; and the formulation of a set of rules for the combination of these concepts. Leibniz's logical calculus, in which letters and numbers were employed to indicate concepts and formulate propositions, therefore provided a sample of how this calculation of thoughts could have been performed.[328]

Even more exciting news was to come from Bouvet, which took this parallel between the *I Ching* and the *characteristica universalis* still further. While he was putting the finishing touches to his essay on the dyadic for

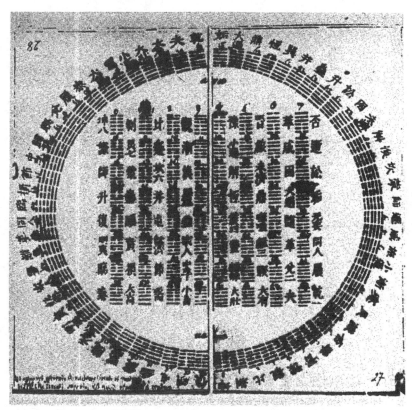

Figure 7.1. As in LBr 105 (Bouvet), Bl. 27 8 (Gottfried Wilhelm Leibniz Bibliothek – Niedersächsische Landesbibliothek Hanover).

the Académie Royale des Sciences, Leibniz wrote a long letter to Bouvet in which he included a detailed exposition of his binary arithmetic, presented as "an admirable representation of Creation" because "following this method all numbers are written by mixing unity and zero, more or less as all creatures come only from God and nothing."[329] Bouvet replied from Peking on 4 November 1701, announcing to Leibniz the discovery of an amazing analogy between the dyadic and the hexagrams of the *I Ching*, where the 0 was represented by the broken line and the 1 by the solid line.[330] In the letter Bouvet included a depiction of the so-called Fuxi order of the hexagrams showing the correspondence between the *I Ching* hexagrams, Leibniz's binary notation, and the decimal notation from 0 to 63 (see Figure 7.1).

Bouvet's letter took a long time to make its way to Germany, but when it finally reached Leibniz on 1 April 1703 it was greeted with great enthusiasm. Not only had the Chinese independently developed a sort of *characteristica*, but this was reducible to a numerical analysis such as that ideally envisaged by Leibniz for his universal calculus of thoughts. Moreover, it was even possible to see in the Fuxi order a representation of the history of creation as narrated in Genesis, with a remarkable symbolic reference to the Trinity due to the fact that the sacred number seven was written in binary notation as 111.[331] For Leibniz this was a wonderful and unexpected confirmation of the existence of a universal truth which was independently discovered or providentially adumbrated in the most diverse cultures. Although not perhaps the sort of "palpable benefits" awaited by the more pragmatic members of the Académie Royale des Sciences, to Leibniz nothing could be more useful than the demonstration of the existence of such profound and fundamental universal truth. Within a week of receiving Bouvet's news, he prepared a new essay on the dyadic for the Académie, specifically mentioning the usefulness of his invention in connection with the discovered analogy with the hexagrams of the *I Ching*.[332] On 7 April the essay was sent directly to the president of the Académie, Jean Paul Bignon, for publication in the *Histoire de l'Académie Royale des Sciences* instead of the previous paper on binary arithmetic.[333] Meanwhile reports on the discovery were sent to the Jesuit Carlo Maurizio Vota and to the secretary of the Royal Society, Hans Sloane.[334]

Sophie Charlotte's Death

Ironically, Sophie Charlotte died in Hanover on 1 February 1705 while Leibniz was in Berlin. She had gone as usual to Hanover for the annual carnival and, during the journey, had contracted a heavy cold which developed into pneumonia. Leibniz had remained in Berlin but was planning to follow her to Hanover. In his last letter of 31 January, although alarmed by the news of the queen's bad health, he was very far from thinking that this illness could prove fatal;[335] but, on the morning of 2 February Joachim Heinrich von Bülow, a nobleman of the Hanoverian court, brought to Berlin the unexpected news of the Queen's demise in the early hours of the previous day.[336] Leibniz was devastated. Shortly after being informed of the tragic turn of events, he described to Sophie Charlotte's lady-in-waiting, Henriette Charlotte von Pöllnitz, his state of shock:

I judge of your feelings from my own. I do not weep, I do not complain, but I do not know where I am. The loss of the queen seems like a dream, but when I awake from my slumber I find it only too real. Your grief in Hanover does not surpass mine in anything, except that you have more vivid feelings and have been struck from close range by the misfortune that we share. This is what encourages me to write to you and to beg you to moderate your sorrow, if you can, so that it does not harm you. It is not by dark dispair that you honour the memory of one of the most accomplished princesses in the world. It is by imitating her that we can do so, and the learned world will do the same. This letter is more philosophical than my heart, but I am the master of my letter, and I am not in a fit state to follow my own advice exactly, though it is not less reasonable on that account.[337]

During the following days his grief grew, if anything, even deeper. Writing to Heino Heinrich von Fleming he remarked,

The sad news stunned me the first day. My resentment grew in proportion to my recovery from the blow which had surprised me, just as wounds when still fresh do not make you feel at first all the pain that they will cause. The kindness of the Queen toward me was a blessing which Her Majesty's constancy gave me the right to promise to myself for my entire life, considering her age and mine. But it was otherwise ordained. It was not interest which governed my attachment, but an uncommon agreement and satisfaction[.][338]

After a month he was still struggling to come to terms with his loss:

Although my reason tells me that regrets are superfluous and that we must honour the memory of the Queen of Prussia instead of mourning her, my imagination always presents this princess to me with all her perfections and reminds me that they have been snatched from us and that I have lost one of the greatest satisfactions in the world, which I could reasonably promise to myself for all my life.[339]

At the beginning of March he eventually returned to Hanover, but for several more months the profound sorrow for the loss of Sophie Charlotte provoked a unique hiatus in his life of ceaseless intellectual work and correspondence.[340] Finally, in July he began to re-emerge from his grief. On 10 July he resumed his correspondence with Lady Masham, explaining the reasons of his long silence with a heartfelt testimony to the outstanding intellectual qualities of the late queen:

My lady. The death of the Queen of Prussia has caused a long interruption in my correspondence and my intellectual work. This great Princess had unbounded good will towards me: she took pleasure in being informed about my speculations, she even deepened them, and I shared with her what came to me from you and what I had the honour of replying to you. There may never have been another Queen at once so accomplished and so philosophical. You can judge, Madame, what pleasure I would have had in often being close to such a Princess and being encouraged by the passion she had for the knowledge of truth. When she departed for Hanover I was due to follow her soon, since she gratiously asked for me very frequently; but what a shock it was for me, and for the whole of Berlin, when we learned of her death! For me in particular it was like being struck by lightning, since my personal loss was the greatest amidst this public misfortune. I thought I would fall ill, since feelings do not depend from reasoning. I have been so terribly distressed by this death, but have finally returned to myself and my friends[.][341]

Notes

1. See respectively Henriette Charlotte von Pöllnitz (Sophie Charlotte's lady-in-waiting) to Leibniz, 2 May 1702 (Klopp X, 146) and Sophie Charlotte to Leibniz, 1 September 1699 (A I, 17, 438).
2. Leibniz to Pierre Bayle, 19 August 1702 (GP III, 63).
3. Georg Ludwig to Sophie, 23 October 1703 (Pertz I, 1, xiv). Isaac Jaquelot (or Jacquelot, 1647–1708) was part of the French Reformed community exiled from France by the revocation of the Edict of Nantes. In 1702 he was called to Berlin by Sophie Charlotte's husband, Frederich I, as court preacher and pastor of the French refugee church. He worked for most of his life at a massive book on the truth and inspiration of the books of the Old and New Testaments (published posthumously in 1715 in Rotterdam). On his exchanges with Leibniz see below.
4. The term 'freethinker' emerged in England in the late seventeenth century to indicate people who refused to assent to doctrines on the basis of authority or revelation, advocating instead the supremacy of reason.
5. Leibniz to Sophie Charlotte, 12 February 1698 (A I, 15, 22).
6. See Müller–Krönert, Leben und Werk, p. 153.
7. See Müller–Krönert, Leben und Werk, pp. 153–154; Lackmann, "Leibniz' Bibliothekarische Tätigkeit in Hannover," p. 338.
8. Klopp VIII, 272.
9. See Ravier 252, 291, 292.
10. See Ravier 43, 48, 49; Scheel, "Leibniz als Historiker des Welfenhauses," pp. 263–4, 273; Müller–Krönert, Leben und Werk, pp. 130, 153, 169; A I, 11, l–lii; Leibniz, Schriften und Briefe zur Geschichte, pp. 230–35. See also Ravier 44, 45 (Leibniz's edition of Albericus Monachus's Trium Fontium Chronicon).
11. See the decisions of the Hauskonferenz of 12 July 1696 (Hanover, Niedersächs. Hauptstaatarchiv, Cal[enberg] Br. 24 Nr. 1628; Celle Br. 68 Nr. 55) and 20 September 1698 (Hanover, Niedersächs. Hauptstaatarchiv, Cal[enberg] Br. 22 Nr. 538 Bl. 6).
12. See Leibniz to Duchess Eleonore, 13 January 1699 (A I, 16, 69–71). See also Leibniz to the prime minister of Celle, Andreas Gottlieb von Bernstorff, 19 July 1701 (A I, 20, 17).
13. Leibniz to Caroline, 3 October 1714 (Klopp XI, 15–17).

14. The fragile son of Princess Anne, the Duke of Gloucester, died at eleven years of age on 7 August 1700.
15. See the undated letter of Sophie to the English ambassador, George Stepney, published in Klopp VIII, 214–15.
16. Cf. Klopp VIII, xxv–lxx.
17. See chap. II. 6.
18. See esp. George Stepney to Sophie, 21 September 1700 (Klopp VIII, 208–13); Leibniz to Stepney, 18 January 1701 (Klopp VIII, 239–44); Leibniz to Cressett (Klopp VIII, 227).
19. See for instance Klopp VIII, 218–25, 227–38, 251–6.
20. See Klopp VIII, 240.
21. See the speech to parliament of 21 February 1701 (Klopp VIII, lii).
22. See Müller–Krönert, *Leben und Werk*, pp. 154–5.
23. See Leibniz to Georg Ludwig, 29 January 1699 (A I, 16, N. 56).
24. See Jablonski to Leibniz, 29 September 1699 (*Deutsche Schriften* II, 107).
25. See Leibniz to the fellows of the Académie Royale des Sciences, 26 February 1700 (Dutens IV, ii, 143).
26. LII XLI, 8.
27. See Jürgen Mittelstraß, "Der Philosoph und die Königin – Leibniz und Sophie Charlotte." In *Leibniz in Berlin*. Ed. by Hans Poser and Albert Heinekamp. Stuttgart: Steiner, 1990, pp. 9–27; Ines Böger, "Der Spanheim-Kreis und seine Bedeutung für Leibniz' Akademiepläne." In *Leibniz in Berlin*, pp. 202–17; Hans-Stephan Brather, "Leibniz und das Konzil der Berliner Sozietät der Wissenschaften." In *Leibniz in Berlin*, pp. 218–30. The essential source for the history of the Berlin Academy of Sciences remains Adolf Harnack, *Geschichte der Königlich Preussischen Akademie der Wissenschaften zu Berlin*. 3 vols. Berlin: Gedruckt in der Reichsdruckerei, 1900.
28. On the intellectual activities of the lively Huguenot community in Berlin see Sandra Pott, Martin Mulsow, and Lutz Danneberg, eds., *The Berlin Refuge 1680–1780: Learning and Science in European Context*. Leiden: Brill, 2003.
29. See Eberhard Knobloch, "Die Astronomie an der Sozietät der Wissenschaften." In *Leibniz in Berlin*, p. 232; Rudolf Vierhaus, "Wissenschaft und Politik im Zeitalter des Absolutismus. Leibniz und die Gründung der Berliner Akademie." In *Leibniz in Berlin*, pp. 199–200; Müller–Krönert, *Leben und Werk*, p. 161.
30. See Harnack, *Geschichte*, II, N. 23–25, pp. 58–68; Harnack, *Geschichte*, I, pp. 73–105; Mittelstraß, "Der Philosoph und die Königin," p. 22; Böger, "Der Spanheim-Kreis," pp. 212, 214; Brather, "Leibniz und das Konzil der Berliner Sozietät der Wissenschaften," p. 222.
31. Harnack, *Geschichte*, II, N. 28, pp. 70–71.
32. See Klopp X, 299–304, 304–10; Harnack, *Geschichte*, II, N. 30a–b, pp. 76–8, 78–81; Brather, "Leibniz und das Konzil der Berliner Sozietät der Wissenschaften," pp. 221–2.
33. Klopp X, 299. Cf. also Klopp X, 304–5.

34. In January 1699 the Académie Royale des Sciences was reorganized and new regulations were introduced.

35. Leibniz to Georg Ludwig, 28 March 1700 (Klopp VIII, 150).

36. See Leibniz to Georg Ludwig, 28 March 1700 (Klopp VIII, 151).

37. See Leibniz to Sophie, 22 May 1700 (Klopp VIII, 151–5); Brather, "Leibniz und das Konzil der Berliner Sozietät der Wissenschaften," pp. 222–3.

38. See Harnack, *Geschichte*, II, N. 50, pp. 104–6; Brather, "Leibniz und das Konzil der Berliner Sozietät der Wissenschaften," p. 223.

39. See Leibniz's series of memos published in Klopp X, 310–25. See also FC, *Oeuvres*, VII, 626, 628–36, 637–43.

40. Klopp X, 325–8 (here 325–6).

41. See Leibniz to Jablonski, 26 March 1700 (*Deutsche Schriften* II, 155). The Society was renamed *Die Königliche Akademie der Wissenschaften* by Friedrich the Great on 29 January 1744 (cf. Harnack, *Geschichte*, II, N. 158, pp. 263–8).

42. Cf. Klopp X, 328–30 (see p. 328); Müller–Krönert, *Leben und Werk*, p. 165. The only member of Leibniz's family elevated to the nobility seems to have been Paul von Leubnitz, a nephew of Leibniz's great-great-grandfather, who was ennobled in August 1600 by Emperor Rudolf II for his merits in the war against the Turks. He died childless. Both Leibniz and his half-brother, Johann Friedrich, adopted his coat of arms. Cf. Müller, "Gottfried Wilhelm Leibniz." In *Leibniz. Sein Leben–Sein Wirken–Seine Welt*, pp. 8–9; Eckhart, *Lebensbeschreibung*, pp. 191, 225.

43. See Klopp X, 330, 331.

44. See Klopp X, 330.

45. See Klopp X, 331–6; Hans-Peter Schneider, "Leibniz und die preußischen Justizreformen im 18. Jahrhundert." In *Leibniz in Berlin*, pp. 281–96.

46. See Jablonski to Gabriel Groddeck, 4 September 1700 (Berlin Staatsbibliothek, Groddecks Nachlaß Bl. 78).

47. The other main founding member, Rabener, died in January 1701. See Brather, "Leibniz und das Konzil der Berliner Sozietät der Wissenschaften," p. 225. Gottfried Kirch, the first astronomer of the Society and the only other paid member, appointed on the recommendation of both Jablonski and Leibniz, never took an active interest in the work of the council. On Kirch and his appointement see Leibniz to Jablonski, 26 March 1700 (*Deutsche Schriften* II, 155); Jablonski to Leibniz, 21 April 1700 (*Deutsche Schriften* II, 167); Knobloch, "Die Astronomie an der Sozietät der Wissenschaften," pp. 234–5.

48. See Brather, "Leibniz und das Konzil der Berliner Sozietät der Wissenschaften," pp. 224–8; Vierhaus, "Wissenschaft und Politik im Zeitalter des Absolutismus," p. 201.

49. See Leibniz to Stepney, 18 January 1701 (Klopp VIII, 239).

50. See Leibniz to Georg Ludwig, 28 March 1700 (Klopp VIII, 151) and Leibniz to Jablonski, 30 August 1700 (Harnack, *Geschichte*, II, p. 124).

51. See Müller–Krönert, *Leben und Werk*, p. 167.

52. See Klopp VIII, xxx.

53. See Müller–Krönert, *Leben und Werk*, pp. 168–9; Ph. Hiltebrandt, "Eine Relation des Wiener Nuntius über seine Verhandlungen mit Leibniz (1700)." In *Quellen und Forschungen aus ital. Archiven u. Bibliotheken*. Vol. 10. Rome, 1907, pp. 238–46. On these last efforts by Leibniz towards a reunification with Rome see below.
54. Klopp VIII, xxxi.
55. See Leibniz to De Volder, 31 December 1700 (GP II, 219).
56. See Ravier 52: *La justice encouragée, contre les chicanes et les menaces d'un Partisan des Bourbons*. Published also in FC, *Oeuvres*, III, 331–44.
57. *Manifeste contenant les droits de Charles III, roi d'Espagne*, published in 1703–4 in four different French editions and a Dutch translation (in FC, *Oeuvres*, III, 377–431; see also FC, *Oeuvres*, III, 360–76; cf. Ravier 55–9, and Klopp IX, xiv). The *Manifeste* is partially translated by Riley in Leibniz, *Political Writings*, pp. 146–63.
58. See Klopp X, 338–46. Cf. also Ravier 53: *De nummis Gratiani Augg. Aug. cum Gloria Novi Seculi dissertatio*, published in Hanover in 1701.
59. A I, 20, 259.
60. See Müller–Krönert, *Leben und Werk*, p. 173.
61. See Leibniz to Claude Nicaise, 24 August 1701 (GP II, 593).
62. See Klopp X, 82–3.
63. Klopp VIII, 288.
64. Sophie to Leibniz, 19 October 1701 (Klopp VIII, 290).
65. See Klopp X, 353–61; 361–6; 366–71.
66. See *Summarische punctation, die Medicinalische observationes betreffend*, 1701 (Klopp X, 346–50). See also Klopp X, 350–53 and LH XXXIV, 25, Bl. 128 (Bodemann, *Handschriften*, pp. 274–6). Cf. Fritz Hartmann and Wolfgang Hense, "Die Stellung der Medizin in Leibniz' Entwürfen für Sozietäten." In *Leibniz in Berlin*, pp. 241–52.
67. See G. Schnath, "Die Überwältigung Braunschweig-Wolfenbüttels durch Hannover und Celle zu Beginn des Spanischen Erbfolgekrieges, März 1702." *Braunschweigisches Jahrbuch* 56 (1975): 27–100; Van den Heuvel, "Leibniz zwischen Hannover und Berlin," p. 275.
68. See Klopp X, 91–2.
69. See Müller–Krönert, *Leben und Werk*, p. 177; Leibniz to Thomas Burnett, 27 February 1702 (GP III, 287).
70. Klopp X, 136.
71. Klopp X, 136.
72. Klopp X, 137.
73. See Leibniz to Sophie Charlotte, 22 April 1702 (Klopp X, 145).
74. Quoted in Guhrauer, *Leibnitz*, II, p. 24 (*Anmerkungen*).
75. Klopp X, 146.
76. See Eckhart, *Lebensbeschreibung*, p. 174.
77. See Leibniz to King Friedrich I (Klopp X, 372–8). Cf. also Klopp X, 371–2; 379–83 and FC, *Oeuvres*, VII, 287–97.

78. See Leibniz's letter probably addressed to Cord Plato von Gehlen, second half of November 1699* (LBr 302, Bl. 4).

79. See respectively Klopp X, 372 and Theodor Distel, ed., "Vorlegung einer Abschrift der in dem Hauptstaatsarchive zu Dresden befindlichen Briefe von Leibniz." In *Berichte über die Verhandlungen der Königlich Sächsischen Gesellschaft der Wissenschaften zu Leipzig. Philologisch-Historische Classe.* Leipzig, 1879, vol. 31, pp. 130–32.

80. See Klopp X, 381–4.

81. Klopp IX, 8.

82. Klopp X, 384. See also the Guelf *Hauskonferenz* of 18 April 1705, where Leibniz was branded as "totus Brandenburgicus" (*Hauptstaatarchiv Hannover*, Cal[enberger] Br[iefschaftsarchiv] 22 V 217). Cf. Schnath, "Die Überwältigung Braunschweig-Wolfenbüttels durch Hannover und Celle," p. 46 and Van den Heuvel, "Leibniz zwischen Hannover und Berlin," p. 278.

83. *Briefe der Königin Sophie Charlotte von Preußen und der Kurfürstin Sophie von Hannover an hannoversche Diplomaten.* Ed. by R. Doebner. Leipzig, 1905 (Publicationen aus den Preußischen Staatsarchiven. 79; new print: Osnabrück, 1965), p. 31.

84. See Van den Heuvel, "Leibniz zwischen Hannover und Berlin," pp. 276–7.

85. LBr F 27, Bl. 124.

86. See Leibniz to Sophie Charlotte, 5 August 1703 (Klopp X, 212).

87. See Sophie to Leibniz, 7 January 1704 (Klopp IX, 71).

88. See Müller-Krönert, *Leben und Werk*, p. 188.

89. See Eduard Bodemann, ed., "Leibnizens Plan einer Societät der Wissenschaften in Sachsen." *Neues Archiv für Sächsische Geschichte und Alterthumskunde* 4 (1883), pp. 180–84.

90. Leibniz to J. R. Patkul, 2 February 1704, in "Leibnizens Plan einer Societät der Wissenschaften in Sachsen," p. 183.

91. See Leibniz to Carlo Maurizio Vota, 4 September 1703 (Bodemann, *Handschriften*, p. 368; "Leibnizens Plan einer Societät der Wissenschaften in Sachsen," p. 180). In June 1697 the elector of Saxony had converted to Catholicism, thereby upsetting the rough balance between Protestant and Catholic electors. See above, chap. I. 6.

92. See FC, *Oeuvres*, VII, pp. 218–29, 234–6, 249–65. See also ibid., pp. 230–33, 237–42, 243–8.

93. See "Leibnizens Plan einer Societät der Wissenschaften in Sachsen," pp. 189–90; Eckhart, *Lebensbeschreibung*, pp. 174–5.

94. See Müller–Krönert, *Leben und Werk*, p. 192.

95. See Leibniz to Le Thorel, 5 December 1698 (A I, 16, 306); Daniel Erasmi von Huldeberg to Leibniz, 9 February 1701 (A I, 19, N. 193); Leibniz to Daniel Erasmi von Huldeberg, 3 April 1701 (A I, 19, N. 293).

96. See Jablonski, 13 June 1699 (A I, 17, N. 165) and Jablonski to Leibniz, 29 September 1699 (*Deutsche Schriften* II, pp. 106–7).

97. See Leibniz to Sophie Charlotte, undated (Klopp IX, 95–6); Sophie to Leibniz, 3 September 1704 (Klopp IX, 96–7); Leibniz to Georg Ludwig, 16 September 1704 (Klopp IX, 101).

98. See respectively Klopp IX, 96 and 97.

99. Klopp IX, 101–2.

100. See Leibniz to Tschirnhaus, 26 December 1704 in "Leibnizens Plan einer Societät der Wissenschaften in Sachsen," pp. 208–9. See also Leibniz for Eckhart, August 1704 in "Leibnizens Plan einer Societät der Wissenschaften in Sachsen," p. 190.

101. See Klopp X, 394–9; Van den Heuvel, "Leibniz zwischen Hannover und Berlin", pp. 277–8.

102. See Leibniz to Sophie Charlotte, 31 January 1705 (Klopp X, 262); Leibniz to Baron von Görtz, 2 February 1705 (Klopp X, 263); Guhrauer, *Leibnitz*, II, p. 24 (*Anmerkungen*).

103. See above, chap. I. 6.

104. For the same reason, he encouraged the use of "Reformed" as opposed to "Calvinist" for the other main Protestant denomination. See esp. Leibniz to Jablonski, second half of September 1698 (A I, 15, 833). Cf. also Leibniz to Landgraf Ernst, 30 January 1692 (A I, 7, 257) and Leibniz to Molanus, 22 February 1698 (A I, 15, 371).

105. See Jablonski, *Kurtze Vorstellung*, in *Labora diligenter*, pp. 128–64, esp. pp. 134–6, 143–7, 154–64.

106. See A I, 14, N. 496; A I, 15, N. 201, N. 202; LH I 9, Bl. 168–73.

107. See LH I 9, 2, Bl. 106–67; LH I 9, 4, 174–315 (fair copy with many corrections in Leibniz's hand); LH I 7, 5, Bl. 95–9. The *Unvorgreiffliches Bedencken*, never published in their entirety, are forthcoming in A IV, 7. The excerpts reproduced in French translation in Dutens I, 735–7 are seriously misleading in their misrepresensation of the spirit of the document, due to the fact that Molanus and Leibniz's criticism of mere toleration amongst the Lutheran and Reformed churches is not placed in the context of their efforts to reach a proper reunification. A very interesting and significant selection of passages edited by Wolfgang Hübener can be found in *Leibniz in Berlin*, pp. 147–67. Cf. also Hartmut Rudolph, "Zum Nutzen von Politik und Philosophie für die Kirchenunion." In *Labora diligenter*, esp. pp. 119–20; Paul Schrecker, "G.–W. Leibniz. Lettres et fragments inédits," esp. pp. 37–9, 49–50; A I, 16, xxxviii; A I, 16 N. 55.

108. See esp. Leibniz to Molanus, 12 February 1698 (A I, 15, N. 208) and the passages of the *Unvorgreiffliches Bedencken* edited in *Leibniz in Berlin*, pp. 147–67.

109. Cf. A I, 16, xxxvii–xxxviii.

110. *Tentamen expositionis irenicae trium potissimarum inter protestantes controversiarum* (LH I 9, 7 Bl. 355–6). See Jablonski to Leibniz, 12 November 1698 (A I, 16, N. 162).

111. See Jablonski to Leibniz, 7 February 1699 (A I, 16, 545). Leibniz's *Tentamen* was published in the posthumous collection of Spener's *Consilia et judicia theologica latina*. Francofurti ad Moenum: Zunner & Jungius, 1709, Pars 1, pp. 105–10. Cf. also ibid., Pars 1, pp. 110–13, Spener's comment (*Reflexiones super tentamen irenicae expositionis*). Important improvements to the text of the *Tentamen expositionis irenicae* published in Spener's volume are offered by Wolfgang Hübener in *Leibniz in Berlin*, pp. 167–9.

112. See Schrecker, "G.-W. Leibniz. Lettres et fragments inédits," pp. 41–2. Contrary to Müller–Krönert, *Leben und Werk*, p. 160, who identified Spener as the author of the *Annotata placida*, these remarks must have been written by a Reformed theologian, as appears clearly from Leibniz's answer to them.

113. See Leibniz's defence of the *Tentamen expositionis irenicae* published in Schrecker, "G.-W. Leibniz. Lettres et fragments inédits," pp. 86–9. In this text, contrary to the opinion expressed on other occasions and possibly influenced by Molanus, Leibniz entertained the possibility of a more complete theological unity.

114. See Leibniz's report on the situation to Ezechiel Spanheim, 2 March 1699 (A I, 16, N. 362). See also Leibniz to Jablonski, 4 September 1699 (A I, 17, N. 273).

115. See A I, 17, xxxix; N. 308; N. 390.

116. See Jablonski to Leibniz, 24 November 1699 (A I, 17, 659).

117. See Leibniz to Molanus, beginning of November 1699 (A I, 17, N. 365 and N. 366); Leibniz to Cressett, 8 December 1699 (A I, 17, N. 404); Leibniz to Jablonski, 8 December 1699 (A I, 17, N. 405).

118. See A I, 17, 722.

119. See Schrecker, "Lettres et fragments inédits," pp. 47–9 and Wolfgang Hübener, "Negotium irenicum. Leibniz' Bemühungen um die brandenburgische Union." In *Leibniz in Berlin*. Ed. by Hans Poser and Albert Heinekamp. Stuttgart: Steiner, 1990, p. 124.

120. Leibniz's criticism of this book is published in J. E. Kapp, *Sammlung einiger Vertrauten Briefe, welche zwischen . . . Leibnitz und . . . Herrn Daniel Ernst Jablonski, auch andern Gelehrten, Besonders über die Vereinigung der Lutherischen und Reformirten Religion . . . gewechselt worden sind*, Leipzig 1745, pp. 368–71.

121. See Franz Julius Lütke, *Christliche unmaßgebliche Gedancken über die Vereinigung Der beyden Protestirenden Kirchen*. In Franz Julius Lütke, *Unvorgreiffliche Doch Wolgemeinte Gedancken Von Vereinigung der Christlichen Religionen*. N. pl., 1703, pp. 38–49.

122. See for instance Leibniz to Jablonski, 26 March 1700 (in Kapp, *Sammlung einiger Vertrauten Briefe*, p. 167; *Vorausedition*: A I, 18, N. 275).

123. Molanus to Leibniz, 5 December 1703 (in Schrecker, "Lettres et fragments inédits," p. 111).

124. See Kapp, *Sammlung einiger Vertrauten Briefe*, pp. 363–5 and Schrecker, "Lettres et fragments inédits," no. XXII.

125. See Schrecker, "Lettres et fragments inédits," no. XXIV (here p. 116). See also Kapp, *Sammlung einiger Vertrauten Briefe*, pp. 405–19. A further, interesting exchange with the Reformed community of French refugees in Berlin is represented by Leibniz's remarks on an irenical writing by Isaac Jaquelot (see Schrecker, "Lettres et fragments inédits," no. XXVI). Leibniz summarized these events in a letter of 1716 to the Princess of Wales, Caroline (Klopp XI, 85–6).

126. One of the strongest expressions of this conviction can be found in a letter to Caroline, Princess of Wales, written in the early spring of 1716 (Klopp XI, 85–90).

127. See Leibniz to Cressett, 16 November 1697 (A I, 14, N. 403). See also Leibniz to Cressett, 10 December 1697 (A I, 14, N. 460), and Leibniz to Caroline, Princess of Wales, spring* 1716 (Klopp XI, 85–90).

128. A I, 14, 690–91.

129. See Cressett to Leibniz, 23 November 1697 (A I, 14, N. 424).

130. A I, 15, 198.

131. See A I, 15, N. 535.

132. See Leibniz to Caroline, 3 October 1714 (Klopp XI, 15–17) and above.

133. See A I, 15, N. 267.

134. Gilbert Burnet to Leibniz, 27 February 1699 (A I, 16, 595).

135. Cf. Michael J. Murray, "Leibniz's Proposal for Theological Reconciliation among the Protestants." *American Catholic Philosophical Quarterly* 76, no. 4 (2002): 623–46 (here esp. pp. 625–6). Jablonski's printed translation (*Gilberti Burneti Dissertatio de praedestinatione et gratia etc., latine versa*, Berlin, 1701) with Leibniz's extensive remarks is found at LH I, 18. An edition and English translation are in preparation by Michael J. Murray and will appear in the series "The Yale Leibniz", published by Yale University Press. Murray's illuminating introduction discusses the deep and complex connections between Leibniz's theological and philosophical positions.

136. See Murray, "Leibniz's Proposal for Theological Reconciliation among the Protestants," esp. pp. 639–40 (quoting Leibniz's commentary on Burnet, § 2).

137. See Reiner von Vlostorff to Leibniz, 25 October 1696 (A I, 13, N. 200). See also A I, 14, N. 374.

138. See Leibniz for Rudolf Christian von Imhoff, 20* May 1698 (A I, 14, N. 375).

139. See A I, 15, N. 386, N. 403, N. 433.

140. See *Project de Leibniz pour faciliter la réunion des Protestants avec les Romains Catholiques*, French version of the *Declaratio Luccensis* written in Loccum on 27 August (O.S.)/6 September (N.S.) 1698 (FC, *Oeuvres*, II, 168–89); Molanus to Leibniz, 21* September 1698 (A I, 15, N. 523); Leibniz (as Molanus) to Georg Ludwig, 21* September 1698 (A I, 15, N. 524); Buchhaim to Leibniz, 27 December 1698 (A I, 16, N. 236); A I, 16, xxxv–xxxvi; Aloys Pichler, *Die Theologie des Leibniz.* 2 vols. Munich: Cotta, 1869–70, vol. II, pp. 492–3. The *Declaratio Luccensis* was published in J. D. Winckler, ed., *Anecdota historico-ecclesiastica novantiqua.* Vol. 1, 3, Braunschweig: Ludolph Schröders Erben, 1757, pp. 313–36. The draft in Leibniz's hand is found at LH I 10 Bl. 55–62.

141. See Buchhaim to Leibniz, 27 December 1698 (A I, 16, N. 236); Buchhaim to Leibniz, 10 January 1699 (A I, 16, N. 272); A I, 16, xxxv–xxxvi.

142. See Hiltebrandt, "Eine Relation des Wiener Nuntius," pp. 238–46. See also Franz Xaver Kiefl, *Der Friedensplan des Leibniz zur Wiedervereinigung der getrennten christlichen Kirchen aus seinen Verhandlungen mit dem Hofe Ludwigs XIV., Leopolds I. und Peters des Großen.* Paderborn: Schöningh, 1903, pp. lxv–lxx; 2nd

ed.: *Leibniz und die religiöse Wiedervereinigung Deutschlands*. Regensburg, 1925, pp. 122–7; Pichler, *Die Theologie des Leibniz*, vol. II, pp. 492–5.

143. See Hiltebrandt, "Eine Relation des Wiener Nuntius," pp. 243–4 and FC, *Oeuvres*, II (2nd ed. 1869), pp. 172–93.

144. See the undated letter of Cardinal Paolucci to Da Via published in Hiltebrandt, "Eine Relation des Wiener Nuntius," pp. 245–6.

145. See A I, 16, N. 114.

146. See A I, 16, N. 17.

147. See A I, 16, xxxvii.

148. See A I, 16, N. 275.

149. See Eisenkopf, *Leibniz und die Einigung der Christenheit*, pp. 71–2, 182–6.

150. Leibniz to Thomas Burnett of Kemney, 14 December 1705 (Klopp IX, 182).

151. FC, *Oeuvres*, II (2nd ed. 1869), 173.

152. See Antonio Magliabechi to Leibniz, [end of] December 1690 (A I, 6, 326) and A VI, 6, xvii.

153. See A I, 11, 516. This letter is identified as Leibniz's first mention of Locke by A VI, 6, xvii. Leibniz owned the first edition of the *Essay* (London: Printed for Th. Basset, 1690) and the French translation of the fourth edition by Pierre Coste (published in Amsterdam in 1700). A second edition of Locke's *Essay* with important additions (including the famous chapter XXVII of book II on identity and diversity) was published in London in 1694. In the letter to Thomas Burnett of Kemney of 3 December 1703, in which he communicated his critical reading of Coste's French translation of the *Essay*, Leibniz acknowledged that before he "had nothing but the old English edition."

154. Maurice Cranston, *John Locke. A Biography*. London: Longmans, 1957, p. 416 notes that "there was one correspondent whom Locke did 'make bold' to ignore; and this, paradoxically, was his only peer among philosophers then living: Leibniz." Cf. Roger Woolhouse, *Locke. A Biography*. Cambridge: Cambridge University Press, 2007, p. 368.

155. See A I, 12, 477 and *Quelques remarques sur le livre de Mons. Lock intitulé Essay of Understanding* (A VI, 6, N. 1₁). A series of further remarks written around 1698 were apparently never sent (*Échantillon des réflexions sur les livres I et II de l'Essay de Locke*; A VI, 6, N. I/2).

156. Note of 13 May (2 June N.S.) 1696 inserted in Burnett's letter to Leibniz of 24 June 1696 (A I, 12, 649).

157. See Leibniz to Thomas Burnett of Kemney, 27 July 1696 (A I, 12, 730).

158. See the very informative introduction in A VI, 6, xviii ff., from which I am drawing.

159. Locke to William Molyneux, 10 April 1697 (O.S.) / 20 April 1697 (N.S.), in John Locke, *The Correspondence*. 8 vols. Ed. by E. S. de Beer. Oxford: Clarendon Press, 1976–89, vol. 6, p. 86. Cf. Woolhouse, *Locke. A Biography*, p. 367.

160. See Thomas Burnett of Kemney to Leibniz, 16 December 1696 (A I, 13, 387–8).

161. See A I, 13, 551.

162. These included his *Letter* to the Bishop of Worchester, Edward Stillingfleet, in which he defended the *Essay on Human Understanding* against the charges of antitrinitarianism levelled by Stillingfleet in his *Vindication of the Doctrine of the Trinity*. Cf. Thomas Burnett of Kemney to Leibniz, 13 May 1697 (A I, 14, 175–6); John Locke, *A Letter to the Right Reverend Edward Lord Bishop of Worcester, Concerning Some Passages Relating to Mr. Locke's "Essay of Humane Understanding": in a Late Discourse of His Lordship, in Vindication of the Trinity.* London: Printed for A. and J. Churchill, 1697; Edward Stillingfleet, *A Discourse in Vindication of the Doctrine of the Trinity*. London: Printed by H. J. for Henry Mortlock, 1697.

163. See respectively GP III, 127–8 and GP III, 130.

164. See Leibniz to Basnage, 13 February 1697 (GP III, 134) and Leibniz to Thomas Burnett of Kemney, 3 September 1697 (A I, 14, 450).

165. De Beer notes in Locke, *Correspondence*, vol. 6, p. 73 that this sentence is a variation of Horace, *Satires* II. iii.

166. Jean Le Clerc to Locke, 30 March (O.S.)/9 April (N.S.) 1697. In Locke, *Correspondence*, vol. 6, p. 73; Jean Le Clerc, *Epistolario*. Vol. 2. Edited by Maria Grazia and Mario Sina. Florence: Olschki, 1991, pp. 232–3. See also Locke to William Molyneux, 3 May 1697 (O.S.)/13 May 1697 (N.S.), in Locke, *Correspondence*, vol. 6, p. 107.

167. *Meditationes de Cognitione, Veritate et Ideis*, published in the *Acta Eruditorum* of November 1684.

168. Locke to William Molyneux, 10 April 1697 (O.S.)/20 April 1697 (N.S.), in Locke, *Correspondence*, vol. 6, pp. 86–7.

169. Locke to William Molyneux, 3 May 1697 (O.S.)/13 May 1697 (N.S.), in Locke, *Correspondence*, vol. 6, p. 107. On Le Clerc's letter to Locke of 30 March (O.S.)/9 April (N.S.) 1697 see above, note 166. Cf. Woolhouse, *Locke. A Biography*, p. 367.

170. GP VII, 487.

171. See GP VII, 488–9. Attention to these letters to Bierling is drawn by Nicholas Jolley in *Leibniz and Locke: A Study of the New Essays on Human Understanding.* Oxford: Clarendon Press, 1984, pp. 12–13.

172. GP I, 361. See also Dutens V, 191. Cf. Jolley, *Leibniz and Locke*, p. 49; Nicholas Jolley, "Leibniz on Locke and Socinianism." *Journal of the History of Ideas* 39, 2 (1978), p. 244; Antognazza, *Leibniz on the Trinity and the Incarnation*, p. 134.

173. GP III, 612.

174. Leibniz to Nicolas Rémond, July 1714 (GP III, 621). See also Leibniz to Caroline, Princess of Wales, 10 May 1715 (Klopp XI, 39–40).

175. Leibniz's *Nouveaux Essais* (1703–5) are published in A VI, 6, N. 2. On their genesis and some of the main issues discussed in them see below.

176. See A I, 13, 383–4. The cover page of the *Vindication* indicated 1697 as the official year of publication.

177. Although *Christianity Not Mysterious* initially appeared anonymously, the second edition (also published in 1696) identified John Toland as the author of the

book. See Giancarlo Carabelli, *Tolandiana. Materiali bibliografici per lo studio dell'opera e della fortuna di John Toland (1670–1722)*. Florence: La Nuova Italia, 1975, pp. 22–3. Recent work on Toland includes the study by Justin Champion, *Republican Learning: John Toland and the Crisis of Christian Culture, 1696–1722*. Manchester: Manchester University Press, 2003.

178. Locke answered Stillingfleet's *Vindication* with *A Letter to the Right Reverend Edward Lord Bishop of Worcester* (London 1697) to which Stillingfleet replied in his *The Bishop of Worcester's Answer to Mr. Locke's Letter* (London 1697). There followed a first *Reply* from Locke (London 1697), a second *Answer* by Stillingfleet (London 1698) and, finally, a second *Reply* by Locke (London 1699). In February 1700 Leibniz wrote to Thomas Burnett (GP III, 268–9), "I now have all the pieces of the debate between the late Monsieur of Worcester and Monsieur Locke, with the exception of the second letter of Monsieur Locke [Locke, *Reply*, 1697] which I am still missing."

179. Thomas Burnett of Kemney to Leibniz, summer 1698 (GP III, 242).

180. See Leibniz to Thomas Burnett, 20/30 January 1699 (GP III, 243–53); Thomas Burnett to Locke, 27 March 1699 in Locke, *Correspondence*, vol. 6, pp. 586–90. Cf. Woolhouse, *Locke. A Biography*, p. 416.

181. See *Réflexions sur la seconde réplique de Locke*, end* 1699–beginning 1700 (A VI, 6, N. I/4); Leibniz to Thomas Burnett, 13 February 1700 (GP III, 265–72); Thomas Burnett to Locke, 23 April 1700, in Locke, *Correspondence*, vol. 7, pp. 57–9. Around the end of 1698 Leibniz prepared a detailed report on Stillingfleet's *Vindication* and Locke's answering *Letter* (*Compte rendu de la Vindication de Stillingfleet et de la Lettre de Locke*, A VI, 6, N. I/3). See also in A VI, 6 *Passages soulignés par Leibniz dans son exemplaire de la Vindication de Stillingfleet* (1697–1700*; A VI, 6, N. I/2*); *Passages soulignés par Leibniz dans l'ouvrage de Stillingfleet* [Stillingfleet's *Answer* of 1697] (end* 1698–beginning* 1700; A VI, 6, N. I/5); *Extrait de la seconde réplique de Locke* (end 1699–beginning 1700*; A VI, 6, N. I/6).

182. As pointed out in A VI, 6, xxii, the author of this review was not Leibniz.

183. See A I, 12, 731. Attention to this letter to Burnett is drawn by Remnant and Bennett in the introduction to their translation of the *Nouveaux Essais* (NE, p. vii). Leibniz might have been overmodest, as shown by the controversial letter to Lord Stamford of 12 January 1706 (see chap. II. 8). I am indebted to the extremely well-documented introduction by André Robinet and Heinrich Schepers in A VI, 6, xxii–xxvii for the identification of a number of texts relating to the history of the composition of the *Nouveaux Essais*.

184. See Leibniz to the Marquis d'Ausson, mid-January–beginning of February 1704 (LBr 977, Bl. 6v); Leibniz to Sophie Charlotte, 17 November 1703 (LBr F 27, Bl. 124v); Leibniz to Thomas Burnett of Kemney, 3 December 1703 (GP III, 291).

185. See Leibniz to Sophie Charlotte, 25 April 1704 (Klopp X, 230) and 17 November 1703 (LBr F 27, Bl. 124v); Leibniz to Isaac Jaquelot, 9 February 1704 (GP III, 466) and 28 April 1704 (GP III, 474).

186. Leibniz to Isaac Jaquelot, 28 April 1704 (GP III, 474).

187. Leibniz to the Marquis d'Ausson, mid-January–beginning of February 1704 (LBr 977, Bl. 6v).

188. Leibniz to Isaac Jaquelot, 28 April 1704 (GP III, 474).

189. LBr F 27, Bl. 124v.

190. See GP III, 291–2.

191. See Cranston, *John Locke*, p. 342.

192. See Thomas Burnett of Kemney, 25 January 1704 (LBr 132, Bl. 137r); Leibniz to Isaac Jaquelot, 28 April 1704 (GP III, 475). See also Lady Masham to Leibniz, 29 March 1704 (O.S.) (GP III, 338).

193. GP III, 466. See also Leibniz to the Marquis d'Ausson, 9 February 1704 (Leyde UB, Ms 293 B fol. 230 sq).

194. See Leibniz to Sophie Charlotte, 25 April 1704 (Klopp X, 230); Leibniz to Isaac Jaquelot, 28 April 1704 (GP III, 474–5); Leibniz to Thomas Burnett of Kemney, 12 May 1704 (GP III, 296).

195. See the *Pièces rectificatives* published in A VI, 6, N. 31–4.

196. GP III, 475.

197. Lady Masham to Leibniz, 3 June 1704 (O.S.) (GP III, 351). Cranston, *John Locke*, p. 417 is obviously mistaken in asserting that "it was only after Locke's death that Leibniz opened a correspondence with Lady Masham."

198. See Leibniz to Lady Masham, 30 June 1704 (GP III, 355–6).

199. See GP III, 361.

200. Leibniz to Lady Masham, September 1704 (GP III, 362).

201. See Philippe Naudé senior, 13 October 1704 (LBr 679, Bl. 12).

202. Respectively, Leibniz to Lady Masham, 10 July 1705 (GP III, 368) and Leibniz to Pierre Coste, 16 June 1707 (GP III, 392). See also Leibniz to Jacques Bernard, January 1706 (LBr 517, Bl. 13); Leibniz to Thomas Burnett of Kemney, 26 May 1706 (GP III, 307); Leibniz to Nicolas Rémond, 14 March 1714 (GP III, 612).

203. See A VI, 6, xxv–xxvi.

204. See Leibniz to Lady Masham, 10 July 1705 (GP III, 366–368).

205. See R. E. Raspe, *Oeuvres philosophiques latines et françoises de feu Mr de Leibnitz*. Amsterdam-Leipzig: Schreuder, 1765, pp. 1–496.

206. See "Introduction," in NE, pp. x–xi. A helpful list of literature in English bearing on the *Nouveaux Essais* can be found ibid., pp. xxxv–xxxvii. For a book–length discussion see Nicholas Jolley, *Leibniz and Locke: A Study of the New Essays on Human Understanding*.

207. See Leibniz to Isaac Jaquelot, 28 April 1704 (GP III, 474).

208. Leibniz to Thomas Burnett, 3 December 1704 (GP III, 291–2). See also Leibniz to Isaac Jaquelot, 28 April 1704 (GP III, 473–4) and Leibniz to Nicolas Rémond, 14 March 1714 (GP III, 612).

209. Cf. Remnant and Bennett's introduction (pp. xvii–xix) to their translation of the *Nouveaux Essais*.

210. This summary is taken from Mugnai, *Introduzione*, p. 53. On the distinction between ideas "in mente Dei" and ideas in human minds, see pp. 42–53, from which I draw here.

211. See Augustine of Hippo, *De libero arbitrio*, 388/391–5, lib. II, cap. iii ff.

212. NE, 447.

213. NE, 106.

214. See respectively A VI, 6, 52 and 144.

215. See the examples of the "*zopyra*" presented in the "Preface" to the *Nouveaux Essais* (NE, 49): "living fires and flashes of light hidden inside us but made visible by the stimulation of the senses, as sparks can be struck from a steel."

216. NE, 49.

217. Ibid.

218. GP VI, 503–4. On the circumstances of the composition of this letter see below.

219. See GP III, 291–2 (quoted above).

220. See A VI, 2, 393 and chap. I. 2.

221. *Nouveaux Essais* (A VI, 6, 111).

222. *Nouveaux Essais* (A VI, 6, 77).

223. For the following remarks on language I am indebted to Mugnai's lucid analysis in *Astrazione e realtà*, esp. pp. 48-59 and *Introduzione*, pp. 239–45.

224. The importance of this metaphysical strand is very well documented in Jolley, *Leibniz and Locke*. Jolley argues that from Leibniz's point of view the central issue at stake between him and Locke was not epistemological but metaphysical: that is, the central issue was materialism or, more precisely, what Leibniz regarded as a pervasive materialistic tendency in Locke's philosophy (see Jolley, *Leibniz and Locke*, pp. 6–10).

225. See for instance Leibniz to Thomas Burnett, 3 December 1704 (GP III, 291–2).

226. See GP VII, 487–9 and GP I, 361. On Leibniz's views on the charge of Socinianism brought against Locke see esp. Jolley, "Leibniz on Locke and Socinianism," pp. 233–50 (early version of chap. II in Jolley, *Leibniz and Locke*), and Antognazza, *Leibniz on the Trinity and the Incarnation*, pp. 132–4.

227. John Toland, *Anglia Libera: or the Limitation and Succession of the Crown of England explain'd and asserted*. London: Printed for Bernard Lintott, 1701. Cf. Leibniz to Thomas Burnett of Kemney, 27 February 1702 (Klopp VIII, 333) and Margaret C. Jacob, *The Newtonians and the English Revolution. 1689–1710*. Ithaca: Cornell University Press, 1976, p. 230.

228. Sophie to Leibniz, 29 October 1701 (Klopp VIII, 294). See also Klopp VIII, 333. Cf. F. H. Heinemann, "Toland and Leibniz." *The Philosophical Review* 54, 5 (1945), p. 439.

229. London, 1699.

230. Leibniz to Thomas Burnett of Kemney, undated (Klopp VIII, 271).

231. Leibniz to Thomas Burnett of Kemney, undated (Klopp VIII, 276).

232. See Klopp VIII, 276.

233. See *Annotatiunculae subitaneae Ad Tolandi Librum De Christianismo Mysteriis Carente* (Dutens V, 142–9) and Leibniz to Thomas Burnett of Kemney, 27 February 1702 (Klopp VIII, 333).

234. See *Annotatiunculae subitaneae Ad Tolandi Librum De Christianismo Mysteriis Carente* (Dutens V, 147): "But to one who calls *Mystery* everything which is

above any created reason, I dare to say that no natural phenomena are above reason, although the comprehension itself of individual substances is impossible for the created mind because they involve the infinite. For this reason it is impossible to provide a perfect explanation [perfecta ratio] of the things of the universe. And nothing prevents certain divinely revealed dogmas from being of this kind." Cf. Maria Rosa Antognazza, "Natural and Supernatural Mysteries: Leibniz's *Annotatiunculae subitaneae* on Toland's *Christianity not Mysterious.*" In *Nihil sine Ratione. Mensch, Natur und Technik im Wirken von G. W. Leibniz. VII. Internationaler Leibniz-Kongress.* Ed. by Hans Poser. 3 vols. Berlin: Leibniz-Gesellschaft, 2001,vol. 1, pp. 17–24.

235. Klopp VIII, 333.

236. Ibid.

237. Klopp VIII, 334. Cf. also Klopp VIII, 356–7 and 357–8.

238. See Klopp VIII, 353.

239. See Klopp X, 82–3.

240. See Heinemann, "Leibniz and Toland," p. 440.

241. See Leibniz to Franz Ernst von Platen, 29 July 1702 (Klopp VIII, 357–8).

242. R. Doebner, ed., *Briefe der Königin Sophie Charlotte von Preußen und der Kurfürstin Sophie von Hannover an hannoversche Diplomaten.* Leipzig, 1905, p. 14.

243. See Heinemann, "Leibniz and Toland," pp. 440–41 and Jacob, *The Newtonians and the English Revolution*, pp. 230–31.

244. See GP VI, 491 and 499.

245. See the texts published in GP VI, 488–519, in particular the *Lettre touchant ce qui est independant des Sens et de la Matiere* (GP VI, 499–508). See also Klopp X, 154–77 and 181–8. Another important text arising from Leibniz's conversations with Sophie Charlotte in Lützenburg in 1702 was his *Considerations sur la doctrine d'un Esprit Universel Unique* (GP VI, 529 38), in which Leibniz defended the existence of individual souls. On the exchange between Leibniz and Toland see Stuart Brown, "The Leibniz–Toland Debates on Materialism and the Soul at the Court of the Queen of Prussia." In *Nihil sine Ratione. Mensch, Natur und Technik im Wirken von G. W. Leibniz. VII. Internationaler Leibniz-Kongress.* Ed. by Hans Poser. 3 vols. Berlin: Leibniz-Gesellschaft, 2001,vol. 1, pp. 147–54 and Chiara Giuntini, *Panteismo e ideologia repubblicana: John Toland (1670–1722)*, Bologna: Il Mulino, 1979, pp. 152–62.

246. See Klopp VIII, 362–3. Leibniz met Toland again in Hanover in December 1707 and March 1708 (cf. GP III, 315 and 317). In 1716 Toland's anonymous "Remarques Critiques sur le Système de Monsr. Leibnitz de l'Harmonie preetablie" (dated Berlin, 14 January 1703 and allegedly written at the behest of Sophie Charlotte) were published in the *Histoire Critique de la République des Lettres* (vol. 11, pp. 115–33). Toland's "Remarques" are reprinted in *The Leibniz Review* 10 (2000): 114–33 together with a translation by Richard Francks and R. S. Woolhouse (ibid., pp. 103–11).

247. GP VI, 501.

248. On the role of imagination see Mugnai, *Introduzione*, pp. 68–76 and Enrico Pasini, *Corpo e funzioni cognitive in Leibniz*. Milan: Angeli, 1996, pp. 146–204. On Leibniz's conception of bodies as well founded phenomena see esp. Adams, *Leibniz*, pp. 219–24.
249. See Heinemann, "Leibniz and Toland," p. 440.
250. See Leibniz to Johann Bernoulli, 29 May 1702 (GM III/2, 696–697).
251. "Lettre de M. Leibnits à l'Auteur, contenant un Eclaircissement des difficultez que Monsieur Bayle a trouvées dans le système nouveau de l'Union de l'âme et du corps." *Histoire des ouvrages des savans* (July 1698): 332–42.
252. See the excerpt from Bayle's letter published in *Histoire des ouvrages des savans* (March 1699): 135–6. See also Leibniz to Pierre Bayle, undated (GP III, 58). A full account and translation of the texts relating to this exchange is given in WF, 68–132.
253. Pierre Bayle, *Dictionaire historique and critique*. 2nd ed. Rotterdam: Reinier Leers, 1702, note H to the article "Rorarius."
254. Leibniz's reply was sent via both Johann Bernoulli and Burchard de Volder (see respectively GM III/2, 712 and GP II, 244). It was eventually published in *Histoire critique de la République des lettres* 11 (1716): 78–114.
255. See Klopp VIII, 357–8 and 359–60.
256. Leibniz to Christoph Joachim Nicolai von Greiffencrantz, 2 May 1715 (GP VI, 12).
257. See *De ipsa natura sive de vi insita actionibusque Creaturarum, pro Dynamicis suis confirmandis illustrandisque*. In *Acta Eruditorum* (September 1698): 427–40.
258. On this correspondence see in particular Roberto Palaia, "Naturbegriff und Kraftbegriff im Briefwechsel zwischen Leibniz und Sturm." In *Leibniz' Auseinandersetzung mit Vorgängern und Zeitgenossen*. Ed. by Ingrid Marchlewitz and Albert Heinekamp. Stuttgart: Steiner, 1990, pp. 157–72.
259. Cf. Johann Christoph Sturm, *Idolum naturae similiumque nominum vanorum ex hominum christianorum animis deturbandi conatus philosophicus*. Altdorf: Heinrich Mayer, 1692 (University Dissertation: Praes. Sturm; Resp. Leonhard Christoph Riederer).
260. See *De ipsa natura* (GP IV, 509).
261. See ibid., 515.
262. See ibid., 509. This principle was endorsed by Leibniz as early as 1668 in *De Transsubstantiatione* (A VI, 1, 508).
263. See chap. II. 6.
264. *De ipsa natura* (GP IV, 511/L 503–4). The term "monad" recurs several times after having been introduced en passant in paragraph 10 (GP IV, 510).
265. GM III, 537. Trans. by Robert M. Adams in *Leibniz*, p. 277, who offers a detailed and insightful commentary on this exchange on pp. 277–82.
266. See Adams, *Leibniz*, p. 265. On corporeal substances see also chap. II. 4.
267. GP II, 252. Trans. by Adams in *Leibniz*, p. 265.
268. On Leibniz's doctrine of primitive and derivative forces and of active and passive forces see chap. II. 6. The claim that this was Leibniz's favoured definition of

monad, and that the alternative definition of monad was designed to appeal to Cartesians, is argued by Pauline Phemister in her key contribution to the current debate on the relation between monads and corporeal substances ("Leibniz and the Elements of Compound Bodies." *British Journal for the History of Philosophy* 7, 1 (1999): 57–78). See also her *Leibniz and the Natural World. Activity, Passivity and Corporeal Substances in Leibniz's Philosophy* (Dordrecht: Springer, 2005) in which she expands the same thesis.

269. On the correspondence between Leibniz and De Volder see in particular the insightful contributions of Paul Lodge, to which I am indebted for this brief discussion ("The Failure of Leibniz's Correspondence with De Volder." *The Leibniz Review* 8 (1998): 47–67; "Leibniz's Close Encounter with Cartesianism in the Correspondence with De Volder." In *Leibniz and His Correspondents*. Ed. by Paul Lodge. Cambridge: Cambridge University Press, 2004, pp. 162–92). See also Paul Lodge, "Burchard de Volder: Crypto-Spinozist or Disenchanted Cartesian?" In *Receptions of Descartes: Cartesianism and Anti-Cartesianism in Early Modern Europe*. Ed. by Tad M. Schmaltz. London: Routledge, 2005, pp. 128–46.

270. See GP II, 148–283.

271. GP II, 270. See Robert M. Adams, "Leibniz's Conception of Religion." In *The Proceedings of the Twentieth World Congress of Philosophy*. Vol. 7: Modern Philosophy. Ed. by Mark D. Gedney. Bowling Green (USA): Philosophy Documentation Center, 2000, p. 61.

272. GP II, 272.

273. See GP II, 442–54.

274. The main texts discussing the doctrine of pre-established harmony and the related issue of freedom are introduced and translated in WF, 171–201.

275. Isaac Jaquelot to Leibniz, 10 March 1704 (GP III, 467; WF, 178).

276. See GP III, 467.

277. Jaquelot's *Système abregé de l'âme et de la liberté* appeared as an appendix to his book on the *Conformité de la foi avec la raison, ou defence de la religion*. Amsterdam, 1705. Leibniz's *Remarque* is published in GP VI, 558–60. See also GP VI, 556–8. On Leibniz and Jaquelot's debate on human freedom see in particular Ursula Franke, "Die Freiheit eines Christenmenschen. Streitgespräch zwischen Leibniz und Jaquelot in der Spannung von Vernunft und Glauben." In *Leibniz in Berlin*, pp. 103–19.

278. See WF, 144. Bayle's suggestion in the second edition of the *Dictionaire* (article "Rorarius", note L) that the expression "pre-established harmony" had been first introduced by Lamy was mistaken, as Leibniz himself pointed out (see WF, 137, note 20). The exchange between Leibniz and Lamy regarding the *Système nouveau* started with Leibniz's *Addition à l'Explication du systeme nouveau touchant l'union de l'ame et du corps, envoyée à Paris à l'occasion d'un livre intitulé Connoissance de soy même* (1698; GP IV, 572–7), written in response to a review of the first edition of Lamy's *De la Connoissance de soi-même* (cf. R. S. Woolhouse and R. Francks, "Leibniz, Lamy, and the 'way of pre-established

harmony'." *Studia Leibnitiana* 26, 1 (1994): 76–90 and Andreas Blank, "Incomplete Entities, Natural Non-separability, and Leibniz's Response to François Lamy's *De la Connoissance de soi-même*." *The Leibniz Review* 13 (2003): 1-17). The texts relating to this exchange between Leibniz and Lamy are introduced and translated in WF, 133–70. Further details of the writings involved in the philosophical discussion between Leibniz and Lamy can be found in the very helpful Introduction by Maria Grazia Zaccone Sina in *La corrispondenza di François Lamy, benedettino cartesiano*. Firenze: Olschki, 2006.

279. Lamy's discussion is found in the second volume, published (together with the first volume) in 1699. In 1701 the entire work was reprinted in six volumes. The first edition of *De la Connoissance de soi-même* appeared in Paris between 1694 and 1698. Cf. R. S. Woolhouse, "Leibniz and François Lamy's *De la Connaissance de soi-même*." *The Leibniz Review* 11 (2001): 65–70. In the same issue of *The Leibniz Review*, pp. 72–100 is also included a reprint of François Lamy's *De la Connoissance de soi-même*. 2nd ed. (Paris 1669/1701), 1699 Title page, 1701 Title page, and volume 2, pp. 224–43 and 387–92.

280. See GP IV, 577–90.

281. See *Réponse de Mr. Leibnitz aux Objections que l'Auteur du Livre de la Connaissance de soi-même a faites contre le système de l'Harmonie Préétablie. In Supplément du Journal des Savans, du dernier de Juin 1709* (1709): 275–81 (GP IV, 590–95).

282. See GP III, 336. As Leibniz wrote to Lady Masham, he had read Cudworth's *System* for the first time at the house of Adrien Auzout during his soujourn in Rome in 1689.

283. GP III, 336–7. Leibniz read and appreciated the *Principia Philosophiae Antiquissimae et Recentissimae de Deo, Christo et Creatura* written in English between 1672 and 1677 by Anne Viscountess Conway, translated and published posthumously in 1690 by Franciscus Mercurius van Helmont. See Leibniz to Thomas Burnett of Kemney, 3 September 1697 (A I, 14, 450); *Nouveaux Essais*, livre I, chap. 1 (A VI, 6, 72). On Anne Conway see Sarah Hutton, *Anne Conway. A Woman Philosopher*. Cambridge: Cambridge University Press, 2004. The relationship between Conway's philosophical doctrines and Leibniz's monadalogy is examined by C. Merchant, "The Vitalism of Anne Conway: Its Impact on Leibniz's Concept of the Monad." *Journal of the History of Philosophy* 17, 3 (1979): 255–69.

284. See GP III, 338–43. Cf. the illuminating paper by Pauline Phemister, " 'All the time and everywhere everything's the same as here': The Principle of Uniformity in the Correspondence Between Leibniz and Lady Masham." In *Leibniz and His Correspondents*. Ed. by Paul Lodge. Cambridge: Cambridge University Press, 2004, pp. 193–213. Leibniz adapted this phrase from Nolant de Fatouville's *Arlequin empereur dans la lune* (Troyes: Garnier, s. d.), as he revealed in a letter of 4 May 1704 to Sophie Charlotte which repeated the arguments presented in the letter to Lady Masham (see GP III, 343 and Phemister, "The Principle of Uniformity," p. 200).

285. GP III, 339.

286. See "Memoire communiqué par Mr. Bayle," *Histoire des ouvrages des savans*, August 1704, art. 7, p. 393 and *Bibliothèque Choisie*, 1705, tome 5, art. 4, p. 301 (this tome of the *Bibliothèque Choisie* appeared before May 1705). Leibniz himself mentioned these two references at the beginning of his *Considérations sur les Principes de Vie* (GP VI, 539). See also GP VI, 546–7.

287. Leibniz's *Considérations sur les Principes de Vie, et sur les Natures Plastiques, par l'Auteur du Systeme de l'Harmonie préétablie* can be found in GP VI, 539–46. See also *Eclaircissement sur les Natures Plastiques et les Principes de Vie et de Mouvement, par l'Auteur du Systeme de l'Harmonie préétablie* (GP VI, 546–55).

288. Klopp X, 212–3. Attention to this letter is drawn by Patrick Riley, "Leibniz's *Méditation sur la notion commune de la justice*, 1703–2003." *The Leibniz Review*. 13 (2003): 67–78 (here p. 67).

289. Cf. Riley, "Leibniz's *Méditation sur la notion commune de la justice*." The *Méditation* was published for the first time by Georg Mollat in *Rechsphilosophisches aus Leibnizens Ungedruckten Schriften* (Leipzig: Verlag Robolski, 1885) and is translated by Riley in Leibniz, *Political Writings*, pp. 45–64.

290. *Méditation sur la notion commune de la justice* in Leibniz, *Political Writings*, p. 45.

291. Ibid., p. 54.

292. The story of the priority controversy in this period is detailed in chapter 6 ("The Outbreak: 1693–1700") and chapter 7 ("Open Warfare: 1700–1710") of Hall, *Philosophers at War*. A shorter account by J. E. Hofmann can be found in A III, 1, xxxvii–xliii. See also the recent contribution by Jason Bardi, *The Calculus Wars. Newton, Leibniz and the Greatest Mathematical Clash of All Times*. London: High Stakes, 2006.

293. L'Hôpital to Leibniz, 13 July 1699 (GM II, 336).

294. See John Wallis to Leibniz, 31 October 1697 (GM IV, 44); Leibniz to John Wallis, 3 April 1698 (GM IV, 44); Leibniz to Johann Bernoulli, 4 August 1699 (GM III, 597); Leibniz to Magliabechi, 30 October 1699 (A I, 17, 596–7).

295. Leibniz to L'Hôpital, 7 August 1699 (GM II, 337).

296. Johann Bernoulli to Leibniz, 1 December 1699 (GM III, 619).

297. Leibniz to Johann Bernoulli, 12 January 1700 (GM III, 620–21).

298. See Nicolas Fatio de Duillier, *Lineae Brevissimi Descensus Investigatio Geometrica Duplex. Cui addita est Investigatio Geometrica Solidi Rotundi, in quod minima fiat Resistentia*. London: Typis R. Everingham, 1699, p. 18. Published also in *Commercium epistolicum D. Joannis Collins et aliorum de analysi promota*. London, 1712 (January 1673 N.S.) (here p. 107).

299. See Fatio de Duillier, *Lineae Brevissimi Descensus Investigatio*, [p. 2] and GM IV, 71–3.

300. See *The Correspondence of Isaac Newton*, vol. 5, p. 96. Cf. also p. 98, note 5.

301. See Ravier 156; GM V, 340–50.

302. See Aiton, *Leibniz*, p. 240.

303. See the letter of Varignon to Johann Bernoulli, appended by Bernoulli to his letter to Leibniz of 5 October 1700 (GM III/2, 641–2).

304. See "Mémoire de Mr. Leibnitz touchant son sentiment sur le calcul différentiel." *Mémoires de Trévoux* (November 1701): 270–72 (GM V, 350).
305. See Pierre Varignon to Leibniz, 28 November 1701 (GM IV, 89–90).
306. Leibniz to Pierre Varignon, 2 February 1702 (GM IV, 91–5). See Ravier 162.
307. GM IV, 104.
308. Leibniz to Pierre Varignon, 20 June 1702 (GM IV, 110).
309. See George Cheyne, *Fluxionum methodus inversa*. Londini: Typis J. Matthews, 1703 and Aiton, *Leibniz*, p. 239.
310. Johann Bernoulli to Leibniz, 29 September 1703 (GM III/2, 724).
311. See "Isaaci Newtoni Tractatus duo, de Speciebus et Magnitudine Figurarum Curvilinearum. Londini apud Samuelem Smith et Benjamin Walford. 1704." *Acta Eruditorum* (January 1705): 30–36.
312. See the extract from a letter of W. Burnet to Johann Bernoulli of the summer of 1712 which Bernoulli copied to Leibniz in a letter of 13 August 1712 (GM III/2, 892–3).
313. See Leibniz to Antonio Conti, 9 April 1716 (GB, 274–5) and A III, 1, xlii–xliii.
314. See Leibniz to Antonio Conti, 9 April 1716 (GB, 275).
315. See Newton to Antonio Conti, 29 May 1716 (GB, 285–6).
316. See Leibniz to Antoine Verjus, end 1698 (A I, 16, N. 242). Cf. also Leibniz to Oldenburg, 28 December 1675 (A III, 1, 331). Around 1698 Leibniz was actively working at the *analysis situs* (see *Analysis Geometrica Propria eique connexus calculus situs*; GM V, 172–8).
317. See G. W. Leibniz, *Lettres et opuscules inédits*. Ed. by Louis Alexander Foucher de Careil. Paris, 1854, pp. 202–203. As Fontenelle explained to Leibniz in this letter, the *Histoire* had been introduced by the new Academy's regulations of 26 January 1699.
318. Cf. Zacher, *Die Hauptschriften zur Dyadik*, pp. 59, 250–61. The essay included tables of series of numbers in binary notation for the calculation of which Leibniz had been helped by Philippe Naudé (see Zacher, *Die Hauptschriften zur Dyadik*, pp. 237–42).
319. Zacher, *Die Hauptschriften zur Dyadik*, pp. 251–2. On dyadic and creation *ex nihilo* see chap. II. 6.
320. See LBr 275. Quoted in Zacher, *Die Hauptschriften zur Dyadik*, p. 65.
321. See Leibniz's letters to Fontenelle of 5 May and 12 July 1702, and Fontenelle's letters to Leibniz of 30 April 1701 and 18 November 1702. Quoted in Zacher, *Die Hauptschriften zur Dyadik*, pp. 66–8.
322. Zacher, *Die Hauptschriften zur Dyadik*, p. 69.
323. Cf. Claudia von Collani, "Gottfried Wilhelm Leibniz and the China Mission of the Jesuits." In *Das Neueste über China*. Ed. by Wenchao Li and Hans Poser. Stuttgart: Steiner, 2000, pp. 90–93. Bouvet and his relationship with Leibniz are discussed in Perkins, *Leibniz and China*, passim.
324. See A I, 14, N. 358 and Joachim Bouvet, *Portrait historique de l'Empereur de la Chine*. 1697.
325. See "Introduction," in Leibniz, *Writings on China*, pp. 20–22 and Collani, "Gottfried Wilhelm Leibniz and the China Mission of the Jesuits," pp. 96–7.

326. A I, 15, 355–6.

327. A I, 16, 375–6.

328. On the origins of Leibniz's pursuit of the *characteristica universalis* or universal formal language see chapters I. 1 and I. 2. On the development of this project and on the logical calculus see esp. chap. II. 4.

329. See Leibniz to Joachim Bouvet, 15 February 1701, in Rita Widmaier, ed., *Leibniz korrespondiert mit China. Der Briefwechsel mit den Jesuitenmissionaren (1689–1714)*, p. 135.

330. See *Leibniz korrespondiert mit China*, pp. 148–63.

331. See Leibniz to Joachim Bouvet, 18 May 1703, in *Leibniz korrespondiert mit China*, p. 187.

332. *Explication de l'Arithmetique Binaire, qui [se] sert des seuls caracteres 0 et 1, avec des remarques sur son utilité, et sur ce qu'elle donne le sens des anciennes figures Chinoises par FOHI.* In Zacher, *Die Hauptschriften zur Dyadik*, pp. 293–301. Leibniz's essay appeared at pp. 85–9 of the *Histoire de l'Académie Royale des Sciences* of year 1703, published in Paris in 1705.

333. See Zacher, *Die Hauptschriften zur Dyadik*, p. 292.

334. See Leibniz to Carlo Maurizio Vota, 4 April 1703 (Zacher, *Die Hauptschriften zur Dyadik*, pp. 287–91) and E. J. Aiton, "An unpublished letter of Leibniz to Sloane." *Annals of Science* 38 (1981): 103–7. As subsequent sinological studies have shown, Bouvet's 'discovery' was in fact a misinterpretation.

335. See Klopp X, 262. See also Leibniz to Caroline, 18 March 1705 (Klopp IX, 116).

336. See Leibniz to Baron von Görtz, 2 February 1705 (Klopp X, 263–4).

337. Klopp X, 264–5.

338. Klopp X, 268. See also Leibniz to Baron von Görtz, 7 February 1705 (Klopp X, 265).

339. Leibniz to Johann Mathias von der Schulenburg, 4 March 1705 (Klopp X, 270). See also Leibniz to Caroline, 18 March 1705 (Klopp IX, 116–17).

340. Around the spring of 1705 Leibniz must have done at least some work on his *Considérations sur les Principes de Vie, et sur les Natures Plastiques* published in May 1705 in the *Histoire des ouvrages des savans*, because they cite an article which appeared in tome 5 of the *Bibliothèque Choisie* of 1705. This reference was undoubtedly part of the text sent by Leibniz to the editor of the *Histoire*, Basnage, as shown by LH IV, 1 2b Bl. 1.

341. Klopp X, 287–8 and GP III, 366–7. See also the letter written by Leibniz on the same day to the Cambridge theologian William Wotton, 10 July 1705 (Klopp X, 287).

8

Light and Shadows: Hanover, Berlin, Wolfenbüttel, Vienna (February 1705–September 1714)

T HE DECADE FOLLOWING the demise of Sophie Charlotte was a mixture of successes and defeats. Leibniz – now a well-known savant in the learned circles of European courts – was aging and acquiring a somewhat eccentric appearance. In public, his old-fashioned and flamboyant outfits looked hilarious to Sophie's youngest son, Prince Ernst August, who compared him to the court jester.[1] In private, his still more extravagant attire surprised those ushered into his private quarters: in an attempt to combat gout and arthritis, he donned a fur-lined nightgown, fur stockings, further large socks of grey felt instead of slippers, and a peculiarly long, dark wig.[2] Yet his affability and friendliness won over most. He was a great conversationalist and almost everybody – even the dour Georg Ludwig to some degree – enjoyed his conversation and company, not least because (as the duchess of Orléans pointed out to her aunt, the electress Sophie) he was one of those rare learned men who "were clean, did not stink, and had a sense of humour."[3]

In these later years in Leibniz's life, a sense of urgency, of needing to finish what he had started, began to grow. Leibniz was in his sixties and sensed that time was short.[4] Once he had gradually recovered from the terrible blow of Sophie Charlotte's death, his philosophical correspondence and intellectual production picked up again. In his correspondence with the Jesuit theologian Bartholomew Des Bosses he revisited the issue of corporeal substances and toyed with the concept of *vinculum substantiale*;[5] and in correspondence with a bright young German, Christian Wolff, he expounded the metaphysical grounds of dynamical laws and properties and the relation between his ethics and metaphysics.[6] In 1710 there appeared anonymously the most voluminous philosophical work published during his life – the *Essais de Théodicée sur la bonté de Dieu, la liberté de l'homme et l'origine du mal.* The issues discussed in the *Theodicy* had been on his mind since his youth, and many of the doctrines and solutions proposed in it could be traced back to his earlier writings. But despite being the bulky fruit of decades of reflections, the *Theodicy* was meant to be merely the popular forerunner of a more specialized work expounding in technical philosophical detail his "entire system."[7] Needless to say, Leibniz's *magnum opus* never saw the light. Rather than producing the specialised Latin exposition of his entire system which he had envisaged, in 1714 Leibniz penned two agile French pamphlets in which he summarised in popular terms his metaphysical views: the *Principes de la nature et de la grâce fondés en raison* and the untitled essay which came to be known after his death as *Monadologie.*

In the meantime the controversy on the invention of the calculus continued to escalate following the formal accusation of plagiarism by John Keill (1671–1721), a Scottish mathematician apprenticed to David Gregory (1659–1708). While vigorously defending himself from this charge, Leibniz busily pursued his longstanding agenda – promoting knowledge through the search for enlightened patronage and the establishment of learned academies or societies. As a consummate networker, he gained the support of the Russian tsar, Peter the Great; continued to enjoy the friendship and protection of the dowager electress, Sophie, and of the duke of Wolfenbüttel, Anton Ulrich; and last but not least, reached a prominent position in Vienna, entertaining cordial relationships with the court of the new emperor, Joseph I (1705–11), and of his successor, Charles VI (1711–40). On the other hand, due to his long absences and unrelenting pursuit of new projects and schemes, he found himself marginalised in the Berlin Society of Sciences and had to weather the mounting anger of the Hanover elector, Georg Ludwig, who clamoured to see the long-awaited Guelf history between hard covers. During Leibniz's most prolonged absence in this period from the Guelf territories – his almost two-year-long sojourn in Vienna from 1712 to 1714 – he was reached by the distressing news of the death of his two closest remaining protectors: Anton Ulrich, on 27 March 1714, and Sophie herself, on 8 June 1714. Sophie had died only a couple of months before succeeding to the crown that she had been so reluctant to accept: on 12 August (1 August O.S.) 1714, the death of Queen Anne of Great Britain and Ireland marked the passage of the throne to the Hanoverian line in the person of Georg Ludwig.

Leibniz Networking

Back in Hanover in March 1705, after six months of absence and with the wound of Sophie Charlotte's death still fresh, Leibniz took advantage of a sojourn of the elector in Celle to disappear again on a visit to his friend and patron in Wolfenbüttel, Anton Ulrich. As he explained to Sophie, the official reason for the trip was to discuss plans for the Wolfenbüttel library. Anton Ulrich had grand ideas for "restoring the ducal library of Wolfenbüttel to its ancient lustre";[8] and between 1705 and 1713 he constructed the first freestanding, purpose-built library of the early modern period. Although the building was erected under the direction of Hermann Korb (1656–1735), Leibniz was in all probability the real inspiration of the mathematically beautifully proportioned design, which combined a square plan with an oval reading room.[9] From Wolfenbüttel he returned to Berlin, where in mid-April he discussed with court officers the composition of Sophie Charlotte's obituaries and himself composed the account of the queen's life before her marriage.[10] By the end of May, Leibniz was back in Hanover, to discover that Georg Ludwig had run out of patience with his employee's wanderings: on 6 June 1705 an ordinance was issued forbidding him from undertaking any further travels without specific permission from the elector.[11] The unavoidable task was intended to be the completion of the Guelf history.

On 28 August 1705, the death of the duke of Celle, Georg Wilhelm, fulfilled the plan envisaged many years earlier by Ernst August through the infelicitous marriage between his oldest son and Sophie Dorothea: the reunion of the Braunschweig-Lüneburg duchies under Georg Ludwig. With the passage of Celle to the ruler of Hanover, the Celle prime minister, Andreas Gottlieb von Bernstorff, assumed responsibility for the entire electorate. On 2 September 1705, the electoral prince, Georg August (1683–1760; after 1727 George II of Great Britain), married Wilhelmine Caroline von Ansbach (1683–1737). Young, charming, and bright, Caroline had been a favourite of Sophie Charlotte, and both Sophie and Leibniz were fond of her as well. Indeed, the previous year, she had managed with Leibniz's help to extricate herself from an arranged marriage to the second son of Emperor Leopold I and Habsburg pretender to the Spanish crown, Charles (1685–1740), which would have required her conversion to Roman Catholicism: while staying in Lützenburg, Leibniz himself had helped her draft the letter explaining her reasons for declining the union.[12]

So she turned down the opportunity to become, eventually, an empress, and had to settle for being a British queen, but was blessed in compensation with a congenial husband and a caring grandmother-in-law. On the other hand, there was no lost love between her and Georg Ludwig, whose dislike for his daughter-in-law was surpassed only by his animosity towards his own son.

Between late 1705 and early 1706, while under strict orders to get on with his historical work, Leibniz managed to whip up quite a storm in the English Channel. Despite the Act of Settlement passed in 1701 by the Westminster parliament nominating the dowager Electress Sophie and her descent as heirs to the crown, the dangers for the Protestant succession were never far away. The Jacobite movement supporting the exiled pretender, the son of James VII and II, James Francis Edward Stuart (1688–1766), maintained support in Scotland, Wales, and Ireland and even found powerful allies in England within the Tory party. Within this loose opposition movement, dynastical, national, and political considerations mingled with religious ones: Roman Catholics at home and abroad fiercely opposed both the Protestant monarchs William III (1689–1702) and Queen Anne (1702–14) and the succession of the Hanoverians, who were mainly supported by the Whig party. In November 1705 the Tory leader, Lord Haversham, proposed that Queen Anne should invite to England the heir presumptive to the throne, the dowager Electress Sophie; but the queen strongly objected to the proposal, fearing the establishment of a foreign court in her own territory. The Whig party sided with the queen and rejected the motion. It was at this point that Leibniz, observing English events from a perilously long distance, took up his pen to castigate what he regarded as the incoherent politics of the Whigs. In his view, their ambivalent, hesitant attitude risked jeopardising the entire Protestant succession, further upsetting the European scene, and even consigning the leading Protestant state to the Catholic and philo-French Jacobites. Leibniz's attack took the form of a letter to the Earl of Stamford allegedly written on 12 January 1706 by the English representative residing in Hanover, Sir Rowland Gwynne. Written in English with Gwynne's help and printed in Holland, it was distributed in March 1706 to some twenty or thirty members of the parliament.[13] To Leibniz's dismay, the pamphlet pleased neither Queen Anne nor parliament: on 8 March a parliamentary vote of 114 against 97 sanctioned the letter as a "scandalous false and malicious libel tending to create a misunderstanding between

Her Majesty and the Princess Sophia."[14] Sophie was advised to distance herself from Gwynne, who, having fallen into disgrace both in Hanover and in London, was forced to resign his post. As for Leibniz, he did not reveal his authorship of the letter, leaving Gwynne alone to bear the consequences of their act; and eventually the storm blew itself out. After all, Queen Anne had other matters on her hands, such as the participation of her country in the War of the Spanish Succession and the constant threat of rebellions by her Scottish subjects. In this latter regard a key move was made during her reign, with the union of the crowns of England and Scotland in 1707.

Throughout this whole affair, Georg Ludwig kept firmly to his policy of strictly abstaining from any intervention in British affairs – a policy which suited both himself and Queen Anne. As a matter of fact, his dynastic and political interests were still focused on the Holy Roman Empire. He continued to be less than enthusiastic about the idea of entanglement in a temperamental parliamentary monarchy, regarded by continental sovereigns as unstable and far too much at the mercy of the whims of its subjects. Despite the relatively small size of their territories, many of the leading German princes suffered few limitations on their authority within their own domains; the Hanoverians' strategy of dynastic aggrandisement was unfolding according to plan; and for the time being Georg Ludwig's priority therefore remained the consolidation of his power base in Germany. In the summer of 1706 another major step in dynastic policy was taken by the courts in Hanover and Berlin through the marriage between Georg Ludwig's daughter (also named Sophie Dorothea, after her mother) and her cousin Friedrich Wilhelm, the crown prince of Prussia, son of Sophie Charlotte and Friedrich I. The match further tightened the blood relations between the two leading families in northern Germany – the Guelfs and the Hohenzollerns – but did little to ease their recurrently strained relationship.[15] As for Leibniz, he hoped that the marriage would give new impetus to the irenical negotiations between the Lutheran and Reformed courts of Hanover and Berlin,[16] but unfortunately rather the opposite proved to be the case. Officially engaged to Friedrich Wilhelm in June 1706, Sophie Dorothea insisted on being granted religious freedom, possibly under the influence of Molanus, who feared the Calvinist proselytism of the Berlin court;[17] and despite strenuous attempts the two courts could not agree on the rite to be adopted for the wedding. To overcome the impasse – and perhaps advance towards church reunification – Leibniz proposed to celebrate the nuptials according to the more flexible rites of the Church of England. As it happened, following the Act of Naturalisation passed by the English parliament in 1705 for the Electress Sophie and her descent, both the bride and the groom could in fact claim the rights of English citizens – Friedrich Wilhelm and Sophie Dorothea being respectively Sophie's grandson and granddaughter. Yet Leibniz's ingenious and broadminded proposal pleased no one; and the wedding proceeded through a less elegant expedient: Sophie Dorothea was married by proxy in a Lutheran service on 14 November in Hanover, with her brother, Georg August, representing the groom; and three days later she travelled to Berlin, where the marriage was ratified on 28 November with a celebration in the royal chapel in the Reformed manner. Meanwhile, in August the king of Prussia ordered Bishop Ursinus to stop irenical correspondence with Hanover, and Georg Ludwig issued an ordinance on 15 November forbidding Leibniz from any further intervention in religious issues regarding his daughter: "you must not interfere or allow yourself to be used either directly or indirectly. We also wish that you withdraw from all negotiations whatsoever regarding the reunification of the Lutheran and Reformed religions[.]"[18] Leibniz could not but face this new situation. As he wrote to Fabricius in January 1708, sadly but not without a hint of his unquenchable optimism: "From irenical negotiations, as things now stand, I do not expect anything further. At some point the thing will be accomplished of its own accord."[19]

Although the marriage between Sophie Dorothea and Friedrich Wilhelm did not bring Leibniz any closer to church reunification, it did at least bring him to Berlin. Georg Ludwig's explicit prohibition of travel notwithstanding, Leibniz managed to stay there for six months, from mid-November 1706 to mid-May 1707, attending to the business of building up the Berlin Society of Sciences. Several meetings of the society council were held under his presidency, devoted, amongst other things, to the election of members and the preparation of the first volume of the Society official publication, the *Miscellanea Berolinensia*. The key desiderata remained, however, securing premises and funding, and on both fronts some progress was made. Leibniz focused much of his efforts on obtaining a monopoly for silk cultivation, which was finally granted on 28 March 1707.[20] One month later, on 28 April, Friedrich I ordered the Berlin *Kammer* to acquire a place for the Society.[21] Yet despite this progress, Leibniz could not but feel frustrated. Seven years after its foundation, the society still existed on little more than paper. His hopes of finding in Sophie Dorothea a patroness of science to replace Sophie Charlotte had been rapidly dashed, and the concrete support from the court which the Society needed to flourish was undermined by a thousand difficulties. On 12 May 1707, shortly before departing from Berlin, Leibniz vented his disappointment to Sophie: "I labour to establish the society of sciences in some reasonable fashion. Yet in doing so I have encountered almost as much difficulty as if I was negotiating for the pope."[22]

In the second half of May, Leibniz left Berlin but did not return to Hanover until mid-June, having taken a detour to Leipzig and the nearby Probstheida, where he visited his nephew, Friedrich Simon Löffler. In the Swedish camp on Saxon estates near Altranstädt he had the opportunity to observe three of the protagonists of the Great Northern War which was still raging in north-eastern Europe for supremacy on the Baltic and the control of Poland-Lithuania: the king of Sweden, Charles XII; the elector of Saxony and now former king of Poland, Augustus II (deposed by the treaty of Altranstädt in September 1706); and the new king of Poland, Stanisłaus Leszczyński, whose election had been forced by Sweden in July 1704. Leibniz waited for over a week in the hope of being granted an audience with Charles XII before withdrawing disappointed.[23] Instead he travelled to Halle, Wolfenbüttel, and finally Hanover.

The return to his main residence was not empty-handed. As he had repeatedly insisted over the years, his travels did not keep him from working on the Guelf history. In June 1707 there appeared in Hanover one of the major fruits of these labours: the first volume of a massive edition of medieval sources relating to the history of the Guelfs and of Lower Saxony, the *Scriptores rerum Brunsvicensium*. Two further volumes followed, respectively, in 1710 and 1711.[24] In total, these three volumes published 157 texts dating before 1500, some eighty of these as first editions. In addition to making a wealth of sources readily available, they also displayed the high editorial standards intended for Leibniz's project from the outset and placed the local history of the Guelfs and their territories firmly in their wider European context.[25] Taken together, they represented a truly remarkable archival, editorial, and historiographical accomplishment; yet they were also not remotely the concise and coherent history of his family which Georg Ludwig had been impatiently expecting for years. The lack of enthusiasm with which he greeted his historiographer's painstaking work was palpable: Leibniz had to battle long and hard to recover the costs of printing and of the research assistants he had employed, not to speak of his honorarium for the work.[26] Further unpleasantness relating to his historiographical office marred the summer of 1708: in June he complained to the Hanover ministers that his former secretary and research assistant at the Guelf history, Johann Georg Eckhart, had published material pertaining to the *Scriptores rerum Brunsvicensium* without his knowledge, thereby compromising the originality of Leibniz's major editorial effort. In July, when Leibniz requested permission to travel to Munich to study further documents relating to the Guelf history, Georg Ludwig called his bluff: permission was granted under condition that Leibniz paid his travel expenses out of his own purse. Since Leibniz did not relish the idea of being out of pocket for the glory of Georg Ludwig – and, for that matter, never displayed a properly philosophical detachment from money – he decided to let the Munich documents rest in peace.[27]

With the Munich trip foiled, his love for travelling and networking devised another scheme which he was careful to keep secret from indiscrete ears, since it had nothing to do with the Guelf history. His accomplice this time was Duke Anton Ulrich of Wolfenbüttel, who agreed to send Leibniz on a secret mission to Vienna aimed jointly at the negotiation of political alliances and at securing part of the estates of the bishopric of Hildesheim for the Guelf house.[28] In addition to these juridical-political tasks, this trip provided Leibniz with the opportunity to see the new emperor, Joseph I (1678–1711), who had ascended to the throne in 1705 at the death of his father, Leopold I. Armed with Anton Ulrich's references for emperor and empress,[29] he departed in late November 1708, misleading even his friend Sophie as to the real destination of his trip.[30] He arrived in Vienna probably at the beginning of December. Besides negotiating about Hildesheim, he gained access to the empress, Wilhelmine Amalie (1673–1742), who happened to be one of the daughters of his old friend and patron, Duke Johann Friedrich. Wilhelmine Amalie was not the only prominent contact that Leibniz was able to gain during his visit: another was the Russian plenipotentiary in Vienna, Johann Christoph von Urbich, who asked Leibniz to prepare a plan for the advancement of the sciences in Russia – something to which Leibniz readily agreed.[31] In the company of Urbich he left Vienna on 28 December, directed to Leipzig. After spending a few days there in early January 1709, he proceeded to Berlin, where he remained until the beginning of March, dealing, amongst other things, with the preparation of the *Miscellanea Berolinensia*. Within a few days of his arrival in Berlin, however, news of his whereabouts inevitably reached Hanover, where the exasperated elector had joked about advertising a reward in the newspapers for anyone able to locate his elusive historiographer.[32] If the discovery of his hideout in Berlin was embarrassing, the revelation of his secret escapade in Vienna was far worse. A report of 26 January from Hanover's envoy in the Imperial city, Daniel Erasmi von Huldenberg, sent to Georg Ludwig, unveiled Leibniz's visit;[33] and when Leibniz called on Sophie's chambers to pay his respects after returning to Hanover on 9 March he encountered the enraged Georg Ludwig instead, who expressed his acute displeasure at the behaviour of his employee in no uncertain terms.[34] Leibniz responded to this tempestuous meeting (as always) by writing a memo – this time concocting a version of events which disguised the premeditation of his visit to Vienna and carefully omitted to mention the Hildesheim affair. After the customary preambles, quite unrepentant and perhaps mindful of the adage that the best defence is attack, he launched himself into a tirade of his own about the unfair way in which his historiographical achievements and discoveries had been treated, not to speak of the paucity of his remuneration in comparison to that of other historiographers with a much easier task on their hands.[35] In an attempt to placate the elector, during the course of the year he offered a sample of the *Annales Imperii Occidentis Brunsvicenses* ("sixteen or seventeen years . . . from the beginning of the reign of Charlemagne to his peace with Wittekind")[36] for the perusal of Prime Minister Bernstorff.[37] Yet the relationship with the Hanover court must have remained strained for some time. Leibniz, for his part, proposed to Anton Ulrich to move into his service.[38] As for Georg Ludwig, if this was the way in which a prince ruled a middle-ranking court official in an absolutist principality in Germany, it is perhaps no wonder that he had reservations about attempting to govern Britain in league with the parliament at Westminster.

1710 was also a mixed year in the relationship between Leibniz and the Berlin Society of Sciences. On the one hand, it was marked by the crisis of Leibniz's presidency, triggered by his discovery that important decisions were being taken without consulting him. On the other hand, it saw the publication in May of the first volume of the *Miscellanea Berolinensia ad Incrementum Scientiarum*.[39] The proud volume contained no less than sixty papers distributed into three sections: the first, "containing literary contributions"; the second, "physical and medical"; and the third, "mathematical and mechanical". Twelve of the papers – one-fifth of the

total – were contributed by Leibniz himself, and these covered a variety
of topics in all three sections: from linguistic studies to the history of
the discovery of phosphorus, from fossils to the aurora borealis, from the
infinitesimal calculus to the description and illustration of the calculating
machine.[40] His essay on the origin of peoples traced through the study
of languages offered a key systematisation of his thought as a linguist and
philosopher of language on a subject central to the second preamble to his
Guelf history.[41] This was followed two years later by another key paper
which was left unpublished, the *Epistolica de historia etymologica dissertatio*
(1712).[42]

The *Miscellanea Berolinensia* were well received in the learned community. Leibniz was understandably proud of this tangible accomplishment
achieved under his presidency, especially since he had contributed to it
directly as well. Yet he was left little time to relish this milestone: a few
months later he was reached by the unsettling news from Berlin that the
king of Prussia had promulgated on 3 June 1710 new regulations for the
Society without Leibniz's knowledge.[43] Worse still, on 7 August Friedrich
I nominated an honorary president of the Society, Marquard Ludwig von
Printzen, again without consulting or even informing Leibniz.[44] When
these facts came to Leibniz's attention in December, he was even led
to believe that the position to which the Baron von Printzen had been
appointed was his own and that he had therefore been unceremoniously
removed from the office of president.[45] On 10 December he wrote to
Sophie Dorothea hoping for her support and complaining of the lack of
consideration shown toward him:

[C]ertain people in Berlin have just played a nasty trick on me . . . [T]his change could
have been made in a gracious way in my regard. The position of president was not
elective: the King gave it to me, and the King can take it away; but I doubt that
His Majesty has ordered that things be done this way. I did nothing to deserve bad
treatment[.][46]

The misunderstanding regarding von Printzen was clarified a few days
later,[47] but Leibniz was still fuming. He corresponded in a perfectly
civilized way with von Printzen regarding the general aims of the Society
and the ways to put them into practice but, pleading a slight ailment,
avoided attending the official inauguration of the Society on 19 January
1711.[48] A month later, however, he travelled to Berlin for what turned
out to be his last visit. As usual, his sojourn lasted longer than expected,

but this time, at least part of the delay was genuinely due to circumstances beyond his control, since a bad fall injured his leg, forcing him to bed for a while. Notwithstanding this incident, his prolonged visit aroused sullenness in both Hanover and Berlin: the former because Leibniz had once again left without seeking the elector's permission, the latter because of the old suspicions of espionage.[49] Yet he was working in the interest of both courts: continuing his historical researches in the libraries of Berlin,[50] and promoting the Society of Sciences. In particular, on 26 March he called a general meeting of the fellows in which he delivered a momentous speech on the tasks to be pursued by the Society.[51] This was in many respects his swan song: he left Berlin at the beginning of May, never to return. His dealings with the members of the Society Council continued in epistolary form, but his position became increasingly marginal, due in no small measure also to his increasing focus on the establishment of other scientific organisations.

Leibniz's pursuit of the advancement of science through enlightened patronage, although waning in Berlin, was waxing in two very different places: the Vienna of the Habsburgs and the Russia of Peter the Great. His most promising contact in Vienna was another Braunschweig-Lüneburg princess: Empress Wilhelmine Amalie. On 22 September 1710, Leibniz addressed a memo to her in which he outlined his plans and wishes, notably his desire to be nominated as a member of the Imperial Aulic Council (*Reichshofrat*), one of the two supreme courts of appeal of the Empire.[52] Before anything could come of it, Emperor Joseph I died of smallpox (17 April 1711) at only thirty-two years of age without fathering a male heir. Fortunately for Leibniz, the Guelf house had another of its daughters waiting in the wings of the imperial palace. On 23 March 1708, a granddaughter of Duke Anton Ulrich of Wolfenbüttel, Elisabeth Christine (1691–1750), had married Charles, the brother of Joseph I and the second son of the late Leopold I; and on 22 December 1711 he was crowned Holy Roman Emperor as Charles VI. Leibniz's friend and protector, Duke Anton Ulrich (who the year before had formally converted to Catholicism), travelled to the coronation and was able to gain assurance from the new emperor that Leibniz would be nominated *Reichshofrat*.[53] It remained unclear, however, whether this was to be a merely honorary title without remuneration; and once again Leibniz enlisted the help of a woman, the new empress, Elisabeth Christine, to resolve the matter. Via R. C. von Imhof (a Privy Counsellor of Braunschweig-Wolfenbüttel), he asked her to intercede with her husband so that a proper salary could be attached to the title, which he otherwise regarded as useless.[54]

On the Russian front, Leibniz's relations with officers and learned men of the entourage of Peter the Great, steadily growing since the Grand Embassy of 1697,[55] culminated in October 1711 with a meeting with the tsar himself. Until the end of his life Leibniz continued to cultivate his relationship with Peter the Great and his court, regarding Russia as a possible key player on the international political, religious, and even scientific scene. Well in advance of the many contemporaries who dismissed Peter's widespread empire as a barbarian and remote country, Leibniz recognised the enormous potential latent in the still backward Russia. Geographically, it was ideally situated to play a role of political and cultural mediation, because it spanned both Europe and Asia and stretched northeast as far as America. Religiously, it could provide the bridge between the Latin (Catholic) and the Germanic (Protestant) churches, thanks to the ancient ecclesiastical tradition of the Greek Orthodox church stretching back to the apostolic times.[56] Scientifically, its backwardness appeared to Leibniz not so much as a disadvantage as an enormous opportunity for starting afresh with modern science on virgin territory.[57] In all of these respects Leibniz felt that he had something important to propose to the tsar; and in turn, Peter the Great's comprehensive programme of modernisation by opening Russia to western influence and wide-ranging reforms – juridical, administrative, economical, technical, scientific, and pedagogical – seemed to provide Leibniz with the enlightened and truly powerful patron that he had not yet been able to find.[58] Now in his sixties, Leibniz saw in Russia the chance to fulfil the urgent task of accomplishing at least part of the grandiose plans he had conceived since his youth.[59]

Prompted by his Viennese meeting of 1708 with Urbich, he therefore prepared a plan for the development of the sciences in Peter's empire. The plan was forwarded by the Russian diplomat to the tsar, together with a glowing reference for its author, which Leibniz himself had drafted.[60] On his way back from Vienna in the company of Urbich, the two men's discussions ranged from science and the advancement of knowledge to issues of dynastic policy, in particular the possibility of arranging a marriage between Peter's son and heir, Alexei, and a Guelf princess.[61] Once again Guelf dynastic plans met with success, and the resulting union, besides sealing a politically useful relationship between the Russian and Guelf ruling families, provided Leibniz with his opportunity to meet the tsar.

The chosen bride was another granddaughter of Duke Anton Ulrich of Wolfenbüttel, the teenager Charlotte Christine (1694–1715). Although far from keen on the union, Charlotte had the misfortune of being perfectly suited for the kind of alliances the tsar was pursuing. In 1708, as noted above, her sister Elisabeth Christine had married the second son of the late Emperor Leopold, shortly to become Charles VI. Moreover, the young girl had been raised at the court in Dresden of Augustus, the Elector of Saxony and (momentarily) deposed King of Poland, who was one of the tsar's closest allies in the Great Northern War. By the time of the wedding, Peter the Great had inflicted a disastrous defeat on the troops of Charles XII at the battle of Poltava (8 July 1709), effectively ending the period of Sweden's "Age of Greatness" in the Baltic region.[62] Augustus, restored to the throne of Poland-Lithuania in 1710 as a result of this victory, was more than happy to host in Torgau the wedding of his protégée, Charlotte, to the son of his mighty ally. Invited by the Duke of Wolfenbüttel to attend his granddaughter's wedding, Leibniz jumped at the opportunity to fulfil his long nursed desire to meet the tsar.[63] On 19 October 1711 he arrived in Torgau where, after the wedding six days later, he was given an audience by Peter the Great on 30 October.[64] Needless to say, he came to the meeting prepared with his usual stack of memos and proposals.[65] In particular the tsar seemed to be taken by the idea of investigating the magnetic declination in his immensely vast territories.[66] Other proposals and schemes followed: for the advancement of science and knowledge in Russia, for the study of the Slavic heritage,[67] for the exploration of Siberia – in search, *inter alia*, of a passage between Asia and America[68] – and for innovative relief maps of Peter's domains.[69] Taken together, Leibniz's proposals for the tsar were a variation of his all-embracing encyclopaedic dream: in a letter addressed to Peter the Great on 16 January 1712 he explained how his programme as a whole a was intended, as ever, to celebrate God's glory through the improvement of the human condition, for which the advancement of the sciences was the key instrument:

Although I have very frequently been employed in public affairs and also in the judiciary system and am consulted on such matters by great princes on an ongoing basis, I nevertheless regard the arts and sciences as a higher calling, since through them the glory of God and the best interests of the whole of human race is continuously promoted. For in the sciences and the knowledge of nature and art, the wonders of God, his power, wisdom, and goodness are especially manifest; and the arts and sciences are also the true treasury of the human race, through which art masters nature and civilised peoples are distinguished from barbarian ones. For these reasons I have loved and pursued science since my youth.... The one thing I have been lacking is a leading prince who adequately embraced this cause.... I am not a man devoted solely to his native country or to one particular nation: on the contrary, I pursue the interests of the whole human race because I regard heaven as my fatherland and all well-meaning people as its fellow citizens.... To this aim, for a long time I have been conducting a voluminous correspondence in Europe and even as far as China; and for many years I have not only been a fellow of the French and English Royal Societies but also direct as president the Royal Prussian Society of Sciences[.][70]

Integral to this grandiose scheme was the achievement of peace and reconciliation, beginning with the far too lacerated Christian world. To this end, it seemed to Leibniz that Christian countries should direct their military efforts against the constantly looming danger of the Ottoman Empire instead of fighting one another. In the same spirit in which he had written his youthful *Consilium Aegyptiacum*, Leibniz repeatedly urged Peter the Great and his entourage to focus on the Turks pressing on Russia's borders rather than waging war against Sweden. If a Christian country had to be fought, then let it be France, since Leibniz held Louis XIV's aggressive imperialism chiefly responsible for Europe's constant unrest.[71] The tsar, however, had his own agenda. Although prepared to give sympathetic hearing to Leibniz's scientific projects, he was unlikely to change the tsars' traditional determination to secure Russia's access to the sea. Since the plan of pushing back the Ottoman frontier to the Black Sea had proved unsuccessful, in 1700 Peter the Great made peace with the Turks in order to concentrate on rolling back Swedish advances southeast of the Baltic. Never long discouraged, Leibniz soon perceived in Peter's Baltic campaigns the possibility of advancing reconciliation between the Orthodox churches, the Catholic church, and the Protestant churches as well. The Great Northern War was being fought out largely in the enormous kingdom of Poland-Lithuania, interposed between Russia and the Baltic. By supporting the rule of Augustus II of Saxony over Poland-Lithuania, Peter found a way of reducing Sweden's hegemony while extending Russia's influence in this vital region. Since courting Poland meant courting Rome, noises of reconciliation were in order;[72] and Leibniz found these noises so encouraging that he soon began discussing with Urbich the possibility of a worldwide ecumenical council convened by the tsar.[73] Perhaps the Eastern Orthodox traditions of Greece and Russia could provide the means of mending the otherwise irreparable divisions of the Latin and Germanic churches. Needless to say, nothing came of these dreams, not least because the rumours of reconciliation between Roman Catholics and Greek Orthodox through the tsar's good will proved to be little more than rumours.

In the autumn of 1712 Leibniz was invited to meet the tsar in Carlsbad, and again he eagerly accepted, having already planned to travel from Carlsbad further south to Vienna to check on the progress of his nomination to the Imperial Aulic Council.[74] While neglecting to divulge anything of these plans in Hanover, he confided his travel arrangements to Duke Anton Ulrich, who entrusted him with the task of negotiating an anti-French alliance between Russia and Austria.[75] From 6 to 10 November Leibniz was in Carlsbad, busily discussing his scientific and political ideas with the tsar.[76] On 11 November, while the tsar removed to Töplitz with Leibniz in tow,[77] the German philosopher was officially nominated Russian privy counsellor of justice as well as adviser to the tsar on mathematical and scientific matters, services to be remunerated by the handsomely rounded sum of 1000 talers per annum. The German draft of the nomination, duly translated into Russian, had been written by Leibniz himself, who took the opportunity to compose his ideal job description: roughly, a minister without portfolio, devoted to the advancement of knowledge, and free to pursue a wide range of reforms and research projects.[78] In particular, the task of working on the reform of the Russian juridical system bestowed upon him by the chancellor, Gavriil Ivanovič Golovkin, made him feel like the Athenian legislator Solon. Yet the task, he believed, could be fulfilled without much expenditure of time and energy, given his juridical background and experience. His plan was to compress the Russian legal corpus by applying principles dating back at least to his juridical work in Mainz, according to which "the shortest Laws, like the ten commandments of God and the 12 tables of ancient Rome, are the best."[79] Whether these bold declarations in a letter to Sophie were intended merely to sooth the Hanoverians' legitimate concerns regarding their historiographer's priorities, or resulted from Leibniz's typical underestimation of the effort needed to turn theoretical principles into practical reforms, they proved unrealistic. From Töplitz, Leibniz followed the tsar to Dresden, where Peter the Great on 24 November boarded a ship bound for Berlin. Instead Leibniz turned south to Prague, from which he announced his imminent arrival in Vienna to Bishop Buchhaim, asking him to keep his visit secret.[80]

By around mid-December 1712 he was in the Imperial capital for a stay which, this time, lasted almost two years.

Private and Public Debates: Mathematical, Scientific, and Philosophical

A Commerce of Light by Correspondence

While networking for the advancement of science (and the advancement of his own career) through enlightened patronage, Leibniz maintained his own outstanding contribution to the prosecution of the scientific and philosophical discussions of his own day through correspondence with mathematicians, philosophers, and learned men. As he hinted to Peter the Great, corresponding with people all over Europe and as far a field as China was not an idle pastime, as Georg Ludwig seemed to think, but a key facet of his commitment to the improvement of the human condition.[81] It represented a model for the advancement of knowledge which pivoted around a dialectical exchange with other minds, cultures, and experiences rather than centring on meditation in splendid isolation. It was "a commerce of light" through which new insights were reached through communication with people who saw the same universe and the same truth from a different perspective. Accordingly, his correspondence continued to be of gigantic proportions.[82] As in the past, some of his most illuminating expositions of his philosophical views and most lucid scientific and mathematical ideas were penned in letters to old and new partners. Letters to Sophie, for instance, respectively of 31 October 1705 and 6 February 1706 were philosophical jewels in which Leibniz expounded for his friend and protector his notions of simple substance and of soul, grounding his conception on considerations of the nature of the mathematical continuum and the physical continuum.[83]

In his epistolary exchange with Pierre Varignon in 1705 and 1706, amongst other mathematical problems, he revisited the issue of central forces and came to realize that his calculation of centrifugal force needed correction. The result was his *Illustratio tentaminis de motuum coelestium causis*, a new version of his essay of 1689 on the causes of the motion of celestial bodies, with a correction of his calculation of centrifugal force and a reply to the criticisms by David Gregory of his astronomical theories.[84] Dispatched in the autumn of 1705 to the editor of the *Acta Eruditorum*,

Otto Mencke, the paper was judged too long to be published in toto, so only an extract of Leibniz's essay appeared in the *Acta* of October 1706.[85] Two other products of the same year were the *Antibarbarus physicus*, attacking the reintroduction into physics of occult qualities or forces reminiscent of the infamous abuse of qualities in scholasticism,[86] and a study of motion in a resisting medium, a topic which featured prominently in his correspondence with Varignon over the following years.[87] In 1706 he also began a remarkable correspondence with the Dutchman Nicolaus Hartsoeker (1656–1715) discussing issues of physics and arguing against the existence of atoms.[88]

Once again in 1706, an exchange with Molanus provided Leibniz with the opportunity to formulate some of his most rigorous pieces on natural law while returning to his criticism of Pufendorf. The abbot of Luccum had asked his Hanoverian friend and collaborator to let him know whether Pufendorf's *De officio hominis et civis juxta legem naturalem* (Lund 1673) was suitable "as a topic of instruction for the young."[89] Leibniz replied that Pufendorf's little book could serve "usefully as a compendium of natural law for those who are satisfied with a superficial smattering (as are the majority of readers), without looking for sound learning" since the author seemed "to have correctly identified neither the end, the object, nor the efficient cause of natural law."[90] In short, Leibniz could scarcely have disagreed more with the legal positivism and voluntarism of Pufendorf, Hobbes, and the like. Indeed, he continued, a doctrine "which makes all law derivative from the command of a superior, is not free of scandal and errors" even if the superior in question is said to be God. "Neither the norm of conduct itself, nor the essence of the just, depends on [God's] free decision, but rather on eternal truths, objects of the divine intellect, which constitute, so to speak, the essence of divinity itself."[91]

In addition to Varignon and Hartsoeker, new entries to the long list of Leibniz's correspondents in the first years of the new century included two other people who merit special mention: Christian Wolff (1679–1754), with whom Leibniz corresponded between 1704 and 1716, and Bartholomew Des Bosses (1668–1738), with whom he exchanged letters between 1706 and 1716. Although their epistolary exchanges with the Hanoverian savant spanned roughly the same period of time, the relationships documented by their correspondence were quite different in kind. Wolff was a clever young man whom Leibniz supported in the early stages of his academic career but never perceived as an intimate friend with deeper insights than others into the secrets of his philosophy. Despite the subsequent philosophical historiography, which came to regard Wolff as the epigone of Leibniz and the systematizer of his philosophy, in life neither Leibniz nor Wolff saw things that way. Indeed their philosophy differed on key points notwithstanding many, sometimes superficial, similarities.[92] On the other hand, Leibniz found in Des Bosses a much closer intellectual partner and friend – and one who prompted him to explore different philosophical paths to a possible solution to the problem of composite substance.

It was Wolff who in December 1704 took the initiative of contacting Leibniz, sending him a copy of his dissertation *De philosophia practica universali methodo mathematica conscripta* (1703). This move was understandable. Wolff, born in 1679 into a Lutheran family in Breslau (in Habsburg-ruled Silesia), was educated in the same Saxon universities as Leibniz – first Jena, then Leipzig, where he achieved his habilitation as *Privat-dozent* in mathematics with the dissertation he sent to Leibniz.[93] As an enterprising young academic, it was only natural that he should seek support from an established and well-connected savant who was likely to be sympathetic towards his philosophical approach. Wolff was not disappointed. Leibniz liked his dissertation, replied with comments meant "to advance rather than correct" Wolff's ideas,[94] and together with Tschirnhaus supported his academic appointment as a professor of mathematics and natural sciences at the University of Halle (1706).[95] In the following years Leibniz and Wolff discussed philosophical, physical, mathematical, and chemical issues both in their personal meetings and in correspondence. Meanwhile the bright newly appointed professor found his footing in the learned and scientific community. Between 1708 and 1711 he reviewed new mathematical publications for the *Acta Eruditorum* under Leibniz's close mentoring;[96] on 25 February 1711 he was elected a member of the Berlin Society of Sciences, as attested in the official document signed by Leibniz and the secretary of the Society, Johann Theodor Jablonski; and in 1713 he published the first book (known as the *German Logic*) in the multivolume series of *Vernünftige Gedanken*, which he continued until 1725. Regarding issues of practical philosophy discussed in Wolff's dissertation, Leibniz and Wolff found themselves in general agreement: both did not tie morality to revealed religion (as testified by Leibniz's outspoken appreciation for Chinese practical philosophy in the preface of the *Novissima Sinica*) and both saw continuous progress towards greater perfection as a fundamental ethical principle.[97] More complex was Wolff's reaction to Leibniz's proposal regarding the metaphysical grounding of dynamic laws and properties. In particular, the correspondence with Wolff of 1710 and 1711 recorded probably the most sustained Leibnizian explanation of the status of derivative forces and their relation to primitive forces.[98] In July 1711, however, the younger partner in the exchange felt that they had reached an impasse and quite boldly declared that due to his own method of philosophising and his own hypotheses on this topic he could not follow Leibniz any further. Rather than entering into long discussions of these differences, he preferred for the moment to add nothing.[99]

The correspondence with Des Bosses began on 25 January 1706 when the learned Jesuit picked up his pen following a recent "tumultuous conversation" between him and Leibniz.[100] At the time the two of them were separated by less than a day's ride, since Leibniz was based in Hanover and Des Bosses taught theology at the nearby Jesuit college in Hildesheim.[101] In all likelihood, the thirty-eight-year-old theologian had travelled the short distance to meet Leibniz in Hanover at the beginning of January and was now following up on their stimulating conversation. Over the next ten years, until barely six months before Leibniz's death, they kept in close contact despite the fact that in 1710 Des Bosses departed from Hildesheim to teach mathematics (and later moral philosophy) at the Jesuit college in Cologne, where, apart from a stint of theology teaching in Paderborn in 1712–13, he resided until his death in 1738. After Leibniz's demise, he published in 1719 the first Latin translation of the *Theodicy*, which he had been preparing during the previous years in close consultation with his friend.[102]

The beginning of their correspondence fell in a period in which Leibniz – especially in his exchanges with Jesuit theologians – was beginning to toy with the idea of a metaphysical union of soul and body, which was not part of his theory of pre-established harmony, but which he did not deny could be admitted.[103] This line of thinking had been stimulated by his belated notice of an article published in the March 1704 issue of the influential Jesuit journal, the so-called *Mémoires de Trévoux*, by one of its editors, René-Joseph Tournemine.[104] In it Tournemine had objected that Leibniz's system of pre-established harmony was no more capable of accounting for a "veritable union" between soul and body than the

occasionalist brand of Cartesianism which the German thinker had criticized. Leibniz's cautious reply to Tournemine, probably sent to the Jesuit
in January 1706 and eventually published in the *Mémoires de Trévoux* of
March 1708, was that with his doctrine of pre-established harmony he
had tried

to account only for the Phenomena, that is to say, for the relation that is perceived
between the soul and the body. But since the metaphysical union added to it is not
a phenomenon, and since we do not even have an intelligible notion of it, I have not
taken it upon myself to seek the reason for it. But I do not deny that there is something
of this nature[.][105]

Tournemine's objection stuck in Leibniz's mind, although in a letter to
De Volder of 19 January 1706 he seemed to dismiss the metaphysical
union desired by Tournemine as some utopian notion for which the
scholastics appeared to be in constant search.[106] Despite his sceptical
remarks to De Volder, Leibniz realized that Tournemine had identified
an unresolved problem in his philosophy, namely the ontological status of
living creatures such as plants, animals, and human beings. According to
the Aristotelian tradition, being and unity were convertible (*ens et unum
convertuntur*): nothing could be *a* being without having a degree of unity.
Following this tradition, Leibniz maintained that one of the fundamental
requisites for qualifying as a substance was to be endowed with an intrinsic
unity, to be *unum per se*. Granted this fundamental requisite, the question
arose of whether the degree of unity of living creatures such as plants and
animals was sufficient for them to qualify, strictly speaking, as substances.
Leibniz had of course often written of living organisms (including human
beings) as corporeal *substances*. But did they really satisfy the substantiality
criterion of being *unum per se*? Or were they called substances only in the
broad sense of enjoying a degree of unity clearly superior to that of a heap
of stones or a flock of sheep? Despite the beautiful economy of his theory
of simple substances, endowed as such with intrinsic unity and activity,
out of which everything else resulted, Leibniz realized that the need for
a metaphysical union stronger than that provided by the system of pre-
established harmony could be a serious problem; and he therefore set
about in his correspondence with Des Bosses to address it, with particular
attention to the key problem of the metaphysical unity of human beings.[107]
In three letters to Des Bosses of 3 September 1708, 24 April 1709, and 8
September 1709 he returned to his response to Tournemine, reiterating

that he did not deny the possibility of a metaphysical union.[108] A high-profile admission of this possibility was included in the *Theodicy* of 1710, which presented the most public face of his thinking.[109]

From 1712 onwards, Leibniz's letters to Des Bosses explored the issue of a metaphysical union which provided the ultimate principle of unity of composite substance through the introduction of the controversial notion of *vinculum substantiale* or substantial bond.[110] This terminology was not unprecedented, especially in seventeenth-century Jesuit metaphysics; but the notion itself was something new in the context of Leibniz's metaphysics of monads and was definitely at odds with his often reiterated fundamental tenet that only monads, and in them perception and appetite, were ultimately real. With the *vinculum substantiale* – that is "a certain union, or rather a real unifier superadded to the monads by God"[111] – he was introducing a further level of irreducible metaphysical reality over and above monads. Whereas his 'standard' theory of monads regarded monadic domination as sufficient to provide the unity of a composite (or corporeal) substance, the theory of the *vinculum substantiale* seemed to postulate the necessity of a stronger principle of unity not simply reducible to the monads. Approaching both the end of his correspondence with the Des Bosses and the end of his life, Leibniz candidly confessed that he was not at all sure that the things he had written in his letters regarding the principle of unity required by composite substances – the *vinculum substantiale* versus his more typical monadological views – were or could be made consistent with one another.[112] And yet doubts about the necessity, at least in certain cases, of a more robust principle of unity superadded to monads seems to have been genuinely nagging at Leibniz's mind. Finding himself unable to produce a theory sufficiently coherent with his previous explanation of phenomena through the doctrine of pre-established harmony, he even proposed that a plausible account of this metaphysical union was above the scope of limited human reason ("It is like in the *mysteries*", he wrote to Tournemine).[113] But he did not deny that something of the sort could be possible or even necessary in certain cases. Interestingly these 'certain cases' belonged to the realm of the mysteries of revealed theology. Although Leibniz famously played with the notion of *vinculum substantiale* in order to provide a possible explanation of the Roman Catholic doctrine of transubstantiation, it seems that the mystery which concerned him most in this regard was rather that of the Incarnation. As a Lutheran he was not committed to the doctrine of transubstantiation, and especially in these later years his youthful sympathies towards it had very noticeably cooled down; but he remained throughout his life committed to the mystery of the Incarnation. The union in Christ of divine and human natures was traditionally explained through the analogy in human beings of the union of soul and body. Leibniz repeatedly endorsed this analogy but never seems to have applied his distinctive theory of the union of soul and body through pre-established harmony to it, probably because it did not seem to provide the robust union of the two natures in one single person required by an orthodox reading of the mystery. In the first place, in Leibniz's monadological conception, mind and body did not represent two radically different 'natures' as they did in the Cartesian framework, with its sharp distinction between *res cogitans* and *res extensa*; and if these natures were not radically different, then their union could not provide an analogy applicable to the union of the divine and human natures in Christ. Second, even if one granted that the distinction between a dominating monad (the 'mind') and an aggregate of corporeal substances resulting, ultimately, from monads (the 'body') was sufficient to serve as an analogy with the union of divine and human natures in Christ, the underlying question still remained of whether Leibniz's metaphysics had the resources for granting the status of single substance to *any* composite entity. Whereas Leibniz could safely remain uncommitted on the vexed issue of whether, strictly speaking, the status of substances could be granted to the unified aggregates of monads which we perceive as living organisms (animals or plants), the same did not apply to an orthodox understanding of the dogma of the Incarnation. So much Leibniz confessed to Des Bosses in a letter of 10 October 1712: "Nor do we need any other thing besides Monads and their modifications, for Philosophy as opposed to the supernatural. But I fear that we cannot explain the mystery of the Incarnation, and other things, unless real bonds or unions are added."[114] In short it seems plausible to think that Leibniz did not regard the theory of the *vinculum substantiale* as something he could endorse in his philosophical explanation of reality; but he nevertheless left open the possibility of such a bond as a truth above but not contrary to human reason since it was needed to account for certain mysteries of revealed religion to which he was committed.[115]

The "Forerunner" of Leibniz's Great Synthesis

In 1710, in the midst of his correspondence with Des Bosses, there appeared in Amsterdam the most voluminous and intentionally popular philosophical work which Leibniz ever published: his *Essais de Théodicée sur la bonté de Dieu, la liberté de l'homme et l'origine du mal*. Although the immediate origin of the *Theodicy* could be traced back to his conversations on Pierre Bayle's *Dictionaire* with Sophie Charlotte and her entourage in Lützenburg, Leibniz's sustained reflections on the main topics discussed within it – God's justice and goodness in relation to the problems of evil and of human freedom – went back to his youth.[116] As early as 1669–71, in fact, he had penned a "meditation" on the freedom of human beings and on God's foreknowledge and grace; and one of the most important writings of his youth, the *Confessio Philosophi* of 1672–3, was a sort of proto-theodicy.[117] During the following years the cluster of problems discussed in the *Theodicy* remained amongst his ongoing concerns.

If the themes of this long-planned work were well established topics of discussion in the literature of his time, the word chosen by Leibniz to signify "the doctrine of God's justice" was new and caused some bewilderment:[118] writing to Des Bosses in January 1712, Leibniz reported that a reviewer had taken it to indicate the name of the book's author ("Theodicaeum") instead of its topic.[119] Leibniz, it appears, had probably penned the term "theodicy" for the first time in its French and Latin forms between 1695 and 1697. On 8 June 1696, writing to Etienne Chavin (a Huguenot refugee who served as preacher to the Reformed community in Berlin and had begun that year to edit the *Nouveau Journal des savants*), he remarked,

Some day I might entertain you with some reflections which I have nurtured and examined for a very long time on my own and with others with a view to including them in my Theodicies [dans mes Theodicées] on the origin of evil and the difference between the necessary and the contingent. There I believe I have also discovered that those who do not regard our good qualities as the last reason of the [divine] decrees in our favour are not as wrong as many people imagine. I flatter myself that these meditations, drawn from theology and natural jurisprudence and grounded in certain philosophical demonstrations reserved to my universal characteristic [Specieuse universelle], might help to establish the greatest truths more incontestably, in a manner which will be as accessible as a dialogue and as precise as geometrical reasoning.[120]

The following year, in a letter of 30 September 1697, he confirmed to Antonio Magliabechi his intention to write "the elements of a Theodicy" ("Theodicaeae . . . elementa").[121] In two letters to Jablonski of 2 February and 26 March 1700 he again turned over the plan to write "a *Theodicy* and to vindicate in it the goodness, wisdom, and justice of God and His supreme power and immutable influence." Amongst other things, this was intended to promote the reunification of the Protestant churches.[122] But perhaps the most interesting of these early uses of the new term is found in a fragment written between 1695 and 1697 in which the Latin term "Theodicaea" appeared probably for the very first time.[123] Hiding behind the pseudonym Guilielmus Pacidius, which he had used in his programmatic work for the *scientia generalis*,[124] Leibniz proposed to write a work entitled *Theodicaea* and conceived as "catholic demonstrations on divine justice" (Demonstrationes catholicae de divina justitia).[125] Clearly, this was meant to be part of the all-embracing plan of his youth, the *Demonstrationes Catholicae*. Indeed, in a letter of October 1710 announcing to Thomas Burnett the imminent publication of the *Essais de Théodicée* and recounting their immediate origins in the conversations with Sophie Charlotte and her entourage, Leibniz presented the *Theodicy* as the "forerunner" ("avantcoureur") of a broader enterprise reminiscent of the *Demonstrationes Catholicae*, later reconceived as the *scientia generalis*, and now finally envisaged as "Elements of general philosophy and of natural theology."[126] In contrast to his youthful conception, in which the mysteries of revealed Christian theology were amply represented, the focus was now clearly on the realm of demonstrative reason, that is, of philosophy proper and of natural theology. As Leibniz saw it, an array of articles published over the years in the learned journals of the European *république des lettres* were also pieces of this perennial scheme:

[Throughout the *Theodicy*] there are also scattered clarifications of my system of preestablished harmony and of many issues of general philosophy and natural theology, where I claim that everything can be determined demonstratively and provide the means of doing so. If I were freed from my historical labours, I would like to work at establishing these elements of general philosophy and of natural theology, which include what is most important in this philosophy for both theory and practice. But this present work can serve as a forerunner, together with all the loose pieces which I have published in the journals of Germany, France, and Holland.[127]

In a letter of November 1710 to Charles Hugony (a native of Languedoc whom Leibniz had met in Berlin), Leibniz returned to the idea of a work expounding his "entire system," of which the *Theodicy* was meant to provide some parts cast in a popular style for the broader public. The fact that the language envisaged by Leibniz for this further work was Latin indicated that it was intended for a more specialised readership able to

grasp the technical subtleties of his philosophical system and thereby to
reach a deeper and richer understanding of it:

> My essays on the goodness of God, the freedom of man, and the origin of evil have
> been printed in Holland, but I did not want to put my name to them. They are woven
> together from what I said and wrote at various times to the Queen of Prussia, who
> enjoyed reading M. Bayle and in whose company the difficulties that he raises on
> these matters were often discussed. [In them] I try to explain one part of my views in
> a rather informal manner. As you know, some of my views cannot be presented in a
> straightforward manner, since people are liable to misunderstand them, not in relation
> to religion (which is strongly supported) but in relation to the senses. I am therefore
> thinking of [writing] a Latin work in which I will try to unfold my entire system.[128]

In the late summer of 1715 he was still nurturing the hope of following
up the *Theodicy* with a rigorously demonstrative exposition:

> I also tried to show that there is in God as much goodness as there is greatness, in
> order to give human beings reason to imitate his beneficent nature as much as possible,
> as the best way to please him[.] If God will grant me more free time, I will attempt
> by means of well-formed demonstrations to impart to a good portion of my views the
> certainty of Euclid's *Elements*[.][129]

Although this more rigorous exposition of his entire system never developed beyond the stage of a long-cherished aspiration, its intended precursor, the *Theodicy*, eventually materialized on Leibniz's desk. The bulk of
the text (checked for linguistic improvement by Charles Ancillon, another
French refugee from the Reformed community in Berlin) was ready by the
end of of spring of 1707.[130] In a letter to Des Bosses of 3 September 1708
Leibniz announced that the work was finished and that he wished to send
it to him for his comment.[131] Des Bosses was delighted to oblige and even
began to search for a suitable publishing outlet.[132] After some unsuccessful
negotiations, Leibniz eventually found a solution of his own, entrusting
his manuscript to the Amsterdam printer Isaac Troyel. Although the
Theodicy was already a very cautious work, targeted to a broad public
which Leibniz did not want to upset with his potentially most controversial philosophical views, he nevertheless deemed it prudent to omit
his authorship from the first edition.[133] But the secret was short-lived:
it was not difficult to guess that the author of the *Theodicy* was Leibniz,
and his name appeared on the title page of the second edition published
in Amsterdam in 1712.[134] By that time, as well, Leibniz's fears of being
taken to task by theologians were proving exaggerated. Already in October

1711 the lively duchess of Orléans, Elisabeth Charlotte, wrote to her aunt Sophie that Leibniz's *Theodicy* had done him much good in dispelling the unjust suspicion, expressed in the *Plattdeutsch* nickname circulating in Hanover, that he was a "Glaubenichts" (a "believe-nothing").[135] Leibniz himself seemed surprised as well as delighted that the *Theodicy* was received with favour by theologians of the three main Christian confessions – something scarcely to be taken for granted in a period of unending religious controversy:

> Curiously enough, this work has pleased excellent theologians of all three main confessions. Our [Lutheran] theologians in Leipzig have been happy with it; a famous professor of theology in Geneva has complimented me over it;[136] [and] the Jesuits themselves have had it reprinted in Paris,[137] . . . since I spoke of Luther and of Calvin in an honourable and appropriate way but do no less justice to the able people of the Roman Church.[138]

In the late summer of 1715 he repeated the point to a Polish diplomat named Biber: "This book has been happy in this respect: that excellent theologians of the three parties of the Empire have been satisfied with it."[139] This gratifying agreement among theologians with disparate views was no doubt due in part to Leibniz's avoidance in the *Theodicy* of presenting explicitly the controversial aspects of his system which might well have bewildered all of them, first and foremost his conception of contingency hinging on the notion of infinite analysis.[140] In discussing contingency he had reverted to the more traditional justification based on the distinction between absolute necessity and hypothetical (or moral) necessity,[141] and had also tried to play down any talk which could ring suspiciously of necessitarianism. He had already had an earful from Arnauld about sliding down that slippery slope, and this even without revealing to the French theologian anything regarding the infinite analysis conception of contingency which he was developing precisely around the time of their correspondence on the *Discours de Métaphysique*.

If, in the *Theodicy*, he was (as usual) not telling the whole story of his philosophy, on the other hand he was convinced of what he was saying and deemed it sufficient for the purpose at hand: defending God's justice and the Christian religion for the general educated public. For all his cautions he had been quite candid in telling some of his correspondents that this work was not the place for an account of the more complex and technical aspects of his philosophical system: the *Theodicy* was just a part of a broader picture, or rather a mere "precursor" of his *magnum opus*. Still, it contained a large part of the complete puzzle. Carefully assembled with the interlocking articles which he had published in learned journals over the years, it was enough to account "at least for the principles" of his system.[142] On the other hand, perhaps no other writing exemplified better than the *Theodicy* Leibniz's view that

Metaphysics should be written with accurate definitions and demonstrations, but nothing should be demonstrated in it that conflicts too much with received opinions. For thus this metaphysics will be able to be received. If it is once approved, then afterwards, if any examine it more profoundly, they will draw the necessary consequences themselves.[143]

This circumspect way to proceed was characteristic of Leibniz the lawyer and diplomat but also of Leibniz the peacemaker and seeker of reconciliation in a time in which intellectual divides and religious controversies served to justify bloodshed and military action. Genuinely convinced both of the existence of a universal truth and that unity could therefore be found through reasoning and dialogue, Leibniz was doing his best to knit back together a lacerated fabric. With such considerations in mind, Leibniz felt compelled to tread carefully on the mined territory of intellectual disputes. When after the publication of the *Theodicy* a Lutheran theologian, Christopher Matthäus Pfaff, let Leibniz know that his book must have been a *jeu d'esprit*, a playful joke, since his alleged refutation of Bayle's scepticism was not effective enough and did in fact confirm it, the Hanoverian thinker might well have felt that it was people like Pfaff who would for ever stand in the way of reconciliation. Instead of entering into a dispute with the theologian about the earnestness of his work, apparently he decided to take Pfaff for a ride. If this latter report has to be credited, he replied to the astonished theologian:

You have hit the nail on the head. And I am amazed there has been no one hitherto who has sensed that this is my game. For it is not for philosophers always to take things seriously. In framing hypotheses, as you rightly point out, they try out the force of their mental talents.[144]

Despite the absence of important aspects of Leibniz's philosophical system from the *Theodicy*, what *was* included in it corresponded to genuine views held by the philosopher, most of them attested in a vast array of private notes and letters penned over the years.

The *Essais de Théodicée* themselves were organized in three main parts, devoted to expounding in detail the matter for discussion, answering Bayle's particular objections regarding the cause of moral evil, and providing Leibniz's solution to the problem of physical evil. They were preceded by an extensive "Preface" followed by a "Preliminary discourse on the conformity of faith with reason" in which Leibniz recapitulated views on the relationship between faith and reason the key features of which he had maintained since his youth. After a detailed index prepared by Leibniz himself, the work featured three appendices: a "summary of the controversy reduced to formal arguments"; Leibniz's reflections on the dispute between Thomas Hobbes and an Arminian bishop, John Bramhall, on freedom, necessity, and chance;[145] and, finally, Leibniz's remarks on *De Origine Mali* (London 1702), written by the Anglican bishop of Derry and (since March 1703) archbishop of Dublin, William King. In the same year in which the *Theodicy* appeared in print, its Amsterdam printer also published an agile Latin pamphlet – the *Causa Dei asserta per justitiam ejus*[146] – in which Leibniz summarized the arguments of his main volume.

Amongst the wealth of topics buttressed by examples and anecdotes which made their way into a voluminous work like the *Theodicy*, one in particular must be mentioned for its enormous resonance in contemporary logic: Leibniz's notion of possible worlds. Its most famous application, popularised by the *Theodicy*, provided Leibniz with the key to his answer to the problem of evil, which hinged on the claim that the actual world is the best of all possible worlds. Despite the presence in it of all sorts of evils, God had a morally sufficient reason for creating (that is, actualizing) this world in preference to any other possible world which his infinite intellect contemplates. But could one not imagine this actual world with all its good features and positive aspects but with at least one less evil occurrence? Leibniz's adamant denial of this possibility was central to his theory. Even the slightest difference of *any* kind – for instance, Leibniz wearing a pair of black socks on 3 June 1710 instead of the grey ones he actually wore on that day – would result in a completely different possible world containing someone who looks very similar to the Leibniz of the actual world but who is in fact another individual altogether; and the same would be true of all other beings in this alternative possible world, due to the universal harmony or universal connection of everything with everything and to the fact that, according to Leibniz, there are no purely extrinsic denominations.[147] A fortiori, the elimination of one evil occurrence from this world would result in another possible world, and God knows that (despite what we might think) this different possible world is not the world which contains the maximum compossible perfection and goodness. In short, all the evils of this actual world are logically necessary for the greater good of the best of all possible worlds.

In the last pages of the *Theodicy* Leibniz made this point by elaborating the story of Sextus Tarquinius narrated by Lorenzo Valla in his famous *Dialogus de libero arbitrio* of 1439.[148] In Leibniz's view, had Sextus behaved in a way different from the one in which he actually behaved (that is, had he not violated the wife of his friend), he would not have been the same Sextus acting in a different way, but another Sextus living in another (albeit very similar) possible world. Despite some oscillations on other occasions, Leibniz here clearly denied the identity of the subjects of counterfactuals (that is, the subjects of conditional statements indicating what would follow if an hypothesis contrary to the facts were true). It does not seem, however, that Leibniz also thought of necessity in terms of truth in all possible worlds, and of contingency in terms of truth in some (as opposed to all) possible worlds. In other words, although authors such as Rudolf Carnap (1891–1970) and Saul Kripke (1940–) were inspired by Leibniz's notion of possible worlds, it would be misleading to regard Leibniz as the first proponent of a possible worlds semantics pivoting around the interpretation of modal notions in terms of truth and falsity in possible worlds.[149]

From Bad to Worse in the Calculus War

Around the time that the *Theodicy* was published and began to send ripples through the learned world, Leibniz continued his logical researches, probably penning a pamphlet on the *Mathesis rationis*,[150] as well as his technical work towards an improved model of the calculating machine. For the latter project he secured the help of Gottfried Teuber, a deacon at the court of Duke Moritz Wilhelm von Sachsen-Zeitz whom Leibniz probably had met during his first visit in Zeitz in May 1711.[151] In the same period he also suffered the most explicit and painful attack so far against his claim of having invented the calculus. The official periodical publication of the Royal Society, the *Philosophical Transactions* for 1708 (actually published in 1710), included a paper by the Scottish mathematician John Keill in which Leibniz was openly accused of having plagiarized

Newton's method of fluxions from the latter's *epistola prior* and *epistola posterior* of 1676. Discussing the law of centripetal force Keill remarked:

All these things follow from the nowadays highly celebrated arithmetic of fluxions, which Mr Newton beyond any shadow of doubt first discovered, as any one reading his letters published by Wallis will readily ascertain,[152] and yet the same arithmetic was afterwards published by Mr Leibniz in the *Acta Eruditorum* having changed the name and the symbolism.[153]

The volume of the *Philosophical Transactions* containing Keill's attack was sent to Leibniz on 28 November 1710 by the secretary of the Royal Society, Hans Sloane.[154] Upon reading Keill's accusations, Leibniz, as a fellow of the Society, officially complained to Sloane on 4 March 1711, hoping that the upsetting incident could be resolved with appropriate apologies as it had been in the case of Fatio de Duillier's charges.[155] To his dismay, this time things went differently. Apparently Sloane took up the matter with the president of the Society, who happened to be Newton himself. In turn Newton approached Keill, who cunningly drew the English mathematician's attention to Leibniz's review in the *Acta Eruditorum* of 1705 of the mathematical treatises appended to the *Opticks*.[156] Newton felt at this point that he was the one being attacked and treated unfairly by the German thinker. With the president of the Society on his side, instead of being pressed for apologies, Keill was invited to vindicate his position in a written account. Keill's piece was read at the Royal Society meeting of 24 May 1711 (O.S.) and subsequently copied to Leibniz.[157] Presented with this further battery of accusations Leibniz sent a dignified defence to Sloane in a letter of 29 December 1711. While acknowledging Newton's own right to claim independent discovery of the calculus, he also reserved the same right for himself. After all, Leibniz pointed out, he had not rushed to publish his results of 1675 but waited nine years.[158] In the meantime Newton could have had all the time to unveil his discovery to the public if he felt so inclined. By now, however, Newton was on the warpath, determined to establish his priority of discovery once and for all. Besides, the *Theodicy* had poured oil rather than water on the smouldering dispute by criticising Newtonian gravitation as involving an occult action at a distance; and Leibniz renewed this charge in a letter of 10 February 1711 to Hartsoeker, which was published in the *Mémoires de Trévoux* of March 1712.[159] To settle the issue, the Royal Society decided to appoint a committee which would look at the documentation and write a final report. On 24 April 1712 (O.S.), less than two months after the nomination of the committee, the job was done – an exemplary exercise in investigative efficiency aided perhaps by the fact that the report was composed by Newton himself. Unsurprisingly, the report's verdict inclined overwhelmingly in favour of the rights of its author and Leibniz was treated as a plagiarist guilty of knowingly appropriating the discovery of another. Peer review by the Royal Society judged it a fair appraisal of the facts and ordered its publication, together with the relevant supporting documents. Newton seized the opportunity to edit the collection in the second half of 1712, annotating the documents with caustic notes and using the documents available to support his side of the story, but neglecting in this case to claim credit for his intellectual work.[160] The resulting *Commercium epistolicum D. Johannis Collins et aliorum de analysi promota* was published in London in January 1713, although the date of publication which appeared on the volume was 1712, following the Julian calendar still in use in England. A copy of the volume was dispatched to Hanover, but by that time Leibniz was in Vienna.[161] It was several months before he was informed of the publication and content of the *Commercium Epistolicum* by his friend Johann Bernoulli.[162]

At the Court of the Emperor (December 1712–September 1714)

Since Leibniz's last visit four years before, Vienna had changed once again. The imperial sceptre was now held by Charles VI (1711–40), the Habsburg pretender to the Spanish throne against the Bourbon King installed in Madrid, Philip V.[163] This very fact proved a turning point of the decade-long War of the Spanish Succession, even more decisive than the battles of the anti-French Grand Alliance against the army of Louis XIV. If the allies had gathered to prevent Spain and its rich colonial empire from being swallowed into the French sphere of influence, none of them relished the idea of having the crowns of Spain and of the Holy Roman Empire sitting on the same head. It was time for peace, at least as far as Charles VI's allies were concerned. Great Britain withdrew from the coalition and a peace congress was opened in Utrecht on 29 January 1712 despite the emperor's efforts to convince the other members of the Grand Alliance to continue fighting.

It was in this climate of transition and uncertainty that Leibniz arrived in Vienna in mid-December 1712 to stake his claim to the nomination as

Reichshofrat agreed upon by the emperor almost one year before thanks
to the good offices of Duke Anton Ulrich. Writing on 23 December to
the Hanoverian Prime Minister, Bernstorff, to announce for the first
time that he was in Vienna – miles and miles away from his desk in
Hanover piled, the minister would have hoped, with drafts of the Guelf
history – Leibniz did his best to describe the outing as another unplanned
excursion brought about by fortuitous circumstances: first a sore foot
delayed his return from Dresden, and then a lucky star had sent him the
opportunity of an almost free ride to Vienna that he could not possibly
forgo. No one could really blame Bernstorff or, for that matter, the elector,
if upon receiving this letter they felt an irritating feeling of déjà vu,
especially because their patience with Leibniz's unauthorized absences
was already stretched to its limits. As it happened, on the same day in
which Leibniz was belatedly informing his employers of his whereabouts,
his amanuensis (J. Fr. Hodann) was writing from Hanover reporting the
deep annoyance of the elector at his absence and Bernstorff's summons to
return.[164] Having weathered such storms before, the unrepentant Leibniz
continued to pursue his own agenda, hoping that in the end he could
persuade Bernstorff and company that his unauthorized sojourn did not
jeopardize the completion of the Guelf history.

Immediately upon arriving, he set about with his usual alacrity preparing to bury the new emperor under a blizzard of memoranda highlighting
his past services, accomplishments, and projects as justification for the formalisation of his appointment as imperial counsellor.[165] In mid-January
1713 Leibniz was granted his first audience with Charles VI. On 18 January
he proudly reported to Bernstorff that the emperor was very interested
in his work on the Guelf history and appreciated the need to set it in
the context of the history of the Holy Roman Empire as a whole: indeed
for this purpose the ruler seemed prepared to grant him the use of his
jealously kept library.[166] Perhaps hoping to have mollified Bernstorff's
attitude with this news, on 1 March he unveiled the ongoing negotiations for his appointment to the Imperial Aulic Council, pleading for the
minister's help in securing Georg Ludwig's permission.[167] Yet despite
Leibniz's protracted secrecy, the impending appointment was already old
news in Hanover. As befitted one of the chief princes of the Empire, Georg
Ludwig was not without means of keeping abreast of affairs in Vienna. On
22 February the Hanoverian envoy in Vienna, Huldenberg, had already
approached the dowager empress, Amalie, with the aim of persuading

her – and through her the emperor himself – of Leibniz's unsuitability
for the proposed office. The portrait of Leibniz painted by Huldenberg
for the benefit of the empress reflected Hanover's exasperation with its
undisciplined *Hofrat*:

In his period [of service] he has neither reviewed [judicial] acts nor made [legal]
judgements and would certainly be very bad at it. His Majesty wishes to warn the
Emperor, lest what has happened to the Elector befall him. For Leibniz, by his
native disposition, wants to achieve everything; and he therefore delights in endless
correspondence and shuttling here and there, striving to satisfy his insatiable curiosity;
but he has either no talent or no inclination to pull anything together and bring it to a
close. It would be regrettable if the Elector were to lose him and yet the Emperor to
gain nothing useful from him.[168]

There is no denying the accuracy of this character sketch; but it is equally
clear that such an unfavourable reference so spontaneously offered ironically betrayed Georg Ludwig's determination to retain Leibniz's services
nevertheless. Leibniz, after all, had a job to finish on which many talers
had already been invested; and his unrivalled juridical and historical competence, greatly increased by protracted research in leading European
archives, might again prove invaluable in promoting Hanover's dynastic
and territorial claims. Exasperating as they were to both parties, Leibniz's
seemingly endless historical researches had fused a bond with the house
of Hanover which neither the elector's impatience with his court historiographer nor the philosopher's impatience with court historiography
could break. Leibniz's sometimes brazen disregard for his employer's
most forceful and explicit orders shows that he was well aware of his
unique value to Georg Ludwig; but he must also have been aware that
this unique value could not be transferred to another princely employer
without another lifetime pursuing the history of another dynasty through
the archives of Europe. In this sense the Guelf history was a chain which
bound Leibniz to the house of Hanover. Despite furious domestic disagreements and Leibniz's perennial flirtation with other employers, this
marriage proved permanent.

   In this particular instance, moreover, Georg Ludwig eventually
relented: after dragging his feet for some time, on 5 April 1713 he granted
permission for the nomination of Leibniz as *Reichshofrat*.[169] Absolute ruler
though he was (in theory) within his own lands, the elector was ill-advised
to cross the emperor; and when the emperor wanted something from him
Georg Ludwig was shrewd enough to arrange a quid pro quo. The day

after granting his gracious permission, the elector requested Leibniz to present to the emperor the claims of the Braunschweig-Lüneburg house to the duchy of Lauenburg.[170] Leibniz dutifully obliged, no doubt glad to be offered a way to ingratiate the elector, demonstrate the value of his connections in the capital, and prolong his stay in Vienna.[171] In mid-April the decree appointing Leibniz a member of the Imperial Aulic Council was finally ready.[172] His nomination was backdated to 2 January 1712, the day on which the emperor had first given his verbal agreement to the appointment, allowing Leibniz to make the case that his pay as *Reichshofrat* of 2000 guilders per annum should also be paid retrospectively. Moreover, Leibniz proposed that his stipend should be increased to 6000 guilders in the event that he settled permanently in Vienna.[173] Before putting forward this suggestion he had taken careful stock of his income. Summing up his various sources – 1800 talers from Hanover including stipend and expenses; 400 talers from Wolfenbüttel; 600 talers from Berlin; 2000 guilders from St. Petersburg; 2000 guilders from Vienna – produced the rough bottom line of a heartening 8000 guilders or about 5400 talers.[174] The trouble was that only too often for Leibniz's taste these nicely rounded figures remained *lettera morta*. His numerous stipends were not paid automatically by direct debit and sometimes remained unpaid for years, whether due to other urgent demands on his employers' funds or to their not so subtle attempts to remind him of his debts to them. Like many of his contemporaries, he therefore had to take action of his own to collect the income needed to afford a life-style in which "investigations, discoveries, and experiments"[175] loomed large in the column of his expenditure. Vienna proved no exception. It was not until July that the emperor gave instructions for the quarterly payment of Leibniz's emoluments in the form of a pension (instead of the regular stipend of a *Reichshofrat*) until a vacancy in the Imperial Aulic Council became available.[176] Whether unsatisfied by an office which had begun to look like an empty title, or simply yielding to his habitual careerism, between August and October 1713 Leibniz tried to gain the support of the dowager Empress Amalie and the emperor himself, among others, for his appointment as chancellor (*Kanzler*) of the recently conquered principality of Transylvania (Siebenbürgen). Nothing came of this rather improbable idea. Amongst other things, Leibniz was not a candidate who could have carried forward the Austrian attempt to establish the Catholic confession in Transylvania.[177] In November 1713, however, he at least had the satisfaction of announcing proudly to the dowager Electress Sophie that the emperor had given him the same rights of audience as one of his ministers, something not ordinarily granted to foreign ministers or imperial court counsellors.[178] In January 1714 more concrete gratification finally arrived in the form of the first quarterly instalment of his stipend as *Reichshofrat*;[179] but this proved the first of a very intermittent line of pay, despite numerous petitions from Leibniz urging that the terms of his imperial appointment be honoured. By 17 May 1714 he still had received only 500 guilders, whereas he had to disburse a tax of over 1300 guilders.[180] Worse still, in October 1713 the Hanover court stopped the payment of his main stipend to impress upon him the need to return at once if he wanted to earn his money. In fact, disbursement of his emoluments in Hanover only resumed on 29 May 1716, almost two years after his return.[181]

Yet in Vienna far too much was going on for Leibniz to cut short his unauthorized visit. To start with, he had the opportunity to network with prominent people on the European scene, such as Prince Eugene of Savoy (1663–1736), who after playing an important role in rescuing Vienna from the great siege of 1683 had become an eminent statesman and general of the Imperial army with a central role at court. Leibniz may already have met him during his visit to Hanover in April 1708,[182] and in Vienna they struck up a mutually stimulating relationship which left Leibniz greatly impressed with the intellectual acumen of the statesman. Two days after lunching with Eugene on 16 February 1713, Leibniz wrote to Duke Anton Ulrich, "The Prince can speak of theology much better than I can speak of war, since he studied in his youth while I have never been in war."[183] The war still on everyone's mind in Vienna was that of the Spanish succession: after protracted negotiations in Utrecht, a peace was signed on 11 April 1713 by the British, the Dutch, and all the other forces of the Grand Alliance with the exception of the emperor. Leibniz was incensed by the defection of the allies and produced a stream of memoranda for Charles VI in which he envisaged ways to continue the war, including a possible alliance with Russia, Prussia, and Denmark.[184] Particularly noteworthy was a long tract he wrote in December 1713 condemning the peace of Utrecht and probably intended to influence above all Prince Eugene, who had been won over by the necessity of signing a peace with France.[185] Amongst Leibniz's reasons for opposing the end of the hostilities with France was the fear that a reconciliation between France and Britain could endanger the Protestant succession, which he considered "the only way to rescue reformed religion and public freedom."[186] The Catholic Pretender in exile in France, he feared, might gain sympathy in the Tory party, whose policy of peace had prevailed in London. It was true that one of the conditions of peace was France's acceptance of the Protestant succession; but if the mood in London towards the Pretender changed, was Louis XIV's word to be trusted? The arrival in January 1714 of a Scottish noble-man, John Ker of Kersland (1673–1726), provided Leibniz with a new (although improbable) idea for undermining France and Spain's military engagement in Europe without major allies or insupportable investment: he proposed to start a privately financed war of piracy against them in the American colonies, to which the emperor would offer his protection in exchange for a share of the pirates's booty.[187] Leibniz, who perceived Ker as an "honest man and a man of merit... who seems to be disin-terested and who does not speak of money and pensions, as most people who offer their services do,"[188] was taken by this scheme and, more gen-erally, by the nobleman's commitment to the Protestant succession; and he did his best to help Ker to gain the emperor's approval. Throughout the Scotsman's extended visit in Vienna the two of them met repeatedly, discussing British politics and the means of dispelling the sneaking sus-picion in London that the Hanoverians were in fact indifferent to the British crown.[189] Notwithstanding Ker's dubious reputation and espi-onage activity probably necessitated by his persistent financial troubles, Leibniz's support went as far as repaying without Ker's knowledge the considerable debts contracted during the Scot's stay in Germany.[190]

No matter how imaginative Leibniz and Ker's schemes for contin-uing the war, or how great Charles VI's dissatisfaction with ending it, the emperor's coffers simply could not sustain it on their own; and on 7 March 1714 the Treaty of Rastatt between France and the Empire put an end to the conflict. Yet the peace was not entirely without its consolations. Although the Bourbon king, Philip V, retained the crown of Spain and its American colonies, he was compelled to divide Spain's other European territories amongst his chief enemies: the Habsburgs regained the Spanish (now Austrian) Netherlands, the duchy of Milan, and the Kingdom of Naples and Sardinia (all once part of the empire of Charles V); the duke of Savoy obtained the kingdom of Sicily and expanded his territories in northern Italy; and Britain acquired Minorca and Gibraltar as well as part of France's colonies overseas. As for Leibniz, he was more than enough of a pragmatist to know when to put a cheerful face on things: whereas at the beginning of 1714 he was still penning anonymous verses warning against the "treacherous peace" emerging from Rastatt, in April he produced a brief Latin poem celebrating the peace.[191]

The end of the hostilities allowed the cash-strapped Imperial treasury some chance to recover and eventually to devote funds to more worthy enterprises than war. In a memo of 23 February 1714 Leibniz urged the emperor to turn his attention to fighting misery:

Conscience, honor, duty and interest equally oblige one to do it ... From which it follows that one must furnish the poor with the means of earning their livelihood, not only by using charity and [charitable] foundations to this end, but also by taking an interest in agriculture, by furnishing to artisans materials and a market, by educating them to make their productions better, and finally by putting an end to idleness and to abusive practices in manufacturers and in commerce.[192]

Moreover, he renewed his efforts towards the establishment of an Imperial Society of Sciences in Vienna, an idea which went back at least to October 1704.[193] Barely two weeks after his arrival in Vienna, a plan for the Society was ready on his desk, awaiting the opportunity of an audience with the emperor granted in mid-January.[194] In subsequent memos Leibniz expanded his project, highlighting for Charles VI the advantages to be derived from such a Society and advising concerning its presidency – an office, predictably, envisaged for himself.[195] In May 1713 he drafted the charter of the Society, penned further advice for the emperor regarding its establishment, and started an epistolary discussion of the project with the imperial cryptanalyst and polymath, the Abbot Giuseppe Spedazzi.[196] Next he tried to secure the support of the chancellor of the imperial court, Philipp Ludwig Wenzel von Sinzendorf, addressing to him a series of remarks relating to the proposed institution and expressing his preference for the name "Society" rather than "Academy."[197] On 14 August 1713 Leibniz was named by the emperor as director of the Society, with a projected stipend of 4000 guilders;[198] but this glorious prospect was destined to remain purely on paper. Despite Leibniz's usual stack of memos, petitions, and proposals directed to the emperor, his ministers, Prince Eugene, the dowager empress and others, no amount of eloquence could summon either the money or the will to transform this would-be Society into a real one.[199] As late as 17 August 1714, two weeks before his unavoidable return to Hanover, Leibniz was still writing to Prince Eugene asking him to promote the cause of the Society with the emperor. Following the blueprint of the *Miscellanea Berolinensia*, his proposal was to divide the society into three sections: "literary" (including history and philology), "mathematical" (spanning pure and applied mathematics, astronomy, architecture, and mechanics), and "physical" (embracing "the three realms of nature: the mineral, the vegetable, and the animal" and devoting special attention to medicine).[200] Alas, this memo, like its predecessors, failed to bear palpable fruit.

Broadsides between Mathematicians

Meanwhile the calculus controversy had escalated into a quarrel in which previous attempts at fairness and courtesy were set aside. This final bitter phase was triggered when a letter of 7 June 1713 by Johann Bernoulli – who had succeeded his elder brother Jakob in the chair of mathematics in Basel – was forwarded from Hanover to Vienna. "My nephew" [201] Bernoulli reported

brought from Paris a single copy of the *Commercium Epistolicum Collinsii et aliorum de Analysi promota*, which the Abbé Bignon had handed to him, having received a number of copies sent from London for distribution to the learned. I have read it, not without a fair amount of attention. This hardly civilized way of doing things displeases me particularly; you are at once accused before a tribunal consisting, as it seems, of the participants and witnesses themselves, as if charged of plagiary, then documents against you are produced, sentence is passed; you lose the case, you are condemned.[202]

If anybody was a plagiarist, Bernoulli continued, it was Newton.[203] According to the Swiss mathematician, what Newton possessed before Leibniz was not a genuine calculus, not a new algorithm. Indeed, in his view, Newton did not "so much as dream of his calculus of fluxions and fluents, or of its reduction to the general operations of analysis in order to serve as an algorithm or in the manner of the arithmetical and algebraic rules"[204] before Leibniz had shown him the way. Having stirred the hornet's nest, Bernoulli promptly retreated and begged Leibniz not to involve him in the dispute lest he appear "ungrateful to Newton", with whom he entertained cordial relations.[205]

Bernoulli's report landed on Leibniz's desk on 27 June 1713, taking him by surprise. He appears to have been quite unaware of the Royal Society's inquiry of the spring of 1712 and certainly did not expect to be sanctioned as a plagiarist as a result of it.[206] The day after receiving Bernoulli's letter, he vented in his response his resentment, now deepened by embracing Bernoulli's thesis that Newton had followed rather than led him to a proper calculus:

I have not yet seen the little English book directed against me; those idiotic arguments which (as I gather from your letter) they have brought forward deserve to be lashed by a satirical wit. They would maintain Newton in the possession of his own invented calculus and yet it appears that he no more knew our calculus than Apollonius knew the algebraic calculus of Viète and Descartes. He knew fluxions, but not the calculus of fluxions which (as you rightly judge) he put together at a later stage after our own was already published. Thus I have myself done him more than justice, and this is the price I pay for my kindness. . . . [A]lthough I have no wish that you should make trouble for yourself for my sake, I expect from your honesty and sense of justice that you will as soon as possible make it evident to our friends that in your opinion Newton's calculus was posterior to ours, and say this publicly when opportunity serves. . . . I would like to know what the Parisians think. I can scarcely doubt that Varignon is on my side but several others, moved by envy, will perhaps gladly seize the opportunity given them of carping, but these people I think will be found only among the undiscerning. For many years now the English have been so swollen with vanity, even the distinguished men among them, that they have taken the opportunity of snatching German things and claiming them as their own.[207]

On the same day he wrote to Varignon seeking his support:

I understand from M. Bernoulli that the book of the English has appeared, in which they claim to prove that M. Newton invented the new calculus. But from what M. Bernoulli sends me, I conclude that, very far from having proved this, they give occasion of thinking that the calculus of points was developed afterwards,[208] and that M. Newton did indeed have the knowledge of fluxions at the same time as us but not the knowledge of the calculus[.][209]

In his reply of 9 August, although profoundly sympathetic toward Leibniz for the unjust trial to which he had been subjected, Varignon did not take up Bernoulli's (and Leibniz's) suggestion that Newton's calculus was invented in the wake of Leibniz's. Instead he simply assured Leibniz that the learned community in Paris was still honouring him for his discovery as it was honouring Newton.[210] By the time Varignon answered, however, Leibniz had decided to take action. On 1 July, Christian Wolff had also written to pass on to Leibniz further details of the *Commercium Epistolicum*, which he had received the day before from the Royal Society.[211] By 29 July Leibniz had prepared a short Latin reply to the English charges – christened by Newton as a *Charta Volans* or "flying paper"[212] – which was entrusted to Wolff for printing and distribution.[213] It appeared in the form of a leaflet intended for broad circulation and was reprinted in French translation in the *Journal Literaire* of The Hague of November–December 1713.[214] In the *Journal Literaire* it was accompanied by some *Remarques* by Leibniz in response to a long "Lettre de Londre [Letter from London]" published in the May–June issue of the same journal. The anonymous author of the *Lettre* was Keill, who recounted in French for the broader public the history of the infinitesimal calculus as reconstructed in the *Commercium Epistolicum*.

Bernoulli did not want to get caught in this vicious crossfire, as his German friend had hoped;[215] and Leibniz did not come out in the open either: the *Charta Volans* was published anonymously as if written by a third person. Without having seen for himself the *Commercium Epistolicum*, Leibniz endorsed Bernoulli's thesis that the Englishman had in effect plagiarised the German's calculus, not the other way around. In order to support this claim, Bernoulli's letter of 7 June was reprinted as the verdict of an unnamed "leading mathematician" who had been asked to pass judgement on the matter.[216] Having spiralled to this level of acrimony, the matter was unlikely to rest. By his own recollection, Newton first became aware of Leibniz's *Charta Volans* in the autumn of 1713 but took no action.[217] When Keill drew his attention to its republication in the *Journal Literaire* of The Hague complete with Leibniz's *Remarques*, however, Newton decided that such a public attack needed an answer.[218] The zealous Keill was again only too happy to act as front man and furthered his attacks against Leibniz in the *Réponse* published in the *Journal Literaire* of The Hague for July–August 1714. Meanwhile, in March 1714 a fellow of the Royal Society, John Chamberlayne, had humbly offered his "Poor Mediation" to bring the "Affair to a happy end."[219] Leibniz left the door to a possible reconciliation open, but not without making clear to Chamberlayne that he felt he had been unfairly treated by the Royal Society: his side of the story had never been heard and yet an official report was making the rounds of the learned European world.[220] Chamberlayne passed on Leibniz's letter to Newton, intending it only for his private perusal; but Newton decided otherwise, preparing an English translation which was read at a meeting of the Royal Society on 20 May 1714 (O.S.).[221] Unfortunately Chamberlayne's laudable attempt fell through: the Royal Society declined to take the matter any further, and Newton remained evidently unmoved by Leibniz's point of view.

Two Pamphlets on Monads

Fortunately, in the midst of all this, Leibniz still found time for philosophy. In February 1714, Charles Hugony had written from Paris that Nicolas Rémond desired some clarifications of Leibniz's doctrine of monads.[222] In his capacity of chief counsellor of the duke of Orléans, Rémond was one of the most prominent politicians of the Parisian scene. Unlike other top courtiers, however, he was also a man of keen philosophical interest and wide learning, as well as a passionate admirer of the *Theodicy*;[223] and Leibniz had corresponded with him since June 1713. Although Hugony's reference to Rémond's wish for clarification was rather vague,[224] Leibniz was intrigued enough to draft a compact explanation in which he tried to gather together the key features of his doctrine. His result – after poring over it for some time, amending and correcting his text – was a small philosophical jewel in which his austere ontology, reducing the 'ingredients' of reality to a minimum, was in full display.[225] "I believe," Leibniz began,

that the whole universe of creatures consists only in simple substances or monads and in their assemblages. These simple substances are what is called spirit in us and in superior rational beings [les Genies], and soul in animals. They all have *perception* (which is nothing other than the representation of multitude in the unity) and *appetite* (which is nothing other than an inclination to pass from one perception to another) and which is called *passion* in animals, and *will* where perception is understanding. It could not even be conceived that there is something other than that in simple substances and as a consequence in the whole of nature. The assemblages are what we call bodies.[226]

This draft letter to Rémond apparently constituted the germ of the *Monadologie*;[227] yet Leibniz remained unconvinced that his short explanation would do. In July he noted on the draft itself that it was still unsent and wrote to Rémond,

I had hoped to include with this letter some clarification on monads that you seemed to request; but it has grown under my hands, and many distractions have prevented me from completing it so soon. And you know very well, Sir, that these sorts of considerations demand concentration.[228]

During the following weeks he continued to work toward an exposition of his doctrine of monads in clear, plain terms, encouraged by another grandee of the *ancien régime* deeply interested in his philosophy – Prince Eugene of Savoy – for whom a more mature and extended presentation of the key features of his metaphysics was written around this time.[229]

This "petit papier" was the famous *Principes de la nature et de la grâce fondés en raison* which Leibniz offered to Eugene before the statesman's departure from Vienna at the end of August 1714, together with several other philosophical papers evidently intended to provide further elements needed for a more rounded picture of his philosophical system.[230] The prince certainly appreciated these efforts: as his friend, the imperial field marshal Claude Alexandre de Bonneval, reported on 6 October 1714, Eugene guarded Leibniz's philosophical gift "as the priests in Naples guard the blood of Saint Gennaro: that is to say, he let me kiss it, and then he locked it back in the casket" from which it had come, thereby preventing his friend from copying it.[231]

On 26 August 1714 a copy of the *Principes* was sent to Rémond via Henry Sully, a capable English watchmaker whom Leibniz had met in Vienna.[232] In the accompanying letter Leibniz explained to Rémond his attitude towards the philosophical doctrines of other thinkers. What might have appeared to some as duplicity and lack of candour was in fact the other side of Leibniz's firm belief that fragments of truth are everywhere. They are facets of the universal truth which ought to be discovered in an open dialogue with the views of others. Referring to religious controversies, Leibniz had vehemently stated, "shame on those who maintain schism through their obstinacy, not wanting to attend to reason, yet wanting to have it always" on their side.[233] Likewise in philosophy he made a genuine effort to see things from the perspective of others so that, in return, they might see his original philosophical proposal not as something foreign but as an improvement on their own tenets. Following an intellectual policy of stressing agreement over disagreement, Leibniz hoped to unearth the perennial truth lying under philosophical debris. As he wrote to Rémond,

I hoped that this little paper might help to make my meditations better understood, together with what I published in the journals of Leipzig, Paris, and Holland. In those of Leipzig I adapt myself somewhat to the language of the school; in the others I adapt myself more to the style of the Cartesians; and in this most recent piece I try to express myself in a way which could be understood by those who are not yet very accustomed to either of these languages. . . . Truth is more widespread than people think but it is very often disguised and very often also enveloped and even weakened, mutilated, corrupted by additions which spoil it or render it less useful. If attention were drawn to these traces of truth in the ancients, or (speaking more generally) in former thinkers, gold would be dug from the mud, diamonds from their mine, and light out of darkness; and it would in fact be *perennis quaedam Philosophia* [a certain perennial Philosophy].[234]

A few months before, on 10 January 1714, Leibniz had already told Rémond, "I have tried to unearth and reunite the truth buried and dispersed under the opinions of the different sects of philosophers, and I believe I have added to that something of my own in order to advance a few steps further. . . . I have found that most sects are right in a good part of what they affirm, but not so much in what they deny."[235] He had expressed himself in similar terms in an unpublished text probably written at the beginning of 1708, at the apex of a pointed dispute between the French orientalist based in Berlin, Mathurin Veyssières de La Croze, and an anonymous Jesuit. Pouring water on the fire of a sterile controversy in which he had become involved against his will, Leibniz remarked,

I am more inclined to excuse than to accuse, and to praise rather than to blame; and I prefer to note the good in people [in order] to benefit from it and to encourage them, than to point out their defects and do them wrong. . . . There are many true and certain things, but sometimes this truth is only known in a confused way until one begins to doubt it. And it is then that it is developed and demonstrated as it should be. . . . [I]nsightful objections are always useful, and serve to better clarify the truth[.][236]

While writing the *Principes*, Leibniz was also working on another paper which expanded on the clarifications of the doctrine of monads wished by Rémond.[237] This text, which had "grown under his hands" and on which he continued to work after his return to Hanover in mid-September 1714, eventually became the untitled essay known as *Monadologie*.[238] This title – destined to have immense fortune and introducing, after Leibniz's death, the term 'monadology' into the vocabulary of Leibnizian philosophy[239] – was the product of a follower of Christian Wolff, Heinrich Köhler, who published in 1720 a German translation of Leibniz's essay based on a lost, intermediate version, dating back to the summer of 1714, which Köhler had probably received from Leibniz in Vienna. The year after Köhler's publication, there appeared in the supplements to the *Acta Eruditorum* a Latin translation of the *Monadology* under the title of *Principia Philosophiae, autore G. G. Leibnitio*. The anonymous translator was in all likelihood Christian Wolff himself, who evidently had been in possession of another independent, preliminary version of the *Monadology*. The final version, prepared by Leibniz in Hanover, was never sent to Rémond or, as far as is known, to any of his correspondents.[240] Despite having pored for months over his compact presentation of the doctrine of monads in laymen's terms, preparing and painstakingly correcting and annotating several different versions in the process, Leibniz left the most mature of these buried in the mass of his papers. The original text of the *Monadology* had to wait for over a century after the German and Latin translations of preliminary texts had announced Leibniz's doctrine of monads to the learned circles of Europe before seeing the light in the edition of his *Opera philosophica omnia* published by J. E. Erdmann in 1840. The *Principes de la nature et de la grâce* fared better: they appeared two years after Leibniz's death in *L'Europe savante*, published in The Hague in November 1718.[241]

Although rightly celebrated, these two compendia of Leibniz's metaphysics did not represent his whole philosophical system and needed to be supplemented by other papers, as Leibniz himself had pointed out explicitly or implicitly to Rémond and Prince Eugene. Moreover, as explanations targeted to laymen, they did not always contain the most brilliant and felicitous formulations of the complex facets of Leibniz's sophisticated metaphysical thought. Yet they were destined to remain masterpieces amongst the classic texts of philosophy, and established Leibniz as the author of a strikingly innovative and beautifully economical metaphysics insofar as it was centred on the notion of simple substances (or monads) from which every other really existing thing resulted. The existence of two treatments of the same topic, of similar size and scope, intended for the same broad lay readership, and written during the same period raises the obvious question of why Leibniz should simultaneously have composed two such similar works. The long and overlapping evolution of the two texts rules out the possibility that one can be regarded as a draft of the other, and the very different fortunes of the two works only deepens the mystery: although Leibniz was confident enough to present the *Principes* to their immediate addressee, Prince Eugene, he effectively suppressed the paper written to satisfy Rémond and sent him instead a copy of the *Principes* while continuing to work at the *Monadology*. Although many conjectural explanations are possible, the most probable may hinge on a crucial distinction between the two works. In the *Principes* Leibniz explicitly acknowledged the existence of two types of substances: simple substances (or monads) and compound substances.[242] In the *Monadology* he avoided any description of "compounds" ("les composés") as substances.[243] In other words, whereas the *Principes* seem to suggest that bodies are substances (albeit conceived as ultimately resulting from monads, that is, as corporeal substances of which bodies as perceived by us are phenomenal manifestations), the *Monadology* leaves undetermined whether an entity which is composed of simple substances can itself properly qualify as a substance.[244] It is possible that Leibniz regarded the *Monadology* as more controversial than the *Principes* or, at the very least, as raising more questions regarding the ontological status of bodies than could safely be entrusted to the lay public for which it was written. It is also possible that the answer to the vexed question of whether bodies (conceived ultimately as aggregates of monads) properly qualify as substances, or whether or not there are corporeal *substances*, was still open in Leibniz's mind. Throughout his philosophical career it appears that, although very certain about the properties a being must have in order to qualify as a substance (notably an intrinsic principle of unity and activity), he was arguably less certain that beings other than indivisible unities could sufficiently satisfy these criteria and therefore be properly called substances.[245]

Important as they were, the *Principes* and the *Monadology* were not the only deeply significant philosophical texts penned by Leibniz during his last weeks in Vienna and his first months back in Hanover. At some point after June 1714, for instance, in a paper on the *Initia rerum matematicarum metaphysica* ("The metaphysical origins of mathematics"), he gave a complex account of the philosophical foundations of the *mathesis generalis*, claiming that "there is an analytical art wider than mathematics, from which the science of mathematics borrows all its most beautiful methods." In this paper elements converged from a lifetime of reflection on issues such as the analysis of concepts as a basis for the creation of a universal language, the development of an *analysis situs*, and the demonstration of the axiomatic parts of Euclid's *Elements*.[246] Most importantly, the *Initia rerum matematicarum metaphysica* were the product of Leibniz's mature reflection on the nature of space, stimulated by his monadology. Although his studies and reflections on space and situational geometry started as early as the *Dissertatio de Arte Combinatoria* of 1666 and continued throughout his life, it was not until his very last years that he reached an accomplished theory and philosophy of space able to account for the relationship between space and substances, matter and extension, phenomena and things-in-themselves required by his mature monadology. At the heart of this reflection was the question of how monads related to the (spatial-temporal) phenomenal world, or, in distinctively Leibnizian terms, how the one was "expressed" by the other. Leibniz's mature theory of space was eventually put forward in his famous correspondence with Samuel Clarke of 1715–16. The arena of a heated debate, however, was not the place to unveil many of the deepest and most daring insights on the nature of space which Leibniz was still in the process of formulating. These remained buried in his Nachlaß in papers and fragments on the *analysis situs* penned between 1712 and 1716.[247]

Return to Hanover

On 30 March 1714 the Hanoverian Prime Minister, Bernstorff, addressed to Leibniz a pressing request to return. The elector was becoming increasingly impatient. "As a friend and a servant," the minister wrote, "I cannot but advise you to satisfy him on this matter."[248] Bernstorff's letter was merely the latest of a long string of similar requests. Given the freezing of his stipend the previous October, the Hanoverian privy counsellor of justice could be in no doubt that the elector's tolerance was wearing dangerously thin. Even his indulgent friend Sophie had joked in December 1713 that the pestilent air of Vienna – currently affected by the plague – seemed to be more dear to him than that of Hanover.[249] Yet Leibniz invariably tergiversated, coming up with excuses, explanations, and special pleadings which would have tried the patience of a saint – let alone that of Georg Ludwig. After March 1714 another stream of letters passed between Leibniz and Hanover, while the rumour began to circulate that he had become a Catholic.[250] On 24 June, J. G. Eckhart conveyed the exasperated ultimatum of Bernstorff: Leibniz had to decide whether he wished to return to Hanover or not.[251]

The truth of the matter was that by the end of the spring of 1714 Hanover had became a distinctly unattractive place for Leibniz. On 27 March his old friend and protector, Duke Anton Ulrich, had died. With him disappeared for Leibniz the welcome respite of Wolfenbüttel from the intellectual aridity of the Hanoverian court. An even worse personal blow came just over two months later: on 8 June 1714 Sophie herself passed away. She had died in the arms of the Countess von Bückeburg and the electoral princess, Caroline, felled by a stroke while taking her customary evening stroll in her beloved gardens of Herrenhausen. As the Countess von Bückeburg recounted in an emotional letter to the Palatine Raugräfin Louise in which the last dramatic moments of the electress's life were recorded in graphic detail, recent events relating to the English succession had deeply upset the still strong eighty-three-year-old.[252] The Hanoverian envoy, Baron Schütz, had addressed to the English chancellor the request for a writ of summons for the son of the elector, the electoral prince Georg August. This request had infuriated Queen Anne, who continued to regard the presence of a member of the Hanoverian family in London during her lifetime as a threat to her sovereignty. Anne had therefore responded on 30 May (19 May O.S.) with three extremely forceful letters addressed respectively to Sophie, the elector, and the electoral prince, in which she threatened to call into question the entire settlement regarding the Hanoverian succession if these plans were not abandoned.[253] The arrival of the letters in Hanover on 5 June threw the palace into agitation and caused great grief to Sophie.[254] Two days before her death she confided to the Countess von Bückeburg, "this affair will certainly make me ill. It will be the death of me."[255] On 20 May, in her last letter to Leibniz, sensing the dark clouds gathering in the sky between Hanover and London, Sophie wrote, "I very much wish that you were here, for I do not write with enough pleasure to enjoy reasoning by letter, in comparison to the pleasure I have in seeing you."[256]

Leibniz was informed of the dowager electress's death in a letter of 13 June from Matthias Johann von der Schulenburg.[257] On 7 July he wrote to Caroline,

The death of Madam the Electress has stirred great feelings in me. It is as if I see her expiring in the arms of Your Most Serene Highness. This death was the one that she desired. It is not her: it is Hanover, it is England, it is the world, it is myself who has lost because of it. . . . [I]f you do not wish, Madam, to receive me like a bad piece of furniture which you have inherited from her, you will banish me from Hanover.[258]

Caroline was indeed the only person close to Leibniz left in the electoral family – after the late Sophie and Sophie Charlotte, the last of the "three people in the world amongst those of your sex whom I not only infinitely honoured with everyone who is reasonable and well-informed, but whom I also cherished the most."[259] With Sophie, Leibniz lost not only a friend and protector but also the presumptive heiress to the British crown. The right rested now with her son Georg Ludwig, who had never been one of his supporters and was now especially annoyed due to his long unauthorized absence. Unsurprisingly, Leibniz did not feel any inclination to rush back. It was not long, however, before events across the Channel forced him into action. On 12 August 1714, scarcely two months after Sophie, Queen Anne also died and Georg Ludwig was proclaimed her successor as King George I. Leibniz, who had been thinking for a while about packing but could not summon the will, saw at this point that if he wanted a place in the Protestant succession for which he had worked so hard, he had to return to Hanover at once. On 3 September he departed from the imperial capital. On the evening of 14 September he arrived in Hanover, only to discover that the king and his court had left for England three days before, leaving him behind.[260]

Notes

1. See the letters of Ernst August to Johann Franz Diedrich von Wendt respectively of 15 July 1707 and of 30 October 1711 (in *Briefe des Herzogs Ernst August [1674–1728] zu Braunschweig-Lüneburg an Johann Franz Diedrich von Wendt aus den Jahren 1703 bis 1726*. Ed. by Erich Graf von Kielmanseff. Hanover and Leipzig 1902, pp. 80 and 264. Quoted in Müller–Krönert, *Leben und Werk*, pp. 206 and 226.

2. See the description reported by one of Leibniz's visitors on 10 January 1710, Zacharias Konrad von Uffenbach, in his book *Merkwürdige Reisen durch Niedersachsen, Holland, und England*. Part 1. Ulm and Memmingen, 1753, pp. 409–411. Quoted by Müller–Krönert, *Leben und Werk*, p. 216. See also Eckhart, *Lebensbeschreibung*, p. 225. According to Eckhart, *Lebensbeschreibung*, p. 196 and Ludwig Grote, *Leibniz und seine Zeit*. Hanover: Buchhandlung von Carl Brandes, 1869, p. 248, Leibniz lost his hair very early and therefore wore a wig from the age of 21 years onward. See also Görlich, *Leibniz als Mensch und Kranker*, p. 28.

3. See *Aus den Briefen der Elisabeth Charlotte von Orléans an Kurfürstin Sophie*. Ed. by E. Bodemann. 2 vols. Hanover, 1891, vol. 2, pp. 112–13.

4. See for instance the memo of Leibniz for Peter the Great on the advancement of science in Russia (September 1712) and Leibniz to Jacob Daniel Bruce, 23 September 1712 (in Guerrier, *Leibniz*, N. 148, p. 217; N. 149, p. 220; N. 157, pp. 236–8).

5. On the epistolary exchange between Leibniz and Des Bosses see the excellent introduction in *The Leibniz–Des Bosses Correspondence*. Translated, edited, and with an introduction by Brandon C. Look and Donald Rutherford. New Haven and London: Yale University Press, 2007. On the *vinculum substantiale* see in particular Brandon Look, *Leibniz and the 'Vinculum Substantiale'*. Stuttgart: Franz Steiner, 1999 and Adams, *Leibniz*, pp. 299–303. On the exchange more generally cf. also Vittorio Mathieu, *Leibniz e Des Bosses (1706–1716)*, Turin: Giapichelli 1960.

6. See Donald Rutherford, "Idealism Declined. Leibniz and Christian Wolff." In *Leibniz and His Correspondents*. Ed. by Paul Lodge. Cambridge: Cambridge University Press, 2004, pp. 214–37 and Adams, *Leibniz*, pp. 383–6.

7. See below.

8. See Klopp IX, 120–21.

9. See Hans Reuther, "Das Gebäude der Herzog-August-Bibliothek zu Wolfenbüttel und ihr Oberbibliothekar Gottfried Wilhelm Leibniz." In *Leibniz. Sein Leben, sein Wirken, seine Welt*. Ed. by W. Totok and C. Haase. Hanover: Verlag für

Literatur und Zeitgeschehen, 1966, pp. 349–60. Another significant contribution of Leibniz in this period was his acquisition in July 1710 of the important collection of manuscripts of Marquard Gudius for the Wolfenbüttel library. Cf. Ravier 179.

10. Leibniz's *Personalien* of Sophie Charlotte are published in Klopp X, 273–84 and Pertz IV, 99–107.

11. "Rescript des Kurfürsten Georg Ludwig an Leibniz" in R. Doebner, "Leibnizens Briefwechsel mit dem Minister von Bernstorff." *Zeitschrift des Historischen Vereins für Niedersachsen* (1881), p. 228.

12. See Klopp IX, 108–9.

13. Cf. Schnath, *Geschichte Hannovers*, vol. IV, pp. 122–36. Contrary to what was previously believed, Schnath found textual evidence that Leibniz drafted not only the French version of the letter published in Klopp IX, 188–200, but also the English printed version. This seems to indicate a better mastery of the English language than he used to claim for himself (cf. Schnath, *Geschichte Hannovers*, vol. IV, p. 127).

14. Quoted by Schnath, *Geschichte Hannovers*, vol. IV, p. 128.

15. On the relationship between the Hanover electorate and the Prussian monarchy see especially Leibniz's long memo of the summer of 1705 for Georg Ludwig (Klopp IX, 127–42). In it Leibniz argued that, despite some conflicts in specific matters, the overall interest of the house of Hanover was to maintain a close alliance with Berlin. Cf. Heuvel, *Leibniz zwischen Hannover und Berlin*, p. 278.

16. See Leibniz to Johann Fabricius, 31 August 1706, in Leibniz, *Epistolae ad diversos*, vol. 1, p. 115.

17. See Hübener, "Negotium irenicum," pp. 136–7 and Weidemann, *Gerard Wolter Molanus*, vol. 2, pp. 144–5.

18. LH I, 7, 5, 8, Bl. 176r–v. Cf. Müller–Krönert, *Leben und Werk*, pp. 201–2; Hübener, "Negotium irenicum," pp. 136–7; Murray, "Leibniz's Proposal for Theological Reconciliation among the Protestants," p. 626; Schrecker, "G.-W. Leibniz. Lettres et fragments inédits," p. 50.

19. Leibniz, *Epistolae ad diversos*, vol. 1, p. 124.

20. See Harnack, *Geschichte*, II, N. 85, pp. 169–72. The monopoly was based on Leibniz's proposals (cf. Klopp X, 407–9).

21. See Bodemann, *Handschriften*, p. 223. Almost one year later, on 17 February 1708, the purchase had yet to take place (cf. J. Kvačala, "Neue Beiträge zum Briefwechsel zwischen D. E. Jablonski und G. W. Leibniz." *Acta et Commentationes Imp. Universitatis Jurievensis*. IV (1899), pp. 169–70). Finally, in March 1708, the Society was able to secure a loan for the acquisition of premises on the basis of the grant of 700 talers for each of the next three years provided by Friedrich I. Cf. Harnack, *Geschichte*, II, pp. 177–8. Quoted by Müller–Krönert, *Leben und Werk*, pp. 208–9.

22. Klopp IX, 281.

23. See Leibniz to Thomas Wentworth (Lord Raby), 1 July 1707 (Guhrauer, *Leibnitz*, II, *Anmerkungen*, pp. 27–8). On the abdication of the Polish crown by Augustus II see Leibniz to Sophie, 2 November 1706 (Klopp IX, 241–4).

24. See Ravier 65, 66, 69.

25. See Scheel, "Leibniz als Historiker," pp. 264–5.

26. See esp. Doebner, "Leibnizens Briefwechsel mit dem Minister von Bernstorff," pp. 232–7, 240–42, 251–5; R. Doebner, "Nachträge zu Leibnizens Briefwechsel mit dem Minister Bernstorff." *Zeitschrift des Historischen Vereins für Niedersachsen* (1884), pp. 213–14.

27. See Doebner, "Leibnizens Briefwechsel mit dem Minister von Bernstorff," pp. 242–3; 244–5.

28. See Müller–Krönert, *Leben und Werk*, pp. 210–11.

29. E. Bodemann, "Leibnizens Briefwechsel mit dem Herzoge Anton Ulrich von Braunschweig-Wolfenbüttel." *Zeitschrift des historischen Vereins für Niedersachsen* (1888): pp. 184–5, 186–7.

30. See Leibniz to Sophie, 29 November 1708 (Klopp IX, 290). Leibniz pretended to be in Carlsbad for thermal cures.

31. See Guerrier, *Leibniz*, N. 73, pp. 95–100.

32. See Sophie to Leibniz, 23 January 1709 (Klopp IX, 294).

33. Müller–Krönert, *Leben und Werk*, p. 213.

34. See Klopp IX, 297.

35. See Klopp IX, 297–300.

36. In 768, at the death of his father, Pepin the Short, Charlemagne shared sovereignty over the Franks with his brother Carloman (d. 771). Wittekind (or Widukind, Witikind) was the leader of the Saxons, who fought fiercely against Charlemagne until submitting and being baptised in 785.

37. Doebner, "Nachträge zu Leibnizens Briefwechsel mit dem Minister Bernstorff," p. 219. See also "Promemoria Leibnizens über Anstellung weiterer Forschungen in Modena" (4 April 1710) for the Hanover privy counsellors (Doebner, "Leibnizens Briefwechsel mit dem Minister von Bernstorff," pp. 254–5).

38. See Guerrier, *Leibniz*, N. 124, pp. 171–2.

39. See Harnack, *Geschichte*, II, N. 94, p. 187. On the *Miscellanea*'s composition see Harnack, *Geschichte*, I, pp. 148–51.

40. For a complete list see Ravier 305.

41. *Brevis designatio meditationum de originibus gentium ductis potissimum ex indicio linguarum.*

42. See Stefano Gensini, "Leibniz Linguist and Philosopher of Language: Between 'Primitive' and 'Natural,'" pp. 111–36. A transcription of the third version of the *Epistolica dissertatio* (Ms IV 469 ff. 68r–104v, f. 255r/v) can be found in Stefano Gensini, *Il naturale e il simbolico. Saggio su Leibniz*. Roma: Bulzoni, 1991, pp. 191–271.

43. See Harnack, *Geschichte*, I, pp. 165–8; II, N. 99, pp. 192–6. Brather, "Leibniz und das Konzil der Berliner Sozietät der Wissenschaften," p. 228 points out that Harnack's description of the new regulations as a "*Statut*" is inappropriate.

44. See Harnack, *Geschichte*, II, N. 98, p. 192.

45. See Charles Ancillon to Leibniz, 6 December 1710 (LBr 12, Bl. 83–4) and Brather, "Leibniz und das Konzil der Berliner Sozietät der Wissenschaften," p. 228 (note 41).

46. Klopp X, 418–19. See also Leibniz to Marquard Ludwig von Printzen, 10 December 1710 (Klopp X, 421–2).
47. See Leibniz to Sophie Dorothea, 17 December 1710 (Klopp X, 423).
48. See Klopp X, 424–9; Müller–Krönert, *Leben und Werk*, p. 222; Brather, "Leibniz und das Konzil der Berliner Sozietät der Wissenschaften," p. 229.
49. See Sophie to Sophie Dorothea, 7 March 1711 (G. Schnath, *Briefwechsel der Kurfürstin Sophie von Hannover mit dem Preußischen Königshause*. Berlin and Leipzig 1927, p. 207); Leibniz to Sophie, 21 March 1711 (Klopp IX, 326–7); Sophie to Leibniz, 25 March 1711 (Klopp IX, 328); Leibniz to Friedrich I, end of March 1711 (Harnack, *Geschichte*, II, N. 114, p. 213).
50. See Klopp IX, 327.
51. See Brather, "Leibniz und das Konzil der Berliner Sozietät der Wissenschaften," p. 229, quoting the Konzilsprotokoll (Zentrales Archiv der Akademie der Wissenschaften der DDR, I–IV-6, Bl. 35–38).
52. Manuscript mentioned by Müller–Krönert, *Leben und Werk*, p. 220. On the Imperial Aulic Council see above, chap. II. 4. A previous attempt to be nominated *Reichshofrat* dated from July 1680 (cf. A I, 3, N. 334 and above, chap. II. 4).
53. See Duke Anton Ulrich to Leibniz, 3 February 1712 (Bodemann, "Leibnizens Briefwechsel mit dem Herzoge Anton Ulrich von Braunschweig-Wolfenbüttel," p. 212).
54. See Leibniz to R. C. von Imhof, 9 September 1712 (Klopp IX, 369–70).
55. See above, chap. II. 6.
56. See in particular Leibniz to Landgraf Ernst, first half of December 1692 (A I, 8, 210).
57. See for instance the memo for the tsar of December 1708 (Guerrier, *Leibniz*, N. 73, pp. 95–100). A wealth of other texts are quoted in Ernst Benz, "Leibniz und Peter der Grosse," 1947, p. 26 ff. Instalment 2 in *Leibniz. Zu seinem 300. Geburtstage 1646–1946*. Ed. by Erich Hochstetter. Instalments 1–8. Berlin: W. de Gruyter, 1946–52. Leibniz repeatedly took inspiration from the foundation in 1703 of the new Russian capital in St. Petersburg, stressing the advantages of a coherent plan which did not have to take into account what had been built in the past.
58. See especially the letters of Leibniz to, respectively, Peter the Great, Jacob Daniel Bruce, and Gavriil Ivanovič Golovkin written on 16 January 1712 (Guerrier, *Leibniz*, N. 143, p. 208 and N. 139, p. 199; FC, *Oeuvres*, VII, 502–3).
59. See for instance Leibniz to Jacob Daniel Bruce, 23 September 1712 (Guerrier, *Leibniz*, N. 157, p. 238).
60. See Guerrier, *Leibniz*, N. 125, pp. 174–6.
61. See Leibniz for Georg Ludwig, beginning of October 1709 (Guerrier, *Leibniz*, N. 99, p. 136).
62. See Robert I. Frost, *The Northern Wars. 1558–1721*. Harlow: Longman, 2000, p. 231. Despite the Swedish defeat at Poltava, the war was to continue for another twelve years.
63. See Leibniz to Sophie, 20 October 1711 (Klopp IX, 349–50).

64. See Leibniz to Sophie, 31 October 1711 (Bodemann, *Handschriften*, p. 259).

65. See in particular Guerrier, *Leibniz*, N. 125–127, pp. 174–83 and FC, *Oeuvres*, VII, 395–418, 459–62, 467–79, 480–88, 489–98.

66. See Leibniz to Johann Fabricius, 8 December 1711 (Dutens V, 294) and Leibniz to Peter the Great, 16 January 1712 (Guerrier, *Leibniz*, N. 143, p. 205).

67. See for instance Guerrier, *Leibniz*, N. 148–149, pp. 217–20; N. 158, pp. 239–49; N. 179, pp. 272–3.

68. See Leibniz to Louis Bourget, 2 July 1716 (GP III, 596).

69. See Guerrier, *Leibniz*, N. 123, p. 169.

70. Guerrier, *Leibniz*, N. 143, pp. 206–8.

71. See for instance Leibniz to Johann Christoph von Urbich, 11 October 1707 (Guerrier, *Leibniz*, N. 58, p. 67).

72. See for instance Johann Christoph von Urbich to Leibniz, 16 November 1707 (Guerrier, *Leibniz*, N. 60, p. 71).

73. See Benz, "Leibniz und Peter der Grosse," pp. 30–38; Kiefl, *Der Friedens-plan des Leibniz*, pp. lxxxvii–lxxxx; and Eisenkopf, *Leibniz und die Einigung der Christenheit*, p. 58. On the role of mediation envisaged for the Greek Orthodox church cf. for instance *Réponse de Leibniz au mémoire de l'Abbé Pirot*, in FC, *Oeuvres*, I, pp. 380–410 (see pp. 398–9, 405); Leibniz to Landgraf Ernst, 14 March 1685 (A I, 4, 356); Leibniz to Landgraf Ernst, first half of December 1692 (A I, 8, 210); Leibniz to Bossuet, 14 May 1700 (A I, 18, N. 368, esp. pp. 636, 638–9).

74. See H. Chr. von Schleinitz to Leibniz, 28 September 1712 (Guerrier, *Leibniz*, N. 160, p. 252) and Leibniz to R. C. von Imhof, 27 September 1712 (Klopp IX, 370).

75. See Bodemann, "Leibnizens Briefwechsel mit dem Herzoge Anton Ulrich von Braunschweig-Wolfenbüttel," pp. 216–17.

76. See Guerrier, *Leibniz*, N. 171, pp. 264–7; N. 179, pp. 272–3.

77. See Leibniz to Gottfried Teuber, 10 November 1712 (Guerrier, *Leibniz*, N. 177, p. 271) and Leibniz to Sophie, 9 November 1712 (Guerrier, *Leibniz*, N. 178, p. 272).

78. See Guerrier, *Leibniz*, N. 174–176, pp. 268–71. The date of 1 November 1712 in the official nomination follows the Julian Calendar (Old Style), adopted in Russia from 1700 onward in lieu of the traditional calendar, which started from the supposed date of the creation of the word.

79. Leibniz to Sophie, 9 November 1712 (Guerrier, *Leibniz*, N. 178, p. 272).

80. See Müller–Krönert, *Leben und Werk*, p. 232.

81. See Leibniz to Peter the Great, 16 January 1712 (Guerrier, *Leibniz*, N. 143, pp. 206–8) and Sophie to Leibniz, 20 September 1704 (Klopp IX, 102).

82. Although the number of Leibniz's correspondents peaked in the decade between 1695 and 1705, his correspondence remained extremely extensive thereafter. See the interesting graphic by Georg Gerber in "Leibniz und seine Korrespondenz." In *Leibniz. Sein Leben, sein Wirken, seine Welt*. Ed. by W. Totok and C. Haase. Hanover: Verlag für Literatur und Zeitgeschehen, 1966, p. 142.

83. See GP VII, 558–70. On simple substances and the continuum see above, chap. II. 6.

84. The *Illustratio tentaminis* is published in GM VI, 254–76. On the *Tentamen de Motuum caelestium Causis* see chap. II. 5. Cf. Bertoloni Meli, *Equivalence and Priority*, pp. 187, 206 and Aiton, *Leibniz*, pp. 290–91.

85. See Ravier, 170–71 and GM VI, 276–80.

86. See *Antibarbarus Physicus pro Philosophia Reali contra renovationes qualitatum scholasticarum et intelligentiarum chimaericarum* (GP VII, 337–44).

87. See *Observatio Mechanica de Resistentia Frictionis* (in Leibniz, *Nachgelassene Schriften*, pp. 115–19).

88. See in particular Leibniz's letter of 30 October 1710 (GP III, 504–10).

89. *Monita quaedam ad Samuelis Puffendorfii principia, Gerh. Wolth. Molano directa* (Dutens IV, iii, 275–83). Trans. by Riley in Leibniz, *Political Writings*, pp. 65–75 (here p. 65). See Riley's brief introduction, pp. 64–5.

90. Leibniz, *Political Writings*, pp. 64–5.

91. Leibniz, *Political Writings*, p. 71.

92. See the illuminating paper by Rutherford, "Idealism Declined. Leibniz and Christian Wolff." Regarding Leibniz's perception of his intellectual relationship with Wolff see the letter of July 1714 to Nicolas Rémond (GP III, 619) to which Rutherford, "Idealism Declined," p. 233 (note 1) draws attention.

93. See *Allgemeine Deutsche Biographie* and L. W. Beck, *Early German Philosophy: Kant and His Predecessors*. Cambridge, MA: Harvard University Press, 1696, pp. 256–61.

94. See Leibniz to Wolff, 21 February 1705 (in *Briefwechsel zwischen Leibniz und Christian Wolff*. Ed. by C. I. Gerhardt. Halle: H. W. Schmidt, 1860, p. 20).

95. In a letter of 25 January 1707 to the imperial counsellor, Michael Gottlieb Hansch, Leibniz mentioned a discussion with Wolff in Berlin in relation to this latter's appointment to the professorship at the University of Halle (cf. Dutens V, 160). Leibniz visited Wolff in Halle in June 1707 (cf. Müller–Krönert, *Leben und Werk*, p. 205).

96. See Ravier, pp. 90–92.

97. See Rutherford, "Idealism Declined," p. 219.

98. Cf. Adams, *Leibniz*, pp. 383–6.

99. Cf. *Briefwechsel zwischen Leibniz und Christian Wolff*, p. 142. Quoted in translation by Rutherford, "Idealism Declined," p. 227. In the following pages Rutherford presents a detailed and convincing discussion of the nature of these differences the root of which, in his view, is to be identified in Wolff's decision to decline Leibniz's specific brand of idealism.

100. GP II, 291.

101. Cf. *Neue Deutsche Biographie* and Look, *Leibniz and the 'Vinculum Substantiale'*, pp. 16–17. Des Bosses was born in 1663 in Herve, near Liège, in the Spanish Netherlands (now Belgium).

102. *Tentamina Theodicaeae de Bonitate Dei, Libertate Hominis et Origine Mali.* Latine versa et Notationibus illustrata a M. D. L. Ab ipso auctore emendata et auctior.

Francofurti: Sumptibus Caroli Josephi Bencard, 1719. From September 1711 onward, the correspondence between Leibniz and Des Bosses was strewn with references to the translation (see for instance GP II, 425, 426, 427, 443–4, 452, 513).

103. Cf. Adams, *Leibniz*, pp. 295–9. In their introduction to *The Leibniz–Des Bosses Correspondence*, Look and Rutherford point out that, although the best–known parts of the exchange between Leibniz and Des Bosses are those devoted to the nature of substance and body, other topics close to the heart of the two correspondents are discussed at length, notably the engagement of the Jesuits in the China mission and the Jansenist controversy.

104. René-Joseph Tournemine, "Conjectures sur l'union de l'ame et du corps." *Mémoires pour l'Histoire des Sciences et des Beaux Arts* 7 (1704): 231–7.

105. GP VI, 595.

106. See GP II, 281. Attention is drawn to this letter by Adams, *Leibniz*, pp. 296–7, and by Look and Rutherford in their introduction to *The Leibniz–Des Bosses Correspondence*, p. xlvi.

107. For an outstanding, nuanced discussion of the conception (or conceptions) of corporeal substance put forward by Leibniz, especially in his correspondence with Des Bosses, see Look and Rutherford, "Introduction," *The Leibniz–Des Bosses Correspondence*.

108. See respectively GP II, 354–5; GP II, 371; GP II, 390. Mentioned by Adams, *Leibniz*, p. 297.

109. See *Theodicy*, "Preface" (GP VI, 45) and "Discours preliminaire," paragraph 55 (GP VI, 81). Cf. Adams, *Leibniz*, 298–9.

110. See Adams, *Leibniz*, pp. 299–303. An illuminating discussion of the changes in Leibniz's conception of the *vinculum* unfolding during his correspondence with Des Bosses is contained in Look and Rutherford's "Introduction" to *The Leibniz–Des Bosses Correspondence*.

111. Leibniz to Des Bosses, 5 February 1712 (GP II, 435). Trans. by Adams, *Leibniz*, p. 299).

112. See Leibniz to Des Bosses, 30 June 1715 (GP II, 499).

113. *Remarque de l'Auteur du Systeme de l'Harmonie préetablie sur un endroit des Memoires de Trevoux du Mars 1704* (GP VI, 596).

114. GP II, 461. Trans. by Adams, *Leibniz*, p. 304.

115. Cf. Antognazza, *Leibniz on the Trinity and the Incarnation*, pp. 35–7; Adams, *Leibniz*, pp. 303–7; and Look and Rutherford, "Introduction," in *The Leibniz–Des Bosses Correspondence*, esp. pp. lxxiv–lxxv, lxxix. On the problems and possible weaknesses unveiled in Leibniz's philosophy by the concept of *vinculum substantiale* see Brandon Look, "On Substance and Relation in Leibniz's Correspondence with Des Bosses." In *Leibniz and His Correspondents*. Ed. by Paul Lodge. Cambridge: Cambridge University Press, 2004, pp. 238–61 (esp. pp. 239, 259) and Look, *Leibniz and the 'Vinculum Substantiale'*, esp. pp. 13–16.

116. See in particular Leibniz to Thomas Burnett, 30 October 1710 (GP III, 320–21). See also Leibniz to Christoph Joachim Nicolai von Greiffencrantz, 2 May 1715

(GP VI, 12). On the Lützenburg conversations of the summer of 1702 see chap. II. 7.

117. Cf. respectively chapters I. 2 and I. 3. The "meditation" seems to correspond to *De Possibilitate Gratiae Divinae* (A VI, 1, N. 19) and *Von der Allmacht und Allwissenheit Gottes und der Freiheit des Menschen* (A VI, 1, N. 20). Cf. Leibniz to Duke Johann Friedrich, early 1671 (A II, 1, 83). On Leibniz's early writings on the problem of evil see the collection of papers edited and introduced by Robert Sleigh (Leibniz, *Confessio Philosophi. Papers Concerning the Problem of Evil, 1671–1678*). A reconstruction of Leibniz's reflections on the problems of evil, freedom, and moral responsibility from Leibniz's earliest texts to 1716 is offered by Gianfranco Mormino, *Determinismo e Utilitarismo nella Teodicea di Leibniz*, Milan: FrancoAngeli, 2005.

118. In the letter to Des Bosses of 5 February 1712 (GP II, 437) Leibniz defined *Theodicaea* as the "doctrine of the justice (that is, the simultaneous wisdom and goodness) of God." The word "theodicy" derives from Greek *theos* ("God") and *dikē* ("justice"). In creating this word Leibniz might have been inspired by the Greek text of Romans 3:4–5 (I owe this information to Herbert Breger).

119. See GP II, 428. Cf. also GP VI, 12.

120. A I, 12, 625. This is probably the first occurrence of the term "theodicy" in French ("Théodicées"). Cf. Mormino, *Determinismo e Utilitarismo nella Teodicea di Leibniz*, p. 165.

121. See Dutens V, 118 and GP VI, 4.

122. See A I, 18, N. 194 (p. 322) and N. 275.

123. *Guillelmi Pacidii. Theodicaea*, Grua, 370–71.

124. See *Guilielmi Pacidii initia et specimina Scientiae Generalis*, spring 1682* (A VI, 4, N. 115). Leibniz also used this pseudonym in early writings (cf. *Wilhelmus Pacidius. Entwurf einer Einleitung*, second half of 1671–beginning of 1672*; A VI, 2, N. 59).

125. Grua, 370.

126. See Heinrich Shepers, entry "Leibniz" in *Neue Deutsche Biographie*.

127. GP III, 321. Cf. also Leibniz's letter to Thomas Burnett of 11 February 1697 (GP III, 196–7).

128. GP III, 680.

129. Leibniz to Biber, LBr 64, Bl. 3r. In his insightful essay on "Demonstration and Reconciliation: The Eclipse of the Geometrical Method in Leibniz's Philosophy," Donald Rutherford argues that Leibniz's choice (especially in his later years) to present his philosophy in terms comprehensible to the broader public rather than focusing on a rigorously demonstrative exposition, which he continued to regard as superior, was motivated by fundamental commitments of his ethics to the values of charity and reconciliation, values which could be better pursued by presenting his philosophy in approachable terms.

130. See Giuseppe Tognon, "Christian Wolff e gli 'Essais de Théodicée.'" In *Leibniz. Tradition und Aktualität. V. Internationaler Leibniz-Kongress. Vorträge*. Hanover: Gottfried-Wilhelm-Leibniz-Gesellschaft, 1988, pp. 962–3.

131. See GP II, 356.

132. See the letters of Des Bosses to Leibniz of, respectively, 11 September 1708 (GP II, 357–8), 28 November 1708 (GP II, 365), and 30 July 1709 (GP II, 374).

133. See Leibniz to Charles Hugony, November 1710 (GP III, 680).

134. See Ravier 70.

135. See Elisabeth Charlotte to Sophie, 22 October 1711 (*Aus den Briefen der Elisabeth Charlotte von Orléans an Kurfürstin Sophie*. Vol. 2, p. 292).

136. Probably the reformed theologian Jean Alphonse Turrettin (1671–1737).

137. This Parisian edition appeared in 1715 with the false indication of Amsterdam as place of publication to avoid the need of censorship approval. See Ravier 73 and GP VI, 12.

138. Leibniz to Christoph Joachim Nicolai von Greiffencrantz, 2 May 1715 (GP VI, 12–13).

139. LBr 64, Bl. 3*r*. Leibniz wrote his answer directly on the space left in Biber's letter of 22 July 1715. Biber had reported that the king of Poland had much appreciated the *Theodicy*.

140. Adams, *Leibniz*, p. 51 notes that the infinite analysis theory of contingency is partly stated in the *Theodicy*, in § 14 of Leibniz's remarks on *De Origine Mali* (London 1702) by William King. Nevertheless that would be insufficient to provide "the uninitiated reader" with an idea of Leibniz's infinite analysis conception (see Adams, "Leibniz's Conception of Religion," p. 61).

141. On these two solutions to the problem of contingency see chap. II. 4.

142. See in particular Leibniz to Thomas Burnett, 30 October 1710 (GP III, 320–21); Leibniz to Charles Hugony, November 1710 (GP III, 680); Leibniz to Nicolas Rémond, July 1714 (GP III, 618).

143. A VI, 3, 573. This text was probably written in 1676. Trans. by Adams in *Leibniz*, p. 52.

144. According to Pfaff's account in the *Acta Eruditorum* of March 1728, this text came from a letter of 2 May 1716 ("Fragmentum Epistolae a Cel. D. Christoph. Matthaeo Pfaffio," pp. 125–7, here p. 127). Trans. by Adams in *Leibniz*, p. 51.

145. See Thomas Hobbes, *The Questions Concerning Liberty, Necessity, and Chance: Clearly Stated and Debated between Dr. Bramhall, Bishop of Derry, and Thomas Hobbes of Malmesbury*. London: Printed for Andrew Crook, 1656.

146. Amstaelodami: apud Isacum Trojel, 1710. See GP VI, 437–62. The *Causa Dei* can be found both as an independent publication and bound together with the first edition of the *Theodicy*.

147. On Leibniz's denial of purely extrinsic denominations see chap. II. 5.

148. See GP VI, 361–5.

149. See Adams, *Leibniz*, pp. 46–50; Mugnai, *Leibniz: Vita*, pp. 14–15, and *Introduzione*, pp. 201–3.

150. See Couturat, 193–202. Cf. also Couturat, 203–6.

151. See Müller–Krönert, *Leben und Werk*, p. 224.

152. On the selection of letters published by Wallis in the third volume of his *Opera mathematica* see chap. II. 7.

153. John Keill, "Epistola . . . de Legibus Virium Centripetarum." *Philosophical Transactions* 26 (1708), p. 185. Trans. by Hall in *Philosophers at War*, p. 145. It should also be noted that, in an obituary for Jakob Bernoulli (d. 16 August 1705) published in the *Nouvelles de la République des Lettres* of February 1706 and later in the *Mémoires de Trevoux*, Fontenelle had erroneously attributed the invention of the calculus to the Bernoulli brothers. In that case, however, Leibniz had easily obtained a published rectification (cf. GM V, 389–92; GP VI, 396–7; Ravier 172, 174, 175).

154. See LBr 871, Bl. 24.

155. See LBr 871, Bl. 25. On Fatio de Duillier see chap. II. 7.

156. On this review see chap. II. 7.

157. See *Commercium Epistolicum*, pp. 110–18; LH 35, VIII, 15, Bl. 1r–5v; A III, 1, xliii; Hall, *Philosophers at War*, p. 169.

158. See *Commercium Epistolicum*, pp. 118–19 and Hall, *Philosophers at War*, pp. 176–7.

159. See *Theodicy*, "Discours preliminaire," § 19 (GP VI, 61–2); GP III, 516–21 (the date of the letter to Hartsoeker given in GP is 6 February 1711); Ravier 181; republished: Ravier 185. Newton prepared a draft for a direct reply although, in the end, the answer came in the preface by Roger Cotes to the second edition of the *Principia* (1713) (cf. *The Correspondence of Isaac Newton*, vol. 5, 298–300; Newton, *Principia*, 1713, "Editoris Praefatio"). See Ezio Vailati, *Leibniz and Clarke. A Study of Their Correspondence*, New York and Oxford: Oxford University Press, 1997, p. 6.

160. See Hall, *Philosophers at War*, pp. 178–80.

161. See Isaac Newton to [T. Johnson (publisher of the *Journal Literaire de la Haye*)] [1714] (*The Correspondence of Isaac Newton*, vol. 6, p. 80); Leibniz to John Chamberlayne, 28 April 1714 (*The Correspondence of Isaac Newton*, vol. 6, pp. 103–4).

162. See Johann Bernoulli to Leibniz, 7 June 1713, GM III/2, 907–12 (extract also in *The Correspondence of Isaac Newton*, vol. 6, pp. 1–3; trans. pp. 3–5) and Leibniz to Pierre Varignon, 28 June 1713 (GM IV, 193–4).

163. Cf. chap. II. 7.

164. See Doebner, "Leibnizens Briefwechsel mit dem Minister von Bernstorff," p. 261 and E. Bodemann, "Nachträge zu 'Leibnizens Briefwechsel mit dem Minister v. Bernstorf und andere Leibniz betr. Briefe'." *Zeitschrift des historischen Vereins für Niedersachsen* (1890), p. 149.

165. See the memoranda written during the first month of his sojourn in Vienna (18 December 1712: Karl L. Grotefend, *Leibniz-Album aus den Handschriften der Königlichen Bibliothek zu Hannover*. Hanover: Hahnschen Hofbuchhandlung, 1846, pp. 18–20; 23 December 1712 and 2 January 1713: O. Klopp, "Leibniz' Plan der Gründung einer Societät der Wissenschaften in Wien." *Archiv für österreichische Geschichte*. Vol. 40. Vienna, 1869, pp. 217–222, 222–224; January 1713: E. F. Roessler, "Beiträge zur Staatsgeschichte Oesterreichs aus dem Leibnitzschen Nachlasse in Hannover." *Sitzungsberichte der philosophisch-historischen*

Classe der Kais. Akademie der Wissenschften zu Wien. Vol. 20 (1856): 267–89, here pp. 271–5). Attention is drawn to these texts by Müller–Krönert, *Leben und Werk*, pp. 233–4 and Nicholas Rescher, "Leibniz Visits Vienna (1712–1714)." *Studia Leibnitiana* 31, 2 (1999), p. 142.

166. See Doebner, "Leibnizens Briefwechsel mit dem Minister von Bernstorff," p. 264.

167. See Doebner, "Leibnizens Briefwechsel mit dem Minister von Bernstorff," p. 267.

168. Doebner, "Leibnizens Briefwechsel mit dem Minister von Bernstorff," p. 217.

169. See Bernstorff to Leibniz, 5 April 1713 (Doebner, "Leibnizens Briefwechsel mit dem Minister von Bernstorff," p. 269).

170. See Doebner, "Nachträge zu Leibnizens Briefwechsel mit dem Minister Bernstorff," pp. 227–8. On the Lauenburg duchy see chap. II. 4.

171. See "Denkschrift . . . über das Anrecht des Hauses Braunschweig-Lüneburg an Lauenburg," April–May 1713 (in Doebner, "Nachträge zu Leibnizens Briefwechsel mit dem Minister Bernstorff," pp. 229–32).

172. Contrary to Aiton, *Leibniz*, p. 312 Leibniz was never appointed Imperial Privy Counsellor. Unlike the *Geheimer Rat* (Privy Council), which advised the emperor on all matters of governance of the Empire, the *Reichshofrat* (Imperial Aulic Council) was one of the two Imperial supreme courts of appeal, and thus part of the judicial system of the Empire rather than the executive. Cf. Gerhard Oestreich, *Verfassungsgeschichte vom Ende des Mittelalters bis zum Ende des alten Reiches.* Stuttgart: Ernst Klett Verlag, 1970, pp. 61–4; Peter H. Wilson, *The Holy Roman Empire. 1495–1806.* London: Macmillan Press, 1999, pp. 45–9.

173. Cf. J. Bergmann, "Leibniz als Reichshofrat in Wien und dessen Besoldung." *Sitzungsberichte der kaiserlichen Akademie der Wissenschaften zu Wien. Phil.– hist. Klasse.* Vol. 26. Vienna, 1858. Fasc. I, pp. 187–204; M. Faak, *Leibniz als Reichshofrat.* Humboldt-Universität Berlin, 1966 (Phil. Dissertation, typw), pp. 79–80.

174. See Klopp, "Leibniz' Plan der Gründung einer Societät der Wissenschaften in Wien," p. 226. According to Leibniz's own calculation, the exchange rate between taler and guilder (*Gulden*) was 1.5 guilder per taler. In his note he equates 2800 talers (the sum of his income from Hanover, Wolfenbüttel, and Berlin) with 4200 guilders.

175. Klopp, "Leibniz' Plan der Gründung einer Societät der Wissenschaften in Wien," p. 226.

176. Ibid., pp. 194, 240–41.

177. See Müller-Krönert, *Leben und Werk*, p. 240 and Faak, *Leibniz als Reichshofrat*, pp. 90–92.

178. See Klopp IX, 414.

179. See Müller-Krönert, *Leben und Werk*, p. 242 and Rescher, "Leibniz visits Vienna," p. 147.

180. See Bergmann, "Leibniz als Reichshofrat in Wien und dessen Besoldung," pp. 195–6, 200–201.

181. See J. Fr. Hodann to Leibniz, 8 October 1713 (Bodemann, "Nachträge zu 'Leibnizens Briefwechsel mit dem Minister v. Bernstorff und andere Leibniz betr. Briefe,'" p. 150); Müller–Krönert, *Leben und Werk*, pp. 240, 258; Rescher, "Leibniz visits Vienna," pp. 146–7. One payment was made in December 1714 in acknowledgement of Leibniz's work for the Lauenburg inheritance (cf. Rescher, "Leibniz visits Vienna," p. 147, quoting W. Junge, *Leibniz und der Sachsen-Lauenburgische Erbfolgestreit*. Hildesheim, 1965, p. 170 (*Quellen und Darstellungen zur Geschichte Niedersachsens*, vol. 65).

182. See M. Braubach, *Prinz Eugen von Savoyen. Eine Biographie*. 5 vols. München, 1963–5, vol. 5, p. 171.

183. Leibniz to Anton Ulrich, 18 February 1713 (Bodemann, "Leibnizens Briefwechsel mit dem Herzoge Anton Ulrich von Braunschweig-Wolfenbüttel," p. 225).

184. See in particular "Projet d'alliance avec les puissances du nord" (1703) in FC, *Oeuvres*, IV, 214–17. See also FC, *Oeuvres*, IV, 148–53, 189–206, 239–47, 255–72, 315–24, 338–44; P. Fransen, *Leibniz und die Friedensschlüsse von Utrecht und Rastatt-Baden. Eine aus größtenteils noch nicht veröffentlichten Quellen geschöpfte Untersuchung*. Purmerend, 1933.

185. "Paix d'Utrecht inexcusable, mise dans son jour par une lettre à un milord tory" (FC, *Oeuvres*, IV, 1–140).

186. Leibniz to Caroline, 7 July 1714 (Klopp IX, 464).

187. See FC, *Oeuvres*, IV, 273–6 and 277–89.

188. See Leibniz to the Palatine Raugräfin Louise, 9 May 1714 (Klopp IX, 441, 443).

189. See ibid., pp. 442–3; Sophie to Leibniz, 20 May 1714 (Klopp IX, 446–7); Leibniz to Caroline, 7 July 1714 (Klopp IX, 463–4). Ker left Vienna in July 1714.

190. See John Ker of Kersland, *Memoirs... Containing His Secret Transactions and Negotiations in Scotland, England, the Courts of Vienna, Hanover, and Other Foreign Parts* [Part I]. London, 1726, p. 117 (a French version appeared in Rotterdam in the same year).

191. See Pertz IV, 346–7.

192. *Moyens* (FC, *Oeuvres*, IV, 150–51); trans. by Riley in Leibniz, *Political Writings*, pp. 106–7 (footnote).

193. Leibniz's writings on the establishment of a Society of Sciences in Vienna are collected in LH XIII, 27, Bl. 109–84. A first mention of this idea is recorded in a paper of 2 October 1704 penned in Lützenburg (LH XIII, 27, Bl. 109–10).

194. See *Societatis Imperialis Germanicae designatae schema*, 2 January 1713 (in Klopp, "Leibniz' Plan der Gründung einer Societät der Wissenschaften in Wien," pp. 222–4).

195. See Klopp, "Leibniz' Plan der Gründung einer Societät der Wissenschaften in Wien," pp. 224–9, 230–31. Cf. also FC, *Oeuvres*, VII, 328–31.

196. Cf. FC, *Oeuvres*, VII, 339–40; 343–7; 373–82; Müller–Krönert, *Leben und Werk*, pp. 238–9; Rescher, "Leibniz Visits Vienna," p. 143.

197. Cf. FC, *Oeuvres*, VII, 343–7 and Müller–Krönert, *Leben und Werk*, p. 240.

198. Klopp, "Leibniz' Plan der Gründung einer Societät der Wissenschaften in Wien," pp. 241–2.

199. Cf. FC, *Oeuvres*, VII, 312–27, 337–42, 367–72; Bodemann, *Handschriften*, pp. 209–13.

200. See Leibniz to Prince Eugene, 17 August 1714, and the attached memo for the emperor (Klopp, "Leibniz' Plan der Gründung einer Societät der Wissenschaften in Wien," pp. 246–7; 247–51).

201. Nikolaus Bernoulli.

202. *The Correspondence of Isaac Newton*, vol. 6, p. 3.

203. See Hall, "Philosophers at War," pp. xii, 198–9.

204. *The Correspondence of Isaac Newton*, vol. 6, p. 4.

205. See GM III/2, 912; *The Correspondence of Isaac Newton*, vol. 6, pp. 3, 5.

206. See Leibniz to Antonio Conti, 9 April 1716 (GB, 275) and Hall, "Philosophers at War," p. 186.

207. Leibniz to Johann Bernoulli, 28 June 1713 (GM III/2, 913–14). Trans. adapted slightly from *The Correspondence of Isaac Newton*, vol. 6, pp. 8–9.

208. Leibniz was referring to Newton's calculus, which from mid-December 1691 employed a dotted notation (see D. T. Whiteside, "The Mathematical Principles Underlying Newton's *Principia Mathematica*." *Journal for the History of Astronomy* 1 (1970), p. 118).

209. Leibniz to Pierre Varignon, 28 June 1713 (GM IV, 193–4).

210. See GM IV, 194–5.

211. See *Briefwechsel zwischen Leibniz und Christian Wolff*, pp. 149–52.

212. See Newton to Pierre Varignon, 19 January (O.S.) 1721 (*The Correspondence of Isaac Newton*, vol. 7, p. 120).

213. See Christian Wolff to Leibniz, 11 December 1713 (*Briefwechsel zwischen Leibniz und Christian Wolff*, p. 154) and Johann Bernoulli to Leibniz, 23 May 1714 (GM III/2, 931).

214. See Ravier 72 ("Epistola qua probatur analyticam artem primum a L[eibnitio] fuisse editam et post complures demum annos a N[ewtono] calculum fluxionem fuisse productum") and 313. The *Charta Volans* appeared (in Latin) also in the *Deutsche Acta Eruditorum* 19 (1713): 590–94 (see Ravier 310).

215. See for instance Johann Bernoulli to Leibniz, 23 May 1714 (GM III/2, 931).

216. See the *Charta Volans* in GM V, 411–13 and *The Correspondence of Isaac Newton*, vol. 6, pp. 15–17. Leibniz first saw the *Commercium Epistolicum* only once he was back in Hanover in September 1714. Cf. his letter of 28 October 1714 to René-Joseph Tournemine, published in the *Mémoires de Trevoux* of January 1715, pp. 154–5 (republished in Dutens III, 441–3).

217. See Newton to Pierre Varignon, 1721* (*The Correspondence of Isaac Newton*, vol. 7, p. 123).

218. See Keill to Newton, 8 February 1714 and Newton to Keill, 2 April 1714 (*The Correspondence of Isaac Newton*, vol. 6, respectively p. 62 and pp. 79–80). Newton prepared his own answer addressed to the publisher of the *Journal Literaire* of The Hague, T. Johnson (cf. *The Correspondence of Isaac Newton*,

vol. 6, pp. 80–90). This answer never appeared in the *Journal*, in all probability because Newton eventually decided not to send it.

219. See John Chamberlayne to Leibniz, 27 February (O.S.)/10 March (N.S.) 1714 (*The Correspondence of Isaac Newton*, vol. 6, p. 71).

220. See Leibniz to John Chamberlayne, 28 April 1714 (*The Correspondence of Isaac Newton*, vol. 6, pp. 103–4).

221. See Newton's translation in *The Correspondence of Isaac Newton*, vol. 6, pp. 105–6 and the letter of Chamberlayne to Newton of 20 May (O.S.)/31 May (N.S.) 1714.

222. See Leibniz to Charles Hugony, 14 March 1714 (GP III, 682).

223. See Nicolas Rémond's letters to Leibniz of 2 June 1713 and 2 September 1714 (respectively GP III, 603 and 626).

224. See GP III, 618, 622, and 682.

225. On Leibniz's 'austere' ontology see Adams, *Leibniz* and Mugnai, *Introduzione*.

226. GP III, 622.

227. Cf. Müller–Krönert, *Leben und Werk*, p. 246 and G. W. Leibniz, *Principes de la nature et de la grâce fondés en raison. Principes de la philosophie ou monadologie*. Ed. by A. Robinet. Paris: Presses Universitaires de France, 1954, p. 14. Robinet's hypothesis that the *Monadology* was written as an outline for the Neolatin poet Claude François Fraguier, a friend of Rémond (cf. GP III, 611–18), has been contested by other scholars. A lively account of the genesis of the *Monadology* is offered by Enrico Pasini, "Cinque storie sulla *Monadologia* di Leibniz." In *Monadi e monadologie. Il mondo degli individui tra Bruno, Leibniz e Husserl*. Ed. by Bianca Maria d'Ippolito, Aniello Montano, and Francesco Piro. Soveria Mannelli: Rubbettino, 2005, pp. 147–67.

228. Leibniz to Nicolas Rémond, July 1714 (GP III, 618).

229. See GP III, 624, 642, 648, and 650.

230. See Leibniz to Nicolas Rémond, 26 August 1714 (GP III, 624). The other papers given to Prince Eugene included the *Système nouveau* and three of the texts which clarified it, especially in relation to Bayle's objections. They were collected in a volume now held at the Österreichische Nationalbibliothek in Vienna (Cod. 10.588). See list in Müller–Krönert, *Leben und Werk*, p. 245, and Antonio Lamarra, Roberto Palaia, and Pietro Pimpinella, *Le prime traduzioni della Monadologie di Leibniz (1720–1721)*. Florence: Olschki, 2001, pp. 54–5. A first edition of the papers contained in the volume is being prepared by Antonio Lamarra.

231. In Leibniz, *Principes de la nature et de la grâce fondés en raison. Principes de la philosophie ou monadologie*, p. 16.

232. See GP III, 624, 642, 648, and 650. Some remarks of Leibniz were appended to Sully's *Regle artificielle du Tems* published in Vienna in 1714. Cf. Ravier 152, and Dutens III, 502–4.

233. Leibniz for Paul Pellisson-Fontanier, end of October 1690 (A I, 6, 121).

234. Leibniz to Nicolas Rémond, 26 August 1714 (GP III, 624–5).

235. GP III, 606–7.

236. LH I 20 Bl. 132. Leibniz was involved in this dispute on the basis of a letter of 2 December 1706 on the origin of Islam published by La Croze in his *Dissertations historiques sur divers sujets*, Rotterdam: Reinier Leers, 1707. For details see Antognazza, *Leibniz on the Trinity and the Incarnation*, chap. 11. Leibniz's letter is published in Dutens V, 479–84.

237. The relation between the *Principes de la nature et de la grâce fondés en raison* and the *Monadologie* has long been a source of equivocations and mistakes, including the identification of the two texts and the erroneous belief that the *Monadologie* was addressed to Prince Eugene. See the illuminating account of Antonio Lamarra in Lamarra, Palaia, and Pimpinella, *Le prime traduzioni della Monadologie di Leibniz*, esp. pp. 1–15 and 107–8, referring also to the decisive studies of Clara Strack, *Ursprung und sachliches Verhältnis von Leibnizens sogenannter Monadologie und den Principes de la nature et de la grâce. I. Teil: Die Entstehungsgeschichte der beiden Abhandlungen*. Inaugural Dissertation. Berlin, 1915 and André Robinet in his edition of the two texts published in 1954. Rudolf Boehm, "Notes sur l'histoire des 'Principes de la Nature et de la Grâce' et de la 'Monadologie' de Leibniz." *Revue Philosophique de Louvain* 55 (1957): 232–51 criticises the conclusion reached by Robinet in his 1954 edition and proposes to regard the *Principes de la nature et de la grâce* and the *Monadologie* as successive stages of (broadly speaking) the same work of clarification of Leibniz's doctrine of simple substances stimulated by both, Prince Eugene and the circle of Rémond.

238. Cf. Robinet in Leibniz, *Principes de la nature et de la grâce fondés en raison. Principes de la philosophie ou monadologie*, p. 12; Lamarra, Palaia, and Pimpinella, *Le prime traduzioni della Monadologie di Leibniz*, pp. 11–12; Pasini, "Cinque storie sulla *Monadologia* di Leibniz."

239. See Lamarra, Palaia, and Pimpinella, *Le prime traduzioni della Monadologie di Leibniz*, p. 5.

240. These conclusions are based on the richly documented essay of Antonio Lamarra "Le traduzioni settecentesche della *Monadologie*." In Lamarra, Palaia, and Pimpinella, *Le prime traduzioni della Monadologie di Leibniz*, pp. 1–117. Köhler and Wolff's translations appeared, respectively, in *Des Hn. Gottfried Wilh. von Leibnitz . . . Lehr-Sätze über die Monadologie, ingleichen von Gott und seiner Existentz, seinen Eigenschafften und von der Seele des Menschen*. Frankfurt and Leipzig, 1720, pp. 1–46 and *Actorum Eruditorum Supplementa* 7 (1721), Sect. xi, pp. 500–514.

241. See Ravier 335.

242. GP VI, 598: "La substance . . . est simple ou composée."

243. GP VI, 607.

244. See Michel Fichant, "La costituzione del concetto di monade." In *Monadi e monadologie. Il mondo degli individui tra Bruno, Leibniz e Husserl*. Ed. by Bianca Maria d'Ippolito, Aniello Montano e Francesco Piro. Salerno: Rubbettino, 2005, p. 61.

245. See the convincing analysis offered by Rutherford and Look in the section devoted to the "Metaphysics of Substance" of the introduction to their edition of the Leibniz–Des Bosses correspondence (pp. xxxviii–xlv).

246. See GM VII, 17–29. Attention is drawn to this text by Mugnai and Pasini in the third volume of Leibniz, *Scritti Filosofici*.

247. These conclusions are reached by Vincenzo De Risi in his impressive doctoral thesis on *The Analysis Situs 1712–1716* (cf. esp. pp. 10–17, 107–11, 288–92). Amongst other things, De Risi offers a history of the *Analysis Situs* (pp. 18–125) and a tentative chronology of Leibniz's major writings on situational geometry (pp. 126–34). An Appendix to the thesis presents a wealth of unpublished texts by Leibniz on the philosophy of space. A revised version of the thesis is now published under the title *Geometry and Monadology: Leibniz's Analysis Situs and Philosophy of Space*.

248. Doebner, "Leibnizens Briefwechsel mit dem Minister von Bernstorff," p. 282.

249. See Klopp IX, 415.

250. This rumour was reported by Elisabeth Charlotte of Orléans to her aunt Sophie in a letter of 8 April 1714 (see *Aus den Briefen der Elisabeth Charlotte von Orléans an Kurfürstin Sophie*, vol. II, p. 346).

251. See Doebner, "Leibnizens Briefwechsel mit dem Minister von Bernstorff," p. 286. Cf. also Leibniz to Bernstorff, 4 July 1714 (Doebner, "Leibnizens Briefwechsel mit dem Minister von Bernstorff," p. 290).

252. See Klopp IX, 457–62. Cf. also Johann Mathias von der Schulenburg to Leibniz, 13 June 1714 (Klopp IX, 481–3).

253. The letters, in English and French versions, are published in Schnath, *Geschichte Hannovers*, vol. 4, pp. 734–40. The French version of the letter to Sophie can be seen in Klopp IX, 454–5.

254. See Caroline to Leibniz, 7 June 1714 (Klopp IX, 452–3). Leibniz was a firm supporter of the necessity for the presence of the Hanoverian family in London. Cf. for instance his last letter to Sophie (24 May 1714; Klopp IX, 448–50), in which the issue of the writ is discussed.

255. The Countess von Bückeburg to the Palatine Raugräfin Louise, 12 July 1714 (Klopp IX, 459).

256. Klopp IX, 448.

257. See Klopp IX, 481–3.

258. Klopp IX, 462.

259. Leibniz to Caroline, 18 March 1705 (Klopp IX, 116–17).

260. See Leibniz to Andreas Gottlieb von Bernstorff, 20 September 1714 (Klopp XI, 12).

9

Epilogue: Last Years in Hanover (September 1714–November 1716)

EIBNIZ'S LAST YEARS were marred by frustration and loneliness. His wish to follow the new king, George I, to London and serve as historiographer of Great Britain was brutally rebuffed. First he had to produce the long-awaited Guelf history. His plans to return to Vienna or to move to Paris did not materialize. Chained to his historical task and unwilling to compromise on his high scholarly standards, he was forced to sideline researches and projects closer to his heart in a last desperate attempt to finish the *Annales Imperii Occidentis Brunsvicenses*. His Hanoverian stipend, suspended in October 1713 due to his unauthorized sojourn in Vienna, recommenced again only in May 1716. In the meantime, upsetting news of reduction or cancellation of his pensions came from both Berlin and Vienna. The bitter quarrel about the calculus continued unabated, eventually spiralling into a clash between competing physical and metaphysical world views: on the one hand, the Newtonian universe defended by Samuel Clarke and characterized by absolute space, gravitational force, and ready divine intervention to repair the world-mechanism; on the other hand, the Leibnizian universe in which the world-clock did not need rewinding or mending, "occult" elements were rejected, and space and time were conceived as relations. Not only did Leibniz not succeed in convincing Clarke; the support of Caroline – the only friend left him in the electoral and now royal family, who acted as intermediary in the correspondence with Clarke – seemed gradually to wane.

Meanwhile his health deteriorated. After several days of illness in which gout and arthritis forced him to bed, Leibniz died peacefully in Hanover on the evening of Saturday, 14 November 1716, with none of his grand plans finished, not even the comparatively minor one of the Guelf history. Around his deathbed in his quarters in Schmiedestraße there were no close relatives, friends, or high-ranking persons – only his amanuensis and his coachman. This best of all possible worlds included neither the permanent post he had hoped for in one of the great cities of culture – Paris, London, or Vienna – nor the realisation of some considerable proportion of his projects and dreams. Yet he maintained an unflinching faith in the unending progress of a world governed by the universal harmony created by the infinite wisdom and goodness of God. The year before dying, broadening his sight to the eschatological contemplation of the future state of all things, he wrote, in one of the very last items added to his mountain of unpublished papers,

Yet one can conclude from this that the human race will not always remain in this state, since it is not consonant with the divine harmony to fiddle away on the same string for ever. And one should believe instead that, due to natural reasons of congruence, things are bound to progress for the better, whether gradually or sometimes even by leaps and bounds. Although at times things do seem to change for the worse, this should be regarded as similar to the way in which we sometimes retrace our footsteps in order to leap forward with greater vigour.[1]

Unfinished Business

On his arrival in Hanover on the evening of 14 September 1714, Leibniz was confronted with the depressing news that the newly created king of Great Britain, George I, was already on his way to England with his son, Georg August (now Prince of Wales), and the Hanoverian court in tow. Caroline was still residing in Herrenhausen, preparing to follow her husband with her daughters, whereas her seven-year-old eldest son, Friedrich, was to remain behind. In the absence of the elector and king, the duchy was entrusted to Georg Ludwig's youngest brother, Ernst August (1674–1728), who regarded Leibniz as a hilarious fossil from past times. Confronting such a bleak homecoming, Leibniz briefly entertained the idea of following the king in the hope of catching up with him in Holland before he crossed the Channel. Upon reflection, however, he thought better of it. More than the discomfort and danger for his health of a hasty journey in the mail-coach at the onset of the autumnal season, he probably doubted his ability to justify such a move in the eyes of the king, not to speak of the reception he was likely to receive after his long, unauthorised absence in Vienna.[2] Instead he went to see

Caroline at Herrenhausen and dispatched hasty letters to Georg August
and Prime Minister Bernstorff to inform the elector that he had at last
returned.[3] He judged it unwise, however, to write directly to Georg Ludwig: conversation with Caroline confirmed his fears that the elector was
still deeply annoyed and had greeted the news of his impeding return to
Hanover with the sarcastic words, "He is only coming now that I have
become King."[4]

Still, Caroline was on his side and wished that he would travel with her
to London.[5] Writing on 8 October to his friend, Ker of Kersland, Leibniz
expressed his firm intention to follow the king. It was only a matter
of deciding exactly when.[6] On the same day, his duplicitous secretary,
Eckhart, wrote to Bernstorff insinuating that Leibniz's true plan was
hurriedly to finish the Guelf history, bag a sizable reward, and disappear
once again in Vienna.[7] In the end, Caroline departed on 12 October,
leaving Leibniz behind.[8] The Princess of Wales's desire to have him at her
side in London was neutralised by Georg Ludwig's dislike for and distrust
of his daughter-in-law, and indeed his own son and heir. The king himself
had no intention of allowing Leibniz to show his face in London until he
could display his Guelf history there as well. So with Caroline gone, the
loneliness of the sociable philosopher grew unmistakable. "Madame," he
wrote in the first letter addressed to her in London, "The departure of
Your Most Serene Highness filled me with sorrow and at first Hanover
was insufferable to me. . . . I am shut in my room working and I hardly
ever leave it."[9]

It must have been some consolation that his prestigious admirers in
Vienna desired his return to the Imperial city. Indeed, notwithstanding
his desire to move to London, he kept other options open, above all
the possibility of returning to Vienna.[10] Yet for all his escapades and
diversions, Leibniz was a dutiful and honourable man. Now he felt that
his time was short and that he owed it to his employers to make the
completion of the Guelf history his first priority. As his letter to Caroline
continued,

the count of Bonneval tells me that Prince Eugene asks why, since I have not gone to
England, I do not return to Vienna, where it is expected that I would not be neglected.
But I want to use this winter to put the bulk of my work in such a state that, even
if I then took my leave of this world to go to the next one, our court would have no
grounds to complain about me[.][11]

It had also occurred to him that the history of the Guelfs might be turned to his advantage in expediting a move to London. Seeking Caroline's support once again, he vented the idea of being nominated historiographer of Great Britain:

> Since in my history I must often touch on that of England and on that of Henry the Lion, the King would not misuse the honour and salary of Historiographer of Great Britain if he were to grant it to me. These kinds of offices are still given to foreigners, since there can be more than one. I have written about this to Mr Bernstorff.[12]

Unfortunately, for the time being neither Bernstorff nor George I had any inclination to humour Leibniz. Quite the opposite. Toward the end of 1714 a cold shower swept across the Channel from London: George I personally prohibited him from travelling and Bernstorff specifically instructed him to abandon any plan to go to London. If he wanted to please the king, the prime minister advised, he should simply keep his head down and prepare a big chunk of the Guelf history for presentation to George I on the occasion of his visit to Hanover planned for the following summer.[13] Leibniz obliged, detailing in his answer to Bernstorff the shape and state of his work. His goal was to finish during the winter the first tome of the *Annales*, covering the period from Charlemagne to 1024, the year of death of Emperor Heinrich II. This period included the beginning of the new Braunschweig line originating from the common ancestor of the Este and Guelf families, Azzo II, who was born before Heinrich II's demise. The result would be a freestanding volume. This way, if God decided to "dispose of him" before he was able to finish the second tome, "the first one will be a complete work." Once the first volume was dispatched, he was planning to return to the preliminary dissertations on the natural history of the earth (his *Protogaea*) and on the origins and migrations of peoples. Having sketched this nicely rounded picture, he broached the subject of his nomination to the office of historiographer of Great Britain.[14] For good measure, on 18 December he addressed a memo to the king in defence of the work done.[15] But George I would have none of it, and required Leibniz to remain in Hanover in order to focus on completing the *Annales*.[16]

For his part, Eckhart continued to fan the court's suspicions regarding Leibniz's real commitment to work on the *Annales*. Perhaps to defend himself from guilt by association with the continuing lack of visible results, he wrote on 5 March 1715 to one of the privy counsellors of justice,

There is nothing lacking in my industry, however; and if Herr von Leibniz were to pull his weight, our historical voyage would soon be over. But when he is not suffering from gout, he is travelling; and he knows how to extend this project (as well as numbers) *ad infinitum*.[17]

Eckhart succeeded so well in his attempt to secure the favour of George I at Leibniz's expense that he was eventually charged with the continuation of the *Annales* after 1024 without the knowledge or consent of Leibniz himself.[18]

In April 1715, Bernstorff conveyed his regrets at not yet being able to give a definite answer to Leibniz's petition for the office of British historiographer: "This is hindered by the King's opinion that, even after such a long wait, he will never see your [historical] works" completed. George I first wanted to see the history of the Guelfs with his own eyes in black and white: then Leibniz could "hope for everything."[19] Caroline also added her voice, confidently predicting that the king would relent and grant Leibniz what he wanted after the work had been finished.[20] But despite his plans to finish the first tome during the winter of 1714–15, in late summer of 1715 he was still working away at it. As he confided in a letter of 17 September to the Venetian physician and mathematician, P. A. Michelotti, this task absorbed virtually all his time. To his chagrin, he was forced to put aside his philosophical, mathematical, and juridical researches and to neglect his correspondence.[21] In September he also reported to Bernstorff on his progress: the preliminary dissertation on the origin of the earth (the *Protogaea*) was finished; the dissertation on the migration of peoples was still to be written but he had already assembled all the materials. Once the *Annales* until the year 1024 were in the hands of the printer, he would return to the two preliminary dissertations in order to complete them.[22]

His letter probably crossed one from Caroline of 13 September heading in his direction. The Princess was doing her very best to mollify her difficult father-in-law and to convince him to grant Leibniz the office he so much desired. Having recently approached George I on the subject, she had received a more encouraging answer: "First he must prove he can write history. I hear that he is diligent." Her overall impression was that George I was now well disposed and she urged Leibniz "to do all that depended on him" to "force the king" to follow through on his good intentions.[23] The main reason behind George I's refusal to accommodate Leibniz was clearly, and not unreasonably, his longstanding annoyance with the continuous delays and unauthorised travels. The prohibition in the Act of Settlement of the new monarch granting official offices to foreigners only applied (Leibniz had argued) to positions requiring naturalisation.[24] In any case this rule had not stopped George I from gratifying his Hanoverian entourage (including his two German mistresses) with titles and favours – with limited regard for the popularity of such measures with his new subjects. So the time had definitely come to complete the *Annales*, and the only thing delaying the project was now (Leibniz argued) its author's unwillingness to compromise his high scholarly standards. Writing on 23 December 1715 to the president of the *Kammer*, Friedrich Wilhelm von Görtz, and on 28 January 1716 to Prime Minister Bernstorff, he declared that the first volume could have been dispatched for publication; but supervising printing would have interrupted the completion of the second volume as well as preventing the insertion of the amendments which were certain to emerge as work on the second volume progressed. Although it would have been easy enough to deceive most readers, such a procedure would never have satisfied his own conscience.[25]

Meanwhile his wages and arrears remained unpaid. The king had made clear that, on account of his services at the Imperial court for the Hanover electorate, he would pay him for three of the months he had spent in Vienna but not for the other eighteen. Beyond these financial losses, Leibniz was hurt by "the bad opinion that His Majesty seems to have of my work." "It has wounded me more than I can say," he wrote to Bernstorff, "to see that, while Europe gives me justice, this is not done where I would have most reason to expect it."[26] Worse still, the rumour that he was ready to disappear to Vienna the moment he pocketed his money caused the Hanover government to tighten his leash. Leibniz's distress at such a base opinion of his character was freely expressed in an emotional letter to Caroline, probably penned in 1715, which remained unsent.[27] For all his delays on the Guelf history, he was unflinchingly loyal to the new king and to the succession of the house of Hanover to the British throne. As if to prove his point, in the year which saw the great Jacobite uprising in the summer of 1715 he once again put his pen to the service of George I. In an "Avis aux Proprietaires Anglois [Notice to the English Proprietors]," an anonymous partisan of the most conservative fringes of the English church and the Tory party had advised the "Freeholders or proprietors of England" against the economical, political, and religious motivations of the new Hanoverian king. The author of the "Avis," Leibniz counter-attacked, despite his protestations to the contrary, was in reality a Jacobite supporter of the Pretender, that is, of the supremacy of the Bourbons in Europe, and of the restoration of the Papists in Britain to the detriment of the Protestant cause.[28]

Further bitter surprises arrived from other quarters. On 6 April 1715 the secretary of the Society of Sciences of Berlin, Johann Theodor Jablonski, informed him that his emoluments as president were being cut in half: from now on he would be paid 300 talers per annum for the expenses incurred in the exercise of his office. In September a letter of Daniel Ernst Jablonski followed, bearing the still less welcome news that for the time being his pay had been suspended altogether.[29] Leibniz's protest of 15 October to the Society's director, von Printzen, was rebutted with the argument that in the past three or four years he had neither written to the Society nor visited Berlin. Although von Printzen's argument was not without force, Leibniz had legitimate cause to resent the decision, since he had spent time and energy planning the second volume of the *Miscellanea Berolinensia*.[30]

Given the souring of his prospects in northern Germany and the lack of any imminent opportunity to join the court in London, it is not surprising that Leibniz continued to consider other possibilities. These included not only Vienna, but also Paris. Around March 1715 the rumour circulated that he intended to transfer to the French capital.[31] The Jesuit Father, René-Joseph Tournemine, later confirmed that Leibniz had indeed sought his help in 1715 for a possible move to Paris. Although Louis XIV was disposed to welcome the famous German savant to his country, nothing came of it.[32] His death on 1 September 1715 put an end to the controversial and yet splendid reign of the Sun King over whose aggressive policies Leibniz had spilled so much ink. Power was placed in the hands of the Regent, the Duke of Orléans, whose wife, Elisabeth Charlotte, and chief counsellor, Nicolas Rémond, were both enthusiastic admirers of Leibniz; but by then it was already too late to take concrete advantage of such prominent supporters in the city which he had so much regretted leaving when he was young.

During the following spring Leibniz was still battling to finish the *Annales* and be free to devote his last intellectual energies to enterprises closer to his heart. On 27 March 1716 he wrote to Rémond, at the moment I am working to complete my Annals of the Western Empire, which embrace almost three centuries, and these amongst the darkest. I am correcting a large number of points even on the history of France. The work will be ready for printing before the end of the year. I have found the means to resolve almost all of the chronological difficulties. Afterwards, if God leaves me more time, it will be [used] to push forward some lines of inquiry and to develop them as far as demonstration.[33]

Writing to Biber in the summer of 1716 he hinted at his desire to return to the grand plan which he had never abandoned: the youthful *Demonstrationes Catholicae*, subsequently reconceived as the *scientia generalis*, then as the "elements of general philosophy and of natural theology", of which the *characteristica universalis* was the key instrument:[34]

[I]t is only my massive historical work which hinders me from executing my idea of presenting philosophy demonstratively. I hope to finish [the history] this year; and if God gives me more strength thereafter, I will try to discharge myself of certain ideas I still have regarding the advancement of knowledge. For I see that it is possible to develop a general characteristic able of achieving, in all fields of inquiry capable of certainty, what algebra does in mathematics.[35]

Other unfinished business remained on his mind as well: the reunification of the Protestant churches and the achievement of durable peace in Europe; the advancement of the arts and sciences through the patronage of Peter the Great; the improvement of the calculator; and the establishment of a Society of Sciences in Vienna. Regarding Europe, Leibniz was still of the opinion that the best chance for peace would have been the consolidation of a *republica Christiana*, a Christian commonwealth built on the 'federative' model of the Holy Roman Empire, in which the various members, although maintaining a degree of autonomy and independence, found their spiritual unity in a reformed papacy and their political unity in the emperor.[36] In more philosophical terms, this harmonisation of rich diversity in federative unity offered the best solution for the continuous unrest which had plagued Europe throughout the seventeenth century. As for church reunification, Leibniz's perennial hopes had been refreshed by the accession of two new monarchs: Friedrich Wilhelm I (1688–1740), crowned King in Prussia in 1713, and George I of Great Britain and Ireland (1714).

The new Prussian king, although the offspring of a dynasty which had consistently adopted the Reformed religion for a century, was the son and the husband of two Lutheran princesses from Hanover, Sophie Charlotte and Sophie Dorothea, and in 1716 he decided to resurrect the efforts to reconcile the Lutheran and Reformed churches. The move was eagerly supported by Daniel Ernst Jablonski and Leibniz, who personally discussed the matter in Hanover as late as October 1716; and Leibniz in particular saw new hope for this old project in events unfolding simultaneously across the English Channel. During his coronation ceremony in Westminster, George I – ostensibly a loyal Lutheran – had communicated according to the rites of the Church of England, of which he was now the head. As Leibniz argued to Caroline, newly established as princess of Wales, the Lutheran ruler's entrance into the Church of England without a change of religion demonstrated that he regarded the Lutheran and Anglican denominations as differing only in liturgy and in nonessential dogmas not required as articles of faith. Surely the English clergy could also be brought to realize that the Augsburg Confession could accommodate the Anglican liturgy, mending in part the rifts caused by the various European reformations.[37] Moreover, as he pressed further in a second letter on this subject, the English church regarded itself as theologically in agreement with the international Reformed church, in Prussia and elsewhere, and this brought an even more exciting implication in its train: on the basis of the logical principle that "two things being the same with a third, are one with one another", Leibniz triumphantly concluded that the Lutheran church was also basically in agreement with the Reformed confession, because both were in basic agreement with Anglicanism. The Church of England, in short, could therefore provide the missing link necessary to reunite the three main Protestant churches.[38] Sadly, in identifying the essential middle term of this argument, Leibniz appeared to overlook the more likely explanation that George I, in taking his first Anglican communion, simply did not care about the fine points of theology and had merely concluded that, if 'Paris was worth a Mass' to the Huguenot who became Henry IV of France, then London was worth a Eucharist.[39]

Meanwhile, Leibniz continued to cultivate his relationship with Peter the Great, presenting him with further proposals and memos on scientific activities and state administration while the tsar sojourned in Bad Pyrmont during the summer of 1716.[40] This effort was Leibniz's last to gain a powerful patron, yet the project for which he sought patronage was the one which he had pursued since his youth: the systematisation and advancement of the whole encyclopaedia of sciences for the improvement of the human condition. "The improvement of arts and sciences in a great empire," he explained to the tsar, "involves the following: (1) making available the necessary resources; (2) instructing people in the sciences already discovered; (3) the discovery of new information."[41] This final redaction of his plans included a noteworthy emphasis on the importance of the education of children. Leibniz advised that even those who were to be employed in manual work and commercial activities should not leave school until twelve to fourteen years of age – a progressive proposal in an era of widespread and persistent illiteracy, once again reminiscent of Comenius. Within these comprehensive plans for the provision of state education, special mention was again made of the necessity of appropriate training for physicians, surgeons, and pharmacists.[42] The last section of the proposal expounded his ideal of the demonstrative encyclopaedia, intended as the key means for the "discovery of new information." Explicitly following blueprints for the organisation of knowledge envisaged by Keckermann and executed by Alsted, Leibniz proposed a tripartite systematic work including (1) an *encyclopaedia major* consisting in a multivolume universal atlas with illustrations and maps; (2) an *encyclopaedia media* of roughly the scope of Alsted's *Encyclopaedia*; and (3) an *encyclopaedia minor* in the form of an agile handbook recording "the quintessence . . . of useful things", such as existed already for mathematics but not yet for medicine or physics. The heart of this project was clearly the *encyclopaedia media*, conceived not merely as a systematic collection of existing knowledge but as a "demonstrative" and "analytical" work, which would include the proofs and methods of past discoveries and which could therefore lead the way toward new scientific developments.[43] His last, indirect communication with Peter the Great via the tsar's physician, Petr Matveevič Areskine, reported on the satisfactory improvements to his most recent model of the calculating machine.[44] Moreover, during these final years and months, the establishment of societies of sciences continued to be close to Leibniz's heart: his last dated letter, written on 3 November 1716, conveyed his hopes that the Society of Sciences of Berlin would flourish under the patronage of the new king.[45] As for the project of an analogous society in Vienna, the disappointing manner in which it had ground to a halt during his recent visit to the imperial capital did not dissuade Leibniz from continuing to turn the project over in his mind.[46]

In September 1716, however, the unnerving rumour arrived from Vienna that his salary as *Reichshofrat* had been cancelled. Leibniz, who was still toying with the idea of returning to Vienna the following year, wrote with alarm to the dowager empress, Amalie, and to her lady-in-waiting,

Mlle. Klencke.[47] The reassuring letter of the Imperial counsellor, Karl Gust. Heraeus, was sadly too late to bring Leibniz any comfort: it was written in Vienna on 18 November 1716, four days after Leibniz's death. At that point, only two decades were missing before the planned end of the *Annales* with the year 1024, and not a single page of them had appeared in print. Only with the three-volume publication of the *Annales* in 1843–6 by Georg Heinrich Pertz did the real magnitude of Leibniz's historical achievement begin to come to light. In clear and economical language the *Annales* presented a history of the Empire in the Middle Ages compressed seamlessly from an enormous mass of information drawn directly from the historical sources.[48] Any other scholar might well have regarded this impressive work as his most important contribution to the world of learning. Yet it is scarcely remembered amongst Leibniz's achievements, eclipsed by so many other brilliant discoveries and innovations. Although unfinished, its final words were, not inappropriately, a reference to further matters "which I leave to the industry of others to retrieve from the darkness."[49]

Last Battles with Newton and the Newtonians

Even after Leibniz returned to Hanover in September 1714, the venomous quarrel on the calculus still had plenty of sting in its tail. Leibniz was finally able to see for himself the *Commercium Epistolicum*, a copy of which had been sent after publication to his Hanoverian address.[50] Moreover, he was still settling in after almost two years of absence when Wolff informed him of the publication, in the Dutch *Journal Literaire* of July–August 1714, of the acrid *Réponse* to Leibniz's own *Remarques* by Keill, who also attacked Leibniz's *Tentamen de Motuum caelestium Causis*.[51] Appalled by the "impudence of the man" and suspecting that he was fighting with weapons supplied by Newton himself, Wolff urged Leibniz "to show, by way of reply, the true origin and nature of the differential calculus."[52] Leibniz toyed with this suggestion, and even drafted a *Historia et origo calculi differentialis*. Amongst other things, in it he recounted that, being away from home in Vienna and then distracted by many activities in Hanover, he did not have the opportunity and the time to search for the relevant papers and defend himself on the basis of his own documents.[53] Eventually, however, he abandoned the idea of publishing his own *Commercium Epistolicum*. Wolff nevertheless persevered in his plea for an answer to Keill, fearing that some people might "conclude from [Leibniz's] silence that the arguments of the English are truly insurmountable."[54] On 2 April 1715 Leibniz answered that he could not bring himself "to reply to that rude man Keill": what he wrote was scarcely worth reading.[55] Still Wolff did not give up: in May he pointed out that the French were also expecting a reply.[56] On 18 May 1715 Leibniz put his foot down: almost uniquely within his immense correspondence, his response to Wolff oozed unmitigated contempt and exasperation towards a fellow human being:

Since Keill writes like a bumpkin, I wish to have no dealings with a man of that sort. It is pointless to write for those who respond only to his bold assertions and boasting, for they do not examine the substance. . . . I think of knocking the man down, some time, with things rather than words. . . . I myself, considering Keill's rudeness, have not yet thought the paper worthy of a thorough reading.[57]

In an annotation to a further letter by Wolff dated 28 July 1715, Leibniz remarked,

I don't know whether I should answer Keill, whose writing is rude and uncivil. It is not my habit to wrestle with such people. I prefer an antagonist to write in such a way that the dispute between us can be joined with pleasure. If some people draw perverse conclusions from my silence, I care little for their judgement.[58]

Wolff could not but graciously concede that, after all, Leibniz was right in refusing to pay attention to a man like Keill.[59] Meanwhile, in the spring of 1715 Newton's anonymous "Account" of the *Commercium Epistolicum* had appeared in the *Philosophical Transactions* for February 1715, causing a new, painful blow to Leibniz's pride.[60]

Keill and Newton's public attacks might well have played a part in his decision to mention for the first time to the Princess of Wales his controversy with Newton and the Newtonians. In a letter to Caroline of 10 May 1715, Leibniz aired his resentment against them, giving to the matter the spin of a nationalistic confrontation between England and Germany with political undertones. His nomination to historiographer of Great Britain – Leibniz argued – offered the perfect opportunity for honouring Hanover and Germany while deflating the arrogance of the English. Moreover, the new philosophy of Newton was "a bit odd": his gravitational attraction with its action at a distance introduced a miraculous element into the explanation of natural events. How then did these people dare to charge the Lutheran Eucharistic doctrine of the real presence with absurdity following their "spirit of contrariety to the house of Hanover"? As for

Locke, he had spoken "with contempt" of Leibniz's remarks on the *Essay on Human Understanding* while proposing all the while a materialistic philosophy in which matter is endowed with thought.[61] Alas, Leibniz's proposal to throw religious disputes and philosophical polemics, political controversies and personal offences into the pot and to mix them energetically together by means of an unsavory confrontation between opposed national prides was at best unwise, and certainly unpromising. Without Leibniz's help, George I had already managed to arouse more than enough unpopularity with his subjects, who suspected him of favouring German interests. As for the Princess of Wales and her husband, they were working hard to gain the trust of their new adoptive country. Accordingly, in her response Caroline did not pick up Leibniz's implicit invitation to set the contentious points in the context of an Anglo-German confrontation, but steered the discussion onto the more interesting territory of the philosophical and theological doctrines of Locke, Newton, and Samuel Clarke (1675-1729).

Dr. Clarke was a divine of the Church of England who served for a time as court chaplain to Queen Anne and, from 1709, as the rector of Newton's parish at St. James's, Piccadilly. In 1704 and 1705 he was appointed to deliver the prestigious Boyle lectures. Although the suspicion of antitrinitarianism caused his fall from grace in the eyes of Queen Anne and his removal from his position of court chaplain, Clarke continued to enjoy esteem and reputation in ecclesiastical and learned circles. An acute and clear thinker, he had been recommended to Caroline by her friend and mentor, the Bishop of Lincoln and later Archbishop of Canterbury, William Wake, as the only person able to carry forward a pet project of the Princess and of her German protégé, the translation of the *Theodicy* into English. Caroline, however, could not fail to notice that Clarke was far too close to Newton and Newton's opinions to serve Leibniz well as a translator: indeed, the English cleric could be regarded as the most capable Newtonian philosopher of his generation.[62] Although his primary intellectual interests lay in natural religion and related philosophical issues, he had enough competence in science and mathematics to translate into Latin the standard textbook of Cartesian physics – the *Traité de physique* of Jacques Rohault (1618-72) – and did the same in 1706 for Newton's *Opticks*.[63]

"Neither Dr Clarke nor Newton want to be included in Mr Locke's party," Caroline confided to Leibniz; "but I cannot, nor do I wish to be, a member of their party. They have a different notion of the soul: they say that God can annihilate the soul. . . . I am of a completely different opinion. I believe that God has made souls immortal."[64] The natural immortality of the soul was of course one of Leibniz's central tenets as well. Implored by Caroline to come to her "aid" because she was "in dispute" with Clarke,[65] Leibniz charged into the fray. In a paper of November 1715 sent to the Princess of Wales, he castigated the "extreme weakening of natural religion in England." The causes of this deplorable state of affairs were spelled out with decisiveness:

1. Many maintain that souls are corporeal; others that God himself is corporeal. 2. Mr Locke and his faction are at least uncertain whether souls are material and naturally perishable. 3. Mr Newton says that space is the organ which God uses to perceive things. . . . 4. . . . According to [Mr Newton and his followers], God needs to rewind his watch from time to time: otherwise its action would stop. He did not have enough foresight to make it a perpetual motion. According to them, in fact, this machine of God is so imperfect that he is forced to clean it from time to time by an extraordinary concourse, and even to repair it, like a watchmaker with his handiwork, who is a worse workman the more he is forced to touch up and rectify it. In my view, the same force and vigour always subsist in it. . . . To think otherwise would be to have a very low opinion of the wisdom and power of God.[66]

Caroline passed Leibniz's paper to Clarke for comment, and with that the famous Leibniz–Clarke correspondence was underway.[67] Between November 1715 and October 1716, five papers from Leibniz and five papers from Clarke passed through the hands of the Princess of Wales, who acted as the intermediary between the two learned men. Although Newton had some indirect involvement in the correspondence, possibly advising Clarke on some points under discussion, the English mathematician was not as interested as Clarke himself in unveiling the metaphysical implications of his ongoing dispute with Leibniz.[68] Clarke's last paper, transmitted by Caroline to Leibniz on 29 October 1716, arrived too late to receive any kind of answer. From 6 November until his death on 14 November Leibniz was bedridden, plagued by gout and arthritis, and unable to write.[69]

For all their disagreements, both Leibniz and Clarke were firm advocates of natural religion against the reduction of nature to a self-sufficient mechanism independent of God; but they had very different ideas on how to counter the ultimately atheistic attack mounted by naturalism. Indeed, Clarke went so far as to claim that, however pious Leibniz's intentions

may have been, he ended up excluding God from his universe. By presenting God as a skilful clockmaker who constructed the clockwork of the
world with such perfection that it continued indefinitely without need of
mending or rewinding, Clarke argued, Leibniz opened the door to "the
notion of materialism and fate." The ultimate result was nothing less than
atheism, since the Leibnizian conception of God as a permanently absen-
tee monarch was only a small step away from regarding the king as useless
and eliminating him altogether.[70] In Clarke's view, Newton's alternative
conception, in which the correct functioning of the world mechanism
required the continual intervention and direction of God, restored the
absolute sovereignty of God over the universe.

Leibniz naturally rejected Clarke's accusations. First, he claimed, the
omnipotent and omniscient God of the Christian tradition could not be
reduced to an unskilled clockmaker who continuously needed to mend and
rewind his handiwork. Second, the fact that the divinely created world-
mechanism did not need correction did not imply that the world could
go on without God. On the contrary, embracing a traditional Thomistic
doctrine, Leibniz maintained that God conserved everything in being
so that nothing could subsist without him.[71] The physical autonomy of
the world mechanism once it had been created did not imply its metaphysical independence from God. In other words, Leibniz resolutely
shifted the dependence of the universe on God from the physical to the
metaphysical level, proposing a radical ontological dependency which
was much more robust than the physical dependency on which Clarke
insisted. In Leibniz's view, God was not only the creator of what exists
but also the source of its conservation in being and the very "root of
possibility."[72] Without the ideas (or essences) of all possible things being
present from all eternity as thoughts in God's mind, not only would nothing be existent, but nothing would even be possible. Contrary to Clarke's
suspicion that the world-clock could continue its regular ticking even if
God was eliminated from the Leibnizian universe, the whole edifice of
Leibniz's ontology strictly required the presence of God as the substantial support of the ideas or archetypes of all possible things and, consequently, as the ultimate foundation of those possible things which actually
exist.[73]

In the process of defending their opposite views regarding the need
of direct divine intervention for the correct functioning of the physical
mechanism, Leibniz and Clarke disputed a wide range of interrelated

issues. Leibniz, for his part, rejected the void and Newtonian gravitation as an occult or miraculous force acting at a distance, proposed his conception of space and time as having a purely relational nature (the one being "an order of coexistences", the other "an order of successions"),[74] opposed Newton's notion of space as *sensorium Dei* (that is, as a sort of organ needed by God to perceive things), reiterated his doctrine of the conservation of the quantity of motive force or *vis viva* (implying, amongst other things, that the world-clock did not gradually wind down), tied contingency to his principle of sufficient reason, and adamantly rebuked the notion of an extended soul interacting with the body. Clarke, by contrast, defended the void and gravitation, embraced the notion of absolute space, accused Leibniz of destroying the contingency of nature and God's free will, and stood by his notion of an extended and yet immaterial soul.

In this by no means exhaustive catalogue of philosophical–theological issues at stake in the dispute, the exchange on the ontological status of space and time is especially famous. Leibniz's attack on the doctrine of absolute space and time was based on theological as well as philosophical principles. Theologically, Leibniz argued, the hypothesis of absolute space and time was unacceptable because either there would be something eternal and absolute in addition to God or space and time would have to be properties *of* God. No orthodox Christian could accept either alternative: the first option implied the eternal existence of some aspects of creation outside the Creator, whereas the second implied that God has parts and therefore denied divine simplicity. Philosophically, Leibniz continued, the existence of absolute space and time clashed with the principles of sufficient reason and the identity of indiscernibles. In absolute space and time, "one point of space" would not "differ in any respect whatsoever from another point of space." In absolute time, two instants would likewise be indiscernible from one another. As a consequence, God would not have a sufficient reason for placing bodies in space "after one particular manner, and not otherwise" or for creating at one time rather than another. On the other hand, conceiving space and time as purely relations amongst things – and therefore as mental entities which do not exist outside the mind considering the order of coexistence and the order of succession of things – would raise none of these problems.[75]

Caroline, who had entered the fray as Leibniz's philosophical disciple, gradually warmed to Clarke's arguments and shifted from a resolute partisan of the views of her German friend to the role of an impartial facilitator of the discussion.[76] Leibniz was not pleased, not least because he felt he needed all the support he could muster across the Channel for countering his Newtonian opponents. For this reason, in the letter to Caroline in which he included his second paper for Clarke, he mentioned the arrival in England of a learned Venetian noble, the Abbé Antonio Conti (1677–1748; alias Antonio Schinella). Conti had written to him from France declaring that he was firmly on his side and would not fail "to uphold his cause in England as he had done in Paris."[77] Leibniz was hoping that he could liaise with Caroline and join forces in his support. By 10 January 1716, Caroline had met Conti and the two of them offered themselves as mediators in the dispute with Newton.[78] On 25 February, Leibniz not only thanked Caroline for the offer but also handed over his olive branch, proposing very reasonable conditions of peace. In essence, they consisted of the official acknowledgment that he was not a callous plagiarist. In his view "this reconciliation can be accomplished" since all the noise was made not by Newton but by "a certain man" (Keill) who was "not considered to be one of the best regulated." If his opponents had been content to maintain that

> Mr Newton was the first to discover the calculus, although he gave no knowledge or hint of it to anyone, I would not be worried, since that is perfectly possible. But it seems that they went so far as to attack my good faith, as if I had learned it from him and had disguised this fact. In order to do me justice, it would therefore be necessary for the Royal Society to declare that there was no intention of casting doubts on my integrity, and that no one will be permitted to do so.[79]

For his part the Abbé Conti had already launched into his mission of peace, acting as intermediary in an epistolary exchange between Leibniz and Newton. In the extensive postscript to a letter to Conti of 6 December 1715, Leibniz laid down for Newton's eyes his remonstrations concerning the *Commercium Epistolicum* and his objections to Newton's philosophy of nature.[80] Newton – who had been, quite rightly, exceedingly annoyed by the *Charta Volans* – replied via Conti in March 1716 defending the *Commercium Epistolicum* as "matter of fact and uncapable of an Answer", while dismissing Leibniz's philosophical objections.[81] Such an unpromising beginning was unlikely to bring about reconciliation. On 9 April 1716, Leibniz penned a long letter (intended for Newton) in his own defence.[82] On the same day he sent a copy to Rémond lamenting the fact that Conti, far from being an impartial mediator, seemed to be increasingly taking

Newton's side.[83] The same complaint landed on Caroline's desk. In a letter of 12 May he wrote to her,

[Conti] is a bit fickle toward me, and I signalled this to him with an answer as dry as his letter.[84] But it doesn't matter. He does not appear to have firm principles, and is like a chameleon which takes (it is said) the colour of the things it touches.... When my answer to Mr Newton's letter appears, people will discover that the bases of his claims against me are imaginary facts and that what can be alleged against him is only too real.[85]

Caroline was decidedly exasperated by Leibniz's either-with-me-or-against-me attitude: "I beg you to use your time in a more profitable way than to dispute with one another," she replied.[86] On 26 June 1716 she insisted: "I regret seeing people of your worth quarrelling for the vanity that you should destroy through the goodness of your reasoning. What does it matter whether you or Sir Newton have discovered the calculus? You are the great men of our age."[87] The Princess definitely had a point, but things had become so sour between Leibniz and Newton by this stage that neither of them seemed to listen any more.

In July 1716, Conti travelled to Hanover with the entourage of George I on the occasion of the king's first trip back to Germany.[88] On 10 December 1716, he reported from Hanover to Newton, "Mr Leibniz is dead and the dispute is finished", proceeding to summarise the dead man's life in such an uncharitable way as to reveal Leibniz's description of him as "a bit fickle" as a charitable understatement: "Mr Leibniz laboured all his life to invent machines which did not work. He wanted to build a kind of windmill for the mines, a carriage moved without horses.[89] ... There are two models of his arithmetical machine, but it is very complicated and they say that it is ultimately nothing but a multiplied version of Pascal's machine."[90] Worse still, the dispute was far from finished. Leibniz's demise did not appease Newton's animosity against him. The partisans of the eminent English mathematician zealously carried forward war beyond death.[91]

Unending Progress

Although the history of the Guelfs consumed most of the last two years of Leibniz's life, some energy was left for other reflections. It was in fact only comparatively that his production of philosophical papers and correspondence diminished somewhat. By almost any standard but his own, his philosophical activities remained truly remarkable even during this last, difficult period. In particular, he turned his attention once again to China and its theological and philosophical tradition, and commented upon the work of George Berkeley (1685–1753). Last but not least, one short year before taking leave of this world he broadened his vision to horizons beyond it, pausing for eschatological contemplation of the future state of all things.

Alongside Clarke, two of the people with whom he maintained regular philosophical correspondence were his friends and admirers, Des Bosses and Rémond. It was in a letter to Des Bosses of 15 March 1715 that Leibniz formulated his most famous criticism of Berkeley: "We correctly maintain that bodies are things [res], for phenomena are also realities [realia]. . . . The man in Ireland who opposes the reality of bodies seems neither to provide convincing reasons nor to explain his view sufficiently. I suspect him to be one of those men who want to be known for their paradoxes."[92] But despite the differences between the Irishman's views and his own, Leibniz realized that his philosophy shared common ground with Berkeley's. In fact, he noted on his own copy of Berkeley's *Treatise Concerning the Principles of Human Knowledge* (Dublin 1710), "Many things here are correct and agree with my views." But the Irishman's doctrines were unnecessarily paradoxical:

For we do not need to say that matter is nothing: it suffices to say that it is a phenomenon like the rainbow. Nor [do we need to assert] that [matter] is a substance, but a result of substances. . . . The true substances are monads or perceivers.[93]

Although it was true, as Berkeley maintained, that bodies were not substances, they could not be dismissed as nothing. They were phenomena resulting from the only true substances (or monads) and, as such, were endowed with their own degree of reality.

Des Bosses had also been the recipient of a series of remarks on "Chinese rites and religion" appended to a letter addressed to the Jesuit savant on 12 August 1709.[94] In turn, both Des Bosses and Rémond learned from Leibniz in January 1716 that he had written a "discourse on the natural theology of the Chinese" which was "almost a small treatise."[95] The occasion of this work had been provided by Rémond himself who, a few months earlier, had sent him the works of two prominent missionaries in China, the Jesuit Nicolas Longobardi (1565–1655) and the Franciscan

Antonio Caballero de Santa Maria (or, as Leibniz referred to him, Antoine de Sainte Marie) (1602–69).[96] Rémond, who had read their works, was eager to hear what Leibniz had to say about them;[97] but despite the announcement in January that the *Discours sur la Theologie naturelle des Chinois* was complete, on 27 March 1716 Leibniz confessed to Rémond that he needed a bit more freedom to put the finishing touches to it.[98] Possibly instigated by the wish expressed by Des Bosses in a letter of 7 March 1716 that the *Discours* would also comment on the philosophy of Fu-Hsi,[99] Leibniz had decided that his treatise needed more work. Unfortunately, neither freedom nor time were forthcoming in the following few months of his life, and his most important philosophical work on China remained on his desk buried in the pile of many other unfinished projects.

In the *Discours*, arguing against Longobardi and Santa Maria, Leibniz defended the so-called accommodationist position championed by the Jesuit Matteo Ricci (1552–1610).[100] Virtually alone amongst the Jesuits, Longobardi shared the views of most Dominicans and Franciscans (including Santa Maria) that Chinese religion and cultural traditions were fundamentally incompatible with Christianity due to their materialism and atheism. In contrast, Leibniz (following Ricci) claimed the presence in ancient Chinese tradition of key elements consonant with Christian doctrine, notably belief in God and in spiritual substances. In order to convert China to Christianity, Chinese rites and religion needed to be accommodated as much as possible, acknowledging in them fragments of a universal religious truth which found its expression in their ancient natural theology.[101] After expounding the traditional views of God, His productions (that is, matter and spirits), and the human soul, Leibniz concluded his "small treatise" reiterating the importance of the parallelism he saw between his dyadic and the hexagrams of the ancient Chinese *Book of Changes* in the context of a justification of the doctrines of the ancient Chinese tradition.[102]

Chinese natural theology was not the only exotic doctrine to capture Leibniz's attention during his last months. Despite the urgency of his historical work, he stole precious moments to meticulously revise and improve the monumental cosmogonical verse epic about divine matters produced at his own encouragement by an old acquaintance, the controversial millenarian Johann Wilhelm Petersen.[103] Leibniz had instigated the idea of this massive poetic project nearly a decade earlier in response to some verses by Petersen sent to him in the autumn of 1706 by Johann Fabricius.[104] This work, which he thought only Petersen capable of composing, should "celebrate in Virgilian measure the city of God and the life eternal."[105] The first part would deal with "God, sufficient in his perpetual and secret eternity; then the creation of the cosmos; and finally the workings of providence in governing the world . . . the second part should treat the future as it pertains to the body and the soul. Here the purification of souls and the restitution of all things, or rather their gradual improvement and elevation, could be discussed . . . the last, but not the least, part of the work will concern the grandeur of the celestial kingdom."[106] Petersen responded to the challenge and in the winter of 1711–12 his massive *Uranias*, in fifteen books of roughly one thousand verses each, landed on Leibniz's desk. Although initially delighted to see it, Leibniz gradually became dismayed to discover that the poem, written in haste, needed many changes and improvements.[107] Unwilling to see it either abandoned or published in such a state, Leibniz – whose first indications of brilliance had been in Latin verse – started amending it himself, though he eventually refused to get directly involved in the revision of the last book, devoted to the doctrine of the *Apokatastasis pantōn*, or (as he himself translated the Greek phrase) the "restitution of all things."[108] His long stay in Vienna in 1712–14 interrupted his work, but upon returning to Hanover he resumed the task. On 15 January 1715 he wrote to Fabricius, "I have expended much effort upon it, in order to polish and recall to order a thing far too quickly written. So I have changed numberless things and sometimes entire pages."[109] In July 1716 he finally returned Petersen's manuscript, urging that more revision was needed.[110]

Leibniz's decision to devote so much effort to Petersen's work at the very moment at which his determination to complete the Guelf history had persuaded him to sideline other interests indicates the extraordinary importance which he attached to this epic poem. Poetry had always figured high in Leibniz's estimation as a powerful means which, through the employment of concrete, vivid, and imaginative language, could move and motivate men far beyond the nonemotive, rational language of philosophy or the abstract formalism of mathematics. Indeed, the primary object of natural language in his view was the *affectus*, that is, the expression of our apprehension of the world via the emotional and sensitive aspects of human nature.[111] When expressed in the metaphorical and evocative language of poetry, moreover, doctrines which were not literally true could be employed to convey truths not easily grasped by nonphilosophers. An outstanding example of this distinctive power of poetry was the employment of the doctrine of the *Apokatastasis pantōn*. Leibniz did not regard as literally true this doctrine of Origenist origin, which expected the final return of all beings to their original state of perfection before the Fall and the universal salvation of all souls.[112] Nevertheless he did not condemn it either, tending to regard it as a metaphor for the "gradual improvement and elevation" of all things or, in other words, for the unending progress in which God's glory was manifested in His creation.[113] At some point during the spring or early summer of 1715, during the last period of work on Petersen's *Uranias*, he decided to reformulate the doctrine of the *Apokatastasis* for himself, penning two versions of a meditation "about the revolution or palingenesis of all things, which would be necessary if humankind were to endure for sufficient time in its present state."[114] In this meditation, a prima facie acceptance of the (pagan) notion of eternal return was bent into the opposite thesis. According to Leibniz, what might appear to be the repetition of identical circumstances was not and could not be the eternal return of all things, due to the fact that individual substances involve the infinite. To the eye able to appreciate the infinite detail of concrete beings and the infinite truths of fact which can be enunciated about them, there is no such thing as a finite number of circumstances which (no matter how great their number) ought to result in a finite number of combinations: "even if a previous century returns for what concerns things which can be sensed [quoad sensibilia] or which can be described by books, it will not return completely in all respects [non tamen redibit omnino quoad omnia]: since there will always be differences although imperceptible and such that could not be sufficiently described in any book [semper enim forent discrimina etsi imperceptibilia et quae nullis satis libris describi possint]."[115] Leibniz's conclusion was that there is, in fact, unending progress towards the best rather than an eternal return: "And for this reason it could be the case that things gradually although imperceptibly progress for the better after the revolutions."[116] As he had suggested some fourteen years earlier in a fragment datable around February–March 1701, the best image to describe this notion of progress was a spiral: "And thus it would be agreeable . . . that the same human being should be brought back not simply by returning to the earth but as if through a spiral or winding way, thence progressing to something greater. This is to go back to leap better forward, as at a ditch."[117] In short, the spiral graphically reconciled the concept of cyclical return with that of unending progress. In Leibniz's view, even the supreme happiness of the beatific vision consisted, not in a static permanence in a final state, but in this unending progress toward the best:

It is true that supreme happiness (irrespective of the *beatifical vision* or knowledge of God which may accompany it) could never be complete because God, being infinite, can never be fully known. Thus our happiness will never consist, and should not consist, in complete satisfaction, where there is nothing else to desire, which would render our mind stupid, but in a perpetual progress to new pleasures and new perfections.[118]

Leibniz turned this metaphysical vision into his own way of living: as he had written nearly a decade earlier in November 1705, "Tranquillity is a step on the path toward stupidity.... One should always find something to do, to think, to plan, concerning ourselves for the community and for the individual, yet in such a way that we can rejoice if our wishes are fulfilled and not be saddened if they are not."[119]

Inclinata Resurget

"The line which declines will rise again" – *inclinata resurget*: with these words symbolized by a spiral and engraved on his coffin Leibniz was accompanied to his eternal rest by a handful of people amidst the general indifference of the city and court of Hanover. Yet the motto and the spiral on his coffin could hardly have been more appropriate. The inescapable pathos of his decline in the cold isolation of Hanover with innumerable unfinished and unpublished projects on his hands was to be relieved by the seemingly inexhaustible fecundity of his thought for the philosophical and scientific progress of future generations.

At the end of July 1716, George I had returned to his German dominions for a visit which kept him away from London for six months. The day after the king's arrival in Hanover on 26 July, Leibniz dined at his table. George I was in good spirits and remarked that Leibniz was not as cheerful as he used to be.[120] Around mid-September Leibniz confirmed to Caroline that he was working hard on the Guelf history, which he expected to occupy him for a good part of the following year: "So I do not hope to be able to go to England soon.... Since I do not hope for it soon, I do not know whether I can hope for it afterward; because for me there are not many 'afterwards' to hope for."[121] Leibniz had turned seventy on 1 July and seemed to know that his time was running out. A month and a half later he fell seriously ill. On 6 November 1716, gout and arthritis forced him to bed, suspending any writing.[122] During the following days, after the administration of a remedy suggested to him by a Jesuit in Vienna, Leibniz suffered from strong colic which compelled him to give up reading as well. Assisted by his amanuensis, Johann Hermann Vogler, and his coachman, Henrich, on the evening of Friday 13 November he consented to seek the advice of a doctor, apparently following Eckhart's counsel. Eckhart recalled visiting Leibniz during the day, hoping to do some work on the Guelf history, but had found his condition worryingly worsened. Although Leibniz had previously insisted that nobody should be informed of his illness, he agreed to see Dr Johann Philipp Seip, whom he had recently met in Bad Pyrmont, who was by chance in Hanover. Dr Seip prescribed a medicine which helped Leibniz somewhat through the night. The following day, calling around noon, Dr Seip prescribed further remedies. Given Leibniz's worsening condition, Vogler suggested he call a pastor and the lawyer Hennings, who lived in the same house; but Leibniz gently declined, replying that it could wait until the next day. In the evening, hearing Leibniz tearing apart some paper, Vogler hurried back to the bedroom to find him holding the paper in the flame of his bedside candle. Fearing that it would catch fire, he removed it from Leibniz's hands. Meanwhile the coachman returned. Around 10 pm the two men became aware of the peaceful death of Leibniz, who quietly slipped away in his sleep.

Vogler informed Leibniz's secretary, Eckhart, who took care of all the formalities. On 15 November Leibniz's Nachlaß was officially put under seal. In the evening, Leibniz's body was taken, in a provisional coffin, to the Neustädter Kirche, where the coffin was covered in sand awaiting a proper burial. Eckhart travelled to Göhrde, a hunting lodge not far from Hanover where George I was staying, to communicate to the king the news of Leibniz's death.[123] On 26 November, after the arrival of Leibniz's only heir (his nephew Friedrich Simon Löffler), a first stock of Leibniz's possessions was taken. In addition to his private library, manuscripts, and calculating machine, a black box containing money and securities possibly totalling some 12,000 talers was found and promptly claimed by Löffler. Books, manuscripts, and calculator were retained by the Königliche Bibliothek in Hanover.[124]

Leibniz's burial was conducted on 14 December in the Neustädter Kirche by the Chief Court Chaplain, H. Erythropel. The new coffin, prepared following Eckhart's instructions, was richly decorated with symbols and sentences.[125] In addition to Leibniz's coat of arms, his date of death, his titles, some verses by Horace, and the motto "Inclinata resurget" symbolized by a spiral,[126] these included Leibniz's motto "Part of life dies whenever a hour is lost", the symbol of the dyadic (the number one inscribed within a zero) with the heading "Omnia ad unum", an image of a rising eagle looking at the sun with the heading "It draws light from the light", and a depiction of a burning phoenix, the mythical bird which is born again from its ashes, with the heading "The ashes will retain the honour."[127] Leibniz's friend Ker of Kersland, who arrived in Hanover the very day of Leibniz's death, bitterly commented,

I must Confess, it afforded me Matter of strange Reflection, when I perceived the little Regard that was paid to his Ashes by the *Hanoverians*; for he was buried in a few Days after his Decease, more like a *Robber* than, what he really was, the Ornament of his Country.[128]

Ker certainly overstated the case, in all probability mistaking for Leibniz's funeral the quiet translation of his coffin to the Neustädter Kirche on the evening of 15 November. This translation was not unusual and did not represent a sign of disregard for Leibniz. On the contrary, the burial of important people normally took place quite some time after their death to give time to prepare an ornate coffin and a proper ceremony. Nevertheless, there can be little doubt that the funeral celebrated on 14 December was a far cry from the honour due to a man of Leibniz's stature. Whereas some eleven years later Newton was buried like a national hero in Westminster Abbey, no one from the court apart from the duplicitous Eckhart came to pay Leibniz their last respects[129] – and this despite the fact that the king was still in Göhrde, within easy reach of Hanover. Moreover, neither the Society of Sciences of Berlin nor the Royal Society of London thought fit to honour Leibniz with an official commemoration. Only at the Académie Royale des Sciences was an "Éloge" read by Fontenelle on 13 November 1717 – the product it seems of initiatives by Leibniz's great admirer, the duchess of Orléans, who had solicited for this purpose a short biographical account from Eckhart.[130]

Sadly, this first biographer was far from being a trustworthy friend to the German savant. The day before Leibniz's death – after the elderly man had already been forced to bed for eight days and Eckhart himself, noting that he was no longer as lucid as usual, had urged that a physician be called at once[131] – Eckhart had written a letter to Minister Bernstorff intimating that, given the opportunity of a new pension by a powerful patron, Leibniz would have sprung out of his bed. As for the history of the Guelfs, Eckhart continued, it would never be finished, "because he is far too much distracted; and since he wants to do everything and to be involved in everything, he can finish nothing, not even if he had angels as assistants. If it should please your royal Majesty to retain me [in your service], you will certainly soon see the difference."[132] In death, of course, everyone becomes a saint; and Eckhart's biographical account was appropriately laudatory. Yet it reported the suspicion circulating amongst Hanover's common folk that Leibniz was at heart a *Loevenix* – a "believes nothing" – due to his irregular church attendance and his very infrequent participation in holy communion. Although Leibniz's coachman reported that he had communicated during the plague outbreak in Vienna, Eckhart claimed never to have seen such a thing in nineteen years.[133] Clearly this was out of keeping with the precedent, established by George I, of communicating according to whatever denomination happened to fit one's purposes; but whether abstemious or indiscriminate participation in the sacraments was the clearer testimony of sincere conviction does not seem to have been considered by those courtiers who questioned Leibniz's commitment to the Christian religion. In Leibniz's extant texts from his earlier years rang unmistakable tones of genuine fervour. The extent of his Christian piety in later periods remains inscrutable. While he continued to regard the institution of the church as a necessary structure for the European religious and political world, he did not seem to consider its practices as essential for his own commitment to the Christian religion.[134] Nor, on the other hand, did he ever call seriously into doubt the truth of the Christian religion, whether in public or in private. Rather, for him Christianity seems to have been a given – a datum which lay at the very foundation of the Western world and which he was happy to accept and hold (often pragmatically) as true because, in his view, there were no philosophical grounds for rejecting its fundamental tenets. Indeed, in his own view his philosophical system supported and confirmed the Christian doctrines. His acceptance of Christianity, far from being duplicitous lip service paid to powerful patrons, was inextricably interwoven with his philosophical doctrines and his practical endeavours.[135] When, a year after Leibniz's death, Fontenelle attempted to summarize for the Académie Royale des Sciences the bewilderingly various endeavours of its recently deceased German fellow, he might have been helped by Leibniz's own formula for pulling together the numerous threads of his extraordinary life's work: "all these things are connected and have to be directed to the same aim, which is the glory of God and the advancement of the public good by means of useful works and beautiful discoveries."[136]

Notes

1. Ἀποκατάστασις, 1715, in G. W. Leibniz, *De l'horizon de la doctrine humaine. Ἀποκατάστασις πάντων (La Restitution Universelle)*. Ed. by Michel Fichant. Paris: Vrin, 1991, p. 74; see also p. 109, n. 4. In the letter to Sophie of 6 February 1706 (GP VII, 568) Leibniz used the same metaphor of retracing one's footsteps in order to leap further.

2. See Leibniz to the Empress Amalie, 16 September 1714 (Klopp XI, 8–9); Leibniz to the Electoral Prince Georg August, 17 September 1714 (Klopp XI, 9–11); Leibniz to Ker of Kersland, 8 October 1714 (in Ker of Kersland, *Memoirs*, [Part I] p. 100).

3. See Klopp XI, 9–11 and 12–14.

4. Klopp XI, 10.

5. See Leibniz to the president of the Imperial court counsellors, Ernst Friedrich von Windischgrätz, 20 September 1714 (Klopp XI, xxi). See also Leibniz to C. A. Bonneval, 21 September 1714 (Klopp XI, 14–15).

6. See Ker of Kersland, *Memoirs*, [Part I] p. 100.

7. See J. G. Eckhart to A. G. von Bernstorff, 8 October 1714 (Bodemann, "Nachträge zu 'Leibnizens Briefwechsel mit dem Minister v. Bernstorff und andere Leibniz betr. Briefe,'" pp. 161–2). Eckhart also kept Bernstorff informed about Leibniz's movements (cf. ibid., pp. 162–3).

8. In a letter of 11 February 1715 to Nicolas Rémond, Leibniz gave his precarious health and recent attacks of gout as the reason for his failure to go with Caroline to London (see GP III, 634). Although this might well have compounded his difficulties, still greater obstacles to moving to London were George I's prohibition of travel and Bernstorff's specific instruction to stay in Hanover to finish to Guelf history (see below). In any case, at the time of Caroline's departure on 12 October, his health did not prevent him from planning to travel to Braunschweig and Helmstedt on 13 or 14 October (cf. Müller–Krönert, *Leben und Werk*, p. 248).

9. Klopp XI, 19.

10. See Leibniz to C. A. Bonneval, 21 September 1714 (Klopp XI, 14). For a different interpretation of the facts see the lively account of the correspondence between Leibniz and Caroline by Gregory Brown ("Personal, Political, and Philosophical Dimensions of the Leibniz-Caroline Correspondence." In *Leibniz and His*

Correspondents. Ed. by Paul Lodge. Cambridge: Cambridge University Press, 2004, pp. 262–92 (esp. pp. 264–5, 267–8).

11. Leibniz to Caroline, undated (Klopp XI, 19–20). See also Klopp XI, 14 and 42.

12. Klopp XI, 20. Cf. Leibniz to Bernstorff, 8 December 1714 (Klopp XI, 24) and Leibniz to Caroline, 29 March 1715 (Klopp XI, 36).

13. Klopp XI, 22. See also George I to the government in Hanover, 30 November 1714 (in Doebner, "Leibnizens Briefwechsel mit dem Minister von Bernstorff," p. 297). In January 1715 rumours were still circulating in Paris that Leibniz had gone to London with Caroline (see Nicolas Rémond to Leibniz, January 1715; GP III, 630).

14. See Leibniz to Bernstorff, 8 December 1714 (Klopp XI, 22–4). See also Leibniz to Bernstorff, 15 March 1715 (Doebner, "Leibnizens Briefwechsel mit dem Minister von Bernstorff," p. 313). On Azzo II see chap. II. 5.

15. See Doebner, "Leibnizens Briefwechsel mit dem Minister von Bernstorff," pp. 301–4.

16. See "Rescript König Georg I an die Regierung zu Hannover," 1 January 1715 (in Doebner, "Leibnizens Briefwechsel mit dem Minister von Bernstorff," pp. 308–9).

17. Bodemann, "Nachträge zu 'Leibnizens Briefwechsel mit dem Minister v. Bernstorff und andere Leibniz betr. Briefe,'" p. 163.

18. See "Rescript König Georg I an die Regierung zu Hannover," 21 February 1716 (in Doebner, "Leibnizens Briefwechsel mit dem Minister von Bernstorff," pp. 362–4).

19. Klopp XI, 36.

20. See Caroline to Leibniz, 16 January and 12 February 1715 (Klopp XI, 32 and 34–5).

21. See Bodemann, *Handschriften*, p. 185.

22. Doebner, "Leibnizens Briefwechsel mit dem Minister von Bernstorff," pp. 333–4. Quoted in Müller–Krönert, *Leben und Werk*, p. 253, and in Scheel, "Leibniz als Historiker des Welfenhauses," p. 255.

23. Klopp XI, 46.

24. See Leibniz to Bernstorff, 8 December 1714 (Klopp XI, 24).

25. See passages from Leibniz's letters quoted in Müller–Krönert, *Leben und Werk*, pp. 254–5 and 256.

26. See Leibniz to Bernstorff, 28 December 1714 (Klopp XI, 26–7). See also Klopp XI, 13.

27. See Klopp XI, 47–8.

28. See *Anti-Jacobite ou Faussetés de l'Avis aux Proprietaires Anglois Refuteés par des Reflexions impartiales*, 1715.

29. See correspondence quoted by Müller–Krönert, *Leben und Werk*, pp. 251, 253.

30. See Klopp XI, 458–64.

31. See Elisabeth Charlotte of Orléans's letters of 3 and 24 March 1715 to Christian Friedrich von Harling (in *Briefe der Herzogin Elisabeth Charlotte von Orléans an ihre frühere Hofmeisterin A. K. v. Harling, geb. v. Uffeln, und deren Gemahl,*

Geh. Rath Fr. v. Harling zu Hannover. Ed. by Eduard Bodemann. Hanover and
Leipzig: Hahn, 1895, p. 90).

32. See *Journal des Sçavans* (1722), p. 213.

33. GP III, 673.

34. On the *Demonstrationes Catholicae* and the *scientia generalis* see especially chapters
I. 2 and II. 4. On the "elements of general philosophy and of natural theology"
see chap. II. 8.

35. LBr 64, Bl. 4r. Leibniz wrote his reply directly on the space still available on
Biber's letter of 22 March 1716. The fact that at the end of his answer Leibniz mentioned Peter the Great's sojourn in Bad Pyrmont ("Le Czar . . . maintenant . . . est
à Pirmont boire les eaux" LBr 64, Bl. 4v) indicates that the letter must have been
written in the summer of 1716.

36. See in particular Leibniz's *Observations sur le projet d'une paix perpétuelle de M.
l'Abbé [Carl Irenaeus Castel] de Saint-Pierre* of February 1715 (FC, *Oeuvres*, IV,
pp. 328–36).

37. See Leibniz to Caroline, undated (Klopp XI, 20–21). Cf. also *Anti-Jacobite*,
pp. 50–60.

38. See Leibniz to Caroline, undated (Klopp XI, 85–90).

39. Caroline herself, in a letter to Leibniz of 26 May 1716, communicated to Leibniz
her fear that George I did not see any utility in talks of church reunification (see
Klopp XI, 112).

40. See Guerrier, *Leibniz*, N. 238, pp. 345–6; N. 239, pp. 346–8; N. 240, pp. 348–60;
N. 244, pp. 364–9.

41. Guerrier, *Leibniz*, N. 240, pp. 348–60 (here p. 349).

42. See Guerrier, *Leibniz*, N. 240, esp. pp. 352, 354.

43. See Guerrier, *Leibniz*, N. 240, pp. 357–8. On Alsted's encyclopaedia see above,
chap. I. 2; on Leibniz's conception of the encyclopaedia see esp. chap. II. 4; on the
German tradition of systematic encyclopaedias see Howard Hotson, *Commonplace
Learning: Ramism and its German Ramifications. 1543–1630*.

44. See Leibniz's letter to Areskine of 3 August 1716 (Guerrier, *Leibniz*, N. 243,
p. 363).

45. See Leibniz to Marquard Ludwig von Printzen (cited by Müller–Krönert, *Leben
und Werk*, p. 261).

46. See for instance the correspondence with Alois Thomas Raymund von
Harrach.

47. See Klopp XI, 191–2; 192–5.

48. See Werner Conze, *Leibniz als Historiker*. Berlin: De Gruyter, 1951, p. 23. A very
helpful overview of the significance of Leibniz's historical works, including the
Annales, is offered by Gerd van den Heuvel, "Einleitung," in Leibniz, *Schriften
und Briefe zur Geschichte*, pp. 13–50.

49. Pertz III, 878.

50. See Leibniz's letter of 28 October 1714 to Tournemine (published in the *Mémoires
de Trevoux* for January 1715, pp. 154–5; Ravier 190; Dutens III, 441–3; extract
in *The Correspondence of Isaac Newton*, vol. 6, N. 1109). See also Isaac Newton

to T. Johnson (publisher of the *Journal Literaire* of The Hague) [1714] (*The Correspondence of Isaac Newton*, vol. 6, p. 80).

51. See Christian Wolff to Leibniz, 3 October 1714 (*Briefwechsel zwischen Leibniz und Christian Wolff*, p. 160). On Keill's *Réponse* and Leibniz's *Remarques* see chap. II. 8.

52. *Briefwechsel zwischen Leibniz und Christian Wolff*, p. 160. Trans. by Hall in *The Correspondence of Isaac Newton*, vol. 6, p. 180. See also Christian Wolff to Leibniz, 11 December 1713 (*Briefwechsel zwischen Leibniz und Christian Wolff*, p. 154) and Johann Bernoulli to Leibniz, 23 May 1714 (GM III/2, 931).

53. See Leibniz to Tournemine, 28 October 1714 (Dutens III, 441–3; Ravier 190). The *Historia et origo calculi differentialis* remained unpublished. It can be seen in GM V, 392–410 (see esp. pp. 394–5).

54. Christian Wolff to Leibniz, February 1715 (*Briefwechsel zwischen Leibniz und Christian Wolff*, p. 162). Trans. by Hall, *The Correspondence of Isaac Newton*, vol. 6, p. 207.

55. *Briefwechsel zwischen Leibniz und Christian Wolff*, p. 162.

56. See *Briefwechsel zwischen Leibniz und Christian Wolff*, p. 164.

57. *Briefwechsel zwischen Leibniz und Christian Wolff*, pp. 168–9. Trans. by Hall in *The Correspondence of Isaac Newton*, vol. 6, pp. 222–3. See also Leibniz to Nicolas Rémond, 22 June 1715 (GP III, 645).

58. *Briefwechsel zwischen Leibniz und Christian Wolff*, p. 174.

59. See Wolff to Leibniz, 1 October 1715 (*Briefwechsel zwischen Leibniz und Christian Wolff*, p. 175).

60. *Philosophical Transactions* 29/342 (February 1715): 173–224. Reprinted in Hall, *Philosophers at War*, pp. 263–314. A French translation appeared the same year in the *Journal Literaire* of The Hague (cf. *The Correspondence of Isaac Newton*, vol. 6, N. 1162).

61. See Leibniz to Caroline, 10 May 1715 (Klopp XI, 37–40).

62. See Caroline's letters to Leibniz of 14 and 26 November 1715 (Klopp XI, 48 and 52) and Ezio Vailati, *Leibniz and Clarke. A Study of Their Correspondence*, pp. 4–5.

63. Respectively *Jacobi Rohaulti Physica*. Latinè reddidit, & annotatiunculis quibusdam illustravit S. Clarke. Londini: Impensis Jacobi Knapton, 1697; *Optice: sive De reflexionibus, refractionibus, inflexionibus & coloribus lucis libri tres*. Latine reddidit Samuel Clarke. Londini: impensis Sam. Smith & Benj. Walford, 1706.

64. Caroline to Leibniz, 26 November 1715 (Klopp XI, 52–3).

65. See Klopp XI, 52.

66. Klopp XI, 54–5. There are a number of editions and translations of the Leibniz–Clarke correspondence, the most widely available of which are Klopp XI and GP VII, 352–440.

67. The key role played by Caroline in the origin and development of the Leibniz–Clarke dispute is recountred by Domenico Bertoloni Meli, "Caroline, Leibniz, and Clarke." *Journal of the History of Ideas* 60, 3 (1999): 469–86 and by Brown, "Personal, Political, and Philosophical Dimensions of the Leibniz–Caroline Correspondence."

68. On Newton's involvement see Caroline to Leibniz, 10 January 1716 (Klopp XI, 71). Apparently Caroline passed on to Newton at least Leibniz's letter of 12 May 1716 (Klopp XI, 100–103) including a postscript on the void and atoms which Newton copied (cf. R. S. Westfall, *Never at Rest: A Biography of Isaac Newton*. Cambridge: Cambridge University Press, 1980, p. 778). See Vailati, *Leibniz and Clarke*, p. 4.

69. See Paul Ritter, "Bericht eines Augenzeugen über Leibnizens Tod und Begräbnis." *Zeitschrift des Historischen Vereins für Niedersachsen* 81 (1916): 247–52 (here p. 248) and Paul Ritter, "Wie Leibniz gestorben und begraben ist." *Preuß. Jahrbücher* 157 (1914): 437–49 (here p. 440).

70. See Clarke's first reply (GP VII, 354–5).

71. See Leibniz's second paper (GP VII, 357–8).

72. *Specimen inventorum de admirandis naturae generalis arcanis* (c. 1688), A VI, 4, 1618.

73. Antognazza, "Leibniz and the Post-Copernican Universe," pp. 319–21.

74. Klopp XI, 80.

75. Quotations from Leibniz's third paper (GP VII, 363–4). Engl. trans. by H. G. Alexander in *The Leibniz–Clarke Correspondence*. Manchester: Manchester University Press, 1956, p. 26. Cf. Vailati, *Leibniz and Clarke*, pp. 109–37 (esp. pp. 122–6; see also pp. 8–15 for a helpful summary of the main issues discussed in the Leibniz–Clarke correspondence). For a comparison between Newton and Leibniz's theories of space see Richard Arthur, "Space and Relativity in Newton and Leibniz." *The British Journal for the Philosophy of Science* 45 (1994): 219–40.

76. See Brown, "Personal, Political, and Philosophical Dimensions of the Leibniz–Caroline Correspondence," pp. 277–89.

77. See Leibniz to Caroline, undated (Klopp XI, 62–3) and Antonio Conti to Leibniz, undated (GB, 258–62; extract in *The Correspondence of Isaac Newton*, vol. 6, p. 215). Conti arrived in London in the spring of 1715. In November he was elected a fellow of the Royal Society.

78. See Caroline to Leibniz, 10 January 1716 (Klopp XI, 71–2).

79. Klopp XI, 78–9.

80. See GB, 262–7; *The Correspondence of Isaac Newton*, vol. 6, pp. 250–53.

81. See GB, 271–4; *The Correspondence of Isaac Newton*, vol. 6, pp. 285–8. See also the draft of a letter written by Newton to Pierre Des Maizeaux in August 1718 (*The Correspondence of Isaac Newton*, vol. 6, p. 460, n. 8) in which Leibniz was accused of "running the dispute into a squabble about a Vacuum, and Atoms, and universal gravity, and occult qualities".

82. Leibniz to Antonio Conti, 9 April 1716 (GB, 274–82).

83. See GB, 284–5.

84. Leibniz was referring to his letter of 9 April 1716 (see GB, 274–84) responding to both Newton's reply of March 1716 (26 February O.S.; GB, 271–4) and Conti's accompanying letter (GB, 269–70).

85. Klopp XI, 100.

86. Caroline to Leibniz, 26 May 1716 (Klopp XI, 112).

87. Klopp XI, 115.

88. See Müller–Krönert, *Leben und Werk*, p. 259.

89. See Leibniz's proposals for improving the productivity of the Harz mines, discussed in chap. II. 4.

90. *The Correspondence of Isaac Netwton*, vol. 6., pp. 376–7.

91. I borrow this expression from Hall, *Philosophers at War*, chapter 11 of which recounts the final stage of the controversy between 1715 and 1722.

92. GP II, 492.

93. Leibniz's annotations on the last page of his copy of Berkeley's *Treatise Concerning the Principles of Human Knowledge* (p. 636 in Willy Kabitz, "Leibniz und Berkeley." *Sitzungsberichte der preußischen Akademie der Wissenschaften. Philosophisch-historische Klasse* 24 (1932): 623–6). According to Kabitz, Leibniz probably received Berkeley's *Treatise* via Caroline during the winter of 1714–15. See also André Robinet, "Leibniz: Lecture du *Treatise* de Berkeley." *Les études philosophiques* (1983): 217–23.

94. *Annotationes de Cultu Religioneque Sinensium*. Critical edition by Wenchao Li and Hans Poser in G. W. Leibniz, *Discours sur la Theologie Naturelle des Chinois*. Frankfurt am Main: Vittorio Klostermann, 2002, pp. 265–70. According to Leibniz's recollection in the accompanying letter to Des Bosses, the remarks were written in 1708. They can be seen also in GP II, 380–84. Trans. in *Writings on China*, pp. 67–74.

95. See Leibniz to Bartholomew Des Bosses, 13 January 1716 (GP II, 508), and Leibniz to Nicolas Rémond, 17 January 1716 (GP III, 665) and 27 January 1716 (GP III, 670).

96. See Nicolas Rémond to Leibniz, 4 September 1715 (GP III, 650), and Leibniz to Nicolas Rémond, 4 November 1715 (GP III, 656, 660). The works sent to Leibniz were, respectively, Longobardi's *Traité sur quelques points de la religion des Chinois* and Santa Maria's *Traité sur quelques points importans de la Mission de la Chine*, both translated into French by Louis Champion de Cicé and published in a volume intitled *Anciens Traitez de divers auteurs sur les ceremonies de la Chine*. Paris, 1701. Leibniz's copy of the volume is preserved at the Deutsche Staatsbibliothek in Berlin. Cf. the introduction to the critical edition of the *Discours* in Leibniz, *Discours sur la Theologie naturelle des Chinois*, pp. 8–9, 12. Together with the treatises of Longobardi and Santa Maria, Rémond sent Nicolas Malebranche's *Entretien d'un philosophe chrétien et d'un philosophe Chinois*. Paris, 1708 (see GP III, 650).

97. See Nicolas Rémond to Leibniz, 12 October 1714 and 1 April 1715 (respectively GP III, 630 and 640).

98. GP III, 675.

99. See GP II, 512 and "Editorische Einleitung," in Leibniz, *Discours sur la Theologie naturelle des Chinois*, p. 7. On the mythological Emperor Fuxi or Fu-Hsi see chap. II. 7.

100. On Leibniz's support of Jesuit accommodationism in relation to the China mission see chap. II. 6.

101. A similar accommodationist position was outlined by Leibniz in his *Annotationes de Cultu Religioneque Sinensium* of 1708. On the composition of the *Annotationes*

see "Editorische Einleitung," in Leibniz, *Discours sur la Theologie naturelle des Chinois*, pp. 9–10. On Leibniz's accommodationism see the illuminating account of Perkins, *Leibniz and China*, esp. pp. 188–94.

102. The *Discours* broke off before Leibniz began to spell out the philosophical and theological implications of this "discovery." For Leibniz's views on this matter see chap. II. 7.

103. On Petersen see chap. II. 6.

104. See Hotson, "Leibniz and Millenarianism," pp. 192–9.

105. See Leibniz to Johann Fabricius, 3 September 1711 (Dutens V, 293–4). Trans. by Hotson in "Leibniz and Millenarianism," p. 194.

106. Leibniz to Johann Wilhelm Petersen, 15 October 1706, in Leibniz, *De l'horizon de la doctrine humaine*, p. 25. Trans. adapted by Hotson, "Leibniz and Millenarianism," p. 193 from Coudert, *Leibniz and the Kabbalah*, pp. 115–116.

107. See Leibniz to Johann Fabricius, 28 January 1712 (Dutens V, 296–7).

108. See Leibniz to Thomas Burnett of Kemney, 27 February 1702 (GP III, 283) and Leibniz to Johann Fabricius, letters of 10 and 17 March 1712 (Dutens V, 297 and 299). Petersen had already extensively discussed the doctrine of the Ἀποκατάστασις πάντων in a large volume published in 1700; two further volumes followed, respectively, in 1703 and 1710. Leibniz published a generally sympathetic but noncommittal review in the *Monatlicher Auszug* of April 1701 (*Deutsche Schriften* II, 342–7). Attention to the letter to Thomas Burnett as ground for translating Ἀποκατάστασις with "Restitution" is drawn by Fichant in Leibniz, *De l'horizon de la doctrine humaine*, pp. 22-3, 111.

109. Dutens V, 301. Trans. by Hotson, "Leibniz and Millenarianism," p. 196. Some of Leibniz's extensive emendations are found in LH XXXIX, 18, Bl. 39–53.

110. See Leibniz to Johann Fabricius, 6 July 1716 (Dutens V, 301). Petersen's poem was published in 1720 under the title of *Uranias qua opera Dei magna omnibus retro seculis et oeconomiis transactis usque ad apocatastasin seculorum omnium... carmine heroico celebrantur.*

111. Cf. Heinekamp, "Ars Characteristica und Natürliche Sprache bei Leibniz," pp. 478–84 and Mugnai, *Astrazione e realtà*, pp. 99–112.

112. Cf. Fichant in Leibniz, *De l'horizon de la doctrine humaine*, pp. 20–21 and Hotson, "Leibniz and Millenarianism," p. 184. For an indication of texts supporting the thesis that Leibniz did not ultimately adopt the unorthodox doctrine of universal salvation see Hotson, "Leibniz and Millenarianism," p. 186, n. 213. For a different interpretation see Coudert, *Leibniz and the Kabbalah*.

113. See in particular Leibniz to Johann Wilhelm Petersen, 15 October 1706 (in Leibniz, *De l'horizon de la doctrine humaine*, p. 25) and Leibniz to Johann Fabricius, 10 March 1712 (Dutens V, 297). Cf. Hotson, "Leibniz and Millenarianism," p. 197.

114. Leibniz to Adam Theobald Overbeck, 17 June 1715 (in Leibniz, *De l'horizon de la doctrine humaine*, p. 86). The first, shorter version of this "meditation" was entitled Ἀποκατάστασις πάντων, the second simply Ἀποκατάστασις. Both are published by Fichant in Leibniz, *De l'horizon de la doctrine humaine*, pp. 60–66, 66–77.

115. Ἀποκατάστασις (in Leibniz, *De l'horizon de la doctrine humaine*, p. 72).

116. Ibid.

117. *Demonstrationes de Universo immenso aeternoque; de Mundis et aevis, deque rerum longiquarum et futurarum statu* (in Leibniz, *De l'horizon de la doctrine humaine*, pp. 56–60, here p. 58). On the metaphor employed here, see note 1 above. Leibniz was not new to the "meditation" of the Ἀποκατάστασις: see the earlier texts published by Fichant, notably the paper *De l'Horizon de la Doctrine Humaine* written in 1693 for the Académie Royale des Sciences (cf. Leibniz, *De l'horizon de la doctrine humaine*, pp. 39–53).

118. These words concluded Leibniz's *Principes de la nature et de la grâce fondés en raison* (1714) (GP VI, 606). Cf. also *De Progressu in Infinitum*, 1694–6[*] (Grua, 94–5) and *An Mundus Perfectione Crescat*, 1694–6[*] (Grua, 95).

119. Leibniz to Louise von Hohenzollern, in Feder, *Commercii Epistolici Leibnitiani Typis nondum vulgati Selecta specimena*, pp. 476–7.

120. See Leibniz to Caroline, 31 July 1716 (Klopp XI, 130).

121. Klopp XI, 189.

122. A number of details traditionally associated with Leibniz's last days, death, and funeral seem to be devoid of foundation in any reliable source. There are two accounts which can be regarded as generally trustworthy. The first is the report by Leibniz's amanuensis, Johann Hermann Vogler, who on 17 November 1716 wrote a letter to his predecessor, Johann Friedrich Hodann, describing Leibniz's last days and death, followed by another letter describing his funeral, published by Ritter as "Bericht eines Augenzeugen über Leibnizens Tod und Begräbnis." The second reliable source is a letter by Eckhart probably written on 29 November 1716 to a friend in Wolfenbüttel (in all likelihood the librarian Lorenz Hertel): the text can be found both in Heinrich Schneider, "Wie Starb Leibniz?" *Braunschweigisches Magazin* no. 2 (1923): columns 28–31 and in Görlich, *Leibniz als Mensch und Kranker*, pp. 199–200. Vogler and Eckhart's early recollections are generally in agreement, although they remembered and/or noted different details. In his *Lebensbeschreibung*, pp. 191, 221–3, Eckhart gave a somewhat different account of Leibniz's last moments, providing the basis for the famous narration of Leibniz's death by Guhrauer (*Leibnitz*, II, pp. 328–30). Given the fact that Vogler was present at Leibniz's death whereas Eckhart was not, and that Eckhart's early private recollection for his Wolfenbüttel friend broadly agrees with Vogler's account, I follow the version given by Leibniz's amanuensis. Eckhart's biographical accounts should in any case be taken with caution since there was no love lost between him and Leibniz. Finally, the account by the physician who assisted Leibniz in his last hours, Dr Johann Philipp Seip (1686–1757), written in 1752, should be mentioned: the text can be found in Andreas Seip von Engelbrecht, *Der Fürstlich Waldeckische Leibmedicus Dr. med. Johann Philipp Seip in Pyrmont und seine Familie*. Eisenach: Kahle, 1938, p. 27, and in Görlich, *Leibniz als Mensch und Kranker*, pp. 200–201. This account tends to diverge in several points from Vogler and Eckhart's early recollections. The fact that it was written thirty-six years after Leibniz's death and that Seip

had a vested interest in presenting his own medical intervention in the best light suggests that (although useful) it is not completely trustworthy (cf. Görlich, *Leibniz als Mensch und Kranker*, pp. 205, 213–14). For medical details of the possible causes of Leibniz's death see Görlich, *Leibniz als Mensch und Kranker*, pp. 205–9.

123. See Vogler to Hodann, in "Bericht eines Augenzeugen über Leibnizens Tod und Begräbnis," pp. 247–51 and J. W. Göbel to Lorenz Hertel, 15 November 1715 (in Guhrauer, *Leibnitz*, II, *Anmerkungen*, pp. 35–6).

124. See Heinrich Lackmann, "Der Erbschaftsstreit um Leibniz' Privatbibliothek." *Studia Leibnitiana* 1, 2 (1969): 126–36. A long dispute arose between Löffler and the Hanover government regarding the "Äquivalent" to be paid by the government to Löffler as compensation for relinquishing Leibniz's private library to the Königliche Bibliothek.

125. See Vogler to Hodann, in "Bericht eines Augenzeugen über Leibnizens Tod und Begräbnis," pp. 251–2, and Eckhart, *Lebensbeschreibung*, p. 191.

126. According to Eckhart, *Lebensbeschreibung*, p. 192, this was Bernoulli's emblem, which Leibniz greatly appreciated.

127. See Vogler to Hodann, in "Bericht eines Augenzeugen über Leibnizens Tod und Begräbnis," pp. 251–2 and Eckhart, *Lebensbeschreibung*, pp. 191–2. Eckhart's description is reproduced in Guhrauer, *Leibnitz*, II, pp. 331–2.

128. Ker of Kersland, *Memoirs*, [Part I] pp. 117–18.

129. See Vogler to Hodann, in "Bericht eines Augenzeugen über Leibnizens Tod und Begräbnis," p. 251, and Eckhart, *Lebensbeschreibung*, p. 192.

130. See Fontenelle, "Éloge de M. Leibnitz," pp. 94–128; Eckhart, *Lebensbeschreibung*, p. 125; *Briefe der Herzogin Elisabeth Charlotte von Orléans an ihre frühere Hofmeisterin A. K. v. Harling*, pp. 102–6.

131. See Eckhart's letter of 29 November 1716* to his Wolfenbüttel friend, in Schneider, "Wie Starb Leibniz?" p. 30.

132. Doebner, "Leibnizens Briefwechsel mit dem Minister von Bernstorff," pp. 370–71.

133. See Eckhart, *Lebensbeschreibung*, pp. 201–2. Cf. also p. 224. According to Eckhart, the nickname *Loevenix* originated from the Hanover pastor, Heinemann, who disliked Leibniz (see ibid., p. 219).

134. I am grateful to Robert M. Adams for a helpful conversation on these matters.

135. See Donald Rutherford, "Introduction: Leibniz and Religion." *American Catholic Philosophical Quarterly* 76, 4 (2002), p. 523.

136. Leibniz to Duke Johann Friedrich, 1678 (A I, 2, 111).

Appendix

Leibniz's own description of his physical appearance, habits, and temperament:

From childhood onward he led a sedentary life with very little physical activity. In his youth he read widely and was an autodidact in most things; and he always wanted to investigate things more deeply than is ordinarily done and to discover new things. – He works deep into the night and gets up late. He does not move much. But occasionally he leaves the city and can walk at a good pace for a long time without getting tired. He lies still while sleeping.

He is of average height, lean, and of pale complexion. He normally has cold hands. He does not often sweat, and has long feet and fingers which are very thin, with innumerable lines running through his hands.

His body is not very hairy. The hair on his head is rather dark (dark brown and straight).

From his youth his eyes did not see well at a distance, which resulted not from studying but from his natural constitution. On the other hand, as he reads and writes constantly, he has no difficulty in exactly distinguishing even the smallest writing at close range, and he therefore finds it easier to read middle-sized than large writing.

He has a faint voice but high and clear rather than strong. . . .

Concerning his feelings, he is never very happy or very sad. He quickly becomes animated by conversation and intellectual activity and sometimes can scarcely contain himself, but soon gets back to normal.

He has a moderate appetite for conversation, preferring to think and read in solitude; but once he enters into conversation he carries it on happily enough, enjoying witty and friendly discussions more than games (of cards) and physical exercise.

His happiness and grief are never excessive. He laughs frequently, with his mouth rather than with his chest shaking. He angers quickly, but only for a short time. He dreads beginning something, but is fearless in continuing it.

He does not have a strong imagination, due to his defective vision. His memory is mediocre. Because of his weak memory and imagination, the smallest present trouble afflicts him more than the greatest past one.

He is superbly gifted in discovery and judgement and does not find it difficult to devise, read, write, and speak on a variety of things extemporaneously and, when called upon, to get to the bottom of any intellectual matter by thorough scrutiny and reflection. It is therefore probable that his brain is dry and spirituous. (Pertz I, 4, 173–5; cf. Leibniz, *Nouvelles lettres et opuscules inédits*, pp. 388–9.)

Description of Leibniz's physical appearance, habits, and temperament by Johann Georg Eckhart, Leibniz's collaborator at the Guelf history since the end of 1698 and first biographer:

Regarding his constitution, he was of medium stature, with a rather large head. In his youth he had black hair, thin and short, but very clear eyesight which lasted until the end. Because he was short-sighted, he preferred to read small rather than big writing, and wrote himself in a very small hand. He became bald at an early age and had in the middle of his crown a cyst the size of a pigeon's egg. He was broad-shouldered, and always walked with his head stooped, so that it looked like he had a high back. His body was thin rather than fat, and he was bowlegged when he walked. . . . He was of strong constitution, ate a great deal and drank little when not obliged to, always mixing water with his wine when he dined out, since otherwise he suffered from heartburn. At home he drank a little beer and always drank sweet and dry wine mixed together, to which he added cherry juice boiled with sugar and a bit of water: it is amazing that he did not upset his stomach with this concoction. Since he never had his own cook, he was not particular about his food, and had things delivered from taverns to his room. He then always ate alone, not keeping regular meal times, but taking a break when it was convenient for his studies. Once he began to suffer badly from gout, he started eating nothing for lunch except a bit of milk; but on the other hand he ate a large meal in the evening, and then went straight to sleep. He joked that in this way he could use his time better, by dining *à la Romaine* [in the Roman fashion], and that the stomach digests better while asleep than while he was awake. He did not particularly suffer from illnesses, apart from the fact that for a time he was inconvenienced by dizziness. He slept deeply and without interruption. He did not usually go to bed before 1 or 2 am. He also often slept in his chair and at six or seven in the morning was again awake. He studied incessantly and often did not leave his chair for several weeks. I think this was the reason that a *fluxion* or open wound formed on his right leg. . . . He did not mind simple women and lost track of time when he had the opportunity to converse with them. Indeed, he could adapt his speech in such a manner that one would not have taken him for a philosopher at all. He was often at court, often dined there, and was certainly an ornament of the royal table. Her Royal Highness used to call him her walking encyclopaedia because nothing came up [in conversation] which he did not discuss in depth. He talked to soldiers, courtiers, and statesmen, artists and similar people as if he were one of their profession; so everyone liked him, except those people who did not understand such behaviour. He spoke well of everyone, saw the bright side of everything, and even indulged his enemies, whom he often could have harmed at court. He read a lot and made extracts of everything, also writing down his reflections on almost every interesting book on small pieces of paper. As soon as he had written them, however, he put them aside and did not consult them again, since his memory was unequalled: in fact, he could recite by heart the most beautiful passages of the ancient poets (especially Virgil), church hymns, and whatever else he had read in his youth, even when he had grown old. He wanted to be involved in all things learned; and when he heard that someone had found something new, he could not rest until he was fully informed about it. His correspondence was very extensive, and took most of his time. All distinguished learned people in Europe corresponded with him, and when also people of lower standing wrote to him, he always replied and gave them information. . . . He was very indulgent with his servants: he tended to get angry quickly, but he also calmed down quickly. He cared for money, and this is why he was almost a bit mean; yet he did not use it for his comfort, but allowed artisans and his servants to cheat it from him. His arithmetical machine, finished shortly before his death, cost him great sums[.] . . . He had good moral principles and followed them well enough[.] (Eckhart, *Lebensbeschreibung*, pp. 196–201.)

Gilbert Burnet's assessment of Leibniz's intellectual gifts in a letter to Leibniz of 27 February 1699:

I doe not wonder to find all languages so familiar to one of so Comprehensive and Universall a Genius. Very often those who deal in many things are slight and Superficiall in them all but it is a very singular character to know so many things and to goe so profoundly to the depth of every thing. (A I, 16, 594.)

FAMILY TREE OF THE HOUSE OF HANOVER

(BASED ON SCHNATH, *GESCHICHTE HANNOVERS, VOL. II*)

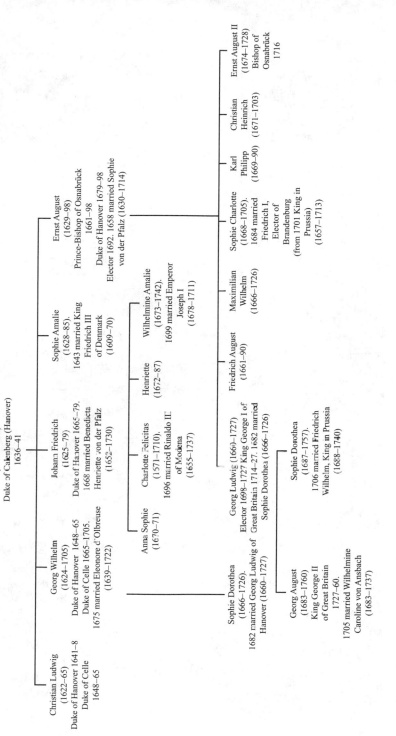

Georg
(1582–1641)
Duke of Calenberg (Hanover)
1636–41

Christian Ludwig
(1622–65)
Duke of Hanover 1641–8
Duke of Celle
1648–65

Georg Wilhelm
(1624–1705)
Duke of Hanover 1648–65
Duke of Celle 1665–1705.
1675 married Eleonore d'Olbreuse
(1639–1722)

Johann Friedrich
(1625–79)
Duke of Hanover 1665–79.
1668 married Benedicta
Henriette von der Pfalz
(1652–1730)

Sophie Amalie
(1628–85).
1643 married King
Friedrich III
of Denmark
(1609–70)

Ernst August
(1629–98)
Prince-Bishop of Osnabrück
1661–98
Duke of Hanover 1679–98
Elector 1692. 1658 married Sophie
von der Pfalz (1630–1714)

Anna Sophie
(1670–71)

Charlotte Felicitas
(1571–1710),
1696 married Rinaldo II
of Modena
(1655–1737)

Henriette
(1672–87)

Wilhelmine Amalie
(1673–1742).
1699 married Emperor
Joseph I
(1678–1711)

Sophie Dorothea
(1666–1726).
1682 married Georg Ludwig of
Hanover (1660–1727)

Georg Ludwig (1660–1727)
Elector 1698–1727 King George I of
Great Britain 1714–27. 1682 married
Sophie Dorothea (1666–1726)

Friedrich August
(1661–90)

Maximilian
Wilhelm
(1666–1726)

Sophie Charlotte
(1668–1705).
1684 married
Friedrich I,
Elector of
Brandenburg
(from 1701 King in
Prussia)
(1657–1713)

Karl
Philipp
(1669–90)

Christian
Heinrich
(1671–1703)

Ernst August II
(1674–1728)
Bishop of
Osnabrück
1716

Georg August
(1683–1760)
King George II
of Great Britain
1727–60.
1705 married Wilhelmine
Caroline von Ansbach
(1683–1737)

Sophie Dorothea
(1687–1757).
1706 married Friedrich
Wilhelm, King in Prussia
(1688–1740)

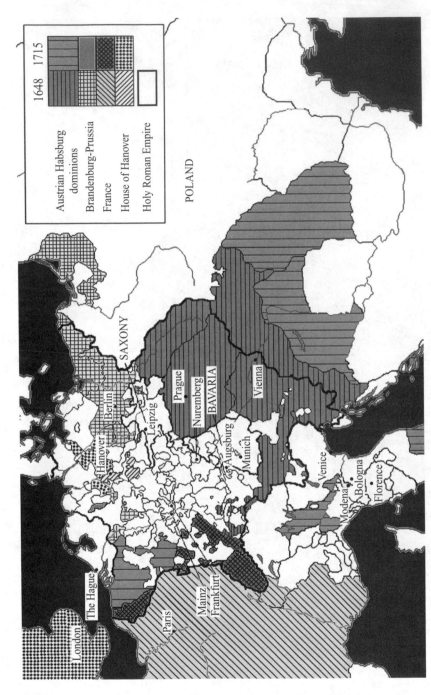

Map 1. Central Europe – 1648–1715 (by Howard Hotson).

Legend:

1648	1715	
		Austrian Habsburg dominions
		Brandenburg-Prussia
		France
		House of Hanover
		Holy Roman Empire

POLAND

SAXONY

Hanover
Berlin
Leipzig
Prague
Nuremberg
BAVARIA
Vienna
Augsburg
Munich
Venice
Modena
Bologna
Florence
London
The Hague
Paris
Mainz
Frankfurt

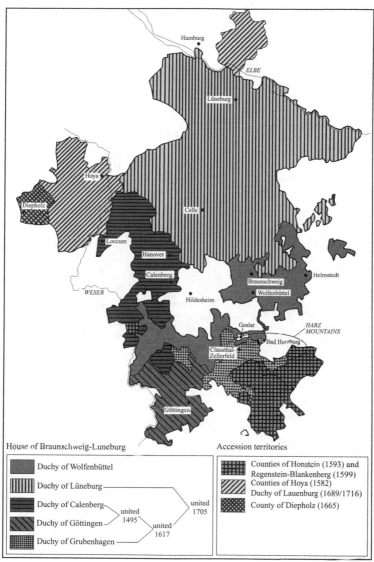

Map 2. Lower Saxony (by Howard Hotson).

Bibliography

In the following sections are listed only works consulted in the preparation of this book. For the main editions of Leibniz's writings, the two main published catalogues of Leibniz's manuscripts, and other frequently cited literature, see the list of abbreviations.

I. Sources

i. Leibniz

Leibniz, G. W. *Codex Juris Gentium Diplomaticus.* Hanoverae: Literis et impensis Samuelis Ammonii, 1693.

Leibniz, G. W. *Oedipus Chymicus.* In *Miscellanea Berolinensia.* Berlin: Sumptibus Johann. Christ. Papenii, 1710, pp. 16–22.

Leibniz, G. W. *Historia inventionis Phosphori.* In *Miscellanea Berolinensia.* Berlin: Sumptibus Johann. Christ. Papenii, 1710, pp. 91–8.

Commercium epistolicum D. Johannis Collins et aliorum de analysi promota. Londini: Typis Pearsonianis, 1712 (January 1673 N.S.)

Leibniz, G. W. *Anti-Jacobite ou Faussetés de l'Avis aux Proprietaires Anglois Refuteés par des Reflexions impartiales.* N. pl., 1715.

Leibniz, G. W. *Collectanea Etymologica.* Ed. by J. G. Eckhart. Hanover, 1717.

Feller, Joachim Friedrich, ed., *Otium Hanoveranum, sive, Miscellanea ex ore & schedis illustris viri, piae memoriae, Godofr. Guilielmi Leibnitii.* Lipsiae: Impensis Joann. Christiani Martini, 1718.

Leibniz, G. W. *Tentamina Theodicaeae de Bonitate Dei, Libertate Hominis et Origine Mali.* Latine versa et Notationibus illustrata a M. D. L. Ab ipso auctore emendata et auctior. Francofurti: Sumptibus Caroli Josephi Bencard, 1719.

Leibniz, G. W. *Epistolae ad diversos.* Ed. by Chr. Kortholt. 4 vols. Leipzig: B. C. Breitkopfius, 1734–42.

Gruber, J. D., ed. *Commercii Epistolici Leibnitiani, ad omne genus eruditionis comparati, per partes publicandi. Tomi prodromi pars altera.* Hanoverae et Gottingae: Apud Io. Wilhelm. Schmidium, 1745.

Kapp, J. E., ed. *Sammlung einiger Vertrauten Briefe, welche zwischen... Leibnitz und... Herrn Daniel Ernst Jablonski, auch andern Gelehrten, Besonders über die*

Vereinigung der Lutherischen und Reformirten Religion . . . gewechselt worden sind. Leipzig, 1745.

Leibniz, G. W. *Protogaea sive de prima facie telluris et antiquissimae historiae vestigiis in ipsis naturae monumentis dissertatio.* Ed. by Ch. L. Scheidt. Göttingen, 1749. (Modern edition: Toulouse-Le Mirail, 1993; introduction by Jean-Marie Barrande, pp. i–xxxi.)

Raspe, R. E., ed. *Oeuvres philosophiques latines et françoises de feu Mr de Leibnitz.* Amsterdam and Leipzig: Schreuder, 1765.

Feder, J. G. H., ed. *Commercii Epistolici Leibnitiani Typis nondum vulgati Selecta specimena.* Hanover, 1805.

Rommel, Chr. von, ed. *Leibniz und Landgraf Ernst von Hessen-Rheinfels. Ein ungedruckter Briefwechsel über religiöse und politische Gegenstände.* Frankfurt am Mein: J. Rütten, 1847.

Leibniz, G. W. *Lettres et opuscules inédits.* Ed. by Louis Alexander Foucher de Careil. Paris, 1854. Reprint, Hildesheim: Olm, 1975.

Foucher de Careil, Louis Alexander, ed. *Réfutation inédite de Spinoza par Leibniz.* Paris, 1854.

Roessler, E. F., ed. "Beiträge zur Staatsgeschichte Oesterreichs aus dem Leibnitzschen Nachlasse in Hannover." *Sitzungsberichte der philosophisch-historischen Classe der Kais. Akademie der Wissenschaften zu Wien* 20 (1856): 267–89.

Leibniz, G. W. *Nouvelles lettres et opuscules inédits.* Ed. by Louis Alexander Foucher de Careil. Paris: Auguste Durand, 1857.

Gerhardt, C. I., ed. *Briefwechsel zwischen Leibniz und Christian Wolff.* Halle: H. W. Schmidt, 1860.

Foucher de Careil, Louis Alexander. *Leibniz, la philosophie juive et la Cabale.* Paris: Auguste Durand, 1861.

Klopp, O., ed. "Leibniz' Plan der Gründung einer Societät der Wissenschaften in Wien." *Archiv für österreichische Geschichte.* Vol. 40. Vienna, 1869, pp. 157–255.

Guerrier, Woldemar. *Leibniz in seinen Beziehungen zu Russland und Peter dem Grossen.* St. Petersburg and Leipzig, 1873.

Doebner, R., ed. "Leibnizens Briefwechsel mit dem Minister von Bernstorff und andere Leibniz betreffende Briefe und Attenstücke aus den Jahren 1705–1716." *Zeitschrift des historischen Vereins für Niedersachsen* (1881): 205–380.

Bodemann, Eduard, ed. "Leibnizens Plan einer Societät der Wissenschaften in Sachsen." *Neues Archiv für Sächsische Geschichte und Alterthumskunde* 4 (1883): 177–214.

Doebner, R., ed. "Nachträge zu Leibnizens Briefwechsel mit dem Minister von Bernstorff." *Zeitschrift des historischen Vereins für Niedersachsen* (1884): 206–42.

Bodemann, Eduard, ed. "Leibnizens Entwürfe zu seinen Annalen von 1691 und 1692." *Zeitschrift des Historischen Vereins für Niedersachsen* (1885): 1–58.

Mollat, Georg, ed. *Rechsphilosophisches aus Leibnizens Ungedruckten Schriften.* Leipzig: Verlag Robolski, 1885.

Bodemann, Eduard, ed. "Leibnizens Briefwechsel mit dem Herzoge Anton Ulrich von Braunschweig-Wolfenbüttel." *Zeitschrift des historischen Vereins für Niedersachsen* (1888): 73–244.

Bodemann, Eduard, ed. "Nachträge zu 'Leibnizens Briefwechsel mit dem Minister v. Bernstorff und andere Leibniz betr. Briefe.'" *Zeitschrift des historischen Vereins für Niedersachsen* (1890): 131–68.

Kvačala, J. *Neue Beiträge zum Briefwechsel zwischen D. E. Jablonski und G. W. Leibniz.* In *Acta et Commentationes Imp. Universitatis Jurievensis* 4 (1899): 11–192.

Bodemann, Eduard, and S. Dickstein, eds. "Korespondencya Kochańskiego i Leibniza." *Prace Matematyczno-fizyczne* 12 (1901): 226–73.

Doebner, R., ed. *Briefe der Königin Sophie Charlotte von Preußen und der Kurfürstin Sophie von Hannover an hannoversche Diplomaten.* Leipzig, 1905 (Publ. a. d. Preuß. Staatsarchiven. 79; new print: Osnabrück, 1965).

Leibniz, G. W. *Nachgelassene Schriften physikalischen, mechanischen und technischen Inhalts.* Ed. by Ernst Gerland. Leipzig: Teubner, 1906.

Child, J. M. *The Early Mathematical Manuscripts of Leibniz.* Chicago and London, 1920.

Schnath, G., ed. *Briefwechsel der Kurfürstin Sophie von Hannover mit dem Preußischen Königshause.* Berlin and Leipzig, 1927.

Schrecker, Paul, ed. "G.-W. Leibniz. Lettres et fragments inédits." *Revue philosophique de la France et de l'étranger* 118 (1934): 5–134.

Leibniz, G. W. *Principes de la nature et de la grâce fondés en raison. Principes de la philosophie ou monadologie.* Ed. by André Robinet. Paris: Presses Universitaires de France, 1954.

Leibniz, G. W. *Reise-Journal. 1687–1688.* Hildesheim: Olms, 1966.

Leibniz, G. W. *Discours de métaphysique et Monadologie.* Texte définitif avec indexation automatisée. Ed. by André Robinet. Paris: Vrin, 1974.

Hartmann, Fritz, and Matthias Krüger, eds. "*Directiones ad rem Medicam pertinentes.* Ein Manuskript G. W. Leibnizens aus den Jahren 1671/72 über die Medizin." *Studia Leibnitiana* 8, no. 1 (1976): 40–68.

Leibniz, G. W. *Novissima Sinica.* [Hanover] 1697 (2nd ed. [Hanover] 1699). Modern edition: *Das neueste von China. Novissima Sinica.* Ed. by Heinz-Günther Nesselrath and Hermann Reinbothe. Cologne: Deutsche China-Gesellschaft, 1979.

Leibniz, G. W. *Generales inquisitiones de analysi notionum et veritatum.* [Latin and German] Ed., trans., and with a commentary by Franz Schupp. Hamburg: Meiner, 1982.

Leibniz, G. W. *Specimen Dynamicum.* Latin and German. Ed. and trans. by Hans Günter Dosch, Glenn W. Most, and Enno Rudolph. Hamburg: Meiner, 1982.

Widmaier, Rita, ed. *Leibniz korrespondiert mit China. Der Briefwechsel mit den Jesuitenmissionaren (1689–1714).* Frankfurt am Main: Klostermann, 1990.

Leibniz, G. W. *De l'horizon de la doctrine humaine.* Ἀποκατάστασις πάντων *(La Restitution Universelle).* Ed. by Michel Fichant. Paris: Vrin, 1991.

Leibniz, G. W. *Phoranomus seu de potentia et legibus naturae: Rome, Juillet 1689.* Prés. par André Robinet. In *Physis* (Florence) 28, no. 2/3 (1991): 429–541 and 797–885. [Extracts from the *Phoranomus* are published by C. I. Gerhardt in *Archiv für Geschichte der Philosophie* 1 (1888): 575–81.]

Fichant, Michel, ed. *G. W. Leibniz. La réforme de la dynamique. De Corporum concursu (1678), et autres texts inédits.* Paris: Vrin, 1994.

Leibniz, G. W. *Die Grundlagen des logischen Kalküls*. [Latin and German] Ed., trans., and with a commentary by Franz Schupp. Hamburg: Meiner, 2000.
Leibniz, G. W. *Discours sur la Theologie naturelle des Chinois*. Ed. by Wenchao Li and Hans Poser. Frankfurt am Main: Vittorio Klostermann, 2002.
Leibniz, G. W. *Schriften und Briefe zur Geschichte*. Ed. with introduction and commentary by Malte-Ludolf Babin and Gerd van den Heuvel. Hanover: Verlag Hahnsche Buchhandlung, 2004.
Leibniz, G. W. *Essais scientifiques et philosophiques*. Les articles publiés dans les journaux savants recueillis par Antonio Lamarra et Roberto Palaia. Préface de Heinrich Schepers. 3 vols. Hildesheim: Olms, 2005.

ii. Translations of Leibniz's Writings

The most frequently cited translations are included in the list of abbreviations. When not otherwise identified, translations are my own.
The Leibniz–Clarke Correspondence. Ed. with introduction and notes by H. G. Alexander. Manchester: Manchester University Press, 1956.
Leibniz, G. W. *Logical papers*. Trans. by G. H. R. Parkinson. Oxford: Clarendon Press, 1966.
Leibniz, G. W. *Philosophical Writings*. Ed. by G. H. R. Parkinson. Trans. by Mary Morris and G. H. R. Parkinson. London: J M Dent & Sons, 1973.
Leibniz, G. W. *The Political Writings of Leibniz*. Trans. and ed. with an introduction by Patrick Riley. 2nd ed. Cambridge: Cambridge University Press, 1988.
Leibniz, G. W. *Confessio Philosophi e altri scritti*. Ed. by Francesco Piro. Naples: Cronopio, 1992.
Leibniz, G. W. *De Summa Rerum. Metaphysical Papers*, 1675–1676. Trans. with an introduction and notes by G. H. R. Parkinson. New Haven and London: Yale University Press, 1992.
Leibniz, G. W. *Writings on China*. Ed. by Daniel J. Cook and Henry Rosemont, Jr. Chicago and La Salle, IL: Open Court, 1994.
Leibniz, G. W. *Scritti filosofici*. Ed. and trans. by Massimo Mugnai and Enrico Pasini. 3 vols. Turin: Utet, 2000.
Leibniz, G. W. *The Labyrinth of the Continuum: Writings on the Continuum Problem*, 1672–1686. Trans., ed., and with an introduction by Richard Arthur. New Haven and London: Yale University Press, 2001.
Leibniz, G. W. *Confessio Philosophi: Papers Concerning the Problem of Evil*, 1671–1678. Trans., ed., and with an introduction by Robert C. Sleigh, Jr. Additional contributions from Brandon Look and James Stam. New Haven and London: Yale University Press, 2005.
The Leibniz–Des Bosses Correspondence. Trans., ed., and with an introduction by Brandon C. Look and Donald Rutherford. New Haven and London: Yale University Press, 2007.

iii. Other Authors

Alsted, Johann Heinrich. *Panacea philosophica*. Herborn, 1610.

Alsted, Johann Heinrich. *Encyclopaedia septem tomis distincta*. 7 tomes in 2 vols. Herborn, 1630.

Althusius, Johannes. *Dicaeologicae libri tres, totum et universum jus . . . methodicè complectentes*. Herborn, 1617, 1618; Frankfurt am Main, 1649.

Arnauld, Antoine and Pierre Nicole. *Logique, ou l'art de penser*. Paris, 1662.

Arnauld, Antoine. *Lettres de Monsieur Arnauld, Docteur de Sorbonne, au R. P. Malebranche, Prêtre de l'Oratoire*. N. pl., 1685.

Bacon, Francis. *Instauratio magna*. London: Apud Joannem Billium, 1620.

Bacon, Francis. *De dignitate et augmentis scientiarum*. London: I. Haviland, 1623.

Baillet, Adrien. *La vie de Monsieur Descartes*. 2 vols. Paris: Horthemels, 1691. Reprint, Geneva, 1970.

Bayle, Pierre. *Dictionaire historique et critique*. Rotterdam: Reinier Leers, 1697; 2nd ed. 3 vols. Rotterdam: Reinier Leers, 1702.

Bayle, Pierre. "Memoire communiqué par Mr. Bayle." *Histoire des ouvrages des savans* (August 1704): 369–96.

Becher, Johann Joachim. *Character, pro notitia linguarum universali. Inventum steganographicum hactenus inauditum*. Frankfurt, 1661.

Becher, Johann Joachim. *Appendix practica, über Seinen Methodum Didacticam*. Munich, 1669.

Becher, Johann Joachim. *Närrische Weisheit und weise Narrheit*. Frankfurt am Main: Johann Peter Zubrods, 1682.

Beck, Cave. *The Universal Character, By Which All the Nations in the World May Understand One Anothers Conceptions*. London, 1657.

Berkeley, George. *A Treatise Concerning the Principles of Human Knowledge*. Dublin: Printed by Aaron Rhames for Jeremy Pepyat, 1710.

Birch, Thomas. *The History of the Royal Society of London*. 4 vols. London: A. Millar, 1756–7.

Bisterfeld, Johann Heinrich. *Elementorum logicorum libri tres [. . .]. Accedit, ejusdem authoris, phosphorus catholicus, seu artis meditandi epitome. Cui subjunctum est, consilium de studiis feliciter instituendis*. Lugduni Batavorum: Ex Officina Henrici Verbiest., 1657.

Bisterfeld, Johann Heinrich. *Philosophiae primae seminarium*. Lugduni Batavorum: Apud Danielem et Abrahamum Gaasbeck, 1657.

Bodemann, Eduard, ed. *Aus den Briefen der Elisabeth Charlotte von Orléans an Kurfürstin Sophie*. 2 vols. Hanover, 1891.

Bodemann, Eduard, ed. *Briefe der Herzogin Elisabeth Charlotte von Orléans an ihre frühere Hofmeisterin A. K. v. Harling, geb. v. Uffeln, und deren Gemahl, Geh. Rath Fr. v. Harling zu Hannover*. Hanover and Leipzig: Hahn, 1895.

Boyle, Robert. *The Origine of Formes and Qualities (According to the Corpuscular Philosophy)*. Oxford: Printed by H. Hall . . . for R. Davis, 1666.

Boyle, Robert. *Some Motives and Incentives to the Love of God*. 5th ed. London: Printed for H. Herringman, 1670.

Boyle, Robert. *The Excellency of Theology, Compar'd with Natural Philosophy*. London: Printed by T. N. for Henry Herringman, 1674.

Boyle, Robert. *Some Considerations about the Reconcileableness of Reason and Religion*. London: Printed by T. N. for H. Herringman, 1675.

Boyle, Robert. *Some Physico-Theological Considerations about the Possibility of the Resurrection*. London: Printed by T. N. for Henry Herringman, 1675.

Bossuet, Jacques-Bénigne. *Exposition de la doctrine de l'Eglise catholique sur les matières de controverse*. Paris: Chez Sebastien Mabre-Cramoisy, 1671.

Bossuet, Jacques-Bénigne. *De scripto qui titulus: Cogitationes privatae ... Episcopi Meldensis sententia*. In *Oeuvres complètes*. Ed. by F. Lachat. 31 vols. Paris, 1862–79, vol. 17, pp. 458–99.

Bossuet, Jacques-Bénigne. *Oeuvres complètes*. Ed. by F. Lachat. 31 vols. Paris, 1862–79.

Bossuet, Jacques-Bénigne. *Correspondance*. Ed. by C. Urbain and E. Levesque. New edition. 15 vols. Paris: Hachette, 1909–25.

Bouvet, Joachim. *Portrait historique de l'Empereur de la Chine*. Paris: Michallet, 1697.

Bruno, Giordano. *De monade numero et figura liber consequens quinque de minimo magno et mensura*. Francofurti: Apud Ioan. Wechelum & Petrum Fischerum consortes, 1591.

Burnet, Gilbert. *Exposition of the Thirty-Nine Articles of the Church of England*. London: R. Roberts, 1699.

Burnet, Thomas. *Telluris theoria sacra*. London: Kettilby, 1681. English translation: *The Theory of the Earth*. 2 vols. London: Kettilby, 1684–90. Modern edition of the 1689–91 English version: *The Sacred Theory of the Earth*. With an introduction by Basil Willey. London: Centaur Press, 1965.

Cavalieri, Bonaventura. *Geometria indivisibilibus continuorum nova quadam ratione promota*. Bononiae: ex typographia de Ducijs, 1653.

Cheyne, George. *Fluxionum methodus inversa*. Londini: Typis J. Matthews, 1703.

Clauberg, Johannes. *Logica vetus et nova quadripartita*. Amstelodami: Apud Ludovicum Elzevirium, 1654.

Comenius, J. A. *Januae linguarum reseratae aureae vestibulum, quo primus ad latinam ed. tiruneulis paratur: cum versione interlineari Germanica*. Leipzig, 1639.

Comenius, J. A. *Via Lucis*. 1641. In *Johannis Amos Comenii Opera omnia*. Vol. 14. Prague: Academia, 1974.

Comenius, J. A. *Unum necessarium*. 1668. In *Johannis Amos Comenii Opera omnia*. Vol. 18. Prague: Academia, 1974.

Conring, Hermann. *De antiquissimo statu Helmestadii et vicinae conjecturae*. Helmstedt, 1665.

Conway, Anne. *Principia philosophiae antiquissimae et recentissimae de Deo, Christo et creatura*. Amstelodami, 1690.

Cordemoy, Géraud de. *Copie d'une lettre ecrite à un sçavant religieux de la Compagnie de Jesus* [Gabriel Cossart]. [Paris: T. Girard, 1669.]

Cudworth, Ralph. *The True Intellectual System of the Universe*. London: Printed for Richard Royston, 1678.

Dalgarno, George. *Ars signorum, vulgo character universalis et lingua philosophica*. London, 1661.

Dalgarno, George. *George Dalgarno on universal language: The art of signs (1661), The deaf and dumb man's tutor (1680), and the unpublished papers*. Ed. with a translation, introduction, and commentary by David Cram and Jaap Maat. Oxford and New York: Oxford University Press, 2001.

Descartes, René. *Principia philosophiae*. Amsterdam: Elzevir, 1644.

Descartes, René. *Geometria*. Ed. by Frans van Schooten. Leiden: Joannes Maire, 1649 (2nd ed. Amsterdam: Elzevir, 1659–61).

Descartes, René. *Opera philosophica*. Editio Secunda ab Auctore recognita. Amsterdam, 1650.

Descartes, René. *Oeuvres*. Ed. by. C. Adam and P. Tannery. Paris: Vrin, 1964–76.

Epictetus. *Enchiridion*. Leiden and Antwerp, 1670.

Fatio de Duillier, Nicolas. *Lineae brevissimi descensus investigatio geometrica duplex. Cui addita est investigatio geometrica solidi rotundi, in quod minima fiat resistentia*. London, 1699. Published also in *Commercium Epistolicum*.

Fatouville, Nolant de. *Arlequin empereur dans la lune*. Troyes: Garnier, s. d.

Fontenelle, Bernard le Bovier de. "Éloge de M. Leibnitz." In *Histoire de l'Académie Royale des sciences. Année 1716*. Paris: Impr. Royale, 1718, pp. 94–128.

Foucher, Simon. *Critique de la recherche de la vérité*. Paris, 1675.

Foucher, Simon. *Réponse pour la critique à la préface du second volume de la recherche de la vérité*. Paris, 1676.

Freke, William. *A Dialogue by Way of Question and Answer, Concerning the Deity. All the Responses Being Taken Verbatim out of the Scriptures. – A Brief, but Clear Confutation of the Doctrine of the Trinity*. London, 1693.

Galilei, Galileo. *Discorsi e dimostrazioni matematiche intorno a due nuove scienze*. Leiden, 1638. In *Opere... in questa nuova editione... accresciute*. 2 vols. Bologna, 1656.

Galilei, Galileo. *Opere*. Edizione Nazionale. 20 vols. Florence, 1890–1909. New reprint, Florence, 1964–6.

Guericke, Otto von. *Experimenta nova (ut vocantur) Magdeburgica de vacuo spatio*. Amstelodami, 1672.

Hessen-Rheinfels, Ernst von. *Der so warhaffte als gantz auffrichtig und discret-gesinnte Catholischer*. N. pl., 1666.

Hobbes, Thomas. *Elementorum philosophiae sectio tertia de cive*. Paris, 1642.

Hobbes, Thomas. *Elementorum philosophiae sectio prima de corpore*. London, 1655.

Hobbes, Thomas. *The Questions Concerning Liberty, Necessity, and Chance: Clearly Stated and Debated between Dr. Bramhall, Bishop of Derry, and Thomas Hobbes of Malmesbury*. London: Printed for Andrew Crook, 1656.

Hobbes, Thomas. *Elementorum philosophiae sectio secunda de homine*. London, 1658.

Hobbes, Thomas. *The English Works of Thomas Hobbes of Malmesbury*. Ed. by William Molesworth. 11 vols. London, 1839–45.

Hobbes, Thomas. *The Correspondence*. Ed. by Noel Malcolm. 2 vols. Oxford: Clarendon Press, 1994.

Hutter, Leonhard. *Compendium locorum theologicorum ex scripturis sacris et libro concordiae collectum*. Wittebergae: Helwig, 1610.

Huygens, Christiaan. "Extrait d'une lettre de M. Hugens à l'Auteur du Journal." *Journal des Sçavans* (18 March 1669): 22–4.

Huygens, Christiaan. "A Summary Account of the Laws of Motion, communicated by Mr. Christian Hugens in a Letter to the R. Society, and since printed in French in the Journal des Scavans of March 18, 1669. St. n." *Philosophical Transactions* 46 (12 April 1669) (O.S.): 925–8.

Huygens, Christiaan. *Horologium oscillatorium*. Paris, 1673.

Huygens, Christiaan. *Oeuvres complètes*. 22 vols. The Hague, 1888–1950.

Jablonski, Daniel Ernst. *Kurtze Vorstellung der Einigkeit und des Unterscheides, im Glauben beyder Evangelischen so genandten Lutherischen und Reformirten Kirchen.* In *Labora diligenter.* Ed. by Martin Fontius, Hartmut Rudolph, and Gary Smith. Stuttgart: Steiner, 1999, pp. 128–64.

Jaquelot, Isaac. *Conformité de la foi avec la raison, ou defence de la religion.* Amsterdam, 1705. (Including Jaquelot's *Système abregé de l'âme et de la liberté.*)

Jaquelot, Isaac. *Traité de la vérité et de l'inspiration des livres du Vieux et du Nouveau Testament.* Rotterdam: Aux dépens de Gaspard Fritsch, 1715.

Jungius, Joachim. *Logica Hamburgensis, hoc est, Institutiones logicae in usum schol*[ae] *Hamburg*[ensis] *conscriptae, & sex libris comprehensae.* Hamburg: B. Offerman, 1638.

Keckermann, Bartholomäus. *Opera omnia.* 2 vols. Geneva, 1614.

Keill, John. "Epistola . . . de Legibus Virium Centripetarum." *Philosophical Transactions* 26 (1708): 174–87.

Ker of Kersland, John. *Memoirs . . . Containing His Secret Transactions and Negotiations in Scotland, England, the Courts of Vienna, Hanover, and Other Foreign Parts.* [Part I]. London, 1726. (A French version appeared in Rotterdam in the same year.)

Kielmanseff, Erich Graf von, ed. *Briefe des Herzogs Ernst August* [1674–1728] *zu Braunschweig-Lüneburg an Johann Franz Diedrich von Wendt aus den Jahren 1703 bis 1726.* Hanover and Leipzig, 1902.

King, William. *De Origine Mali.* London, 1702.

Kircher, Athanasius. *Polygraphia nova et universalis ex combinatoria arte detecta.* Rome, 1663.

Kircher, Athanasius. *Ars magna sciendi sive Combinatoria.* 2 vols. Amsterdam, 1699.

La Croze, Mathurin Veyssières de. *Dissertations historiques sur divers sujets.* Rotterdam: Reinier Leers, 1707.

Lamy, François. *De la connoissance de soi-même.* 1st ed. Paris, 1694–8. 2nd ed. Paris, 1669/1701.

Le Clerc, Jean. *Epistolario.* Ed. by Maria Grazia and Mario Sina. 4 vols. Florence: Olschki, 1987–97.

L'Hôpital, Guillaume François Antoine de. *Analyse des infiniment petits, pour l'intelligence des lignes courbes.* Paris: de l'Imprimerie royale, 1696.

Locke, John. *An Essay Concerning Humane Understanding: in Four Books.* London: Printed for Th. Basset, 1690; 2nd ed. London: Printed for Awnsham and J. Churchill, 1694; critical ed. by P. H. Nidditch in *The Clarendon Edition of the Works of John Locke.* Oxford: Clarendon Press, 1975.

Locke, John. *A Letter to the Right Reverend Edward Lord Bishop of Worcester, Concerning Some Passages Relating to Mr. Locke's "Essay of Humane Understanding": In a Late Discourse of His Lordship, in Vindication of the Trinity.* London: Printed for A. and J. Churchill, 1697.

Locke, John. *Reply to the Right Reverend the Lord Bishop of Worcester's Answer to His "Letter Concerning Some Passages Relating to Mr. Locke's Essay of Humane Understanding": In a Late Discourse of His Lordship, in Vindication of the Trinity.* London: Printed for A. and J. Churchill, 1697.

Locke, John. *Reply to the Right Reverend the Lord Bishop of Worcester's Answer to His Second Letter.* London: Printed for A. and J. Churchill, 1699.

Locke, John. *Essai philosophique concernant l'entendement humain.* Trans. from the 4th ed. by Pierre Coste. Amsterdam: Schelte, 1700.

Locke, John. *The Correspondence.* Ed. by E. S. de Beer. 8 vols. Oxford: Clarendon Press, 1976–89.

Longobardi, Nicolas. *Traité sur quelques points de la religion des Chinois.* In *Anciens traitez de divers auteurs sur les ceremonies de la Chine.* Paris, 1701.

Lütke, Franz Julius. *Christliche unmaßgebliche Gedancken über die Vereinigung Der beyden Protestirenden Kirchen.* In Franz Julius Lütke, *Unvorgreiffliche doch Wolgemeinte Gedancken von Vereinigung der Christlichen Religionen.* N. pl., 1703, pp. 38–49.

Lull, Ramon. *Ars magna generalis ultima.* Venice, 1480.

Lull, Ramon. *Opera.* Strasbourg, 1598.

Luther, Martin. *De servo arbitrio.* (1525) In *D. Martin Luthers Werke. Kritische Gesamtausgabe.* Weimar, 1883 ff., vol. 18, pp. 600–787.

Luther, Martin. *Der kleine Catechismus für die gemeine Pfarherr und Prediger.* Leipzig: Hartung, 1860. (Reprint of the 1st ed. Erfurt, 1529.)

Malebranche, Nicolas. *Conversations chrétiennes dans lesquelles on justifie la vérité de la religion et de la morale de Jésus-Christ.* Mons: G. Migeot, 1677. (Nouvelle édition corrigée et augmentée, Bruxelles: impr. de J. Fricx, 1677.)

Malebranche, Nicolas. *De la recherche de la vérité.* Quatriéme edition reveuë et augmentée. Paris, 1678–9.

Malebranche, Nicolas. *Traité de la nature et de la grace.* Rotterdam, 1684.

Malebranche, Nicolas. *Trois lettres de l'auteur de la Recherche de la verité, touchant la défense de Mr. Arnauld contre la réponse au livre des vrayes et fausses idées.* Rotterdam, 1685.

Malebranche, Nicolas. *Entretien d'un philosophe chrétien et d'un philosophe Chinois.* Paris, 1708.

Mariotte, Edme. *Essay de logique contenant les principes des sciences.* Paris, 1678.

Matthaeus, Anton. *Collegia juris.* Franekerae, 1647.

Mengoli, Pietro. *Novae quadraturae arithmeticae.* Bologna, 1650.

Meyer, Lodewijk. *Philosophia s. scripturae interpres; Exercitatio paradoxa, in qua, veram philosophiam infallibilem s. literas interpretandi normam esse, apodictice demonstratur, & discrepantes ad hac sententiae expenduntur, ac refelluntur.* Eleutheropoli [Amsterdam], 1666.

Molanus, Gerhard Wolter. *Cogitationes privatae de methodo reunionis Ecclesiae protes-tantium cum Ecclesia Romano-Catholica*. (1691) In Jacques-Bénigne Bossuet, *Oeuvres complètes*. Ed. by F. Lachat. 31 vols. Paris, 1862–79, vol. 17, Paris, 1864, pp. 294–431.

Molanus, Gerhard Wolter and Hermann Barckhausen. *Methodus reducendae unionis ecclesiasticae inter Romanenses et Protestantes*. (1683) In R. A. Nolte, *Commercium litterarium clarorum virorum*. Brunsvigae: Renger, 1737–8, pp. 327 ff.

More, Henry. *Enchiridion ethicum*. London, 1668.

Newton, Isaac. *Philosophiae naturalis principia mathematica*. Londini: Jussu Societatis Regiæ ac Typis Josephi Streater, 1687.

Newton, Isaac. *Opticks: or, A treatise of the reflexions, refractions, inflexions and colours of light. Also two treatises of the species and magnitude of curvilinear figures*. London: Printed for Sam. Smith 1704. (Including *De quadratura curvarum* and *Enumeratio linearum tertii ordinis*.)

Newton, Isaac. *Optice: sive De reflexionibus, refractionibus, inflexionibus & coloribus lucis libri tres*. Latine reddidit Samuel Clarke. Londini: impensis Sam. Smith & Benj. Walford, 1706.

Newton, Isaac. "An Account of the Book entituled Commercium Epistolicum Collinii et aliorum." *Philosophical Transactions* 29, no. 342 (1715): 173–224.

Newton, Isaac. *The Correspondence of Isaac Newton*. 7 vols. Cambridge: Cambridge University Press, 1959–77.

Nolte, R. A. *Mathematischer Beweis der Erschaffung und Ordnung der Welt in einem Medallion*. Leipzig: Langenheim, 1734.

Nye, Stephen. *Considerations on the Explications of the Doctrine of the Trinity, by Dr. Wallis, Dr. Sherlock, Dr. S-th, Dr. Cudworth, and Mr. Hooker*. London, 1693.

Oldenburg, Heinrich. *The Correspondence of Henry Oldenburg*. Ed. by A. Rupert Hall and M. Boas Hall. 13 vols. Madison: University of Wisconsin Press and London: Taylor and Francis, 1965–86.

Pascal, Blaise. *Lettres de A. Dettonville*. Paris, 1659.

Pellisson-Fontanier, Paul. *Reflexions sur les differends de la religion*. Paris: Chez Gabriel Martin, 1686.

Pellisson-Fontanier, Paul. *Reflexions sur les differens de la religion. Quatrième partie. Ou réponse aux objections envoyées d'Allemagne, sur l'unité de l'Eglise, et sur la question, si elle peut tolérer les sectes*. Paris: chez la Veuve de Gabriel Martin, 1691.

Pellisson-Fontanier, Paul. *De la tolerance des religions, lettres de M. de Leibniz et réponses de M. Pellisson, Ou quatrième partie des Reflexions sur les differends de la religion*. Paris: Jean Anisson, 1692.

Petersen, Johann Wilhelm. *Uranias qua opera Dei magna omnibus retro seculis et oeconomiis transactis usque ad apocatastasin seculorum omnium . . . carmine hero-ico celebrantur*. Francofurti et Lipsiae: sumptu Novi Bibliopolii, 1720.

Pfaff, Christopher Matthäus. "Fragmentum Epistolae a Cel. D. Christoph. Matthaeo Pfaffio." *Acta Eruditorum* (March 1728): 125–7.

Pufendorf, Samuel (pseudonymous: Severinus de Monzambano). *De statu imperii germanici*. Geneva, 1667.

Pufendorf, Samuel. *Disquisitio de republica irregulari ad Severini Monzambano Cap. IV de forma imperii Germanici*. N. pl., 1669.

Pufendorf, Samuel. *De jure naturae et gentium*. Lund, 1672.

Pufendorf, Samuel. *De officio hominis et civis juxta legem naturalem*. Lund, 1673.

Rays, John. *Miscellaneous discourses, concerning the dissolution and changes of the world*. London, 1692.

Rohault, Jacques. *Physica*. Latinè reddidit, & annotatiunculis quibusdam illustravit S. Clarke. Londini: Impensis Jacobi Knapton, 1697.

Rojas y Spinola, Cristobal de. *Regulae circa christianorum omnium ecclesiasticam reunionem* (1682/1683). In J. C. Lünig, *Publicorum negotiorum sylloge*. Frankfurt and Leipzig, 1694, pp. 1092–1124.

Ronsard, P. *Le tombeau du feu Roy Tres-Chrestien Charles IX*. Paris, 1574.

Rosenroth, Christian Knorr von. *Kabbala denudata, seu doctrina Hebraeorum transcendentalis et metaphysica atque theologica*. Sulzbaci: Typis Abrahami Lichtenthaleri, 1677.

Rosenroth, Christian Knorr von. *Kabbalae Denudatae tomus secundus: Id est Liber Sohar Restitutus . . . cui adjecta Adumbratio Cabbalae Christianae ad captum Judaeorum*. Francofurti: Sumptibus Joannis Davidis Zunneri, 1684.

Saint-Vincent, Grégoire de. *Opus geometricum quadraturae circuli et sectionum coni*. Antwerp, 1647.

Santa Maria, Antonio Caballero de. *Traité sur quelques points importans de la mission de la Chine. In Anciens traitez de divers auteurs sur les ceremonies de la Chine*. Paris, 1701.

Scherzer, Johann Adam. *Collegium anti-socinianum*. Leipzig: F. Lanckisius, 1672.

Scherzer, Johann Adam. *Heptas Catholica, seu de Catholico, quatenus fidei et ecclesiae tribuitur, VII. dissertationes academicæ*. Leipzig: Typis Christiani Götzi, 1683.

Scherzer, Johann Adam. *Anti-Bellarminus*. Leipzig, 1703.

Scherzer, Johann Adam. *Collegium anti-Calvinianum*. Leipzig: Zschau, 1704.

Schulenburg, J. Chr. *Unvorgreiflicher Vorschlag zur Vereinigung d. Fest-Zeit*. Frankfurt and Leipzig, 1724.

Schwenter, Daniel and Georg Philipp Harsdörffer. *Deliciae physico-mathematicae*. Vol. 1 (by Schwenter). Nuremberg, 1636. Vols. 2–3 (by Harsdörffer). Nuremberg, 1651–3.

Spener, Philipp Jakob. *Consilia et judicia theologica latina*. Francofurti ad Moenum: Zunner & Jungius, 1709.

Spinoza, Baruch. *Opera posthuma*. [Amsterdam], 1677.

Spinoza, Baruch. *Opera*. Ed. by Carl Gebhardt. 4 vols. Heidelberg: Carl Winters Universitätsbuchhandlung, 1925.

Spinoza, Baruch. *Tractatus Theologico-Politicus*. (1670) In C. Gebhardt, ed. *Spinoza Opera*. Vol. 3. Heidelberg: Carl Winters Universitätsbuchhandlung, 1925.

Spinoza, Baruch. *The Correspondence*. Trans. and ed. by A. Wolf. London: George Allen and Unwin, 1928.

Spizelius, Theophilus [Spitzel, Gottlieb]. *De atheismo eradicando ad virum praeclarissimum Dn. Antonium Reiserum Augustanum etc. Epistola.* Augustae Vindelic.: apud G. Goebelium, 1669.

Stahl, Daniel. *Compendium metaphysicae in XXIV tabellas redactum.* Jena, 1655.

Stensen, Niels. *De solido intra solidum naturaliter contento.* Florence, 1669.

Stillingfleet, Edward. *A Discourse in Vindication of the Doctrine of the Trinity.* London: Printed by H. J. for Henry Mortlock, 1697.

Stillingfleet, Edward. *The Bishop of Worcester's Answer to Mr. Locke's Letter.* London: Printed by J. H. for Henry Mortlock, 1697.

Stillingfleet, Edward. *The Bishop of Worcester's Answer to Mr. Locke's Second Letter.* London: Printed for J. H. for Henry Mortlock, 1698.

Sturm, Johannes. *Academicae Epistolae.* Strasbourg: Rihel, 1569.

Sturm, Johann Christoph. *Idolum naturae similiumque nominum vanorum ex hominum christianorum animis deturbandi conatus philosophicus.* Altdorf: Heinrich Mayer, 1692. (University Dissertation: Praes. Sturm; Resp. Leonhard Christoph Riederer.)

Sully, Henry. *Regle artificielle du Tems.* Vienna: André Heyinger, 1714.

Thomasius, Jakob. *Philosophia practica.* Leipzig, 1661.

Thomasius, Jakob. *De sectarum conciliationibus. Praemissa disputationi, habitae Anno 1668. d. 20. Junii. De quaestione: an Deus sit materia prima? Resp. Joh. Friderico Hekelio, Gerano.* In Jakob Thomasius, *Praefationes sub auspicia disputationum suarum in Academiâ Lipsiensi, recitatae, argumenti varii.* Lipsiae: Apud Johann. Fuhrmannum & Matthaeum Ritterum, 1681.

Thomasius, Jakob. *Adversus philosophos novantiquos.* In Jakob Thomasius, *Dissertationes LXIII: Varii argumenti magnam partem ad historiam philosophicam & ecclesiasticam pertinentes.* Halae Magdeburgicae: Impensis J. F. Zeitleri, 1693.

Toland, John. *Christianity Not Mysterious: Or, a Treatise Shewing, That There Is Nothing in the Gospel Contrary to Reason, Nor above It: And That No Christian Doctrine Can Be Properly Call'd a Mystery.* London, 1696.

Toland, John. *Anglia Libera: Or the Limitation and Succession of the Crown of England Explain'd and Asserted.* London: Printed for Bernard Lintott, 1701.

Toland, John. "Remarques critiques sur le systême de Monsr. Leibnitz de l'harmonie préetablie." *Histoire Critique de la République des Lettres* 11 (1716): 115–33. Reprinted in *The Leibniz Review* 10 (2000): 114–33. Trans. by Richard Francks and R. S. Woolhouse (ibid., pp. 103–11).

Tournemine, René-Joseph. "Conjectures sur l'union de l'ame et du corps." *Mémoires pour l'Histoire des Sciences et des Beaux Arts* 7 (1704): 231–7.

Turmair, Johannes [Aventin]. *Annalium Boiorum lib. VIII.* Basel, 1580.

Turnbull, H. W., ed. *James Gregory Tercentenary Memorial Volume.* London: G. Bell & Sons, 1939.

Uffenbach, Zacharias Konrad von. *Merkwürdige Reisen durch Niedersachsen, Holland, und England.* Part 1. Ulm and Memmingen, 1753.

Walenburch, Adrian and Peter van. *Tractatus generales de controversiis fidei.* Coloniae Agrippinae: Apud Ioannem Wilhelmum Friessem juniorem, 1670.

Walenburch, Adrian and Peter van. *Tractatus speciales, de controversiis fidei*. Coloniae Agrippinae: Apud Ioannem Wilhelmum Friessem juniorem, 1670.

Wallis, John. *Arithmetica infinitorum*. Oxford, 1656.

Wallis, John. "Dr Wallis's opinion concerning the Hypothesis Physica Nova of Dr. Leibnitius, promised in Numb. 73. and here inserted in the same tongue, wherein it was written to the Publisher, April. 7. 1671." *Philosophical Transactions* 74 (14 August 1671) (O.S.): 2227–31.

Wallis, John. *Opera mathematica*. Vols. I, II, III. Oxford, 1695, 1693, 1699.

Whiston, William. *New Theory of the Earth*. London, 1696.

Wideburg, J. B. [Praes.] *Diss. math. De praestantia arithmeticae binariae*. Jena, 1718.

Winckler, Johann Joseph. *Arcanum Regium*. Frankfurt, 1703.

Wilkins, John. *Essay towards a Real Character and a Philosophical Language*. London, 1668.

Winckler, J. D., ed. *Anecdota historico-ecclesiastica novantiqua*. Braunschweig: Ludolph Schröders Erben, 1757.

Wolff, Christian. *Vernünftige Gedanken: Von den Kräften des menschlichen Verstandes und ihrem richtigen Gebrauch in der Erkenntnis der Wahrheit* [German Logic]. Halle, 1712. In Christian Wolff, *Gesammelte Werke. 1. Abt., Deutsche Schriften*. Vol. 1. Hildesheim: Olms, 1965.

Woodward, John. *Essay towards a Natural History of the Earth*. London, 1695.

II. Main Biographies of Leibniz

Aiton, E. J. *Leibniz: A Biography*. Bristol and Boston: Adam Hilger, 1985.

Eckhart, Johann Georg. *Lebensbeschreihung des Freyherrn von Leibnitz*. In *Journal zur Kunstgeschichte und zur allgemeinen Literatur*. Ed. by Chr. G. von Murr. Nürnberg 7 (1779): 123–321. (Reprinted in Eberhard, J. A., and J. G. Eckhart. *Leibniz-Biographien*. Hildesheim: Olms, 2003.)

Guhrauer, Gottschalk Eduard. *Gottfried Wilhelm Freiherr von Leibnitz. Eine Biographie*. 2 vols. Breslau: Hirt, 1842. 2nd enlarged ed. Breslau: Hirt, 1846. Reprint, Hildesheim: Olms, 1966.

Hirsch, Eike Christian. *Der berühmte Herr Leibniz: Eine Biographie*. Munich: Beck, 2000.

Hochstetter, Erich. "Zu Leibniz' Gedächtnis. Eine Einleitung." In *Leibniz. Zu seinem 300. Geburtstage 1646–1946*. Ed. by Erich Hochstetter. Instalments 1–8. Berlin: W. de Gruyter, 1946–52. Instalment 3, 1948, pp. 82.

Mackie, J. M. *Life of Godfrey William von Leibnitz on the basis of the German work of Dr. G. E. Guhrauer*. Boston (Mass): Gould, Kendell and Lincoln, 1845.

Müller, Kurt. "Gottfried Wilhelm Leibniz. Sein Leben und Wirken." In *Leibniz. Sein Leben, sein Wirken, seine Welt*. Ed. by W. Totok and C. Haase. Hanover: Verlag für Literatur und Zeitgeschehen, 1966, pp. 1–64.

Müller, Kurt, and Gisela Krönert. *Leben und Werk von Gottfried Wilhelm Leibniz. Eine Chronik*. Frankfurt am Main: Klostermann, 1969.

Schepers, Heinrich. "Leibniz." In *Neue Deutsche Biographie*. Berlin: Duncker and Humblot, 1985, Vol. 14, pp. 121–31.

III. Main Bibliographies of Leibniz

Bibliographie des oeuvres de Leibniz. Ed. by Émile Ravier. Paris: F. Alcan, 1937. Reprint, Hildesheim: Olms, 1966.
Schrecker, Paul. "Une bibliographie de Leibniz." *Revue philosophique de la France et de l'étranger* 126 (1938): 324–46.
Leibniz-Bibliographie. Die Literatur über Leibniz bis 1980. Ed. by Albert Heinekamp. Frankfurt am Main: Vittorio Klostermann, 1984.
Leibniz-Bibliographie. Die Literatur über Leibniz 1981–1990. Ed. by Albert Heinekamp. Frankfurt am Main: Vittorio Klostermann, 1996.
Leibniz-Bibliographie at http://www.leibniz-bibliographie.de.

IV. Secondary Literature

Leibniz à Paris (1672–1676). *Symposion de la G. W. Leibniz-Gesellschaft*. 2 vols. Wiesbaden: Steiner, 1978.
Adams, Robert Merrihew. *Leibniz. Determinist, Theist, Idealist*. New York and Oxford: Oxford University Press, 1994.
Adams, Robert Merrihew. "Leibniz's Examination of the Christian Religion." *Faith and Philosophy* 11, no. 4 (1994): 517–46.
Adams, Robert Merrihew. "Leibniz's Conception of Religion." In *The Proceedings of the Twentieth World Congress of Philosophy*. Vol 7: Modern Philosophy. Ed. by Mark D. Gedney. Bowling Green: Philosophy Documentation Center, 2000, pp. 57–70.
Ahsmann, Margreet. "Teaching in Collegia: The Organisation of Disputationes at Universities in the Netherlands and Germany during the 16th and 17th Centuries." In A. Romano, ed., *Università in Europa. Le istituzioni universitarie dal Medio Evo ai nostri giorni*. Soveria Mannelli: Rubbettino, 1995, pp. 99–114.
Aiton, E. J. "An Unpublished Letter of Leibniz to Sloane." *Annals of Science* 38 (1981): 103–7.
Angelelli, Ignacio. "Leibniz's Misunderstanding of Nizolius' Notion of 'multitudo.'" *Notre Dame Journal of Formal Logic* 6, no. 4 (1965): 319–22.
Antognazza, Maria Rosa. "Inediti leibniziani sulle polemiche trinitarie." *Rivista di Filosofia neo-scolastica* 83, no. 4 (1991): 525–50.
Antognazza, Maria Rosa. "*Immeatio* and *emperichoresis*. The Theological Roots of Harmony in Bisterfeld and Leibniz." In *The Young Leibniz and His Philosophy, 1646–1676*. Ed. by Stuart Brown. Dordrecht: Kluwer, 1999, pp. 41–64.
Antognazza, Maria Rosa. "The Defence of the Mysteries of the Trinity and the Incarnation: An Example of Leibniz's 'Other' Reason." *British Journal for the History of Philosophy* 9, no. 2 (2001): 283–309.

Antognazza, Maria Rosa. *"Debilissimae Entitates?* Bisterfeld and Leibniz's Ontology of Relations." *The Leibniz Review* 11 (2001): 1–22.

Antognazza, Maria Rosa. "Natural and Supernatural Mysteries: Leibniz's *Annotatiunculae subitaneae* on Toland's *Christianity Not Mysterious.*" In *Nihil sine Ratione. Mensch, Natur und Technik im Wirken von G. W. Leibniz. VII. Internationaler Leibniz-Kongress.* Ed. by Hans Poser. 3 vols. Berlin: Leibniz-Gesellschaft, 2001, vol. I, pp. 17–24.

Antognazza, Maria Rosa, "Leibniz and Religious Toleration: The Correspondence with Paul Pellisson-Fontanier." *American Catholic Philosophical Quarterly* 76, no. 4 (2002): 601–22.

Antognazza, Maria Rosa. "Leibniz and the Post-Copernican Universe. Koyré Revisited." *Studies in History and Philosophy of Science* 34 (2003): 309–27.

Antognazza, Maria Rosa. *Leibniz on the Trinity and the Incarnation: Reason and Revelation in the Seventeenth Century.* New Haven, CT: Yale University Press, 2007. Revised version of *Trinità e Incarnazione: Il rapporto tra filosofia e teologia rivelata nel pensiero di Leibniz.* Milan: Vita e Pensiero, 1999.

Antognazza, Maria Rosa, and Howard Hotson, eds. *Alsted and Leibniz on God, the Magistrate and the Millennium.* Texts edited with introduction and commentary. Wolfenbütteler Arbeiten zur Barockforschung, vol. 34. Wiesbaden: Harrassowitz Verlag, 1999.

Ariew, R. "G. W. Leibniz, Life and Works." In *The Cambridge Companion to Leibniz.* Ed. by Nicholas Jolley. New York and Cambridge: Cambridge University Press, 1995, pp. 18–42.

Arthur, Richard. "Russell's Conundrum. On the Relation of Leibniz's Monads to the Continuum." In *An Intimate Relation. Studies in the History and Philosophy of Science.* Ed. by J. R. Brown and J. Mittelstrass. Boston, Dordrecht, and London: Reidel, 1989, pp. 171–201.

Arthur, Richard. "Space and Relativity in Newton and Leibniz." *The British Journal for the Philosophy of Science* 45 (1994): 219–40 (also in *Leibniz.* Ed. by Catherine Wilson. Dartmouth, 2001, pp. 61–82).

Arthur, Richard. "Infinite Aggregates and Phenomenal Wholes: Leibniz's Theory of Substance as a Solution to the Continuum Problem." *Leibniz Society Review* 8 (1998): 25–45.

Arthur, Richard. "The Enigma of Leibniz's Atomism." *Oxford Studies in Early Modern Philosophy* 1 (2003): 183–227.

Asch, Ronald G. *The Thirty Years War: The Holy Roman Empire and Europe, 1618–1648.* Basingstoke: Macmillan, 1997.

Badur, Klaus, and Wolfgang Rottstedt. "Und sie rechnet doch richtig! Erfahrungen beim Nachbau einer Leibniz-Rechenmaschine." *Studia Leibnitiana* 36, no. 2 (2004): 130–46.

Bardi, Jason. *The Calculus Wars: Newton, Leibniz and the Greatest Mathematical Clash of All Time.* London: High Stakes, 2006.

Bardout, Jean-Christophe. "Johannes Clauberg." In *A Companion to Early Modern Philosophy.* Ed. by Steven Nadler. Oxford: Blackwell, 2002, pp. 129–39.

Barnett, Frances Mason. *Medical Authority and Princely Patronage: The Academia Naturae Curiosorum, 1652–1693*. University of North Carolina at Chapel Hill, 1995. (Unpubl. Ph.D. dissertation.)

Becco, Anne. "Aux sources de la monade: Paléographie et lexicographie leibniziennes." *Les Études Philosophiques* 3 (1975): 279–94.

Becco, Anne. "Leibniz et François-Mercure van Helmont: Bagatelle pour des monades." In *Magia Naturalis und die Entstehung der Modernen Naturwissenschaften. Symposion der Leibniz-Gesellschaft Hannover, 14. und 15. November 1975*. Studia Leibnitiana Sonderheft, vol. 7. Wiesbaden: Steiner, 1978, pp. 119–41.

Beck, Lewis White. *Early German Philosophy: Kant and His Predecessors*. Cambridge, MA: Belknap Press of the Harvard University Press, 1969.

Beeley, Philip. *Kontinuität und Mechanismus. Zur Philosophie des jungen Leibniz in ihrem ideengeschichtlichen Kontext*. Stuttgart: Steiner, 1996.

Beeley, Philip. "Mathematics and Nature in Leibniz's Early Philosophy." In *The Young Leibniz and His Philosophy, 1646–1676*. Ed. by Stuart Brown. Dordrecht: Kluwer, 1999, pp. 123–45.

Beeley, Philip. "A Philosophical Apprenticeship: Leibniz's Correspondence with the Secretary of the Royal Society, Henry Oldenburg." In *Leibniz and His Correspondents*. Ed. by Paul Lodge. Cambridge: Cambridge University Press, 2004, pp. 47–73.

Belaval, Yvon. "Premières animadversions de Leibniz sur les *Principes* de Descartes." In *Mélanges Alexandre Koyré t. II: l'Aventure de l'esprit*. Paris: Hermann, 1964, pp. 29–56.

Belaval, Yvon. *Leibniz: Initiation à sa philosophie*. 3rd ed. Paris: Vrin, 1969.

Benz, Ernst. "Leibniz und Peter der Grosse," 1947, pp. 1–88. Instalment 2 in *Leibniz. Zu seinem 300. Geburtstage 1646–1946*. Ed. by Erich Hochstetter. Berlin: W. de Gruyter, 1946–52. Instalments 1–8.

Berg, Wieland, and Benno Parthier. "Die 'kaiserliche' *Leopoldina* im Heiligen Römischen Reich Deutscher Nation." In *Gelehrte Gesellschaften im mitteldeutschen Raum (1650–1820)*. Part I. Ed. by Detlef Döring and Kurt Nowak. Vol. 76, 2 of *Abhandlungen der Sächsischen Akademie der Wissenschaften zu Leipzig. Philologisch-historische Klasse*. Leipzig: S. Hirzel, 2000, pp. 39–52.

Bergmann, J. "Leibniz als Reichshofrat in Wien und dessen Besoldung." *Sitzungsberichte der kaiserlichen Akademie der Wissenschaften zu Wien. Phil.–hist. Klasse*. Vol. 26. Vienna, 1858. Fasc. I, pp. 187–215.

Bernstein, Howard. "*Conatus*, Hobbes, and the Young Leibniz." *Studies in History and Philosophy of Science* 11 (1980): 25–37.

Bertoloni Meli, Domenico. *Equivalence and Priority: Newton versus Leibniz*. Oxford: Clarendon Press, 1993.

Bertoloni Meli, Domenico. "Caroline, Leibniz, and Clarke." *Journal of the History of Ideas* 60, no. 3 (1999): 469–86.

Bireley, R. A. "The Thirty Years War as Germany's Religious War." In *Krieg und Politik 1618–1648*. Ed. by K. Repgen. Munich: R. Oldenbourg, 1988, pp. 85–106.

Blank, Andreas. "Incomplete Entities, Natural Non-separability, and Leibniz's Response to François Lamy's *De la Connoissance de soi-même*." *The Leibniz Review* 13 (2003): 1–17.

Boas Hall, Marie. "The Royal Society's Role in the Diffusion of Information in the Seventeenth Century." *Notes and Records of the Royal Society of London* 29 (1975): 173–192.

Boas Hall, Marie. "Leibniz and the Royal Society. 1670–76." In *Leibniz à Paris (1672–1676). Symposion de la G. W. Leibniz-Gesellschaft.* 2 vols. Wiesbaden: Steiner, 1978, vol. 1, pp. 171–82.

Bodéüs, R. *Leibniz–Thomasius, Correspondance, 1663–1672.* Paris: J. Vrin, 1993.

Boehm, Rudolf. "Notes sur l'histoire des 'Principes de la nature et de la grâce' et de la 'Monadologie' de Leibniz." *Revue philosophique de Louvain* 55 (1957): 232–51.

Böger, Ines. "Der Spanheim-Kreis und seine Bedeutung für Leibniz' Akademiepläne." In *Leibniz in Berlin*. Ed. by Hans Poser and Albert Heinekamp. Stuttgart: Steiner, 1990, pp. 202–17.

Bos, H. J. M. "Differentials, Higher-Order Differentials and the Derivative in the Leibnizian Calculus." *Archive for History of Exact Sciences* 14 (1974): 1–90.

Bos, H. J. M. "The Influence of Huygens on the Formation of Leibniz's Ideas." In *Leibniz à Paris (1672–1676). Symposion de la G. W. Leibniz-Gesellschaft.* 2 vols. Wiesbaden: Steiner, 1978, vol. 1, pp. 59–68.

Bradley Bassler, O. "Towards Paris: The Growth of Leibniz's Paris Mathematics out of the Pre-Paris Metaphysics." *Studia Leibnitiana* 31, no. 2 (1999): 160–80.

Brambora, Josef. "Comenius und Leibniz." In *Akten des [I.] Internationalen Leibniz-Kongress Hannover, 14.–19. November 1966.* Vol. 5. Wiesbaden: Steiner, 1971, pp. 55–71.

Brather, Hans-Stephan. "Leibniz und das Konzil der Berliner Sozietät der Wissenschaften." In *Leibniz in Berlin*. Ed. by Hans Poser and Albert Heinekamp. Stuttgart: Steiner, 1990, pp. 218–30.

Braubach, M. *Prinz Eugen von Savoyen. Eine Biographie.* 5 vols. Munich, 1963–5.

Breger, Herbert and Friedrich Niewöhner, eds. *Leibniz und Niedersachsen.* Stuttgart: Steiner, 1999.

Brown, Gregory. "Personal, Political, and Philosophical Dimensions of the Leibniz–Caroline Correspondence." In *Leibniz and His Correspondents*. Ed. by Paul Lodge. Cambridge: Cambridge University Press, 2004, pp. 262–92.

Brown, Stuart. "Leibniz's *New System* Strategy." In *Leibniz's New System (1695)*. Ed. by Roger S. Woolhouse. Florence: Olschki, 1996, pp. 37–61.

Brown, Stuart. "The Proto-monadology of the *De Summa Rerum*." In *The Young Leibniz and His Philosophy, 1646–1676*. Ed. by Stuart Brown. Dordrecht: Kluwer, 1999, pp. 263–88.

Brown, Stuart. "The Leibniz–Toland Debates on Materialism and the Soul at the Court of the Queen of Prussia." In *Nihil sine Ratione. Mensch, Natur und Technik im Wirken von G. W. Leibniz. VII. Internationaler Leibniz-Kongress*. Ed. by Hans Poser. 3 vols. Berlin: Leibniz-Gesellschaft, 2001, vol. I, pp. 147–54.

Brown, Stuart. "The Leibniz–Foucher Alliance and Its Philosophical Bases." In *Leibniz and His Correspondents*. Ed. by Paul Lodge. Cambridge: Cambridge University Press, 2004, pp. 74–96.

Bruyère, Nelly. "Leibniz, lecteur de Ramus." In *Leibniz et la Renaissance*. Ed. by Albert Heinekamp. Wiesbaden: Steiner, 1983, pp. 157–73.

Bruyère, Nelly. *Méthode et dialectique dans l'oeuvre de la Ramée*. Paris: J. Vrin, 1984.

Bussman, Klaus and Heinz Schilling, eds. *1648: War and Peace in Europe*. 3 vols. Munich: Bruckmann, 1998.

Burkhardt, H. *Logik and Semiotik in der Philosophie von Leibniz*. Munich: Philosophia Verlag, 1980.

Busche, Hubertus. "Die drei Stufen des Naturrechts und die Ableitung materialer Gerechtigkeitsnormen beim frühen Leibniz. Zur Vorgeschichte der 'caritas sapientis.'" In *Realität und Begriff*. Ed. by Peter Baumanns. Würzburg: Königshausen & Neumann, 1993, pp. 105–49.

Busche, Hubertus. *Leibniz' Weg ins perspektivische Universum: Eine Harmonie im Zeitalter der Berechnung*. Hamburg: Felix Meiner Verlag, 1997.

Carabelli, Giancarlo. *Tolandiana. Materiali bibliografici per lo studio dell'opera e della fortuna di John Toland (1670–1722)*. Florence: La Nuova Italia, 1975.

Chaitin, Gregory. "Leibniz, Information, Math and Physics." In *Wissen und Glauben/Knowledge and Belief. Akten des 26. Internationalen Wittgenstein-Symposiums 2003*. Ed. by Winfried Löffler and Paul Weingartner. Vienna: ÖBV & HPT, 2004, pp. 277–86.

Chaitin, Gregory. "Leibniz, Randomness and the Halting Probability." *Mathematics Today* 40 (2004): 138–9.

Champion, Justin. *Republican Learning: John Toland and the Crisis of Christian Culture, 1696–1722*. Manchester : Manchester University Press, 2003.

Clarke, Desmond. *Descartes: A Biography*. Cambridge: Cambridge University Press, 2006.

Collani, Claudia von. "Gottfried Wilhelm Leibniz and the China Mission of the Jesuits." In *Das Neueste über China*. Ed. by Wenchao Li and Hans Poser. Stuttgart: Steiner, 2000, pp. 89–103.

Conze, Werner. *Leibniz als Historiker*. Berlin: De Gruyter, 1951.

Cook, Alan. "Leibniz and the Royal Society." *Notes and Records of the Royal Society of London* 50, no. 2 (1996): 153–63.

Coudert, Allison P. *Leibniz and the Kabbalah*. Dordrecht: Kluwer, 1995.

Couturat, Louis. *La logique de Leibniz*. Paris, 1901. Reprint, Hildesheim: Olms, 1969.

Cover, J. A. and John O'Leary-Hawthorne. *Substance and Individuation in Leibniz*. Cambridge: Cambridge University Press, 1999.

Cranston, Maurice. *John Locke. A Biography*. London: Longmans, 1957.

Davídek, V. "G. W. Leibniz oriundus Lipnicky." *Revue internationale d'onomastique* 17 (1965): 93–8.

Davillé, Louis. *Leibniz historien*. Paris: Félix Alcan, 1909.

De Melo, Wolfgang David Cirilo and James Cussens. "Leibniz on Estimating the Uncertain: An English Translation of *De incerti aestimatione* with Commentary." *The Leibniz Review* 14 (2004): 31–53.

De Risi, Vincenzo. *The Analysis Situs 1712–1716. Geometry and Philosophy of Space in the Late Leibniz*. Pisa, 2005 (Ph.D. dissertation). Revised version published under the title *Geometry and Monadology: Leibniz's Analysis Situs and Philosophy of Space*. Basel, Boston, and Berlin: Birkhäuser, 2007.

Distel, Theodor, ed. "Vorlegung einer Abschrift der in dem Hauptstaatsarchive zu Dresden befindlichen Briefe von Leibniz." In *Berichte über die Verhandlungen der Königlich Sächsischen Gesellschaft der Wissenschaften zu Leipzig. Philologisch-Historische Classe*. Leipzig, 1879, vol. 31, pp. 104–54; "Nachtrag." Leipzig, 1880, vol. 32, pp. 187–9.

Döring, Detlef. *Der junge Leibniz und Leipzig: Ausstellung zum 350. Geburtstag von Gottfried Wilhelm Leibniz im Leipziger Alten Rathaus*. Berlin: Akademie Verlag, 1996.

Dohmke, Emil. "Die Nikolaischule zu Leipzig im siebzehnten Jahrhundert." In *Programm des Nicolaigymnasiums in Leipzig*. Leipzig: Edelmann, 1874, pp. 1–43.

Drischler, William Fr. *The Political Biography of the Young Leibniz in The Age of Secret Diplomacy*. Charleston, SC : BookSurge Publ., 2006.

Duchesneau, François. *Leibniz et la méthode de la science*. Paris: Presses Universitaires de France, 1993.

Duchesneau, François. *La dynamique de Leibniz*. Paris: Vrin, 1994.

Duchesneau, François. "Leibniz's Theoretical Shift in the 'Phoranomus and dynamica de potentia.'" *Perspectives on Science* 6, nos. 1–2 (spring–summer 1998). 77–109.

Duchesneau, François. *Les modèles du vivant de Descartes à Leibniz*. Paris: J. Vrin, 1998.

Dürr, Karl. *Neue Beleuchtung einer Theorie von Leibniz. Grundzüge des Logikkalküls*. Darmstadt: Reichl, 1930.

Eisenkopf, Paul. *Leibniz und die Einigung der Christenheit. Überlegungen zur Reunion der evangelischen und katholischen Kirche*. Munich, Paderborn, and Vienna: Schöningh, 1975.

Erler, Georg. *Die jüngere Matrikel der Universität Leipzig (1559–1809)*. 3 vols. Leipzig: Giesecke and Devrient, 1909.

Eulenburg, Franz. *Die Frequenz der deutschen Universitäten*. Leipzig, 1904; repr. Berlin, 1994.

Faak, M. *Leibniz als Reichshofrat*. Humboldt-Universität Berlin, 1966 (Phil. Dissertation, typewr.)

Fichant, Michel. "*Actiones sunt suppositorum*. L'ontologie Leibnizienne de l'action." *Philosophie* 53 (1997): 135–48.

Fichant, Michel. "De la puissance à l'action: La singularité stylistique de la dynamique." In Michel Fichant, *Science et métaphysique dans Descartes et Leibniz*. Paris: Presses Universitaires de France, 1998, pp. 205–43.

Fichant, Michel. "Leibniz et l'exigence de démonstration des axiomes: 'La partie est plus petite que le Tout'." In Michel Fichant, *Science et métaphysique dans Descartes et Leibniz*. Paris: Presses Universitaires de France, 1998, pp. 329–73.

Fichant, Michel. "Mécanisme et métaphysique: Le rétablissement des formes substantielles. (1679)." In Michel Fichant, *Science et métaphysique dans Descartes et Leibniz*. Paris: Presses Universitaires de France, 1998, pp. 163–204.

Fichant, Michel. "La costituzione del concetto di monade." In *Monadi e monadologie. Il mondo degli individui tra Bruno, Leibniz e Husserl*. Ed. by Bianca Maria d'Ippolito, Aniello Montano, and Francesco Piro. Soveria Mannelli: Rubbettino, 2005, pp. 59–81.

Findlen, Paula, ed. *Athanasius Kircher. The Last Man Who Knew Everything*. New York and London: Routledge, 2004.

Fischer, Kuno. *Gottfried Wilhelm Leibniz. Leben, Werke und Lehre*. 4th ed. Heidelberg: Winter, 1902.

Fischer, Rudolph. "Der Name Leibniz." In *Leipziger Namenkundliche Beiträge II*. Berlin, 1968 (Sitzungsberichte der Sächsischen Akademie des Wiss. Vol. 113. Issue 4), pp. 7–18.

Foucher de Careil, Alexandre. *Mémoire sur la philosophie de Leibniz*. Paris: F. R. de Rudeval, 1905.

Fouke, Daniel C. "Metaphysics and the Eucharist in the Early Leibniz." *Studia Leibnitiana* 24 (1992): 145–59.

François, E. "Géographie du livre et réseau urbain dans l'Allemagne moderne." In *La Ville et l'innovation*. Paris, 1987, pp. 59–74.

Franke, Ursula. "Die Freiheit eines Christenmenschen. Streitgespräch zwischen Leibniz und Jaquelot in der Spannung von Vernunft und Glauben." In *Leibniz in Berlin*. Ed. by Hans Poser and Albert Heinekamp. Stuttgart: Steiner, 1990, pp. 103–19.

Fransen, P. *Leibniz und die Friedensschlüsse von Utrecht und Rastatt-Baden. Eine aus größtenteils noch nicht veröffentlichten Quellen geschöpfte Untersuchung*. Purmerend (Holland): Muusses, 1933.

Freudenthal, J. *Die Lebensgeschichte Spinoza's in Quellenschriften, Urkunden und Nichtamtlichen Nachrichten*. Leipzig: Verlag Von Veit, 1899.

Friedberg, Emil. *Die Leipziger Juristenfakultät, ihre Doktoren und ihr Heim, 1409–1909*. Leipzig, 1909.

Friedmann, G. *Leibniz et Spinoza*. 2nd ed. Paris: Gallimard, 1962.

Frost, Robert I. *The Northern Wars. 1558–1721*. Harlow: Longman, 2000.

Garber, Daniel. "Motion and Metaphysics in the Young Leibniz." In *Leibniz: Critical and Interpretative Essays*. Ed. by Michael Hooker. Manchester: Manchester University Press, 1982, pp. 160–84.

Garber, Daniel. "Leibniz and the Foundations of Physics: The Middle Years." In *The Natural Philosophy of Leibniz*. Ed. by Kathleen Okruhlik and James Robert Brown. Dordrecht: Reidel, 1985, pp. 27–130.

Garber, Daniel. "Leibniz: Physics and Philosophy." In *The Cambridge Companion to Leibniz*. Ed. by Nicholas Jolley. New York and Cambridge: Cambridge University Press, 1995, pp. 270–352.

Garber, Daniel. "Leibniz and Fardella. Body, Substance, and Idealism." In *Leibniz and His Correspondents*. Ed. by Paul Lodge. Cambridge: Cambridge University Press, 2004, pp. 123–40.

Garber, Daniel. *Enchanting the World: Leibniz on Body, Substance and Monad*. Oxford: Oxford University Press (Provisional title; Forthcoming.)

Gaukroger, Stephen. *Descartes: An Intellectual Biography.* Oxford: Clarendon Press, 1995.

Gensini, Stefano. *Il naturale e il simbolico. Saggio su Leibniz.* Rome: Bulzoni, 1991.

Gensini, Stefano. "Leibniz Linguist and Philosopher of Language: Between 'Primitive' and 'Natural'." In *Leibniz and Adam.* Ed. by Marcelo Dascal and Elhanan Yakira. Tel Aviv: University Publishing Projects Ltd., 1993, pp. 111–36.

Gerber, Georg. "Leibniz und seine Korrespondenz." In *Leibniz. Sein Leben, sein Wirken, seine Welt.* Ed. by W. Totok and C. Haase. Hanover: Verlag für Literatur und Zeitgeschehen, 1966, pp. 141–71.

Giuntini, Chiara. *Panteismo e ideologia repubblicana: John Toland (1670–1722).* Bologna: Il Mulino, 1979.

Giusti, Enrico. "Le Problème des tangentes de Descartes à Leibniz." In *300 Jahre "Nova Methodus" von G. W. Leibniz (1684–1984). Symposion der Leibniz-Gesellschaft ... 28. bis 30. August 1984.* Ed. by Albert Heinekamp. Stuttgart: Steiner, 1986, pp. 26–37.

Görlich, Ekkehard. *Leibniz als Mensch und Kranker.* Hanover, 1987. (Dissertation for the Doctorate in Medicine, typewr.)

Goldenbaum, Ursula. "Leibniz as a Lutheran." In *Leibniz, Mysticism and Religion.* Ed. by Allison P. Coudert, Richard H. Popkin, and Gordon M. Weiner. Kluwer: Dordrecht, 1998, pp. 169–92.

Goldenbaum, Ursula. "Die Commentatiuncula de judice als Leibnizens erste philosophische Auseinandersetzung mit Spinoza nebst der Mitteilung über ein neuaufgefundenes Leibnizstück." In *Labora Diligenter.* Ed. by M. Fontius et al. Stuttgart: Steiner, 1999, pp. 61–107.

Goldenbaum, Ursula. "Transubstantiation, Physics and Philosophy at the Time of the Catholic Demonstrations." In *The Young Leibniz and His Philosophy, 1646–1676.* Ed. by Stuart Brown. Dordrecht: Kluwer, 1999, pp. 79–102.

Gotthard, Axel. "'Politice seint wir bäpstisch': Kursachsen und der deutschen Protestantismus im frühen 17 Jahrhundert." *Zeitschrift für Historische Forschung* 20 (1993): 275–319.

Gottschalk, Jürgen. "Der Oberharzer Bergbau und Leibniz' Tätigkeit für Verbesserungen." In *Leibniz und Niedersachsen.* Ed. by Herbert Breger and Friedrich Niewöhner. Stuttgart: Steiner, 1999, pp. 173–86.

Grote, Ludwig. *Leibniz und seine Zeit.* Hanover, 1869.

Grotefend, Karl L. *Leibniz-Album aus den Handschriften der Königlichen Bibliothek zu Hannover.* Hanover: Hahnschen Hofbuchhandlung, 1846.

Grua, Gaston. *Jurisprudence universelle et Théodicée selon Leibniz.* Paris: Presses Universitaires de France, 1953.

Grua, Gaston. *La Justice humaine selon Leibniz.* Paris: Presses Universitaires de France, 1956.

Guicciardini, Niccolò. *Reading the Principia. The Debate on Newton's Mathematical Methods for Natural Philosophy from 1687 to 1736.* Cambridge: Cambridge University Press, 1999.

Guicciardini, Niccolò. "Newton's Method and Leibniz's Calculus." In *A History of Analysis*. Ed. by Hans Niels Jahnke. History of Mathematics, vol. 24. Providence: American Mathematical Society, 2003, pp. 73-103.

Hall, Rupert. "Leibniz and the British Mathematicians." In *Leibniz à Paris (1672–1676)*. *Symposion de la G. W. Leibniz-Gesellschaft*. 2 vols. Wiesbaden: Steiner, 1978, vol. 1, pp. 131–52.

Hall, Rupert. *Philosophers at War. The Quarrel between Newton and Leibniz*. Cambridge: Cambridge University Press, 1980.

Harnack, Adolf. *Geschichte der Königlich Preussischen Akademie der Wissenschaften zu Berlin*. 4 vols. Berlin, 1900.

Hartmann, Fritz, and Wolfgang Hense. "Die Stellung der Medizin in Leibniz' Entwürfen für Sozietäten." In *Leibniz in Berlin*. Ed. by Hans Poser and Albert Heinekamp. Stuttgart: Steiner, 1990, pp. 241–52.

Heinekamp, Albert. *Das Problem des Guten bei Leibniz*. Bonn: H. Bouvier u. Co. Verlag, 1969.

Heinekamp, Albert. "Ars Characteristica und Natürliche Sprache bei Leibniz." *Tijdschrift voor Filosofie* 34, no. 3 (1972): 446–88.

Heinekamp, Albert, ed. *300 Jahre "Nova Methodus" von G. W. Leibniz (1684–1984)*. *Symposion der Leibniz-Gesellschaft . . . 28. bis 30. August 1984*. Stuttgart: Steiner, 1986.

Heinekamp, Albert. "Das Glück als höchstes Gut in Leibniz' Philosophie." In *The Leibniz Renaissance. International Workshop (Firenze 1986)*. Florence: Olschki, 1988, pp. 99–125.

Heinemann, F. H. "Toland and Leibniz." *The Philosophical Review* 54, no. 5 (1945): 437–57.

Heinemann, O. von. *Die Herzogliche Bibliothek zu Wolfenbüttel*. 2nd ed. Wolfenbüttel: Zwissler, 1894.

Hertrampf, Hans-Dieter. "Höe von Höenegg – Sächsischer Oberhofprediger 1613–1645." *Herbergen der Christenheit. Jahrbuch für deutschen Kirchengeschichte*. [= Beiträge zur Kirchengeschichte Deutschlands, vol. 7] Berlin, 1969, pp. 129–48.

Hess, Heinz-Jürgen. "Die unveröffentlichten naturwissenschaftlichen und technischen Arbeiten von G. W. Leibniz aus der Zeit seines Parisaufenthaltes. Eine Kurzcharakteristik." In *Leibniz à Paris (1672–1676). Symposion de la G. W. Leibniz-Gesellschaft*. 2 vols. Wiesbaden: Steiner, 1978, vol. I, pp. 183–217.

Hess, Heinz-Jürgen, ed. *Der Ausbau des Calculus durch Leibniz und die Brüder Bernoulli: Symposion der Leibniz-Gesellschaft und der Bernoulli-Edition der Naturforschenden Gesellschaft in Basel, 15.–17. Juni 1987*. Stuttgart, 1989.

Heuvel, Gerd van den. "Leibniz zwischen Hannover und Berlin." In *Leibniz in Berlin*. Ed. by Hans Poser and Albert Heinekamp. Stuttgart: Steiner, 1990, pp. 271–80.

Hill, C. *Intellectual Origins of the English Revolution*. Oxford: Oxford University Press, 1965.

Hiltebrandt, Ph. "Eine Relation des Wiener Nuntius über seine Verhandlungen mit Leibniz (1700)." In *Quellen und Forschungen aus italienischen Archiven und Bibliotheken*. Vol. 10. Rome, 1907, pp. 238–46.

Hofmann, J. E. "Vom öffentlichen Bekanntwerden der Leibnizschen Infinitesimalmathematik." In *Sitzungsberichte d. Österr. Akad. d. Wiss. Mathem.-naturw. Kl.* Section II. 175, nos. 8–9 (1966): 209–54.

Hofmann, J. E. *Leibniz in Paris 1672–1676. His Growth to Mathematical Maturity.* Cambridge: Cambridge University Press, 1974.

Hotson, Howard. "Leibniz and Millenarianism." In Maria Rosa Antognazza and Howard Hotson, eds. *Alsted and Leibniz on God, the Magistrate and the Millennium.* Texts edited with introduction and commentary. Wiesbaden: Harrassowitz Verlag, 1999, pp. 127–214.

Hotson, Howard. "A Dark Golden Age: The Thirty Years War and the Universities of Northern Europe." In *Ships, Guns and Bibles in the North Sea and Baltic States, c. 1350–c. 1700.* Ed. by Allan I. Macinnes, Thomas Riis, and Frederik Pedersen. East Linton: Tuckwell Press, 2000, pp. 235–70.

Hotson, Howard. *Johann Heinrich Alsted 1588–1638: Between Renaissance, Reformation, and Universal Reform.* Oxford: Clarendon Press, 2000.

Hotson, Howard. "Irenicism in the Confessional Age: The Holy Roman Empire, 1563–1648." In *Conciliation and Confession: Struggling for Unity in the Age of Reform.* Ed. by Howard Louthan and Randall Zachman. Notre Dame: University of Notre Dame Press, 2004, pp. 228–85.

Hotson, Howard. *Commonplace Learning: Ramism and Its German Ramifications, 1543–1630.* Oxford-Warburg Studies. Oxford: Oxford University Press, 2007.

Hotson, Howard. *The Reformation of Common Learning: Post-Ramist Method and the Reception of the New Philosophy, 1618–1670.* Oxford-Warburg Studies. Oxford: Oxford University Press, forthcoming.

Huber, Kurt. *Leibniz.* Munich: Oldenbourg, 1951.

Hübener, Wolfgang. "Leibniz und der Renaissance-Lullismus." In *Leibniz et la Renaissance.* Ed. by Albert Heinckamp. Wiesbaden: Steiner, 1983, pp. 103–12.

Hübener, Wolfgang. "Negotium irenicum. Leibniz' Bemühungen um die brandenburgische Union." In *Leibniz in Berlin.* Ed. by Hans Poser and Albert Heinekamp. Stuttgart: Steiner, 1990, pp. 120–69.

Hutton, Sarah. *Anne Conway. A Woman Philosopher.* Cambridge: Cambridge University Press, 2004.

Iltis, C. "Leibniz and the *Vis Viva* Controversy." *Isis* 62, no. 1 (1971): 21–35.

Israel, Jonathan I. *Radical Enlightenment: Philosophy and the Making of Modernity, 1650–1750.* Oxford: Oxford University Press, 2001.

Israel, Jonathan I. *Enlightenment Contested: Philosophy, Modernity, and the Emancipation of Man, 1670–1752.* Oxford: Oxford University Press, 2006.

Jacob, Margaret C. *The Newtonians and the English Revolution. 1689–1710.* Ithaca: Cornell University Press, 1976.

Jolley, Nicholas. "Leibniz on Locke and Socinianism." *Journal of the History of Ideas* 39, no. 2 (1978): 233–50.

Jolley, Nicholas. *Leibniz and Locke: A Study of the New Essays on Human Understanding.* Oxford: Clarendon Press, 1984.

Jolley, Nicholas. *Leibniz*. London and New York: Routledge, 2005.

Joly, Henri. "Thomasius et l'Université de Leipzig pendant la jeunesse de Leibniz." *Revue philosophique de la France et de l'étranger* 6 (1878): 482–500.

Jordan, G. J. *The Reunion of the Churches: A Study of G. W. Leibnitz and His Great Attempt*. London: Constable & Co., 1927.

Jürgensmeier, F. *Johann Philipp von Schönborn (1605–1673) und die römische Kurie*. Mainz: Selbstverlag der Gesellschaft für mittelrheinische Kirchengeschichte, 1977.

Junge, W. *Leibniz und der Sachsen-Lauenburgische Erbfolgestreit*. Quellen und Darstellungen zur Geschichte Niedersachsens, vol. 65. Hildesheim, 1965.

Kabitz, Willy. *Die Philosophie des jungen Leibniz. Untersuchungen zur Entwicklungsgeschichte seines Systems*. Heidelberg: Carl Winter's Universitätsbuchhandlung, 1909.

Kabitz, Willy. "Die Bildungsgeschichte des jungen Leibniz." *Zeitschrift für Geschichte der Erziehung und des Unterrichts* 2 (1912): 164–84.

Kabitz, Willy. "Leibniz und Berkeley." *Sitzungsberichte der preußischen Akademie der Wissenschaften. Philosophisch-historische Klasse* 24 (1932): 623–36.

Kauppi, R. *Über die Leibnizsche Logik*. Helsinki: Societas philosophica, 1960.

Kiefl, Franz Xaver. *Der Friedensplan des Leibniz zur Wiedervereinigung der getrennten christlichen Kirchen aus seinen Verhandlungen mit dem Hofe Ludwigs XIV., Leopolds I. und Peters des Großen*. Paderborn: Schöningh, 1903; 2nd ed. *Leibniz und die religiöse Wiedervereinigung Deutschlands*. Regensburg, 1925.

Knapp, Hans. *Matthias Hoe von Hoenegg und sein Eingreiffen in die Politik und Publizistik des dreissigjährigen Krieges*. Halle, 1902.

Koenigsberger, H. G. *The Habsburgs and Europe, 1516–1660*. Ithaca: Cornell University Press, 1971.

Korthaase, Werner, Sigurd Hauff and Andreas Fritsch, eds. *Comenius und der Weltfriede*. Berlin: Deutsche Comenius-Gesellschaft, 2005.

Knobloch, Eberhard. "Die Entscheidende Abhandlung von Leibniz zur Theorie linearer Gleichungssysteme." *Studia Leibnitiana* 4 (1972): 163–80.

Knobloch, Eberhard. "Studien von Leibniz zum Determinanten Kalkül." *Studia Leibnitiana Supplementa* 13 (1974): 37–45.

Knobloch, Eberhard. *Der Beginn der Determinantentheorie*. Hildesheim: Gerstenberg, 1980.

Knobloch, Eberhard. "Zur Vorgeschichte der Determinantentheorie." *Studia Leibnitiana Supplementa* 22 (1982): 96–118.

Knobloch, Eberhard. "Die Astronomie an der Sozietät der Wissenschaften." In *Leibniz in Berlin*. Ed. by Hans Poser and Albert Heinekamp. Stuttgart: Steiner, 1990, pp. 231-40.

Knopf, Sabine, and Volker Titel. *Der Leipzig Gutenbergweg. Geschichte und Topographie einer Buchstadt*. Leipzig: Sax-Verlag Beucha, 2001.

Kroker, Ernst. "Leibnizens Vorfahren." *Neues Archiv für sächsische Geschichte* 19 (1898): 315-38.

Kroll, M. *Sophie, Electress of Hanover: A Personal Portrait*. London, 1973.

Kulstad, Mark. *Leibniz on Apperception, Consciousness, and Reflection.* Munich: Philosophia, 1991.

Kulstad, Mark. "Exploring Middle Ground: Was Leibniz's Conception of God Ever Spinozistic?" *Americam Catholic Philosophical Quarterly* 76, no. 4 (2002): 671–90.

Lach, D. *The Preface to Leibniz' Novissima Sinica.* Honolulu: University of Hawaii Press, 1957.

Lackmann, Heinrich. "Leibniz' Bibliothekarische Tätigkeit in Hannover." In *Leibniz. Sein Leben, sein Wirken, seine Welt.* Ed. by W. Totok and C. Haase. Hanover: Verlag für Literatur und Zeitgeschehen, 1966, pp. 321–48.

Lackmann, Heinrich. "Der Erbschaftsstreit um Leibniz' Privatbibliothek." *Studia Leibnitiana* 1, no. 1 (1969): 126–36.

Lamarra, Antonio. "The Development of the Theme of the 'Logica Inventiva' during the Stay of Leibniz in Paris." *Leibniz à Paris (1672–1676). Symposion de la G. W. Leibniz-Gesellschaft.* 2 vols. Wiesbaden: Steiner, 1978, vol. 2, pp. 55–71.

Lamarra, Antonio, Roberto Palaia, and Pietro Pimpinella. *Le prime traduzioni della Monadologie di Leibniz (1720–1721).* Florence: Olschki, 2001.

Lampe, Joachim. *Aristokratie, Hofadel und Staatspatriziat in Kurhannover. 1714–1760.* Göttingen, 1963.

Leinkauf, Thomas. *Mundus combinatus: Studien zur Struktur der barocken Universalwissenschaft am Beispiel Athanasius Kirchers SJ (1602–1680).* Berlin: Akademie Verlag, 1993.

Leinsle, Ulrich G. *Reformversuche protestantischer Metaphysik im Zeitalter des Rationalismus.* Augsburg: Maro Verlag, 1988.

Lenzen, Wolfgang. *Calculus Universalis: Studien zur Logik von G. W. Leibniz.* Paderborn: Mentis, 2004.

Leube, Hans. *Kalvinismus und Luthertum im Zeitalter der Orthodoxie.* Leipzig: A. Deichert, 1928.

Lewalter, E. *Spanisch-jesuitische und deutsch-lutherische Metaphysik des 17. Jahrhunderts.* Hamburg, 1935.

Lewis, Rhodri. *Language, Mind and Nature. Artificial Languages in England from Bacon to Locke.* Cambridge: Cambridge University Press, 2007.

Lynn, John A. *The Wars of Louis XIV.* Harlow: Longman, 1999.

Lodge, Paul. "The Failure of Leibniz's Correspondence with De Volder." *The Leibniz Review* 8 (1998): 47–67.

Lodge, Paul. "Leibniz's Close Encounter with Cartesianism in the Correspondence with De Volder." In *Leibniz and His Correspondents.* Ed. by Paul Lodge. Cambridge: Cambridge University Press, 2004, pp. 162–92.

Lodge, Paul. "Burchard de Volder: Crypto-Spinozist or Disenchanted Cartesian?" In *Receptions of Descartes: Cartesianism and Anti-Cartesianism in Early Modern Europe.* Ed. by Tad M. Schmaltz. London: Routledge, 2005, pp. 128–146.

Lodge, Paul. "Garber's Interpretation of Leibniz on Corporeal Substance in the 'Middle Years.'" *The Leibniz Review* 15 (2005): 1–26.

Loemker, E. "Boyle and Leibniz." *Journal of the History of Ideas* 16, no. 1 (1955): 22–43.

Look, Brandon. *Leibniz and the 'Vinculum Substantiale.'* Stuttgart: Steiner, 1999.

Look, Brandon. "On Substance and Relation in Leibniz's Correspondence with Des Bosses." In *Leibniz and His Correspondents.* Ed. by Paul Lodge. Cambridge: Cambridge University Press, 2004, pp. 238–61.

Malcolm, Noel and Jacqueline Stedall. *John Pell (1611–1685) and His Correspondence with Sir Charles Cavendish. The Mental World of an Early Modern Mathematician.* Oxford: Oxford University Press, 2005.

Malortie, C. E. von. *Der Hannoversche Hof unter dem Kurfürsten Ernst August und der Kurfürstin Sophie.* Hannover: Hahn, 1847.

Masser, Karin. *Christobal de Gentil de Rojas y Spinola O.F.M. und der lutherische Abt Gerardus Wolterius Molanus: Ein Beitrag zur Geschichte der Unionsbestrebungen der katholischen und evangelischen Kirche im 17. Jahrhundert.* Münster: Aschendorff, 2002.

Mathieu, Vittorio. *Leibniz e Des Bosses (1706–1716).* Turin: Giapichelli, 1960.

Mathieu, Vittorio. "Introduzione." In G. W. Leibniz, *Teodicea.* Bologna: Zanichelli, 1973, pp. 3–56.

Matzat, Heinz-L. "Die Gedankenwelt des jungen Leibniz." In *Beiträge zur Leibniz-Forschung.* Ed. by G. Schischkoff. Reutlingen: Gryphius-Verlag, 1947, pp. 37–67.

McIntyre, J. Lewis. *Giordano Bruno.* London: Macmillan, 1903.

Meier, Ernst von. *Hannoversche Verfassungs- und Verwaltungsgeschichte. 1680–1866.* Leipzig, 1898–9.

Menk, Gerhard. *Die Hohe Schule Herborn in ihrer Frühzeit (1584–1660): Ein Beitrag zum Hochschulwesen des deutschen Kalvinismus im Zeitalter der Gegen-reformation.* Wiesbaden: Selbstverlag der Historischen Kommission für Nassau, 1981.

Merkel, F. R. *G. W. Leibniz und die China-Mission.* Leipzig: Hinrichs, 1920.

Merchant, C. "The Vitalism of Anne Conway: Its Impact on Leibniz's Concept of the Monad." *Journal of the History of Philosophy* 17, no. 3 (1979): 255–69.

Mercer, Christia. "The Seventeenth-Century Debate between the Moderns and the Aristotelians: Leibniz and Philosophia Reformata." *Studia Leibnitiana Supplementa* 27 (1990): 18–29.

Mercer, Christia. "Mechanizing Aristotle: Leibniz and Reformed Philosophy." In *Studies in Seventeenth-Century European Philosophy.* Ed. by M. A. Stewart. Oxford: Clarendon Press, 1997, pp. 117–52.

Mercer, Christia. "The Young Leibniz and His Teachers." In *The Young Leibniz and His Philosophy, 1646–1676.* Ed. by Stuart Brown. Dordrecht: Kluwer, 1999, pp. 19–40.

Mercer, Christia. "Clauberg, Corporeal Substance, and the German Response." In *Johannes Clauberg.* Ed. by T. Verbeek. Dordrecht: Kluwer, 1999, pp. 147–59.

Mercer, Christia. *Leibniz's Metaphysics: Its Origins and Development.* Cambridge: Cambridge University Press, 2001.

Mercer, Christia. "Leibniz and His Master. The Correspondence with Jakob Thomasius." In *Leibniz and His Correspondents.* Ed. by Paul Lodge. Cambridge: Cambridge University Press, 2004, pp. 10–46.

Mercer, Christia and R. C. Sleigh, Jr. "Metaphysics: The Early Period to the *Discourse on Metaphysics.*" In *The Cambridge Companion to Leibniz.* Ed. by Nicholas Jolley. New York and Cambridge: Cambridge University Press, 1995, pp. 67–123.

Mesnard, Jean. "Leibniz et les papiers de Pascal." *Leibniz à Paris (1672–1676). Symposion de la G. W. Leibniz-Gesellschaft.* 2 vols. Wiesbaden: Steiner, 1978, vol. 1, pp. 45–58.

Mikkeli, Heikki. *An Aristotelian Response to Renaissance Humanism: Jacopo Zabarella on the Nature of Arts and Sciences.* Helsinki, 1992.

Mittelstraß, Jürgen. "Der Philosoph und die Königin – Leibniz und Sophie Charlotte." In *Leibniz in Berlin.* Ed. by Hans Poser and Albert Heinekamp. Stuttgart: Steiner, 1990, pp. 9–27.

Moll, Konrad. *Der junge Leibniz.* 3 vols. Stuttgart-Bad Cannstatt: Frommann-Holzboog, 1978–96.

Mondadori, Fabrizio. "A Harmony of One's Own and Universal Harmony." *Leibniz à Paris (1672–1676). Symposion de la G. W. Leibniz-Gesellschaft.* 2 vols. Wiesbaden: Steiner, 1978, vol. 2, pp. 151–68.

Mormino, Gianfranco. *Determinismo e Utilitarismo nella Teodicea di Leibniz.* Milan: FrancoAngeli, 2005.

Moss, Ann. *Printed Commonplace-Books and the Structuring of Renaissance Thought.* Oxford: Clarendon Press, 1996.

Most, G. W. "Zur Entwicklung von Leibniz' *Specimen Dynamicum.*" In *Leibniz' Dynamica.* Ed. by Albert Heinekamp. Studia Leibnitiana Sonderheft, vol. 13. Wiesbaden: Steiner, pp. 148–63.

Mugnai, Massimo. "Der Begriff der Harmonie als metaphysische Grundlage der Logik und Kombinatorik bei Johann Heinrich Bisterfeld und Leibniz." *Studia Leibnitiana* 5 (1973): 43–73.

Mugnai, Massimo. *Astrazione e realtà. Saggio su Leibniz.* Milan: Feltrinelli, 1976.

Mugnai, Massimo. *Leibniz' Theory of Relations.* Stuttgart: Steiner, 1992.

Mugnai, Massimo. *Introduzione alla filosofia di Leibniz.* Turin: Einaudi, 2001.

Mugnai, Massimo. "Leibniz on Individuation: From the Early Years to the 'Discourse' and Beyond." In *Studia Leibnitiana* 33 (2001): 36–54.

Mugnai, Massimo. "Leibniz: Vita di un genio tra logica, matematica e filosofia." *Le Scienze* 5, no. 29 (2002): 1–103.

Mugnai, Massimo. "Review of Lenzen, *Calculus Universalis,* 2004." *The Leibniz Review* 15 (2005): 169–81.

Murray, Michael J. "Leibniz's Proposal for Theological Reconciliation among the Protestants." *American Catholic Philosophical Quarterly* 76, no. 4 (2002): 623–46.

Nadler, Steven. *Spinoza: A Life.* Cambridge: Cambridge University Press, 1999.

Nadler, Steven, ed. *A Companion to Early Modern Philosophy*. Oxford: Blackwell, 2002.

Nischan, Bodo. "Reformed Irenicism and the Leipzig Colloquy of 1631." *Central European History* 9 (1976): 3–26.

Nischan, Bodo. *Prince, People, and Confession: The Second Reformation in Brandenburg*. Philadelphia: University of Pennsylvania Press, 1994.

Nunziante, Antonio-Maria. *Organismo come armonia. La genesi del concetto di organismo vivente in G. W. Leibniz*. Trento: Verifiche, 2002.

Oestreich, Gerhard. *Verfassungsgeschichte vom Ende des Mittelalters bis zum Ende des alten Reiches*. Stuttgart: Ernst Klett Verlag, 1970.

Ohnsorge, T. H. "Leibniz als Staatsbediensteter." In *Leibniz. Sein Leben, sein Wirken, seine Welt*. Ed. by W. Totok and C. Haase. Hanover: Verlag für Literatur und Zeitgeschehen, 1966, pp. 173–94.

Olgiati, Francesco. *Il significato storico di Leibniz*. Milan: Vita e Pensiero, 1929.

Ong, S. J. Walter. *Ramus and Talon Inventory: A Short-Title Inventory*. Cambridge, MA: Harvard University Press, 1958.

Otto, Rüdiger. "Leibniz' Aktivitäten für die sachsen-lauenburgische Erbfolge." In *Leibniz und Niedersachsen*. Ed. by Herbert Breger and Friedrich Niewöhner. Stuttgart: Steiner, 1999, pp. 53–75.

Palaia, Roberto. "Naturbegriff und Kraftbegriff im Briefwechsel zwischen Leibniz und Sturm." In *Leibniz' Auseinandersetzung mit Vorgängern und Zeitgenossen*. Ed. by Ingrid Marchlewitz and Albert Heinekamp. Stuttgart: Steiner, 1990, pp. 157–72.

Palaia, Roberto. "Unità metodologica e molteplicità disciplinare nella *Nova Methodus Discendae Docendaeque Jurisprudentiae*." In *Unità e Molteplicità nel Pensiero Filosofico e Scientifico di Leibniz*. Ed. by Antonio Lamarra and Roberto Palaia. Florence: Olschki, 2000, pp. 143–57.

Papineau, David. "The Vis Viva Controversy." In *Leibniz: Metaphysics and Philosophy of Science*. Ed. by R. S. Woolhouse. Oxford: Oxford University Press, 1981, pp. 139–56.

Parker, Geoffrey, ed. *The Thirty Years War*. 2nd ed. London: Routledge, 1997.

Parkinson, G. H. R. "Leibniz's Paris Writings in Relation to Spinoza." In *Leibniz à Paris (1672–1676). Symposion de la G. W. Leibniz-Gesellschaft*. 2 vols. Wiesbaden: Steiner, 1978, vol. 2, pp. 73–89.

Parkinson, G. H. R. "Sufficient Reason and Human Freedom in the *Confessio Philosophi*." In *The Young Leibniz and His Philosophy, 1646–1676*. Ed. by Stuart Brown. Dordrecht: Kluwer, 1999, pp. 199–222.

Parkinson, G. H. R. "Review of Leibniz, *Sämtliche Schriften und Briefe*, vol. VI, 4." *Studia Leibnitiana* 31, no. 1 (1999): 109–22.

Pasini, Enrico. *Il reale e l'immaginario: La fondazione del calcolo infinitesimale nel pensiero di Leibniz*. Turin: Sonda, 1993.

Pasini, Enrico. *Corpo e funzioni cognitive in Leibniz*. Milan: Angeli, 1996.

Pasini, Enrico. "Cinque storie sulla *Monadologia* di Leibniz." In *Monadi e monadologie. Il mondo degli individui tra Bruno, Leibniz e Husserl*. Ed. by Bianca Maria d'Ippolito, Aniello Montano, and Francesco Piro. Soveria Mannelli: Rubbettino, 2005, pp. 147–67.

Perkins, Franklin. "The Theoretical Basis of Comparative Philosophy in Leibniz' Writings on China." In *Das Neueste über China*. Ed. by Wenchao Li and Hans Poser. Stuttgart: Steiner, 2000, pp. 275–93.

Perkins, Franklin. *Leibniz and China. A Commerce of Light*. Cambridge: Cambridge University Press, 2004.

Perkins, Franklin. "Leibniz's Exchange with the Jesuits in China." In *Leibniz and His Correspondents*. Ed. by Paul Lodge. Cambridge: Cambridge University Press, 2004, pp. 141–61.

Petersen, P. *Geschichte der aristotelischen Philosophie im protestantischen Deutschland*. Leipzig: Verlag Felix Meiner, 1921.

Phemister, Pauline. "Leibniz and the Elements of Compound Bodies." *British Journal for the History of Philosophy* 7, no. 1 (1999): 57–78.

Phemister, Pauline. "'All the time and everywhere everything's the same as here': The Principle of Uniformity in the Correspondence between Leibniz and Lady Masham." In *Leibniz and His Correspondents*. Ed. by Paul Lodge. Cambridge: Cambridge University Press, 2004, pp. 193–213.

Phemister, Pauline. *Leibniz and the Natural World. Activity, Passivity and Corporeal Substances in Leibniz's Philosophy*. Dordrecht: Springer, 2005.

Pichler, Aloys. *Die Theologie des Leibniz*. 2 vols. Munich: Cotta, 1869 70.

Piro, Francesco. "Jus – Justum – Justitia. Etica e Diritto nel giovane Leibniz." *Annali dell'Instituto Italiano per gli Studi Storici* 7 (1981/2): 1–54.

Piro, Francesco. *Varietas identitate compensata. Studio sulla formazione della metafisica di Leibniz*. Naples: Bibliopolis, 1990.

Piro, Francesco. "Leibniz and Ethics: The Years 1669 72." In *The Young Leibniz and His Philosophy, 1646–1676*. Ed. by Stuart Brown. Dordrecht: Kluwer, 1999, pp. 147–67.

Piro, Francesco. *Spontaneità e ragion sufficiente. Determinismo e filosofia dell'azione in Leibniz*. Rome: Edizioni di Storia e Letteratura, 2002.

Platzeck, E. W. "Gottfried Wilhelm Leibniz y Raimundo Llull." *Estudios Lulianos* 16, nos. 2–3 (1972): 1–193.

Poser, Hans. "Leibniz's Parisaufenthalt in seiner Bedeutung für die Monadenlehre." *Leibniz à Paris (1672–1676). Symposion de la G. W. Leibniz-Gesellschaft*. 2 vols. Wiesbaden: Steiner, 1978, vol. 2, pp. 131–47.

Poser, Hans. "Leibnizens *Novissima Sinica* und das europäische Interesse an China." In *Das Neueste über China*. Ed. by Wenchao Li and Hans Poser. Stuttgart: Steiner, 2000, pp. 11–28.

Pott, Sandra, Martin Mulsow, and Lutz Danneberg, eds. *The Berlin Refuge 1680–1780: Learning and Science in European Context*. Leiden: Brill, 2003.

Prívratská, J. and V. Prívratská. "Language as the Product and Mediator of Knowledge: The Concept of J. A. Comenius." In *Samuel Hartlib and Universal Reformation. Studies in Intellectual Communication*. Ed. by Mark Greengrass, M. Leslie, and T. Raylor. Cambridge: Cambridge University Press, 1994, pp. 162–73.

Raab, Heribert. "Der 'Discrete Catholische' des Landgrafen Ernst von Hessen-Rheinfels (1623–1693)." *Archiv für mittelrhein. Kirchengeschichte* 12 (1960): 175–98.

Raab, Heribert. "'De Negotio Hannoveriano Religionis.' Die Reunionsbemühungen des Bischofs Christoph de Rojas y Spinola im Urteil des Landgrafen Ernst von Hessen-Rheinfels." In *Volk Gottes.* Ed. by Remigius Bäumer and Heimo Dolch. Herder: Freiburg, 1967, pp. 395–417.

Rathmann, Lother, ed. *Alma Mater Lipsiensis. Geschichte der Karl-Marx-Universität Leipzig.* Leipzig, 1984.

Rescher, Nicholas. "Leibniz Finds a Niche (Settling in at the Court of Hannover: 1676–77)." *Studia Leibnitiana* 24, no. 1 (1992): 25–48.

Rescher, Nicholas. "Leibniz Visits Vienna (1712–1714)." *Studia Leibnitiana* 31, no. 2 (1999): 133–59.

Reuther, Hans. "Das Gebäude der Herzog-August-Bibliothek zu Wolfenbüttel und ihr Oberbibliothekar Gottfried Wilhelm Leibniz." In *Leibniz. Sein Leben, sein Wirken, seine Welt.* Ed. by W. Totok and C. Haase. Hanover: Verlag für Literatur und Zeitgeschehen, 1966, pp. 349–60.

Richter, Arndt, and Weert Meyer. "Gottfried Wilhelm Leibniz (1646–1716). Pedigree and Ancestors." *Knowledge Organization* 23 (1996): 103–6.

Riley, Patrick. *Leibniz's Universal Jurisprudence. Justice as the Charity of the Wise.* Cambridge, MA: Harvard University Press, 1996.

Riley, Patrick. "Leibniz's *Méditation sur la notion commune de la justice*, 1703–2003." *The Leibniz Review* 13 (2003): 67–78.

Risse, Wilhelm. *Die Logik der Neuzeit.* 2 vols. Stuttgart-Bad Cannstatt: Frommann, 1964–70.

Risse, Wilhelm. *Bibliographia logica: Verzeichnis der Druckschriften zur Logik mit Angabe ihrer Fundorte.* Vol. 1: 1472–1800. Hildesheim: Olms, 1965.

Ritschl, Otto. *Dogmengeschichte des Protestantismus: Grundlagen und Grundzüge der theologischen Gedenken- und Lehrbildung in den protestantischen Kirchen.* 4 vols. Leipzig: J. C. Hinrichs, 1908–27.

Ritter, P. "Wie Leibniz gestorben und begraben ist." *Preuß. Jahrbücher* 157 (1914): 437–49.

Ritter, P. "Bericht eines Augenzeugen über Leibnizens Tod und Begräbnis." *Zeitschrift des Historischen Vereins für Niedersachsen* 81 (1916): 247–52. Republished as P. Ritter, "Bericht eines Augenzeugen über Leibnizens Tod und Begräbnis." In *Leibniz. Zum Gedächtnis seines 200jährigen Todestages.* Hanover: Gersbach, 1916, pp. 83–8.

Robinet, André. *Malebranche et Leibniz. Relations personnelles.* Paris: Vrin, 1955.

Robinet, André. "Leibniz: Lecture du *Treatise* de Berkeley." *Les études philosophiques* (1983): 217–23.

Robinet, André. "Dynamique et Fondements Métaphysiques." *Studia Leibnitiana Sonderheft* 13 (1984): 1–25.

Robinet, André. *Architectonique disjonctive, automates systémiques, et idéalité dans l'oeuvre de G. W. Leibniz.* Paris: Vrin, 1986.

Robinet, André. *G. W. Leibniz. Iter Italicum.* Florence: Olschki, 1988.

Robinet, André. "L' 'Accademia matematica' de D. Quartaroni et le 'Phoranomus' de G. W. Leibniz (Rome, 1689)." *Nouvelles de la république des lettres* 2 (1991): 7–18.

Rohrbasser, Jean-Marc and Jacques Véron. "Leibniz et la mortalité. Mesure des 'apparences' et calcul de la vie moyenne." *Population* 1–2 (1998): 29–44.

Roncaglia, Gino. *Palaestra Rationis. Discussioni su natura della copula e modalità nella filosofia 'scolastica' tedesca del XVII secolo.* Florence: Olschki, 1996.

Ross, George MacDonald. "Leibniz and the Nuremberg Alchemical Society." *Studia Leibnitiana* 6 (1974): 222–48.

Ross, George MacDonald. "Alchemy and the Development of Leibniz's Metaphysics." In *Theoria cum Praxi, Akten des III. Internationaler Leibniz-Kongresses.* Vol. 4 (Naturwissenschaft, Technik, Medizin, Mathematik). Wiesbaden: Franz Steiner Verlag, 1982, pp. 40–45.

Ross, George MacDonald. "Leibniz's Exposition of His System to Queen Sophie Charlotte and Other Ladies." In *Leibniz in Berlin.* Ed. by Hans Poser and Albert Heinekamp. Stuttgart: Steiner, 1990, pp. 61–9.

Rossi, Paolo. *The Dark Abyss of Time: The History of the Earth and the History of Nations from Hooke to Vico.* Trans. by Lydia G. Cochrane. Chicago: University of Chicago Press, 1984.

Rudert, Otto. "Der Raid des Grafen Holck im Jahre 1633." In *Schriften des Vereins für die Geschichte Leipzigs.* Vol. 16. Leipzig: Selbstverlag des Vereins, 1933, pp. 45–50.

Rudolph, Hartmut. "Zum Nutzen von Politik und Philosophie für die Kirchenunion." In *Labora diligenter.* Ed. by Martin Fontius, Hartmut Rudolph, and Gary Smith. Stuttgart: Steiner, 1999, pp. 108–27.

Ruestow, Edward G. *Physics in 17th and 18th-Century Leiden.* The Hague: M. Nijhoff, 1973.

Russell, Bertrand. *A Critical Exposition of the Philosophy of Leibniz.* 2nd ed. London: G. Allen & Unwin, 1937.

Rutherford, Donald. *Leibniz and the Rational Order of Nature.* Cambridge: Cambridge University Press, 1995, pp. 36–40.

Rutherford, Donald. "Metaphysics: The Late Period." In *The Cambridge Companion to Leibniz.* Ed. by Nicholas Jolley. New York and Cambridge: Cambridge University Press, 1995, pp. 124–32.

Rutherford, Donald. "Demonstration and Reconciliation: The Eclipse of the Geometrical Method in Leibniz's Philosophy." In *Leibniz's 'New System' (1695).* Ed. by R. S. Woolhouse. Florence: Olschki, 1996, pp. 181–201.

Rutherford, Donald. "Introduction: Leibniz and Religion." *American Catholic Philosophical Quarterly* 76, no. 4 (2002): 523–30.

Rutherford, Donald. "Idealism Declined. Leibniz and Christian Wolff." In *Leibniz and His Correspondents.* Ed. by Paul Lodge. Cambridge: Cambridge University Press, 2004, pp. 214–37.

Salomon-Bayet, Claire. "Les académies scientifiques: Leibniz et l'Académie Royale des Sciences. 1672–1676." In *Leibniz à Paris (1672–1676). Symposion de la*

G. W. Leibniz-Gesellschaft. 2 vols. Wiesbaden: Steiner, 1978, vol. 1, pp. 155–70.

Savile, A. *Leibniz and the Monadology.* London: Routledge, 2000.

Scheel, Günter. "Leibniz als herzoglicher Bibliothekar in Leineschloß." In G. Schnath, *Das Leineschloß.* Hanover: Hahn, 1962, pp. 249–56.

Scheel, Günter. "Hannovers politisches, gesellschaftliches und geistiges Leben zur Leibnizzeit." In *Leibniz. Sein Leben, sein Wirken, seine Welt.* Ed. by W. Totok and C. Haase. Hanover: Verlag für Literatur und Zeitgeschehen, 1966, pp. 83–115.

Scheel, Günter. "Leibniz als Historiker des Welfenhauses." In *Leibniz. Sein Leben, sein Wirken, seine Welt.* Ed. by W. Totok and C. Haase. Hanover: Verlag für Literatur und Zeitgeschehen, 1966, pp. 227–76.

Scheel, Günter. "Fürstbistum und Stadt Osnabrück im Leben und Werk von G. W. Leibniz." In *Osnabrücker Mitteilungen* 74 (1967), pp. 146–90.

Scheel, Günter. "Leibniz als politischer Ratgeber des Welfenhauses." In *Leibniz und Niedersachsen.* Ed. by Herbert Breger and Friedrich Niewöhner. Stuttgart: Steiner, 1999, pp. 35–52.

Schepers, Heinrich. "Non alter, sed etiam Leibnitius." *The Leibniz Review* 14 (2004): 117–35.

Schmid, Alois. "Die Herkunft der Welfen in der bayerischen Landeshistoriographie des 17. Jahrhunderts und bei Gottfried Wilhelm Leibniz." In *Leibniz und Niedersachsen.* Ed. by Herbert Breger and Friedrich Niewöhner. Stuttgart: Steiner, 1999, pp. 126–47.

Schmidt-Biggemann, Wilhelm. *Topica Universalis: Eine Modellgeschichte humanistischer und barocker Wissenschaft.* Hamburg: Meiner, 1983.

Schnath, Georg. *Geschichte Hannovers im Zeitalter der neunten Kur und der englischen Sukzession 1674–1714.* 4 vols. Hildesheim and Leipzig: August Lax, 1938–82.

Schnath, G. "Die Überwältigung Braunschweig-Wolfenbüttels durch Hannover und Celle zu Beginn des Spanischen Erbfolgekrieges, März 1702." *Braunschweigisches Jahrbuch* 56 (1975): 27–100.

Schneider, Hans-Peter. "Leibniz als Jurist." In *Leibniz. Sein Leben, sein Wirken, seine Welt.* Ed. by W. Totok and C. Haase. Hanover: Verlag für Literatur und Zeitgeschehen, 1966, pp. 489–510.

Schneider, Hans-Peter. *Justitia Universalis. Quellenstudien zur Geschichte des "christlichen Naturrechts" bei Gottfried Wilhelm Leibniz.* Frankfurt am Main, 1967.

Schneider, Hans-Peter. "Der Begriff der Gerechtigkeit bei Leibniz." In *Pensamiento jurídico y sociedad internacional.* Vol. 2. Madrid: Centro de Estudios Constitucionales, Univ. Complutense, 1986, pp. 1089–1113.

Schneider, Hans-Peter. "Leibniz und die preußischen Justizreformen im 18. Jahrhundert." In *Leibniz in Berlin.* Ed. by Hans Poser and Albert Heinekamp. Stuttgart: Steiner, 1990, pp. 281–96.

Schneider, Hans-Peter. "Leibniz und der moderne Staat." In *Leibniz und Niedersachsen.* Ed. by Herbert Breger and Friedrich Niewöhner. Stuttgart: Steiner, 1999, pp. 23–34.

Schneider, Heinrich. "Wie Starb Leibniz?" *Braunschweigisches Magazin* no. 2 (1923): columns 28–31.

Schneider, Martin. "Leibniz' Konzeption der *Characteristica Universalis* zwischen 1677 und 1690." *Revue Internationale de Philosophie* 48, no. 2=188 (1994): 213–36.

Schröder, Peter. "Reich versus Territorien? Zum Problem der Souveränität im Heiligen Römischen Reich nach dem Westfälischen Frieden." In Olaf Asbach et al., eds., *Altes Reich, Frankreich und Europa*. Berlin: Duncker and Humblot, 2001, 123–43.

Shapiro, Barbara J. *John Wilkins. 1614–1672: An Intellectual Biography*. Berkeley and Los Angeles: University of California Press, 1969.

Siefert, Arno. "Das höhere Schulwesen: Universitäten und Gymnasien." In Christa Berg et al., eds., *Handbuch der deutschen Bildungsgeschichte*, vol. 1: *15. bis 17. Jahrhundert*. Ed. by Notker Hammerstein. Munich, 1996, 197–374.

Seifert, Arno. *Der Rückzug der biblischen Prophetie von der neueren Geschichte. Studien zur Geschichte der Reichstheologie des frühneuzeitlichen Protestantismus*. Vienna and Cologne: Böhlau, 1990.

Seip von Engelbrecht, Andreas. *Der Fürstlich Waldeckische Leibmedicus Dr. med. Johann Philipp Seip in Pyrmont und seine Familie*. Eisenach: Kahle, 1938.

Selge, Kurt-Victor. "Das Konfessionsproblem in Brandenburg im 17. Jahrhundert und Leibniz' Bedeutung für die Unionsverhandlungen in Berlin." In *Leibniz in Berlin*. Ed. by Hans Poser and Albert Heinekamp. Stuttgart: Steiner, 1990, pp. 170–85.

Sierksma, Gerald and Wybe Sierksma. "The Great Leap to the Infinitely Small: Johann Bernoulli; Mathematician and Philosopher." *Annals of Science* (Paris) 56 (1999): 433–49.

Sleigh, R. C. Jr. *Leibniz and Arnauld. A Commentary on Their Correspondence*. New Haven: Yale University Press, 1990.

Staemmler, Heinz. *Die Auseinandersetzung der kursächsischen Theologen mit dem Helmstedter Synkretismus: eine Studie zum "Consensus repetitus fidei vere Lutheranae" (1655) und den Diskussionen um ihn*. Waltrop: Spenner, 2005.

Stein, Ludwig. *Leibniz und Spinoza. Ein Beitrag zur Entwicklungsgeschichte der Leibnizschen Philosophie*. Berlin: Georg Reimer, 1890.

Steinberg, S. H. *The 'Thirty Years War' and the Conflict for European Hegemony, 1600–1660*. London: Edward Arnold, 1966.

Stieda, Wilhelm. *Professor Friedrich Leubnitz, der Vater des Philosophen*. Leipzig: Teubner, 1917.

Stoye, John. *The Siege of Vienna*. London, 1964.

Strack, Clara. *Ursprung und sachliches Verhältnis von Leibnizens sogenannter Monadologie und den Principes de la nature et de la grâce. I. Teil: Die Entstehungsgeschichte der beiden Abhandlungen*. Berlin, 1915. (Inaugural Dissertation.)

Strasser, Gerhard F. *Lingua universalis: Kryptologie und Theorie der Universalsprachen im 16. und 17. Jahrhundert*. Wiesbaden: Harrassowitz Verlag, 1988.

Swoyer, Chris. "Leibniz's Calculus of Real Addition." *Studia Leibnitiana* 26, 1 (1994): 1–30.

Thijssen-Schoute, C. Louise. *Nederlands cartesianisme*. Amsterdam: Noord-Hollandsche Uitg. Mij., 1954.

Tognon, Giuseppe. "Christian Wolff e gli 'Essais de Théodicée.'" In *Leibniz. Tradition und Aktualität. V. Internationaler Leibniz-Kongress. Vorträge*. Hanover: Gottfried-Wilhelm-Leibniz-Gesellschaft, 1988, pp. 961–71.

Torresetti, Giorgio. *Crisi e rinascita del diritto naturale in Leibniz*. Milan: Giuffrè, 2000.

Totok, Wilhelm, and Carl Haase, eds. *Leibniz. Sein Leben, sein Wirken, seine Welt*. Hanover: Verlag für Literatur und Zeitgeschehen, 1966.

Trevisani, Francesco. *Descartes in Germania. La ricezione del cartesianismo nella facoltà filosofica e medica di Duisburg 1652–1703*. Milan, 1992.

Turnbull, H. W., ed. *J. Gregory Tercentenary Memorial Volume*. London, 1939.

Utermöhler, Gerda. "Die Literatur der Renaissance und des Humanismus in Leibniz' privater Büchersammlung." In *Leibniz et la Renaissance*. Ed. by Albert Heinekamp. Wiesbaden: Steiner, 1983, pp. 221–38.

Utermöhlen, Gerda. "Die Rolle fürstlicher Frauen im Leben und Wirken von Leibniz." In *Leibniz in Berlin*. Ed. by Hans Poser and Albert Heinekamp. Stuttgart: Steiner, 1990, pp. 44–60.

Utermöhlen, Gerda. "Leibniz im kulturellen Rahmen des hannoverschen Hofes." In *Leibniz und Niedersachsen*. Ed. by Herbert Breger and Friedrich Niewöhner. Stuttgart: Steiner, 1999, pp. 213–26.

Vailati, Ezio. *Leibniz and Clarke. A Study of Their Correspondence*. New York and Oxford: Oxford University Press, 1997.

Vasoli, Cesare. "Enciclopedia, pansofismo e riforma 'metodica' del diritto nella 'Nova Methodus' di Leibniz." *Quaderni fiorentini per la storia del pensiero giuridico moderno* 2 (1973): 37–109.

Vasoli, Cesare. *L'enciclopedismo del Seicento*. Naples: Bibliopolis, 1978.

Verbeek, Theo, ed. *Johannes Clauberg (1622–1665) and Cartesian Philosophy in the Seventeenth Century*. Dordrecht: Kluwer, 1999.

Verbeek, Theo. "Dutch Cartesian Philosophy." In *A Companion to Early Modern Philosophy*. Ed. by Steven Nadler. Oxford: Blackwells, 2002, 167–82.

Vermeulen, Bernhard. "The Metaphysical Presuppositions of Nieuwentijt's Criticism of Leibniz's Higher-Order Differentials." In *300 Jahre "Nova Methodus" von G. W. Leibniz (1684–1984). Symposion der Leibniz-Gesellschaft . . . 28. bis 30. August 1984*. Ed. by Albert Heinekamp. Stuttgart: Steiner, 1986, pp. 178–84.

Vierhaus, Rudolf. "Wissenschaft und Politik im Zeitalter des Absolutismus. Leibniz und die Gründung der Berliner Akademie." In *Leibniz in Berlin*. Ed. by Hans Poser and Albert Heinekamp. Stuttgart: Steiner, 1990, pp. 186–201.

Voigt, Georg. "Über den Ramismus an der Universität Leipzig." *Berichte über der Verhandlungen der königlichen sächsischen Gesellschaft der Wissenschaften zu Leipzig, Philologisch-historische Klasse* 40 (1888): 31–61.

Wallmann, Johannes. "Zwischen Reformation und Humanismus: Eigenart und Wirkungen Helmstedter Theologie unter besondere Berücksichtung Georg Calixts." *Zeitschrift für Theologie und Kirche* 74 (1977): 344–70.

Ward, A. W. *Leibniz as a Politician*. Manchester: At the University Press, 1911.

Waschkies, Hans-Joachim. "Leibniz' geologische Forschungen im Harz." In *Leibniz und Niedersachsen*. Ed. by Herbert Breger and Friedrich Niewöhner. Stuttgart: Steiner, 1999, pp. 187–210.

Weber, Hans E. *Reformation, Orthodoxie und Rationalismus*. Gütersloh: Bertelsmann, 1951.

Weidemann, Heinz. *Gerard Wolter Molanus, Abt zu Loccum: Eine Biographie*. 2 vols. Göttingen: Vandenhoeck & Ruprecht, 1925 and 1929.

Westfall, R. S. *Never at Rest: A Biography of Isaac Newton*. Cambridge: Cambridge University Press, 1980.

Whiteside, D. T. "The Mathematical Principles Underlying Newton's *Principia Mathematica*." *Journal for the History of Astronomy* 1 (1970): 116–38.

Wiedeburg, Paul. *Der Junge Leibniz. Das Reich und Europa*. Wiesbaden: Steiner, 1962–70.

Wilson, Catherine. "De ipsa natura. Sources of Leibniz's Doctrines of Forces, Activity and Natural Law." *Studia Leibnitiana* 19, no. 2 (1987): 148–72.

Wilson, Catherine. *Leibniz's Metaphysics. A Historical and Comparative Study*. Princeton: Princeton University Press and Manchester: Manchester University Press, 1989.

Wilson, Catherine. *The Invisible World. Early Modern Philosophy and the Invention of the Microscope*. Princeton: Princeton University Press, 1995.

Wilson, Peter H. *The Holy Roman Empire. 1495–1806*. London: Macmillan Press, 1999.

Winae, Rolf. "Zur Frühgeschichte der Academia Naturae Curiosorum." In *Der Akademiegedanke im 17. und 18. Jahrhundert*. Ed. by Fritz Hartmann and Rudolf Vierhaus. Bremen, 1977, pp. 117–37.

Woolhouse, R. S. and R. Francks. "Leibniz, Lamy, and the 'Way of Pre-established Harmony'." *Studia Leibnitiana* 26, no. 1 (1994): 76–90.

Woolhouse, R. S. "Leibniz and François Lamy's *De la Connaissance de soi-même*." *The Leibniz Review* 11 (2001): 65–70.

Woolhouse, R. S. *Locke. A Biography*. Cambridge: Cambridge University Press, 2007.

Wundt, M. *Die deutsche Schulmetaphysik des 17. Jahrhunderts*. Tübingen: Verlag von J. C. B. Mohr (Paul Siebeck), 1939.

Zaccone Sina, Maria Grazia, ed. *La corrispondenza di François Lamy, benedettino cartesiano*. Florence: Olschki, 2006.

Zacher, Hans J. *Die Hauptschriften zur Dyadik von G. W. Leibniz*. Frankfurt am Main: Klostermann, 1973.

Index